THE MISSIONS OF NEW MEXICO, 1776

REREDOS OF OUR LADY OF LIGHT, 1776

THE MISSIONS OF
NEW MEXICO, 1776

A DESCRIPTION BY

FRAY FRANCISCO ATANASIO DOMINGUEZ

WITH OTHER CONTEMPORARY DOCUMENTS

TRANSLATED AND ANNOTATED BY

ELEANOR B. ADAMS & FRAY ANGELICO CHAVEZ

DRAWINGS BY HORACE T. PIERCE

SUNSTONE
PRESS

SANTA FE

Sunstone books may be purchased for educational, business, or sales promotional use.
For information please write: Special Markets Department, Sunstone Press,
P.O. Box 2321, Santa Fe, New Mexico 87504-2321.

_____

Library of Congress Cataloging-in-Publication Data

Domínguez, Francisco Atanasio, fl. 1776.
  The missions of New Mexico, 1776 / translated and annotated by Eleanor B. Adams
and Angélico Chávez.
    p. cm.
  Originally published: Albuquerque : University of New Mexico Press, c1956.
  Includes index.
  ISBN 978-0-86534-869-1 (softcover : alk. paper)
  1. Missions--New Mexico--Early works to 1800. 2. Franciscans--New Mexico--Early works
to 1800. 3. New Mexico--Description and travel--Early works to 1800. I. Adams, Eleanor B.
(Eleanor Burnham) II. Chavez, Angelico, 1910-1996. III. Title.
  D799.D64 2012
  978.9'02--dc23
                                        2012001303

_____

www.sunstonepress.com
SUNSTONE PRESS / POST OFFICE BOX 2321 / SANTA FE, NM 87504-2321 /USA
(505) 988-4418 / ORDERS ONLY (800) 243-5644 / FAX (505) 988-1025

FRANCE VINTON SCHOLES

HIS BOOK

Preface

New Mexico is fortunate in the wealth of published material about its history from the time of the early explorers to the end of the seventeenth century. By comparison, the readily available material for the century after the Reconquest is meager indeed. The publication of Fray Francisco Atanasio Domínguez' report and the documents that accompany it should provide some much needed background for an understanding of the later colonial history of this frontier of the Spanish Empire in America.

The preparation of this volume has been a lengthy and arduous task, and the authors are most grateful for the generous cooperation of many persons.

At the University of New Mexico, William M. Dabney, W. W. Hill, Richard G. Huzarski, John E. Longhurst, and Frank D. Reeve were kind enough to give assistance on various problems. The efficiency and patience of the staff of the University Library have, as always, helped to smooth the path of research.

Some difficult passages have been illuminated by Arthur Bibo's intimate knowledge of the Acoma country. Gordon Ferguson, of Albuquerque, discussed the interpretation of architectural terms. To Alfred V. Kidder thanks are due for reading and commenting upon the Pecos portion of the manuscript.

Stanley A. Stubbs and Bruce T. Ellis, of the Laboratory of Anthropology, Santa Fe, rendered valuable service by sharing the results of their investigations at the Chapel of San Miguel and at the site of the Castrense before publication. Arthur J. O. Anderson, of the Museum of New Mexico, advised in the translation of certain words of Nahuatl origin.

Greatly appreciated is the kindness of the Minister Provincial of the Franciscan Province of Cincinnati, the Very Reverend Vincent Kroger, O.F.M., not only for giving Father Angélico permission to publish, following the recommendation of the Reverend Lambert Brockman, O.F.M., provincial examiner, but for previously allowing him the lengthy period spent in research and writing, as well as the considerable travel expenses involved. To the Archbishop of Santa Fe, the Most Reverend Edwin Vincent Byrne, D.D., very special thanks are due for readily granting his license upon the recommendation of his examiner, the Reverend O. A. Coggiola, and, in addition, for graciously extending the full use of heretofore unpublished material in the archdiocesan archive.

In re-creating the missions as they might have looked in 1776, Horace T. Pierce made every effort to combine historical accuracy with effective illustra-tion. His drawings are based on careful study of Domínguez' descriptions, photographs, and other sources. Laura Gilpin deserves particular gratitude for making and contributing a superb photograph of the reredos now at Cristo Rey, upon which Father Angélico based his interpretation, in color, of its original appearance in the Chapel of Our Lady of Light.

Copies of Bernardo de Miera y Pacheco's Map of the Interior Province of New Mexico are preserved in the Archivo General de la Nación, Mexico, the Academia de la Historia, Madrid, and the British Museum. The reproduction of this map and its sections is derived from the Academia de la Historia copy, but photographs of all three versions have been used to supply and clarify details. The Joseph de Urrutia Plan of Santa Fe and Miera y Pacheco's Map of the Río del Norte are based on photographs of the originals in the collections of the British Museum and of the Academia de la Historia, Madrid, respectively. The painstaking work of preparing these maps for press was done by Jan Alfidi Cleveland and Roland F. Dickey.

This, however, is but a small part of Mr. Dickey's contribution as designer and editor of this volume for the University of New Mexico Press. His intelligent interest and wholehearted participation have placed the authors deeply in his debt.

E.B.A.   Fr. A.C.

October, 1955

Contents

RELATED MATERIALS

LETTERS AND OBSERVATIONS

DOCUMENTS

FRANCISCANS AND SETTLERS

ILLUSTRATIONS

REREDOS OF OUR LADY OF LIGHT, 1776
Frontispiece, in color

SEAL OF THE CUSTODY OF THE CONVERSION OF ST. PAUL
Title Page

DRAWINGS OF THE MISSIONS

ABBREVIATIONS USED IN THIS WORK

AASF: Archive of the Archdiocese of Santa Fe.

AB-1634: F. W. Hodge, G. P. Hammond, and A. Rey, eds., *Fray Alonso de Benavides' Revised Memorial of 1634 (Coronado Historical Series,* vol. 4, Albuquerque, 1945).

AGI: Archivo General de Indias, Sevilla.

AGM: Archivo General de la Nación, Mexico.

AT: E. B. Adams, ed., *Bishop Tamarón's visitation of New Mexico, 1760* (Historical Society of New Mexico, *Publications in History,* vol. 15, Albuquerque, 1954).

BL: Bancroft Library, University of California.

BNM: Biblioteca Nacional, Mexico.

DHM: *Relaciones de Nuevo-Mexico,* in *Documentos para la historia de México,* Tercera sér., tomo 1 (Mexico, 1856).

DII: *Colección de documentos inéditos relativos al descubrimiento, conquista y organización de las posesiones españolas de América y Oceanía,* 42 vols. (Madrid, 1864-84).

GK: G. Kubler, *The religious architecture of New Mexico in the colonial period and since the American occupation* (Colorado Springs, 1940).

HB: C. W. Hackett, ed., *Historical documents relating to New Mexico, Nueva Vizcaya, and approaches thereto, to 1773. Collected by Adolph F. A. Bandelier and Fanny R. Bandelier,* 3 vols. (Carnegie Institution of Washington, *Publication No. 330,* Washington, 1923-37).

HS: C. W. Hackett and C. C. Shelby, eds., *Revolt of the Pueblo Indians of New Mexico and Otermin's attempted reconquest, 1680-1682,* 2 vols. *(Coronado Historical Series,* vols. 8, 9, Albuquerque, 1942).

JS: Capt. John Stevens, *A new Spanish and English dictionary* (London, 1706, 1726).

MN: Museo Nacional, Mexico.

NMF: Fray Angélico Chávez, *Origins of New Mexico families in the Spanish Colonial Period.* (Historical Society of New Mexico, Santa Fe, 1954).

NMHR: *New Mexico Historical Review.*

SANM: R. E. Twitchell, *The Spanish Archives of New Mexico,* 2 vols. (Cedar Rapids, 1914). When possible, Twitchell's document numbers have been used to refer both to his calendar and to the original documents.

A NOTE ON THE FRONTISPIECE

The frontispiece is a restoration of the stone reredos of the Chapel of Our Lady of Light in Santa Fe as it may have looked in 1776, some fifteen years after it was installed. This chapel, also known as the Castrense or military chapel, no longer exists. The reredos was housed for many years in the sanctuary of the old adobe Parroquia and Cathedral and it is now the chief ornament of the church of Cristo Rey in Santa Fe.

The restoration is based on a black-and-white camera study made at Cristo Rey by Laura Gilpin. This photograph was tinted to match the colors faintly visible on the stone carving. Walls surrounding the altar screen were sketched in accordance with Father Domínguez' measurements of the Castrense sanctuary. Although the original chapel walls may have been decorated in another manner, the *tierra amarilla* painted wainscot follows the custom of New Mexico churches.

The arching top border is copied from a photograph taken by Charles F. Lummis after the reredos was transferred to the old Parroquia. The border probably was destroyed when the present Cathedral sanctuary was built in 1895, at which time the adobe sanctuary behind it, which held the reredos, was fitted with a lower ceiling. In Lummis' photograph it appears to be a continuous border of plaster with a crude design of leaves and roses, quite different in spirit and execution from the remainder of the reredos. While the border rounded out the lateral arcs and the lunette of the Eternal Father, it did not hide the unfinished look of the double pilasters on either side of the upper Madonna panel, which seem to await a stone arch and finials.

Domínguez tells us that the representation of Our Lady of Light in the central niche was a painting. Here, it has been copied from an old canvas at Loretto Convent in Santa Fe. This painting is much too large for the niche, but two vertical lines impressed on it are spaced to the exact width of the niche. Folded to these proportions, the picture would appear as now reproduced. It could well be that this is the very painting originally installed in the central niche. Bishop Lamy gave it to the Sisters of Loretto, together with the stone plaque from the façade, when the Castrense was sold and its reredos removed.

The altar frontal is restored on the basis of supposition. Domínguez mentions an oval of St. Anthony carved on white stone, but says that the table itself was of wood, a good indication that this lower section, like the top of the reredos, was never finished. Lacking the solid support that a stone altar table would have provided, this frontal eventually collapsed. The Museum of New Mexico exhibits two pieces of a plaque of St. Anthony which may be the original from Our Lady of Light. It is of the same kind of stone, similar workmanship, and the right height for an altar. Although the date is 1791, this could well be a mistake for 1761, especially when carved around an oval by a perhaps illiterate person.

The fact that both the altar table and the upper part of the altar screen itself appear to have been left unfinished leads one to conjecture that the sculptor, who may have been a gifted Mexican Indian, was a member of the household of the donor, Governor Marín del Valle, and returned to New Spain with his lord and master.

Historical Introduction

While the Second Continental Congress was drafting at Philadelphia the Declaration that marked the birth of a new nation, in the west a dying empire had summoned a final spurt of energy to expand and consolidate its North American borderlands. Within less than three generations the United States of America was to inherit the fruit of the labors of the last explorers and pioneers in the great Spanish tradition who risked everything they had to establish new outposts for the glory of God and the King.

The long northern frontier of New Spain was menaced from all directions by the middle of the eighteenth century. Fear of British encroachments on the east forced Spain reluctantly to acquire Louisiana and its problems from the French. On the Pacific coast, fear of the Russians in Alaska inspired the Spanish advance into Upper California. Meanwhile, the old problem of holding in check the hordes of marauding Indians who harried without mercy the scattered settlements of the vast interior provinces was hourly becoming more acute.

An intensive search for more effective means to safeguard this hard-won fringe of the empire began in the 1760's. Louisiana passed into Spanish hands in the early part of the decade. In 1765, Charles III sent José de Gálvez to Mexico, entrusting to him the enormous task of reorganizing the whole administrative system of New Spain. During 1766-68, the Marqués de Rubí surveyed conditions in the northern provinces from East Texas to Sonora. In 1769, Gálvez promoted the colonization of Upper California under the first governor, Gaspar de Portolá. In that very year Fray Junípero Serra founded the first mission at San Diego, and Monterey was established in 1770.

As a result of all these activities, the problems were both clarified and increased. In Louisiana the Spanish authorities found no alternative but to carry on as best they could the conciliatory methods of their French predecessors in attempting to win the allegiance of the obstreperous tribes there. They adopted the same course in dealing with the less belligerent Indians of eastern Texas. But in order to subdue the hostile nations within Spain's older boundaries, it was obvious that the military and governmental system of the interior provinces needed drastic revision. In accordance with Rubí's recommendations, the work of improving the military organization in the north was begun by Commandant Inspector don Hugo O'Conor in the early 1770's. Then, on August 22, 1776, the Crown created a new governmental unit by placing the provinces of New Vizcaya, Coahuila, Texas, New Mexico, Sinaloa, Sonora, and the Californias under a Commandant General who was, in the beginning, directly responsible to the King and exercised jurisdiction in civil and ecclesiastical as well as military affairs. Don Teodoro de Croix was the first to hold the office of Commandant General of the Interior Provinces, and under his able direction an integrated policy for the defense of the whole region began to develop.

In California, from the moment the first handful of colonists occupied Monterey, it became clear that permanent settlement in that area could not be achieved unless new land supply routes were discovered without delay. The days of blind enthusiasm and wild hopes of gold and glory had long since passed. Years of wresting a precarious living from the barren lands of the north and a never-ending struggle to survive in the face of the unremitting hostility of barbaric infidel tribes had led to general disillusionment and demoralization. But even in this era of decline the Spanish genius could and did produce leaders worthy to stand beside the conquistadores and missionaries of a more glamorous age. At Tubac on the Sonora border, a great American soldier and frontiersman named Juan Bautista de Anza was quick to realize the possibilities when the news of the white men on the Pacific coast filtered inland via the Yuma and Pima Indians. From San Xavier del Bac nearby, a Franciscan successor to the exiled Jesuit missionaries, Fray Francisco Garcés, was making solitary journeys of reconnaissance to the north and west. The friar and the soldier soon found that they shared a common aspiration. The opening of a road between Sonora and California would assure new domains for the King of Spain and the spread of the Gospel among innumerable pagan peoples.

When Anza's proposals to this effect reached Mexico City, Viceroy Antonio Bucareli submitted them for searching examination and criticism to all who might be qualified to express an opinion. Bucareli was one of the most competent administrators of eighteenth-century New Spain, but bureaucratic procedure and slow communications made inevitable delay between the conception of a plan and permission to put it into effect. Yet once the ponderous machinery was in motion, it left nothing undone to complete the picture, and this led to careful investigation of all possible solutions to the problem at hand. By 1774, when Anza and Garcés finally set forth on the first expedition, the prospects of further uniting the frontier settlements by discovering direct routes from the key province of New Mexico to Sonora and to the sea were under review.

From the days of Cortés and the "Twelve Apostles of Mexico," Franciscan missionaries had marched in the van of Spanish progress in America. Now, in the last decades of the eighteenth century, Fathers Serra, Garcés, Palóu, and Font were making outstanding contributions to the California enterprise. Fray Agustín de Morfi was to render invaluable service by recording his own observations during his travels in Texas and elsewhere on the northern frontier with the Caballero de Croix, as well as using every means to gather other pertinent information. In New Mexico, after nearly two centuries of constant turmoil and frustration, the flaming ardor of earlier times had been all but extinguished in many of the latter-day friars, who considered their assignment to the troubled and understaffed Custody of the Conversion of St. Paul a hopeless exile. But the old spark was by no means dead, and when the viceregal authorities called upon the Province of the Holy Gospel for assistance in the new projects and explorations, there were still talented and fervent religious eager to sacrifice themselves for a good cause. In the summer of 1775, Fray Silvestre Vélez de Escalante, missionary at Zuñi, who had once hoped to find peace "in this out-of-the-way place," traveled to the Hopi pueblos for the double purpose of making another attempt to evangelize these stubborn infidels and of getting all the information he could about the route to Monterey.

In June, 1776, the efforts of the California pioneers culminated in the beginnings of the great city of St. Francis by the Golden Gate. Meanwhile, in Santa Fe, Father Vélez de Escalante and Fray Francisco Atanasio Domínguez, who had arrived in New Mexico as Commissary Visitor of the missions a few months before, were planning another expedition to find a road to Monterey.

Fray Silvestre Vélez de Escalante was born in the Montañas of Santander, but crossed the ocean at an early age, for he took the Franciscan habit in the Convento Grande at Mexico City when he was seventeen years old. Father Domínguez' report adds at least two years to the age recorded in the two lists of friars of the Province of the Holy Gospel on which Vélez de Escalante's name appears. In the first, dated 1769, we find him among the brothers studying philosophy, nineteen years old and two in the Order. On the second, dated October 6, 1772, he appears among the theological students and candidates for the priesthood, twenty-two years old and five in the habit. He must have received ordination and traveled to New Mexico shortly thereafter, for someone with a different handwriting has changed the "Hermano Chorista" before his name to "Padre," and added "missionary in New Mexico" after it. As for those extra years he had acquired by 1776, perhaps, like so many of his time, he really did not know exactly how old he was. His first entry in the extant mission records of New Mexico is at Laguna on December 21, 1774. In January, 1775, he was at the pueblo of Zuñi, and he continued to be its minister until after the Commissary Visitor summoned him to Santa Fe the following year.

Fray Francisco Atanasio Domínguez was born in Mexico City about 1740 and joined the Franciscan Order in the Convento Grande about 1757 at the age of seventeen. The first reference to him that we have found places him at the Convent of Veracruz as Commissary of the Third Order there in October, 1772, when he was thirty-two years old and had been in the Order fifteen years.

In 1775, he was sent to New Mexico from

the Mexican Province of the Holy Gospel to make a visitation of the Custody of the Conversion of St. Paul, which, 177 years after its foundation as a mission, was still dependent on the mother Province. The office of canonical visitor, we know, was given only to clergymen of the highest caliber, and there can be no doubt that Father Domínguez enjoyed esteem at headquarters for his learning and mature judgment.

The instructions he received ordered him to make a complete, detailed report on both the spiritual and economic status of the New Mexico missions, and this entailed the gathering of much geographical and ethnological data as well. By so doing he would serve "both Majesties," as he himself put it, for such a report would be as useful to the royal authorities in formulating their frontier policy as to the Lord's Franciscan ministers in promoting the spiritual welfare of this distant and little understood region. Moreover, he was commissioned to further the search for new routes to connect the northern provinces, and thus open new missionary fields.

Father Domínguez arrived in El Paso, at this time the headquarters of the Custody, on September 4, 1775. Two months later he wrote to his Provincial, Fray Isidro Murillo, describing the wretched panic-stricken state to which Apache and Comanche attacks had reduced the settlements and missions of New Mexico. Nevertheless, he was all the more determined to go on to the interior missions at the first opportunity, for under these circumstances the need for his services and for a trustworthy eyewitness report was even more urgent. He left El Paso March 1, 1776, and arrived in Santa Fe on the twenty-second of the same month, accompanied by Fray José Mariano Rosete y Peralta and Fray José Palacio, who was to act as his secretary during the visitation. Between April 10 and May 5 he made formal visitations of the missions from Santa Fe north as far as Taos, and on May 13 he turned his attention to the missions of the Río Abajo.

He was also making preparations to perform the second task laid upon him by his instructions and was gathering all the information he could about the route to Monterey. This involved considerable labor, since, in Father Domínguez' opinion, the statements made by the local inhabitants required the most searching appraisal: "The people here are very light in their speech and there is no rhyme or reason to what they say." Although the governor of New Mexico, Don Pedro Fermín de Mendinueta, discouraged his hopes of finding material of value in the fragmentary archives of the government at Santa Fe, the good father insisted upon making arrangements to examine it. Not long afterward a letter from Father Morfi arrived, asking permission for Fray Silvestre Vélez de Escalante to use these papers.

On April 15, Father Domínguez had ordered Father Vélez de Escalante, who, as we already know, had been working on the problem of a route to Monterey for about a year, to join him as soon as possible for discussion of this project. Fray Silvestre arrived in Santa Fe on the night of June 7, eager to undertake the expedition that same summer. The two friars saw eye to eye immediately and lost no time in formulating plans for their journey. They notified the governor of their decision, and he guaranteed all the support he could manage to give them. They also enlisted the services of a few local citizens. Don Bernardo Miera y Pacheco, who was to take observations and map the new discovery, was the most prominent of these.

Various circumstances made it impossible for them to carry out their original intention to leave Santa Fe on July 4, 1776. As it turned out, this disappointment was all to the good, for on July 3 Fray Francisco Garcés sent an Acoma Indian called Lázaro from Moqui with a letter to the mission father at Zuñi, and this armed our explorers with essential information, short and incoherent though it was. Father Garcés excelled in action, but hardly with his pen.

When Anza left Yuma with the San Francisco colonists on his second expedition, Father Garcés had parted from them to renew relations with some of the tribes he had visited before and to test his conclusions about better communications with Monterey by doing some more independent exploring. Another hard-working Franciscan, Fray Tomás Eixarch, remained at Yuma to carry on the work of evangelization at this lonely half-way post. Father Garcés first went up the Colorado to the Mojave country, and from there he traveled hundreds of miles through new territory to the San Joaquín Valley and back before heading toward the Hopi country and Santa Fe with a Mojave guide.

The viceregal authorities and everyone concerned with the search for new routes to the establishments on the Pacific coast had long been impatiently awaiting news from Father Garcés, and the arrival of his letter was an event of major importance. When the Indian courier, Lázaro, reached Zuñi on July 6, Fray Mariano Rosete, who had been assigned to that mission in April as Vélez de Escalante's assistant, was well aware of its significance. After questioning Lázaro, he sent the Indian on to Santa Fe with the Garcés letter and letters of his own to Father Domínguez and the governor.

The tidings that Father Garcés had, in effect, opened a trail from the coast to Santa Fe via Moqui forced the two New Mexican friars to review their own plans. Vélez de Escalante's experiences had inclined him to believe that the way to Monterey did not lie through the Hopi pueblos, but through the Ute country to the west-northwest of Moqui. Therefore he and Domínguez had based their project on this assumption. After consulting the governor and discussing the matter at length in the light of this recent development, they came to the conclusion that their own expedition would still be useful, whether or not they reached Monterey (and Vélez de Escalante had never been very sanguine about this possibility). Their stated aims in their prospectus for the journey were to learn what other tribes in addition to the Yutas inhabited the region between New Mexico and Monterey, and, on the way back, to confirm the Cosninas in their desire for conversion to Christianity and to examine this region and that around the Hopi province with the idea of establishing future missions and settlements. On July 29, 1776, they set forth on their memorable adventure.

The present work is chiefly concerned with Fray Francisco Atanasio Domínguez' description of the conditions he found in New Mexico in 1776. To make the story complete, there is a good summary of the Domínguez–Vélez de Escalante expedition in their letters. Some of those translated here have not previously appeared in print, while others are published for the first time in English. For a detailed study of the route and a translation of the Diary, we defer to H. E. Bolton's *Pageant in the Wilderness*, which appeared in 1950. Professor Bolton personally retraced the friars' trail and thus added immeasurably to the enduring value of that account.

But, like all historians up to the present, Dr. Bolton was inclined to minimize Father Domínguez' contribution to the enterprise. After prolonged and intensive study of this conscientious friar's career in New Mexico, we feel obliged to emphasize the fact that Fray Francisco Atanasio Domínguez was not only a full partner, but the senior partner, in the "Splendid Wayfaring" for which Vélez de Escalante has long received the lion's share of the credit. We have no desire to detract from Fray Silvestre's achievements. On the contrary, we have the most sincere and profound admiration for this capable and dedicated Franciscan. It is high time, however, that Father Domínguez received a just meed of appreciation for his heartbreaking and thankless labors, which even his own contemporaries and superiors denied him. Domínguez was a perfectionist, and perfectionists can be very irritating when they persist in harping upon flaws almost impossible to remedy in this imperfect world. But this very trait of his character, his habit of meticulous attention to the most minor details, and his strong personal sense of duty make it incredible that he could ever have delegated to a younger man, his subordinate, however much he respected and trusted him, full responsibility for recording the observations they made during explorations of major importance. Father Vélez de Escalante would have been the first to deplore this time-worn misconception. He himself never referred to their account of the expedition except as *our* diary, things "of which the Reverend Father Custos and I spoke in the diary of the journey we made through those regions in the year '76." A careful reading of the Diary itself confirms this. It is greatly to the credit of both men that they recognized each other's qualities, that they were willing to cooperate wholeheartedly in a cause for which they had received separate instructions, and that they remained fast friends under conditions calculated to mar the best of human relationships.

Cold and weary to death, they arrived in Zuñi on the night of November 24 after nearly four arduous months of charting new trails through unknown regions. They had failed in their ultimate objective, to reach Monterey, but they could feel well satisfied that what they had accomplished was more than worth the doing. And today their achievement is considered one of the outstanding peaceful journeys of exploration in American history.

On November 25, the day after their arrival, they sent preliminary reports to the governor and to their Franciscan provincial. They remained at Zuñi until December 13, and Father Domínguez made his visitation of the mission during this period. He visited Acoma and Laguna on the way back to Santa Fe. They reached the capital on January 2, 1777, and on the following day they presented their Diary to the governor.

During the Father Visitor's absence, a few of his disgruntled brethren, who resented the standards and reforms he imposed, had been stirring up trouble and had even forwarded charges against him to Mexico City. Not all of the details are clear, but the Domínguez report and letters leave no doubt that there was good reason for this earnest, conscientious father's anguish of mind in his struggle to better conditions that horrified and appalled him. For Father Domínguez it was very difficult to compromise with regard to lapses that shocked him to the innermost depths of his being. "Jupiter rains calamities upon me, but with the favor of Heaven I keep insisting that there is a remedy for everything and that it can be applied without making a din." It is not surprising that he made himself disliked in some quarters and that he himself suffered from an increasing sense of frustration. We must remember, too, that Mexico City, "the delightful and alluring cradle" of his birth, was then the most cosmopolitan center of culture in North America, if not the Western Hemisphere. The contrast with New Mexico in those harsh, enemy-infested times could hardly have been greater. Little wonder that he found it difficult to adjust himself to this primitive way of life and that he was severely critical of it. Nevertheless, his report was as honest and complete as he knew how to make it. There is no doubt that he fulfilled his instructions to the letter —more literally, as it turned out, than was pleasing to his superiors.

It can justly be said that the Domínguez description of 1776 is to the eighteenth century what the Benavides Memorials of 1630 and 1634 are to the seventeenth. But here the comparison ends. For while Benavides painted a very general picture, really a hopefully exaggerated prospectus of what was to be done, Domínguez gives a factual statement of what had become of these sanguine hopes almost a century and a half later. Readers with romantic ideas of halcyon Spanish colonial days will be disappointed by the progressive decadence found in the missions (and in a few of the missionaries), as well as with the material and cultural backwardness prevalent among the colonists. To one who can place himself in a remote frontier province in a land already poor by nature, not only isolated by oceans of land from the rest of the civilized world, but also from his nearest neighbor, the picture is not quite so bad. Indeed, one can only feel the highest admiration for the majority of the padres, who kept the missions going in the face of utter poverty and loneliness, and for the Hispanic folk who for generations had survived among perils and hardships that might have driven other peoples to desertion, if not extinction.

The rest of Father Domínguez' story is soon told. Now Custos of New Mexico, he set out for El Paso on May 5, 1777, leaving at San Ildefonso his good companion, Fray Silvestre Vélez de Escalante, to act as his vice-custos in the interior missions, for "he is the only person who can carry out my just plans and decisions." The attacks upon his integrity and the increasing opposition he encountered had destroyed his peace of mind. He begged Father Murillo to allow him to resign as custos, quoting St. Francis: "I do not wish to be my brothers' executioner." In August, after he had finished his visitation of the El Paso missions, he started for Chihuahua to have his faculties to hear confessions renewed by the episcopal authorities. On the second day he met a friar bearing the necessary dispatches, and he returned to El Paso. He was still there in October, 1778, by which time another custos had succeeded him. This is the last direct word we have from him for about eighteen years. A note in the Provincial records indicates that he was assigned to the Presidio of Carrizal as chaplain very soon thereafter. It is unlikely that he was ever permitted to return to the City of Mexico which he loved so well. Other entries in the Provincial records place him at Zia, Jémez, and Santa Ana in 1788, and at Isleta in 1791, although his name does not appear in the New Mexico mission registers. After that the Provincial records have him at the Presidio of Janos. And it was from Janos, in 1795, that he wrote the last pathetic letter included in this volume. He had indeed been correct in his suspicion that his faithful conduct was considered superfluity. His reward was permanent exile to the northernmost limits of the Province of the Holy Gospel and deprivation of any chance for further advancement in the Order and the Church. The last time his name appears as chaplain at Janos is in 1800, and we know that he had died before the spring of 1805.

His lengthy report was filed away with a sarcastic notation and forgotten. To our good fortune, it survived time and the weather through destructive periods of social unrest and revolution to find its way into the National Library of Mexico among bundles of unsorted papers from the past. There it was discovered in 1928, a historical mine of information about life and society in eighteenth-century New Mexico. The meticulous record of the most commonplace appurtenances of everyday life makes this document uniquely valuable, for these are the vital details least often passed on to posterity, being, to the man of the time, too obvious to mention.

We owe the discovery and publication of this remarkable document to the patience, learning, and discernment of Dr. France V. Scholes, outstanding historian of colonial Hispanic America. Digging in the mountains of countless dusty and disheveled manuscripts that illuminate our human past seems to require a special flair not granted to every scholar. Dr. Scholes is exceptionally gifted with a talent for recognizing treasures at first sight. This is by no means the only unique document he has found to revise the time-worn conventions of history. We dedicate this volume to him because, in view of his discovery of the manuscript and his unselfish encouragement of the authors when other obligations prevented him from giving it to the world himself, we feel that in a very real sense this is indeed his book.

E.B.A.   Fr. A.C.

Instructions

which the Father Visitor of New Mexico, Fray Francisco Atanasio Domínguez, shall carry out.[1]

The said father shall constantly remember that the confidence and commission that we have reposed in him are for the sole purpose of the welfare of that Custody [of the Conversion of St. Paul of New Mexico]. With this in mind he shall proceed with his visitation in the most disinterested fashion, avoiding extraordinary expenditures in his transportation from one mission to another and contenting himself with the frugal sustenance that those regions and the poverty of the missionary religious have to offer. His conduct must be prudent and pacific, and his reprimands must not be vociferous lest the defects of his brethren become known to the public. Except in a most urgent and unavoidable case, let there be no noisy judicial proceedings. Under such circumstances the matter shall be dealt with according to the Sacred Canons and Laws of the Order. He shall establish harmonious relations with the principal authorities and their subordinates and with the rest of the lay population, and he shall direct his thoughts wholly to the service of God and of our Catholic Sovereign, who supports the missionaries out of his royal exchequer with munificent liberality for the benefit of those vassals of his for whom we are answerable

to both tribunals [divine and royal]. This responsibility falls more heavily upon the Father Visitor, because by his conscience he will discharge the weighty burden laid upon ours.

At the time of the visitation he shall draw up as clear and accurate a description of the location of the missions as may be possible, noting the distances from their capitals and from one to another; he shall note the languages of each pueblo and mission; their arable lands, waters, and fruits; their population and the number of families, distinguishing among Spaniards, Europeanized mixtures,[2] and Indians, with the approximate number of individuals in each group, which will be easy to discover from the censuses. And he shall set up a system whereby the Reverend Father Custos will remit to us annually a well-made census for presentation to the Most Excellent Lord Viceroy, as he has ordered us.[3]

The visitor shall inspect the valuables and furnishings each mission may have belonging to its little convent, or dwelling, of the missionary; and in each one the number of such items as may be considered useful and necessary shall be prescribed and a formal inventory made so that the outgoing religious may hand them over and the newcomer receive them. He shall endeavor to put the same system into practice with regard to some provision of produce and livestock in the manner that seems best. This is done in the convents of the Province [of the Holy Gospel of Mexico] with the result that the incoming religious finds something available for food and maintenance while he is becoming acquainted with the place.

He shall also give us an itemized memorandum of the valuables in the church and sacristy: the vessels, vestments, and other things pertaining to Divine Worship. The visitor shall take care that the material edifices, however poor, shall not be permitted to deteriorate and shall be repaired and put in order, and that there shall be the necessary rooms and offices to make a comfortable abode for the religious, compelling the remiss to supply this lack, but without imposing any prejudicial burden on the Indians, and with the consent of their governors and principal men.[4]

The retention of the missionaries in the same missions so that they may learn the language shall be sought, and if there is

reason to transfer them, let it be to other missions where the same tongue is spoken. Inquiry shall be made whether (as they have been commanded) they faithfully administer the Holy Sacraments to their parishioners, whether they teach them Christian doctrine and the other things needful for the good of their souls; also whether they are careful to record baptisms, marriages, and burials in the books where they belong and with due clarity in accordance with the method used in the diocese.

A list of the religious, their native places, ages, years in the Order, length of residence in the Custody and in the mission where they dwell and serve at present shall be sent to our office and to that of the procurator of the Custody. When they are transferred, the Custos shall notify us so that we may record it in the registers and know where they are employed, and be able to give a complete and accurate report where necessary.

Finally, our visitor shall undertake to find out whether the Father Custos, or any of our missionaries, received a letter from the Reverend Father Garcés, apostolic missionary, written from the junction of the Gila and Colorado Rivers, which the Indians offered to take to the New Mexico missions. If it has been received, he shall notify us at once so that the information may be transmitted to the Most Excellent Lord Viceroy, to whom this news will be most welcome in view of the project to open communications, not only with the provinces of Sonora but with the new establishments at Monterey, in the service of both Majesties [divine and human]. And if this letter has not arrived, as I suspect, our visitor shall undertake to write one to the aforesaid Father Garcés and find out whether any of the Indians of our settlements of converts will take the risk of carrying it and bringing back a reply. The accomplishment of this would be one of the greatest services that could be rendered to our Catholic Monarch (God keep him) in these times.

1. BNM, leg. 10, no. 86. Not dated.

2. [Gente] "de razón." Although this term is sometimes erroneously translated as "whites," it was generally applied to all those of mixed blood, including mestizos and mulattoes, whose way of life followed Spanish rather than indigenous customs. By contrast the Indians were on occasion referred to as "sin razón." The distinction among Spaniards, i.e., individuals of pure European blood, but not necessarily of European birth, *gente de razón*, and Indians was commonly used in censuses and reports concerning population. Cf. AT, p. 34. For detailed information about the terminology used to describe the various classes and blood mixtures that made up the population of New Spain, see N. León, *Las castas del México colonial, o Nueva España* (Mexico, 1924).

3. Cf. HB, 3: 479.

4. In the colonial period the term *principal* was applied to any Indian of recognized noble status and in some cases to one who held a municipal office.

A DESCRIPTION
OF NEW MEXICO

by Fray Francisco Atanasio Domínguez

Plano de la Provincia interna de el Nuebo Mexico que hizo por
mandado de el tte. Coronel de Caballeria, Gobernador, y Comte. General
de dha Prova. Don Juan Bapta. de Anza. Dn. Bernardo de Miera, y Pacheco
Soldado Extinguido deel Real Presidio de Santa fe. con sus Poblaciones en el esta
do que a la presente se hallan, mui malformadas y dispersas unas de otras las
Cassas de los Vezinos que las componen, y de esta mala disposicion conque se han Ra
dicado, cada yndividuo en el pedazo de tierra que se le á Mercenado, fabricando su
havitacion, se han Originado muchos daños, desastres, y desolacion de Poblaciones
que han caussado los enemigos Cumanchis y Apaches que circumbalan dha Provincia y pron
Matando y llebandose muchas familias, a lo que se hace preciso que con Exactitud y pron
ta Obediencia se ejecute la Orden que con toda prudencia, Caridad y celo á el Real servicio, dió
dho Señor Gobernador, luego que Reconocio todas su Poblaciones, y su desorden para poner el Re
medio y que permanescan en estavilidad civilidad y Politica Christiana haciendo sus plazas
quadradas comodas á lo menos de veinte familias cada una en forma de Reductos, las pequeñas con
dos Baluartes, y las grandes con quatro en medio de las cortinas, para el Alcanse de las escopetas
cortas que se usan, no conviene se hagan torreones á lo antiguo, pues debajo de ellas se cubre el Ene
migo, los ahora y prende fuego, como se tiene experiencia, A una legua corta de el Pueblo de taos, en la
Margen de el Rio que llaman de Dn. Fernando estaban Radicados doze familias, y sus Cassas como han
acostumbrado, tubieron noticia venian las Cumanchis á ynsultarlos, se recogieron todos á una Cassa
grande con sus torreones de Pablo de Villa alpando catorze hombres con Armas de fuego con muchas
municiones, atacaron los Enemigos con vigor y ntrepido dha Cassa; se mitieron debajo de las tro
neras, del pretil, y torreones, cubiertos á su salvo, emperaron por barias partes abrir brechas y á in
troducir fuego; los Sitiados para ympedir dha maniobra descubrian sus cuerpos sobre el parapeto, y entre
lograron dhos enemigos heridos con balas, y flechas, los que todos perecieron, y se llebaron sesenta y que
tro personas chicas y grandes de ambos sexsos. de ellos murieron mas de ochenta. Pongo esta narra
tiba, para que se vea con el tieson que estos enemigos Pelean. los Pueblos de Indios Christianos
se mantienen, en aquel modo de Politica union y Zivilidad que en su Gentilidad los halla
ron los Españoles en su primer Puebla, con sus Cassas unidas de dos y tres altos,
formando Plazas, y todas con Escaleras portatiles a qualquiero ymbazion las
suben; y los Cubiertos y terrados, altos y bajos contraneras en los parapetos,
para su defensa y de el enemigo, ofensa.
Echo en la Villa de Santa fee, Capital de dha Pro
vincia. Año de 1779.

37
36
35
Grados de Latitud

Sierra de las Gru llas
frontera de los tieras

Nacimiento
Ventana

Explicazion para
su ynteligencia
Villas . . . .
Poblaciones dispersas de
los Españoles . . . .
Arruinadas pr. los Enemigos
Pueblos de los Indios
Christianos . . . .
Pueblo antiguo assumados
ojos de Agua . . . .
Rancherias de Gentiles . . . .

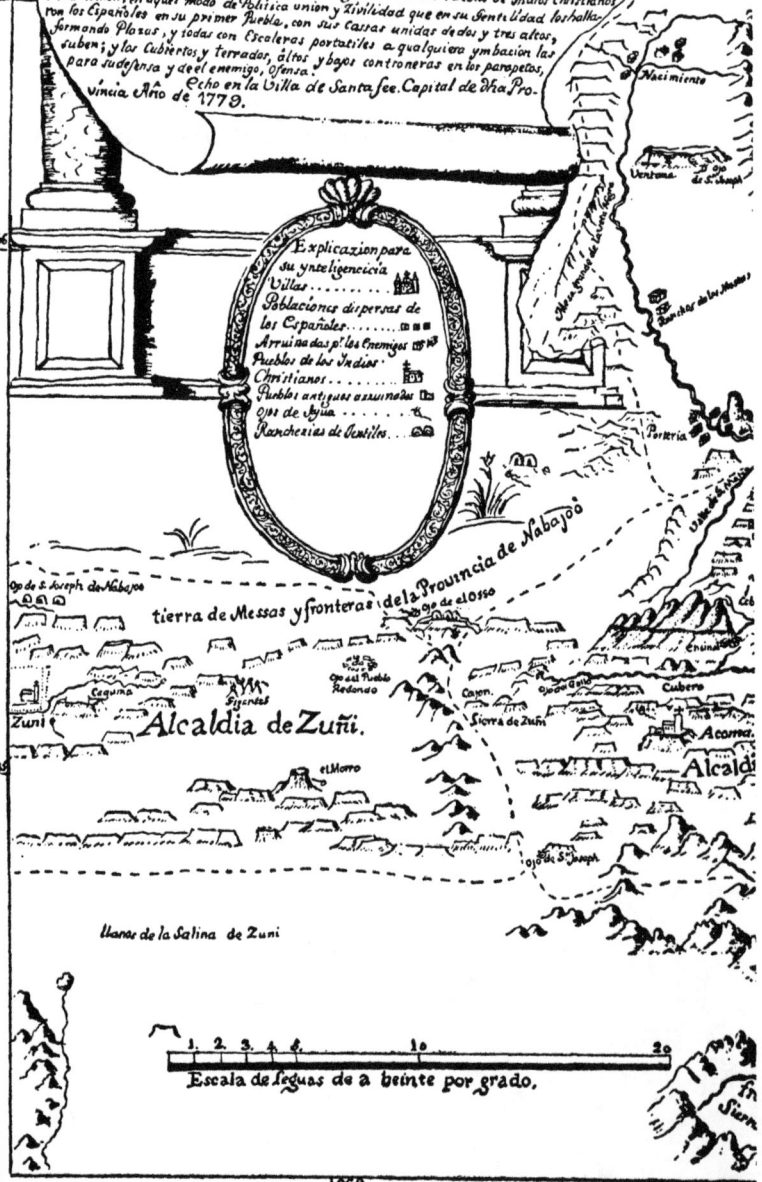

Posteria

Provincia de Nabajoó

Ojo de S. Joseph de Nabajoo
Ojo de el Osso
tierra de Messas y fronteras de la Provincia de Nabajoó

Caguina
Gigantes
Ojo del Pueblo Redondo
Cajon
Sierra de Zuñi
Cubero
Acoma
Zuni
Alcaldia de Zuñi.
Alcaldi

el Morro
ojo de S. Joseph

llanos de la Salina de Zuni

1 2 3 4 6   10   20
Escala de Leguas de a beinte por grado.

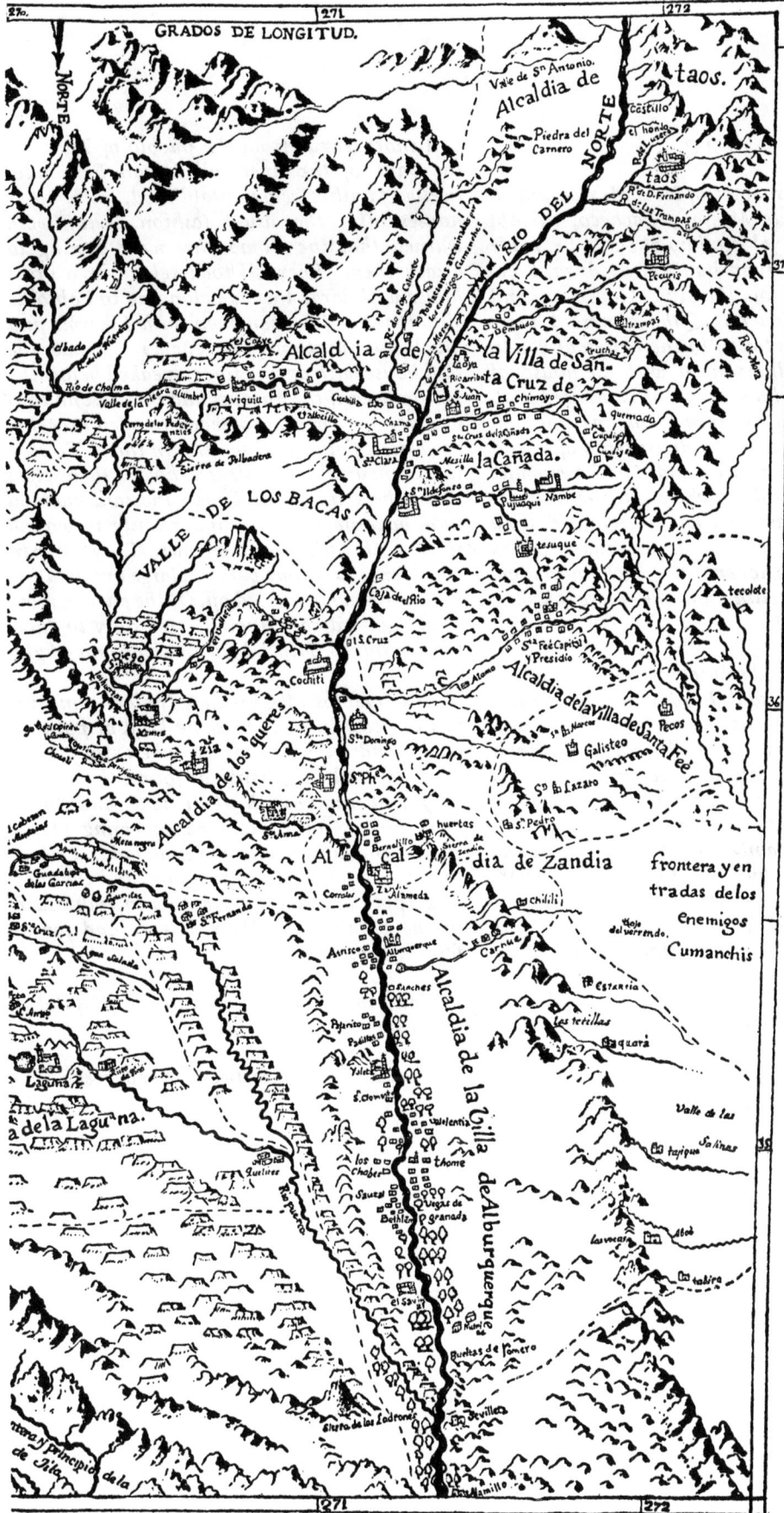

GRADOS DE LONGITUD.

NORTE

Valle de Sn Antonio.

Alcaldia de

taos.

Castillo

El hondo

Piedra del Carnero

Rio del Pueblo

RIO DEL NORTE

taos

Rio de Dn Fernando de las Trampas

Picuris

Alcald ia de

la Villa de San-

Embudo

trampas

truchas

ta Cruz de

Ricaribita

Sn Juan

Chimayo

Rio de Chama

Aviquiu

Cuchillo

la quemada

Valle de la Piedra alumbra

Sta Cruz de la Cañada

Cerro de los Pedos nales

Valloalto

Sierra de Polbadera

Mesilla la Cañada.

Sta Clara

Sn Ildefonso

Nambe

Pojuaqui

VALLE DE LOS BACAS

tesuque

A

tecolote

Caja del Rio

S Cruz

Los Alamo

Sta Fee Capital y Presidio

Cochiti

Alcaldia de la Villa de Santa Fee

Pecos

Diego

Santa Fee

Sto Ds Marcos

Galisteo

MADR

Alcaldia de los queres

Sn Domingo

Sn Phe

Sto Lazaro

huertas

Sto Sn Pedro

Sn Ana

Sierra de

Al

cal

dia de Zandia

frontera y en

Barnalillo

Sandia

tradas de los

Corrales

Alameda

Chilili

enemigos

Cumanchis

Atrisco

Alburquerque

Carnue

Hoja del verrendo.

Ranchos

ESTANCIA

Pajarito

Pueblito

Las tetillas

tazquará

Yeletta

Valentia

S. Clemente

Valle de las

Salinas

los Chabes

thome

tajique

Saurzal

Abot

Vegas de

Betleta

granada

Alcaldia de la villa de Alburquerque

Rio Puerco

las vocas

tabira

el Saviyal

Nabri

Pueblitas de Somero

Sevilleta

Elista de los Ladrones

Sta Amillo

Rio Puerco

Quelues

a de la Lagu na.

Laguna

Cebolleta

Guadalupe de las Garcias

Sn Fernando

Sn Cruz

Agua Salada

Sn Arys

tutra y Principio de la

de Jila

MAP

of the Interior Province of New Mexico, which Don Bernardo de Miera y Pacheco, exempt soldier of the Royal Presidio of Santa Fe, made by order of Don Juan Bautista de Anza, Lieutenant Colonel of Cavalry, Governor and Commandant General of the aforesaid province. Showing its towns in their present condition, extremely ill arranged, with the houses of the settlers of whom they are composed scattered about at a distance from one another. Many evils, disasters, and destruction of towns, caused by the Comanche and Apache enemies who surround said province, killing and abducting many families, have originated from this poor arrangement in accordance with which they have taken root, each individual building his dwelling on the piece of land granted to him.

Therefore it is absolutely necessary that the order which the said Lord Governor issued, with all prudence, charity, and zeal in the royal service, as soon as he had viewed all their towns and their disorder, be put into effect with exactitude and prompt obedience, in order to impose the remedy and so that they may endure in stability, civil government, and Christian polity, building their ample square plazas of at least twenty families each in the form of redoubts, the small ones with two bulwarks, and the large with four, between the ramparts, for the range of the short firelocks that are in use. It is not wise to build large towers in the old style, for the enemy takes cover below them, pierces them, and sets fire to them, as has been learned by experience.

A short league from the pueblo of Taos, on the bank of the river called Don Fernando, twelve families were established, with their houses after the usual fashion. They were warned that the Comanches were coming to attack them. They all took refuge in a great house with large towers belonging to Pablo de Villalpando—fourteen men with firearms and much ammunition. The enemy attacked the said house with daring force, sneaked below the embrasures of the parapet and towers, and thus safely under cover, proceeded to open breaches at various points and set fires in them. To stop this maneuver, the besieged showed themselves upon the parapet, and then the said enemies took advantage of the opportunity to wound them with bullets and arrows. They all perished, and sixty-four persons, large and small of both sexes, were carried off. Of the enemy, more than eighty died. I include this story to show the constancy with which these enemies fight.

The pueblos of Christian Indians continue to live according to the same kind of political unity and civilization as when they were heathens and the Spaniards found them when they first came—with their two- and three-story houses joined together, forming plazas, and all the houses with portable ladders which they pull up in time of invasion, and the roofs and upper and lower terraces with embrasures in the parapets for their defense and for offense against the enemy.

Made in the Villa of Santa Fe, Capital of said Province. Year 1779.

Scale of leagues, twenty per degree.

I. INTRODUCTION

Introduction

The Province of the Holy Gospel of Franciscan Observants of New Spain has in its charge in the Kingdom of New Mexico the Custody of the Conversion of St. Paul. This Custody has two branches, a smaller one at El Paso del Río del Norte and a larger one in the interior of the aforesaid kingdom.[1]

The El Paso branch consists of a Spanish villa and four Indian pueblos. Both the villa and the pueblos are supplied with water by the said river and are established on its west bank. The distance from the villa to the last pueblo downstream is 10 to 12 leagues.

The New Mexico branch consists of three Spanish villas and twenty-two Indian pueblos, distributed and established on both sides (east and west) of the river mentioned. It should be noted that some lie near it on its meadows, and that others are far from it in different directions and distances. It is true that the three villas are on the east side, and although one of them (Santa Fe) is about 8 leagues from the river, the other two lie in full view of it. The distance from the first settlement to the last is about 40 leagues, almost in a straight line from south to north.

This New Mexico branch is divided into two sections: Río Arriba,[2] which runs from San Ildefonso to Taos and includes the places which lie on either side of the line between them; and Río Abajo,[3] which runs from Cochiti to below Isleta, the inclusion of the outlying places being understood as above. This designation arises from the fact that some missions and their subordinate settlements are upstream and others downstream along the Río del Norte.

The river is called the Río del Norte because it comes from the north many leagues beyond Taos (sometimes entering mesas, where it forms canyons, sometimes flowing through plains, broadening out more in some places than in others, winding in still others, but always tending toward the south). It is so many leagues long that even though the settlers of these regions have penetrated very far north for various purposes again and again, they have not found the source of this river. Moreover, the heathens in these regions, like the great wanderers they are, have gone even farther in than the settlers, and in spite of this give no account of its source.

From the places where the headwaters on this river are to be seen, one observes a great abundance of water. As it declines toward the south it acquires more and more water from the many rivers (large and small) that keep joining it from the east and west from above Taos to below El Paso, where it joins still others. This is why they call it La Junta de los Ríos.[4]

There are various kinds of fish, some in some places, others in others, and a mixture in still others. They are caught either with a hook or with a *chinchorro*,[5] as it is called here. This is a net of agave fiber up to 12 varas long, or even longer, and up to 4 varas wide, with stones tied at intervals on the lower edge so that the weight will keep it straight in the water, and with gourds tied at intervals to the upper edge to prevent it from sinking to the bottom.

When it is ready, about thirty men take it and enter the river, and dragging it against the current they make a barrier as far as the river bank. Now that the fish have been caught in the net, they put in their hands, grab them, and, pulling them out quickly, they throw them to the meadow, where there are people ready to seize them and kill them promptly for division after the maneuver (which they repeat or abandon as they see fit). This operation usually takes place in March, because then the water is muddy with the earth which the melted snow brings down and the river is not too high. It is also done in summer when it has rained a great deal, after the river has subsided leaving the water muddy.

This river is in flood from mid-April to the end of June. The force of the freshets depends upon whether the winter snows have been heavy or light, but they never fail, for it always snows more or less. In a very rainy year the flood season lasts a long time, and

1. BNM, leg. 10, no. 43. The title page which precedes the manuscript of the report is in an unidentified hand and probably of later date: "Report that is intended in part to be a description of New Mexico, but its phraseology is obscure, it lacks proportion, and offers little to the discriminating taste. Still it may serve for the information of the superior prelate, or prelates, for the narrator did his best to perform the ministry entrusted to him. It deals with degrees of latitude and longitude, lands, rivers, settlements, churches and their belongings, censuses, religious and secular administration, juridical visitations, etc. etc. etc." The superior and sarcastic tone of this statement does little justice to Domínguez' conscientious and detailed account of his observations.

2. Upstream.

3. Downstream.

4. The junction of the rivers.

5. *Chinchorro* is the Spanish term for a kind of small dragnet. In American usage it frequently means a net hammock and sometimes a small drove of animals. These meanings are current in New Mexico today. Domínguez' phraseology indicates that he had no previous acquaintance with the word in the sense of fishing net.

the longer it lasts, the greater damage it does, whether to people or cattle who are drowned, or to farmlands that are swept away, or even to nearby houses that are carried off. This damage is so extreme that they assure me that in the year '69 of this century the river flooded (turning east) the greater part of Tomé, to the total destruction of houses and lands. It follows this course to this day, and as a joke (let us put it so), it left its old bed free for farmland for the citizens of Belén, opposite Tomé (and they still have it, and Father Claramonte, from whom I heard this story, has seen it planted).

This kingdom of New Mexico has no sworn patron saint like those of other kingdoms, provinces, cities, villas, etc. Although it is commonly said that Our Lady of the Rosary is the patron, this is not true. This popular opinion originates from the events of the years 1770 to this one of 1777, a more detailed account of which will be found in the place destined for miscellaneous bits of information.[6] The saint who might most properly hold the title of patron is the one from whom the Custody takes its appellation, but even this cannot be said with certainty, for the only corroboration is immemorial custom among the missionary fathers, who have handed down from the beginning the custom of observing his feast, January 25, with the rite of the first class without octave; and they keep it as a Spanish

feast day, as is done with St. Hippolytus in Mexico.[7]

I, Fray Francisco Atanasio Domínguez, then, entered upon my visitation of this Custody in March, 1776, by order and commission of our Very Reverend Father Minister Provincial of the above-mentioned Province, Fray Isidro Murillo. Since in his orders as superior his Very Reverend Paternity enjoins and bids me not to fail to tell him everything I find worth noting, as a submissive son of Obedience I am therefore doing everything I can to attain the desired end, endeavoring to fulfill his instructions and justify the confidence his Very Reverend Paternity has placed in my conduct.

In view of all the foregoing I have thought it well to start in this manner, for in the light of this compendious introduction, the

6. See p. 240 infra.

7. St. Paul in his Conversion was the patron of the Franciscan missions from their founding, while St. Francis of Assisi was that of the Spanish colonists. The Oñate itinerary of 1596-98 tells how, on August 11, 1598, irrigation ditches were begun "for the city of Our Father St. Francis [at or near San Juan Bautista, the first Indian mission], whom the Spaniards take for their patron, while the Indians in their chapel choose the Lord St. Paul in the Feast of his Conversion, and the latter remains patron of the whole land of New Mexico as St. Joseph is in New Spain. Therefore these provinces are called the Evangelical Conversion and [the missions] have the Conversion of St. Paul for their seal." Translated

from AGI, Patronato, leg. 22, ramo 13. Cf. DII, 16: 262; G. P. Hammond and A. Rey, *Don Juan de Oñate, colonizer of New Mexico, 1595-1628* (Albuquerque, 1953), pt. 1: 322. In every Spanish kingdom and province, both at home and in the colonies, the Virgin Mary always shared a general patronage, even when not specifically chosen. Thus the royal standard used in the Conquest and in the Reconquest almost a century later depicted Nuestra Señora de los Remedios. Her appearance on the standard when used as a civil banner made her a sort of patroness of the government, and as a battle flag, of the military forces. Likewise, the *parroquia* (parish church as distinct from a mission) of Santa Fe went under the titles of the Assumption and Conception of Mary consecutively until the 1680 Rebellion, thus obscuring the patronage of St. Francis over the Spaniards; yet the same parish was named for St. Francis immediately after the Reconquest. Meanwhile we find Our Lady of the Rosary, title of the chief image of Mary in the parish church, considered the Queen and Patroness of the Kingdom of New Mexico and its villa of Santa Fe before and after the Reconquest, a patronage which was renewed in 1770. See Fray Angélico Chávez, *Our Lady of the Conquest* (Santa Fe, 1948). Since the choice of any of these celestial patrons probably was made without the requisite formalities, Domínguez' observation that there was no formal "sworn" patron saint is correct.

account of my visitation of the body of the Custody can be read with understanding, because a knowledge of its division into branches, the number of missions, the distances between the first and the last one in each branch, and of the Río del Norte and its course and other details about it [is indispensable]. Since this river is mentioned for different reasons almost at every step (as will be seen), it cannot but arouse curiosity and a desire to know more about it. Finally, I point out that although I began, carried on, and finished the visitation as suited my convenience (as will be noted from the dates of the writs of visitation), the narrative is in consecutive order as follows.

INTRODUCCION.

La Provincia del S. Evang. de Franciscanos Observantes de Nueva España, tiene en el Reyno del Nuevo-Mexico, y à su cargo la Custodia de la Conversion de S. Pablo, la qual tiene dos ramos, uno menor en el Paso del Rio del Norte, y otro mayor en lo interior de dho Reyno. El ramo del Paso consta de una Villa de Españoles, y quatro Pueblos de Indios: y asi la Villa, como los Pueblos estan amparados de dho Rio, fundado todo por la vandas que de este Rio corresponde al Occidente: y ai de distancia desde essa Villa al ultimo Pueblo aguas abajo de diez à doce leguas.

THE OPENING LINES OF DOMINGUEZ' DESCRIPTION OF NEW MEXICO,
IN THE HANDWRITING OF FRAY ANDRES CLARAMONTE

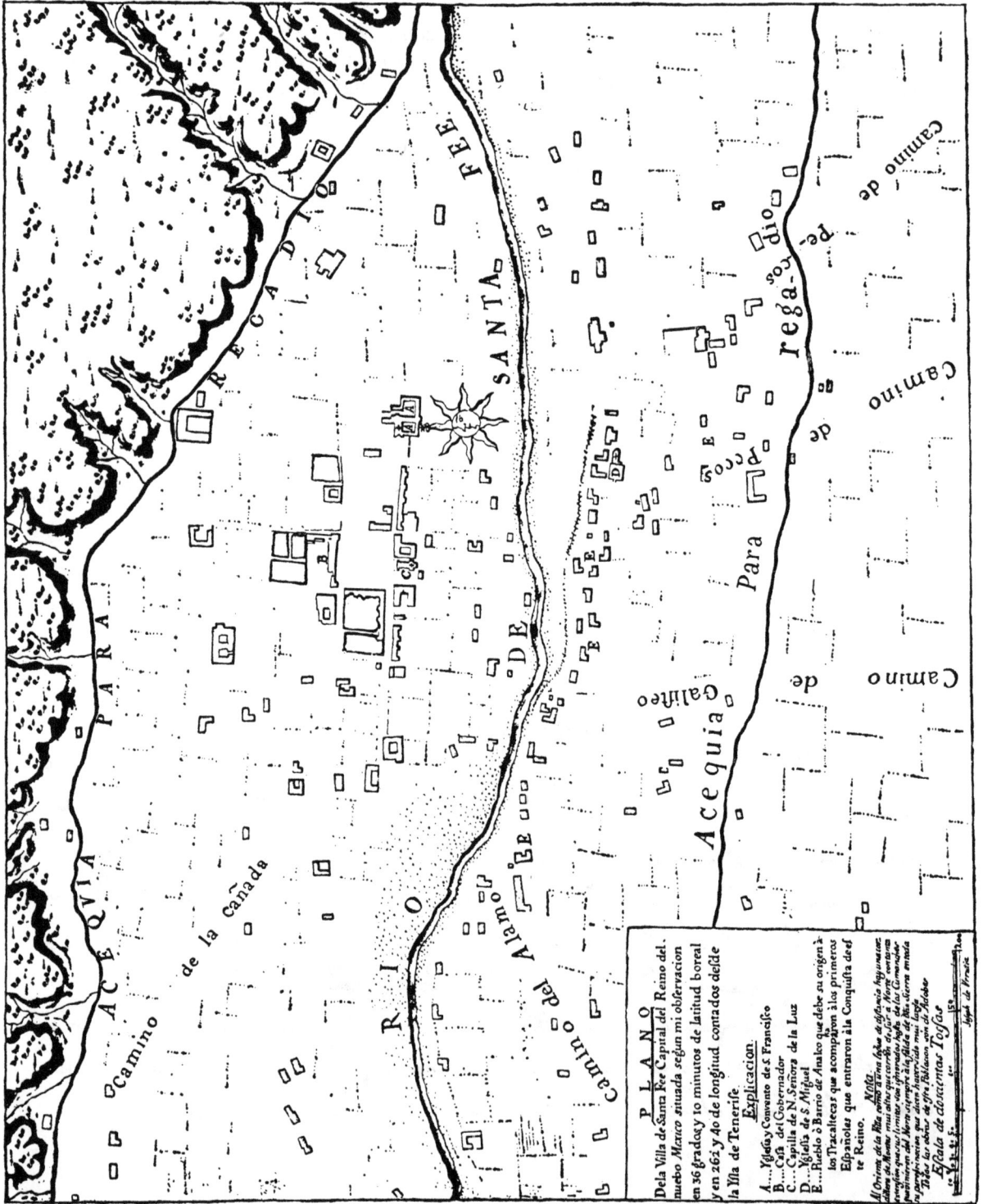

ACEQUIA PARA RECADIO

Camino de la cañada

ACEQUIA PARA

Camino de la cañada

RIO DE SANTA FEE

Camino del Alamo

Acequia Para Pecos Galileo

Camino de

Camino de Pecos

Camino de regadio

PLANO
De la Villa de Santa Fee Capital del Reino del
nuebo Mexico situada segun mi observacion
en 36 grados y 10 minutos de latitud boreal
y en 261 y 40 de longitud contados desde
la Ysla de Tenerife.

Explicacion.

A... Yglesia y Convento de S Francisco
B.... Casa del Gobernador
C.... Capilla de N. Señora de la Luz
D.... Yglesia de S Miguel
E.... Pueblo ò Barrio de Analco que debe su origen à
los Tlaxcaltecas que acompañaron à los primeros
Españoles que entraron à la Conquista de es
te Reino.

Nota.

Escala de doscientas Toesas

PLAN

of the Villa of Santa Fe, Capital of the Kingdom of New Mexico, situated according to my observation at 36 degrees and 10 minutes north latitude and 262° and 40′ longitude, reckoned from the Island of Tenerife.

Legend

A.   *Church and Convent of St. Francis*

B.   *House of the Governor*

C.   *Chapel of Our Lady of Light*

D.   *Church of St. Michael*

E.   *Pueblo or Suburb of Analco which owes its origin to the Tlascalans who accompanied the first Spaniards who entered in the Conquest of this Kingdom.* [*See n. 2, p. 304 infra.*]

Note

To the east of the Villa, about a league distant, there is a chain of very high forested mountains which reach so far from south to north that its limits are unknown even to the Comanches, who came from the north, ever along the base of said sierra during their entire migration, which they say was very long.

All the buildings of this place are of adobes.

Scale of two hundred toises.

Joseph de Urrutia

[*C. 1766-68*]

II. THE CENTER & CAPITAL OF THE KINGDOM

Villa of Santa Fe

This is the capital of the kingdom and as such the seat of political and military government and of a royal presidio. It is about 700 leagues to the north of the great city of Mexico, the delightful and alluring cradle of my birth, for which no praise is ever adequate. The latitude is 36°11′ north and the longitude 271°.[1] It is established and located on a very beautiful site which lies at the foot of a sierra (it is called the Sierra Madre here) which is to the east of this villa and not very far from it.[2] The view to the north, west, and south is open. I begin my description with the

CHURCH

It is almost in the center of the villa, and its titular patron is Our Seraphic Father St. Francis.[3] It has adobe walls more than a vara thick, and the main door faces west. It is 44 varas long from the door to the high altar, 9 varas wide, and 10 high to the bed molding.[4] It has a regular transept; this occupies 6 varas of the 44, and is 15 varas wide and 11 long varas high, for across the church at the mouth of the nave a clerestory rises to light the transept and the sanctuary. The approach to the sanctuary consists of three steps made of wrought beams[5] (which occupy about a vara of the floor of the transept) and another beam level with the sanctuary floor, and this ascent is about a vara high. The upper end of the sanctuary is as high as the transept, and the difference in height at the back can be gathered from the height of the floor. It is in the form of a square 6 varas wide and 6 varas long, so it is not as wide as the nave of the church. There is no vaulted arch in the sanctuary, but the substitute for it will be seen later.[6]

This church has a choir loft in the usual place which occupies the full width and projects 5 varas into the nave.[7] It is supported by fourteen wrought beams which rest on a thick wrought and corbeled cross timber embedded in the side walls. It is about 7 varas above the floor of the church, and the height from its floor corresponds to the remainder of the 10 varas from the floor

of the church to the bed molding. The choir loft has a balustrade, or railing, more than a vara high. The entrance is below it near a corner, like a trap door, reached by a ladder inside the church. Its furniture, or adornment, is the entire absence of any, for there is not even a bench for the singers. The floor

1. Undoubtedly Domínguez obtained these figures from Don Bernardo Miera y Pacheco, the soldier-cartographer who accompanied him and Father Vélez de Escalante on their famous expedition into Utah. Although the figures are not exact, they are reasonably close. The latitude of Santa Fe is 35° 41′ 11″ N. A number of prime meridians were used in the eighteenth century. Miera apparently made his computations from Tenerife Peak, about 17° west of Greenwich, the prime meridian almost universally used today. Counting eastward to Santa Fe, we obtain approximately 271° E longitude from Tenerife. In 1782, Father Morfi, most of whose data for his *Description of New Mexico* was assembled for him by Vélez de Escalante, stated that "New Mexico extends from this kingdom [of Nueva Vizcaya] from thirty-four degrees to thirty-seven degrees, thirty minutes northern latitude. By careful calculation [it extends] from two hundred and sixty-eight degrees to two hundred and seventy-two of longitude computed from the meridian of Tenerife, although both are liable to many errors because the longitudes have not been observed and because the instruments with which latitude has been taken, up to now, do not inspire confidence in the observations." A. B. Thomas, *Forgotten frontiers* (Norman, 1932), p. 87. The undated plan of Santa Fe by Joseph de Urrutia (British Museum, Add. Ms. 17.622) reproduced on p. 10 *supra*, gives the latitude as 36° 10′ and the longitude from the Island of Tenerife as 262° 40′. This plan usually is assigned to the late eighteenth century. It actually was made about 1766-68. In those years Lieutenant Urrutia accompanied Captain Nicolás de Lafora, cartographer of the Marqués de Rubí for the latter's inspection of the presidios on the northern frontier. He assisted Lafora with his map of the northern frontier and also made a number of maps of presidios and villas. See N. de Lafora, *Relación del viaje que hizo a los Presidios Internos situados en la frontera de la América Septentrional perteneciente al Rey de España. Con un liminar bibliográfico y acotaciones por Vito Alessio Robles* (Mexico, 1939), pp.

12, 17, 98; W. Lowery, *The Lowery Collection, a descriptive list of maps of the Spanish possessions within the present limits of the United States, 1502-1820* (Washington, 1912), pp. 347-48; P. Torres Lanzas, *Relación descriptiva de los mapas, planos, &, de México y Floridas existentes en el Archivo General de Indias* (Sevilla, 1900), 1: 174-75.

2. The name "Sangre de Cristo" appears to be of later date. Cf. GLOSS., Blood of Christ.

3. This church was at the site of the pre-Revolt parish church destroyed by the Indians in 1680. Begun in 1714, remnants of it survive in the present cathedral built in the nineteenth century. These are the north Conquistadora chapel, the sacristy, and the sanctuary directly behind the rear cathedral wall. See GK, pp. 100-01; Chávez, "Santa Fe church and convent sites in the seventeenth and eighteenth centuries," NMHR, 24 (1949): 85-93. As L. B. Bloom pointed out in 1945 (NMHR, 20: 108, 187), both the civil and ecclesiastical documents of the colonial period invariably refer to Santa Fe simply as "Santa Fe" or "la villa de Santa Fe." The erroneous belief that the original complete name was "La Villa Real de la Santa Fe de San Francisco de Assisi," or some variant of this, stems from Twitchell, W. W. H. Davis, and Josiah Gregg, who jumped to this conclusion because the parish church was known as San Francisco, although St. Francis did not become the patron until after the Reconquest. Cf. n. 7, p. 8 *supra*. In accordance with correct Spanish practice, "Fe" carries no accent.

4. "The bed moldings underneath the corbel courses of the roof, and upon which the corbels rest, are wooden poles carved usually with a rope motive derived from the Franciscan cord symbolizing the vow of chastity . . . [They] serve more than a plastic purpose; they seem also to strengthen the wall courses at the point of greatest load." GK, p. 63.

5. "Vigas labradas." The Spanish verb *labrar* has wide application and in this connection can mean any treatment of the rough timber to make it more suitable for its purpose, from dressing, hewing, or squaring it, to carving it.

6. "Arco toral." See GK, pp. 38-39, 63, for discussion of reasons for the avoidance of arches and domes in New Mexico mission architecture.

7. In New Mexico mission churches the choir loft was a gallery across the nave at the façade.

is bare earth packed down like mud. This is the usual floor throughout these regions.

This church has three windows on the Epistle side. All are more than a vara square with reveals splayed to the inside and outside on three sides, that is, at the bottom and on either side, for they did not know how to arrange the lintels at the top. They are in the center of the wall. They have wooden gratings. They look to the south over the flat roof of the cloisters, and one is in the end wall of the transept which faces in this direction and the other two back in the nave. Toward the middle of the wall of the choir loft there is a window door to a balcony which we will describe below.

The nave of the church is roofed by thirty-five wrought beams with multiple corbels. The one opposite the sanctuary is the place where the clerestory, which I mentioned in the beginning when describing the transept, rises. The roof of the transept consists of nineteen beams. Although they are round, they are quite new and have been planed by a carpenter. They rest on the old multiple corbels. They run at right angles to the beams in the church, and for this reason there are three beams joined together over the mouth of the sanctuary to support the weight of the beams in the transept which end there. The foremost of these three joined beams has multiple corbels, and this is what serves as the substitute for the vaulted arch[8] which I mentioned above when I was describing the sanctuary. The sanctuary roof has ten beams like those of the church across its width.

The door of this church is squared,[9] and a strong wooden frame takes the place of masonry. It is up to 5 varas high by 3 wide. It has two paneled leaves, each with a wicket, and a latch and keys. Immediately inside is a paneled wooden vestibule 6 varas high, 4 wide, and 1½ deep. In the center it has a

double-leaved door with a latch. This door is high enough and wide enough to permit the passage of processions. As we enter this vestibule, there is an ordinary postern door to the right. The whole floor of the church, such as it is, is carefully covered with planks.[10]

Now that we have seen what amounts to the hull of the church, we shall describe its exterior. Two thick buttresses about two varas square jut from the outside front corners and extend toward the main door in the center. Where they join the façade near the door they form two tower buttresses, upon each of which is a little square turret continuing up from the façade. Each of these has four arches with balustrades embedded in them. In the one on the corner on the Epistle side there are three fairly large bells and a little one. All are cracked (like many in most of these missions because of the extreme cold).

From tower buttress to tower buttress and above the main door is a balcony (which was mentioned in connection with the choir loft). It consists of fourteen projecting corbels with a wooden balustrade, and its area is that compassed by the distance between the tower buttresses and the wall already mentioned. Over this balcony, and quite high, is its roof, or jacal,[11] of the same construction and form as its floor. From this

8. In Domínguez' mind, the arching line of opposite tiers of corbels approaching each other simulated an arch.

9. Not arched. Domínguez' eye expected to find the arch of dressed stone common in southern colonial churches and was disturbed by straight planes.

10. Most of the churches in New Mexico had earthen floors.

11. Nahuatl, *xacalli.* In Mexico the word usually refers to an adobe hut with a thatched roof or to a hut of upright posts or interwoven wattles packed with mud. Here the ceiling and roof are evidently of wattled construction, which still is found in old Pueblo Indian homes and in sections of the older missions, with thin branches or osier twigs laid over the vigas and packed with mud. "The meaning of the term 'jacal' varied geographically. In the Spanish southwest, particularly in Texas, the term was applied to palisaded construction." G. Kubler, *Mexican architecture of the sixteenth century* (New Haven, 1948), 1: 175n.

balcony all the view the villa has to offer to the north, south, and west can be easily surveyed.

The cemetery projects a proportionate distance from the outside corners of the church, measuring 45 varas from north to south and 38 from east to west. It is surrounded by an adobe wall about two-thirds of a vara thick and not quite 3 varas high. It has two gates, one on the south and the other on the west. Around the inside against the wall, or fence, there are nine little adobe tables like altars at regular intervals. Above each is a small adobe niche, or shrine, in the form of an arch, each holding a wooden cross for the *Via Crucis*. At the side where this cemetery projects from the corner on the Gospel side is a little door to the burial ground.[12] This runs 20 varas along the outside of the nave of the church and is 12 varas wide from the outside wall of the church on the same side, so that it is overshadowed by a very high adobe wall. The settlers and the father shared the cost of construction.

At the side where this cemetery reaches the corner on the Epistle side, the first thing is the baptistery, the entrance to which is under the choir loft immediately to the right as we enter the church. This, then, is a room joined to the church on the outside at the corner which we have just described. It is 6 varas square and 4 high, and has seven round

beams. The door has two leaves and is $2\frac{1}{2}$ varas high and not quite 2 varas wide. The latch is on the outside in the nave of the church. In the middle of this room is a square balustrade with a gate to match, and in the center a small adobe column to hold the baptismal font. The font is large, with a cover but no lock, and it is lined with soldered copper. Behind this baptistery is the porter's lodge,[13] which will be discussed later, for now the adornment of the church demands our attention. Its interior may not be cheerful, but it is not gloomy either.

HIGH ALTAR: The altar screen is of the kind of wood common in this kingdom, which is fir,[14] or pine. Although it is not gilded and burnished, it is nevertheless reasonably ornamental as things go in this kingdom, for it is all painted green in tempera and oil and to simulate jasper in places. There are cornices and little pilasters all painted green with gilt veins. It is in two harmonious sections, and although it does not reach the top, it begins at the floor on a base of joined panels more than a vara high and prettily jasperized. These terminate in a cornice which extends to the lateral walls

12. "Campo Santo." See GLOSS., Cemetery.

13. "Portería." The main entrance and vestibule, or entrance court, to separate the outer door from the interior rooms and serve as a reception room. In New Mexico it usually took the form of an open or semi-enclosed portico with pillars at the front. GK (pp. 73-76) suggested that these might be "open chapels."

14. "Pinabete." Used in New Mexico to refer to all long-needled pines.

and holds the altar screen. The first section has three niches with jasperized interiors, and the borders of the arches are outlined and painted in green and gold. Beneath the center niche is the tabernacle, as is customary on altar screens. The one they have has a little door with a lock and key, and an oil painting of the Holy Face (commonly called Veronica), and an ordinary veil. Within this tabernacle are an altar stone, corporals, and a little curtain.

The center niche in the first section is wider than those on either side. In it is a pretty carved wooden image[15] of Our Lady of the Pillar [of Saragossa] two-thirds of a vara high, not counting the pillar, which is about half a vara high. The niche on the Gospel side holds a very nice Our Father St. Dominic, and the niche on the Epistle side holds a St. John Capistran with a crucifix in his hand and a heretic at his feet. Although the latter is not very pretty, it is not ugly. These two saints are carved and about a vara and a half high, and both belong to the Confraternity of Our Lady of the Rosary.

The second section has a niche in the center decorated like those below. In it is an Our Father St. Francis all carved in wood and about a vara and a half high. On the right is an oil painting on canvas of St. Joseph, and on the left a similar oil painting of St. Didacus. Above, to crown the whole, is a small oil painting of Our Lady of Guadalupe in a triangular jasperized wood frame. The cornice at the top has four large pear-shaped ornaments spaced to correspond to the little pillars and painted like the altar screen.

The altar table is of wood, movable and strong, with a gradin of the same material

carved in half relief and painted mother-of-pearl in tempera. On this are six candlesticks of gilded wood, six little branches of small paper leaves curved like the rainbow, and in the center a medium-sized lacquer crucifix. The altar is always vested in its cloth, pall,[16] and a lacquered framework frontal embossed with paste, painted in oil, and gilded to highlight the contrast between the painted and embossed parts. In the center is a small oval with St. Philip Neri. Other permanent fixtures are a small wooden missal stand, two little bells, and a rather large frieze carpet. The sanctuary is closed in by a turreted balustrade with a gate, and the processional candleholders, which are of gilded wood, stand on this as on pedestals. In addition there are three armchairs in the sanctuary, upholstered in green satin, very old and torn, and a wheel of little bells.

TRANSEPT: There are two altars in the transept, one on the Gospel side and the other on the Epistle side, but they are not at the end walls facing each other, but against the walls that face the nave. The one on the right, or Gospel, side[17] is dedicated to Our Lady of Guadalupe. The little altar screen is 3½ varas high from the altar table up and ends in an arc. It is quite new, all gilded and carved, with a proper small tabernacle. It has six little oil paintings on canvas, three below, of which the center one is that of the appellation of the altar, and three above.[18] Over this little side altar is a framework like a canopy, covered with green satin with a valance of the same material, and now old. The altar table is wood,

15. "Imagen . . . de talla." Colonial descriptions usually make a distinction between images "de bulto" and the more specific "de talla." *Bulto* can refer to any image in the round, however made, but those so described usually were dressed in actual clothing. *Talla* refers to works completely carved in wood or stone.

16. "Palia." Here probably an altar dust cover. See GLOSS., Pall.

17. Domínguez is facing the nave. Whenever he mentions the Gospel, Epistle, right, or left side, etc., it is advisable to determine where he is standing. He does not always describe buildings or places from a fixed place or direction. See GLOSS., Epistle side, Gospel side.

18. One picture showed the image of Our Lady of Guadalupe; the other five doubtless depicted her apparitions. See GLOSS.

vested in cloths, etc., with dais and carpet.

The altar on the other side is of St. Anthony of Padua, with an altar piece like the foregoing. The only difference is that the patron saint is very nicely carved in wood. It has a canopy like that of its counterpart, and the altar table, which is wooden, is vested with what is necessary, including dais and carpet. These two side altars were presented by Don Bernardino Bustamante and his wife, Doña Feliciana Coca. The aforesaid benefactor is captain of the Presidio of Goajoquilla, and years ago when he was stationed in this kingdom with the same office, he married the aforesaid lady.[19] These little side altars were made in Mexico City (that is why they are so attractive and seemly). These gentlefolk, through their attorney, paid the expenses of installing them from beginning to end, including manufacture, transportation, etc.

On the wall opposite the altar of Our Lady of Guadalupe and toward the mouth of the nave of the church is the lord governor's seat.[20] This is an armchair (it belongs to the government, but I mention what is there) of fine wood upholstered in crimson velvet with galloon and fringe of fine gold, all affixed by nails of gilt metal. The cushion matches the chair, with tassels at the corners. The whole thing stands on a little dais facing the high altar. On the wall above is a picture of the King (it looks more like a portrait of the first St. Louis) painted in oils

on canvas, but so old that in addition to lacking a stretcher it is now breaking out in scabs like smallpox.

NAVE OF THE CHURCH: There are four altars in the nave, two on each side. The first one on the Gospel side is dedicated to St. Michael and is furnished with a rather large oil painting on canvas in perspective. Its composition, or design, represents the following: A St. Michael in the center, Purgatory below, and the Most Holy Trinity in glory above; on either side of St. Michael are our fathers St. Francis and St. Dominic and other saints taking souls from Purgatory to Heaven. This canvas is almost new, and the donor is not mentioned. The table of this altar is of wood and vested like the above, although it is all in a mess. There is a dais and carpet.

The second altar on the side of which I am speaking is about 3 varas below the aforesaid. It is dedicated to Our Father St. Francis and belongs to the Third Order. Its furnishings consist of a clothed image in the round of Our Father [St. Francis][21] a vara and a half high, an Our Father St. Dominic just like Our Father [St. Francis], another tiny Our Father, also clothed, a tiny St. Louis, King [of France], carved in wood, and five large paintings on buffalo skin, which they call white elkskin here. (When I mention paintings on elkskin elsewhere, it should be understood that reference is made to the same kind of thing described here.)[22] They depict various saints in tempera. The altar table is like those previously described down to the carpet.

The first altar on the Epistle side is dedicated to Our Lady of Light. Its furnishings consist of a little oil painting on canvas of Our Lady of Light about a vara high placed

---

19. The presidio of Nuestra Señora de las Caldas of Goajoquilla was founded in 1752. Alessio Robles locates it at the present Ciudad Jiménez, Chihuahua. P. Tamarón y Romeral, *Demostración del vastísimo obispado de la Nueva Vizcaya, 1765. Con una introducción bibliográfica y acotaciones por Vito Alessio Robles* (Mexico, 1937), pp. 122, 126; N. de Lafora, *Relación del viaje que hizo a los presidios internos... Con un liminar bibliográfico y acotaciones por Vito Alessio Robles* (Mexico, 1939), p. 65. For Bustamante and his wife, see SETTLERS.

20. The governor's traditional throne in the north transept on the Gospel side. AB-1634 (p. 129) describes its use at the reception of Father Benavides in 1626.

21. "Un Nuestro Padre de bulto vestido." See n. 15 *supra*.

22. In view of this comment, *anta blanca* will be translated buffalo skin when it refers to paintings. It is interesting to note that JS defines *anta* as "a sort of Buffalo." Domínguez' reference is to the American bison.

in a small arch in the wall with a little curtain of old silk. Arranged about it at regular
intervals are eleven little paintings of saints,
some in oils and others in tempera on buffalo skin. Most of these belong to the Confraternity of the Rosary. The table of this
altar is exactly like those mentioned above.

The second altar on this side is about
3 varas below the aforesaid and embedded
in an arch in the wall. It is a Holy Sepulcher and belongs to the Confraternity of
the Rosary. It is furnished with a Holy Sepulcher in a casket of ordinary wood painted
in ochre mixed with oil and not otherwise
adorned, a clothed image in the round
of Jesús Nazareno, and a medium-sized
clothed image in the round of Our Lady of
Solitude. The table of this altar is like the
rest.

The pulpit is in the usual place.[23] It is of
ordinary wood on a base, or pillar, of the
same material not too badly carved. Its rostrum is octagonal with the angles profiled
and the centers of the panels on the eight
sides carved in half relief. It is all painted
green, partly in oil. The sounding board
matches it, and it is all very pretty, subject
to the limitations of the region. This pulpit
was formerly approached from the church,
but now one goes from the sanctuary

through the sacristy[24] and cloister (as we
shall see later) to reach the church and enter the pulpit by a balustrade of unpainted
boards like the balustrade of the pulpit in
the Convento Grande of Mexico City.
Father Zarte designed this. There are four
confessionals in the nave of the church, two
on each side. They are very rude. Six
benches are arranged in the same way, and
they are as well finished as the confessionals.

THIRD ORDER

While I am discussing the church it will
be well to recount its affiliates. Since our
Third Order is so closely connected with it,
let it come first. Its establishment in this
church doubtless dates back to the early
days of the conquest of the kingdom, and
it has here the altar mentioned in the description of the altars in the nave of the
church, but nothing else, for it borrows
what is necessary to celebrate its feasts. The
body of this Order is composed of members
so dry that all its juice consists chiefly of
misfortunes.

ITS FEASTS: Annually, St. Louis, King
[of France], with vespers, procession, Mass,
and sermon. The Anniversary of the deceased brethren with office of the dead, Mass,
and responsory. In some years they are ac-
customed to observe two more; they are the
Blood of Christ, with Mass, sermon, and
procession, and the procession of the Three
Falls with sermon. Monthly on their Sunday, Mass and procession.

ITS EXPENDITURES AND RECEIPTS: This
Third Order has no books in which any of
this is recorded. The fullest account is of
expenditures and it is based on the opinion
of a good man. For the feast of St. Louis,
50 pesos in kind, such as chile, onions, and
similar things. For the Anniversary of the

23. In his functional analysis of the Franciscan
buildings, Montgomery states: "Although there are
no ecclesiastical prohibitions as to pulpit location,
custom and precedent prescribe the Gospel side.
This would apply particularly in the smaller *Custodia* churches without transepts..." R. G. Montgomery, W. Smith, and J. O. Brew, *Franciscan
Awatovi* (Cambridge, Mass., 1949), pp. 195-96.
Nevertheless, Domínguez states here that the pulpit
is in "the usual place," and it is clear that it is on
the Epistle side. The "custom," indeed, seems to be
honored as much in the breach as the observance.
Parish churches in Europe and America often have
the pulpit on the Epistle side, sometimes towards
the middle of the nave. The old New Mexico
churches that still keep their ancient pulpits have
them on the Epistle side, *e.g.*, San Felipe, Zia, Laguna, Isleta, old Santa Clara (photo of destroyed
church), Trampas, and even Guadalupe del Paso
(Ciudad Juárez).

24. This entrance from the sacristy, walled up
since the new cathedral sanctuary was built in 1895,
is in a small chalice closet of the sacristy and could
be seen some eight years ago, before the interior of
the closet was replastered.

[deceased] brothers, 15 pesos of the same sort. For the other feasts (when they are observed), 83 pesos of the same kind for both together. For the monthly Sunday, 6 of the same pesos. I will go into the subject of these pesos in detail in the place I am reserving for miscellaneous information since there has been indirect reference to them in my visitation.[25]

For the present, in order that these pesos may be completely understood, I shall say that they are pesos in name only, for actual coins do not exist; and they weigh as much as the ring of the word. The only sound so many pesos make comes down to the fact that 50 of them may be worth 6 or 8 real ones, and this value is estimated from the effects in which payment is made. I do not make this statement from self-interest but as a curiosity.

Returning to the matter of expenses and receipts, I say that during my visitation I ordered the members of the board of the Third Order to keep account books since this is very necessary. But I have observed that up to now, when I am preparing to make an accounting of my visitation, not a thing has been put in order. Nevertheless the remedy will be applied. In the place reserved for miscellaneous information a certification by the present Chief Brother, Don Miguel de Alini, signed by the members of the board, will be found.

CONFRATERNITY OF
THE BLESSED SACRAMENT

Although the direction of this confraternity is subject to the Sacred Mitre [of Durango], nevertheless, since its administration is in charge of the missionary in this villa, I shall give the relevant information about it. I have discovered no instrument founding it, although I have made a meticulous search. I have also questioned the old people in the kingdom, and no one has any

information.[26] My observations about it will be told elsewhere, for here I confine myself to what pertains to the visitation of the missionary.

Its Feasts: Annually, Corpus Christi and its octave with Mass before the Blessed Sacrament exposed; Ascension of the Lord, vespers and Mass with the Blessed Sacrament exposed; Anniversary of the [deceased] members of the confraternity with office of the dead, Mass, and responsory. Easter procession. And weekly on the Thursdays of the year sung Mass of renewal [of the Eucharist].

Its Expenditures: The majordomo of this confraternity (at present the office is held by one Tomás de Sena) spends for the foregoing: For Corpus Christi with its octave, 40 pesos like those mentioned in connection with the Third Order. For Ascension Day, 15 pesos of the same kind. For the Anniversary [of deceased members], 15 pesos. For Easter, 16 pesos 4 tomines. For each Thursday, 3 pesos. And although these sums (as is inferred, and even definitely known, from the schedule, which will also be recorded in a separate place) should be presented in reales in specie, or their equivalent, the fathers nevertheless resign themselves to accepting what is available for these payments as for all others like poor Franciscans.

25. Cf. pp. 245-46 *infra.*

26. The "cofradías del Santísimo Sacramento" are mentioned in accusations against former governor Juan de Eulate made by Fray Pedro Zambrano, guardian of Galisteo, before Fray Alonso de Benavides as Commissary of the Holy Office on April 20, 1626. Father Zambrano stated that under Eulate's bad influence the settlers had abandoned the confraternities and preferred to gamble in his house. The document also mentions the "cofradía de la Madre de Dios de la Concepción." AGM, tomo 356, f. 278 v. Unlike the Third Order, which was directly under the First Order of Franciscans, these church societies were subject to the bishop's approval and supervision. Early in the eighteenth century this Confraternity of the Blessed Sacrament had been united with that of Our Lady of the Rosary, or La Conquistadora. SANM, 1: no. 860.

Note: The statement about feasts and expenditures for them is absolutely based on the assumption of the confraternity's existence; but coming down to current particulars, the whole thing is in such a state of decline that scarcely the minimum is done. This will be clearly seen from the statement elsewhere, and from a certification by Don Manuel Arteaga, former majordomo of this confraternity. The valuables of this confraternity will be described along with those in the sacristy of the parish church.

DEVOTION OF THE POOR SOULS

Here this devotion is most improperly called a confraternity, and this designation is accepted even by persons of the upper classes. In actual truth it is only a simple devotion, for the exercise of which there is a small legacy at interest, responsible to the Ordinary. That it is a devotion and not a confraternity is evident from the fact that there are no brothers or other characteristics of a confraternity. The exercises of this devotion, then, are for the succor of departed souls in this church with the following

SUFFRAGES: Annually on the sixth or seventh day of November, Anniversary with office of the dead, Mass, and responsory, all with tolling of the bell. On the evening of the same day there is sermon on the poor souls, after which a procession of the Rosary goes forth with vested celebrant. While the procession reciting the Rosary goes through the street, the passing bell tolls. On the first Tuesday of each month, sung Mass and responsory. And for all of the foregoing there are the following

EXPENDITURES: For the Anniversary as described, 15 pesos and the offering of bread, wine, and wax, all of which might amount to 4 pesos, and 3 pesos to the singer. Twenty-five pesos for the sermon. For the Rosary (really a procession), 16 pesos. Eight pesos for each Tuesday of the month and 1 peso

to the singer. These suffrages are now going downhill. A more detailed account will be included elsewhere, since the foregoing suffices as far as the visitation is concerned.[27]

FABRIC AND ITS INCOME

This is paid as follows: [Burials] under the choir loft, 5 pesos; from there to the mouth of the transept, 9 pesos; from there to the steps of the sanctuary, including all the transept, 17 pesos; inside the chapel of the Rosary (which will be described shortly) 25 pesos. Everything is paid in regional pesos, and according to the present majordomo of the fabric, who is Miguel Sandoval (I have proof that he holds this office), they pay the foregoing in little strips of hide, *punche*[28] (which is the local tobacco), chile, onions, and once in a while a fanega of maize. In view of this poor pay, no one wants to accept this position (the present one keeps it because of the father minister's entreaties), for with such bagatelles it is impossible to meet

EXPENDITURES: Twelve bottles of wine a year. Each bottle costs 6 pesos at the cheapest, and 8 pesos or more when dear. Wax, 92 ocote candles a year, 4 to a pound, at 1 peso per candle. For the altar breads, a fanega and a half of wheat, which is worth 6 pesos (4 pesos for the whole fanega and 2 for the half) plus 12 pesos which are given to the woman who makes them for a year. She is called María Domínguez, and she always keeps the iron at her house although it belongs to the mission. Fifty-one pesos a year are given to the sacristan.

In addition to this routine expenditure, the church, sacristy, and chapel of the Rosary (with its sacristy) must be kept in repair.

27. See p. 242 *infra.*
28. "Punchi." For a discussion of the nature of *punche* and its use in New Mexico, see L. A. White, "Punche: Tobacco in New Mexico history," NMHR, 18 (1943): 386-93; L. Kinniard, "The Spanish tobacco monopoly in New Mexico, 1766-67," NMHR, 21 (1946): 328-39.

When repairs are necessary, the workers are unwilling to receive the same kind of payment that the majordomo of the fabric took, but only the most useful objects, not observing fair play as the majordomo did with them when he accepted such objects. The aforesaid must also see to the laundering of the church linen, and he pays for this work; and when he has no funds, he goes begging.

TABLE FEASTS

To show due respect to the government, since this villa is the capital of the kingdom, there are table feasts in this church.[29] They are so called because the governor goes forth at the head of all the soldiers, with banner and drum, and marches from the palace to the church door. There the father minister, vested, meets him, and, sprinkling holy water on him with the aspergillum, conducts him to his seat, which is as I described it when I discussed the transept. These feasts, then, are as follows:

MOVABLE FEASTS: Palm Sunday. Holy Thursday, Friday, and Saturday at the offices only; and the key of the repository is hung about the governor's neck. Ascension of the Lord at vespers, Mass, and nones. Corpus Christi at vespers and Mass. Its octave, at Mass only. Saint's day of our Sovereign, at Mass only. Saint's day of the lord governor, at Mass only.

FIXED FEASTS: *January:* First day, the Circumcision of the Lord, at Mass only. Sixth day, the feast of the Kings [Epiphany], at Mass only. Twenty-fifth day, the Conversion of St. Paul, at vespers and Mass. *February:* Second day, the Purification of Our Lady, at vespers and Mass. *March:* Twenty-fifth day, the Incarnation, at Mass only, with a salvo at the *Incarnatus est.*[30] *July:* Twenty-fifth day, St. James the Apostle, at Mass only. *August:* Fifteenth day, the Assumption of Our Lady, at vespers and Mass. *September:* Eighth day, the Nativity of Our Lady, at vespers and Mass. Fourteenth day, the Exaltation of the Holy Cross, at vespers and Mass. *October:* Fourth day, Our Father St. Francis, at vespers and Mass. The feast of the Rosary at vespers and Mass. *November:* First day, the feast of All Saints, at Mass only. *December:* Eighth day, the Conception of Our Lady, at vespers and Mass. Twelfth day, the Apparition of Our Lady of Guadalupe, at Mass only. Twenty-sixth day, St. Stephen, at Mass only.

On these feasts the garrison fires a salvo at the beginning and end of vespers when there are any; and at the beginning, at the Elevation, and at the end of Mass. At the end of each function the father minister (no longer vested) accompanies the governor to the place where he received him. From

---

29. "Fiestas de tabla." Although New Mexico had no cathedral of its own, because Santa Fe was the capital of the kingdom and the residence of a royal governor, both the secular and ecclesiastical authorities were obliged to celebrate these table feasts with extraordinary observances. In many cathedrals of Spain and the Indies there was a dignitary known as the "canónigo magistral." The precise nature of his duties varied somewhat, but one of them was to preach the sermons on these feasts. The regular clergy also appear to have had some obligations in this respect, for a cedula of Philip IV dated at Madrid, July 17, 1631, directs their prelates to have the religious of their Orders "preach without stipend in the metropolitan churches and cathedrals on Septuagesima Sunday, Sundays, Wednesdays, and Fridays of Lent, and on other table days." *Recopilación de leyes de los Reinos de las Indias*, (5th ed.; Madrid, 1841), Bk. 1, Tit. 14, Law 79. The exact nature of the courtesies due the governor from the Franciscans at such public functions in New Mexico was often a subject of controversy. In Spanish colonial society, matters of precedence and etiquette were always taken with extreme seriousness. Since definite regulations to cover the unusual situation in New Mexico were never formulated, the ecclesiastical and lay authorities found even more occasion than usual to complain when their private notions of the respect and honor justly due them were violated. See AT, pp. 25-26, and SANM, 2: no. 634, for examples of such disagreements in the two decades preceding the Domínguez visitation.

30. The phrase, "and He was made Flesh," in the Nicene Creed, at which all kneel when it is sung at a High Mass.

there the latter marches to his palace[31] in the manner in which he came to the church.

SACRISTY

The sacristy adjoins the church on the Epistle side of the sanctuary and runs east, being 14 varas long, 6 very long ones wide, and 5 high, with twenty round corbeled beams. The door to the cloister is in the corner where the sacristy and cloister are against the church. It has two strong leaves with lock and key. It is about 3 varas high and about 2 wide. At the end, or wall, that faces east there is a large window with a wooden grating. There is a rather large door on the north wall which leads to a room used for old lumber and other things. It runs behind the sanctuary. On this same wall, toward the corner where the principal door to the sacristy is and to the left as we enter it, are some little stairs to a small passage (which exists because the wall of the church is so thick) that leads to the sanctuary. It has a small painted screen toward the sanctuary. The preacher enters and leaves through this little passage (as I said when I was describing the pulpit). This sacristy is dim because it has only the window mentioned.[32]

In the middle of this sacristy is an ordinary table without a cover, and the chalices, missals, cruets, etc., are placed on it. Along the head, or end, wall, below the window mentioned, is a strong table from wall to wall. The vestments are placed on it for vesting. It has six large drawers without lock or handles. In a row upon it are four small crucifixes in the round and the box in which the monstrance is kept. Beneath this table there is a dais which extends its full length, and the whole floor of the sacristy is laid with wood. In this sacristy there are also two chests resembling cellarets with locks, keys, hinges, and handles. Each rests upon a small table. In the drawers of the vesting table, and also in the aforesaid chests, the things pertaining to divine worship are kept. All this is as follows, and what the King gave is noted.[33]

Vestments Belonging to the Church: A complete set of vestments with dalmatics, etc., of red satin with narrow silver galloon. Another set with accessories like the foregoing of white satin and narrow gold galloon; it lacks only the humeral veil and frontal. Another set of black satin, complete like the first, with narrow gold galloon. A separate purple silk cope. Two red damask chasubles with silk galloon; one does not have the appurtenances for the chalice. Four more of white satin with accessories; one has little silver flowers. Another of white lustrine with accessories, in fair condition. Another of green satin with accessories. Another of black satin flowered in gold with narrow

31. The Palace of the Governors, or Casas Reales, believed to have been built in 1610 when Santa Fe was founded, and where the people took refuge during the Indian siege of August, 1680. It was recorded in 1731 that Governor Bustamante "built at his own expense the Casas Reales where the governors reside today." BL, N.M. Originals, Bustamante Residencia, 1731, ff. 79 v., 102 v., 108. This probably means, as was the case with many mission churches, that the entire roof and top tiers of adobes were removed and renewed upon the old walls, a major operation that made the restorers appear like the actual builders to their contemporaries.

32. This is still the main sacristy of the cathedral. The vigas are covered with a ceiling of stamped sheet metal, and a modern skylight in the center supplements the light of the single east window. The ancient corbels on their "Franciscan cord" bed moldings may still be seen. The doorway leading into the old sanctuary (until lately a "Cathedral Museum") is still there. Cf. n. 24 *supra*.

33. This does not imply a direct gift from the King. The phrases "from the King," "the gift of the King," "belonging to the King," etc., mean that the items in question were purchased out of funds provided by the royal treasury for such purposes. In the seventeenth century, each friar going to New Mexico for the first time was assigned a complete set of vestments and other things for use in Divine Worship, as well as all kinds of supplies and tools. See F. V. Scholes, "The supply service of the New Mexican Missions in the seventeenth century," NMHR, 5 (1930): 93-115, 186-210, 386-404.

galloon to match. Another of white damask with narrow silver galloon. Another of purple silk; its only accessory is the burse for the chalice. Two more of purple loose silk, one with narrow silver galloon and the other with blue ribbon; both have accessories. Four frontals of mother-of-pearl satin with silk galloon and fringe. Two more of white satin with silk galloon and fringe. Three more of framework. Of all these, some are on the altars and the rest are in the sacristy. A small cape of mother-of-pearl satin with narrow gold galloon. Two frontals of black baize. Three acolytes' cassocks.

LINEN: Four seemly amices with their ribbons. Six fairly good albs without lace. Eight altar cloths (including those which are on the altars), torn and very old. Five pairs of good double corporals. Several purificators. Three cotton cinctures. A surplice, or cotta. Three more for the acolytes.

SILVER AND OTHER METAL:[34] Two silver chalices with patens and spoons. Three more, with patens and spoons, presented by benefactors. One of these three patens is designated San Juan's. A separate spoon. A middle-sized silver ciborium and a little coffer like a ciborium. Two more ciboria like those mentioned, the gifts of benefactors. A small rayed halo. A pax. A plate and cruets without cover. Another plate with cruets and a little bell, all very good and paid for by benefactors. Two separate patens. A thurible with incense boat and spoon. A wafer box. A baptismal basin. Three little chrismatories for the oils, and they are kept in a little cedar box with a key. A small wide cup with baptismal salt. Thirteen small coins and a ring for arras. A

middle-sized lamp with chains like a censer (it is hanging in the vaulted arch).[35]

The baptismal font in the baptistery as has been said. Six small candlesticks. A holy-water pot with an aspergillum of wood and bristles. Two processional crosses. A hand candle-socket. Three old missals with our [Franciscan] saints. A usable *Manual* by Osorio.[36] The iron for making altar breads as described under fabric, and the keys as mentioned in their respective places.

THINGS BELONGING TO THE CONFRATERNITY OF THE BLESSED SACRAMENT: A white satin chasuble with narrow silver galloon, with accessories. Six cloth humeral veils. A small cape of net over mother-of-pearl ribbed silk. Two veils which Governor Mendinueta[37] gave for the ciborium, one of blue cloth and the other of white cloth. Three cloth cinctures given by the aforesaid gentleman. Three more old cloth ones and one silk one. A blue dossal curtain emboidered in gold and silver for the little throne. A small blue ribbed silk curtain which the aforesaid governor gave for the little throne. Another, of blue and white, which a pious woman gave for the same purpose. A canopy of mother-of-pearl satin with silver fringe which the said gentleman gave. A banner of crimson velvet, now old, with an iron cross. Another of white satin, now old, with a silver cross. Two ordinary mirrors that are on the little throne. The aforesaid gentleman gave one, and his treasurer, Don Mateo Peñaredonda, gave the other.[38] An umbelline which Don Diego

34. "Plata y azófar." Although *azófar* means brass in the strict sense, it is frequently used as a general term to refer to base metals. JS defines it: "Brass, or Copper, for I find it often indifferently us'd for both. From the *Arabick çufar,* Shining. Arabick."

35. Lamp with a glass vase of olive oil kept always burning before an altar where the Eucharist was reserved.

36. Fray Diego Osorio, *Manual para administrar los Santos Sacramentos arreglado al Ritual Romano* (Mexico, 1748).

37. Don Pedro Fermín de Mendinueta, governor of New Mexico, 1767-78.

38. Peñaredonda and Borica were not New Mexico settlers, but members of Governor Mendinueta's staff and household. The first was his secretary; the second, a lieutenant who appears to have been a merchant on the side, for he sold a brand-new vestment to Father Fernández of Abiquiu. SANM, 1: nos. 368, 460, 592, 877; 2: no. 699; AASF, no. 19.

Borica gave. The little throne is of framework with a little gradin to match.

Linen: Brittany alb with lace. A cotta. A cambric hood which the Lord Governor Mendinueta gave.

Silver and other metal: An ordinary silver-gilt monstrance; it is kept in a case made to fit it, as is done with others. A thurible with its appurtenances. Key to the tabernacle for solemn occasions. The cross which was mentioned with the white banner.

Two glass vases to fit into the sanctuary lamp. A little bell. The cross for the crimson banner. Ordinary key to the tabernacle.

CHAPEL OF THE ROSARY

For the sake of order and system, I reserved my description of this chapel for this place. It is, then, on the Gospel side of the main church at the head of the transept, extending beyond it like the Zuleta chapel in the church of our convent in Mexico City.[39] It is of adobes with walls nearly a vara thick. Its door is an arched opening in the wall at the place mentioned, and from there to the wall of the high altar it is 20 varas long, 7 wide, and 9 high. Its beams are on the same level, and there is no clerestory like that in the church. There are twenty-four new round ones (like those in the transept of the church), and they rest on the old corbels. The sanctuary is marked off by two small stairs, and from the upper one it is 4 varas long through the center and as wide as the nave of the chapel. Its choir loft is above the entrance on twelve flying corbels, with a little balustrade, or railing. It is 3 varas deep and as wide as the chapel. The floor is newly laid with wood. The door has two

paneled leaves of proportionate height and width, with a bolt. There are two windows with wooden gratings on the Epistle side spaced at proportionate distances, and they face east. Its furnishings, or adornment, are as follows:

HIGH ALTAR: There is no altar piece, but a large niche resting on a shelf serves the purpose, along with two brackets on either side of the niche to hold two small niches (these and the large one are like shrines). All is painted mother-of-pearl with yellow fillets as if in tempera. In the large niche is an image in the round of Our Lady of the Rosary (or, as others say, of *La Conquistadora*) a vara tall.[40] Although it is old, it has recently been retouched. She has many fine adornments, but as these are always being changed her present finery is not mentioned now. Indeed, the only things she wears constantly are a wig; a small tortoise-shell staff wound about with threads of solid silver and spattered with the same, with a silver-gilt handle; and a silver half-moon at her feet over the dress. Her adornments will all be described later, and thus there will be no confusion with regard to which she is wearing and which she is not, since assuming that she is dressed, she will be wearing some of them, and the rest will be put away except for the things I have just mentioned that she wears constantly.

The niches on the brackets contain little saints in the round. Arranged at regular intervals on the walls of the sanctuary are ten oil paintings on canvas without frames and four on buffalo skin, all large, representing various saints. Between these at equal distances are twenty small canvases. The altar table is of wood and movable. It is vested with the essentials, including dais and carpet, noting that the frontal is made of wood carved in relief and painted like the afore-

---

39. Don Cristóbal Zuleta built a chapel of the Immaculate Conception for the Convento Grande in 1629. It no longer exists. See R. G. Montgomery, et al., *Franciscan Awatovi* (Cambridge, Mass., 1949), pp. 258-61. The outer half of this Conquistadora Chapel now serves as the north chapel of the cathedral.

40. See Chávez, *Our Lady of the Conquest* (Santa Fe, 1948); "La Conquistadora is a Paisana," *El Palacio*, 57: no. 10; *La Conquistadora, the autobiography of an ancient statue* (Paterson, N. J., 1954).

said niches. The interior of this chapel is quite attractive.

NAVE: There are two altars in the nave. The one on the Gospel side is of the Blood of Christ with a very nice large crucifix in the round over a silk dais, now old. At the feet of the Lord is a clothed Mater Dolorosa in the round about a vara high. To one side of this Lady is a middle-sized Lord St. Joseph carved in wood. The altar table is wood and vested like the high altar even to the carpet on the dais. The other altar is on the Epistle side and is of St. John Nepomuk. Father Cuellar erected it, and the titular saint was placed there at his expense. It is carved in wood, about 24 inches high, and is in a niche painted in colors in tempera. Spaced around it as if on an altar piece are six large colored prints. The altar table is wood and vested like the foregoing. The frontal is of painted framework. The said father also bore the expense of the little carpet in addition to that of the saint and his niche and of the prints. The rest belong to this chapel. This altar has a gradin, and on it are a small St. Anthony of Padua carved in wood and two lacquer statues of the Child Jesus. A confraternity entitled the Rosary is founded in connection with this chapel, and I will discuss it as soon as I finish the account of the

SACRISTY: The sacristy[41] is on the Epistle side a little below the sanctuary and runs to the east, being 5 long varas in length, 3½ in width, and the same in height. Its ceiling consists of eight round beams. The door which leads to it is in the chapel. It is an ordinary door with one leaf and no lock. It has a little window with a wooden grating facing east. There are two tables in the sacristy, each with a drawer, two common trunks, and an ordinary box. Each of these three items has a lock, and the belongings of Our Lady of the Rosary are kept in all of

them, as will be related, noting that the confraternity paid the expenses of the fabric.

Vestments: A complete set of new vestments with dalmatics, etc., of white satin with gold galloon. The cost of this was shared by the Confraternity of the Blessed Sacrament and that of the Rosary, and so both use it. Another exactly like the foregoing; the only difference is, it is worn and belongs to the Confraternity of the Rosary alone. Another complete set like those mentioned; it is of white cloth and quite new. Governor Mendinueta gave it to Our Lady of the Rosary. A blue chasuble embroidered in silk, with accessories. Another of white satin with accessories. Two more of mother-of-pearl satin with accessories.

Linen: Eight amices; of these five are old and three usable; one of the latter three is cambric. Three more fine ones that Lord Governor Mendinueta gave. Eight usable cloths; some of these are on the altars. Two more that Lord Governor Mendinueta gave for altar and pulpit. Eight good albs and one old one, all with lace. Three more of fine Brittany that the said gentleman gave. Three cloth cinctures which the said gentleman gave. Everything mentioned as having been given by this gentleman was presented along with the aforesaid cloth vestment and other things that will be noted. Two usable pairs of double corporals. Another which the said gentleman gave. Eighteen palls of various stuffs and colors. Three new cassocks of red cloth with their cottas for the acolytes; these serve the confraternities of the Blessed Sacrament and of the Rosary since they shared the cost.

Silver: A chalice with paten and spoon. A pair of cruets without a plate. Two middle-sized candlesticks. Two more small ones. A candle socket.

Brass: A large brazier. Four middle-sized candlesticks. A small bell. Another tiny one.

Other things: A curtain of plain mother-of-pearl ribbed silk. Another crimson one with gold point lace and braid trimmings

---

41. It no longer exists. The door which led to it now opens to the rear yard of the cathedral.

and silk cords which the Confraternity of the Rosary paid for. An iron rod to hang the curtain over Our Lady's niche when one is used. A canopy of mother-of-pearl silk with gold galloon and fringe. Two red banners, one with a silver cross and the other with a wooden cross. A black banner with an iron cross.

Adornments of Our Lady of the Rosary: Some are to dress her underneath, others for her outer garments, and still others are ornaments. Everything will be set down in order.

Linen: Two good Brittany chemises that her confraternity paid for. Two more that Lord Governor Mendinueta gave; they are cambric with lace. Five pairs of petticoats, consisting of one pair of cambric, two of Brittany, and two of Rouen linen; all five pairs at the confraternity's expense. Two more pairs of cambric which the said gentleman gave with the chemises. Two little cambric tunics which the aforesaid gentleman gave for Our Lady's Child Jesus. Another tunic of the same material for the same Child which the confraternity furnished. Another for another separate Child, and it is of Brittany. Two Brittany sheets and two small pillows which the Confraternity of the Rosary made for the Holy Sepulcher. Although all this linen is kept in the sacristy of this chapel, María Ignacia Salas, Our Lady's sacristan, takes care of it.

Outer garments: A tunic and mantle of white satin with gold galloon. Another tunic and mantle, all of blue cloth of silver with gold trimming, which Lord Governor Mendinueta gave.[42] Another with a mantle of plain mother-of-pearl satin. Two more and their mantles of plain blue ribbed silk. Three more of the aforesaid with contrasting mantles. Another separate tunic of green ribbed silk. Two little tunics for the Child Jesus to match the blue cloth dress,

for the said gentleman gave them together. Two small purple tunics and a little green cape. A small black velvet hat for Our Lady. Three jícaras. A cloth pillow sham which Doña Juana Sáenz de Garviso gave to use as a coverlet for the Holy Sepulcher. The same woman who takes care of the linen takes care of the outer garments.

Jewels: All these are in the care of the majordomo of this confraternity who is (as well as of the Confraternity of the Blessed Sacrament) Tomás de Sena. They are as follows: A curled wig. Silver-gilt crown. Another of silver alone. Two pairs of gold earrings with strands of fine pearls. Another pair of silver gilt with strands of fine pearls. Another of plain silver with strands like those mentioned. Another like it with pearls which Antonia López gave. Some drop earrings with gold hoops which Doña Juana Sáenz Garviso gave. A choker of fine pearls in six strands. Another of six strands which the aforesaid Garviso gave. Another of six strands of fine pearls mixed with black beads. Sixteen strings of fine small pearls which serve as bracelets. Two gold rings with rather poor stones. A gold baby lamb. Two little crosses of gold and one of silver. A bracelet of gilt metal. Nine silver-gilt reliquaries and fourteen plain silver ones. A rosary of silver filigree given by Lugarda Montoya. Three more rosaries with silver links. Another of fine pearls. Two little swaddling bands with various silver trinkets; only four are gold. A silver-gilt nimbus. Another of plain silver. A dagger, all silver, and the handle of another. A small tortoise-shell trunk trimmed with silver. Another of silver alloy inlaid with stones. The half-moon and staff which were mentioned that she wears constantly. Three nine-rayed aureoles of silver gilt and three plain silver ones.

HER CONFRATERNITY: I have had the same difficulty in finding out about the founding of this confraternity that I had with regard to the Confraternity of the

---

42. For this dress, see "Noticias de Juan Candelaria," NMHR, 4 (1929): 296-97.

Blessed Sacrament; and just as I failed in the other case, I was equally unsuccessful in this. Like the other it is dependent on the Sacred Mitre [of Durango], and I shall deal with this one in similar fashion.

Its feasts: Annually: The Purification, with vespers, Mass, and procession. Incarnation of the Lord, Mass and procession. Assumption, with vespers, Mass, and procession. Nativity of Our Lady, vespers, Mass, and procession. Feast of the Rosary, vespers, Mass, and procession. Conception of Our Lady, vespers, Mass, and procession. Anniversary of deceased brethren, office of the dead, Mass, and responsory. Cope service on the afternoon of Good Friday. Monthly: Sung Mass and procession on the Sunday assigned to this confraternity. Weekly: On Mondays, a low Mass with sung responses. Saturdays, sung Mass.

Its expenditures: For the Purification, 16 pesos. For the Incarnation, 16 pesos. For the Assumption, 16 pesos. For Nativity, 16 pesos. For the feast of the Rosary, 16 pesos. For the Conception, 16 pesos. For the Anniversary, 16 pesos. For the ceremony of Good Friday, 16 pesos 4 tomines. For the monthly Sunday, 6 pesos. For each Monday, 3 pesos. For each Saturday, 3 pesos. I do not itemize its receipts, since they pertain to the Mitre. Although it also takes an accounting of the expenditures, I mention them in connection with the missionary friar. With regard to these functions and their alms I refer to the note I made concerning the Confraternity of the Blessed Sacrament, and more extensive comments will be found in a separate place.

CONVENT

When I was speaking of the church, my description of it indicated that the convent is next to it on the Epistle side. Coming down to its construction, I say that it has adobe walls about two-thirds of a vara thick, and, viewing it from the porter's lodge, it forms a square which adjoins the sacristy. Its arrangement is as follows: The porter's lodge begins at the back of the baptistery (as was indicated in the description of the latter). The porter's lodge is a little portico 8 varas long and correspondingly high and wide. It is rather dim. It has seats against the wall, and the door, which gives on the cloister, is in the middle of the center wall. This porter's lodge lies within the cemetery (as I pointed out when I described the latter), for the wall reaches one side of it. This convent was built at Governor Cubero's expense.[43]

Beyond the porter's lodge is a cell, and its inner cell is at an outside corner. Around this corner on the south side there are two cells with inner cells. In the second, which is on an outside corner, is a passage to what I shall describe later. A gallery runs from the corner of this passage to a side wall of the sacristy, and its door (as I said when describing the sacristy) forms a nook between cloister and church. All these rooms are large with good windows, and everything was well designed when it was first built, but the neglect by those who should have taken care of it has left it in such a state that it has been necessary for some careful friars to repair what others have torn down. Father Cuellar renovated the porter's lodge and cloister; another father installed cross timbers to support the beams in the cells; still another furnished new doors with locks.

The cloister of this convent is enclosed. It is square, with eight windows, two in each

43. Don Pedro Rodríguez Cubero, governor of New Mexico, 1697-1703. The original Cubero document is in AASF, 1697, no. 1 [13] and has been translated in Chávez, "Santa Fe church and convent sites in the seventeenth and eighteenth centuries," NMHR, 24 (1949): 85-93. In 1698 Cubero donated additional land to the convent. AASF, 1698, no. 2. Shortly after the Santa Fe parish was secularized, the friars sent copies of these Cubero documents to Durango, and the bishop allowed them to keep title to the convent for the time being. AASF, 1798, no. 21; 1799, nos. 3, 10.

corner, with wooden gratings. It is large, and processions go through it when severe weather or some occurrence prevents their going out through the cemetery. On the wall, or side, of this cloister that is against the church is the door of grace.[44] It stands at the head of the transept opposite the door to the chapel of the Rosary. A little below this door is the entrance to the pulpit, as I mentioned, or noted, in its place.

The aforesaid cloister is dim, even though it has eight windows. The reason for this is probably the little apricot trees in the small patio. As we enter the porter's lodge and turn right toward the corner, there is a little stairway in this cloister with steps of squared beams on an adobe wall. This is the ascent to the new part of the building erected by Father Zarte from the stairway on up. All of this is as follows, and it has an earthen floor like that below.

The stairway has a little landing and turns without a handrail since it is like a tower stair. Its opening at the top resembles a trap door between beams, and it has a little adobe railing like the very many rubble-work walls on flat-roofed outbuildings. From the corner of this stairway to the wall of the church (over the cloister as one would suppose) there is a beautiful portico facing east. It has small wooden balustrades between pillars of the same material. It must be noted that at the corners communication with the flat roofs on the sides is left open so that one may walk around the cloister roof. A little portico also runs to the east from the opening on the right side which faces in that direction.

Three or four paces beyond the mouth of the stairway is the door to the cell. It has two leaves, or doors, and when we enter it we see a handsome salon with two windows to the west. Beyond it is another salon with a balcony over the porter's lodge, and behind this salon, over the baptistery, is an ordinary kitchen, but the entrance is from the portico I have just mentioned. On the left is a small inner cell with a little balcony to the south, and to the left of this inner cell, which is on the corner and faces south, there is another cell. The latter is divided in half by a little board screen to form another small inner cell. All the principal doors of this dwelling have locks. And even though the said apartment is so new (when I reached this convent the finishing touches were just being applied), it is already on the point of falling. The ceiling of the whole new part is the nearest to going, for the beams are not only slender, but they were green when installed.

The little passage hinted at in the description of the cloister leads to a patio with ruined rooms that once served as kitchen, strawlofts, and stables. Today there are only a good stable, a strawloft, and a woodshed, but these rooms are not at hand but some considerable distance away. Here in this old patio is the gate to the burial ground, which faces east. The gate is large, good, strong, and well secured, and it resembles a vestibule. With regard to both the ruined and the new part, because the latter threatens to fall like the rest and needs repairs, I have now left orders for the mission father to exert himself and get on with it.

ITS FURNISHINGS: In the corner room of the new upper apartment there is a cupboard with doors and lock that serves for the archive. A little oil painting on canvas in a gilded frame of Our Lady of Sorrows, all old. Another with a black frame and ordinary glass with a very pretty image of the Blessed Virgin Mary; her title is not ascertainable. A little tablet on which the table feasts are written down. An ordinary table without a drawer. Four crude little arm-

44. Probably called the "puerta de gracias" because the fathers used it as a direct entrance from the refectory to the church for their customary grace after meals before the Blessed Sacrament. This door later served as an entrance from the transept into a south chapel built opposite the Rosary chapel.

less chairs. Two crude armchairs. Another which serves for certain natural functions. A wooden bed with legs like pillars. With the exception of the images, Father Zarte was the benefactor who provided all this. A little crystal vial in a cloth case with a ribbon, which is used for the [holy] oil for the sick; Father Quintana furnished it.

ITS LANDS AND FRUITS: On the side of the convent facing south is a plot with an adobe wall erected by Father Zarte. It runs 274 varas up from the corner of the convent and 172 varas from the wall of the convent. It is irrigated by water (and this is very plentiful) from a little spring that is right there on the east. Many settlers use this water for irrigation, taking it from the same ditch that serves the land I am describing. If wheat is sown, it takes a fanega and a half, which yield 15 fanegas; if maize, about 3 almudes, which usually yield 12 fanegas. The sowing is up to the missionary.

MISSION FATHER

By order of Our Mother the Holy Province, a religious is maintained in this villa for the spiritual succor of the souls there; and by disposition of the Most Excellent Superior Government of Mexico, he does not have a royal allowance but is supported by obventions.[45] The incumbent at the time of my visitation is Father Fray Francisco Zarte, native of Puebla de los Angeles. He is thirty-three years old, has been in the Order fourteen years, and the Custody as a missionary for four. These are divided as follows: a year and some months in the Realito of El Paso, and two years and some months in Santa Fe. He has general faculties issued in Durango and revocable at will.[46]

ADMINISTRATION OF THE MISSION: From what has already been said about the Third Order, confraternities, poor souls, table feasts, and chapels, which I will discuss later (since that will be a better place), one may gather how these things are managed. In addition, I state that he is always busy in the administration, now going out to console the sick, now hearing confessions in the church; daily Mass except when some untoward happening may prevent; doctrinal sermon in the afternoon on Sundays during Lent; *Via Crucis* on the Fridays of Lent. The missionary preaches the sermons, of which there are usually some in addition to those mentioned; other religious preach

45. From the early seventeenth century, when the Spanish authorities decided to maintain New Mexico for the sake of the missions, the Franciscan friars who labored there were supported by the royal treasury. At this period the royal allowance *(real sinodo)* was a fixed annual amount provided for each missionary at a definite list of missions. The number of missions and the number of friars assigned to each (seldom more than two to a mission and usually one) varied somewhat over the years. During the eighteenth century the ecclesiastical revenues at Santa Fe and one or two other Spanish towns increased and were considered sufficient for the support of the ministers stationed at them, so the royal allowance for these was withdrawn. The revenues collected by the Franciscans in addition to their allowances consisted of obventions and first fruits. See GLOSS. The question of the collection of tithes in New Mexico at this period is obscure. By the time of Domínguez' visitation the Franciscans seem to have finally resigned themselves to accepting the jurisdiction of the Bishopric of Durango, although no final legal decision bringing the long controversy to a definite conclusion has been found as yet. Presumably the tithes were administered by the episcopal authorities. See AT, pp. 17-18n, 27-29.

46. "Licencias generales por el tiempo de la voluntad en Durango." Although the regular clergy enjoyed certain privileges and exemptions in the New World, various decrees of the Church Councils, including those of the Mexican Church, required them to have express permission from the Ordinary to hear confessions, preach *extra claustra*, etc. As missionaries and parish priests, the New Mexico Franciscans obtained such faculties from the Bishop of Durango, who usually issued them for the period the friars remained in the province. Cf. F. A. Lorenzana, *Concilios Provinciales Primero, y Segundo . . . 1555, y 1565* (Mexico, 1769), pp. 54-55; M. Galván Rivera, *Concilio III Mexicano, celebrado en México el año de 1585* (Mexico, 1859), pp. 290-91.

others; and those during Lent are gratis.

OBVENTIONS: There is a schedule of these imposed by Don Benito Crespo, a copy of which will be found in a separate place.[47] Although this is prescriptive, the settlers do not abide by it, but expect the missionary to accept what they are willing to give, not paying in accordance with the dispositions of the schedule. For not only do many say, *I bet according to my hand,* but some *show their hands as unwillingly as they bet,*[48] not paying their pledges (this custom of pledging the obvention is usual in these parts, and it leads perniciously to other things that are obvious to the discerning) or not paying them when they fall due, or paying a smaller amount. Others do pay, and this is as follows:

For baptism they offer 3 regional pesos in chile or seeds or something else instead of the customary christening fee. For a marriage between Spaniards, 33 pesos like the foregoing, and they exempt themselves from the arras, although the said schedule lists them. For a marriage between people of the lower classes, 10 or 12 pesos as described, and the arras are omitted. For a burial of Spaniards, 33 pesos of the same kind; in addition to not paying for many items that the

schedule includes and regulates in this regard, they are unwilling for the missionary to omit the Mass. For the burial of the lower classes, 10 pesos. For the burial of a Spanish infant, 16 pesos, or 12. For the same of one of the lower classes, 6 pesos. In all these cases they exempt themselves from the other expenses regulated by the schedule. And since the aforesaid schedule will be examined, I point out that the full amount ordered by it is not paid here. I also point out that the alms for any sermon is 25 pesos of the kind mentioned.

FIRST FRUITS: According to the custom of the kingdom they are paid as follows: When the grain harvest amounts to or exceeds 6 fanegas, each harvester contributes half a fanega of each kind of grain he harvests. If the number of strings of chile, onions, or garlic reaches six, one of each is contributed as first fruits; if none of these come to six, they give what they prudently adjust to their consciences. When the livestock born come to six, one head is for the first fruits, and the wool of one sheep at the time of shearing. Cattle are not included, for this is the custom, but there is usually someone who once in a long while gives a calf as an act of piety.

The foregoing establishes a general rule for what I have to say about the rest of the missions. Coming down to particulars with regard to this villa, I say that the amount the missionary collects is not always the same, varying according to good or bad years, plagues of locust, and the larger or smaller number of those who sow. Nevertheless, at the time I prepared this account of my visitation, I received a statement from the mission father that his first fruits amounted to about 100 fanegas of maize, about 60 of wheat, about 8 all together of various kinds of vegetables. This amount was due to the good year and large number of people who planted, for otherwise there would have been much less, as happened in the year '75

47. See p. 244 *infra.* Bishop Crespo drew up this schedule during his visitation of New Mexico in 1730, in accordance with a royal order of 1725. See AT, pp. 104-05. AASF contains several documents concerning the Crespo schedule: (1730), no. 3, fragment, letter of Don Benito Crespo about the schedule as applied in New Mexico; 1730, no. 2, fragment of broadsheet copy of Crespo schedule; 1731, no. 3, schedule for New Mexico by Crespo, dated Oct. 23; 1760, no. 4, Bishop Tamarón to Vicar Roybal, December 29, commenting on Crespo schedule. In 1813, Father Guerra of Albuquerque made copies (AASF, 1730, nos. 4, 5) of the following items relating to the Crespo schedule: Arancel, Santa Fe, August 22, 1730; Crespo letter, Durango, October 23, 1731; Sánchez de Tagle letter, Durango, July 5, 1753; Tamarón letters, Valle de San Buenaventura, December 29, 1760, Isleta, July 6, 1760.

48. "Como me paro, me pinto, unos pintan tan mal como se paran."

when there were 15 fanegas of maize and everything else was proportionately less.

About 12 strings of chile (I continue to refer to a good year), about 200 onions, a certain amount of other stuff. An official (*primiciero*) is appointed to collect this offering of first fruits, and he brings it in carts or any way he can; and 12 fanegas of grain in wheat and maize are assigned to him in payment if he likes.

His SERVICE AND EXPENDITURES: On these points the religious who serves in the administration of this villa is tied and encircled by the weighty and unavoidable chain of inevitable consequences from inescapable antecedents, because he must spend for necessary service in order not to suffer or perish if he makes no outlay for it. Therefore he has the following service and expense: cook,[49] 12 pesos a month in good merchandise; bell ringer, 6 of the same; girl who makes tortillas, 6 of the same; stableboy, 6 of the same; boy for letters or errands, who is paid according to the journey; and all receive their board. In addition, in summer, 1 peso per fanega for grinding wheat; and in winter when the water freezes and the mills do not work, the one who grinds it by hand is paid amount for amount, that is, a fanega is given for the grinding of a fanega.

How HE ACQUIRES NECESSITIES: [He obtains them] by trading one thing for another. For example, for a sheep, which is worth 2 regional pesos, he gives a vara of Brittany or other linen, or a pound of chocolate, or a pair of shoes, or something else that may be equivalent to the 2 pesos the aforesaid are worth. So according to the number of sheep, an equivalent number of varas of linen, or pounds of chocolate, or a mixture of different commodities sufficient to make up the amount, is given. For half a fanega of wheat or maize, or for a string of chile, each of which is worth 2 pesos, he makes the same kind of exchange, and the same system holds true for everything. To pay the father for Masses they give him 2 pesos for each low Mass and 6 pesos for a sung Mass. This payment is usually made in chile, or something which does not oblige them to give the best, or even the fairly good. Here I interpolate the observation that this is not true of the Masses for the confraternities, for they have so resolved against reason and justice, as is clear if one compares the schedule of fees with the statements about confraternities. All the foregoing reveals how much malice there is; the worst is for the father and the best for themselves. The most disillusioning and fullest account of this will be given in a separate place along with a brief explanation of commerce in these parts and the distribution and use of its pesos.[50]

CONVENT PROVISIONS: This has been prescribed and recorded in the Inventory book of the convent, where there is also a record of the following

WRIT OF VISITATION

Mission of Our Father St. Francis of the Villa of Santa Fe, June 8, 1776. In prosecution of the juridical visitation of this Custody of the Conversion of St. Paul of New Mexico which our Reverend Father Fray Francisco Atanasio Domínguez, one of the appointed preachers[51] in the Convento Grande of Our Father St. Francis in Mexico City and commissary visitor of this aforesaid Custody, is making by order of our Very Reverend Father Minister Provincial Fray Isidro Murillo, he proceeded to examine and did examine this inventory, which faithfully and legally agrees with what ex-

---

49. These cooks were always women, and Domínguez uses the word *cocinera*. For a later New Mexican term, *conventera*, see GLOSS., Convent.

50. See p. 245 *infra*.

51. "Predicador del numero." One of a limited group holding specific appointments as preachers.

ists and was seen during this visitation. However, his Reverend Paternity finds that the rooms of the convent and their furnishings are not recorded, and he therefore orders and commands the present mission father, Fray Francisco Zarte, to make a list of everything, noting clearly and specifically the rooms and furnishings that he has added to this mission at his expense. Thanks for this, for the religious demeanor he has displayed in every way, and for the beautifully harmonious relations he has maintained with the Lord Governor and with his parishioners are given him, and he is enjoined to continue and persevere.

His Reverend Paternity then proceeded to determine the provisions this convent should have and assigned the following to it: 10 fanegas of wheat, 10 of maize, 10 sheep, 10 strings of chile, half a fanega of frijoles, a jar of lard, 2 almudes of salt, 50 onions, 12 tallow candles. Neither the Reverend Custos nor his Vice-Custos can dispense with or omit any of this but only, indeed, add what they may see fit for the benefit of the mission and missionary. At the time he takes over from his predecessor the latter shall take great care to find out whether anything pertaining to the church, sacristy, convent, or provisions is lacking, and also whether the parish books have the number of folios stated in the writ concerning them. And if any of the foregoing is missing, he shall advise the Reverend Custos or his Vice-Custos at once, and they shall have the deficiency made up, for this is the intention of our Reverend Superior Provincial Prelate, who so orders and commands *ratione officii* and therefore validly for all time.

Our Reverend Father Commissary Visitor so provided, ordered, and signed before me, the undersigned secretary, to which I attest. Fray Francisco Atanasio Domínguez, Commissary Visitor. In my presence, Fray José Palacio, secretary.

The parish books were examined and approved, and the corresponding decrees were recorded in them. Their foliation is complete and nearly filled, but new books will be supplied as soon as they are needed.

CHAPEL OF OUR LADY OF LIGHT

Now that we have finished with the church and convent, it will be well to speak of other ecclesiastical matters in so far as the

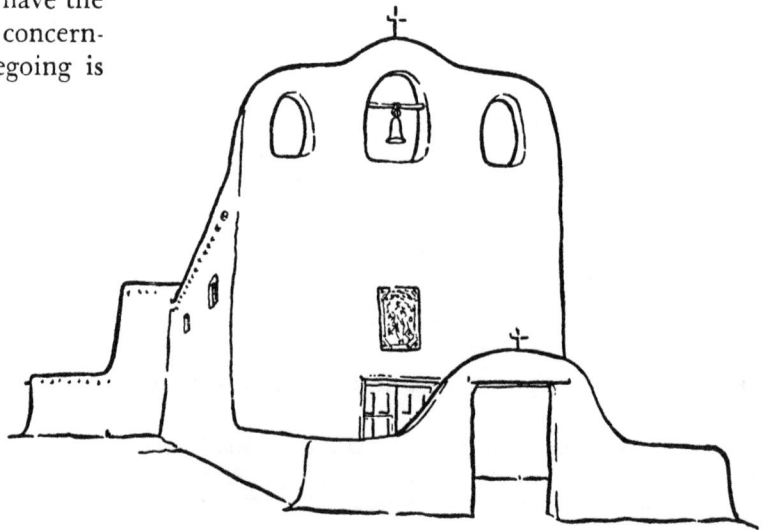

services of the missionary are concerned. We shall deal with this before we say anything about secular matters. Let the chapel mentioned in the heading, then, be first. In the year 1760 Don Francisco Marín del Valle, then governor of this kingdom, displayed the glowing and fervent ardor of his devotion to Our Lady and Mother of Light by his plan to build a chapel for her in this Villa of Santa Fe. For this purpose he bought a site and built the aforesaid chapel on it at his personal cost, solicitude, and expense.[52] I will speak of its dedication and other details elsewhere, for here I merely discuss what is essential because of the services rendered by the missionary and other matters that cannot be omitted because they pertain to his collation.[53]

In relation to our principal church, the location of this chapel is to the west, down the street, and about two musket shots from the west gate of the cemetery. It stands on a block, or side, of the *plaza mayor* of this villa (as will soon be clearer from the description of the plaza) directly opposite the government palace. It has adobe walls about a vara thick. Its door faces due north, and a little above it is a white stone medallion with Our Lady of Light in half relief.[54] At

52. A fragmentary document in AASF (1758), no. 3, concerns the purchase by Governor Marín del Valle and his wife from Jacinto Pineda of a Santa Fe house and lot in order to erect on it a chapel to Our Lady of Light. For history of this church, see E. B. Adams, "The chapel and cofradía of Our Lady of Light in Santa Fe," NMHR, 22 (1947): 327-41; A. von Wuthenau, "The Spanish military chapels in Santa Fe and reredos of Our Lady of Light," NMHR, 10 (1935): 175-94. The Adams article was based in part upon the Domínguez report. Bishop Tamarón also mentions the chapel in his account of his visitation. AT, p. 47. On the basis of Twitchell's erroneous interpretation of a passage from a letter of Governor Otermín to Father Ayeta, describing the siege of Santa Fe by the Indians in 1680, [R. E. Twitchell, *Old Santa Fe* (Santa Fe, 1925), pp. 54, 57-58, 154] von Wuthenau has kept alive the dubious legend of a pre-1680 tower chapel dedicated to Our Lady of Light in the *casas reales*, "the doors of which resisted the attacks of the Indians who attempted to set fire to them during the siege of the palace in 1680." Hackett has translated this passage as follows from AGI, Aud. de Guadalajara, leg. 138: "The Indians were so dexterous and so bold that they came to set fire to the doors of the fortified tower of Nuestra Señora de las Casas Reales, and, seeing such audacity and the manifest risk that we ran of having the casas reales set on fire, I resolved to make a sally into the plaza of the said casas reales with all my available force of soldiers, without any protection, to attempt to prevent the fire which the enemy was trying to set." HS, 1: 101. As Chávez points out ["Santa Fe church and convent sites," NMHR, 24 (1949): 90n] von Wuthenau confuses a chapel which de Vargas arranged in an estufa with a temporary parish church located on the road to Tesuque, outside the town wall. The custos was unwilling to use the estufa chapel because the place had been used for idolatrous rites. J. M. Espinosa,

Crusaders of the Río Grande (Chicago, 1942), pp. 152-54. Von Wuthenau was also misled by Twitchell's unwarranted statement that a military chapel of Nuestra Señora de la Luz was built on the south side of the plaza by Governor Valverde between 1717 and 1722 (*Old Santa Fe*, pp. 50, 154). Governor Valverde did contribute to the building of a chapel at San Ildefonso.

Pál Kelemen has contributed a very interesting study of the iconography of the reredos in "The significance of the stone retable of Cristo Rey," *El Palacio*, 61 (1954): 243-72. In March, 1955, the contemporary buildings on the Castrense site were razed to make way for new commercial construction. Before drastic excavation began, a careful exploration by Bruce Ellis and Stanley Stubbs brought to light the foundations of the old military chapel, and these tally closely with the Domínguez measurements. Indications of a post-1776 rebuilding of the front wall, with added buttresses on either side, corroborate mid-nineteenth century descriptions of the façade. S. A. Stubbs and B. Ellis, *Archaeological investigations at the Chapel of San Miguel and the site of the Castrense, Santa Fe, New Mexico*. (Monographs of the School of American Research, no. 20, 1955).

53. That is, are included in his parish duties. *Colación* usually means benefice, and since the Military Chapel was neither a mission nor a parish church, to the Franciscan chaplain it was a quasi-benefice.

54. Bishop Lamy gave this plaque to the new Academy of Our Lady of Light in 1859. At first it was embedded above the entrance to the Sisters' adobe convent, and later it was removed to the old sanctuary of the parish church, where the great

the very top on the flat roof are three arches, a large one in the center with a good middle-sized bell, and a small one on either side without anything.

From the door to the mouth of the transept it is 24 varas long, 8 wide, and 9½ high up to the bed molding. From the mouth of the transept to the sanctuary there are 7 varas, with 15 in width and 11 in height because of the clerestory which is like that I described in the principal church. The ascent to the sanctuary consists of four octagonal stairs of white stone. The whole sanctuary is tiled with said stone, and there are three sepulchers in it. Its area is 7 varas square, and it is as high as the transept. There is a choir loft across the chapel in the usual place, and it projects 5 varas into the chapel with a balustrade. It rests upon fourteen wrought beams which are supported by a large wrought and corbeled cross timber embedded in the lateral walls.

On the Gospel side there are three windows like those of the principal church. They face east, and one is at the head of the transept and the remaining two are in the nave of the chapel. I have already said that the main door faces north, but I have not mentioned that it is squared, set in a strong wooden frame, has two paneled leaves with a wicket in one, and good locks. It is 3 varas high and correspondingly wide. The cemetery is a little enclosure, or wall, of adobes, more than a vara high, with a gate opposite the chapel door. Its area is that sufficient for a small cemetery.

The ceiling of this chapel is of wrought and corbeled beams on corbels, and there are twenty-eight like this in the body of the chapel. The aforesaid clerestory is on the one which faces the sanctuary. In the transept there are nineteen like the aforesaid

running crosswise from those in the nave. In the sanctuary there are ten exactly like those mentioned, but across the width like those of the nave of the chapel, and a false vaulted arch like that mentioned in the sanctuary of the principal church. The furnishings of this chapel are as follows:

HIGH ALTAR: The altar screen is all of a white stone (about which I will give information in a separate place) very easy to carve.[55] It consists of three sections. In the center of the first, as if enthroned, is an ordinary oil painting on canvas with a painted frame of Our Lady of Light, which was brought from Mexico at the aforesaid Lord Governor Marín's expense.[56] He also provided the curtain it has, which is of crimson damask with silver braid. On the right side of this image is St. Ignatius of Loyola, and on the left St. Francis Solano. Toward the middle of the second section is St. James the Apostle, and beside him, St. Joseph on the right and St. John Nepomuk on the left. The third section has only Our Lady of Valvanera, and the Eternal Father at the top.

All these images, with the exception of Our Lady of Light, are in medallions of the same stone of which the altar screen is made and carved in half relief, painted as is suitable, and this work resembles a copy of the facades which are now used in famous Mexico. The altar table is of wood and vested with cloths, pall, wooden missal stand, and altar card[57] which Father García gave, a bronze crucifix with silver corner plates that Don José Moreno gave, altar stone of the same stone as the altar screen, and a frontal of the same stone carved like the screen, with a little oval of St. Anthony of Padua in the center. There are also six candlesticks of

---

stone reredos also had been taken. When the reredos was installed in the church of Cristo Rey in 1940, this plaque was installed in the central panel, although it does not fit.

55. See p. 60 *infra,* and FRONTIS.

56. This seems to be the framed painting of Our Lady of Light which Bishop Lamy also gave to the Sisters of the Academy in Santa Fe. For years it has hung in the Sisters' reception room.

57. "Palabrero." See GLOSS., Altar card.

rough wood like small holders for wax ta-
pers, dais, and carpet. There is a table in the
sanctuary for the chalice, cruets, etc., an ordinary bench, and two processional candleholders of rough wood.

TRANSEPT: There are two altars on the
walls that face the nave of this chapel. The
one on the right side is dedicated to Our
Lady of the Conception with an oil painting
on canvas with a gilded frame and a white
linen curtain. The one on the left side is
dedicated to St. Francis Xavier with a canvas like that of the Immaculate Conception
in everything except curtain.[58] Both altars
are equipped with what is necessary for the
celebration of Mass. The altar stones of
these altars, and another separate altar
stone, are of stone like the high altar. All
four were consecrated by the Most Illustrious [Bishop] Tamarón, who was in this
kingdom on a visitation at the time this
chapel was under construction. Its interior
is very attractive.

NAVE: The Ecclesiastical Judge Don Santiago Roybal, native of this kingdom, presented the pulpit, which is in the usual
place.[59] It is made of stone like the altar
screen, carved in the same manner, and oc-

tagonal with a little wooden stairway like
many others. The confessional is on the
Gospel side; it is of wood and well made. At
proportionate distances along both sides are
thirteen little oil paintings on canvas that
Don José Reaño and his wife, Doña Ana
Ortiz, gave. One represents Our Lady of
Valvanera, and the others the Twelve Apostles. Two wooden screens given by Doña
Juana Roybal. Two large benches. Stoup
for holy water of the aforesaid stone.

With regard to what I have already said
and still have left to say about this chapel, I
point out that I am not repeating, or making explicit reference to the fact that Lord
Governor Marín was the donor of this or
that, for assuming that he was the prime
mover, it is absolutely clear who probably
gave everything. Therefore I have only specified and shall specify other benefactors.

SACRISTY: The sacristy is on the Gospel
side at the head of the transept. It is a room
7 varas long, 5 wide, and 4 high, with ten
ordinary beams in the ceiling. The window
is on the south side, and the door, which is
ordinary, is in the chapel. There is a table
in it that occupies the whole front and has
four good drawers without locks, although
they do have iron handles. On either side
there is a cupboard with doors and a
wooden cross on top. A little bench, a small
stand for a bowl, four maps and two globes
of the world which Lord Governor Mendinueta gave, a vial for the wine for celebrating Mass, and a clay brazier.

On the aforesaid table are: an image in
the round about 24 inches tall,[60] and it represents Our Lady of Light; a medium-sized
niche containing a small oil painting on
canvas representing the same subject; a
small Lord St. Joseph carved in wood; a
small St. Anthony of Padua carved in wood,
made in Madrid; eight silvered wooden
candlesticks which Don José Moreno gave;
and on the wall two middle-sized mirrors

58. These two paintings, their frames later lacquered white, now hang on either side of the altar
in the Conquistadora chapel.

59. Don Santiago Roybal (or Roibal) was the eldest son of Ignacio de Roybal y Torrado of Caldas
de Reyes near Compostela and of Francisca Gómez
Robledo, a New Mexican of a prominent pre-
Revolt family. He was sent to Mexico City for his
education, and from there the Archbishop sent him
to Bishop Crespo of Durango for ordination. Crespo
used him as an opening wedge to introduce the
secular clergy and episcopal jurisdiction into Franciscan New Mexico by making him his vicar at
Santa Fe. Although the validity of his title was long
in question, Roybal exercised this office from 1730
until his death in 1774, with the exception of a
period as vicar at Guadalupe del Paso from 1733 to
1736. For further details, see Chávez, "El Vicario
Don Santiago Roybal," *El Palacio*, 55: no. 8, pp.
231-52; NMF; AT, pp. 15, 28, 29, 30, 44, 52, 77-78,
79, 104.

60. "De a tres cuartas."

for the use of the priests when vesting which Doña Juana Roybal, the said Moreno's wife, gave. The following things are kept in the table drawers and in the cupboards:

Vestments: A chasuble of mother-of-pearl silver lustrine with galloon to match, with the necessary accessories. Another of black lustrine and silver galloon, with accessories. Another of whitish silver lustrine with gold galloon, with accessories including frontal and pall; Don Juan Francisco Arroniz Riojano gave it.[61] Two humeral veils like the white chasuble. Another of towelling woven in squares which Doña Josefa Bustamante gave. A pall of mother-of-pearl ribbed silk with silver spangles and fringe. A blue and white banner which Don Juan Ortiz gave.

Linen: Two amices of fine Brittany with ribbons and lace. Another that Arroniz gave. Another of cambric which Vicar Don Santiago Roybal gave. Another of Brittany which Vicar Don Lorenzo Rivera[62] gave. Another of Brittany with embroidered corners which Juana Padilla gave. Two albs of fine Brittany like the first amices. Another to match the amice which Arroniz gave. Another like the amice Vicar Rivera gave. Two pairs of double corporals of cambric. Another double pair of Brittany which Arroniz gave. Three silk cinctures. One of cloth which Vicar Rivera gave. Another of cloth which Father Cuellar gave. Another of cotton which Doña Juana Roybal gave. A Chinese carpet embroidered in silk which the aforesaid Moreno gave on account for 100 pesos he owed this chapel.

61. Not a New Mexico settler but an official in Governor Marín del Valle's household.

62. Don José Lorenzo de Rivera was the vicar in Santa Fe in 1775 (Bishop's Pastoral in AASF, Bur-3, Albuquerque), succeeding Roybal who had died the previous year. In this capacity he performed two weddings of prominent citizens at Isleta in May, 1779 (AASF, M-49, Isleta). He might have been a member of a Rivera family then prominent in Santa Fe, but since there is no evidence of a connection, it is more likely that he came from Durango.

Silver and other metal: A silver-gilt chalice with paten and spoon, chased and set with Bohemian stones. A pair of cruets with a little bell and plate just like the chalice except for the stones.

Two ordinary candlesticks and two more which Doña Juana Roybal gave. A small china plate with glass cruets which the aforesaid Moreno gave.

Other things: Three coverlets embroidered in wool which benefactors have presented. Another like those mentioned, which Don Santiago Roybal gave. A new missal with our [Franciscan] saints.

Its CONFRATERNITY: By a legal instrument it is of record that in the aforesaid year of 1760 the Confraternity of Our Lady of Light was founded with all solemnity, since everything took place in the presence of the Lord Bishop Tamarón. The following year, 1761, on the twenty-fourth day of May the chapel was dedicated and inaugurated with all the solemnity conditions in the kingdom at that time permitted. I shall speak of all this in more detail in the appropriate place. It is dependent on the Sacred Mitre [of Durango], but the missionary of this villa has charge of and administers the following

Feasts: All are annual, and the first is May 21, Our Lady of Light, with vespers, Mass, sermon, and procession. Twenty-second day of the same month, Anniversary of deceased brethren, with office of the dead, Mass, and responsory. August 15, Mass and procession with plenary indulgence and remission of all sins conceded by Our Most Holy Father Clement XIII to those who perform the customary obligations. The aforesaid Lord Bishop designated this fifteenth day because His Holiness had conceded it and other favors at the instance of Lord Governor Marín. September 10, Our Lady of Valvanera, with vespers, Mass, and procession.

Its Expenditures: For May 21, 25 pesos in sheep. For the Anniversary, 15 pesos in the same. For August 15, 12 pesos in 6 sheep.

For September 10, 25 pesos in sheep. For the sermon on May 21 the preacher is given 25 pesos in sheep. One arroba of wax per year. About two jugs of wine. And what wine and wax is left over belongs to the confraternity.

Note: Although I am reserving information concerning this chapel and its confraternity for a separate place, by reason of my visitation of the missionary's connection with it, I find it essential to state here that the indulgence of August 15 has been considered a jubilee in this kingdom. As a result, with the knowledge and toleration of the ecclesiastical and secular judges, and of the father ministers (who, out of respect for the aforementioned judges, kept silent, fearful of not finding protection in those who should have upheld their proper zeal) the Most Divine Eucharistic Bread was taken in procession from the parish church to this chapel on the morning of the fifteenth, and such a Sovereign Majesty remained exposed in the chapel until sunset so that the obligations to win the aforesaid indulgence might be performed. Then Our Best Sun, Light, Love, and Life returned in procession to His house, or tabernacle.

I immediately opposed this abuse and illegal practice. After a thorough study of the brief by which our aforesaid Most Holy Father concedes this indulgence (it was issued at Rome on March 22, 1764, and passed upon by the Council, Commissary of the Crusade,[63] and Mitre of Durango) and commits to the lord diocesan bishop the regulation of everything contained in it, I made known to the members of the board of the confraternity that no such jubilee exists and that the Blessed Sacrament should not and would not be exposed on the said day until they showed me a valid license for it. And if there were such a license, now or in future, it would not permit our Sacramental God-Man to leave His tabernacle, but that Mass would be celebrated on the fifteenth in the chapel for the solemn exposition. In the afternoon He would be placed in His tabernacle right there, and would be consumed on the following day at another celebration of Mass. There is no such license, and therefore in order to avoid this unwarranted function, I left a patent containing a superior order for the missionary of this villa, forbidding him to consent to the abuses I specify in it. This will be found in the separate place I have reserved for it.

CHAPEL OF SAN MIGUEL

I made the same effort to find an instrument founding the chapel mentioned in the heading that I did with regard to the confraternities of the Blessed Sacrament and the Rosary, and I found nothing.[64] Never-

63. The Bull granting indulgences known as the Bull of the Crusade (*Santa Cruzada*) was originally conceded to the Spanish monarchs in very early times to subsidize war against infidels, and later for the building and maintenance of churches and other pious purposes.

64. For the past century this chapel has been known as the "Oldest Church in the United States," a claim based originally on the totally discredited myth that Coronado's "Tiguex" of 1540 was at the site of Santa Fe, where some of his men remained to found a town in 1543. Old San Miguel and "The Oldest House in the United States," just north of it, were supposed to be remnants of that Tiguex. Strange how such an unusual settlement of Tlascalans or Spaniards from Coronado's army should have been completely overlooked by the succeeding expeditions of Rodríguez in 1581, Espejo in 1582, and Oñate in 1598. The claims of the early boosters of this legend, like DeFouri and Ritch, were long ago questioned by Read and summarily scorned by Bancroft. Benjamin Read, *Illustrated history of New Mexico* (Santa Fe, 1912), pp. 168-69; H. H. Bancroft, *History of Arizona and New Mexico* (San Francisco, 1889), p. 158n. The great mass of New Mexico documents discovered within the past few decades fully supports these and later historians, but the myth has still been fostered. The first chapel was built some years after the founding of Santa Fe in 1610. In 1640 Governor Luis de Rosas had this Hermita de San Miguel, then used as an infirmary, torn down and the beams carried away, but it is impossible to say whether the building, or buildings, there were completely destroyed at that time. See

theless, I shall not omit the statement that in relation to our parish church this chapel is to the south, in line with it, and more than a musket shot away. It is of adobes, the walls not very thick, single-naved, 8 varas high up to the bed molding, not quite as

ty-one as far as a clerestory like those mentioned elsewhere. The choir loft is across the width of the chapel over the main door on fourteen round beams which rest on a heavy cross timber. Its projection, or depth, is 3½ varas, and it has a balustrade. There

wide, and 23 varas long from the door to the high altar. Its ceiling consists of round beams without corbels, and there are twen-

F. V. Scholes, *Church and State in New Mexico 1610-1650* (Albuquerque, 1937), pp. 138-39, 141, 150, for details about this episode. San Miguel apparently was rebuilt sometime before 1680, when the rebellious Indians burned it. It was built anew in 1710. During the early months of 1955, Stanley Stubbs and Bruce Ellis, of the Laboratory of Anthropology, Santa Fe, thoroughly explored the walls, sanctuary flooring, and timbers of San Miguel. The verdict is that the present four walls of the entire chapel date 1709-10. Stubbs and Ellis, *Archaeological investigations at the Chapel of San Miguel.*

Therefore, on the basis of the historical and archaeological evidence, there is no doubt that the present chapel of San Miguel dates from the eighteenth century and that the surviving seventeenth-century mission churches, especially Isleta and Acoma, have far better claim to the title of the "oldest church." Several eighteenth-century churches, such as Laguna, are also older than San Miguel. Older and different foundations within the present chapel are the only remains of a smaller seventeenth-century San Miguel. The present reredos, cleaned and restored by E. Boyd, disclosed its date, 1798, and its donor, Antonio José Ortiz.

are three windows in this chapel, two on the Epistle side that face south, and one to the west in the choir loft over the main door, which also faces west. The door is squared, set in a wooden frame, has two leaves and no key, but it does have a crossbar. Over the main door is a small arch with a little bell. The cemetery is like the one mentioned at the Chapel of Our Lady of Light. The adornment of this chapel is as follows, and it looks like the granary of an hacienda.

HIGH ALTAR: A St. Michael carved in wood, a vara tall including the pedestal. It stands on an adobe ledge like a pediment. Around it are eight not very large oil paintings on canvas of saints. The altar table is of adobes with an altar stone and an old missal stand. Wooden pulpit and sounding board in the usual place.

SACRISTY: It is on the Gospel[65] side and is a room almost 16 varas long. It runs along the side mentioned and is proportionately

65. The archaeological investigations mentioned in n. 64 *supra* show that there was a room on the

wide and high with twenty beams in the ceiling. Its window to the east, an ordinary one-leaved door into the chapel, another like it to the street, with a key. In it there is an ordinary table with a drawer but no lock of any kind.

Antonio Domínguez takes care of this chapel with the title of majordomo. He has a book recording what belongs to it. Although the said book lists a few things, the following, which the aforesaid keeps in his house, are all that exist.

Vestments: A chasuble of white satin and narrow false galloon, with accessories. A frontal to match the said chasuble. Another of mother-of-pearl frontal. All the aforesaid are extremely old.

Linen: An amice of poor Brittany. Another of Rouen. A Rouen alb. Two Rouen altar cloths. Two Brittany palls embroidered in silk. Another of mother-of-pearl satin with narrow false galloon. A Brittany hand towel. And all old.

Silver: A small nimbus. A little sword, like a dagger, 8 inches long.

Its Feasts: May 8, the Apparition of the Lord Archangel, sung Mass. September 29, vespers and Mass, sometimes a sermon.

Its Expenditures: For May 8, 6 pesos, usually in firewood. For September 29, 25 pesos in woolen stockings and firewood. When some pious person wishes that there

be a sermon he gives 25 pesos to the preacher.

To take care of the cost of wax and other things for the two feasts mentioned, the aforesaid majordomo has two little plots of arable land of 30 varas each, and the expense is met with the harvest they yield, but it should always be understood that the sermon which is usually given is paid for by some pious person.

VILLA

Surely when one hears or reads "Villa of Santa Fe," along with the particulars that it is the capital of the kingdom, the seat of political and military government with a royal presidio, and other details that have come before one's eyes in the perusal of the foregoing, such a vivid and forceful notion or idea must be suggested to the imagination that the reason will seize upon it to form judgments and opinions that it must at least be fairly presentable, if not very good. But as soon as its description is seen, the reason will recognize the fantasy of the imagination and rightly replace it with the true facts. The location, or site, of this villa is as good as I pictured it in the beginning, but its appearance, design, arrangement, and plan do not correspond to its status as a villa nor to the very beautiful plain on which it lies, for it is like a rough stone set in fine metal.

To make my point clearer, take for example a suburb, or quarter, of Mexico City, such as the pueblo of Tlatelolco, which, although a pueblo (a less pretentious title than villa) has the very greatest advantages over this villa; not superficially, as one might suppose, but indeed in its actual appearance, design, arrangement, and plan, for in it there are streets, well-planned houses, shops, fountains; in a word, it has something to lift the spirit by appealing to the senses. This villa is the exact opposite, for in the final analysis it lacks everything.

---

south, or Epistle, side of San Miguel with measurements that match closely those of the sacristy described by Domínguez as being on the Gospel, or north, side. According to Stubbs, the room on the south is "definitely of later construction than the church." The doorway through the church wall and contiguous "sacristy" wall has log lintels. A log on the church side gave a tree-ring date of 1709, which corresponds with the 1709-10 dating of the main portion of the church, while the lintel on the "sacristy" side gave a date of 1714. A closed doorway, also 1710, discovered on the north (or Gospel) wall, near the choir loft, seems too far to the front to have been used as a sacristy entrance. Therefore, it is possible that Domínguez, or his amanuensis, may inadvertently have substituted Gospel for Epistle in locating the sacristy.

Its appearance is mournful because not only are the houses of earth, but they are not adorned by any artifice of brush or construction. To conclude, the Villa of Santa Fe (for the most part) consists of many small ranchos[66] at various distances from one another, with no plan as to their location, for each owner built as he was able, wished to, or found convenient, now for the little farms they have there, now for the small herds of cattle which they keep in corrals of stakes, or else for other reasons.

In spite of what has been said, there is a semblance of a street in this villa. It begins on the left facing north shortly after one leaves the west gate of the cemetery of the parish church and extends down about 400 or 500 varas. Indeed, I point out that this quasi-street not only lacks orderly rows, or blocks, of houses, but at its very beginning, which faces north, it forms one side of a little plaza in front of our church. The other three sides are three houses of settlers with alleys between them. The entrance to the main plaza is down through these. The sides, or borders, of the latter consist of the chapel of Our Lady of Light, which is to the left of the quasi-street mentioned, as has been said, and faces north between two houses of settlers. The other side is the government palace, which, with its barracks, or quarters for the guard, and prison, is opposite the said chapel facing south. The remaining two sides are houses of settlers, and since there is nothing worth noting about them, one can guess what they are like from what has been seen. The government palace

is like everything else here, and enough said.

The sierra that lies to the east of this villa abounds in the firewood and timber needed by the population. There is a lake in it,[67] from which a river with the most crystalline water takes its source. Its current is so swift that in times of freshet it has done some damage, and although this was not extreme, measures have been taken to avoid further harm by installing a stone embankment. It runs from east to west, winding almost through the center of the villa, and although it carries enough water to be called a river, it is not overabundant. Indeed, it is usually insufficient, and at the best season for irrigating the farms, because there are many of them it does not reach the lowest ones, for the first, being higher up, keep bleeding it off with irrigation ditches, and only in a very rainy year is there enough for all. In such seasons ranchos 5 leagues downstream benefit as much as the rest. The water of this river runs three mills[68] which are located from the foot of the sierra to just below our convent. Although they do not grind large quantities, at least they lighten the labor of grinding by hand. There is trout fishing above in the canyon.

ITS LANDS AND FRUITS: On the assumption that this villa consists of many ranchos scattered over a large area, it is clear that there must be a good deal of farmland. Some have more, others less; some of all this land is poor, some not quite so bad, and some is good. There are all kinds in every direction. This, although briefly put, is sufficient to convey the idea that the crops (taking into consideration the contributing factors such as good and bad years and other farming

66. It might be misleading to translate *rancho* as ranch in view of the present association of the word in the United States with large establishments for grazing and breeding horses, cattle, or sheep. The rancho was a hut, or group of huts, outside the settlement used by farmers and herdsmen, or, by extension, a very modest farm or hacienda. The term originally referred to a mess, usually a military one, and to the tents or huts used for the lodging of soldiers.

67. Not either of the two modern reservoirs in Santa Fe Canyon, but Santa Fe Lake farther up.

68. One of these mills was built by Vicar Roybal just above the villa and was donated by him in 1756 to Felipe Sandoval, a grandnephew and godchild whom he reared. SANM, 1: no. 857.

matters) must be as large and good as has been implied. But without going into detail, they are usually sufficient, and I refer to my statement about first fruits for more specific information. The harvest consists of wheat, maize, legumes, and green vegetables, and also fruits such as melon, watermelon, and apricots, of which there are small orchards.

ITS DISTRICTS

A number of settlements of ranchos recognize this villa as their headquarters. Assuming that the capital is as well adorned as I have said, it is clearly evident what the outskirts must be like. Therefore, omitting their description, I will speak of their locations and the distances to them.

One league to the west and at the very outskirts of this villa is Quemado, which was an Indian pueblo in the old days, and because it was purposely burned, it preserves to this day the name of the reason for its end.[69] It has farmlands fertilized by the aforesaid river.

Two roads go down from Quemado like a V, and they lead to two settlements, also of ranchos, both of which are to the southwest in relation to the point from which I am speaking (that is, in relation to each other, one is to the north and the other to the south), one up and one down, with 2 leagues between them. They are about 5 leagues from Santa Fe. The higher settlement is in a canyon that comes down from the San Ildefonso Springs, and in this locality the channel of the villa's river enters it. The farms are made fertile by this water when it gets that far. A little below this settlement near the nooks between some little rock mesas, a number of springs arise (they are probably a resurgence, or outcrop, of the Santa Fe River) and run to the west in little ravines. Since this water flows downhill between rocks, they cannot change its course in order to use it for irrigation instead of the Santa Fe River. The water from these springs forms a river called Las Bocas which takes a very winding course for about 2 leagues to the west through a valley between mesas (so broad that there is a highway through it to the missions of Río Abajo) to join the Río del Norte from the plain above the mission of Our Father Santo Domingo. This settlement is called Cieneguilla.

The lower settlement lies in a kind of nook between two cañadas.[70] None of the rivers mentioned reach it, nor does it have any water except some springs which suffice for the irrigation of the little farms, for watering the cattle, and for the use of the settlers. Here it is called Ciénega Grande, and that is just what it is, for there is a good swamp. Outlines of ancient ruins are visible at the site of this settlement, and perhaps they were pagan pueblos. These two settlements have sufficient land and water as I have explained. These lands and those of Quemado usually yield fairly good crops in accordance with what I said about the villa.

About 2 leagues to the north this villa has another settlement called Río de Tesuque. It is in a little valley which hangs from the sierra of the villa and runs from east to west. It is sprinkled with ranchos and their arable lands, and for the most part these are good. They are watered by a very scanty river of good water which rises in the aforesaid sierra and runs the length of the valley in which the settlement lies. The crops are very good and sufficient.

---

69. *Quemado* means "burned." The settlement near this place was later called Agua Fría. The burned pueblo was excavated by archaeologists after the Santa Fe River laid part of it bare. See S. A. Stubbs and W. S. Stallings, Jr., *The excavations of Pindi Pueblo* (Santa Fe, 1953).

70. As used in the Southwest and by Domínguez in this document, *cañada* refers to the land that lies between two elevations at no great distance from one another.

All the parishioners of this villa, including the settlements described, as I shall explain, speak the Castilian tongue simply and naturally among themselves, with the exception of the Europeans and other people from lands educated in speaking with courtly polish.[71] This applies to the Spaniards, most of whom have servants of different classes, for only as a last resort do they serve themselves. My remark that "speaking Spanish in a simple manner applies to the Spaniards" was made with due reflection, for there are a number of genízaro Indians in this villa, who, after being ransomed from the pagans by our people, are then emancipated to work out their account under them.[72] Although they are servants among our people,

they are not very fluent in speaking and understanding Castilian perfectly, for however much they may talk or learn the language, they do not wholly understand it or speak it without twisting it somewhat. The aforesaid parish, such as it is, is enumerated in the following summary:

CENSUS[73]

VILLA

1 The lord governor and his family with 6 persons
229 Spanish families with 1,167 persons
42 families of genízaros with 164 persons

QUEMADO

57 families with 297 persons

71. In New Mexico, the Spanish folk who had not been out of the region spoke a very simple Castilian full of archaisms as a result of the lack of schools and the fact that cultural contact with the rest of Spanish America was largely limited to the friars and provincial officials. It is the very language found in documents of the sixteenth and seventeenth centuries. A comparison of these with Father Domínguez' Gongoristic style shows how much the language elsewhere had progressed towards more involved phrasing and bigger Latin words. The simple New Mexican tongue, now fast disappearing, has charmed the modern linguist with its Cervantes flavor.

72. The term "genízaro" has been derived from the Turkish *yeni*, new, and *cheri*, troops; hence the English "Janizary," a member of a body of Turkish infantry made up of slaves, conscripts, and subject Christians. In Spanish the word came to be applied specifically in different periods and situations to various non-typical groups or blood mixtures. In New Mexico it was used to designate non-Pueblo Indians living in more or less Spanish fashion. Some of them were captives ransomed from the nomadic tribes, and their mixed New Mexico-born descendants inherited the designation. Church and civil records reveal such varied derivations as Apache, Comanche, Navajo, Ute, Kiowa, Wichita, and Pawnee. Many had Spanish blood, clandestinely or

otherwise. They all bore Christian names from baptism and Spanish surnames from their former masters; belonging no longer to any particular Indian tribe, they spoke the broken Spanish observed by Domínguez. At this period most of the Santa Fe genízaros dwelt in the Barrio of Analco near the chapel of San Miguel. As is evident from the marriage records, the bulk of the Mexican Indians who had been living there up to the time of the 1680 Rebellion remained at Guadalupe del Paso instead of returning to New Mexico with de Vargas in 1693.

73. A census in BL, Mex. Mss. no. 167, dated at Santa Rosa, September 3, 1776, varies considerably from the figures given by Domínguez. In view of Father Domínguez' careful attention to detail, however, it seems likely that the ones he gives for 1776 are reasonably trustworthy. If he had had any reason to doubt them, he most certainly would have mentioned it. Internal evidence in the census dated September 3, 1776, and signed by Antonio Bonilla, who made a report on New Mexico history in that year, indicates clearly that whoever was responsible for it had access to a copy of Father Varo's estimates of 1749-50 and did not trouble to go further. Most of the figures correspond exactly. For census figures 1749-60, see AT, *passim*.

CIENEGUILLA

25 families with 185 persons

CIÉNEGA GRANDE

16 families with 101 persons

RÍO DE TESUQUE

17 families with 94 persons

SUM TOTAL

387 families with 2,014 persons

SUPPOSITION

Having recorded, then, that the Villa of Santa Fe is the capital of the kingdom, for a perfect description of the whole kingdom one should use it as the center and describe the various directions from this point of view. Therefore, setting out from it to the north to inspect the group of missions this Custody has in Río Arriba, I shall begin with the following.

Valle de Sn Antonio.

Alcaldia de taos.

Piedra del Carnero

Castillo

el honda

R. del Lucero

RIO DEL NORTE

taos

R de D. Fernando

de las Trampas

Pecuris

trampas

Embudo

truchas

el Cogte

Alcald ia de

La Mesa

Laoya

La Villa de San-

Poblaciones arruinadas por los enemigos Cumanches

ta Cruz de

R do el ojo Caliente

Rio arriba

S. Juan

Chimayo

quemada

Aviquiu

Cuchilla

Chama

Sta Cruz de la Cañada

Cundiyo

Valtecillo

Mesilla la Cañada.

Cundiyo

Polbadera

Sta Clara

Sn Ildefonso

Pujuaqui Nambe

LOS BACAS

tesuque

Caja del Rio

S. Cruz

Sta Feé Capital y Presidio

Alamo

Alcaldia de la Villa de Santa Fee

Pecos

Sn Marcos

Galisteo

III. RIO ARRIBA

Tesuque

The pueblo and mission of San Diego de Tesuque is not quite 4 leagues north of the villa along the highway, which runs through woods and cañadas, but the journey is not tiring or troublesome. The pueblo lies on a good level site at the mouths of several cañadas. The most important of these runs from east to west, and this is the one in which there is a settlement upstream [Río de Tesuque], as I have just finished saying. Since the matter has come up, I note here that the aforesaid settlement is somewhat more than 2 leagues upstream east of Tesuque, and because it was founded up the river and cañada above the pueblo long after the Reconquest it bears the name of the pueblo's river, as has already been mentioned. Tesuque is the number of leagues north of the villa that I have stated.

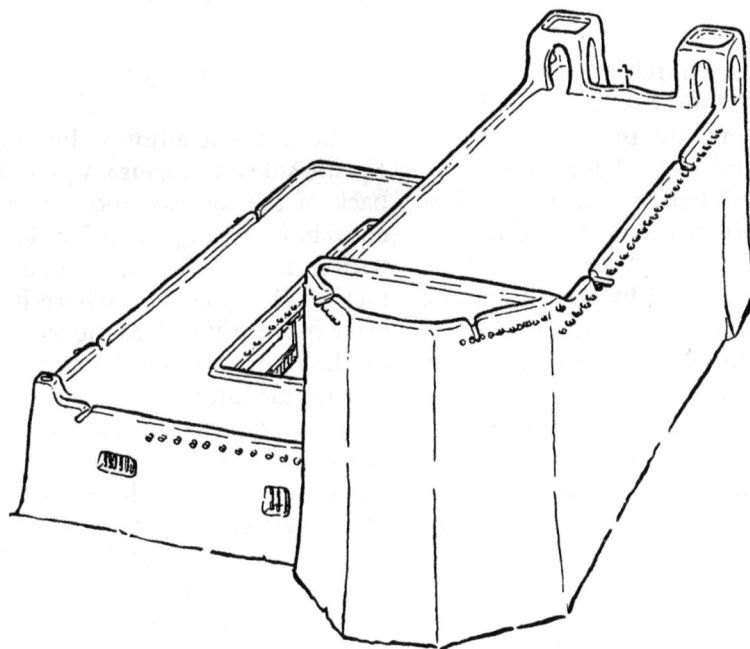

CHURCH

The church[1] is of adobes with thin walls, single-nave construction, about 30 varas long from the door to the high altar, a good 7 varas wide, and 8 high as far as the bed molding. The sanctuary, which is octagonal,[2] is marked off by two steps made of beams, and there are about 3½ varas from the steps to the center. There is no choir loft. As far as the clerestory, which is like those mentioned elsewhere, the ceiling consists of thirty beams with a little carving which rest on small corbels (three of them are ready to fall). From the clerestory to the sanctuary there are ten beams in all, like the others. On the Epistle side, or wall, there are two windows that look to the south over the little convent, and they have wooden gratings. The door faces west, is squared and has two leaves, but the only lock is a crossbar. It is about 3 varas square. The floor of the church is bare earth.

Two buttresses jut from the front corners (like those I described at the Santa Fe church). On each there is a little tower with four arches but no grating. In the tower on the Epistle side there are two medium-sized bells given by the King; they are good, and one has a very commanding tone. As in Santa Fe, there is a grating over the main door extending from one tower buttress to the other. It is so ugly that it would be better if it were not there. The cemetery is very small, with a high adobe wall and a gate opposite the church door. Essentially this church looks like the great granary of an hacienda.

Here are its furnishings:

HIGH ALTAR: Toward the middle of the blank wall hangs an oil painting on canvas about 2 varas high and a little more than 1 wide with a painted wooden frame. It is a pleasing representation of St. Didacus of Alcalá, but quite old, and the King was the donor. It is surrounded by seven small old paintings on buffalo skin (like that I mentioned when describing the second altar

1. This church no longer exists, although the present church, built about 1915, may be on the same site. The church described by Domínguez dated to before 1706. Cf. HB, 3: 375.

2. "Ochavado." Domínguez consistently uses this term to describe the polygonal plan of the sanctuary. He seems to have supplied mentally the missing sides which would have continued and completed the octagon.

in the nave of the church at Santa Fe) of various saints. The altar table is of adobes, and above it there are three ugly adobe gradins that ascend to St. Didacus as if he were enthroned. There is the usual altar stone, an ordinary cross, a poor lectern, a little bell, and two small brass candlesticks; all old and all presented by the King. The only dais is the sanctuary floor, and the rug is a blanket lent by the father when he celebrates Mass.

SACRISTY: The sacristy is on the Epistle side of the sanctuary and has a high, narrow little one-leaved door. This sacristy is about 5 varas square and a little more than 3 high. There are eight rough beams in the ceiling. There is a little window with a wooden grating and no shutters facing east. In a corner beside this window and beyond the street wall there is a small room like an alcove which serves as the baptistery. Near one wall there is a pillar-like step and on this a large earthenware bowl for the baptismal font, covered by another. The door to the convent is almost like the one leading to the sanctuary. There is a poor table in the sacristy with the following in its drawer:

Vestments: An old damask chasuble with two faces (white and crimson), with accessories. A frontal, all trimmed with narrow silk galloon; from the King. Another chasuble of black damask with the necessary appurtenances except frontal and pall for the chalice, trimmed with galloon of yellow chamois. Father Camargo donated this.

Silver and other metal: A very old chalice with a paten but no spoon, which the King gave. Three chrismatories in a little cedar box with a lock but no key. The King gave them.

A doll's spoon. A broken cruet. An extremely old missal. Cardboard box for altar breads.

Linen: An old amice of plain Brittany. An alb like the amice. A cotton cincture. An old altar cloth. An old pair of double corporals. A purificator. A finger towel. An old pall of net over silk stuff.

CONVENT

The convent adjoins the church on the Epistle side and forms a square between the back of the sacristy and the corner of the church. Its arrangement is as follows: A cell, with its inner cell, runs from the back of the sacristy to the corner, where it has a southern exposure as well as the western exposure on the right. Around the corner beyond this cell are the kitchen and storeroom; then the porter's lodge, which is a semi-enclosed little portico. The stable is on a corner below the porter's lodge, and there are two small old rooms between it and the wall of the church. There is an open cloister with little railings below. Even the living quarters have very low ceilings, and nothing is carefully planned. The floor is earth.

NOTE: In the old days the administration of this mission was in charge of the father whom the minister at Santa Fe then had to assist him. Under these circumstances it amounted to a visita of Santa Fe, and as such (apparently) little attention was paid to keeping up [the convent]. And when there was perhaps a resident missionary, it was for a short time, so that even if he was willing to undertake repairs, he could not do so. At the same time this pueblo provided servants for the Santa Fe convent. In the year 1769, during the administration of the Reverend Custos Varo, this service was done away with. Since then this mission has been a visita of Nambe most of the time and still is to this day.[3]

3. This statement probably is substantially correct, although the records of the Province of the Holy Gospel (BNM, leg. 9; MN, Asuntos, legs. 179, 186) do record assignments of missionaries to Tesuque between 1729 and 1772. Some of these friars never came to New Mexico, while others were employed in missions where the need for their services was more urgent owing to the lack of sufficient personnel to maintain a resident minister in each mission. Fray Andrés Varo, who was then about eighty-six years of age, was custos for the fourth time in 1769. MN, Asuntos, leg. 165. The single sacramental register of Tesuque dates from November

In view of the foregoing, my visitation of this mission was made to the father minister of Nambe, who showed me the aforesaid well-kept furnishings and the other things described. With regard to the administration of this mission, he has ordered the fiscal mayor to see that the children come to recite the catechism together in the church morning and evening; and that on Saturdays and feast days the whole pueblo gathers in the church at the peal of the bell to recite the rosary. When he can, he says Mass for them in their own church on feast days; and when he cannot, many go to Nambe. He goes to hear their confessions when they summon him. Baptisms are performed at Nambe. Sometimes, however, he performs one here when he comes to say Mass or hear confessions. If anyone dies, he comes to bury him. Marriages are usually performed at the head mission. As a result, some of the corresponding records are in the books at Santa Fe and others in those at Nambe, but I gave him three new books for use in this mission from the supply that has just come from the Holy Province.

With regard to other visitation matters, there is nothing more here, for I shall speak of the convent lands elsewhere. As for service, there is none at all, since they do not even give the father who visits them a single load of firewood. Even if he asks for it, there is always some petty authority to oppose the gift, for they do not realize that it is not only a minor offering, but seems no more than

a just return to him who cares for their souls without any subsidy in the form of a royal allowance. The missionary overlooks this and other things in order to avoid a breach in harmonious relations, allowing the other party to break them by manifestations of dislike and lack of respect, as well as their bad example.

ITS LANDS AND FRUITS: According to the fiscal mayor's statement, there are two separate plots in the midst of the Indians' lands. More than a fanega of wheat can be sown in these, and almost 2 almudes of maize. According to his statement, they are fairly good, and there is some harvest from them when the father sows; and when they sow them on loan (as the father who now visits them has had them do), they harvest a goodly amount, for they look on it as their own. The planting for the father is entrusted to the pueblo up to the harvest, and since stealing and carelessness prevail, it goes ill for the priest. These lands are irrigated by the river mentioned above through ditches belonging to the Indians, for they run through their lands. This mission has no settlers to administer.

PUEBLO

At the beginning I noted that it is established, or located, at the mouths of several cañadas; the most important and noteworthy of these is the one that comes from the east, for the pueblo lies in the open at its mouth since this cañada widens more and more to the north and northwest. The location, then, of the pueblo buildings must be considered south in relation to the church and convent. In front of the convent there is a little plaza surrounded by three blocks joined together; and the fourth side, which closes in the square plaza, consists of two sections. The first and upper half is the convent, and the lower half is a separate tenement. There are three passages: one on the corner above the convent, another separat-

---

19, 1694, when it was presented to the first missionary assigned there after the Reconquest, Fray José Díez, by Vice-Custos Fray Francisco de Vargas. AASF, B-53, Tesuque. Cuyamungué was attached to Tesuque as a visita. Father Díez baptized twenty-eight children and some adults and was building a church when rumors of an impending revolt led to the recall of the missionaries to Santa Fe in March, 1696. Shortly thereafter he and two other friars who had been on loan from the Franciscan Province of Michoacán left New Mexico. BNM, leg. 3, no. 6, leg. 4, no. 23. Although Tesuque did not join the Rebellion of 1696, there is no evidence that it again had a resident friar for any length of time thereafter.

ing the convent and the tenement, and the third on the corner below the tenement.

It is obvious from the foregoing that the church is outside this little plaza, and this is true. Yet it stands at the end of a blind alley, for there are some small new houses a little farther down facing the back of the aforesaid tenement; and still farther down, beside the highway which passes near here, the community house stands crosswise, and this and other adjoining things are across the street from the block on the west side of the plaza. The highway runs through this street.

It can now be assumed that the houses of which the pueblo is composed are adobe and like other Indian houses in these parts. All have upper and lower dwellings, but they are built like a dovecot, for the patio is communal like the plaza and street. The entrance to some houses is by little doors on the street; others have ladders, and some of these ascend to a door which resembles a little window torn in the wall of the upper apartment, while others rest on a portico-like jacal or on the roof of a small room that juts out from the lower dwelling and has a little flat roof which provides access to the upper dwelling. The fastenings are a wooden lock and key.

The ceilings are quite low. Some dwellings are more spacious than others, and as a general rule all are poorly whitewashed. They have a *coi* (the singular is *coi,* the plural, *cois*), and this is nothing but a gap opened in the floor of the upper dwellings between two beams for use as a trap door to give access to the lower apartment via a ladder.[4] The kitchen is in any room the owner

pleases and it contains several metates (three or four) fixed to the floor with mud (these are generally found after this fashion in the houses of both Indians and settlers), all boxed in with boards, and divided from one another by another small board set crosswise so that the wheat, maize, or other things being ground by hand may not spill, nor may the contents of one metate get mixed with those of another.

The interior decoration of these houses varies according to the owner, but they usually have two or three prints, a wooden cross, some kind of chest, either plain or painted. The arms of the men and the harnesses of the horses are hung from stakes, and there are some *matlacahuitl*[5] on which, like the secondhand dealers of Mexico, they hang their skins of buffalo, lion, wolf, sheep, and other animals, and also their cloaks if they have any, and the rest of the clothing belonging to both men and women. Outside are the little ovens, like those of the bakeshops, and the henhouses. Around the pueblo, but not very near to it, there are corrals to confine livestock of various kinds, and small corrals for fattening pigs.

ITS LANDS AND FRUITS: In comparison with the small population of this pueblo (which will be seen later) there is a good deal of land, for they have a whole league up the cañada, even though it is narrow. Below, where the cañada opens out more and more, as I said when I started to talk about the pueblo, they have about three-quarters of a

---

4. In connection with this word, there is an interesting document concerning a murder investigation at Santa Cruz de la Cañada in 1713, which turned on the question whether a husband beat his wife to death in their "coy" or whether she fell into the "coy" when descending the interior ladder with a water jar on her head. SANM, 2: no. 187. This term, almost obsolete in New Mexico today, is ap-plied to an outbuilding for storing grain or farm articles.

5. *Matlaquauitl,* a Mexican word translated by Molina as *varal* (a long pole), and by Rémi Siméon as *perche* (pole), *pieu* (stick, post), and *bâton pour filet* (a staff for a net). This was probably a sort of pole and net, or rope, arrangement used to hang the skins and clothing where they would be safe from damage from mice, etc. Alonso de Molina, *Vo-cabulario en lengua castellana y mexicana* (Mexico, 1571; facsimile ed., Madrid, 1944); Rémi Siméon, *Dictionnaire de la langue nahuatl ou mexicaine* (Paris, 1885).

league, which occupies most of the open, or wide, part. All are under irrigation, for although the river is short, as I have already said, the Indians are long in ingenuity, and therefore they draw off fairly good irrigation ditches. The land is fairly well suited to grain production and usually yields a good deal of grain of all the kinds sown there. There are also small orchards with apricot trees, chabacanos, and peaches[6] which belong to the Indians.

The sons of this pueblo built the church and convent, and they belong to the nation called Tegua, whose native tongue they speak. The tribe and the language have the same name. They also speak our Castilian, but not very well, for if we and they manage

6. "Albaricoques, chabacanos y duraznos." The chabacano is a variety of apricot.

some mutual explanation and understanding, it is in such a disfigured fashion that it is easier for our people to adjust to their manner of speaking than for them to attempt ours, for if one speaks to them rapidly, even without artifice, they no longer understand. Their customs in general will be described elsewhere when I speak of Indian matters as a whole. With regard to the particular characteristics of this pueblo, I say for now that they manifest a docile disposition; they have some knowledge of good, and to that extent they are inclined toward it. All are included in the following summary.

CENSUS

45 families with 194 persons

Nambe

The pueblo and mission of Our Father San Francisco de Nambe is 3 leagues' journey from Tesuque in the same northerly direction. (Two leagues over level ground, and one over broken and troublesome little hills, with a range of hills running from Tesuque to the right toward the Sierra on the east, and three or four more on the left toward the west.) Nambe is about 7 leagues from Santa Fe and lies north quarter north-northeast from it, located on a site that I shall describe later.

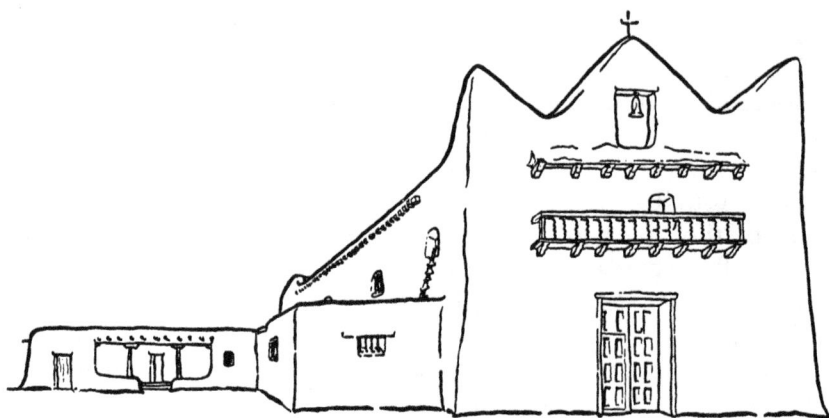

CHURCH

The church is adobe with walls about a vara thick. The main door faces east-northeast, and from the door to the approach to the sanctuary it is 30 varas long by 9 wide and 8 high up to the bed molding. It is single-naved and the sanctuary is closed in like the head of a transept. The ascent to the sanctuary consists of seven steps made of poorly wrought raised beams which occupy a long vara on the floor of the nave. The sanctuary is 5 varas square, and it is a vara higher than the nave because there is a clerestory like those I have described before.

This church has a choir loft in the usual place, which occupies the whole width, projects 6 varas into the nave, and rests on a strong crossbeam set in the lateral walls with corbels. This choir has a railing, or balustrade, which has a medium-sized cross turned on a lathe on it at the center. The entrance is from the flat roof of the convent by a low, little one-leaved door without a key. The furnishings are complete emptiness. On the crossbeam is this inscription: *The Lord Governor Don Juan Domingo Bustamente built this church at his own expense. Year of 1725.*[1]

1. According to a report by Custos Fray Juan Alvarez dated at Nambe on January 12, 1706, the church was then under construction. HB, 3: 375.

On the Gospel side this church has two windows with wooden gratings, so ill-made that they look like holes. They face southeast over the convent. At the front, in the choir loft, there is a window door to a balcony which we shall soon see from the outside. The main door is squared, with a strong wooden frame instead of masonry, and it has two paneled leaves with a wicket in one. It is 3½ varas high and 2 long varas wide. The only lock is the crossbar.

Beginning at the center of the choir, there are thirty-four wrought beams with multiple corbels in the nave, and the clerestory rises from the one opposite the sanctuary to

There was a mission at Nambe as early as 1613, and a church was built in 1617. Undoubtedly it suffered considerable damage in the 1680 Revolt, but in view of similar cases, it is not unlikely that Father Alvarez' statement means that he repaired, or rebuilt, the pre-Rebellion structure. AB, 1634, pp. 236, 310; HS, 1: 96. In his description of the convent Domínguez suggests that a spacious cell was formerly the church, and this is probably the one to which Father Alvarez referred. The church built by Governor Bustamante is mentioned in his *residencia* in 1731. To celebrate its completion, comedies, laudatory speeches, and Indian dances were given in it. BL, N.M. Origs. Bustamante served as governor 1722-31. See SETTLERS. This church collapsed in 1909, and the eighteenth-century timbers, including the dated beam mentioned here, are now in the Gerald Cassidy house at Santa Fe. GK, pp. 120-21, erroneously gave 1729 for 1725.

admit light. Beyond there are 3 open varas to substitute for a vaulted arch, and, imitating a vault, or transept, they have a ceiling made of thirteen small carved beams set crosswise to those in the nave. They have corbels only where they rest on the vaulted arch, and the latter consists of boards fixed in the wall with no attempt at ornamentation except the rough boards in the form of an arch. The sanctuary is roofed by six small beams with corbels on both sides. The floor of the church is the bare earth.

On the left, then, under the choir as we enter the main door is the entrance to the baptistery, which is outside the church walls. This room is 5 varas square and 3 high, with seven rough beams in the ceiling and a little window with a wooden grating to the east-northeast. The door to the church is of ordinary size and has two leaves with wooden gratings from the middle up. In the center of this room there is a round adobe pedestal, upon which stands a thick little pillar of wood, hollowed out to make a drain. This holds a large earthen bowl for a baptismal font, covered by a round piece of wood.

The cemetery juts out from the corners of the church and adjoins the corner at the rear of the baptistery on the southeast. It is almost 32 varas square, with a narrow adobe wall more than a vara high, and two gates, one to the east-northeast toward the pueblo and the other on the southeast to make the turn to the convent. The balcony I mentioned when describing the choir is over this cemetery and above the main door of the church. It consists of eight flying corbels with a wooden balustrade, and the floor is a vara deep by 6 wide, for it does not extend to the corners. It has a jacal overhead of corbels like the floor, and it has an extensive view in the directions its location offers.

On top of the wall above this balcony are three monstrous adobe battlements like the peaks of a biretta; in the center one a square opening which serves as a bell tower. It therefore contains a middle-sized bell with a clapper; it has a poor tone, however, because it is somewhat cracked. Anticipating something I shall have to say when I describe the convent, I point out now that the baptistery does not reach to the corner of the church on the side where it stands, but is set about a vara back from the corner, leaving a recess. Returning to the church, I will describe its furnishings, which are as follows:

HIGH ALTAR: Toward the center of the wall there is an oil painting on canvas of Our Father St. Francis, 2 varas high and a little over a vara wide, with a painted wooden frame. The King gave it and it is now old. Above it hangs an oil painting on canvas without a frame, 2½ varas square. This represents Our Lady of Guadalupe, with her apparitions at the corners. It is now old, and there is no mention of who gave it. The whole wall is painted like a tapestry, but it is ugly. The altar table is adobe with the usual altar stone, and although it is not vested except for Mass, it always holds a missal stand and two small brass candlesticks, which were given by the King, along with the altar stone and a little bell. There is a dais but no carpet, for a blanket belonging to the father is put down for the celebration of Mass.

From wall to wall above the altar table three gradins of poorly wrought beams rise in imitation of a throne. On the first is a rather large old lacquer crucifix, and higher up another bronze crucifix with silver cornerplates, INRI, and Dolorosa. Father Llanos says that these crucifixes were put there through his efforts. Two dozen ugly old candleholders of rough wood which Father Toledo provided and three prints on their little boards are distributed on these three gradins.

NAVE: Below the sanctuary, facing the nave on either side, are two hideous adobe tables for altars. The one on the Gospel side has only a large painting on buffalo skin which represents Our Father St. Francis in the regional manner. Above the one on the Epistle side there is a poor niche (with doors and no key) that looks like a tabernacle, and in it a small image in the round which Father Toledo made. Its title is the Immaculate Conception of Our Lady, and it is ugly enough, but very much adorned with little ribbon flowers and ordinary small medals just like the little saints the Mexican Indians carry when they beg for alms for pious purposes. The pulpit is large, wooden, octagonal, and very old. The confessional is a chair of earth with boards at the sides and poorly grated openings. The interior of this church looks like a dark wine cellar.

SACRISTY: The sacristy is along the nave on the Gospel side about 4 varas from the sanctuary. This room runs along the nave and is 7 varas long, 4 wide, and 3 long varas high, with eleven ordinary beams in the ceiling. The door to the church is small, with two leaves and no key. The window, with its wooden grating, is on the same side as the convent, to which there is an ordinary single-leaved door without a key. In this room there are two little cupboards with doors but no fastenings. These hold things used for divine worship. Also, a big table with a good drawer without a key, containing the following:

Vestments: A usable damask chasuble trimmed with silk galloon, with two faces (white and red), with its accessories; the King gave it. Although the frontal is falling to pieces, it has to do, for there is no other. Another good chasuble of mother-of-pearl damask trimmed with semi-embroidered ribbon, with accessories except for the frontal. Another of white damask exactly like the preceding, and they say that Father Cayuela provided both sets. Another old one of white China cloth trimmed with false gold galloon, with accessories except frontal. Another old one of blue damask with a green orphrey; and the only accessories are stole and maniple. It is said that former fathers provided these two. Another new one of black damask with imitation gold galloon, with accessories including cope and a sheath for the cross. Father Ca-

margo donated this. An extremely old unlined cope of mother-of-pearl satin and narrow silk galloon.

Linen: A good lawn amice with ordinary lace and the usual ribbons. Another fairly good plain Brittany amice. An old and mended alb. A fairly good one of Brabant linen. A new Brittany alb with narrow lace; and Father Llanos says it was furnished through his efforts. An old Rouen altar cloth. Two cinctures of linen and silk that Father Llanos says he supplied. Three fairly good pairs of double corporals of Brittany. Eight purificators. Two Brittany finger towels. A long Brittany cloth for use as a yoke in marriage ceremonies. Two little cloths for use as hood and towel at baptisms. Three old palls of various stuffs and colors. Two linen palls for the chalice and two like them for the paten. Another new one of blue flowered silk for the chalice and one to match for the paten, lined with cambric. It is said that certain fathers have supplied all the foregoing.

Silver and other metal: A chalice with paten but no spoon which the King gave. A middle-sized ciborium with a lid and no inner paten; it has a veil of plain mother-of-pearl satin. Three oilstocks that the King gave; they are in a very well made little tin-plate box, but it has no key. Twelve very old small coins for arras, which the King gave, and two metal rings to go with them. There is no mention of who gave the ciborium.

A broken tin processional cross that the King gave. Two pewter plates furnished by a father. A censer with a broken incense boat and no spoon, which a father supplied. Two unmatched brass candlesticks. A glass cruet. A very ordinary baptismal basin. A very old missal. A *Manual* by Osorio.

CONVENT

The convent adjoins the church on the southeast on the Gospel side. In order to describe it clearly I must reiterate that the sacristy and baptistery are on this same side, the former above and the latter below the convent, with the recess I pointed out when I described the bell tower. Therefore, between the end wall of the sacristy and the side wall of the baptistery there is a room used as an office, or storeroom, with a wretched door and an iron key as bad as the door. Another room runs from the wall where this door is to the porter's lodge. It should be noted here that this is how the back of the baptistery came to stand free and leave a recess against the convent, making two recesses in the wall between the corner of the church and the convent.

Today there is only the first recess at the aforesaid corner, for the one back of the baptistery was filled by a room which Father Guzmán built in the year '68 as an inner cell for the cell already mentioned. He opened a door where the window used to be. This room is very large, with two windows on the two walls, and it makes a corner next to the porter's lodge, thus mitigating the ugliness that the former recess must have had.

The porter's lodge extends from the end wall of the cell I have just mentioned. It faces east-northeast like the church and is a very pretty little portico 5 varas long. Four steps lead from the entrance to the center, with recesses, or adobe seats. In front there are two pillars with corbels at the top to support the cross timber, which, corbeled like the pillars, holds the beams of the roof. As a result of this arrangement there are three archlike openings, although the one in the center is wider than those at the sides which are partly closed in by a railing and balustrade like those at San Cosme.[2]

Running from the end wall of the porter's lodge there is a cell which corners on the southeast. It is very spacious, with an inner cell and a beautiful mirador all tumbled down. Father Llanos says that he has

2. The recollection friary of Nuestra Señora de la Consolación, popularly known as San Cosme, in Mexico City.

heard that this cell was once the church (this is believable in view of the length as far as the inner cell) before the church just described was finished. In this cell and its inner cell there are windows and doors, and a most wretched key in the outer one. On the southwest corner beyond the aforesaid inner cell is another little cell. The latter is hemmed in because the next room is the kitchen, a small room, but adequate for the purpose. There is a brazier on the floor with a wooden hood plastered with mud.

Then there is a little passage (I will speak of it very soon), and then an ordinary stable with a strawloft that extends far enough to join the church behind the sacristy. There is no cloister in this convent, but only a little portico facing southeast, with three pillars like those in the porter's lodge. It runs from the first cell I mentioned to the wall of the strawloft I have just mentioned. This shows that the sacristy, storeroom, and door to the first cell are all under this portico. The missionary now lives in this cell because it is the most usable, the others being greatly in need of repair. The little passage leads to a corral which runs from the southwest corner to the only corner at the back of the sanctuary. It has a rather high adobe wall and is large enough for two hundred sheep. The Indians built the whole edifice.

Its Lands and Fruits: There are three plots of land. One, right in sight of the convent to the southeast, is a kitchen garden with an adobe wall that Father Esparragoza had built. It is 105 varas long and 100 wide. Green vegetables are usually planted, and the harvest is large and good. But when it is sown with wheat, it will take 5 or 6 almudes, which yield about 25 fanegas. It will take a longish almud of maize, which yields about 15 fanegas, proof that the land is good. Above this kitchen garden, beyond the wall, is another better piece of land, much longer than the foregoing, if, indeed, the same width. A fanega of wheat can be sown in it, and usually yields 50, and it will take 2 almudes of maize, which yield about 30 fanegas, or less. To the northeast above this (or rather, to one side, but I say above because it is on a rise) is the third plot. Compared with the others, it is almost 200 varas square, but not as good, for although 2 fanegas of wheat, or a little more, are sown, it usually yields 20 to 25 fanegas; about 3 almudes of maize yield 13 fanegas at most, and this not as good as the crops on the other plots. The sowing is entrusted to the pueblo, who care for it until it is brought in. It is watered from the communal irrigation ditch of the pueblo.

Its FURNISHINGS: Two ordinary tables, without drawers and very poor. Two rough chairs. An ordinary bench, badly made. Three bed boards on adobe legs. A buffalo skin table cover of superlative antiquity. An ebony crucifix with the paint gone from the Christ.

Its SERVICE: All together it consists of a fiscal mayor, three subordinates, eight little sacristans and the chief sacristan, four cooks, and four bakers; but in detail: weekly, one fiscal, two little sacristans, one cook who has another woman to bring water, two bakers. The father gives them what they need, and they leave as soon as they have finished, for their work lasts two days; and they do not return until they are summoned again, which is two weeks later because the other two come during the intervening week, and so these take turns like the others. All eat what the father is able to give them at the convent, and at night they go home until the next day. Only the sacristans sleep in the convent.

In addition, the whole pueblo takes turn as shepherds for the father's lambs, to take care of his horse, and the women to care for the hens. And they take turns in bringing the firewood necessary for the kitchen, the bread oven, and the hearths in the cells in which the father lives in winter. The weekly household servants bring the utensils for use in the father's kitchen and cell and take them away with them as they come and go. There are other utensils that remain in the

convent, such as cups, plates, etc., as will be seen in the writ of visitation with regard to convent provisions.

MISSION FATHER

He who is now serving at this mission by order of Our Holy Province is Father Fray Juan Llanos, a native of Toluca. He is thirty-nine years old, twenty-two in profession, and five in the Custody as a missionary, all at Nambe. He has faculties to preach and to hear confessions of men and women, and they were given to him by the Reverend Custos Hinojosa (although he does not state for what period) by authority from the Most Illustrious and Reverend Lord Don Fray José Díaz Bravo, Bishop of Durango, because his Lordship concedes this authority to him in order that he may qualify friars who come to serve in these missions.[3]

ADMINISTRATION OF THE MISSION: On feast days the whole pueblo comes to Mass, which is said at a regular hour because the settlers are expected. Sometimes they recite the catechism or the rosary with the father before or after Mass, and he always gives them a short explanation. On Saturdays the pueblo assembles and recites the rosary with the father in the church, after Mass when there is one. Daily, morning and afternoon, the bell is rung (as also for the foregoing) for catechism at a regular hour. The unmarried men and women come to it and recite with the father, and he explains something to them. They hear Mass on the days when there is one; he teaches them something; and after half an hour, or an hour, depending upon what has taken place, they go home.

OBVENTIONS AND FIRST FRUITS: I spoke at length about this with regard to the villa of Santa Fe. On this basis, since this kingdom is subject to a single government in spiritual and temporal matters, I need not

3. Fray Juan José de Hinojosa was custos when Domínguez came to New Mexico. See FRANCISCANS.

do more than refer to what I said about the aforesaid villa. There is nothing special to say about obventions.

In general I say the same about first fruits, but in regard to this particular mission, they usually amount to 10 fanegas of wheat, the same of maize, about 3 of all kinds of legumes together, 5 strings of chile made up from the pieces they give, some little quantities of green stuff. Of livestock, perhaps a kid; of cattle, nothing. It is understood that the Indians pay nothing of what has been mentioned.

His EXPENDITURES: Not counting what is consumed by the household, the father who now serves at this mission has the following expense: about 20 wax candles, at 3 to a pound; 2 jugs of wine; more than 200 altar breads, for which he gives the chief sacristan of San Ildefonso, where there is an iron for making them, 2 almudes of wheat. The foregoing is annual expenditure.

How He Acquires Necessities: This has been adequately explained in connection with the mission father at Santa Fe, and although that item is also included in the economic management of each mission and is therefore part of the visitation of the missionary, the system here is the same as that I described there, to which I refer, and merely add that if there were anything characteristic of this place, it is that wheat or maize are also used for barter.

Convent Provisions: When Father Llanos took over this mission, he received only 2 fanegas of wheat and 1½ of maize. But during this visitation, in accordance with what the aforesaid father told me and is evident from what has been said about lands and crops belonging to the convent of this mission, I determined the appropriate amount, recording the following in the inventory:

WRIT OF VISITATION

This book was examined and agrees with what our Reverend Father Commissary Visitor saw and found with regard to the belongings of the church, vestments, and convent furnishings, but he enjoins the mission father to make a new list in this same book of these valuables, etc., in the same manner which he saw used when they were examined in the course of the visitation so that it may thus agree with the individual instruction on this point. And because our Reverend Father Commissary Visitor realizes the experience the aforesaid father has had of this mission and of what the convent lands can produce, in accordance with his report and by virtue of the authority and instructions his Reverend Paternity has, by a formal precept of holy obedience he orders and commands the friar who is, or in future may be, missionary of this mission of Nambe that when he hands the mission over to another, he shall leave the following: 10 fanegas of wheat; 8 of maize; half a fanega of chick peas; a jar of lard; 6 sheep; 4 wax candles; a flask of wine; 2 strings of chile; 12 tallow candles; an almud of frijoles; half an almud of salt; 25 onions; 6 plates, 6 cups, 2 jars, and 4 candlesticks, all these of clay and manufactured in the pueblo.

In addition, the outgoing friar will leave and the newcomer receive the convent furnishings; that is, two tables, one with an old buffalo skin cover, two chairs, one bench, three bed boards, two locks with key. This and the rest must be handed over and a receipt given, specifying whether anything is lacking. If there is, the newcomer shall notify the Reverend Custos or his Vice-Custos promptly so that the lack may be supplied. And we order by holy obedience by virtue of the Holy Spirit that they perform this with integrity, for our Mother the Holy Province so orders, as we have explained. This decision is valid for all time and emanates from the superior of said province *ratione officii*, and therefore it does not expire when his term of office comes to an end. We again charge and command the fulfillment of so just a decision, since it is for the mutual benefit of the religious. Ordered and commanded in this mission of Our Father San Francisco de Nambe, signed by our hand and name, sealed with the great seal of this our Custody, and countersigned by our secretary, on April 10, 1776. Fray Francisco Atanasio Domínguez, Commissary Visitor. By order of his Reverend Paternity, Fray José Palacio, secretary.

The three parish books were examined and approved, and the corresponding decrees were recorded in them, ordering that in future the sections pertaining to the pueblo and mission of Tesuque shall be recorded in separate books for the guidance of the missionary who may occupy that mission. I therefore gave the books I mentioned in my report of the said mission.

These parish books which I inspected at Nambe are new, and Father Llanos provided them. They have been authorized by presentation to the Father Vice-Custos Fray Mariano Rodríguez de la Torre, who holds authority for this from the Reverend Custos Hinojosa. The aforesaid father also supplied two quarto books with few pages. Their decrees of presentation are addressed to the said Reverend Custos, and one is for the inventory, in which I recorded the above decree, and the other for patents, none of which is to be seen, because the Father Custos considers this advisable, but I will decide after the visitation what should be done in this regard. In addition to these books there is a book at this mission of Nambe comprising three parochial registers. That of Baptisms begins with the year 1725 and ends with 1764; that of Marriages begins in the same year and ends with the year '59; that of Burials begins like the aforesaid and ends with the year '57.

PUEBLO

The site, or hole, in which the pueblo of Nambe is established, which I mentioned when I began the account of my visitation,

has the Sierra Madre first noted at Santa Fe on the east-northeast. To the northeast, north, and northwest are some broken, rugged, red hills, with cañadas here and there. From the point where they begin, which is at the aforesaid sierra, these hills lie in the directions mentioned, forming a very extensive enclosure for the site of the pueblo, which lies near the middle of the site in relation to these hills. To the southeast of the pueblo there is a ridge of hills which, although they are essentially similar to the others, do not curve as they do, but run straight down from the sierra in the aforesaid direction. These hills are as near, or close, as a musket shot to the pueblo. At their foot a small river with a swift current full of crystalline water comes from the aforesaid sierra. Higher up in the little canyon of this river there is trout fishing. With regard to its water, Father Llanos says that he has been told that Governor Don Tomás Vélez[4] took samples of all the waters of this region to Mexico, and that while all the others became fetid, that of this river remained the same (if this is true, a good test).

Now that the location of the pueblo has been explained, its plan remains to be told. In front of and in the foreground looking from the church and convent, the pueblo all lies to the east-northeast, around a plaza enclosed by three blocks on the southeast, east-northeast, and northeast [sic]. The other side of the plaza consists of half a block plus the cemetery and the adjacent area in the corresponding direction in relation to the foregoing. There are three little alleys in the plaza; a large one, which is the one by the cemetery; another to the east-northeast, and the third to the southeast. In the center of this plaza there are three dwellings dating from ancient times and some mounds of ruins. Because of these obstacles its ample size cannot be fully seen, but it is obvious that it is large enough. Father Llanos says that the bones of human beings have been

4. Don Tomás Vélez Cachupín was governor of New Mexico 1749-54 and again 1762-67.

removed from the mounds of ruins on occasions when their earth was needed to make adobes. Fearing lest they might be the remains of pagans, he has ordered that they be interred in unconsecrated ground.[5]

Since the houses that form this plaza are entirely like those described at Tesuque, within and without, in decoration and everything else, I refer to that description to avoid needless repetition. The only difference is that in Nambe some houses have little porches on the upper dwellings, which are used for sleeping in summer, and at that season their owners keep their utensils and clothing hanging there in the way I described at Tesuque. The corrals for their little herds of livestock are at a good distance behind the church and convent.

Its Lands and Fruits: They have almost as much land above the pueblo as below it, and it occupies most of the site mentioned, although a great arroyo that arises in the east-northeast and runs to the southwest until it enters the pueblo's river behind the church and convent and in front of the corrals mentioned divides them. They irrigate the upper lands with a mother ditch from well upriver, and they take water for the lower lands from the same ditch a little before the said arroyo empties into the river.

The lands are fairly fertile and everything sown in them yields a crop, with a sufficient harvest of everything. In sight of the porter's lodge there are six little chabacano trees with very delicious fruit, and they belong to an Indian.

The natives of this pueblo are Teguas and speak their native language as in Tesuque. They are a little more fluent in speaking Spanish, since they confess (many of them more than once a year) without an interpreter, whom the former do use. But on the whole the same thing happens to them as to the others in failing to understand rapid Spanish. In general their customs are like all the rest, but the people of this particular pueblo are docile, obedient, somewhat inclined to goodness, and very lively and gay. They are all included in the following summary.

CENSUS

50 families with 183 persons

Some ranchos of citizens are attached to this mission for spiritual administration. They comprise two very small branches called Cundiyó[6] and Pojoaque. In relation to the pueblo, the first is up east-northeast at the foot of the aforementioned sierra in a small cañada which runs from south to north there with a rapid little river through the center. The water is crystalline and good, and there is trout fishing. It has sufficient farmlands for the number of inhabitants. They are fairly good, are irrigated by the said river, and although there is a fairly good harvest of all that is sown in them, they do not yield frijol and ripe chile because it is so near the sierra that cold weather comes early, and they gather the chile when it is green. It is 2 leagues from the pueblo.

The citizens of this Cundiyó pass for Spaniards. They speak their simple Spanish,

5. These remains were probably Christian; indeed, those of settlers killed by the Indians in the uprising on June 5, 1696. Their padre, Fray Antonio Moreno, was visiting San Ildefonso, where he was killed with Fray Francisco Corvera. The Spanish folk killed at Nambe were Juan Cortés, his daughter, and his son-in-law José Sánchez, all of whom had come from Mexico City two years before. A fourth victim was a New Mexican youth, Andrés Baca, whose mother, brother, and a married sister with her two children were killed at San Ildefonso. The Indians left the four naked corpses by the church door, where they were found by Governor de Vargas and his troops on June 7. They were in such bad condition that he had them buried at once in a ruined house close by. Evidently they were placed inside the ruins and then the adobe walls were toppled over them. R. E. Twitchell, "The Pueblo Revolt of 1696," *Old Santa Fe,* 3 (1916): 347. See also NMF, Sánchez and Baca.

6. A 1759 entry in the Nambe baptismal register has "Puesto de Santo Domingo de Cundiyó."

as do their servants, who are of various classes. They are all included in the following summary:

CENSUS

9 families with 36 persons

The other branch is about a league below Nambe. Its lands adjoin this pueblo, and its farmlands are like those of Nambe and on the same site. They yield the same harvest and are watered by the same river, but through their own ditch, which is necessary because of their location. But they do share with the little pueblo that I will soon mention. The citizens of this branch are also accepted as Spaniards; their servants are light colored; and they all speak Spanish as related above. They are all included in this

CENSUS

25 families with 162 persons

DIGRESSION
WITH INFORMATION

For clearer explanation I reserved this note for this place, reminding the reader by saying that the white stone of which the reredos at Our Lady of Light is made was obtained from some little hills that lie to the northwest of this settlement which I have just mentioned. They are about a league from it to the left of the highway as we travel to La Cañada.[7]

7. This was the original Roybal grant of San Antonio de Jacona made by Governor Cubero in 1702 to Ignacio de Roybal, father of the Vicar and of four other sons and four daughters. The main rancho was willed to one son, Mateo Roybal, who also acquired the adjoining portions belonging to two other brothers. The active part played by Vicar Santiago Roybal and his married sisters in Santa Fe in the beginnings of the Chapel of Our Lady of Light is further illustrated by this connection. See NMF.

Pojoaque

A league down the Nambe River from Nambe, after one crosses from the northeast side of the river to the southwest, is the little pueblo of Nuestra Señora de Guadalupe de Pojoaque. It is almost the same distance from Santa Fe as Nambe, and to the north of the villa. It lies, then, on the opposite side of the river from Nambe when one goes from there to Pojoaque, as I have said, but when one goes from Santa Fe, it is not necessary to cross the river. I will describe the site as soon as I finish with my report of the visitation.

CHURCH

The church[1] is adobe with walls nearly a vara thick. The outlook and main door are due north. It is 30 varas long from the door to the ascent to the sanctuary, 7 wide, and 7 high to the entablature. It is single-naved, with the sanctuary marked off like the head of a transept, with two badly laid beams for steps. The sanctuary is about 4 varas square and a little higher than the nave because of the clerestory as described in other places. There is a choir loft in the usual place, which occupies the width of the church and extends 3 varas into the nave. It is supported by twelve carelessly wrought beams which rest on a strong crossbeam set into the side walls without corbels. It has no railing. The

1. Governor Cuervo y Valdés refounded the little pueblo of Pojoaque with a few families in 1707. Since it was always very small and attached to the mission of Nambe, there is no real evidence that it had a church before the one described by Domínguez, which was built in 1765-73. This was abandoned after 1915. HB, 3: 380; GK, pp. 120-21, fig. 205.

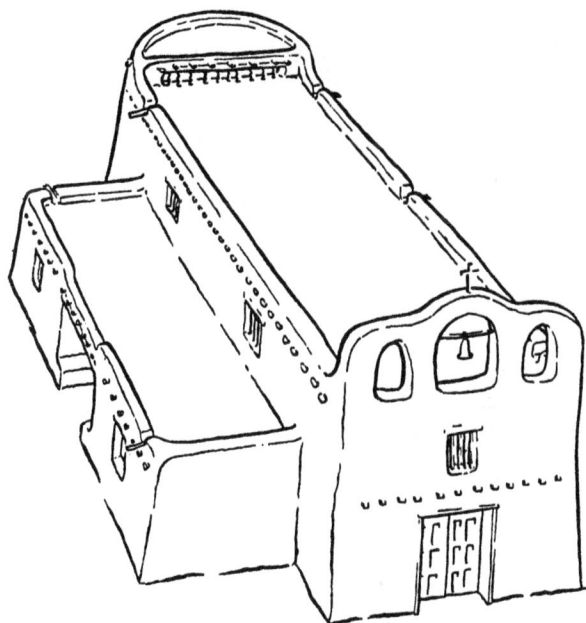

ascent to it is a ladder which stands in a corner.

There are two ugly windows with wooden gratings on the Gospel side of the nave, and another in the wall of the choir. The former face east, and the latter, north. The main door is squared, with a strong wooden frame. It has two roughly paneled leaves, and the only lock is the crossbar. The size of this door is 3 varas high and 2½ wide. The roof of the nave consists of thirty-five wrought beams with small corbels, and the clerestory is on the one facing the sanctuary. From here to the sanctuary there are three beams like those in the nave, and there are six of the same in the sanctuary, but there is no semblance of a vaulted arch. The floor of the whole church is bare earth.

There is no cemetery, but a very small area has, indeed, been designated for making one. Above the main door there are three arches, a large one in the center with a good, sonorous middle-sized bell. The other two arches are rather small, and empty. All this that I have mentioned is very new, for Father Esparragoza began it, with the help of the natives of the pueblo, in the year 1765, and Father Llanos finished it with their help in the year '73. The adornment of this church is as follows:

HIGH ALTAR: Toward the center, or middle, of the blank wall hangs an image of Our Lady of Guadalupe, on canvas like those mentioned in the preceding missions and a present from the King. A little above it there is another canvas, about a vara in size, with St. Anthony in oils. Still higher is another, about a third of a vara in size, with Our Lady of Guadalupe aforesaid in oils. Arranged at regular intervals around these are fourteen medium-sized prints on their little boards. These and the small paintings were donated by benefactors. The altar table is adobe, with an ordinary altar stone, a small cross with a bronze crucifixion and corner plates set on a little pedestal of the white stone mentioned in the recent note, two small brass candlesticks, an ordinary wooden missal stand, a dais made of beams, and a little bell. A borrowed blanket serves as a carpet when Mass is celebrated.

NAVE: On the walls that face the nave like those of a transept there are two altars with small adobe tables. The one on the right side has a small oil painting on canvas about a vara in size of St. Anthony of Padua. The one on the other side has a St. Nicholas of Tolentino exactly like the aforesaid. Doña Josefa de Bustamante gave them both.[2] The pulpit in its usual place, of wood, new, and very ugly. Confessional opposite the pulpit, and fully as ugly.

SACRISTY: The sacristy is on the Gospel side toward the nave of the church and about 3 varas from the sanctuary. It is a little room 4 varas square and 3 high, with seven round beams in the ceiling, a little window with a wooden grating on the east, and two doors, one leading to the church and the other to the street under a little portico which I shall soon describe. Both doors are single-leaved, without keys. Here there is a rough table of boards on an adobe base, at which the priest vests while contemplating a middle-sized print of the Immaculate Conception which hangs on the wall. An old unpainted chest with hinges, lock, and key, given by the said Bustamante. The following are kept in it:

Vestments: A usable damask chasuble with two faces (white and crimson), with accessories, all with silk galloon, the gift of the King. Another new one of crimson damask with ribbon galloon, with accessories except for frontal. And the Indians say that the same father who provided the two I mentioned at Nambe also provided these.

Linen: A usable Brittany amice. A very old Rouen alb. An extremely old Rouen altar cloth, and the aforesaid was the gift of the King. Another new Brittany altar cloth with narrow lace which the aforesaid Bustamante gave. A pair of usable double cor-

porals which the King gave. A thread and silk cincture given by a father. A purificator. Two finger towels. A pall of green ribbed silk with silk fringe.

Silver and other metal: A chalice with paten but no spoon. Three small vessels with the holy oils, and they are kept in a little cedar box with a lock but no key. The King gave the aforesaid. A pewter plate, which a father provided. A glass cruet. The missal is very old and has our [Franciscan] saints.

CONVENT

There is no convent, but the following substitutes for it. I spoke of a little portico when I was describing the sacristy. It is attached to the outside wall down the nave of the church on the same side as the sacristy. It measures 4 varas from the entrance to the center and is 5 varas long, with adobe seats around it. It serves both as cloister and porter's lodge. In the upper corner there is a door to the sacristy, and in the lower corner an ordinary door without a key to a small cell with a little adobe vestibule and a small window facing east. Farther down, and joined to the same wall, there is a room without a door which serves for the use of the moment. All is quite new, built by the Indians, and faces due east.

ITS SERVICE: This little pueblo has been a visita of Nambe in perpetuity. Here there are assigned to the minister of Nambe a fiscal mayor, a subordinate fiscal, three little sacristans and their chief. The latter take care of sweeping the church and convent, ringing the bell on the usual occasions, and serving the father when he comes to visit them. Sometimes the father comes to say Mass for them, and when they go to Nambe to hear it, they take small loads of firewood. The administration is organized in accordance with the mission's status as a visita, and I examined the parish records at Nambe as head pueblo. Therefore they are kept in the

---

2. Probably in memory of her husband, Nicolás Ortiz, who had been alcalde of Pojoaque some years before his death. See SETTLERS.

same books, but with the place to which they belong indicated.

ITS LANDS AND FRUITS: The fiscal mayor says that there are two plots, each about 80 varas square. And because they are among the lands belonging to the natives of the pueblo, and in order to avoid confusion in describing them, I refrain from giving their location at this time. They are fairly fertile; they are irrigated from the communal ditch; and they yield good crops, although the father does not specify the quantity since he has never measured it. The planting is entrusted to the pueblo, who take care of it and harvest it, until it is brought in.

PUEBLO

The hills I first mentioned at Nambe that come from the Sierra Madre as a ridge to the southeast, with the river at their foot, offer in this locality a rather high little level site with a pleasanter view than that at Nambe. Here, then, the little pueblo of Pojoaque and its church are located. The pueblo forms a plaza in front of the church, but not exactly opposite it, for it faces the church near the corner on the Epistle side. The four sides of the plaza consist of four tenements, which leave a large space in the middle, with three passageways, one near the aforesaid corner of the church, another at the corner below the tenement to the east of the church, and the third on the corner below the tenement that faces north. The foregoing shows that the church is outside the pueblo near the corner of the plaza that faces southwest. As for the houses, I refer to Tesuque.

NOTE: The Spanish settlement that I referred to as Pojoaque when I was describing Nambe is opposite this little pueblo, below it to the north, and on the other side of the river. Because of its location opposite it, it bears the same name as the pueblo.

ITS LANDS AND FRUITS: They are really surrounded because of the nearness of the aforesaid Spanish settlement, whose lands encircle them above and below. (The confusion that I mentioned when speaking of the convent lands resulted from all this that I am saying now.) Moreover, they are scanty, but they live off them. Their description is the same as that of those belonging to the Spanish settlement, for all grow grain. They are irrigated by ditches used by both Indians and settlers because they are in the same vicinity; and the harvest they yield is like that of the lands belonging to the citizens.

This pueblo belongs to the Tegua nation, but not all those who live together in it are Teguas, because about a third of the inhabitants are newcomers from various places.[3] But all speak the language of this tribe, and Spanish in the same way as other pueblos that I have already described. The same is true of their customs. They are all included in the following

CENSUS

27 families with 98 persons

3. Cf. HB, 3: 380. "In the following year [1707] he reduced some families of Tehuas Indians to the old pueblo of Pujuaque, called Nuestra Señora de Guadalupe; some of these families had been among the heathen and others were from various of the Tehuas pueblos."

San Ildefonso

The pueblo and mission of San Ildefonso[1] is on the same side of the river as Pojoaque and on the opposite side from Nambe. It is 2 leagues west of Pojoaque a little before one reaches the Río del Norte. It is about the same distance from Santa Fe as Nambe and lies to the northwest of the villa. I will describe the site as soon as I finish with the most important part of the visitation.

CHURCH

The church[2] is adobe with walls nearly a vara thick. The outlook and main door are due south. It is 35 varas long from the door to the high altar, 7 wide, and 8 high as far as the bed molding. The sanctuary is partly enclosed like the head of a transept, and the ascent to it consists of five steps made of beams, like a catafalque. The steps occupy more than a vara in the nave. The sanctuary measures 4 varas square and is higher than the nave because of the clerestory mentioned in other places. This church is dark.

The choir loft of this church is in the usual place and occupies the full width, flying 7 varas into the nave. It is supported by fourteen wrought beams that rest on a strong crossbeam with corbels set into the side walls. It has a balustrade, and the entrance is now from the flat roof of the convent through an ordinary door with a key. There is no furniture. The church has two very ill-made windows on the Epistle side facing east. There is also one in the choir which gives on a balcony like that at Nambe, so there is no need to describe it again.

As far as the clerestory, the roof consists of thirty-six beams with multiple corbels. From here on there are four like those in the nave, and seven of the same in the sanctuary. There is a vaulted arch made of adobe. The main door is squared, with a strong wooden frame instead of masonry. It has two well-paneled leaves with a wicket in one and is nearly 3 varas high by more than 2 wide. The only lock is a crossbar. There is a little adobe arch over the main door, and this holds a good middle-sized bell with a clapper. The cemetery is 30 varas square, with an adobe wall about a vara high, or a trifle higher, with two gates, one to the south and the other to the east.

As we enter the church, the baptistery is on the right under the choir with its walls extending beyond those of the church. This room is 6 varas square and 3 high and has

1. The pueblo of Bove was named in honor of the first commissary of the New Mexico missions, Fray Alonso Martínez, in July, 1598. G. P. Hammond and A. Rey, *Don Juan de Oñate* (Albuquerque, 1953), 1: 320. "Alonso" and "Alfonso" are variants of "Ildefonso." See GLOSS., St. Ildephonse.

2. The first church at San Ildefonso was built early in the seventeenth century. F. V. Scholes and L. B. Bloom, "Friar personnel and mission chronology, 1598-1629," NMHR, 19 (1944): 328. It may have been destroyed in the 1680 Revolt. There was a church there after the Reconquest, either a new one or the pre-Revolt structure repaired and rebuilt. This was burned in the Rebellion of 1696. J. M. Espinosa, *Crusaders of the Río Grande* (Chicago, 1942), p. 246. In 1706 a church was under construction at a site a mile north of the present church (HB, 3: 374) and it was dedicated in 1711. This church was destroyed about 1910, and the present church, which dates from 1905, may be at the location of the seventeenth century church. GK, pp. 122-23.

nine ordinary beams. The usual window with its wooden grating faces south over the cemetery, and there is an ordinary two-leaved door without a key to the church. On one wall there is an empty cupboard, and in the middle of the room a little wooden pillar, hollowed out to make a drain, and on it the baptismal font, which is a large earthenware bowl covered with a round piece of wood. The furnishings of the church are as follows:

HIGH ALTAR: The whole wall around the sanctuary is painted blue and yellow from top to bottom like a tapestry, and not too badly. This was done at Father Tagle's expense (and he did the most here as will be noted). In the center there is a painting of St. Ildephonse like those mentioned in the previous churches, and the King gave it. Above this there is another oil painting of the same size in a finely gilded frame of Our Lady of the Kings, with a curtain (on a rod) of blue ribbed silk embroidered and garnished with ribbon of another color. Governor Mogollón gave all this.[3] A small wooden tabernacle with a key, the outside upholstered with blue China satin and the inside with green China taffeta, with a little canopy and curtain of mother-of-pearl satin, and a small altar stone. Father Tagle made this. Twelve middle-sized colored prints, which the said father provided, hang at regu-

lar intervals on either side of St. Ildephonse.

The altar table is adobe with an ordinary altar stone. On a little step that imitates a gradin and holds the aforesaid small tabernacle, there are six small brass candlesticks which the King gave. The cross is just above the tabernacle and looks like a Jerusalem cross, but it is not. Three altar cards like those usually found on altars. A small bell and a wheel with seven more, and a bell crank such as is used on others. There is no dais, and the carpet is painted buffalo skin, now old but large and serviceable. The missal stand is painted [lacquer?] from Michoacan. A very pretty tin-plate lamp hangs from the vaulted arch. It is of medium size and is drawn up by a silk cord which has large tassels of the same material at the ends. Father Tagle provided everything mentioned from the tabernacle cross to the lamp.

NAVE: There are two altars on the walls that face the nave. The one on the right side has an old oil painting on canvas of Our Lady of Sorrows, about a vara in size, hanging on the wall. Above this is another, but a large one. This was given by the King and represents St. Michael in oils in a painted wooden frame. Still higher is another large one, but on buffalo skin, with the Crucifixion. Four small oil paintings on copper[4] with little black frames hang at regu-

3. Don Juan Ignacio Flores Mogollón was governor of New Mexico 1712-15.

4. "Laminitas al óleo." JS defines *lámina* as "a Plate of any metal. It is also taken for any Picture painted upon Copper."

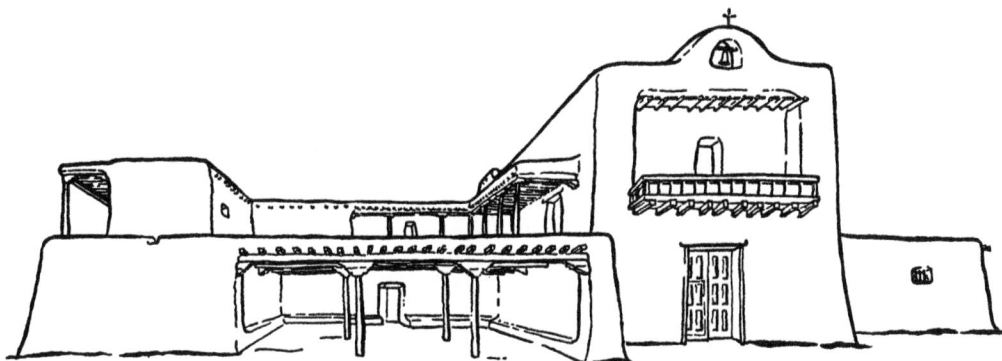

lar intervals on either side of Our Lady of Sorrows.

The other altar is dedicated to the Immaculate Conception, with a small image in the round. It is clothed and I will describe its adornment when I get to the sacristy. Above this Lady there is a large oil painting on canvas in a painted wooden frame, presented by the King, which represents Our Father St. Francis. Still higher there is another large painting on buffalo skin of St. Ildephonse. On either side of the Immaculate Conception there are two paintings on copper in black frames. The tables of these altars are adobe, and each one has an altar stone presented by the King.

With the exception of what was given by the King, everything on these two altars is owed to Father Tagle's solicitude. He also provided five large paintings on buffalo skin that hang around the vaulted arch. These represent various holy subjects. On the Gospel side there is a monstrous, but well arranged, tribune with a balustrade, lattices with wickets above and below like a covered balcony, and all painted blue and yellow. It flies more than a vara into the nave and is about 3 varas wide. It rests on six multiple corbels. Under this tribune is a monstrous confessional, and the resemblance is so great that the tribune might be its mother. Perhaps that is why they put it under it. On the Epistle side there is a very ugly pulpit, which is entered from the following

CHAPEL OF ST. ANTHONY: The door to this chapel is in the nave of the church, where it forms an arch in the wall. The two leaves are made of balusters from top to bottom and have no key. The chapel is outside the church wall toward the east. It is 16 varas long from the door to the wall of the high altar, and 7 varas in width and height. There is a window on the south face like those I have mentioned in other places. The ceiling consists of twenty-two wrought beams on small corbels. The furnishings are a carved St. Anthony about a vara high, adobe altar table, and nothing else. This chapel was built by the charity of Father Tagle and Governor Valverde.[5]

SACRISTY: The sacristy is on the Gospel side, joined to the nave of the church about 3 varas from the sanctuary. This room is 6 varas long, 3 wide, and 3 high, with ten wrought beams, an ordinary single-leaf door to the church with no key, another like it to the cloister, and a window in the end wall looking north. There are two cupboards in the wall with rough board doors with small latches, and these contain odds and ends belonging to the church. Along the whole width of the end wall, under the aforesaid window, is a plank table with legs, all very well made like a proper table, and the front painted to look as if it had drawers with locks and handles. Stretched tight above is a white buffalo skin painted with flowers and very pretty. This provides a place for the priest to vest.

This sacristy room is adorned as follows: At the foot of the said window on the aforesaid table is a little mirror in a black frame. Stanzas and prayers for vesting are arranged at regular intervals above the window and on either side. In the rest of the sacristy there are an old oil painting on canvas of Our Lady of Guadalupe; two middle-sized paintings on buffalo skin representing the Ecce Homo and Dolorosa; a standard print[6] with the Calvary illuminated; an ebony cross and painted crucifixion. The little niches are well touched with paint. One serves as a [rubrical] lavatory and the other to hold the little holy-water pot. There is a paper in a little black frame stating that the church and convent were built and founded by Father Tagle and dedicated on June 3, 1711. Two unpainted chests with keys, and in them the following:

Vestments: Two usable damask chasubles trimmed with the silk galloon, with two

---

5. Captain don Antonio Valverde y Cosío served as governor of New Mexico ad interim 1717-22. Hodge (AB-1634, pp. 235-36) confused this chapel with the church.

6. "Estampa de marca."

faces (white and crimson), with accessories, presented by the King. Another chasuble of blue plush, without accessories. Another of blue velvet, without accessories. Another of white lamé, without accessories. Another of blue camlet, with accessories except frontal. Another of white satin with accessories but no frontal. It is said that former fathers provided all these. Another of black damask with accessories including cope and cross sheath, all with imitation gold galloon, and Father Camargo provided this. An old white damask cope with narrow silk galloon. An old white satin humeral veil with silk galloon. Six palls of various colors and stuffs. It is also said that everything mentioned from the white cope on was provided by the aforesaid fathers.

Linen: Two good plain linen amices. Two usable Brittany albs. Two Rouen albs that the King gave. A fine altar cloth with lace provided by Father Tagle. Two more of Rouen with embroidered edges, which Father Ezeiza provided. A new thread cincture and another old one. Seven purificators. Two finger towels. A Rouen surplice.

Silver and other metal: A chalice with paten but no spoon, which the King gave. A small ciborium that Father Tagle provided, together with a small tabernacle fumed with gold, its monstrance, and glass. Two large cruets with their little plate which Governor Valverde gave at the request of the aforesaid father. Three little vessels for the holy oils, which the King gave, and these are kept in a little cedar box with a key. Thirteen small coins and two rings for arras, given by the King.

A thurible with incense boat and spoon, all of bronze. Two table candlesticks. A china plate. A processional cross which the King gave.

Other things: A white damask canopy with silk galloon and fringe. There is no mention of the donor. A mother-of-pearl shell for baptisms. A usable missal. Another very old one. Two old breviaries, which, along with the aforesaid missal and some

papers with introits, etc., written in musical notes, are for the use of the choir singers. Three armchairs upholstered in painted buffalo skin. Lectern for the ministers. A candelabra for the offices of Tenebrae and the wood for the catafalque, now all in ruins. Five sackcloth cassocks of various colors for the acolytes. A processional cross with a ragged yellow sheath, and processional candleholders of unpainted wood.

Adornments of the Virgin: They are more like dolls' things than adornments. Two little chemises of ordinary linen. Three little dresses (with tunic and mantle) of various colors and materials; they are all mixed up and very old. A small silver crown. A little wig. A little necklace of black pearls. A small pair of earrings of the same with black beads. Little coral bracelets. A little rosary of black beads. Three little jet amulets in the shape of a hand.[7] Three ribbons. A satin cincture. The things I mentioned when I spoke of the second altar in the nave of the church have now been noted in the sacristy.

CONVENT

The convent is joined to the church on the Gospel side and extends to the west. It forms a square between one side of the sacristy and the place where it joins an end wall of the porter's lodge. The latter deforms the square, for it juts out like a bulwark between the church and convent. Even so, I resign myself to beginning my description with this very thing in order to get out of this difficulty in haste. The aforesaid [porter's lodge] stands, then, in the cemetery facing south. It is so out of proportion that it is 15 varas square with adobe seats around it. In the middle are two wooden pillars

7. "Higuitas." An ancient charm against the evil eye. JS describes *higa* as: "a little Hand made of Jet, which in *Spain* they hang about Children to keep them from evil Eyes. A superstitious Custom. The Hand is made with the Finger clench'd and the Thumb sticking out between them."

with corbels to support the crossbeam which holds up the roof in the middle. At the entrance there are two more with corbels to support the crossbeam that receives the beams there. This arrangement results in its being like naves from within and like a portico from outside. The door is in the front wall. It is rather low, has two leaves, and the only lock is the crossbar.[8]

The cloister is very pretty and cheerful, for it is square and open, with adobe pillars at the four corners and others in between at regular intervals, but of wood, carved and with corbels above to imitate arches. Below there are balustrades between the pillars, and the patio is bare. There are rooms on all four sides. As we enter, the first thing on the right in a corner is the well for the stairs that formerly led to the choir. Today it is in such bad shape that it is used as a privy and even as a dunghill. The ascent, or entrance, to the choir is as I described it in its proper place.

Up beyond this stair well, along the church, is a dark room, and then the sacristy, the door to which is in a corner. Around this corner is a long room which runs to a big door which is the entrance to the upper part. Beyond this door there is another corner, and around it there are two rooms separated by a little passage that leads to the kitchen garden. From the lower room on this side a cell with its inner cell, which has a bolt, runs to the porter's lodge. All the foregoing except the sacristy are very tumble-down.

The great door I have just mentioned has two leaves, which are grilled with little balusters from top to bottom. It opens on a well like that of the stairway used by our Reverend Fathers Commissary in the Convento Grande of Mexico City to enter the little patio we call the patio of Jerusalem, and although the plan is not the same, there is a resemblance.[9] It has, then, a stairway of heavy planks with a balustrade and three little landings with balustrades on the open side, and, as we ascend, the father's dwelling is located on our right, and what I will soon describe is on our left.

At present the father's dwelling consists of the following: Three rooms, a large one in the middle with a vestibule of rough boards at the entrance, and one on either side. The one on the left as we enter is very narrow and is used as an inner cell with its tiny board alcove and bed of the same made by Father Guzmán. Here in this room there is a *coi* (see the description of the houses at Tesuque), which the father who now resides here installed as the entrance to the storeroom which he has below as a better and safer room. The middle cell is more used as a passageway than as a cell, for it is seldom, if ever, lived in. The room on the right is very livable because it is cheerful and well arranged.

This last room has a mirador in the form of a corridor which looks west and north over the kitchen garden, and a little to the east over the corral, for it goes around the walls that face in these directions. There are two doors to it, one facing west and the other north. This mirador projects about a vara and a half, and it is as high as the aforesaid room, with little balustrades between pillars.

On the left as we go up is the entrance to a portico with two arches on the open side, because there is a pillar in the middle. It looks south over the whole cloister below, and it is over the room that extends from the corner of the sacristy. It runs as far as the church and then turns forward, with another arched portico like the aforesaid, and runs to the corner of the church, facing west over the cloister above that dark room near the privy. Father Ezeiza built all these living quarters, and the father who lives here today has installed his kitchen in the corner

8. GK, pp. 75, 140, fig. 111, discusses the possibility that this was once an open chapel.

9. Unfortunately this patio is not identified by name in the plan of the Convento Grande reproduced in R. G. Montgomery, et al., *Franciscan Awatovi* (Cambridge, Mass., 1949), pp. 259-62.

the said porticos make over the sacristy (as has been seen). Nevertheless, this friar is of a mind to build a new dwelling in a more convenient place, for all the foregoing are badly cracked. The corral and stable are not fit to mention.

ITS FURNISHINGS: The board alcove and bed. A very large strong table and drawer that Father Irigoyen made. Two small chairs and a little bench that Father Vega installed.

ITS SERVICE: All together, a fiscal mayor, three subordinates, eight sacristans, eight cooks, four bakers, and they are allotted weekly as described at the mission of Nambe. In addition, a shepherd for the sheep, a herdsman for the horses, a woman to care for the hens. Carting of firewood for all purposes I have already described in the aforesaid mission, and to this I refer in order to avoid prolixity.

ITS LANDS AND FRUITS: There are five plots scattered among the milpas of the Indians and so small that some have about 20 varas, others little more, and the largest may have 60, but among them the annual harvest is usually 30 fanegas of wheat, a like amount of maize, and some legumes. This, although scanty, suffices for the maintenance of the missionary. The most important thing this convent has is a large kitchen garden surrounded by an adobe wall, from which they get a great many green vegetables. This kitchen garden is on the west and is reached from the convent as I said when I was describing it. The mirador mentioned is over it. At the foot of it, below the northwest corner of the mirador (inside the kitchen garden, of course) is a great pool with a very leafy poplar at its rim.

By artificial means a great deal of water is collected in the said pool to water the garden and one or another little milpa nearby. This water is brought from a little swamp (which lies about a musket shot to the west) by a ditch made of turfs. Father Vega installed this through the little milpas for the common good. The sowing, cultivation, and harvest are all in the father's care until the crops are taken in.

MISSION FATHER

The priest whom our Mother the Province has here now is Father Fray Manuel Vega, native of Mexico. He is forty-three years of age, twenty-three in profession, eleven and some months as a missionary in this Custody, divided as follows: Three years at Pecos, three more at Taos, four months in Santa Fe, five years at San Ildefonso where he now is. He has general faculties in Durango, revocable at will.

ADMINISTRATION OF THE MISSION: Daily at regular hours, morning and afternoon, the bell is rung for catechism. The unmarried men and women come, recite with the father, and afterwards he explains something to them, spending about half an hour. On feast days the whole pueblo comes to Mass; they recite either before or after it, and perhaps some little explanation is given them. The latter is not always done because of what I shall explain with regard to the administration of the mission of San Juan.

OBVENTIONS AND FIRST FRUITS: I refer to the general rule described at Santa Fe. With special reference to this place, there is sometimes a cow or a horse. The mission father says that the first fruits at this mission usually consist of 6 fanegas of wheat, a like amount of maize, about a fanega and a half all together of all kinds of legumes, 3 or 4 strings of chile, small amounts of green stuff. The Indians pay nothing.

EXPENDITURES: Food used for those serving in the household is not counted. About 2 jugs of wine. About 6 pounds of wax. A little more than 200 altar breads, for which a benefactor gives a half a fanega of wheat annually. The iron mold for making altar breads was given by the King, and at the time of my visitation it was at this mission, but now that I am drawing up my report, it is in Nambe as the result of a petition made to me by the father who now resides in that mission. And he gives altar breads to San Ildefonso weekly (without any subsidy from the aforesaid half fanega).

HOW HE ACQUIRES NECESSITIES: In order not to trouble ears worthy of respect, I refer to what I said at length in regard to Santa Fe.

CONVENT PROVISIONS: The following have been assigned to this mission by the Reverend Custos Fray Jacobo de Castro: 10 fanegas of wheat, 10 of maize, 10 sheep, 6 strings of chile, a pot of lard, half a fanega of frijoles, half an almud of salt. To this I added 2 wax candles and a bottle of wine. All is confirmed by the following

WRIT OF VISITATION

Mission of San Ildefonso, May 4, 1776. In prosecution of the juridical visitation which our Reverend Father Fray Francisco Atanasio Domínguez, one of the appointed preachers in the Convento Grande of Our Father St. Francis in Mexico City, Commissary Visitor for our Very Reverend Father Minister Provincial Fray Isidro Murillo, is making of this Custody, his Reverend Paternity proceeded to examine and did examine this inventory. Finding that it does not agree with the existing state of affairs because it dates from the year 1711, and in so long a time many things belonging to the church and convent have necessarily worn out, his Reverend Paternity therefore orders and commands the present missionary, Fray Manuel Vega, to record separately and clearly in the blank pages remaining in this inventory what actually exists now pertaining to the church, the sacristy, and the convent, including the rooms and furnishings of the latter, so that the inventory may agree with the one to be remitted to the Province and in order to avoid the confusion and difficulty there has now been in finding out what is gone and what actually exists.

With regard to the convent provisions, his Reverend Paternity approves and confirms what the Reverend Custos Fray Jacobo de Castro determined, adding only a bottle of wine and two wax candles. All this, as well as the convent furnishings, to wit: board bed, two small chairs, a table, and a little bench, must be handed over by the outgoing friar and received by the incoming one, who shall notify the Reverend Custos or his Vice-Custos of anything missing, and we order them to supply the lack. And the said Custos and his Vice-Custos cannot dispense with or take away anything included in this list, but they may, indeed, add all they find proper for the benefit of the mission and missionary, for this is the intention and will of our Superior Provincial Prelate, who so orders and commands *ratione officii* and therefore validly for all time. His Reverend Paternity so ordered, commanded, and signed before me, the undersigned secretary, to which I attest. Fray Francisco Atanasio Domínguez, Commissary Visitor. Before me, Fray José Palacio, secretary.

PUEBLO

Those hills that I first mentioned at Nambe as coming to the southeast and which I said sloped to a small level site at Pojoaque begin to deviate from the latter place. Therefore, about three-quarters of a league before reaching the Río del Norte they open up more and more like the mouth of a cañada to the west while the hills recede to the southwest. These hills, together with other separate ones that lie to the east-northeast, northeast, and north (in which are the little mounds of white stone mentioned before in the description of Pojoaque) offer a very reasonable plain before the meadows of the aforesaid river.

In relation to this plain, or depression, the pueblo with its church and convent lies almost in the center, extending toward the Río del Norte about a quarter of a league away and hemmed in by hills in the directions mentioned, with quite a view to the west and northwest, where there are sierras. Now then, the pueblo itself is to the east in relation to the church, with a sort of street between it and the church on the Epistle side, with the Chapel of St. Anthony lying across it. For better understanding and comprehension, the latter can be seen above.

Said pueblo is in the form of a very large plaza, clean and without any impediments. It consists of four tenements with three large passageways to the east, south, and north at their respective corners, and a small one to the west to lead to the church. The houses are arranged as I said at Tesuque, but larger and better kept than there. Therefore I say no more. Around the plaza at proportionate distances are the corrals, ovens, and henhouses.

ITS LANDS AND FRUITS: The Indians of this pueblo have lands in all four directions, but not divided equally, for to the east, north, and south there are a little less than three-quarters of a league. To the west, indeed, they have even more than a league, occupying both banks of the Río del Norte, since it runs through them. Those on the west side of the river are irrigated from this very river through adequate ditches taken from it where necessary. Some of those on the east side, where the pueblo is, are irrigated from the river, and others from the spring in the little swamp I mentioned when I was speaking of the convent lands. Still others are irrigated from the Nambe River, which is very scanty by the time it reaches these parts, because everyone located beyond Nambe bleeds it,[10] as is understood, and when it dries up, there are hardships for those of these lands. Here it is well to mention that the aforesaid small river flows behind and well in sight of the pueblo, i.e., near it and to the north, for it is to the rear of the pueblo and within a short distance it joins the Río del Norte.

These lands are very fertile and produce an abundant and very fine harvest of everything planted in them. Father Vega says that the melons and watermelons gathered here are better and larger than those from the Tierra Caliente. In this pueblo there are ten orchards of two varieties of peaches[11] and an occasional apricot tree. They are to the south in a canyon formed by mesas on both banks of the Río del Norte, and they are watered from a little spring that is at the foot of the east mesa. Even though the harvests are as plentiful as I have said, it happens that they complain that for five years past they have diminished because of the locust. Therefore the Indians have found themselves obliged to go out to seek food, and they return with but a poor supply, for this plague has been almost universal, and those who have had bonanzas have been cautious and have hardened their hearts.

The natives of this pueblo belong to the Tegua nation, whose native tongue they speak. With regard to Spanish, it is the same as with those mentioned before from Tesuque on. With regard to their pueblo in particular, they are affable, businesslike, fairly good, gay, and more inclined to cleanliness, as the good condition of their plaza, etc., shows. They are included in the following summary.

CENSUS

111 families with 387 persons

This mission has a very small number of settlers to administer. In relation to it they are on the east in six ranchos beginning where the citizens of Pojoaque end, although, indeed, they are not on the same bank, but on the same side as Pojoaque. They have their corresponding farmlands— not very good, since they are nearer to being poor. These are irrigated by the aforesaid Nambe River. Since these lands are very

10. "Le van sangrando." To this day a minor ditch off a main one is called a *sangría*.

11. "Durazno" and "prisco." According to F. J. Santamaría, *Diccionario general de americanismos* (Mexico, 1942), *prisco* is a small variety of *durazno*, indigenous to America.

sterile, it will be understood how scarce the crops must be, but the settlers redouble the sowing by efficient cultivation, and so they do very reasonably well in the harvest. They have servants of low class, whereas they themselves have the name and reputation of being Spaniards. Both masters and servants speak the Spanish current in these parts. They all are included in this summary.

CENSUS

14 families with 70 persons

Santa Cruz de la Cañada

Going north from San Ildefonso, the road leads for a while among broken hills, with a little mesa halfway (it is called the Mesilla de San Ildefonso) which stands on the left side of the road. It always runs upriver and in sight of the Río del Norte and finally comes out on the plain, where, 2 leagues from San Ildefonso, the mission of the Villa Nueva de Santa Cruz de la Cañada lies.[1] It is about 9 leagues from Santa Fe and to the north, quarter north-northwest, of the capital. It is established and located as I shall soon describe.

CHURCH

The church[2] has adobe walls more than a vara thick, and its appellation is the Holy Cross. The main door faces due east. From the door to the mouth of the transept, for there is a real one, it is 33 varas long, 9 wide, and 10 high to the bed molding. The transept is 7 varas long from the aforesaid opening to the first step, or riser, of the sanctuary, 15 varas wide, and more than a vara higher than the nave because of the clerestory, as described in other places. The ascent to the sanctuary consists of three little stairs made of beams, and they do not encroach on the transept since they are embedded in the well of the sanctuary itself, which is 7 varas square.

The singers in this church do not have their usual place to intone *Gloria Patri*, because the choir was moved forward to *Sicut*

1. This area became known as La Cañada in the seventeenth century when a number of scattered ranchos and haciendas were established there. After the Reconquest some of the former Spanish settlers reclaimed their lands, and in 1695 Governor de Vargas ordered the Indians to vacate the pueblos of San Lázaro and San Cristóbal to permit the founding of a Spanish town. The Villa Nueva de Santa Cruz was founded on the south bank of the Santa Cruz River at the site of the Tano pueblo of San Lázaro with some of the families brought to New Mexico by Fray Francisco Farfán in 1694, and also twenty families from Zacatecas. SANM, 1: nos. 132, 817, 818, 882; J. M. Espinosa, *Crusaders of the Río Grande* (Chicago, 1942), pp. 224-27; *Old Santa Fe*, 2:58. Some years later the town was moved to its present location on the north side of the river.

erat in principio. That is to say, there is none, except for the strong cross timber across the width of the church set on corbels.[3] This church has four windows with wooden gratings. One is located in the end wall of the transept on the Gospel side; there are two in the nave on the same side, and another over the main door. The latter is squared and entirely like those described before.

The roof of this church is arranged differently from the usual, for there are five cross timbers consisting of three strong beams each at regular intervals as far as the mouth of the transept. They are wrought

2. There was already a small chapel at San Lázaro when the Villa de Santa Cruz was founded there in 1695. In 1706, Cañada had "a small church and a bell," and was visited by the missionary stationed at San Juan. HB, 3: 374. During the first decades of the eighteenth century the new villa led a very precarious existence because of attacks by enemy Indians. The contemporary accounts conflict, and it is difficult to disentangle the facts about the settlement and its church. Cf. DHM, pp. 193-94. The church described here, which is still in existence, although alterations and additions have been made, was begun in the 1730's. On July 14, 1732, Governor Gervasio Cruzat y Góngora wrote to the viceroy that Fray José Irigoyen intended to build a new church at Cañada to replace the parish church. Because Father Irigoyen had not observed the legal formalities required by the royal patronage, the governor had refused his petition for Indian workmen. But since the old church was beyond repair, Cruzat y Góngora referred the matter to the viceroy, who, in a license dated Mexico City, October 31, 1732, granted his permission to build. In June, 1733, the license was remitted to the alcalde mayor of Santa Cruz, Captain Juan Esteban García. SANM, 2: no. 382b. In 1744 Father Menchero mentioned that the missionary was building "a sumptuous church" (HB, 3: 399), and it was not finished before the late 1740's.

3. A typically clerical witticism on the Latin doxology, which was often sung by the choir, especially at vespers. The singers cannot even start the first part (Glory be to the Father, etc.) because the choir loft has been moved to the second part (As it was in the beginning, etc.). And since there was nothing in the beginning when God began the creation, we have no choir loft and a wretched pun.

and have multiple corbels. In each of the five spaces between these cross timbers there are twelve wrought beams running lengthwise of the church. The roof of the transept is necessarily in the regular form and consists of twenty-four wrought and corbeled beams. The sanctuary has nine of the same in the natural position, with a vaulted arch made of boards. Of these ceilings, the one in the nave is owed to the person who built the church, who was Captain Juan Esteban García, citizen and native son of the kingdom. The others were the responsibility of the building funds and Father Fray Andrés García.

A buttress juts out from the front corner on the Epistle side as a tower buttress to hold a little tower with four arches and a balustraded balcony, which contains three rather middle-sized bells, very broken and minus clappers, that belong to the King. Father García made this little tower. The cemetery used today was arranged by Father Rojo, the present missionary, who made it very spacious, 32 varas square, with a wall about 2 varas high and two little gates on the south and east. The interior furnishings of this church are as I shall now describe them.

HIGH ALTAR: The altar screen is of the kind of wood common in the kingdom, and it is exquisitely made, for it is painted with white earth and consists of two sections that look like the boxes of a bull ring, for the niches are squared and, except for the chief one, all have little balustrades below as is customary in the aforesaid boxes. This altar screen begins at an adobe ledge like a gradin and does not reach the ceiling. It is 6 varas high and occupies the width of the sanctuary, which is 7 varas.

The principal niche is in the first [lower] section, and there is a large image in the round of Our Lady of the Rosary in it. Her entire apparel consists of the following: Dress of blue ribbed silk with fine silver lace. Hoop earrings of seed pearls. A small

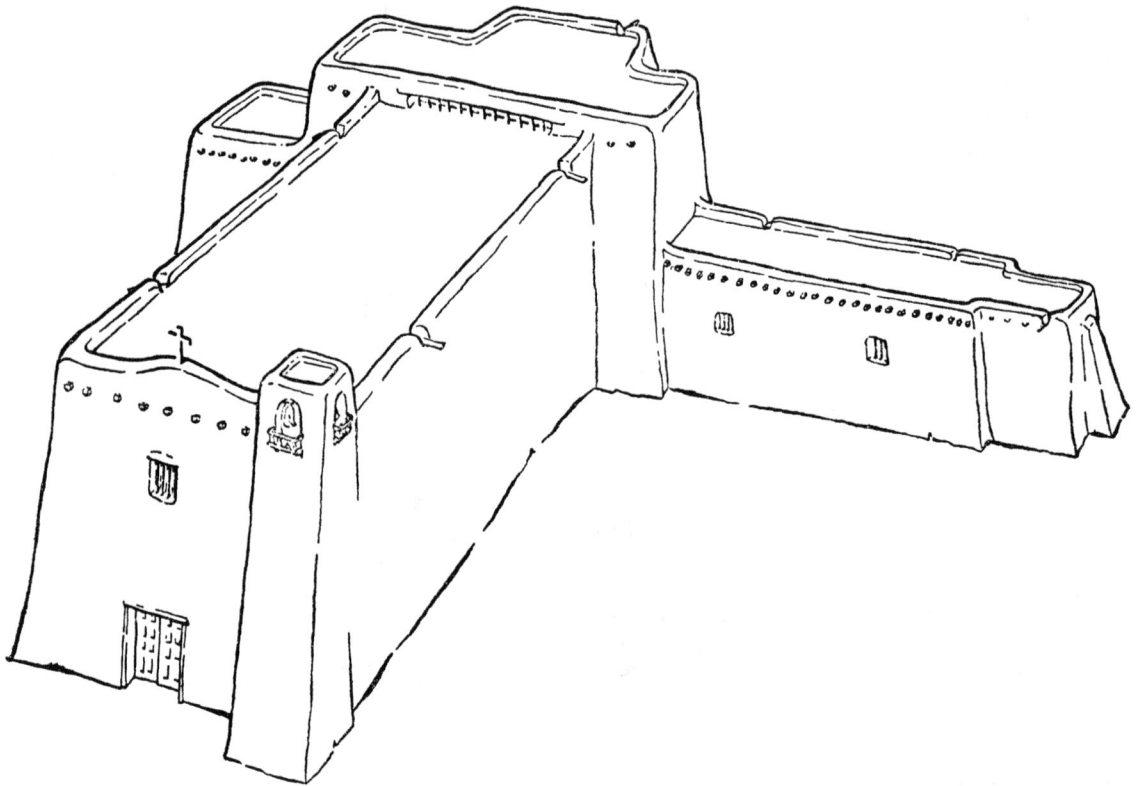

rope of little pearls with silver beads and black beads. Several ribbon flowers for the dress. Wristbands with lawn ruffles. A small silver rosary presented by Rita Romero. Another little strand of paper pearls given by Rita Martínez. Father García made the image, and perhaps for the shame of her being so badly made they left the varnish on her face very red. The articles of apparel have been given by benefactors.

On each side of the main niche is a large old oil painting, one representing the Immaculate Conception and the other the Rosary. On the second [upper] section of the altar screen in the center niche there are two little paintings on buffalo skin so old that their subjects cannot be distinguished. On each side hangs a large painting on buffalo skin, one of St. Louis, King of France, and the other an Ecce Homo. The following articles are on the aforesaid ledge that resembles a gradin.

Below the main niche a tabernacle of painted, silvered wood lined with blue satin, with a small curtain of the same material with silver fringe. It has doors with a key. Beside and above this tabernacle there are: First, above it, a lacquer crucifix with silver cornerplates, INRI, and nails. A small Jesús Nazareno. A similar St. Anthony. A lacquer Child Jesus which Francisca Atienzo gave together with a little Dolorosa, clothed and adorned with a small silver radiance and dagger, and a small string of paper pearls.

The altar table is wood, movable, and has an ordinary altar stone. It is always vested in old altar cloths, pall, frontal, wooden missal stand. There are also a small bell and a carpet, all wool with white flowers on a black ground, on the floor, for there is no dais. On one side there is a small table to hold what is necessary for sung Masses, and an unpainted chair. On the other side is the lantern used when the lamp is taken out; this is a small plain box like the case of a hall clock, with three ordinary panes above, one of which is a door. The sanctuary is enclosed by a little balustrade, and since there are little balconies at the corners as if it were a praetorium, they can be considered the pulpits on either side of the high altar. Father García made it.

TRANSEPT: The altar of the Third Order is on the Gospel side on the wall facing the nave of the church. It is dedicated to Our Father St. Francis, whose image is carved and about a vara high on a very ordinary litter. On this same altar, on either side of Our Father, there are a very large image in the round of Jesús Nazareno clothed in ribbed silk tunics, a white one underneath and a purple one over it, ordinary crown, cross, and rope, and a rather large Dolorosa in the round clothed in half cloth, but everything old. She has a silver radiance and a silver reliquary on her dress, two more of brass, one of lead, a shell cross, and three ordinary medals. These images belong to the church, not to the Third Order, although they are on its altar. Mass is never celebrated on the altar table on which the foregoing stand. It is of wood, movable, and belongs to the Third Order, together with [the image of] Our Father [St. Francis] and other trifles.

NAVE: On the right side there is an atrocious adobe table, the only furnishing of which is a Holy Sepulcher, with hinges, in a poor casket, but it does indeed have a little coverlet, three pillows, and a new Rouen sheet. Down below this table is a badly made confessional. The pulpit is in the usual location and is a horror. There are various mixed-up odds and ends in the rest of the nave, but they will be described in due course under *Other things*.

NOTE: The altar screen, the image of Our Lady of the Rosary, the large Jesús Nazareno, the Holy Sepulcher, casket, and the balustrade in the sanctuary were made and designed by Father Fray Andrés García, who worked day and night with his own

hands. So Juan José Bustos and Juan Manuel Hurtado, native sons and citizens of this Cañada, assured me.

THIRD ORDER

It is founded in this church and has the aforesaid altar with right to the bench mentioned in that place. In addition: A wooden cross of the kind used by the Third Order, a very old frontal of blue ribbed silk, and a bench. All the rest listed in the inventory is presumed to be worn out, for none of it is to be seen. Therefore writs of visitation were recorded in this and the other books pertaining to the Third Order commanding them to draw up new ones and with the clarity specified there.

ITS FEASTS: Annually, St. Louis, King of France, with vespers, Mass, procession, and sermon. Our Father St. Francis, with vespers, Mass, and procession. Our Lady of the Conception, the same as Our Father. Anniversary of the brethren, with office of the dead, Mass, and responsory. Monthly on their Sunday, Mass, procession, and responsory. For this annually:

EXPENDITURES: For the feast of St. Louis, 50 pesos in kind: wheat, maize, chile, etc. For the feast of Our Father [St. Francis], 25 pesos in the same. For the Conception, 25 pesos of the same kind. For the Anniversary, 15 pesos. For each monthly Sunday, 7 pesos. To this the following is added: Two arrobas of tallow for candles for the annual feasts, which cost 12 pesos. Two pounds of powder for the salvo on St. Louis' day, 8 pesos. Eighteen loads of pitch pine and firewood for the three aforesaid feasts at six loads each, 36 pesos. Forty candles of the worst kind of wax, 40 pesos. All amounts to 295 pesos per year.

RECEIPTS: These funds come from the membership of Tertiaries, who number 127, including both sexes. Each member contributes 3 pesos annually in whatever commodity he can, and so they collect 381 pesos. Subtracting from these the 295 for expenses, there are 86 left over. But it should be noted that for the past six years twelve brothers have not contributed because of their extreme poverty. Therefore 36 pesos a year must be subtracted from the 86 mentioned, leaving 50 pesos net in the hands of the chief brother, who says that for three years past he has received 750 pesos in wheat, maize, chile, etc.

CONFRATERNITY OF THE BLESSED SACRAMENT

At the time when the visitation was made the majordomo of this confraternity had gone to Mexico, and so the present mission father was called upon for the accounting. He says that it is completely bankrupt and that 420 pesos are due him. Nevertheless, the Masses on all the Thursdays and Sundays of the year have not been given up. Under these circumstances and in view of the absence of the majordomo, the majordomo of the Confraternity of Carmel obligated himself to donate wine and wax for the Masses until the other returns. The amount that the majordomo of this confraternity must give is the same as that given by the Carmel majordomo and will be seen when we discuss the latter.[4]

FABRIC AND ITS RECEIPTS

The majordomo is one Cristóbal Madrid, who says he receives the following: For

4. The Carmel chapel was already in existence in 1776, but the chapel of the Third Order is post-Domínguez and was built at the south end of the transept sometime before 1798. GK, p. 103. AASF contains a few documents concerning the confraternities at Santa Cruz: 1740, no. 1, Fragment of book of Blessed Sacrament Confraternity at Santa Cruz; Petition to establish it remitted by Vicar Roybal to Bishop Elizacoechea, approved at Durango, January 9, 1741; Re-erection and affiliation with Archconfraternity in Rome by Bishop Tamarón, n.d.; 1759, no. 1, Fragment of account book, 1759-60; 1794, no. 11, Fragment, relation of founding of Carmel and Blessed Sacrament Confraternities in Santa Cruz.

burial in the nave of the church, 4 pesos. In the transept, 16 pesos. In the Carmel chapel, 25 pesos. This is spent on the following

EXPENDITURES: A jug of wine, which costs 15 pesos. Of wax, 40 pitch pine candles, which amount to 40 pesos. Wheat for altar breads, 2 fanegas, which are worth 8 pesos; and the mission has an iron for making them, which the Father Vice-Custos Fray Agustín de Iniesta assigned to it at the King's expense. The majordomo of the fabric is under obligation to repair anything in bad shape and to mend and wash the linen. And since payment is so punctual (according to the statement of the majordomo of the Confraternity of Carmel), even the choir remains as I described it in its proper place. Moreover, for a whole year the majordomo of the fabric has not provided what is necessary for celebrating Mass, such as wine, etc.; instead the aforesaid majordomo has given it, according to his own statement.

CARMEL CHAPEL

It is at the head of the transept on the Epistle side, outside the walls of the church and extending to the north. Now then, the entrance is from the church by a squared door in a strong wooden frame, with two leaves and no key, grated from a third of the way up. It is 3 long varas high and more than 2 wide. The chapel is single-naved and is [20] varas long from the door to the wall of the high altar, 6 wide, and 8 high. The sanctuary is marked off by two stairs made of wrought beams, and it occupies 6 of the 20 varas mentioned.

The choir loft is over the door, occupies the width of the chapel, and flies a long vara into the nave. It is supported by eight strong corbels. There is no railing because it fell down. There are two windows with wooden gratings on the Epistle side, and they face east. The ceiling consists of twenty-six wrought and corbeled beams. The floor is the bare earth. The furnishings are as follows:

HIGH ALTAR: There is no altar screen, but on a wooden bench that runs the width of the wall like a gradin there is a rather pretty gilded and painted tabernacle lined with blue satin, with a curtain to match. It has doors with a key. On this tabernacle there is a rather middle-sized image in the round of Our Lady of Carmel dressed in purple lustrine, with a little wig, silver crown, scapulary of the material mentioned with its small silver shield, and a tiny Child Jesus. Four large oil paintings of holy subjects on buffalo skin are arranged at regular intervals on the wall, along with four others of medium size. The altar table is nothing more or less than a console, but of unpainted wood and bare.

ITS CONFRATERNITY: A legal instrument attests that it was founded in this villa when Father Fray Juan Mingues was missionary here, with faculty and license from the Reverend Father Provincial of the Carmelites of New Spain, Fray Miguel de Santa Teresa, issued on April 3 of the year 1710. I will give a more extensive account of all this in a separate place, since this mention suffices for the present until I have said what strictly pertains to my visitation, because it is in charge of the religious.

ITS FEASTS: Annually, Our Lady of Carmel with vespers, Mass, sermon, and procession. Anniversary of deceased members of the confraternity with office of the dead, Mass, and responsory. Each month on the Sunday assigned to them, sung Mass, procession, and responsory. Every Saturday, sung Mass and responsory. It spends the following on these and other things.

EXPENDITURES: The feast of Our Lady, 50 pesos. For the Anniversary, 16 pesos. For the monthly Sunday, 6 pesos. For each Saturday, 6 pesos. All this amounts to 306 pesos a year, which are given to the father annually in a fixed amount of 50 sheep and the remainder in seeds. No account is kept of the wax except that the majordomo brings the amount used. A jug of wine at 15 pesos. A pound and a half of powder for salvos on the day of Our Lady, 6 pesos. Firewood for the same day, 8 pesos. Forty pesos a year to the sacristan. Forty pesos to the singer for the same period. All mounts up to 415 pesos a year, which are paid in sheep and seeds.

ITS RECEIPTS: These come from the members of the confraternity, who are numerous, through the majordomo's hands. The present majordomo is Don Juan Bautista Vigil. They contribute a peso each in whatever the land has to offer, but since not all of them contribute (those who live around Albuquerque are now four years in arrears), as a consequence no proper account can be drawn up. I have already described the furnishings of this chapel, and I will give further details in the following:

SACRISTY OF THE CHURCH

It is joined to the church on the Gospel side at the head of the transept, where there is an ordinary one-leaved door without a key. From there to the front it is 7 varas long and 5 wide, with twelve round beams in the ceiling. There is no window, but there is an ordinary single-leaved door with a good key to the convent. It serves as the baptistery, and for this reason the baptismal font is near a corner on a small adobe pillar. On one side of this room there is an irregular wooden table with three drawers in a row, and there is a key to the middle one. On the wall above this table hang eight middle-sized prints in their little black frames. The following is kept in the said drawers.

Vestments: A complete set of vestments with accessories, including dalmatics, etc., of white half wool in usable condition, which Father Camargo gave. A white satin chasuble trimmed with narrow gold galloon, with accessories. Another of mother-of-pearl satin trimmed with silver galloon, with accessories. Another of green satin with gold galloon, with accessories. Another of purple satin trimmed with ribbon galloon, with accessories. It is not known who gave these, and they are usable. Another of black satin trimmed with silver galloon, with accessories, which Ventura Mestas gave. A satin cope that serves for two, white with silver galloon, and purple with white chamois; and Father Campo Redondo provided it. Another of mother-of-pearl satin with silver galloon, now old, which Father Gabaldón provided. Another of black satin with silver galloon which Father Camargo gave. A frontal of mother-of-pearl satin with narrow imitation galloon. A yellow one like it. A purple humeral veil with silver fringe only. Three palls of blue ribbed silk. There is no mention of who gave this last.

Linen: A fairly good amice of plain Brittany. An alb to match. Two extremely ancient Rouen altar cloths. Three pairs of double corporals with their palls. Seventeen purificators of various kinds of linen. Five finger towels.

Silver: A chalice with paten and spoon that probably came from the King. A rather middle-sized ciborium. A middle-sized tabernacle, gilded and with glass. A little radiance. Three small vessels for the holy oils in a little Michoacán box with a key. Thirteen small old coins with their two rings for use as arras; they are kept in a little wooden chest without a key. There is no reference to whether the King or others gave the foregoing.

Other metal: The baptismal font. Two small candlesticks. A little plate. A thurible with accessories. A holy-water pot. Shell for baptizing. A small cup with salt for the same purpose. The same situation as above occurs with regard to the donor.

Other things: An old missal. Another worse one, and a breviary for the singer. A *Manual* by Osorio and another one by Vetancurt.[5] An old banner of white satin. A canopy to match. A processional cross of wood painted black with a brass Christus

and cornerplates. Two plain wooden processional candleholders, turned on a lathe. A coffin. A very large cross with its wheel inlaid at the top. Another one, not quite so large, with wooden nails. Two unpainted chests with keys, and in them the following:

BELONGING TO THE CONFRATERNITY OF CARMEL: An old chasuble of white satin with accessories. Three old frontals of various colors and materials. Fourteen palls of various colors and materials. A cloth cincture.

Linen: Two fairly good Brittany amices. Three similar albs. Two altar cloths. Two pairs of double corporals with purificators. Two little cross sheaths for the image of Jesús Nazareno. A tear cloth.

Silver and other metal: A chalice with paten and spoon. Two cruets with covers. A crown in addition to the one for Our Lady. A separate spoon. An amulet in the shape of a hand. Two small candlesticks. Six candlesticks. Some snuffers. Five little bells.

Other things: Five mantles of various colors and materials. Two little curtains. A missal. A little canopy. A pair of paper pearl earrings with brass hoops. A boxwood comb. Two small brushes.

Note: First: Antonio Martín, citizen of a small place (now abandoned because of the enemy Indians) called Ojo Caliente, gave this Carmel chapel an old white satin chasuble with accessories and also a chalice with paten and spoon and an old missal. These ornaments were used in a chapel (which still exists) which served the pious citizens of that place.[6] But as soon as it was abandoned, the same Martín, owner and patron of that chapel, applied the aforesaid for the use of this one. Later, in his testament, he made

---

5. Fray Agustín de Vetancurt, *Manual de administrar los santos sacramentos, conforme a la reforma de Paulo V y Urbano VIII. Sacado de los Manuales de los Padres Fr. Miguel de Zarate, Fray Pedro de Contreras, etc.* (Mexico, 1674, and later editions).

6. HB, 3: 399, describes Ojo Caliente in 1744. In 1748 the settlers of Ojo Caliente, Santa Rosa de Abiquiu, and Pueblo Quemado petitioned the governor for permission to move to a safer location because of Ute and Comanche attacks. Governor Codallos granted them permission to do so for the duration of the danger. Ojo Caliente was resettled in 1768-69. SANM, 1: nos. 28, 655, 656.

the provision that if the place mentioned should again be settled, the ornaments should return to the old chapel. In view of this I consider that the aforesaid is on loan, and therefore I do not mention it in the inventory, but only state how it happens to be here.

Second: The following were not recorded in the inventory: Two middle-sized paintings on buffalo skin, and these are the ones I mentioned that hang one above the other on the altar screen of the church. The little Dolorosa which is on that altar, a gift of the Atienzo woman. The two large crosses I mentioned under *Other things.* The five little bells I mentioned under the metal belonging to the Carmel chapel. I ordered that all this should be recorded in the new inventory which is to be made by my command.

The third thing to be noted is: In the time of the Mission Father Campo Redondo, a sacristan ran away with various things which have not since been recovered. For this reason some items are missing, but I record (as everywhere) what actually exists.

CONVENT

The convent[7] is joined to the church on the Gospel side and extends to the south, forming a square between the head of the sacristy and the corner of the church on the side mentioned. The porter's lodge is there, lies inside the cemetery, and faces east. This is a room with the aspect of a low little portico, for its floor is below the level of the cemetery. It is 12 varas long by 5 wide, with fourteen rough beams in the ceiling. The pillars that divide the archlike openings are two great rough beams which leave the center substitute for an arch entirely open, while the side ones are partly closed by an adobe railing below. The door is in the middle of the façade and is very small, with two leaves and no key.

As we enter, the east is behind us, and on our left there are two cells, each with an inner cell and a lock. The first one is now used as a storeroom, and Father Gabaldón put a lock on it. The second is the present kitchen. Father Rojo installed a lock. It is on a corner. Around the corner from here, facing south, is a salon with an ordinary two-leaved door with a key, which Father Rojo has. Today it really serves as a passage, for as we enter there is a very small board stairway with an adobe railing near the corner immediately to our right. This is used for what I shall explain as soon as I finish saying that there is no window in this salon, for the one it had to the south has been closed up, and Father Rojo opened a door to the street in the corner opposite the aforesaid stairway and made something like a tower buttress there outside which permits one to attend to the demands of nature without being overlooked, even from the salon, since he installed a door.

The little stairway mentioned ascends to the entrance of a cell which, with its inner cell, reaches to the corner. Father García erected it like a rampart halfway up the walls, with a little mirador to the south which is now covered because Father Rojo, seeing that it was rather low near the street and fearing that the enemy [Indians] might harm him from there, reduced it to the status of a little hall and opened a window on the convent patio. In the inner cell an adobe dais serves for a bed, with its partition wall as a screen. This inner cell is on a corner, and the other side of the building runs from it with two separate rooms, and then the stable adjoins the sacristy.

There is no cloister except for a portico, but there is a clear patio between the aforesaid sides of the convent and the church. It is 30 varas square. Father Gabaldón built most of this convent. Father Campo Redondo finished the little that remained to be done. Father García built the aforesaid, and

7. By 1808 the convent was in very poor condition and a new one was built. GK, p. 103.

Father Rojo made quite a high breastwork with an embrasure for defense if the occasion should arise.

Its FURNITURE: An ordinary table with a drawer but no key. A small old cabinet with a key on a little table. A small chair. A little bench.

Its LANDS AND FRUITS: These amount to nothing more than a small plot which is almost at the foot of the condemned mirador. It is so small that it has 15 varas on one side and 5 on the other. It is used as a little kitchen garden, and I will tell you why there is no more on a more opportune occasion.

MISSION FATHER

By order of our Mother the Holy Province, and without a royal allowance because of the disposition mentioned in regard to Santa Fe, Father Fray Manuel Rojo serves this Villa of Cañada. He is a native of Mexico, fifty-eight years of age, forty-two in profession, and twenty-six as a missionary in the Custody, divided as follows: Pecos, four months, Santa Fe, one year, nineteen years in Albuquerque, and four in La Cañada. He says that when he came, he was detained in El Paso for six months for lack of transportation, and that after he was here in the interior, obedience transferred him to the missions at La Junta de los Ríos, but it came to nothing because of the failure of the escort Captain Rubí de Celis had promised for those missions.[8] And therefore he was detained another six months in El Paso waiting for a new convoy. I did not see his faculties for confession because, *inscio prelato,* he had remitted them to Durango.

ADMINISTRATION OF THE MISSION: In addition to the requirements of the Third Order and the other matters shown above, the work of administration is constant, now in the villa, now outside it. And the settlers assured me that the said missionary was their father indeed and that if they had not been struck by lightning, the father was responsible. Every Sunday, explanation of Christian doctrine. On Sundays and feasts of Our Lady, rosary of seven decades in the afternoon. The monthly Sundays of the Third Order and Carmel as assigned to them, general communion. The nineteenth of each month, sung Mass in honor of Lord St. Joseph, at which very many take communion. Sundays of Lent, sermon in the afternoon. Mondays, Wednesdays, and Fridays of Lent and Advent, exercises of the Third Order with their homilies. Palm Sunday, sermon on the Passion. All this gratis.

The following is paid for. Patron saint on May 3, 50 pesos in seeds and chile. Holy Wednesday, sermon on the Blood of Christ, a small jug of wine. Sermon of the Three Falls on that day, a little jar of corn syrup. The day of the Descent from the Cross, a calf on that day. Sermon on the night of the feast of Our Lady of Solitude, a jug of wine.

When it is necessary to give the Most Holy Viaticum, if the place is far from the church, Mass is said on the portable altar in the sick person's house. The Most Illustrious [Bishop] Tamarón gave permission for this.[9] And meanwhile guards and spies are posted in case there might be an attack by enemy [Indians]. If it is near the church, Mass is celebrated there and afterwards Our Lord goes forth. The Confraternity of St. Michael donates the wax for this function.

There is a very small school for children in the father's charge. Their parents give the master an annual sum, and the father

8. Don Alonso Victores Rubí de Celis was in command of the presidio and alcalde mayor of El Paso as early as 1738. F. Ocaranza, *Establecimientos franciscanos en el misterioso Reino de Nuevo México* (Mexico, 1934), pp. 168-69. We also find references to him there in 1744 and 1750. HB, 3: 406, 407, 455. He led an expedition to La Junta in 1750-51 and, according to C. E. Castañeda, a second one in 1759-60. See J. C. Kelley, "The historic Indian pueblos of La Junta de los Ríos," NMHR, 27 (1952): 273-75. In 1760 Captain Manuel de San Juan was in command of the presidio at El Paso. AT, pp. 29, 35.

9. Cf. AT, pp. 63-64.

gives him food, drink, and clothing within reason. At present it looks as if the school is about to come to an end, because the master is on the point of death.

OBVENTIONS AND FIRST FRUITS: For the general rule I refer to what I said with regard to Santa Fe. In regard to this villa in particular, it comes out almost the same as there. And therefore a certification signed by the alcalde mayor and the most important citizens will be included in the proper place.

There is complaint about the first fruits because the locust levies its toll, but not counting this, there are usually collected 80 fanegas of maize, almost an equal amount of wheat, about 6 fanegas of all kinds of legumes, about 20 strings of chile, about 400 heads of onions, some fruit, because there are many orchards near this villa and they give an almud of each kind and a bunch of grapes. The method of collection is by carts at the rate of 15 pesos each, and each carter earns a peso per day. The job usually takes fifteen or twenty days, but it is true that the carts cost the aforesaid amount for the whole of that period.

ITS SERVICE AND EXPENDITURES: The missionary here has the same pension as the one at Santa Fe, and the same holds true for service and expenditure. Cook, 8 pesos; sacristan, 8 pesos; stableboy, 6 pesos; bearer of letters, 6 pesos; two wood gatherers in winter, which lasts seven months, and one in summer, which lasts five months, at 4 pesos each. All payment is in local produce and by the month, and they eat in the household at the expense of their master, the father. With regard to grinding wheat, the same thing holds as in Santa Fe. In addition the tortilla-maker for so many servants earns 8 pesos a month in the same.

HOW HE ACQUIRES NECESSITIES: To avoid delay on this point, I refer to what was said about Santa Fe, but with regard to the present friar in particular, I state that he says that since the fifty sheep he receives from the Confraternity of Carmel are very small and sickly, he finds himself obliged to give three for one large *and healthy* one. At the same time this friar showed me a paper from a certain merchant[10] of this kingdom lending the father a pound of chocolate. Not only is this a forced loan, but he demands in return 6 pounds from the dispatch, alleging loss of profit. These loans usually occur because the dispatch is detained for a long time in El Paso (God knows why), as I saw when I came in the year '76 when the back shipment due from the year '74 finally went forward to these poor friars. By that time many were drinking *atole* rather than get into debt under such tyranny.

CONVENT PROVISIONS: Father Rojo received this mission without any provisions, and when I wanted to assign a reasonable and proper amount in proportion to the receipts, the said father alleged and made frivolous excuses. Although I am obliged not to give these any weight, I nevertheless dissimulated and used prudence, putting off to a more favorable occasion the determination of an amount in accordance with the foregoing. And this will be done with the necessary force and efficacy. It is not, therefore, included in the following

WRIT OF VISITATION

Villa of La Cañada, April 17, 1776. This inventory was examined by our Reverend Father Visitor Fray Francisco Atanasio Domínguez, and in view of the fact that many things belonging to the Confraternity of Carmel are mixed up with those belonging to the main church and because his Reverend Paternity had difficulty in finding out which belonged to which, to avoid further confusion his Reverend Paternity therefore commands and orders the present mission father, Fray Manuel Rojo, to make a new inventory in the same book, recording separately and clearly the things belonging to each, noting who gave them, so that this in-

10. Pedro José Pino. See SETTLERS.

ventory may agree with the one to be remitted to the province. For the rest, he thanks the said father for his punctilious fulfillment of his duty and charges him to continue thus for the benefit of souls, the upholding of his honor, and the credit of our holy habit. His Reverend Paternity so provided, ordered, and signed before me, the undersigned secretary, to which I attest. Fray Francisco Atanasio Domínguez, Commissary Visitor. Before me, Fray José Palacio, secretary.

The parish books were examined, and, finding that the entries are not in the father's hand, although they bear his signature, and that whoever writes them puts one year for another, causing great confusion by this mistake and carelessness, I therefore ordered and commanded by the decrees I recorded in the said books that he should write them himself, and if not, that he should examine and correct them before signing them in order to avoid mistakes. At the same time I noted that these books had not been presented to the prelate of this Custody. Therefore I left orders to continue them with my permission, and that when the foliation is complete, he take prompt action to submit them to the prelate of the Custody.

In addition to these books there are two folio volumes in this mission, one of Marriages, which begins in the year 1726 and ends in '68, another of Burials, which begins in the year 1727 and ends in the same year as the other. Two separate books, one of Marriages, which begins in the year 1716 and ends in '25, the other of Burials, which begins in the year 1711 and ends in '25. Four parchment leaves in the latter contain the elections of majordomo of the Carmel Confraternity for the year 1710. Two separate books, one with the license patent of the Reverend Provincial of the Carmelite Order, list of founders, expenditure and receipts from the year 1720 to 1749; another containing the same accounts from the year

'21 to '60, and in this the contribution of sheep and funds by the Confraternity of Carmel are recorded.

VILLA

In view of the fact that the Villa of Santa Fe is not as golden as the glitter of its name, in spite of the circumstances mentioned that it is the capital, etc., it will be apparent that this Villa of La Cañada, which does not have such an ostentatious aspect, is probably tinsel. It is established and located at the wide mouth of a cañada which comes from east to west, running 3 long leagues from the Sierra Madre, and then, widening like the mouth of a clarion, its hills wheel to the north around some gravelly places without breaking from the aforesaid sierra. To the south there are other hills joined to those that have the little mounds of the fine white stone.

At the same time the said hills overlook a beautiful plain which runs from their foot toward the Río del Norte. Speaking of this villa, this situation permits its location at the wide mouth I mentioned before one reaches the river mentioned, which is about half a league from it. The church, then, is in the place I described, with eight small houses like ranchos to keep it company. The rest of the villa is nothing more than ranchos located at a distance as I described them at Santa Fe. Some of them lie down the highway to the south in the direction of San Ildefonso, others to the west on the meadows of the Río del Norte, and still others, the least in number, to the north.

Up the cañada there is a river, which, although it arises in the aforesaid sierra from three not very large springs, is joined from very high up by three or four rivulets which feed it more water than it brings from its source, and therefore it is permanent. This river takes various names from the little places through which it flows, so when it comes to La Cañada, it takes that name, and, passing in sight of the convent to the south, it flows into the Río del Norte very far downstream. Upriver it flows through the settlement, and so some ranchos are on one bank and others on the other—that is to say, some are north of it and some south. There is trout fishing along all of it where there are deep places. And in addition to drinking its delicious crystalline water, this villa has the use of it for irrigation.

ITS LANDS AND FRUITS: In view of the location as described, it is obvious that what comprises the villa will have lands in accordance with the site, since it offers such, noting that some settlers use the aforesaid water for their irrigation and others find the Río del Norte more convenient. As a result of the fine location described, some lands are better than others, and therefore (barring accidents) there is a copious harvest. Here there are good orchards of fruits such as pears, grapes, peaches, and others that resist the cold, and there is also a fine crop of these.

ITS DISTRICTS: Their location and the distances to them are:

Chimayó, up the Cañada somewhat to the east northeast in relation to the villa, is about 2 leagues from it. It is a large settlement of many ranchos like those mentioned in all the foregoing, with good lands and many more orchards than the Villa of Cañada, but there are no pears. This whole settlement uses the aforesaid river, which is called Chimayó around here, and the settlers, who usually harvest a great deal, water their lands with it. In some nooks like cañadas which there are near Chimayó to the south, there are some ranchos with different place names, but they are so small that they have been included under what I have just said. There are two small mills in this Chimayó.[11]

Quemado,[12] a league above Chimayó and in the same direction, is about 3 leagues from the aforesaid villa. This large settlement is so near the foot of the Sierra Madre that it lies in one of its cañadas. This runs about half a league from north to south, and its width offers very good level sites of farmland. These are planted on either side of a pretty good river with a rapid current and very clear, delicious water that runs from north to south until it joins the one that flows to La Cañada in an appropriate place. The settlers of Quemado use its river for irrigation and harvest well and abundantly from their good lands. There is no fruit. The fish in the river, small trout.

Truchas, much higher up the cañada than Chimayó, is to the east-northeast in relation to the above villa and about 4 leagues from it. This settlement is on a high level site provided by a ridge of the aforesaid sierra, with very good lands, although there is no river. But since the Almighty gave man what he needs, those interested in these lands, with prodigious labor, dammed up in a small canyon the water of a little rivulet that came through it, which arises in the east in the sierra itself. By making it rise in the dam to a height of 60 or more varas, they succeeded in using it very freely for irrigation by means of a good ditch (which must be a league from the settlement). They have a copious harvest of good wheat and legumes. Maize does not usually ripen because of the cold, and for this reason they sow the former heavily and very little of the latter. This settlement is not of ranchos, but around two plazas because Governor Vélez Cachupín issued orders to this effect since they are almost on the borders of the Comanche tribe, whose people make incursions from that vicinity.[13]

12. Referred to in 1750 as "San Francisco Xavier del Pueblo Quemado, Partido de Chimayó." SANM, 1: nos. 766, 767, 768.

13. Governor Vélez founded the settlement of Nuestra Señora del Rosario de Truchas in 1754 by making land grants, chiefly to members of two families, the Romeros of Santa Cruz and the Espinosas of Chimayó. Chimayó and Quemado just grew, while Truchas had some official establishment.

11. Long afterwards Chimayó won fame for its weaving and its shrines. Settlement there began after the 1696 Rebellion and gradually increased to the seventy-one families residing there in 1776.

The whole population that comprises the parish administered from this Villa of Cañada, who live in various places as described, are people of different classes which I refrain from describing in order to avoid prolixity and save confusion. Suffice it to say that most of them pass for Spaniards. Some necessarily have servants while others do not, but all speak the Spanish current and accepted here. All are included in the following summary.

San Juan

Two leagues north of La Cañada, in sight of and upstream on the Río del Norte, along the same good plain I have just mentioned in my description of the aforesaid villa, is the pueblo and mission of San Juan. It is 11 leagues from Santa Fe and lies to the north of it. I will describe the site later.

CHURCH

The church[1] has adobe walls nearly a vara thick, and the outlook and main door are to the east. The nave is 36 varas long from the door to the first step of the sanctuary, 8 varas wide, and 8 high up to the bed molding. The sanctuary is closed in like the head of a transept, and the ascent to it consists of three poor steps. It measures 4 varas, almost in a square, and is a little higher than the nave because of the clerestory. The choir loft is in the usual place, occupies the width of the nave, and flies 5 varas into it. It is supported by fourteen wrought beams that rest on a strong cross timber set into the side walls with corbels. It has a balustrade, but no furniture, and the entrance is from the flat roof of the convent. On the Gospel side there are two poor windows with wooden gratings that face south over the convent, and there is another in the choir which serves as a door to a balcony like the one described earlier at Nambe.

The ceiling of the church consists of forty corbeled beams in the nave and the clerestory rises from the one facing the sanctuary. Beyond this there are three more of the same. The sanctuary has six beams like those mentioned and a vaulted arch like the one at Nambe. The main door is squared, with a strong wooden frame instead of masonry. It has two paneled leaves, is 3 varas high by 2½ wide, and the lock is a crossbar. Above the main door is a poor arch containing two good middle-sized bells without

extends outside the church wall to the north. It is 5 varas square, 4 high, and its ceiling consists of ten round beams. There is a window to the east, and the door to the church is an ordinary two-leaved one with a grating and no key. In the middle of this room stands a small adobe pillar with an earthen bowl upon it for the baptismal font.

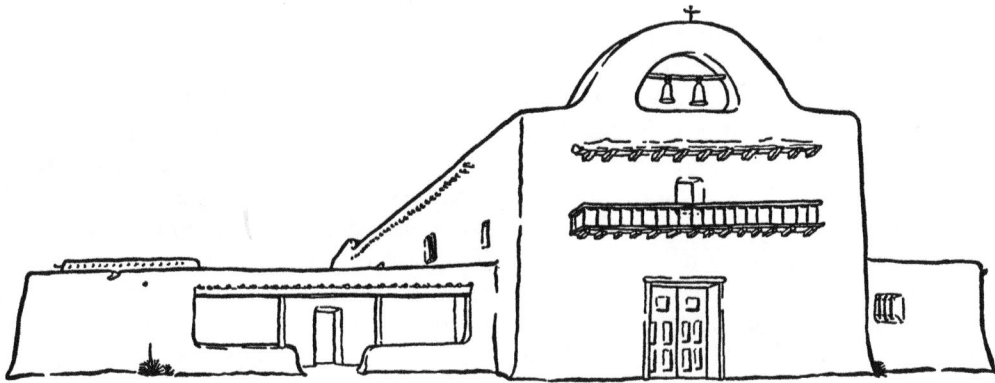

clappers, but they are rung with stones. The cemetery measures 22 varas not very square, with an adobe wall much more than a vara high and three little gates to the north, east, and south.

As we enter the main door, the baptistery is on our right underneath the choir, and it

1. The church described by Domínguez no longer exists, for the present pseudo-Gothic brick structure dates from the late nineteenth or early twentieth century. Father Alvarez tells us that a church was under construction in 1706 (HB, 3: 374), and in this case it is probable that there was little, if anything, left of the pre-Revolt structure. Domínguez, however, says that Father Juan José Pérez de Mirabal built the church he describes here. Although the Provincial records assign Father Mirabal to San Juan in 1726, the parish books show that he was at Taos from October, 1722, to July, 1727. He actually resided at San Juan, March to October, 1746, and from April, 1747, to February, 1763, including his term as custos, 1747-49. There is no doubt that there was an eighteenth-century church at San Juan before the period of Mirabal's residence there, but he may well have erected a new one or made such extensive improvements that he was considered the builder. See FRANCISCANS, Pérez de Mirabal.

There are some old pieces of wood for a catafalque and a bench in this room. The whole floor is the bare earth. The church looks like a gallery, and its furnishing is as follows:

HIGH ALTAR: The altar screen extends from top to bottom. Governor Vélez Cachupín paid for it and left the design up to Father Junco. The result is a great hulk like a monument in perspective, all painted yellow, blue and red. In the center hangs an old oil painting on canvas of St. John the Baptist, 2 varas high by 1½ wide, with a frame of painted wood. The King gave this. At the foot of this canvas is a cross a vara high on a chunk of a pedestal, painted like the altar screen. Below this cross is a tabernacle like the altar screen. Then there is an adobe gradin, on which there are six pieces of iron that look like buckets, for candlesticks, and they are fastened there. On the gradin and below the altar screen are the following:

An image in the round entitled Our Lady of the Rosary. It is small, and its adornment amounts to nothing more than the following gewgaws. Dress and mantle of tatters of mother-of-pearl satin. A moth-eaten wig. Tin-plate crown. Paper pearl earrings. Necklace and bracelets of black glass beads. Rosary of ordinary pearls. Rouen apron. A little shield of silver plate with Our Lady of Guadalupe engraved on it. Two ordinary medals. Now for the altar:

An ebony cross with a bronze crucifix and silver corner plates, INRI, and Dolorosa. A small St. John, old and unseemly. And two brass candlesticks given by the King. The altar table is adobe, with an altar stone given by the King. A very ordinary missal stand and two small bells. The only dais and carpet are the earth floor.

NAVE: On the walls that face the nave are two hideous adobe tables. Hanging on the wall on the right side is a large painting on buffalo skin of Lord St. Joseph, and on the left a similar one of St. John the Baptist. On the right side of the church is another adobe table with a canopy of the same design as the altar screen. Above it dangle two wooden spiders (they are so ugly that this is what they look like).[2] A small Jesús Nazareno clothed in old rags is under this canopy. Lower down on this same side is an extremely ugly confessional and then a bench. The pulpit on the usual side in the usual place. This piece is so exquisite that there is none other to equal it in any mission, since it is adobe and looks like a cathedra without a back. Father Junco made it. Father Mirabal built the church.

NOTE: During the time when the aforesaid Junco was missionary at this mission, a woman called Catarina Pando gave this church the image of Jesús Nazareno which I have just mentioned, just as it is, with its canopy, and the image of Our Lady of the Rosary that was mentioned on the high altar. Both of them are so unworthy that

2. The pun cannot be translated. *Araña,* literally "spider," is also the word for chandelier in Spanish.

they do not deserve the titles of the Most Holy Personages they wish to represent. Therefore I ordered that they be consumed by fire and that the trifles for their adornment be preserved for whatever use they may have. There is no mention of the donor of the cross with the silver trimmings nor of the St. John, which will go into the fire immediately.

SACRISTY: The sacristy is joined to the church on the right side and is about 4 varas from the sanctuary. This room is 5 varas square and 3 high, with nine ordinary beams in the ceiling. Its little window faces west, and the door to the church is a small arch. The door leading to the convent is an ordinary single-leaved one without a key. Near one wall of this room is an adobe table for the use of the priest when vesting, and an unpainted chest with a key, in which the following is kept.

Vestments: A new chasuble of flowered white silk trimmed with fine gold galloon, with accessories, which the aforesaid Governor Vélez gave. Another very old one of damask with two faces (white and crimson), trimmed with silk galloon, with accessories, which the King gave. Another very old one of mother-of-pearl satin with a green orphrey, and its only accessory is a maniple. Another worse one of striped satin, the only accessories of which are a stole and a pall for the chalice. Another still worse one of green silk lustrine, with accessories consisting of stole, maniple, and burse. A green frontal in equally bad condition. The King gave all this a long time ago. A new black damask chasuble with accessories, including cope, frontal, and cross sheath, all trimmed with false gold galloon. Father Camargo gave this. A new cope of China satin without fringe, which Father Abadiano provided.

Linen: The aforesaid Governor Vélez gave a Brittany amice with lace and mother-of-pearl ribbons. Alb of the same with very wide lace below, and a cloth cincture, all presented with the chasuble mentioned before, and all new. Two old Brittany amices.

Two mended Rouen albs. Two altar cloths like the albs. A pair of Brittany corporals with embroidered edges and a flowered pall for the chalice. The assumption is that Governor Vélez must have given them. A purificator. A Rouen surplice. Three palls of different colors, materials, and kinds.

Silver and other metal: A chalice with paten and spoon. A small ciborium. The diminutive arras with their rings given by the King with the aforesaid. A pair of cruets that Father Junco made out of silver gewgaws collected from the settlers when the Holy Bishop gathered up ugly images.[3] Three little vessels for the holy oils given by the King, and they are kept in a small cedar box with a key.

A thurible with accessories, all of bronze. Tin processional cross which the King gave. An iron mold for making altar breads which the King gave.

Other things: A usable missal. Another old one. *Manual* by Osorio. A piece of shell for baptizing. An altar stone, the consecration of which is in doubt.

Note: In the inventory of this mission there is an entry in Father Junco's hand of a baptismal font belonging to the King which had been lent to this mission. The font is not here, nor did Father Abadiano hand it over to Father Salas, nor does the latter account for it. Possibly it is at the mission of Santo Domingo with other things belonging to the King that are being held for the Navajo missions.[4]

CONVENT

The convent is on the right side of the church, extending to the south and forming a square between the head of the sacristy and the corner of the church. The porter's lodge begins on the said corner. It lies outside the cemetery and faces east. It is a little portico exactly like the porter's lodge at La Cañada, even to the door. This convent has a cloister on three sides, for the one on the church side has been turned topsy-turvy and is partly closed by walls that jut out from the corners.

As we enter the porter's lodge, a large cell and its inner cell run to the left, with the inner cell on a corner. Here there is a key. There is a small cell around that corner, then a small passageway which looks like a cave because it no longer leads anywhere. The entrance to the small cell is on one side of it and that to the kitchen on the other. The latter is ordinary and continues forward. Behind the kitchen is a beautiful storeroom on an inside corner and through it is the entrance to a roomy cell which corners on the head wall. There is no inner cell, but the ascent to the upper apartments is in it.

From the inside corner containing this cell two rooms extend to the sacristy. These are the strawloft and stable. The upper story consists of some tumble-down rooms, and even though they are in such condition, it would not take much work to put them in order if any attention had been paid to this. To be exact, [the deterrent] has been fear lest it be said that the fathers want to live in palaces. The stairway that leads to this upper story is of boards and very badly arranged, with a little railing at the opening like those on the flat roof of outbuildings.

ITS FURNITURE: A very large table, and it suffices without a drawer. Three rough benches. A small chair without arms, which Father Abadiano provided.

ITS SERVICE: All together, a fiscal mayor, three subordinates, eight sacristans, eight cooks, four bakers, and they are assigned weekly as I described at Nambe. The pueblo also alternate as caretakers of sheep, horses, cows, pigs, and hens, and for carting of wood.

ITS LANDS AND FRUITS: They are among the milpas of the Indians and are quite large, for it is said that 3 fanegas of wheat, 3 almudes of maize, and an almud of each legume can be sown in all. They are good

3. Probably Bishop Tamarón in 1760.
4. The items brought by Father Menchero. See pp. 136-37, 220, 274-76 *infra.*

because they are on the meadow of the Río del Norte, and as such they yield in harvest 60 fanegas of wheat, about 30 of maize, and some legumes. All this is sufficient to maintain the friar. They are irrigated by a community ditch, and the sowing, cultivation, and harvest are in charge of the pueblo. A citizen at this mission called Francisco Sánchez says that when he was lieutenant this convent had a very large kitchen garden for green vegetables, but that because of the fathers' neglect (neglect is bad, but here it proves disinterest and love for the Indians) the Indians have taken it over little by little.

MISSION FATHER

The one whom our Mother the Province has assigned here to this mission for the present is Father Fray Ramón Salas, native of Seville, who is forty-eight years old, twenty-nine in profession, and thirteen a missionary in this Custody, divided as follows: Picuris, one and a half months; Taos, one year and seven months; Jémez, four years and four months; Acoma, ten months; Santo Domingo, ten months; Santa Ana, four years; San Juan, where he resides today, April 19, '76, two years. He has general faculties from Durango revocable at will.

ADMINISTRATION OF THE MISSION: Daily, morning and evening, the bell is rung for catechism at regular hours. The unmarried men and women come to it, recite with the father, and in the mornings they hear Mass if there is one. Afterwards he commands, teaches, or reproves them as necessary, and this takes half an hour or more according to circumstances. On feast days the whole pueblo comes to Mass, and while the Indians are reciting the settlers assemble to hear Mass, and when it is over they leave.

There are no explanatory discourses on feast days for the reason noted at San Ildefonso and deferred until now. This is why: Father Salas says that when Father Hinojosa (now Custos) was missionary at Sandia, they raised false testimony against him, alleging that he had said in his talk that the married women were living in concubinage. Therefore, when the men returned to their houses (they must have been the settlers), they half-killed their wives with blows. In view of this the aforesaid Hinojosa promised not to preach again, and fathers Vega and Salas have followed his example.

OBVENTIONS AND FIRST FRUITS: Assuming that what I said at Santa Fe is the general rule in this regard, the only particular thing here is that sometimes when an Indian dies, they pay for a Mass. This alms consists either of one or more buckskins, or a cow or a horse. The Mass is sung or said in accordance with the alms, and it is like obsequies, for there are responsory and an offering of little gourds of maize, tortillas, and a tallow candle.

The first fruits of this mission amount to about 60 fanegas, or a little more, of all kinds of grain, 8 to 10 strings of chile, about 200 onions, small amounts of green vegetables, 3 or 4 small head of livestock, but no cattle. The Indians pay nothing.

HIS EXPENDITURES: Food consumed by the household is not counted. About 2 jugs of wine; about 30 wax candles at 3 to a pound for all that pertains to the administration of the mission. The father gives the Indian chief sacristan a fanega of wheat a year, and there are no dependents[5] to give them to.

HOW HE ACQUIRES NECESSITIES: I refer to Santa Fe. Father Salas says that here he usually goes out in person to seek what he needs.

CONVENT PROVISIONS: The following has been designated and recorded in the inventory of this mission by the Reverend Custos Fray Jacobo de Castro: 10 fanegas of wheat, 10 of maize, 10 sheep, a pot of ordinary lard, 6 strings of chile, half a fanega of frijoles, half an almud of salt. I confirmed this and as a sequel I inserted the following

5. "Ahijados," godchildren. If the wheat was for altar breads, the statement must mean that they did not supply them for any other mission.

WRIT OF VISITATION

San Juan de los Caballeros,[6] April 19 of the year 1776. In prosecution of the juridical visitation which our Reverend Father Fray Francisco Atanasio Domínguez, one of the appointed preachers in the Convento Grande of Mexico City and Commissary Visitor of this Custody for our Very Reverend Father Minister Provincial Fray Isidro Murillo, is making of this Custody, his Reverend Paternity proceeded to examine and did examine this inventory. Finding it confused and that many things listed in it as belonging to church and sacristy have been used up, he ordered and commanded the present mission father, Fray Ramón Salas, to make a new one, recording the existing items with the clarity and complete detail that he saw his Reverend Paternity use in his visitation so that it may agree with the one to be remitted to the Holy Province. And until there is an opportunity to make the said new inventory, he orders him for the present to record it in this same one on the fourth leaf, since there are sufficient blank pages to draw it up. Our Reverend Father so provided, ordered, and signed before me, the undersigned secretary, to which I attest. Fray Francisco Atanasio Domínguez, Commissary Visitor. Before me, Fray José Palacio, secretary.

The parish books were examined and approved, and the corresponding decrees were recorded in them. But it should be noted that the book of Baptisms is new, consists of ninety-seven folios, and that the present missionary, Salas, provided it. The other two are nearly finished. I therefore ordered the said father to apply to the Father Vice-Custos for new books out of the supply that came from our Mother the Province for that purpose. These books begin with the year 1726 and continue up to the present year of '76, and they will be remitted to the archive of this Custody, which is at the mission of Our Father Santo Domingo, for the aforesaid missionary was told to do so.

PUEBLO

The same plain that comes from La Cañada continues northward and, extending beyond the mission of San Juan, makes it possible to say that this mission pueblo is almost in the middle of the plain and within a quarter of a league of the Río del Norte. It is located at the edge of the bluff where this plain falls to the meadows of the aforesaid river. It has a wide and very cheerful outlook, because the plain extends 5 or 6 leagues from north to south with the pueblo in the middle. The plain, indeed, extends about a league to the east, and from that point hills rise gradually to the sierra. To the west, in addition to the view of the aforesaid river with poplar groves and woods from one end to the other, one sees far more than a league on the side of the river in the last mentioned direction.

In relation to the church, the buildings of the pueblo are to the north. Three tenements, separated from one another at the corners, and the Epistle side of the church enclose a plaza of ordinary size. In addition, opposite the church and about a pistol shot from that façade are two small tenements that make a kind of street, for one is back of the other and both face south. The plan, furnishings, and other things are the same as those at Nambe even to the neatness and care.

ITS LANDS AND FRUITS: The Indians have lands above and below the pueblo and cor-

6. San Juan Bautista was the name given to this pueblo in 1598 when it was Oñate's headquarters. Although Villagrá said that it was called San Juan de los Caballeros "in memory of those noble sons who first raised in these barbarous regions the bloody Tree upon which Christ perished for the redemption of mankind," it is more likely that those who named the pueblo were thinking of St. John the Baptist as the ancient patron of the Knights of Malta. Gaspar Pérez de Villagrá, *History of New Mexico* (Alcalá, 1610), tr. by Gilberto Espinosa (Los Angeles, 1933), p. 147.

responding lands on the other bank of the Río del Norte. They extend for a league above the pueblo and a league below it, and the same distance along the other bank. All are on the meadows of the aforesaid; they are very fertile; and they are irrigated by a ditch common to settlers and Indians, for they take it from the said river very far up, about 2 leagues or more. From this ditch they keep taking off water as they have the right and need. These lands usually produce (barring accidents) copious fruits at the time of harvest. There is a small fruit orchard that belongs to an Indian.

The natives of this pueblo are Teguas, whose native tongue they speak. They use Spanish more freely than those of the pueblos described before, and they do not employ an interpreter, but the same thing happens with them as with those mentioned when one speaks to them rapidly. Their customs are the usual ones, and they are exactly like Nambe in particular. They are all included in this

CENSUS

61 families with 201 persons

A very large group of settlers recognize this mission for their spiritual administration. They are as follows:

Río Arriba is a league north of the mission and up the same plain. It consists of a number of ranchos like those mentioned before. These settlers live by the help of the afore-mentioned river, with whose waters they make fruitful the very fertile lands that the meadows of that river offer. As such they produce copious harvests. There are three or four little fruit orchards of apples, peaches, and apricots.

In this little place there is a small chapel of Our Lady of Solitude. Its patron was one Sebastián Martín. Today his substitute and heir is a son of his called Marcial Martín.

This little chapel is adobe and resembles a small bodega. It faces west and is 14 to 16 varas long, 5 wide, and 6 high. There is no choir loft. There is a poor window on the Epistle side facing south, and the door is squared with one leaf and a key. The roof is of wrought beams; there is a small belfry with its brass mortar [bell], and a little cemetery.

The altar screen is nothing more than a middle-sized niche like a cupboard in the wall and in this there is a middle-sized image in the round whose title is Our Lady of Solitude, although her dress is a mother-of-pearl tunic and blue mantle, all of smooth ribbed silk, silver radiance, and linen apron. On the whole wall where the high altar is there are some large paintings of saints on buffalo skin in the local style. The altar table is adobe, with its altar stone, cross, candlesticks, and a little bell. It has old vestments of flowered cloth with all accessories, including linen. Chalice, paten, and spoon, all of silver, and glass cruets on a Puebla plate, and an old missal.

The only functions here are two novenas and a Mass annually. The alms for this are collected from all the settlers in the mission's jurisdiction. The citizens of this Río Arriba are of different classes: some are masters, others, servants, and still others are their own masters and servants. They all speak the local Spanish. They are included in the following:

CENSUS

51 families with 299 persons

Moya[7] is more than 2½ leagues from the mission in the same direction. To be brief, the circumstances are in every way the same as described at Río Arriba, although it is not as large, as the following shows.

---

7. A mistake by Domínguez or his secretary. In contemporary mission registers the name is "La Hoya," with its patron St. Raphael.

CENSUS

5 families with 38 persons

Bosque Grande[8] is also to the north, on the opposite bank across from Río Arriba. The distance from the mission is the width of the river plus more than a league and a half, for it lies back beyond the meadow. It consists of ranchos like those described, and the circumstances are the same, for not only does it have its little fruit trees, but the people are of the same classes. Its individuals are included in this

CENSUS

36 families with 187 persons

Canoa[9] is also to the north on the opposite bank. It is diagonally above Bosque Grande, nearer the Río del Norte opposite Moya, and almost at the foot of a mesa, but it has good lands, a little fruit, and water from the aforesaid river. It is some 3 leagues from the mission across the river. The settlers are like those mentioned and are included here:

CENSUS

7 families with 30 persons

Embudo is 5 leagues to the east-northeast in relation to the mission. Three leagues to beyond Moya are flat, and 2 are uneven, turning eastward. The Río del Norte does not reach this Embudo, as the great bend described shows. It is in a beautiful cañada that comes from the Sierra Madre in the east and runs west for nearly 3 leagues where it ends in mesas at the Río Grande Canyon. I should like to fly, but I cannot hasten over the dullness of this place, for although I entered quickly as in a *Funnel,*

I do and will come out slowly through the little canyon that goes to Picuris.[10]

This place is not entirely populated by settlers, but somewhat less than half. They live in the lower part. The remainder up above belongs to the Indians of the pueblo I have just mentioned. The boundary line is a twist of the river that runs from east to west (this river is that of Picuris which comes here after it has been joined by others as we shall see there) and enters the Río del Norte far downstream. It comes through the cañada above, providing the Indians with good arable land on both banks. Below the mid-point it makes a very short turn to the north, and then, returning to its natural course, flows almost at the foot of some hills that are south of it. Therefore the settlers do not have many lands on this bank, but it does leave them more on the other side.

These lands are especially good and are irrigated by the said river, which at this point must be considered quite abundant with good crystalline water, and every crop yields a plentiful harvest. There are little fruit trees of apricot and very delicious plums. The latter are a different species from those outside, for the pit is like that of an apricot. On the north bank toward the middle of the cañada belonging to this place a wide cañada, called the Cañada de Apodaca, opens, and the best highway leads through it to Taos. The route to Picuris is to the east above the cañada in which Embudo lies. The fishing in this river is for rather middle-sized trout. The settlers here are like those mentioned above in every way, and they are included in this

CENSUS

14 families with 69 persons

8. Bosque, or San José del Bosque.
9. La Canoa, the home of Angela Martín (widowed daughter of Sebastián Martín), faced La Hoya. BL, N.M. Origs., 1766.

10. San Antonio del Embudo, site of present-day Dixon. *Embudo* means "funnel." Other place names found in the 1774-98 baptismal book of San Juan are: Angeles, Otra Banda, Plaza de San Francisco, Chamita, Nuestra Señora de Guadalupe, San Antonio del Río Arriba, San Pedro, and Quemado.

Picuris

The pueblo and mission of San Lorenzo de Picuris lies to the northeast in relation to Santa Fe; and since there are two roads to it from that place, there are necessarily two distances, which I do not fail to record. Going north from Santa Fe via Tesuque, Nambe, Cundiyó, Quemado, and Truchas, all of which (see the notes on them) are along the aforesaid Sierra Madre, which keeps taking its name from the places near it, Picuris is about 15 leagues from Santa Fe. Via Tesuque, Pojoaque, Cañada, San Juan, Río Arriba, Moya, and Embudo, the distance is about 19 long leagues.

North from San Juan, within sight of and upstream on the Río del Norte, there are 3 leagues to beyond Moya, and 2 to Embudo make 5. From there one enters a little canyon, which is higher up (as I mentioned earlier), and, leaving the Embudo River on the right, one travels 2½ leagues in the sierra and then a flat half league up the cañada to the east to reach the afore-mentioned pueblo and mission, which is some 8 leagues from San Juan. Therefore the location of Picuris must be thought of as in a sierra as I shall soon explain; and in order to discuss this with perfect clarity, the following is inserted here.

NOTE

The inventory of this mission, newly made by the present mission father, Fray Andrés Claramonte, shows that there is no church or convent, for the present lord governor, Don Pedro Fermín de Mendinueta, ordered that it be torn down because the pueblo is isolated and therefore indefensible against the continual incursions which the Comanche enemy is making. These raids are so daring that this father I have mentioned assures me that he escaped by a mira-cle in the year '69, for they sacked the convent and destroyed his meager supplies; yet he considered them well spent in exchange for his life and freedom from captivity.

In view, then, of this, and fearing another irreparable attack, the aforesaid governor made the foregoing decision. But since there is a formal church consisting of the faithful and their minister, I will give an account of it at length. First, as for the church, I say that at the same time when orders were given to tear down the one mentioned, orders were also issued for the erection of a new building in a safe place. This is near one block of, but outside, one plaza of the pueblo, with the intention that the convent shall be in that block. But according to the plan, all is to be defensible as a unit, for the present space between the church and the block where the convent is to be built will be a cloister. The new church is adobe with quite thick walls, single-naved, with the outlook and main door due south. It is 24 varas long, 7 wide, and what has been built is now 3 varas high.

In the same inventory I found the following statement in substance, signed by the present lieutenant, Don Nicolás Leal: That on December 31 of last year, 1775, the aforesaid Father Claramonte entrusted to him the collection from various persons of alms amounting to 134 regional pesos, the sum due for the personal labor of the said father, or his obventions. The said lieutenant affirms over a signature in his hand and writing that the said father applied this amount to the new building under construction in order to help and alleviate the Indians somewhat, for although they do not reciprocate the father's love, in the final analysis they are few and poor.

For the present, this missionary lives and maintains himself in the community house, which is in one of the blocks of the aforesaid plaza; and in one of three rooms (the most decent one) he has made an oratory in which he celebrates Mass, etc. It is kept with great cleanliness, care, and neatness, but it is very inadequate and poverty-stricken.[1] The things pertaining to divine worship are kept in this oratory, as follows:

LIST

An oil painting on canvas measuring about 2 varas with a painted frame, and it represents St. Lawrence. The King gave it.

It is handsome and in very good condition. Another canvas which serves as a canopy. It is a vara in size, old, without a frame, and represents Our Lady of Guadalupe in oils. A father gave it. On each side of St. Lawrence is a painting on buffalo skin measuring about a vara in a narrow frame. Ana Montaño gave them. Another very old painting on buffalo skin representing Our Lady of the Angels. Another small one with Our Lady of Bethlehem, pretty, but old. An old lacquered Child Jesus.

The altar table is an ordinary new one of wood, which Father Claramonte provided, and on it is an ordinary altar stone provided by the King. A middle-sized wooden cross. Missal stand of the same sort. Two small old candlesticks given by the King. Two little bells. The dais is a good wrought plank which the said father installed, and he lends a blanket for use as a carpet.

There is a very badly made confessional here. The baptismal font is an earthen bowl with a board for a cover. Another like it serves for a holy-water pot, with a very pretty wooden aspergillum that the said father provided. Under the altar table is an ordinary new unpainted chest without a key, which the said father provided, and it contains the following:

Vestments: An old but usable damask chasuble with two faces (white and crimson), trimmed with narrow silk galloon, which the King gave. A very old satin one, with accessories except for frontal, which the King gave. The following are said to have been provided by various fathers: An old but usable purple satin chasuble with stripes and silk galloon; of its accessories the burse is missing, for the Comanches carried it off, without the corporals, at the time of the sack mentioned. Another of green satin trimmed with narrow imitation gold galloon, with the necessary appurtenances. Another new one of black damask, with accessories including cope and cross sheath, all trimmed with false gold fringe. Father Camargo gave it. A separate stole and maniple.

1. This account adds to the chronology of the churches at Picuris even though it does not completely clarify the situation. GK (pp. 108-09) and Hodge (AB-1634, pp. 279-81) have good summaries of the available sources up to the 1750's. In 1759 Governor Marín del Valle took the remains of Fray Ascensio de Zárate, who had died at Picuris in 1632, from "the ruins of the old church of San Lorenzo de Picuris" and transferred them to Santa Fe where they were reinterred in the parish church. J. B. Salpointe, *Soldiers of the Cross* (Banning, Calif., 1898), pp. 99-100. In June, 1760, Bishop Tamarón visited Picuris and found the church in good condition. AT, pp. 55-56; pp. 249-50 *infra*. This means that Father Zárate's remains must have been found in the ruins of the seventeenth-century church, which had been replaced by a post-Reconquest structure, perhaps the one mentioned by Father Alvarez in 1706. HB, 3: 375. In 1769 this latter church was deliberately razed and a new church in a safer location begun, as we learn from Domínguez.

A very small altar stone, which has been consecrated.

Linen: An amice of very poor quality Brittany with lace, which Father García gave. A much mended alb. A fairly good altar cloth. A plain corporal of new lawn with lace, which Father García provided. A very old double one of Brittany. An almost new plain Rouen surplice. Three linen palls embroidered in silk. A Brittany towel with lace, which Father García provided. Four very old purificators. And Father Claramonte has provided the following: Three Brittany purificators. Two white cloths that serve as hood and towel in baptisms.

Silver and other metal: A chalice with a broken base, and a paten, which the King gave. Three little vessels for the holy oils in a small cedar box without a key, which the King gave. Thirteen reales which Father Claramonte provided along with the rings for arras. Small chalice spoons that he also provided.

Tin processional cross, which the King gave. Plate of the same, which Father Claramonte provided. Two glass cruets to the credit of the same father.

Other things: An old missal with thongs for bookmarks, repaired by Father García. A *Manual* by Vetancurt which this father gave. A middle-sized bell from the King. It is good, has no clapper, and is hung on high poles like a gallows, but for the present there is no other recourse.

The usable lumber that was in the old church and convent has been kept. It consists of the door, a latch with no lock or key, the balustrade of the choir loft and its small beams, along with the little balustrade of the high altar. Much from the convent has been lost among the Indians themselves, but there are an ordinary table, three small chairs, three doors, and four windows—but all gone to ruin.

The things recorded up to here exist at present as I saw and noted in my juridical visitation today, April 20, 1776. And finding the mission father living in extreme poverty, discomfort, and indigence, I observed his great will and desire to acquire what is lacking or what he might obtain for divine worship. I also found the books of Inventory and Patents very carefully renovated by Father Claramonte. Moreover, he was resolved to provide the parish books himself, but in view of his great poverty, I left orders for him to apply to the Father Vice-Custos for three new books out of the supply which came for that purpose from our Mother the Province, for which purpose they are applied to this mission. Here the missionary has the following

SERVICE: All together, a fiscal mayor, three subordinates, eight little sacristans; four cooks, four bakers, who are allotted weekly as described in other missions. In addition, stableboy for the little horses used in administering the parish, a shepherd for the sheep, and a woman to care for the hens. Those who serve in the house eat there, and at night they go (except the sacristans). They bring their utensils and take them away with them as they come and go. I add that if something is broken while it is being used in the service of the present missionary, he pays for it in seeds. The father helps them with the wood, either by providing a farm cart or horses, and gives them an axe; and the Indians also cart theirs at his expense.

ITS LANDS AND FRUITS: In relation to the location of the pueblo, its lands are to the east, facing the said plaza near the new church. They are just across an arroyo which runs from north to south, arising in a sierra on the north. Turning to the east, they end at another arroyo like the first. They are bounded on the north side by some hills of the aforesaid sierra, and on the south side by a river that runs along the foot of more hills on the south. There are about 300 square varas in this area, but not all of it is arable. Therefore the following are sown in the usable parts: 1 fanega of wheat, which yields about 20 fanegas; 4 almudes of maize, which yield about 14 fanegas; half a fanega of all legumes together, which yield a total of about 8 fanegas. There is a little kitchen garden for green stuff in these lands. It does not grow ripe chile (because of the coldness of the sierra) but does grow green chile. The same is true of frijoles.

There is a plot about 70 varas square below the pueblo among the milpas of the Indians, so well situated that its fault is that it makes a very damp hollow and the ripening of the crop is endangered. It takes a fanega of wheat, which yields 20, and a long almud of maize, which yields about 12 fanegas. The convent has another milpa in the Embudo lands (mentioned earlier) about 200 varas long and 60 wide. It is the best of all, but what I shall presently relate happens with regard to it. All are watered with the pueblo's river by a general irrigation ditch, from which other ditches are run where necessary.

The pueblo does part of the sowing, cultivation, and harvesting, but for the time being the present missionary bears most of the work. When I remonstrated with him, citing the custom among the Indians, he replied: That since they are so lazy, even in their own affairs, they are even more inclined to let what belongs to the father be lost, and so to avoid animosities, gossip, etc., he considers it a pleasure to do it himself, even to threshing the wheat with six of his own animals. In proof of the weakness of the Indians and of the harmonious relations he maintains with them, I now tell the circumstances about the Embudo milpa.

Father Claramonte says: That his first year as missionary he planted this milpa, using the labor of the pueblo, giving them seed (as all do), and that it went pretty well for him. Therefore, other years when he has been in Picuris he has undertaken to plant it, giving them farm oxen and helping them when he could, but with no success because of their frivolous excuses. Seeing this, he made them an offer that in addition to what he was already giving them, as has been said, that if anyone in particular would be willing to take care of the irrigation alone, he

would give him half the crop afterwards at harvest time; and not even by this means did he accomplish anything. Therefore, in order not to lose the sowing of his milpa entirely, and to avoid animosities, he let it out to a settler for a fanega and a half of frijoles (which do not grow at Picuris), so that he might receive at least that much from this milpa. In consideration, then, of this indifference, he has managed in the way stated in his reply.

MISSION FATHER

The one who exercises the apostolic ministry here at present is Father Fray Andrés Claramonte, native of Mexico City, thirty-seven years and some months of age, seventeen years and a few months in profession, twelve years as a missionary in the Custody, divided thus: One year in Picuris; Laguna, three years, four months; Picuris again, one year and six months; San Ildefonso, two months; Taos, four years; Picuris again, two years, and he lives here now. He has general faculties, revocable at will, in the kingdom only; the Reverend Custos Castro gave them to him by authority from the Most Illustrious [Bishop] Tamarón to qualify friars who might enter to serve in these missions.

ADMINISTRATION OF THE MISSION: The same regime as at Nambe. The only addition here is that the Indians are more frequently instructed in matters of politeness, good breeding and customs. On feast days, when some settlers come, there is a sermon on Christian doctrine. He has taught two Indians in the pueblo how to administer baptism in cases of great urgency, and he has instructed four settlers in his jurisdiction for the same purpose. He has eased his mind by enabling these same settlers to assist the dying to make a good end. For this last hour he applies for the benefit of his parishioners a plenary indulgence which the Most Illustrious Tamarón granted, which is recorded in the decree he inserted in the book of Baptisms. A copy of this will be found in a separate place.

OBVENTIONS AND FIRST FRUITS: I refer to what has been said before. With regard to the first fruits at this place in particular, the mission father says that all of them together amount to about 16 to 18 fanegas. The Indians do not even pay for a Mass. The only livestock here are cattle, and no payment is made.

HIS EXPENDITURES: Food consumed by the household is not counted. Wax, about 7 pounds a year in everything pertaining to the administration of the mission, wine, about 12 or 13 pints, a few more than 200 altar breads, and the father at Taos gives them weekly without any subsidy in wheat, for this religious at Picuris says that he found this custom in force and that they have never asked him for anything in return. In this regard, Father Claramonte says: That with respect to this weekly trip, because the winter is so severe in these places and there is so much snow in the sierra where this pueblo is, travel to Taos is extremely difficult, and it sometimes happens that the altar breads do not arrive in time and consequently there is no Mass on a feast day. And Picuris is so much in the sierra that if they think of going to San Juan or to La Cañada, the situation is the same. In view of this, this friar assures me that it is very necessary to have an iron for making them here, which he intends to provide as soon as he can.

HOW HE ACQUIRES NECESSITIES: Although it comes out the same everywhere according to the usual method and by exchange, this father says that here, in order not to deprive himself of the little grain he acquires by harvest and first fruits and perhaps an obvention or two, most of it comes out of the royal alms in chocolate, linen, or winding sheets.

CONVENT PROVISIONS: What Father Claramonte received came down then to 6 fanegas of wheat and a like amount of maize, but now, in accordance with what this religious frankly states, at my command the amount shown by the following has been recorded in the inventory.

WRIT OF VISITATION

San Lorenzo de Picuris, April 20 of the year 1776. In prosecution of the juridical visitation which our Reverend Father Fray Francisco Atanasio Domínguez, one of the appointed preachers in the Convento Grande of Our Father St. Francis of Mexico and Commissary Visitor for our Very Reverend Father Minister Provincial Fray Isidro Murillo, is making of this Custody, his Reverend Paternity proceeded to examine and did examine this inventory, which faithfully and legally records all his Reverend Paternity saw, examined, and inspected belonging to church, sacristy, and convent of this mission of San Lorenzo de Picuris. Therefore his Reverend Paternity approved it and thanked the present mission father, Fray Andrés Claramonte, both for the neatness and cleanliness of this inventory and other books and for his great disinterestedness and close attention to divine worship, and also for his fine conduct in his dealings with the Indians and their instruction in Christian doctrine. And he charges him to continue and persevere in the same course that he has observed up to now. And our Reverend Father Visitor trusts to the judgment and piety of the said father that he will continue to encourage the Indians so that they may finish the new church and also build a comfortable dwelling for the missionary.

And since it is his Reverend Paternity's duty to see to it that each mission has a corresponding supply of provisions so that the incoming father may have something for his immediate use, he decides, orders, and commands that it be the following: 6 fanegas of wheat, 6 of maize, 6 sheep, 12 cuartillos of lard, half a fanega of broad beans, half a fanega of vetch, 2 strings of chile, 100 onions, a bottle of wine, 2 wax candles. In addition, the outgoing father must hand over with the mission the belongings of the church and sacristy and the convent furniture, to wit: an ordinary table, three small chairs, three doors, four windows. The incoming friar shall receive this in accordance with this inventory, giving a receipt to his predecessor, and if anything is lacking, he shall notify the Reverend Custos or his Vice-Custos at once.

With regard to all this they cannot make any innovations, changes, or reductions, but they may, indeed, add all that may seem necessary for the benefit of the mission and missionary, because the aforesaid is the order of our superior prelate, who so commands *ratione officii*. His Reverend Paternity so provided, ordered, and signed before me, the undersigned secretary, to which I attest. Fray Francisco Atanasio Domínguez, Commissary Visitor. Before me, Fray José Palacio, secretary.

The parish books were inspected and approved, and the corresponding decrees were recorded in them without need for remark. And since they are nearly full and Father Claramonte wishes to provide new ones, I gave him the orders already mentioned in full at the end of *Other things,* again charging him to remit these old ones and their equivalents for Inventory and Patents to the archive at Santo Domingo, since there would now be new ones of all kinds.

PUEBLO

When I began to describe Picuris I pointed out that there were two roads to it, both of which pass through mountainous country to the pueblo, which is established and located in the sierra in a cañada which runs from east to west and is about a league long from beginning to end. This cañada comes from the Sierra Madre I have been talking about ever since Santa Fe. Another sierra comes from this one, following the same course as the pueblo's cañada. It is north of the pueblo and runs to the west, continuing until it is broken by the canyon of the Río del Norte beyond Embudo. It is called the sierra of Picuris.

To the south of this cañada are some hills that come in a ridge from the Sierra Madre. They extend to the west and are broken by mounds closing the cañada. There is quite a good river in this cañada, and its swift current of very good crystalline water runs through it from top to bottom. The river does not run through the center of the cañada, but along the foot of the hills on the south. Therefore its only bank is the north one on which the pueblo stands, located in the foothills of the sierra I said was on that side of the pueblo.

Three tenements, separate but near to one another, are to be seen on some little elevations in these foothills. Below these hills on a small level site near the river is a square plaza with two entrances, a large one to the river and a small one to communicate with the tenements. The plaza is the one I mentioned above that has the new church on the side facing east, etc. But not all the tenements and plaza described are inhabited, for there are no people in a great part of them.

Said tenements are shaped like a sugar loaf, and the houses are heaped there one upon another as if they had tried to build the Tower of Babel. The ascent to them is by ladders which begin at the communal lower floor, with a landing on the flat roof of the lower dwelling. On this flat roof there is another small ladder that rests on another flat roof, and so another and another up to the top, the flat roof of one house being the terrace of another and serving as a landing between one ladder and the next.

Although there is an occasional very small door in these houses, the entrance to most of them is a *coi* (I refer to Tesuque) on the flat roof, and inside there are others from room to room to the bottom. Now in view of this heap of houses, it is obvious that the dwellings, or rooms, in the heart of these tenements are totally dark, and therefore they are entered by the light of brands. The height of these sugar loaves, or honeycombs, must be about 25 to 30 varas, and there will be five or six dwellings from bottom to top, one over the other.

On one corner of the plaza there is a tenement like those described, and the rest is in blocks, or sides, like the plazas of the pueblos described before, although, indeed, there is no little portico. All the dwellings, both the tenements and those on the plaza are so incommodious that an ordinary man can hardly stand erect, and the space will scarcely hold twelve to fourteen men standing quite near to one another. With regard to their cleanliness, I state with disgust that they abound in filth, for they attend to every one of their needs there without even excepting the demands of nature right in sight and scent of everyone. In a separate place I will describe their indomitable customs at length, but for the present I leave them to the imagination in accordance with what has been said. And I cite the report on the father's planting.

THEIR LANDS AND FRUITS: From top to bottom throughout the cañada where the pueblo lies, the Indians have lands of all kinds, that is, bad and good, but all on the same bank because of what I said concerning the location. They are watered by the pueblo's river. To the south, beyond the hills I mentioned as being on that side of the pueblo, there is another cañada that arises and runs in the same directions as that of the pueblo. It is wider and has a river like the one described except that it runs through the middle and leaves better lands on both banks than there are in the other. They are watered by this river. In Embudo (as I said in that place) they have many lands, and much better ones than these, and they irrigate them from the river there.

Frijol and chile do not yield a crop in the Picuris lands because of the cold. Maize usually freezes, but not consistently. There is a very pretty harvest of everything else. The Embudo lands yield a crop of everything sown in them (this is proved by the harvest of its settlers). But even though the Picuris Indians have so many lands, they do not have enough to live on through the year because of their excessive laziness, which is proved by Father Claramonte's statement. Below the pueblo's lands and those in the cañada to the south, the rivers of the two cañadas meet, and far below they are joined by another of which I shall speak later. There is very good trout fishing in all of them.

The natives of this pueblo bear its name and speak a different language from that of the pueblos described before. The language also has the same name as the pueblo, and it is almost nasal. Very few speak the Spanish language, and only two of these with any clarity. At the time of the Reconquest they were brought from a place they call Cuartelejo, and this is said to be toward the east in relation to this kingdom.[2] They are included in the present

CENSUS

64 families with 223 persons

The settlers administered by this Picuris mission are to the south of the pueblo and about 2½ leagues away in the sierra. The place is called *Trampas*[3] and is about the same distance from Truchas as from the pueblo. This little settlement is in a cañada of the Sierra Madre. It runs from southeast to

2. Hodge (AB-1634, pp. 279-81) summarizes the history of the Picuris Indians, their contacts with the Plains Indians, and opinions about the location of Cuartelejo. This word is a diminutive of *cuartel*, or quarters for soldiers. Twitchell erroneously tried to make it mean "far-off post" by dividing it into *cuartel* and *lejos* (far). SANM, 2: 236.

3. This place was settled in 1751 by Governor Vélez Cachupín with twelve families and was named Santo Tomás Apóstol del Río de las Trampas. SANM, 1: no. 975. Among the settlers were some children and grandchildren of Sebastián Rodríguez, de Vargas' African drummer. See NMF. Not to be confused with another Río de las Trampas, now Ranchos de Taos.

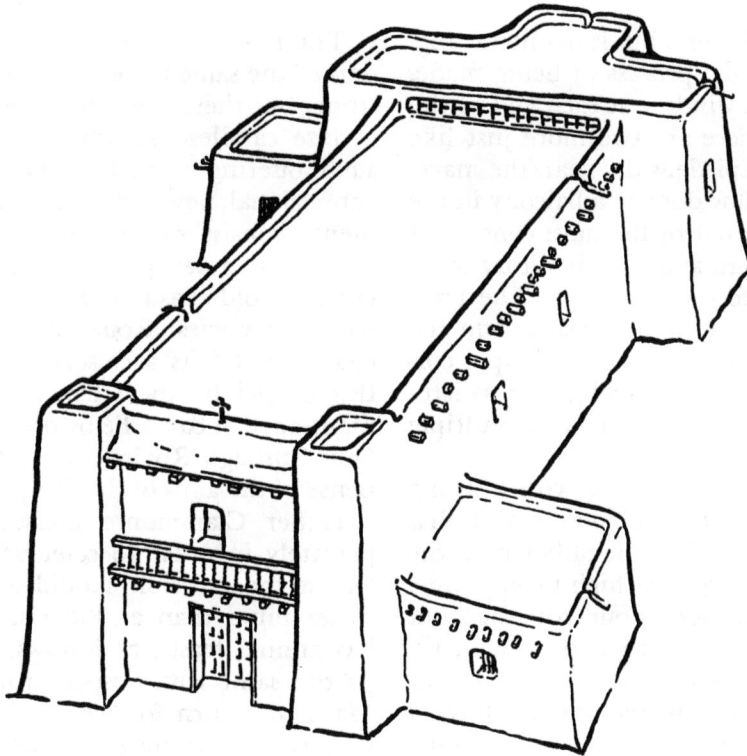

northwest, with a small river with a very rapid current of good crystalline water in the middle. It is not half a league long, but since it is rather wide, it has fairly good farmlands on both banks of the river. Watered by this river, they yield quite reasonable crops with the exception of chile and frijol. This is the river I mentioned in connection with the one at Picuris.

These settlers do not live in ranchos but in a plaza like a neighborhood house. For the most part they are a ragged lot, but there are three or four who have enough to get along after a fashion. They are as festive as they are poor, and very merry. Accordingly, most of them are low class, and there are very few of good, or even moderately good, blood. Almost all are their own masters and servants, and in general they speak the Spanish I have described in other cases. The following includes them all.

CENSUS

63 families with 278 persons

NOTE

There is a chapel in this Trampas. Because what there is to say about it is lengthy, I did not tell it in the same section with the settlers as I did with the one at Río Arriba. In the year 1760, when the Holy Bishop Tamarón visited this kingdom, at the petition of the settlers he left a license (a copy of which will be included elsewhere) for them to build a chapel here to Lord St. Joseph. It is adobe with walls more than a vara thick, and there is a transept. The outlook and main door are to the southwest, and it is 20 varas long from the door to the mouth of the transept, 7 wide, and 8 high up to the bed molding. The transept is 6 varas long, 15 wide, and more than 9 high because of the clerestory. The ascent to the sanctuary consists of five poor steps made of beams, and its area is 4 varas square, the height being equal to that of the transept.

There is a choir loft in the usual place, and, to be brief, it is like those in the missions described before, but it has no railing, for it is still in the process of being made. There is a good window at each end of the transept, and there are two more just like them on the Epistle side near the nave. There is a window door to a balcony in the choir loft. The roof of the nave consists of twenty-five beams, and the clerestory is on the one opposite the sanctuary. The transept is roofed by nineteen beams, and the sanctuary by seven. All have multiple corbels as well as being wrought. The sanctuary has a false vaulted arch with multiple corbels.

The main door is squared with a strong wooden frame instead of masonry. It has two paneled leaves, but the only lock is the crossbar; and it is 3 varas high by 2½ wide. Two tower buttresses jut out from the front corners like those I mentioned at Santa Fe, and on them there is no more than the beginning of towers. On the outside, toward the middle of one of them, there is a frame[4] with a middle-sized bell in it. There is a balcony almost like the one in Santa Fe over the door from one tower buttress to the other. The cemetery is very small, with an adobe [wall] and a gate.

As we enter, the baptistery is on the right under the choir. It is like those described before, with an adobe pillar in the middle, but no font. At the end of the transept on the Gospel side is the sacristy, a very ordinary room without a key. There is a new table with a drawer but no key in this sacristy. The only altar in this chapel is the high altar. Its furnishing consists of a board niche painted and spattered with what they call *talco*[5] here (it is like tinsel, but very flexible). In this niche there is a middle-sized image in the round of Lord St. Joseph. There are many paper prints around the niche, and little candlesockets, like ferules used in school, fixed in the wall with brads.

The altar table is adobe with a gradin and dais of the same material. There is no altar stone, but there are a cross and rather new bronze candlesticks which came out of a small offering we shall see later. Pulpit and confessional, new and badly made. The vestments consist of nothing more than an amice with a new plain Brittany alb, cotton cincture, old chasuble of white China satin with accessories, Rouen altar cloth. This chasuble and its accessories were given to this chapel by the Chapel of the Rosary mentioned at Santa Fe by order of the Vicar Don Santiago Roybal. The rest at the expense of the alms of the Holy Patriarch.[6]

Father Claramonte blessed the chapel privately in order to celebrate Mass there (when the occasion should arise) with an easier mind than at Picuris. Therefore it has annual feasts, as follows: That of the patron saint with vespers, procession, and Mass, in return for which they give what they can by arrangement with the father. Christmas novenary,[7] 6 pesos for each Mass; and the father provides a good deal of wax for all this, because his affection leads him to do so, as well as the wine and altar breads. Baptisms, marriages, and burials are also performed in this chapel (the said license permits it) when necessity demands, and what is necessary for all this is brought from the mission.

This chapel has been built by alms from the whole kingdom, for the citizens of this place have begged throughout it. The chief promoter in all this has been one Juan Argüello, who is more than eighty years old, and this man asked me for alms for the said chapel during my visitation of Picuris. And since I have nothing, I gave him that, with

4. "Morillo." In Mexico, a jamb-post or beam resting on beams set in brick columns.
5. Still the New Mexican word for mica, which abounds in the granite mountains of the area.
6. St. Joseph.
7. "Novenario de Aquilando [Aguinaldo]." Nine Masses before Christmas, "Misas de la Virgen," or "de Nuestra Señora de la O," from the pre-Nativity antiphons, which begin with "O." According to the 1783 Dictionary of the Spanish Academy, *aguinaldo,* or *aguilando,* is a gift made at Christmas or Epiphany.

many thanks for his devotion. Father Clara-monte entrusted the collection of the first fruits of this settlement for one year to this Argüello so that he might try to convert them into reales in cash to be used for sacred necessities for the chapel. When this was done, they netted 16 pesos 1 tomín in addition to 2 actual pesos that the two new bronze candlesticks I spoke of on the altar cost.

To these 16 pesos 1 real are added 9 pesos 6 reales which have been collected by various alms, and the sum total is 25 pesos 7 reales in cash, which are in the keeping of the father as the most trustworthy person. At the same time the chapel has 119 pesos in seeds according to the regional custom, but the safest of these are 22 which the aforesaid father is holding, because one Blas Trujillo owes the rest that goes to make up this amount, and this is of record in a writing he has made before the ecclesiastical tribunal and which the said father is keeping for the chapel. Father Claramonte intends that all shall be converted into reales in cash in order to use them for the greatest needs of the altar and thereby save bringing things from the mission.[8]

8. Bishop Tamarón made the following statement in his report: "A midday stop was made at the site of Trampas, where there are some settlers. License to build a church was left for them. This license was also drawn up to provide that the church should be inside their walled tenement and that it should be thirty varas long including the transept." AT, pp. 55-56. This measurement corresponds exactly to those given by Domínguez. GK (pp. 104-05, 126-27) is under the impression that the chapel, like the settlement, was originally dedicated to St. Thomas, but it is clear that St. Joseph was the titular patron of the church from the beginning. See also pp. 250-51 *infra*.

San Jerónimo de Taos

Going north from Picuris across the sierra to the north of the pueblo (which I mentioned in my account of Picuris), there are about 4 leagues of rough going before one comes out on a very beautiful plain. Three leagues' journey along this (which make 7) bring one to the pueblo and mission of San Jerónimo de Taos, which is near the nook where two sierras meet. I shall describe its location better later. There are two roads [to Taos from Santa Fe] just as there are from the capital to Picuris, and likewise two distances depending on the road used. And so, going from Santa Fe straight along the sierra by the first route to Picuris which I mentioned, the distance from the said villa to Taos will be about 22 leagues (according to the number of leagues noted). By the lower road through San Juan and Embudo, taking the cañada named Apodaca I mentioned in my account of the latter, the distance will be 25 to 30 leagues because of the frequent bends in the road. In relation to Santa Fe, Taos lies to the northeast in latitude 37° plus minutes north, longitude 271°40′.[1] In completely precise and exact terms of travel to it, it is the last mission in this direction, for there is no other even halfway to one side of it like some we shall see elsewhere.

CHURCH

The church[2] is adobe with very thick walls. The main door faces due south, and from it to a balustrade in the nave which substitutes for a transept it is 33 varas long, 8 wide, and 9 high to the bed molding. There are 8 varas from this balustrade to the wall of the high altar, which is one side of an octagon. That is, 4 varas from the balustrade to the first step of the ascent to the sanctuary, 1 occupied by four steps made of beams, and 3 in the sanctuary itself. This balustrade runs the width of the nave, and from here the nave and sanctuary are more than a vara higher because of the clerestory.

The choir loft is in the usual place and like those of the missions described before. It is reached by a ladder which stands in a corner. On the Epistle side of the nave there are two poor windows facing east, and in the choir there is a window door to a balcony so close to tumbling down that one is more likely to look out lest one fall than at the beautiful plain of which its location offers a view. The ceiling is all of well-wrought beams with multiple corbels, numbering thirty-seven from the choir to the clerestory, which runs the width of the nave, and eleven from there to the wall of the high altar. These become shorter because of the octagon. The following inscription is on the

1. Cf. n. 1, p. 13 *supra.*
2. According to an inscription in this church, it was built by Fray Juan José Pérez de Mirabal in 1726, and we know that Father Mirabal was stationed at Taos 1722-27. On May 6, 1725, the Custos granted a petition by Taos, Fray Juan José Mirabal, missionary, for a large bell at Santa Clara, which Taos claimed by virtue of a royal donation. AASF, 1725, no. 2. According to Father Alvarez, work on a church at Taos began in 1706. HB, 3: 374. As at San Juan, we have no way of being sure whether Father Mirabal continued and completed a building begun before his time, or whether he was responsible for a completely new building. In any case, the eighteenth-century church was destroyed by the American forces during a battle at Taos in 1847, and the ruin is on the outskirts of the pueblo to the west.

beam that holds the clerestory: *Fray Juan Mirabal built this church to the greater honor and glory of God. Year of 1726.* The floor is all covered with beams from front to back. The main door has two paneled leaves with no lock except the crossbar, in a strong, squared frame. It is 3 varas high and 2 wide. The cemetery [wall] begins at the front corner on the Gospel side and ends at the front corner of the convent, its area being 40 varas almost in a square. Therefore it must be realized by now that the convent is on the Epistle side to the east, and thus its entrance is through the cemetery, which has a high adobe wall around it and a single gate near the convent on the east.

In the corner where this cemetery meets the church there is a hideous adobe buttress with a tower buttress rising from it and a small tower with four arches on top. The ascent to it is from the flat roof of the church, and it contains two very small bells

which the King gave. One is quite broken to pieces and has no clapper; the other is badly cracked and has a small clapper. The adornment of the church is as follows.

HIGH ALTAR: Altar screen of ordinary wood, and although it is in false perspective, it is not so unworthy as the one at San Juan. It consists of two sections with three arches in each and half-pillars between the arches that make three nichelike openings in each section. These are painted with earth as iridescent as cinnabar and flowered with mica. This altar screen is supported by a wrought beam like a gradin which extends from wall to wall, and it occupies the width, or face, of the wall above, rising 4½ varas without reaching the ceiling.

In the center niche of the first [lower] section there is a large image in the round of Our Lady of Sorrows with a crown, and I shall describe her adornment presently. In the right-hand niche in this section is an

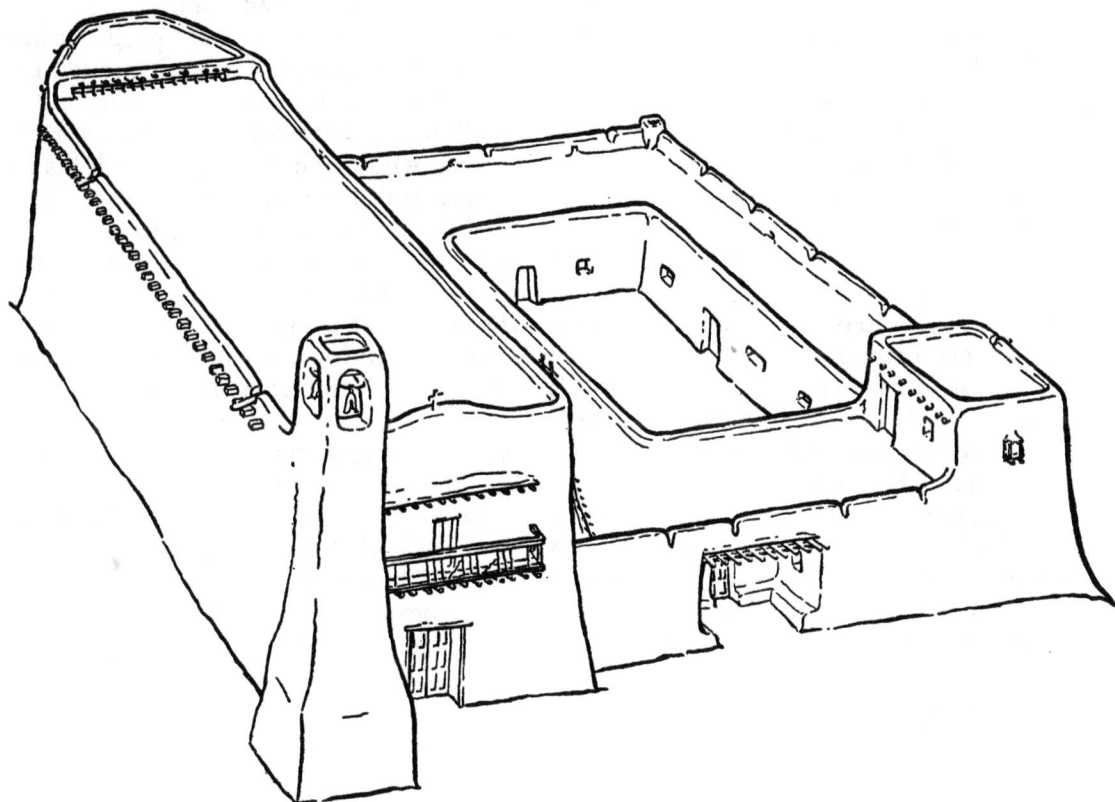

image in the round of Jesús Nazareno dressed in a tunic of sleazy purple silk (it was a skirt given by a pious woman) with fine silver lace, silk cord, ordinary crown, new wig, which a benefactor gave through Father Olaeta's efforts, and a cross. In the left-hand niche is a middle-sized image in the round of St. Michael, all carved. Behind these three aforesaid images are three large paintings on buffalo skin, and they serve as a hanging to cover the wall. Although they are old, they are not torn.

The center niche of the second [upper] section has an oil painting on canvas 2 varas high and 1½ wide with a frame of painted wood. It represents St. Jerome, and the King gave it. The side niches contain two large paintings on buffalo skin, old but good. On the side walls at regular intervals there are four middle-sized paintings on buffalo skin, old and good. The altar table is adobe, with an altar stone given by the King, two small candlesticks given by the same, but they are now broken, cross and missal stand of wood, small bronze bell, and coarse frieze carpet that Father Claramonte provided.

NAVE: On each side there are two monstrous adobe tables that Father García installed. And on the first one on the right side (a piece with gradins which I shall soon describe) there is a canopy over a gradin, lined with buffalo skin painted blue. In this there is a large hinged crucifixion with iron nails, a moth-eaten wig, ordinary crown, and a new Brittany loin cloth with lace which José Hurtado gave at Father Olaeta's request. On the table farther down there is a large niche with little pillars and three openings in a frame, which contains a small image in the round of the woman Veronica, very broken, and Jesus' face on canvas in her hands. Between these tables is a very pretty, though poor, confessional.

One of the two altars, or tables, on the left side has a casket for the Holy Sepulcher (which is completed with the hinged crucifixion mentioned just above), which is of painted wood. In it there is a little coverlet of blue silk serge and a white sheet, both of which pieces the present alcalde, Don Manuel Vigil, gave. The other altar has two gradins like the canopied one, the sections of which are joined together in one piece. Above them there is a very pretty tabernacle with doors and a silver key, and in it a little blue curtain embroidered in silk with silver fringe and lined with China satin. This was made from one face of a vestment (the companion pieces are in the sacristy) with two faces. And Father García deprived the sacristy of it in order to vest the tabernacle.

The pulpit is on the same side as always and it is very pretty. Two little wooden chandeliers with eight branches and candleholders, all of wood, hang from the beam with the inscription. Between these two there is a leather lamp, but very well made and spattered with so much mica that it has a silver sheen, and at the bottom it has a little basket[3] of artificial flowers. The altar screen, all the images in the round which have been mentioned, canopy with three gradins, tabernacle, casket, pulpit, confessional, lamp, chandeliers, balustrade of the false transept, beams on the floor, and the small tower were all provided by Father García, who made the images with his own hands. And it is a pity that he should have used his labor for anything so ugly as the said works are—as bad as the ones mentioned at La Cañada. The adornments of the images of Jesus and of the Virgin, and also the paintings of saints on buffalo skin, have been given by benefactors.

ADORNMENT OF OUR LADY: A gilded cardboard crown with a little silver cross on top. A new wig provided by Father Olaeta. A gauze headdress, now old, that Father García provided. Small silver earrings, which Father Claramonte provided, with drops of paper pearls on little wires, which the Lady had before. A little necklace of blue glass

3. "Chiquibitito." Diminutive of *chiquihuite,* from Nahuatl *chiquihuitl,* "basket."

beads, bugle beads, and spangles which Father Claramonte put on mother-of-pearl ribbon, and from it hang five very ordinary crosses that the Lady had before. Silk dress with embroidery of the same in colors. Wristbands with cambric ruffles edged in gold. A new Brittany chemise which José Hurtado gave. For a mantle she has a small silk towel with blue and white stripes, now worn, which a devout person gave and Father Claramonte made into a mantle, putting ordinary narrow lace around it. A dress and mantle of black ribbed silk, which Doña Gertrudis Armijo gave in Father García's time, are kept for her in the sacristy. Scattered all over her dress she has the following:

Toward the neck, two strings of fat paper pearls which Juan Torres gave at the instance of Father Olaeta. Six ordinary silver reliquaries. Another large one of tin plate, which Teodora Romero gave. Eight little silver shields, which Father Claramonte arranged on rosettes of blue and mother-of-pearl ribbon so that they would show up more. Two reliquaries with silver frames on similar rosettes. A rosary of silver filigree, which Pablo Pando gave and Father Claramonte arranged nicely on a broad heart-shaped mother-of-pearl ribbon, adding eleven small silver medals at his own expense. A jet cross set in silver. Sixteen ordinary medals. An openwork silver cross, which Father Claramonte placed in a nosegay in the Lady's hands. A small reliquary of ordinary metal, well gilded and with oil paintings, which the same father hung from the Lady's hands on a blue ribbon. With regard to these little jewels the following note is inserted.

Note: A few months after Father Olaeta came to this mission of Taos, he informed the Alcalde Mayor Don Manuel Vigil and his lieutenant, Don Nicolás Leal, as well as the Indian principal men of the pueblo, that he was desirous of making a small silver ciborium and cruets out of the pieces of that metal which the Lady had. Since this pro-

posal was agreeable to those mentioned, all the bits of silver were removed by the father, who left only a small cross on her crown. A little silver bell which one Mónica Martín had given to the church and a small box belonging to this father were added to this silver. All this was weighed in the presence of those mentioned, and it amounted to 18 ounces, the cost of [making] the new pieces being assumed by the same father.

Father Olaeta then reported his intention and what he had done to the Father Vice-Custos, asking his permission to proceed. When this was given, everything was sent to Chihuahua with a letter from the aforesaid father to Don Carlos de la Tornera asking him to take charge of having the aforesaid new pieces made. The latter replied that they would be sent in the next convoy. Then when the occasion for the departure of the settlers of this kingdom arose,[4] the father again wrote to the aforesaid under date of November 30, 1775. But when the father's letter reached Chihuahua, the said Tornera had already died. Therefore, his testamentary executor, Don Pedro Velarde,[5] received the letter, and his reply is as follows: "The little vessel and cruets which your Paternity has ordered have not been made, and the silver destined for that purpose, which consists of frames of reliquaries and other things of that kind, is, indeed,

4. Domínguez refers to the cordon which went annually in November or December from New Mexico to Nueva Vizcaya to trade. Bishop Tamarón tells us that five or six hundred settlers usually went. AT, p. 92.

5. Doña Josefa Bustamante, the benefactor of the churches mentioned at Santa Fe and Pojoaque, mortgaged her Pojoaque rancho to her nephew and stepson, Antonio José Ortiz, for 804 pesos which she owed to Don Pedro Velarde, merchant of Chihuahua. SANM, 1: no. 120. This Velarde appears to have been a son of Juan Antonio Pérez Velarde, a Spaniard who settled in El Paso and served as lieutenant governor there under Governor Bustamante. There were further business and marital connections between these El Paso Velardes and the merchant Ortiz and Bustamante families of Santa Fe. See NMF.

here in a *chacual*[6] with a memorandum that they belong to your Paternity and that the aforesaid deceased had advised you by his letter. When the silver is returned, I am ready to hand it over to the person your Paternity pleases." The date of this letter is February 4, 1776, and it remains in the keeping of the said father for his protection.

SACRISTY: The sacristy is joined to the church on the Epistle side. It is 7 varas wide and 6 high, with ten corbeled beams in the ceiling. There are adobe seats on two sides, and the floor was laid with beams by Father García. There is a window to the south over the convent patio, a good two-leaved door to the church, and another very inconvenient one in a corner which gives on the convent through a small cellar. On one wall there is a great adobe table, divided in the center to leave room for an ordinary wooden table with a drawer and a very poor key. On the wall over this great table is a large painting on buffalo skin with eight small ones at its sides. All are very old. The following are kept in this drawer.

Vestments: An old damask chasuble with two faces (white and crimson), with accessories, which the King gave. Another old purple one (this is the other face of the one Father García spoiled), with accessories except frontal. Another of China silk, with accessories except for frontal, extremely old, but Father Olaeta took the trouble to mend it. Another almost new one of black damask, with accessories including cope and cross

6. As a Mexicanism, *chacual* is defined as a leather *cesta* used in the game of pelota by the Mexican Indians. F. J. Santamaría [*Diccionario general de americanismos* (Mexico, 1942)] and I. Alcocer [*El español que se habla en México* (Tacubaya, 1935)] derive it from Nahuatl *tzacualli*, "that which covers, or stops." Santamaría also tells us that in some parts of South America *chacual* is a vessel made from the husk of a fruit and used to assay alloys. L. Islas Escarcega [*Vocabulario campesino nacional* (Mexico, 1945)] defines it as "tecomate" (cup made of a gourd) and says it is used in Michoacán. A similar word, *chacuaco*, formerly was used in Mexico in the sense of a small smelting furnace for silver. Opinions on the derivation of this word vary.

sheath, all with imitation galloon; and Father Camargo gave this one. A usable cope of white tapestry in a foliage design, which was provided through Father Olaeta's efforts. A usable humeral veil of purple damask, which Father Olaeta provided.

Linen: An old openwork cambric amice without lace. Another like it of plain Brittany. Another new one of plain Brittany. A very old Rouen alb. Another of the same material with very wide lace net. An extremely old Rouen altar cloth. Another new one of fine Brittany, 5 varas long with wide lace of medium quality, all of which Father Claramonte provided. Two pairs of old plain Brittany corporals. Two more, almost new, of plain lawn, which Father Olaeta provided. Six usable purificators of various linens. Four more of Brittany, which Father Olaeta provided along with four finger towels to match. Two Rouen finger towels and a hood. An old but usable cincture of thread and silk. A usable plain Brabant linen surplice. A new pall of scarlet cloth with lace flounces and blue ribbon, which Father Claramonte provided. Two more, which Father Olaeta provided, and they are silk with narrow silver point lace. Still another, given by a benefactor, and it is of Brittany with very wide finely embroidered edges on crimson China taffeta with lace flounces. A silk cord, which Father Olaeta provided as a yoke for bridal couples.

Silver and other metal: Chalice with paten, which the King gave, and three spoons provided by other persons. Three little vessels with holy oils, which the King gave, and they are in a small cedar box with a key. Thirteen reales and two rings which Father Claramonte provided for arras, because (so the inventory made by this father says) what there was for that purpose consisted of eight small pieces of silver with a cross etched on them and a socket from the handle of a chisel. The little key to the tabernacle.

Thurible with accessories. Two little cups with a small plate, which Father García provided for cruets. A processional cross from the King. Iron for making altar breads, which the King gave.

Other things: A very old missal. *Manual* by Osorio. A small crystal vessel, which Father García provided. Canopy of painted buffalo skin. Two processional candleholders of unpainted wood. Lectern for the ministers. Three litters that Father García provided. Usable war drum. Useless violin and guitar. Small earthen bowl for a holy-water pot, and another for a baptismal font with a little gourd cup to pour the water. Two wooden boxes for altar breads.

CONVENT

When I spoke of the cemetery I mentioned the location of the convent, which forms a square in that very place, beginning at the upper corner of the sacristy and ending at the lower corner of the church. The porter's lodge lies within the cemetery and is a portico without pillars. It measures 7 varas from mouth to center, 5 varas wide, and 3 very long varas high, with adobe seats around it. Toward the center of the middle wall there is a good ordinary paneled one-leaved door, which Father Claramonte installed, and the lock is a crossbar.

As we enter the porter's lodge there is a room on the left between it and the church which serves for contingencies. Most of the building is on the right and arranged as follows: The cell which had been the chief one from the very beginning is very large, with its inner cell on the corner against the cemetery wall, but Father García wrought such havoc in this convent that it has been necessary for the careful to restore it. Therefore, today the said room is a very fine storeroom with all conveniences, as I saw and observed, everything, even the roof, being new.

At present the inner cell contains a stairway to a little upper story with two rooms which Father García built. They are on what was formerly the flat roof of the said room, and they are on a corner. This stairway is now here inside to avoid the obstruction which the said father had placed in the inside corner here between the cloister and the stairway he built. In order not to get confused by describing two things at once, even though I have noted the foregoing as a matter of principle, I will speak later of this new arrangement, which closes the circuit of the convent.

A room arranged as a very convenient kitchen runs from this inside corner, and through it is the entrance to a small room which lies under the said upper story. Another room runs from this kitchen, then a passage that leads to the enclosed corral, and then another room on a corner. Around the corner is an old room which is used for wood, and Father Olaeta installed a door to it. Beyond this is the stable, the interior of which the same father arranged completely; then the straw loft, and then the little cellar that serves as a passage to the sacristy.

There is a cloister with three sides which adjoins a side wall of the sacristy above and ends below against the church. It is impossible that there be a fourth side of the cloister along the side of the church because the window of the sacristy facing the convent patio would be under it and consequently without light, and a window giving on the open country would not be expedient because of the danger from the enemy. It is enclosed by three walls. And now that I have made the rounds, this is a very good time to explain what I hinted at when I spoke of the inside corner.

Father Claramonte came to Taos as missionary in the year 1770. Finding everything going from bad to worse, he immediately set to work, almost entirely at his own expense, although the Indians did help him a little, and often doing the labor himself, and made the following repairs. He removed various props that encumbered the porter's lodge, and although he left the old roof, he strengthened it with a thick cross timber in the center until such time as a new one should be furnished. He put in the door I mentioned in the porter's lodge. In order to do away with the pool of rain water that formed inside the patio and was soaking in, seriously endangering the walls, he opened a conduit, which drains into the cemetery, and covered it all with planks to prevent falls.

Because of the dampness, the wall facing the entrance to the porter's lodge threatened such ruin that it was held up by seizings and props against the roof. Therefore he built it anew from the foundation up and from beginning to end, with three windows, and he practically put a new roof on this facade. The office which I mentioned in the beginning and the arrangements in it. He removed the awkward stairway in the inside corner, and, in order to make use of the upper story, he broke the corner wall of the inner cell and built and installed a medium-sized staircase through the middle of the wall, with a small landing a short way up; and turning it to the left, he continued it to the cell, in which he installed an ordinary single-leaved door, paneled and without a key. He fixed the walls and built a bay window out over the cemetery. From this there is a full view of the plain to the south and the adjoining areas on the east and west sides.

As we stand looking south through the said window, the inner cell is on the right over the flat roof of the convent with its back to the stairway mentioned. He put a door in it like the one outside, a small fireplace for winter, an adobe bookcase with boards across it, a plain window, and a very neat adobe bed. The passage at the mouth of the stairway leads to the flat roof. There is an adobe railing at this opening and an ordinary door without a key. The ascent to the church and tower is over the flat roof. From all this there is a good view of the Taos plain in all directions, and it is all surrounded by a good railing and embrasures for defense.

The staircase is made of well-wrought beams with an adobe railing, and there is a skylight in the roof to admit light. It is true that the cloister is dark, but it has remained so because human reasons arising from impertinent influences suspended the aforesaid father's desire to continue the work, even at his own expense and labor. Everything is very well made.

Its Furnishings: An ordinary table, which Father Claramonte restored. Two small chairs which the same provided. Two more and a small table which Father Olaeta provided together with a box for certain indispensable business. Kneading trough for breadmaking. Two benches which Father García provided. Metate which Father Claramonte provided for the kitchen.

Its Service: All together, a fiscal mayor, three subordinates, eight sacristans, four cooks, four bakers, who are allotted weekly as has been said at earlier missions. Caretakers of horses, hens, etc.; and carting of wood. There are eight singers for the church.

Its Lands and Fruits: In relation to the location of the church, they are to the west and well in sight. They consist of eight plots distributed in this manner: Four large milpas, in each of which 3 fanegas of wheat can be sown, and they yield 60 to 80 fanegas. If maize is sown in them, they take 3 almudes each, which yield about 40 fanegas. But they are not sown with one thing at a time, but always with everything, and the father usually lends small plots. Three little plots for legumes, of which (except frijol) the usual harvest is 12 to 15 fanegas of all kinds together. Another small plot for green vegetables, of which (except chile) the necessary amount is usually harvested with ease. There is a good pool in this little kitchen garden, like the one mentioned at San Ildefonso even to the poplar tree on the rim. But here there is more than there, and the additional consists of some small trees of fine plums. And the water collected in the pool comes from the pueblo's river and is used to water the garden stuff. The sowing and all other work are in the charge of the pueblo.

MISSION FATHER

The one whom our Mother the Province has here to exercise the apostolic ministry is Father Fray José Olaeta, native of Mexico City, forty-seven years of age, twenty-nine in profession, two years and two months as a missionary in the Custody, all in Taos, where he is now. He holds general faculties from Durango, *sede vacante,* revocable at will.

ADMINISTRATION OF THE MISSION: Mass on feast days at a convenient hour. After it is over the Indians recite the catechism. And on these days there is sometimes explanation of doctrine to the whole congregation during Mass. Daily at a regular hour, morning and evening, recitation of the catechism by unmarried men and women. Sometimes they recite with the father, who expounds some point with the aid of an interpreter.

OBVENTIONS AND FIRST FRUITS: Not to omit the general report given above, yet there is sometimes a horse, cow, or ox here, or a mixture of this kind of offering and grain.

Some 30 fanegas of grain, including all kinds (except frijol and chile), are usually collected as first fruits; a small amount of onions and calabashes.

No small livestock, because there are none. Two or three head of cattle, and sometimes the devout give a calf. The Indians usually pay for a Mass, as I said at San Juan.

EXPENDITURES: Food consumed by the household is not counted. About 8 pounds of wax for all administrative purposes. About 20 cuartillos of wine. More than 500 altar breads, since some are given to Picuris as I stated at length there, and they are made here under Father Olaeta's eyes with the required care.

HOW HE ACQUIRES NECESSITIES: The usual method is taken for granted. This friar says that here in order to save the large amount of grain and other things he used for repeated purchases of lard, he acquired four pigs in order to supply himself with lard from the offspring, and he gave a fanega of wheat each, and . . . [*sic*][7]

CONVENT PROVISIONS: Father Olaeta received with this mission from Father Claramonte (who himself had received half a fanega of refuse as maize from another) a very abundant provision, even of supererogatory things, but I leave in the new inventory that Father Claramonte made here the amount determined as recorded in the following

WRIT OF VISITATION

San Jerónimo de Taos, April 24 of the year 1776. In prosecution of the juridical visitation which our Reverend Father Fray Francisco Atanasio Domínguez, one of the appointed preachers in the Convento Grande of Our Father St. Francis of Mexico City and Commissary Visitor for our Very Reverend Father Minister Provincial Fray Isidro Murillo, is making of this Custody, his Reverend Paternity proceeded to examine and did examine this inventory of valuables belonging to church, sacristy, and convent, and he thanked the present mission father, Fray José Olaeta, for his exactitude and performance in having recorded all the things belonging to this mission and their present condition, as well as for the neatness and cleanliness of the cells and other things. And he is charged to convey thanks to the benefactors who have contributed the additional items this inventory mentions.

And in order that his good conduct may be of record for all time, he shall enter in this inventory the silver jewels that belonged to the Virgin and that, with the consent of the alcalde and others, were sent to Chihuahua so that a small ciborium and cruets might be made from them as is stated in the aforesaid letter of Don Pedro Velarde dated February 4, 1776, in whose possession these jewels remain.

And, proceeding to the provisions this convent must have for the friar who may be

7. The sentence is incomplete in the original.

sent there by the prelate, our Reverend Father Commissary Visitor Fray Francisco Atanasio Domínguez, by virtue of instructions and authority which our Very Reverend Father Minister Provincial Fray Isidro Murillo has conferred upon him, therefore orders and commands the following: 14 fanegas of wheat, 12 of maize, 10 sheep, 6 strings of chile, half a fanega of frijol, half a fanega of broad beans, a cuartilla of vetch, another of chick peas, an almud of salt, a fat hog or sow—and if this is not possible, there shall be 20 cuartillos of lard—12 tallow candles.

In addition, the outgoing friar must hand over and the incoming one receive the convent furnishings and other things as listed in the inventory, and give a receipt for them, and in case of anything missing, the incoming friar shall notify the Father Vice-Custos (or Custos) so that he may have the lack supplied. And the Reverend Custos or his Vice-Custos shall not be able to dispense with or take away anything ordered by us up to here, and only, indeed, add all they may consider necessary for the benefit of the mission and missionary, since we know for a fact that this is the intention and mind of our Superior Provincial Prelate, who so orders and commands *ratione officii* and therefore validly for all time. Our Reverend Father Commissary Visitor so decreed, ordered, and signed before me, the undersigned secretary, to which I attest. Fray Francisco Atanasio Domínguez, Commissary Visitor. In my presence, Fray José Palacio, secretary.

The parish books were examined and approved, and the corresponding writs of visitation were recorded in them. But, although there is nothing to note about them, since they are nearly finished I ordered there in the decrees that Father Olaeta should promptly provide new books and file the others in the archive he intends to make in this convent. If this is not finished within a month, let the said books be remitted to the archive at the mission of Our Father Santo Domingo. The Inventory and Patent books are new and have many folios. They were examined, etc. And Father Claramonte provided them.

PUEBLO

The pueblo of Taos and all I have described stand in a very beautiful valley that comes from the Sierra Madre in the east and from another sierra to the north which slopes from the Sierra Madre and, turning north, runs in that direction to the lands of the pagans. It is, then, near the place where these sierras meet and on the eastern end of the plain, being about 2000 varas from the Sierra Madre and 1000 varas from the other sierra. Therefore I say that it is near them, with a very open view to the south as far as the sierra north of Picuris. Turning from there to the southwest, there is a very broad outlook to the southwest and west to north, with sierras in the far distance.

Its plan resembles that of those walled cities with bastions and towers that are described to us in the Bible. I use this simile to explain myself more clearly with regard to its labyrinthine arrangement, but nevertheless I resign myself to describing it. For greater clarity it should be noted that from that same place between the aforesaid sierras a very decent river arises. It has a rapid current of good crystalline water and runs from the east toward the southwest until it joins another which I shall describe in due course, almost in the middle of the plain.

In relation to the church and convent the pueblo is to the east, and the aforesaid river runs through the middle of it. There are walls to cross it (they are of adobe), with their openings underneath. On each side of the river there is a tenement, or sugar loaf or honeycomb, exactly like the ones described at Picuris. On the east a very high wall extends from the end of one to the end of the other, and there is a gate in this wall facing the said direction. The gate is on the north side of the said river, and on the corner of the tenement facing east on this bank there is a fortified tower.

Continuing along this same bank, below the tenement and at the corner of it, is another fortified tower. Then there is a wall that makes an inside corner, and then a small block of houses which faces south, and, making another inside corner below, turns with its back to the corral of the convent (which is beside it) and faces east. It runs around the corner and turns again to the south, ending about 12 varas before the cemetery gate, which faces east as I said in the proper place. On this north bank the convent and church are joined to the aforesaid.

The tenement on the south side has its fortified tower on the upper corner. Then the wall continues without turning, and then a small block of houses that end with the *casas reales,* which are like all the rest. A wall runs from the end of these *casas reales,* and, crossing the river nearby, joins a small block of settlers' houses (I will very soon say why they live here), which are back to back, and consequently some face east on the plaza and others west away from the plaza, but the entrances are from within the plaza for safety's sake. There is another fortified tower on the *casas reales.*

This settlers' block ends at the main gate, which faces west, and as we stand in it facing that direction, a small block of settlers runs on our right to a corner with a fortified tower facing the cemetery. Around the corner there are other small houses almost to the foot of the church tower. Inside, just beyond the main gate toward the convent, there are other houses on the left against the cemetery wall as far as its gate. The corrals in which the cattle are kept are in the plaza. There is a bridge made of beams to cross from one bank to the other.

For clearer understanding of what remains to be said, I reiterate that: The Taos valley is very pleasant, for in addition to its wide view, it is watered by four fair-sized rivers, one called the Taos River after the pueblo. Another rises from the sierra north of Taos and runs proportionately with good and crystalline water to the south, and they call this river Lucero and it is the one I mentioned a little while ago that joins the pueblo river in the middle of the plain. Another which rises in the Sierra Madre like that of the pueblo and follows the same course exactly to the points of the compass, is about a league below the pueblo and joins the Lucero River.[8] Another river lower down, which rises and runs from east to west with a very rapid current of crystalline water, belongs to the settlers (as we shall see there). It is called the Río de las Trampas de Taos and joins the Lucero River, which, in this vicinity, already carries with it the ones mentioned above. From here down they run together in a rock canyon until they join the Río del Norte, which in relation to Taos and its plain draws back very far to the west in a rock canyon, although there is a plain above on both banks.

There is a very extensive swamp quite near the pueblo on the west. It has so much *zacate* that the enclosed cattle are pastured in it, a very large amount is cut for the herds of horses, and there is so much left over that in the spring it is necessary to set fire to the old so that the new may come up freely. When the Comanches are at peace and come to trade, they bring a thousand or more animals who feed there two days at most, and in spite of this great number repeatedly during the year, there is no lack of fodder.

LANDS AND FRUITS: In relation to the location of the pueblo they run from south and east to the north and approach the aforesaid sierras, extending far from their base. In short, they are excessively large.

8. The Lucero River and the Río de Don Fernando were named for two seventeenth-century landholders of Taos Valley who lost their families here in the Revolt of 1680. The Trampas was below these two streams. Diego Lucero de Godoy and Don Fernando Durán y Chaves did not return to New Mexico at the time of the Reconquest. See NMF.

They are very fertile indeed, and those in the south and east and some of those in the north are watered by the pueblo's river; and those on the north are watered by the Lucero River.

With the exception of frijol and chile, everything yields such an abundant harvest that when (as happened in the year '74) there is scarcity in most of the kingdom, everyone goes to Taos and leaves there well supplied, not just once, but many times. Whether they are at peace or at war, the Comanches always carry off all they want, by purchase in peace and by theft in war. Every year many poor wretches come day by day to work for the little daily wage in grain they get (to say nothing of beggars). Finally, in spite of such great consumption, and not counting the food used, the new grains are gathered with the old.

The natives of this pueblo bear its name. They speak the Picuris language, although in a different manner and not as thickly, but although it is the same, they do not call it Picuris, but Taos. They came down from Cuartelejo with the Picuris, with whom they agree in customs, arrangement of houses, etc. Many more than the latter speak Spanish and not so stammeringly as they do. Here is the

CENSUS

112 families with 427 persons

This mission has charge of the administration of a small settlement called *Trampas de Taos*. In relation to the pueblo it is to the south, about 3 leagues away over the plain. It lies in a cañada that starts from the Sierra Madre and, running about a league from east to west, makes a depression in the plain between ridges of low hills that slope down from the Sierra Madre to north and south. Therefore I say that it comes from the Sierra Madre. A river runs the length of it through the very middle (I have already counted it and mentioned it a short time

ago), which serves to water the very good lands it has on both sides. And with the exception of chile and frijol, the harvest is like those I described in the pueblo. The settlement consists of scattered ranchos, and their owners are the citizens who live in the pueblo.[9]

While speaking of the pueblo I cited the explanation, or reason, why they live there, and it is as follows. Formerly these settlers had a small plaza near the west side of the pueblo on the river and near the said swamp.[10] This, built with the consent of the Indians, came to be a sort of hospice for the settlers when they visited Taos, and they stayed there as long as they liked as owners of the houses. Among these houses, one end of the plaza served for the *casas reales*, and the natives of the pueblo bought it from a citizen for this purpose. Here the alcalde

9. The site of present Ranchos de Taos. According to Bishop Crespo, a settlement of tame Apaches had been attempted here in Father Mirabal's time. BL, *Memorial ajustado . . . que siguió el Illmo. Sr. Don Benito Crespo . . . con la Religión de N. P. S. Francisco . . .* (Mexico, 1738). In Domínguez' time, however, it consisted of some scattered Spanish folk who dared to farm away from the pueblo despite the Comanche menace. Among them were the Vigil and Romero families mentioned in this section, whose ancestor, Diego Romero, had acquired the seventeenth-century "Ranchos de Don Fernando" from a post-Reconquest grantee, Cristobal de la Serna. SANM, 1: no. 240. Later, the name of this village reverted from Trampas back to Ranchos de Don Fernando de Taos, still later shortened to Ranchos de Taos. It will be noted that in 1776 neither the plaza of this village nor its now famed church of St. Francis had yet been started.

10. Site of the present town of Fernández de Taos. Sebastián Martín Serrano had acquired lands in Taos Valley, including some close to the pueblo. The property passed to his daughter, Margarita Martín, wife of Juan Padilla, and then to her daughter, Josefa Padilla, who married a newcomer from Spain, Don Carlos Fernández. This seems to be the answer to the name "Fernández de Taos," mistakenly called "San Fernández" and "San Fernando de Taos." If, however, the name was originally Don Fernando de Taos, it must have come from the nearby stream of Don Fernando de Chaves. See n. 8 *supra*, and NMF.

mayor lived with the settlers, for they lived there most of the year.

Later, when the Comanche raids became more troublesome, because this plaza was about two musket shots away from the pueblo and therefore cut off for purposes of mutual defense of pueblo and plaza, the settlers abandoned it and moved to the pueblo with the consent of the Indians in the year '70 when Father Claramonte was missionary. When the Lord Governor don Pedro Mendinueta was informed of this move, the aforesaid plaza was torn down with his consent and that of the Indians, and all that I have described was built in the pueblo, the aforesaid father being the one who went with the citizens, planning their dwellings for the greater protection of all, along with the church and convent.

But although this is so, it does not mean that they will always live here, but only until the plaza which is being built in the cañada where their farms are is finished.[11] This is being erected by order of the aforesaid governor, Knight [of the Order of Santiago], so that when they live together in this way, even though they are at a distance from the pueblo, they may be able to resist the attack the enemy may make. These settlers are people of all classes. Some are masters, others servants, and others are both, serving and commanding themselves. They speak the local Spanish, and most of them speak the language of the pueblo with ease, and to a considerable extent the Comanche, Ute, and Apache languages. Here is the

CENSUS

67 families with 306 persons

11. Apparently at the site of Ranchos de Taos and perhaps the beginnings of its church and plaza, for the much later town of Fernández de Taos is on a small plateau, not in a cañada.

Santa Clara

In regard to what I have been saying about this part of the Río Arriba, and since we are on the east bank of the Río del Norte, I say that: Near San Ildefonso, or higher up, according to circumstances, one crosses, or fords, the said river to the opposite bank, on which the pueblo and mission of Our Mother Santa Clara stands a short distance away. It is located and established on a fairly good plain almost like the one that extends from the Villa de la Cañada to San Juan; but this one lies at the foot of a sierra which is on the west and is called the Sierra of Santa Clara. This mission is about 9 leagues from Santa Fe and lies to the northwest of the villa. I will soon describe its location, and the following is inserted with regard to the visitation.

NOTE

Because the old church had fallen down, beginning in the year 1758 Father Fray Mariano Rodríguez de la Torre started to build the present one and finished it.[1] We shall see what it is like. Although the Indians and settlers of the mission assisted in this project, no levy was made for the purpose, since most of it was at the father's expense, as is shown by the fact that he supplied twenty-one yoke of oxen to cart the timbers and he fed the laborers gratis. When the lumber was being carted, it happened that an Indian killed an ox belonging to a third person, and the said father paid for it with a shroud. And although the owner (his name is Joaquín Mestas) did not want payment, he finally accepted it.

When the roof of the nave of the church was finished, the Indians and the settlers left the rest up to the father alone and to his industry. Therefore, what was necessary to roof the transept and sanctuary was taken from his alms, and with this he roofed it. The carpenters, in addition to being well paid, ate, drank, and lived in the convent at the father's expense for a period of two months in the winter, when the days are very short in this region. And since these workmen were very gluttonous and spoiled (in this land, when there is work to be done in the convents, the workers want a thousand delicacies, and in their homes they eat filth), the gravy cost the father more than the meat (as the saying goes). That is to say, they ate more and were paid more than they worked.

While this new building was being finished, Mass was said in a very small chapel, or shrine, because there was no other convenient place since the passing years had leveled the old church to the ground. And the reward which has been given to the said shrine for its holy service is that it serves as a stable for dumb beasts that gather in it of their own accord. Keeping this in mind:

CHURCH

Obviously it is new, of adobe with very thick walls, with the outlook and main door to the east. From the door to the mouth of its formal transept it is 30 varas long, 5 wide, and 7 high. The transept is 4 varas long to the mouth of the sanctuary, 13 varas wide, and 8 long varas high because of the clerestory which rises at its mouth. The ascent to the sanctuary consists of three stairs made of wrought beams which stand on the floor of the transept. And it is 6 varas long to the center by 5 wide like the nave of the church, which looks like a culverin.[2] It was necessary to make it so narrow for lack of heavy timbers to support the width it would ordinarily have had like the churches described before.

The choir loft, after all, was superfluous, since there are no nuns to go up to it, and therefore there is none.[3] There are two windows in the transept, one at each end, and there are two on the right side of the nave facing south. The nave is roofed by forty-seven wrought and corbeled beams, and the clerestory rises on the one opposite the sanctuary. The main door is squared, with a wooden frame, two paneled leaves, and a crossbar for a lock. It is somewhat more than 3 varas high by 2½ wide. The floor is earth. Cemetery and baptistery like the choir. On the flat roof over the main door there is a small bell tower containing a ra-

---

1. This church is no longer in existence, for the present one dates from 1918. The pre-Revolt church at Santa Clara was founded by Fray Alonso de Benavides. AB-1634, p. 69. Another church was being built in 1706, but as we learn here, it collapsed, and a new one was started in 1758.

2. "Cerbatana." The original meaning is blowgun. In the sixteenth and seventeenth centuries it also came to be applied to a culverin, or long narrow cannon.

3. A Domínguez witticism prompted by the fact that this church was named for St. Clare, the foundress of Franciscan cloistered nuns who spent much of their time in the choir.

ther medium-sized bell which the King gave. It is a good one and speaks with its own tongue, unlike others that are rung with stones. The church is adorned thus:

HIGH ALTAR: Near the center of the blank wall hangs a painting of Our Mother St. Clare of the same description as those mentioned in previous missions. It is old and the King gave it. There are seven paintings around it, all a vara in size. Four of them are oil paintings and three tempera on buffalo skin. The altar table is adobe with

chief resemblance is to a culverin because of its length and narrowness, it also resembles a wine cellar, and it contains two poor benches provided by Father Fray Sebastián Fernández. There are signs of life, however, and one of these is the walled-up door to the future baptistery, and this is in the right-hand corner on the Epistle side as we enter the main door. Toward the middle of the Gospel side there is a little grating for a confessional, which is inside the sacristy like a confessional for nuns, but the difference is

an altar stone given by the King. Wooden cross and missal stand, and a small bronze bell. And behind the table is a large adobe gradin, on which the following small images in the round stand:

Our Mother St. Clare, given by Antonio Bernal; Our Lady of Loreto, given by Don Carlos Mirabal, and it is quite ugly. The following were given by one Carlos López: Child Jesus with an old ribbed silk tunic; Our Father St. Francis; St. Anthony of Padua, Our Lady of Sorrows, with a very old dress, and she has a silver radiance and dagger, two small strings of ordinary pearls, tin plate reliquary with wax saints, small silver shield with Our Lady of Guadalupe engraved on it, a small cross of ordinary stones, and two half reales.

There is no heading for the nave of this church, because its adornment is so soulless that I consider it unnecessary to describe anything so dead. Nevertheless, although its

that in that case the nuns are inside and the priest outside, and here the reverse is true, for the monk is within and the penitents without.

SACRISTY: The sacristy is joined to the church on the Gospel side, and, beginning at the upper corner of the transept, it ends in the middle of the aforesaid side of the nave. It is 14 varas long, a little more than 4 wide, and 3 long varas high, with seventeen wrought beams in the ceiling. There is a window to the west in the end wall, an ordinary single-leaved door without a key to the church at the head of the transept, and another to the convent on one side. On the wall adjoining the nave there is a hole for the confessional, as I have just said. Against one wall there is an ordinary wooden table with a drawer and key to hold the following:

Vestments: A damask chasuble with two faces (white and crimson), with accessories, trimmed with silk galloon, which the King gave. The frontal is considered worn out, for the whole thing is nothing but raveled threads. Another usable white damask chasuble with the necessary accessories, trimmed with embroidered ribbon galloon, and Father Rodríguez provided this one. Another old blue one, presumably the gift of the King. Another of black damask trimmed with imitation silver galloon, with accessories including cross sheath. It is said that the prelates gave it. Separate stole and maniple. A frontal of blue and white satin, which Carlos López gave, but Father Rodríguez mended it where it had been frayed. Four burses for corporals and two palls for the chalice of various colors and materials, but in regard to age they are all the same.

Linen: An old Brittany amice. Another new one of the same material with narrow lace, which Father Rodríguez provided. An old Rouen alb. Another new one of Brittany, which the said father provided. An old Rouen altar cloth. Another new one of Brittany trimmed with lace, which the said father provided. Four pairs of double corporals, fairly good though rather small and of poor linen. Five purificators. Two finger towels. Two old Rouen palls. Two more of the same material, given by a pious woman. A cotton cincture which the said father provided. Another amice which the prelates gave along with an alb and purificator, and all are of Brittany. Another new Brittany amice which Diego Martín gave.

Silver and other metal: Chalice with paten but no spoon, which the King gave. Three little vessels with holy oils, given by the same, and they are kept in a small box with a key. Another for the oil for the sick. Thirteen small coins and two rings which the aforesaid Father Rodríguez provided for arras.

Two small brass candlesticks that the King gave. The base of a plate for some broken glass cruets. Thurible without chains (but it does have thongs) or other accessories. A dolls' spoon for the chalice. A bowl which Father Fernández provided for a baptismal font.

Other things: An old missal with thong bookmarks, which Father Zambrano gave when he was Vice-Custos. Another older one. *Manual* by Osorio. A completely nondescript tabernacle with little doors and a key. A small carpet of ordinary frieze, which Father Fernández provided.

CONVENT

The convent is joined to the church on the Gospel side and extends to the south in the form of a square full of rooms. One of them begins where the sacristy ends on the said side of the church and ends against a side wall of the sacristy. There is a square cloister. Father Rodríguez built it all; it is new, and is as I have described. A gallery runs from the wall where the sacristy ends against the church. This is used as a storeroom. It has a window to the east in the wall which joins the corner of the church below, and an ordinary two-leaved door with a key to the cloister.

The porter's lodge is beside the said gallery, faces east, and resembles the one at Nambe. As we enter it, the living quarters are at the left, and they consist of three rooms: a very spacious cell with a key, an inner cell on the corner, and another room around the corner. Behind this there are two more rooms as far as the other corner, and there is a key to the first door. Beside the room on this corner there is a single cell, then a passageway, of which I shall soon speak, and the kitchen beyond it against the sacristy.

One must ride from this passage on a hobbyhorse, because the stable, strawloft, oven, and hencoop are not connected with the convent and church. In the inside corner of the sacristy against the church there is a board stairway used to ascend to the flat roof. As soon as we leave the passage on our hobbyhorse there is a mirador like a cage on our left. It begins at the corner, or edge, of the passageway and ends on the west corner.

Its Furnishings: Two nondescript old tables. Two small chairs. A large measure for grain.

Its Service: The same and in the same manner I described at San Ildefonso.

Its Lands and Fruits: In relation to the location of church, convent, and pueblo, there are several small plots to the south, five of which are of moderate value, since a fanega of wheat can be sown in each, or if maize is sown, an almud each. Three other small plots are used for legumes. The amount ordinarily produced by all is not stated, for the present missionary says he has not bothered to measure the grain; but he does, indeed, affirm that there is sufficient to provide a rather comfortable living. They are irrigated by the water from a small river that comes from the sierra to the west which I mentioned a while ago. Later I will describe its course and other details. The sowing, cultivation, and harvest are in charge of the pueblo.

MISSION FATHER

Our Mother the Province employs Father Fray Buenaventura Hermida in the apostolic ministry of this mission. He is a native of Galicia in the bishopric of Tuy, thirty-nine years of age, fifteen in profession, six years in the Custody as a missionary, as follows: Realito of El Paso, two years; El Paso, a year and a half; Senecu, three months; Isleta at El Paso, three months; Santa Clara, where he now is, two years. He holds general faculties from Durango, revocable at will.

Administration of the Mission: I find nothing to note about this, and so I refer to the general custom with regard to Mass and catechism as in the other pueblos.

Obventions and First Fruits: In general I refer to the foregoing. With regard to the first fruits at this mission, the father says that they amount to something like 30 fanegas, including everything, plus a small amount of chile, onions, and other green vegetables. The Indians give nothing.

Expenditures: Annually, about 6 pounds of wax, about 2 jugs of wine, about 200 altar breads, and these are brought from La Cañada although the father gives nothing in return. Food consumed in the household is not counted.

How He Acquires Necessities: The usual method may be taken for granted. This father has nothing in particular to say, and so I refer to the statements of other fathers.

Convent Provisions: In the inventory of this mission it is recorded that the Reverend Custos Fray Jacobo de Castro determined and authorized the following: 10 fanegas of wheat, the same amount of maize, 10 sheep, 6 strings of chile, a jar of ordinary lard, half a fanega of frijol, half an almud of salt. This is confirmed, and I added to it the amount shown by the following

WRIT OF VISITATION

Mission of Our Mother Santa Clara, May 2 of the year 1776. In prosecution of the juridical visitation which our Reverend Father Fray Francisco Atanasio Domínguez, one of the appointed preachers in the Convento Grande of Our Father St. Francis of Mexico City and Commissary Visitor of this Custody for our Very Reverend Father Minister Provincial Fray Isidro Murillo, is making of this Custody, his Reverend Paternity proceeded to examine and did examine this inventory, which he pronounces to be accurate and legal, but he notes that the old black chasuble, stole, maniple, pall, and burse, and also the white chasuble with blue stripes that this inventory records no longer exist. Therefore, the friar who may take over this mission in future shall not recover them.

He also notes that the purple chasuble with accessories recorded in this inventory is the blue one with accessories in the sacristy of this church and mission. This affirmation is made because there is no other color that can serve for purple. In accordance with the foregoing, the outgoing missionary must hand over, and the newcomer receive, because the aforesaid is what is now in existence. And in order to avoid any misunderstanding about this and other things, his Reverend Paternity orders and commands the present mission father, Fray Buenaventura Hermida, or his successor, to be most careful and attentive in recording each thing in the place where it belongs, avoiding all notes, tedious discourse, and words that mean nothing and only cause confusion and great difficulty.

And in order that this mission may have the necessary supply of provisions, our Reverend Father Visitor orders and commands that it be the amount designated by the Reverend Custos Castro, which is recorded in this inventory on folio 2 v., to which his Reverend Paternity adds the following: 4 wax candles, 6 cuartillos of wine, half a fanega of chick peas, half a fanega of vetch, 50 onions. The outgoing friar must hand over all this, along with the convent rooms and furnishings recorded in this inventory, and the incoming one receive it, giving a receipt. And if anything is missing, the prelate of the Custody shall be notified, and he shall have the lack supplied. The Reverend Custos, or his Vice-Custos, shall not be able to dispense with any part of what has been ordered in the foregoing, but only, indeed, add to it for the benefit of the mission and missionary, since this is the intention and will of our Superior Provincial Prelate, who so orders and commands *ratione officii*, and therefore validly for all time. Our Reverend Father Commissary so decreed, ordered, and signed before me, the undersigned secretary, to which I attest. Fray Francisco Atanasio Domínguez, Commissary Visitor. In my presence, Fray José Palacio, secretary.

The parish books were examined, approved, and signed by the secretary. They are folios bound in red sheepskin. They are good and have enough blank paper for two years, judging by the earlier records. They were begun in the year 1726 by Father Fray Juan del Pino and are now being kept by Father Hermida. The books of Inventory and Patents are quarto volumes like the aforesaid.

PUEBLO

The plain I mentioned in the beginning, where the mission I am describing is located and established, offers an extensive view to beyond San Juan and below La Cañada, but above Cañada there are obstructions. Moreover, although it is in full sight of the Río del Norte, it does not lie on its meadows, but on a site above the said river like the rim of the plain, and likewise it slopes down from the foot of the sierra which I mentioned at the very beginning. As the plain spreads out above, it covers a good deal of territory, and below it extends to the milpa lands of the San Ildefonso Indians on the west. But the said mission is not visible from Santa Clara because the little mesa I mentioned when I was telling about the road from San Ildefonso to La Cañada obstructs the view.

Toward the west of the plain mentioned here, there is a cañada that comes from the said sierra, runs to the east, and ends near the north side of the church, with its mouth at a distance from the settlement. The pueblo consists of a plaza which lies to the south of the convent and church, and it is composed of four small blocks with two passages on opposite corners. There is a fortified tower on one corner and five little houses outside the plaza on one side. The kind, decoration, and distribution of the houses are like those of the pueblo of Nambe, to which I refer.

Its Lands and Fruits: Some of these lands occupy the greater part of the cañada I have just mentioned. There are others on the plain. And there are some small milpas on what little meadowland there is by the Río del Norte. All the foregoing are watered by a small river that runs through the middle of the cañada. When there is no rain, this dries up and presents difficulties, since there is no way of using any other irrigation because of the high location. The land by the Río del Norte is watered from it, and all in all there is a decent harvest. There are peach, apricot, and plum trees, in the cañada mentioned.

The natives of this pueblo are Teguas like those mentioned from Tesuque to San Juan inclusive, and therefore they speak the same language, resembling them both in the manner of speaking Spanish and in customs, even to small things. It is said that the Santa Clara people came from Moqui, where the same Tegua language is spoken, but nevertheless this must be untrue, because the Sandia Indians came from there, and they absolutely do not speak the Tegua language. They are included in the following

CENSUS

67 families with 229 persons

The administration of a group of settlers is attached to this mission. They live to the north in scattered ranchos extending about 3 leagues. They have their farmlands which produce good crops of everything, and these are irrigated by the water from a river which comes from Abiquiu (it will be mentioned there too) and winds north-northwest to below San Juan where it joins the Río del Norte. This is called the Chama River. Its water is dirty because of the large amount of red earth throughout its course and because of the muddy bottom. This extensive settlement is divided into four sections, each bearing its own name, but this is nothing but a whim, for it all continues without even a middling break between place and place like those under the administration of San Juan, and this is obvious from the comparison of one with the others.[4] And therefore I do not stop to particularize when they give me no reason to do so. The individuals are like the ones I mentioned at San Juan, and all speak the Spanish described everywhere else. In addition to this mixed populace, there are here nine families of genízaros like those in the Villa of Santa Fe. They have no true home, because hunger and the enemy [Indians] pursue them from every side as a reward for their levity, weakness, etc. But for now these vagrants are included with the majority of this settlement since they are attached to it. The present includes them.

CENSUS

69 families with 340 persons

4. The Spanish settlement most often mentioned in the Santa Clara records of this period is La Cuchilla.

Abiquiu

The pueblo and mission of Santa Rosa de Abiquiu is 9 very good leagues northwest of Santa Clara over a rough road with small hills and arroyos between them, all sandy, and with an occasional small level place. The pueblo stands on a triangular hill which I will describe more fully later. It is some 18 leagues from Santa Fe and lies to the northwest of the villa. This mission was recently founded by Don Tomás Vélez for Christian genízaro Indians. He had it named the pueblo and mission of Santo Tomás de Abiquiu, but the settlers use the name Santa Rosa, as the lost mission was called in the old days. Therefore, they celebrate the feast of this female saint, and not of that masculine saint, annually as the patron. At the same time, to keep the thread of the narrative, the following remarks are inserted.

NOTE

In the year 1772, Obedience sent Father Fray Sebastián Fernández to Santa Clara as missionary, and under the same obligation he was requested to take care of the Abiquiu mission as a visita. And he immediately began to serve the latter with such attention that he became its own minister with the aim of applying himself to the matters we will mention. When he came, he found that Father Toledo had built the church walls halfway up on all sides. Finding it in this state, he put his hand to it so firmly that he took the food from his own mouth and used his royal alms to finish the work and build what I now begin to describe.[1]

CHURCH

The church is adobe with very thick walls and a transept. Its outlook and main door are to the south, and from the door to the mouth of the transept it is 22 varas long, 8 wide, and 9 high. The transept is 6 varas long, 14 wide, and is higher than the nave because of the clerestory. The ascent to the sanctuary consists of three steps of wrought beams on the transept floor. The choir loft is like those of the missions that have them, to avoid stopping to describe it. The floor is bare earth, but the building is very good.

There is a good window at each end of the transept. There are two more in the nave of the church on the Epistle side, and one in the choir loft. The roof of the nave consists of thirty-three wrought beams with multiple corbels. The transept has eighteen of the same, and the sanctuary eight like them, but there is no substitute for a vaulted arch. The main door is squared, in a wooden frame, with two paneled leaves and a crossbar for a lock. It is 3½ varas high by 2½ wide. At the top of the wall above this door there is an adobe arch containing a medium-sized bell, whole, good, and new, the gift of the King. The cemetery is 30 varas square, and the porter's lodge and convent are inside it. It is marked off by an adobe wall a long vara high, with a gate opposite the church door. The adornment of the church is as follows.

HIGH ALTAR: There is no altar piece or image of the titular saint of the mission, but Father Fernández arranged five large, al-

most new paintings on buffalo skin on the blank wall, with a small, not very old oil painting on canvas of St. Raphael in an unpainted wooden frame at the top. On the floor behind the altar table is an adobe table which serves as a gradin. On it there are three adobe stairs, like a throne, culminating in a well-adorned niche in the form of a litter with a canopy. In this there is a very pretty medium-sized image in the round of Our Lady of the Conception which Father Fernández provided.

I will describe the adornment of this image at greater length later. Meanwhile, she is very well adorned at the said father's expense. The altar table is adobe, with an altar stone given by the King. On it, and on the gradin, stand a wooden cross, missal stand of the same, ten unpainted candlesticks of the same material, a painting on copper of Our Lady of Sorrows in a black frame, two ordinary bouquets. There is no dais, but there is a frieze carpet provided by the said father and a small metal bell, per-

---

1. Domínguez' account of the mission and Spanish settlement at Abiquiu helps to clarify the story of this area. According to Fray Miguel Menchero, in 1744 there were twenty Spanish families living at Santa Rosa de Abiquiu, 10 leagues west of Santa Fe, and they were in the spiritual charge of the missionary at San Ildefonso. HB, 3: 399. This area was greatly harassed by enemy Indians, and the settlers were forced to abandon the place more than once in the decade that followed. The center of the Spanish settlement of Santa Rosa, which must originally have consisted of the usual widely scattered ranchos until the need for defense compelled some of them to live in a plaza, was probably 3 miles southeast of the modern town of Abiquiu, where the ruins of their chapel, which Domínguez describes, may still be seen. As we learn here, this chapel antedated the church at the pueblo of Abiquiu. In the late 1740's an attempt to establish a settlement of Christian genízaro Indians in the area failed. This may have been at the site of the modern town, where Governor Vélez Cachupín succeeded in founding a mission for them in 1754. Although the governor named the mission Santo Tomás for his name saint, the inhabitants of the area, both Indian and Spanish folk, appear to have given their first allegiance

to St. Rose of Lima. At modern Abiquiu, the feasts of both saints are observed. The mission church was begun by Fray Juan José Toledo, who came to Abiquiu in 1755 and was there in 1760 when Bishop Tamarón made his visitation (AT, p. 64), but it was not finished until the 1770's. The mission may have been abandoned for a time in the 1760's. It was at the site of the present church, which dates from the 1930's. See also SANM, 1: nos. 28, 36, 1100; 2: nos. 483, 497, 529.

haps from the King. The transept is empty. The nave has very little, and I relate it here without making a separate heading.

Pulpit in the usual place; new, of wood, with the rostrum balustraded, very pretty. Confessional on the other side, not too badly made and new. Arranged throughout the nave, the *Via Crucis* in small paper prints on their little boards. As we enter the main door there is a small adobe pillar in the corner on our left with the covered baptismal font on it, all copper and the gift of the King.

SACRISTY: The sacristy is joined to the church on the Epistle side against the end wall of the transept. It is a room 5 varas square, with a window on the convent patio and an ordinary single-leaved door without a key to the same. The entrance to the church has no doors. In this room there is an ordinary wooden table with a drawer and key, but it should be noted that it is a loan from a settler called Juan Pablo Martín. On the wall over this table there is a print of Our Lady of Guadalupe in an unpainted wooden frame, and a little above it a cross of painted wood. There is a small colored blanket on the table, which the aforesaid father put there as a cover to keep it clean. The following things for divine worship are kept in the drawer of the said table, and because I find something to note here, the following remarks seem pertinent.

Note: The mission of Abiquiu was founded in the year 1754. Its first minister was Father Ordóñez, who (from what I observed) made no inventory of what was consigned to this mission at the King's expense, which came out of what Father Menchero brought for four new missions at the expense of the King. I did find an inventory made by Father Toledo, successor to the said father, and although he does not record the date in day, month, and year, I infer that the said inventory was made in the year '55 by the said Father Toledo, who, after all, did make an inventory of the following, noting what came from the King.

Vestments: A white damask chasuble trimmed with fine gold fringe, with all the necessary accessories. Another red one of the same material trimmed like the aforesaid, with accessories. Another of the same stuff, purple in color, with fringe like those mentioned, with accessories. Another, with accessories and trimmed with the same kind of fringe, but it serves for green. Another black one fringed with fine silver, with accessories. A cope which serves for white and mother-of-pearl and matches the first vestments even to the fringe. Cross sheath to match the cope in every way. Cape belonging to the black chasuble and with the same fringe. A frontal of the said purple-colored stuff with fine gold fringe. Palls to match the said ornaments, one for each. All came from the King and have been exceedingly abused.

Father Fernández has added the following: A crimson velvet chasuble with all the necessary accessories, all new and trimmed with very wide, fine gold galloon. Another of fine silver cloth with all the necessary accessories, with fine gold fringe and braid to match. A frontal of mother-of-pearl silver lustrine with lace to match. Pall like the aforesaid. Canopy like the said frontal, with fringe to match, which serves for processions.

Linen: Amice, alb, surplice, two purificators, two pairs of double corporals, and a finger towel. To this is added an altar cloth so poor that it only covers half the table, and two ragged cotton cinctures. The rest of the aforesaid is of Brittany, the King gave it, and it serves for the time being.

Father Fernández has provided the following: A new alb of fine Brittany with very good lace at the bottom, top, and sleeves. Two altar cloths like the alb. A plain cambric corporal with very fine lace.

Silver and other metal: Chalice with paten and no spoon, but the chalice is in three pieces, and one of them, for it is a loan by the settlers, is used for a little shrine they have. A small ciborium with veil. Pyx for the Viaticum. Cruets and a small bell on their plate. Shell and salt receptacle for baptisms. All came from the King.

A bronze thurible with accessories. Processional cross. Baptismal font, as I said in the church. Bell that I have already mentioned. And then the iron mold for making altar breads. A saw. A lever. Two crowbars, so worn out that they are no longer useful. A plane. All came from the King, and the said inventory so records them. Still another crowbar. Adze. Chisel, but Father Fernández did not find this, for they say it is lost, and so there is nothing but what has been listed before.

Other things: Usable missal. A banner. Two nondescript wooden processional candleholders.

Valuables of Our Lady: It is better for me to repeat myself. Father Fernández installed the niche with the litter and image at his own expense. Its adornment consists of: A wig. Silver crown. Silver hoop earrings with strings of fine seed pearls. A choker with two strings of the same pearls mixed with coral. Another of the same without the coral and with three large pearls hanging from it. A dress of mother-of-pearl silver lustrine with lace to match. Another plain one of mother-of-pearl damask. Four silver reliquaries. Nine ordinary small crosses. Three fine French stones set in metal. The saint's adornment is changed, and what she is not wearing is kept in a small chest which the said father, who sells everything he has for the sake of divine worship, provided with all the rest.

CONVENT

The convent was newly built by Father Toledo. It is joined to the church on the Epistle side and extends to the east, forming a square between the end of the sacristy and the lower corner of the church. The porter's lodge is here, inside the cemetery (as I have already said). It faces south and is exactly like the one at Nambe. As we enter it, there is a cell on the right, with its inner cell on a corner. On the side around the corner there are some rooms used for a storeroom and other necessary offices. The kitchen is in an inside corner, then the stable, with the sacristy beyond it.

There is no cloister, but there is a portico, or a jacal like a portico, which begins at the entrance to the porter's lodge and ends on the same corner as the principal cell and its inner cell. It is made of forked poles with round beams that support some small beams, on which there is a poor covering of branches and earth. The little bread oven is in the patio.

Its Furnishings: An ordinary table. Two benches. Four small chairs. A middle-sized latch with a key in the chief cell.

Its Service: All together, like that in the missions described before; but weekly, a fiscal, a sacristan, a cook, a baker, a shepherd. Here they do not bring their utensils as elsewhere, for since they do not know how to make pottery, the father supplies what is necessary. For carting wood he has supplied them with a farm cart, as well as many other necessities which I shall mention in due course.

Its Lands and Fruits: There are four small plots of reasonable fertility. A fanega of wheat can be sown in them, and this yields 18 to 20 fanegas in the best year. Under the same conditions as the wheat, a long almud of maize yields 12 to 14 fanegas. This small quantity is not the fault of the poor land, but of the character of the Indians, sometimes lazy, sometimes thievish. The lands are watered by a river which runs from west to east here, and it is the one I mentioned in connection with the settlers at Santa Clara. The Indians take care of the sowing and cultivation through the harvest, but the father gives them (in addition to seed as all do) the necessary implements, and I will speak of them in one place later.

MISSION FATHER

The friar, who, under obedience, exercises the apostolic ministry here is Father Fray Sebastián Fernández, native of Asturias, thirty-four years of age, sixteen years and six months in profession, four years as a missionary in the Custody, divided as follows: One and a half at Santa Clara; two and a half at Abiquiu, where he now is. He holds general faculties in the diocese of Durango for the time he resides in it and faculty for [the absolution of grave sins] reserved [to superiors] by the synodal decrees.

ADMINISTRATION OF THE MISSION: Every day, morning and evening, the unmarried people to catechism, which they recite with the father, and there is always an explanation of some point in their recitation. On feast days, the same recitation before or after Mass, during which there is usually a doctrinal sermon to settlers and Indians. Saturdays and feasts of Our Lady, rosary with the father in the church. Fridays of Lent, *Via Crucis* with the father, and later, after dark, discipline attended by those who come voluntarily, because the father merely proposes it to them, and, following his good example, there is a crowd of Indians and citizens.[2] He is very attentive to the needs of the dying and very zealous for the honor of God.

OBVENTIONS AND FIRST FRUITS: In general, as before. But so far as obventions are concerned, it is evident to me that this friar does almost everything without exception for nothing, because his great disinterestedness prevents him from noticing whether they pay him or not.

During the most profitable year the first fruits probably amount to 35 fanegas of all kinds of grain together. Of other things, nothing, for the enemy [Indians] keep the settlers in such a state of terror that they sow their lands like transients and keep going and coming to the place where they can live in less fear. The Indians give nothing.

EXPENDITURES: Annually in administration of the mission: 7 pounds of wax, 2 jugs

2. Was this a manifestation of the "Penitentes"? Domínguez does not mention them. For a radical theory on their origin see Chávez, "The Penitentes of New Mexico," NMHR, 29 (1954): 97-123.

of wine, about 300 altar breads, which are made here and for which half a fanega of wheat is provided. Food for the household is not counted by this friar, and he gives food not only to his servants but to all Indians and settlers who pretend to have an invitation.

HOW HE ACQUIRES NECESSITIES: Although barter is customary everywhere, here drudgery is the rule, in keeping with all I have had to say in my account of this mission. But the father's love is so great that he is well content to do it, because he deprives himself of everything here for the sake of his pueblo, to which he has presented the following

BENEFACTIONS: He provided them with five yoke of oxen; a farm cart. Another, nearly finished. Seventeen milch cows. Thirty goats for the same purpose. And the two shepherds who care for the foregoing are natives of the pueblo, but the father pays them as if they were outsiders; moreover he watches over their work to prevent them from losing everything. Four large hoes. Two ploughs with their shares; these are used with the father's small animals. Moreover, in addition to all this, he doses anyone who needs it as if he were his son. Reatas and lassos necessary for the oxen and carts.

CONVENT PROVISIONS: There was nothing assigned to this mission, and only what was given voluntarily was handed over, but I determined a proper amount, authorizing it in the inventory in accordance with the following

WRIT OF VISITATION

Mission of Santa Rosa de Abiquiu, April 29 of the year 1776. In prosecution of the juridical visitation of this Custody which our Reverend Father Fray Francisco Atanasio Domínguez, one of the appointed preachers in the Convento Grande of Our Father St. Francis in Mexico City and Commissary Visitor of this Custody for our Very

Reverend Father Minister Provincial Fray Isidro Murillo, is making, his Reverend Paternity proceeded to examine and did examine this inventory, and, finding it in agreement with what exists and what his Reverend Paternity personally examined, he gave repeated thanks to the present father missionary, Fray Sebastián Fernández, for his meticulous attention, application, and care in regard to the cleanliness and increase of the things pertaining to divine worship, and also for his punctilious fulfillment of his apostolic religious tasks and the well-known disinterest with which he has conducted himself up to the present, fervently charging him to persevere in every way and in the religious behavior which has been the basis of his good management, not forgetting the teaching given him by our Mother the Province.

And in order that this mission may have the necessary and corresponding provisions, after inspecting its produce, our Reverend Father Visitor decides, orders, and commands as follows: 4 fanegas of wheat, 4 of maize, 2 sheep, 8 strings of chile. In addition, the outgoing friar must hand over and the newcomer receive the convent furnishings, tools, and other belongings listed in the inventory revised by Father Fernández. And if anything is missing, the Father Vice-Custos shall be notified at once. And the Reverend Custos, or his Vice-Custos shall not be able to dispense with or take away anything decided here, but, indeed, may add all they think necessary for the benefit of the mission and missionary. For this purpose they shall see to the restoration of any item missing among those prescribed, for this is the intention and will of our Very Reverend Provincial Prelate, who so orders and commands *ratione officii,* and therefore validly for all time. Our Reverend Father Visitor so ordered and signed before me, the undersigned secretary, to which I attest. Fray Francisco Atanasio Domínguez, Commissary Visitor. In my presence, Fray José Palacio, secretary.

The parish books were examined, etc., and an order to bind them was issued. They are usable. Father Toledo began them under various dates, and Father Fernández has continued them to the present time.

In addition to these three parish books and the inventory which Father Toledo made, a book of Baptisms which Father Ordóñez began in the year '54 and Father Toledo finished in the year '63 is still at this mission. There are also some edicts of Bishop Tamarón with regard to explaining Christian doctrine and listing those who receive communion, and the notice that Our Lady of the Conception is the patron saint of the Spanish dominions.[3]

PUEBLO

The triangular eminence on which the pueblo stands is rather high. It is in the open and has no others near it in the east, north, and west, where there is a broad view over a plain. But all along the south the view is blocked by a mesa and other hills, although they are not very near. Therefore, some milpas that lie to the east at the foot of the hill where the pueblo is can be watered by a stream which runs from southwest to east between the mesas and hills. Its water is very dirty because it carries the earth from the said hills and from some little mounds beyond them.

In addition to the fact that the said hill is open to the directions mentioned, it is very

---

3. A translation of Bishop Tamarón's edicts is included in AT, pp. 81-87. The Immaculate Conception of Mary was declared a dogma of faith for Spain and all her possessions in 1617. The office of the feast, used by the Franciscans since 1480, was extended to all the Spanish clergy in 1761. See C. Morelli, *Fasti novi orbis et ordinationum apostolicarum ad Indias pertinentium breviarum* (Venice, 1776), Ordinatio DCIII, Anno 1760, 10 Nov. and Ordinatio DCIV, Anno 1761, 25 Jan. for the Immaculate Conception of the Blessed Virgin Mary as principal patroness of Spain and the Indies and for the use by all clergy of the Franciscan office on this day.

broad on top, and from all points there is a view of everything to be seen in these directions. The pueblo consists of a large square plaza with a single entrance to the north between the convent and the corner of a tenement. There are three tenements in front of the church and convent, and the latter buildings enclose the plaza on the north. As a result the pueblo is visible from the church and convent, with the cemetery inside the plaza. The approach to the pueblo is a rather steep slope on the north side of the hill on which it stands. At its foot there are two little springs of very good water, and since it is good, it is used for drinking. The houses in which the Indians live are arranged in accordance with their poverty and lack of interest.

Its Lands and Fruits: On the open sides the pueblo has many good farmlands, which are irrigated by the river they call Chama (I mentioned it in connection with the settlers at Santa Clara, making a reference to this place). It runs from north-northwest to southeast, and has very fine meadows on both banks, with corresponding groves of beautiful poplars. The lands are extremely fertile, but their owners, the Indians, are sterile in their labor and cultivation, so they do not yield what they might with attention, and as a result so little is harvested that the Indians are always dying.

Those who have taken root here and their progeny speak Spanish in the manner described with regard to the Santa Fe genízaros, for they all come from the same source, and these were taken for this pueblo. There is nothing to say about their customs, for in view of their great weakness, it will be understood that they are examples of what

happens when idleness becomes the den of evils. They are included in the following

CENSUS

46 families with 136 persons

This mission has charge of the administration of some settlers, part of whom live in farms scattered to the west and north, and part live to the east (all in relation to the pueblo) in a small plaza. In this direction there is a shrine of St. Rose of Lima belonging to the settlers, where they buried their dead when there was no church in the pueblo. It is almost like the one I described at Río Arriba near San Juan. Its furnishing consists of a paper print of the said Lady and nothing else. The settlers built it and provided the set of vestments, which is mother-of-pearl satin, but it is so old that even to look at it is indecorous. The most decent thing is the chalice with its paten, and this is the one in use at the mission for the time being.

I say the same thing about the lands of this settlement as about those of the pueblo, and like them they are watered by the same Chama River since they begin where the others leave off. Indeed, they do yield more and better crops than the others because the settlers work at it. Some are masters, others servants, others serve in both capacities as I have said in other settlements. What I have said in other places about their characteristics holds true here, and all speak the same kind of Spanish. They are included in this

CENSUS

49 families with 254 persons

RETROSPECTIVE NOTE

Up to this point we have seen the missions the interior branch of this Custody has in the Río Arriba area. In the main, all my observations about them have been recorded. The most important consideration is the sum of 7,480 Christian souls who are under the spiritual care of nine priests. Of these said missions, the Villa of Santa Fe is neither *Arriba* nor *Abajo,* and yet, although it is neither, it still belongs to both because (in accordance with the location of all the missions) it is really the middle or center.

Including this villa, there are ten missions in the Río Arriba, comprising the said Santa Fe, Villa de la Cañada, and eight Indian pueblos, to which is added the little pueblo of Pojoaque (which is subject to Nambe as a visita). The last completes the number of twenty-two Indian pueblos that I mentioned in the beginning as being in this interior branch. I now turn to the Río Abajo area, always considering the Villa of Santa Fe as the central point. Taking the highway down from there, I find it necessary to refer to the description of its outlying districts down river, because through them the road forks into two like the consonant V.

One road leads up through Cieneguilla, and in this vicinity a mesa rises, which, flattening out on top, continues for about 2 leagues to a very steep slope that leads down to the plain where that Río de las Bocas which I mentioned under Cieneguilla flows out and continues until it joins the Río del Norte. The other road leads from Quemado down to Ciénega Grande, and from there it enters the canyon between mesas mentioned in that place, crossing the Río de las Bocas many times until it joins the road down from the mesa that I have just described. Now that the roads have joined, they run over a high plain for more than a league until they go down a gradual slope which descends toward the meadows of the Río del Norte about a league farther on.

Now that I have explained this, I shall not cause confusion when it is necessary to mention directions or refer to something said before. Moreover, the missions I am about to describe will be taken in the order, or sequence, in which they are located in relation to the Río del Norte. That is, those on one bank will be taken in sequence, and those on the other side in a separate sequence, because it would be vexatious to keep crossing the aforesaid river every other moment, and, even more important, it would tangle the thread of the story and upset the extremely clear and harmonious style my narrative seems to demand since it is intended for the ears of superiors, to whom humble veneration and the deference of forethought is due.

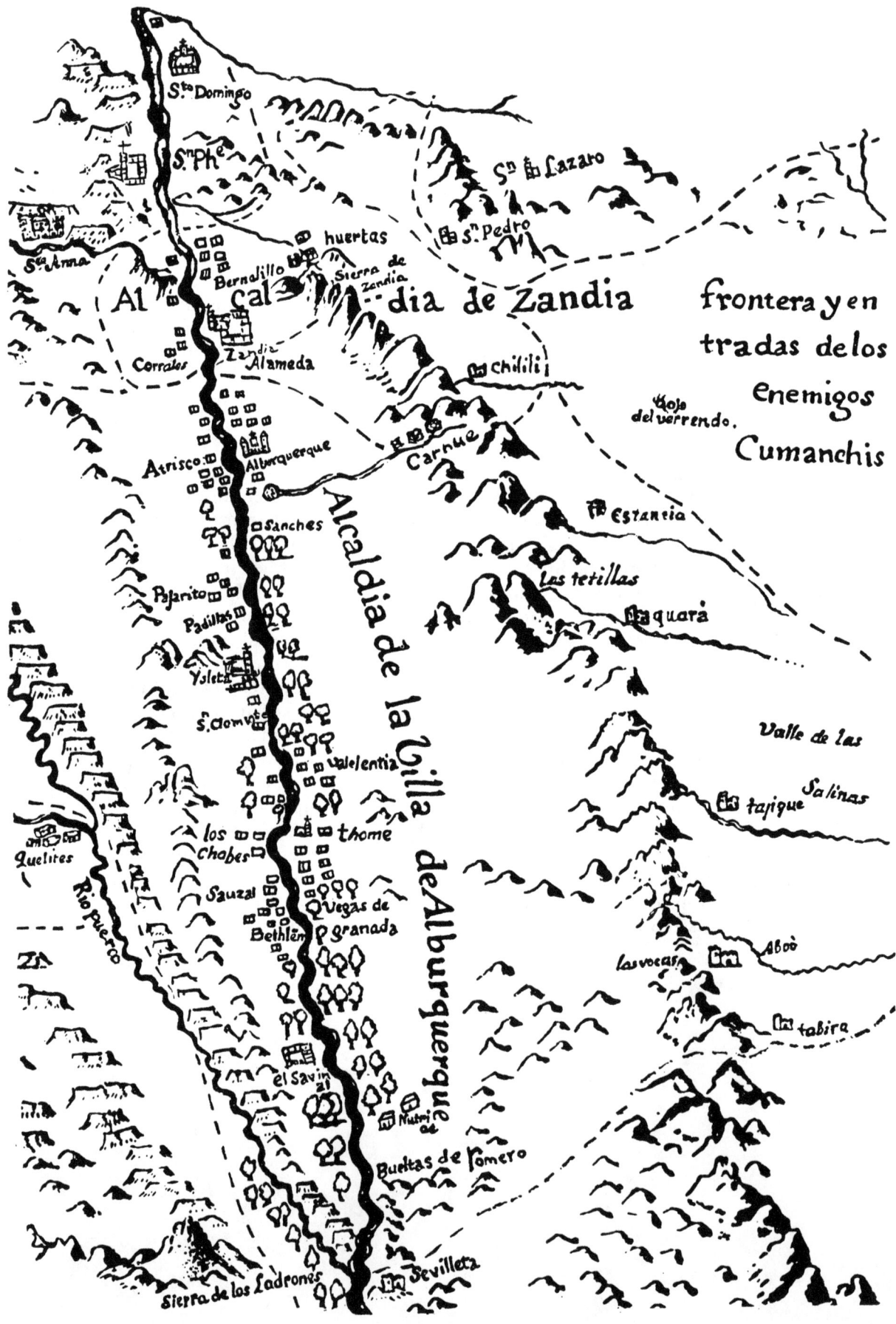

Sto Domingo

SnPhe

SnLazaro

SnPedro

huertas

SnAnna

Bernalillo

Sierra de Zandia

Al cal dia de Zandia

frontera y en
tradas de los
enemigos
Cumanchis

Corrales

Zandia
Alameda

Chilili

Ojo
del verrendo.

Atrisco

Alburquerque

Carnue

Estantia

Sanches

Alcaldia de la Villa de Alburquerque

Las tetillas

aquara

Pajarito

Padillas

Ysleta

Valle de las
Salinas

tajique

S. Clemente

Valentia

Quelites

los
Chabes

thome

Rio puerco

Sauzal

Vegas de
granada

las vocas

Aboo

Bethlen

tabira

el Savinal

Nutri

Bueltas de Romero

Sevilleta

Sierra de los Ladrones

IV. RIO ABAJO

Santo Domingo

The pueblo and mission of Our Father Santo Domingo is reached by traveling a good 9 leagues down from Santa Fe to the southwest over either of the roads just mentioned. It is established and located in full view of the Río del Norte, as I shall explain later, and lies the given distance southwest of the aforesaid Villa of Santa Fe.

NOTE: There are two churches at this mission, one old and the other new. For the present the old one must detain us, for in order to convey a clear understanding of everything, as I am trying to do, I cannot omit to say that it is in good condition but is used only for burying the dead and as a passageway to the new one. Its location makes this necessary since it has always been joined to the convent along the wall on the Epistle side, with its outlook and principal door to the south. The new one is beside it, with about a vara and a half between the Gospel wall of the old church and the Epistle wall of the new. This little alley is closed by walls at both ends and roofed over, but it is so dark that it is really a cellar. One crosses this to enter the new church.

CHURCH

Father Zamora built it out of his alms.[1] It is adobe with very thick walls, single-naved, and the outlook and main door are due south. From the door to the ascent to the

1. The present church at Santo Domingo dates from about 1890, for the buildings described by Domínguez were swept away by flood in 1886. A pre-1886 photograph (GK, fig. 149) shows a general view of both churches and the convent. Another [C. F. Lummis, *Mesa, Cañon and Pueblo,* (New York, 1925), p. 421] shows the paneled doors of the older church with the fleur-de-lis cross escutcheon of the Order of St. Dominic on the left and the escutcheon of the Franciscan Order on the corresponding panel on the right. The Franciscan panel is preserved at the Cathedral in Santa Fe (GK, fig. 197). The first church at Santo Domingo dated from the early seventeenth century. Although there is a statement in the 1681 documents that the church had been "demolished," the same source informs us that, "The principal side of the church building at Santo Domingo had been rebuilt for a fortress and living quarters by the said apostates." HS, 2: 260, 269. A church was being "built" in 1706 (HB, 3: 375), but whether it included any of the pre-Revolt fabric is difficult to determine. This was probably the "old church" described here. The new church must have been built sometime in the 1740's to 1760's. The Provincial records assign Fray Antonio Zamora, who built it, to Santo Domingo in 1760, but these are not always completely reliable, for circumstances in the Custody sometimes led to changes in such assignments. The extant parish books preserved in AASF place Zamora at various missions in the vicinity in the 1740's and 1750's. See Franciscans.

sanctuary it is 30 varas long, 9 wide, and 8 high. The approach to the sanctuary consists of three steps made of beams, all of which are imbedded at the center. It is closed in like the head of a transept. It is 6 varas long, a little over 4 wide, and is more than a vara higher than the nave because of the clerestory.

The choir loft is in the usual place and like those of the Río Arriba missions, and the entrance is an ordinary single-leaf door with a key. It is approached by a stairway of small beams between the walls of the two churches mentioned. This begins from the front corners of both and is open toward the cemetery. In the choir there is a good large bench for the musicians, who, at Father Zamora's expense, keep two guitars and three violins there. A military snare drum which Father Aguilar furnished is also kept there. There is another better one and two good bugles which Father Zamora donated.[2]

2. Bugles and snare drums, plus the firing of musketry or artillery, were military features at vespers and Masses on major feast days. The custom is still prevalent at "Military Masses" all over the world, including those of the U.S. Army. A relic of the custom remains in New Mexico country churches when firearms are discharged when the Elevation and Sanctus bells are rung on the patronal feast, and also at vespers the evening before. At the Indian pueblos a snare drum, not the Indian drum, is played, and at Santo Domingo the snare drum is still accompanied by a battered, screeching bugle.

The roof of the entire nave as far as the sanctuary consists of thirty-six wrought beams with multiple corbels, mortised and painted, and the clerestory rests on the one facing the sanctuary. The sanctuary has nine beams of the same kind, and it has no vaulted arch or semblance of one. On the Epistle side there are two windows with reveals and wooden grills which face east over the old church and convent.

Two tower buttresses like those I described in Santa Fe project from the front corners, but, although they have no towers nor even the beginning of any, they leave space for a very neat balcony, which is better planned than the one described in said villa. It is reached from the choir and has a very pleasant view of all that can be surveyed in the direction of the meadows of the Río del Norte along both banks and downstream.

The main door is squared, with a wooden frame and two paneled leaves with a stout latch. It is more than 3 varas high by 2½ wide, with adobe seats on either side. Above these, two escutcheons have been painted, the one on the right with the arms of the Catholic Church, and the one on the left with those of the King. Each has an inscription, one declaring the Pope's power and the other the Sovereign's dominion. As we enter, the door to the baptistery is on our left under the choir. It is outside the wall of the church and measures 5 varas square. It has a window to the south and a double-leaf grilled door with a latch to the church. In the middle is a small adobe column with a hollow center which serves as a drain. It holds a bowl for a baptismal font, the lid of which is a round piece of wood.

Above the main door is an adobe arch with two bells, a good middle-sized one with clapper and a smaller one, cracked and with half-clapper. They were provided by the King. The cemetery is in front of the new church only and is only 30 varas long by 15 wide. It does not begin at the walls of the church but takes the form of a narrow adobe corridor running from the corner of the baptistery to that of the convent. In front of the church itself it ends in a little stairway, and this approach resembles the one in the choir of the Cathedral of Mexico City near the railed passage between it and the sanctuary (there are probably others elsewhere).

The cemetery fence is adobe, about a vara and a half high, with three gates, one on each side. The church floor is the earth, but the aspect of the interior is very pleasant. Its adornment is as follows.

HIGH ALTAR: For further adornment of the good work which I have been describing, Father Zamora had a small altar screen in perspective painted on the wall at his own expense. Although it is an ordinary painting in tempera, it is very pretty and carefully done. It is in two sections and does not reach the ceiling. Undertaking to describe it, I say: At the base there is a great adobe table which extends from wall to wall like a gradin. In the center is a big adobe niche like a small alcove (this only disfigures it), with a large image in the round of Our Father St. Dominic completely carved in wood and very pretty. It has a large curtain of blue ribbed silk, in good condition and bordered with mother-of-pearl ribbon, complete with rod and valance. Father Camargo donated all this and sent it from Mexico.

Painted on either side of the screen as though in niches are Our Father St. Francis and St. John Nepomuk. In the corners of the aforesaid niche are a small canvas of Lord St. Joseph and two small images in the round. Near the center of the second section is the monstrance in the form of a medallion, and a little above it the Holy Ghost in the guise of a dove. On either side, hanging on painted niches, are two small oil paintings on canvas which were formerly used in the old church and were provided by Father Aguilar's devotion. At the top, not touching the ceiling, is a middle-sized crucifix in a canopy, now old, which the said Aguilar provided, and on either side two middle-sized mirrors in gilt frames newly furnished by Father Zamora.

The altar table is adobe with an altar stone given by the King, a middle-sized cross like a Jerusalem cross, two small brass candlesticks given by the King, a wooden missal stand, and three small bronze bells. There is a well-made platform of small beams and a very large carpet, dyed scarlet with the stuff called cochineal, in little squares (of the kind ordinarily used for tablecloths), which Father Zamora furnished.

NAVE: On the walls which face the nave as if there were a transept, there are two adobe tables which Father Zamora arranged for altars. The one on the right has a large oil painting on canvas in a wooden frame of Our Lady of the Conception. This was painted at the said father's expense by an incompetent craftsman, but it serves for devotional purposes. Above it hangs a middle-sized oil painting on canvas of the Apostle St. Peter, which Father Aguilar had provided for the old church, and there are three small canvases around it. The other altar has an oil painting on canvas of Our Father St. Dominic, which belongs to the King under the same circumstances as those of the patron saints of the Río Arriba missions. Above it there is a canvas representing the Apostle St. Paul, which Father Aguilar gave with the St. Peter, and there are three small canvases around it like those at the other altar. There is an image of Our Father St. Dominic on the left-hand altar, all carved in wood and a vara high. The natives of the pueblo bought it. It is a product of this kingdom and by the same hand that painted the above-mentioned Immaculate Conception. And my statement about the said painting will indicate that this work is not very fine. There is no pulpit, but there is a wooden confessional, and not one of the worst ones.

SACRISTY: The statement in the preliminary note makes it evident that the sacristy is separate from the new church. But even so, I point out that it is joined to the old church up on the Epistle side. It does not, however, have any door to the old church, for it is boxed in between the walls of the convent cloister, as I shall soon explain at more length in order not to cause confusion now by trying to explain everything at once. Boxed in thus, it stands at the head of the cloister on the aforesaid side. It is 6 varas long, 4 wide, and proportionately high, with a nondescript ceiling. The window overlooks one side of the convent patio and there is a good single-leaf door with a key to the cloister, which Father Zamora installed.

This room is adorned with an old middle-sized oil painting on canvas of Jesús Nazareno which Father Muñiz provided; a smaller one on buffalo skin of the Immaculate Conception, covered with little painted paper flowers. Father Aguilar provided all this. Another old one of the same size of St. Vincent Ferrer which this same father provided. Below Jesús Nazareno there is an adobe table on which the necessary things are put for the priest to vest. There are three unpainted chests with keys in this room, which Father Aguilar provided for the storage of what is necessary. All this is as follows.

Vestments: An old damask chasuble with two faces (white and crimson) and all accessories, which the King gave. Another older one of the same fabric with two faces (green and blue), the accessories of which consist of stole and maniple. There is no record of the donor. Another old one of white satin with accessories consisting of stole and maniple. Another new one of white satin with accessories except for frontal. Another new one with all accessories, even a cope, and this is of white satin trimmed with blue ribbon braid, on which there is fine gold braid. Father Zamora provided it. Another new one with all accessories like the foregoing. The same father gave it, and it is of mother-of-pearl satin with gold braid. Another one, almost new, of black damask trimmed with imitation galloon, with all accessories including cope and cross sheath; and Father Camargo gave it. A usable tapestry frontal in foliage design, and there is no record of the donor. A cloth of gold pall edged with ribbon. Another of mother-of-pearl satin with imitation gold galloon.

Linen: Two usable Brittany amices. Three more, now old. Three good Brittany albs; and Father Zamora gave one of them. Two more, now old. Three Malacca altar cloths. Another of Brittany with lace, which Father Zamora provided. Two good cinctures. Three more old ones. Eight usable purificators of various kinds of linen. Six finger towels like the purificators. Three small cloths for the cruets. Four usable pairs of double corporals with their silk palls for the chalice. Two usable Brittany surplices. All this has been provided by different fathers.

Silver and other metal: Chalice with paten and spoon. Three little vials with the holy oils. Thirteen old coins and two rings for arras. The King gave all this. A cruet without a stopper, which a father provided.

Holy-water pot. Thurible with accessories. Plate for cruets. Two processional crosses. Shell for baptizing. A box for altar breads. This was provided by some fathers. Iron mold for making altar breads, which the King gave.

Other things: An altar stone; perhaps it is from the King. A new missal of our Order, which Father Zamora provided. Two very old *Manuals* by Vetancurt. An ordinary blue woolen cassock with embroidery, used by the sacristan who serves at mass.

CONVENT

Since my preliminary note the assumption has been that the convent stands on one side of the old church (in accordance with what I have already said about the latter's location between the convent and the new church). It extends to the east, and although it is square, there are rooms on two sides only, as follows: The porter's lodge, which faces south, is in that little corridor I mentioned when I was describing the cemetery. It is a very charming and pleasant little por-

tico, 4 varas long from the mouth to the center, 6 wide, and proportionately high. There are two small pillars which look as if they had been turned on a lathe, with corbels to hold up the cross timber across the roof at the mouth.

Near the middle of the center wall is an ordinary two-leaved door without a key. There are adobe seats around the walls, and the floor is neatly paved. Outside in front there is a small stairway for an approach like the one mentioned in the cemetery. As we enter the porter's lodge, a room like a galley runs on the left to join the old church farther down. On the right there is a very long cell, which, with its inner cell, is on a corner.

There is no room around the corner here as in other convents I have described, but behind the inner cell there is a passageway with a back door to the east. (This was formerly a tumble-down passageway, but Father Rodríguez arranged it in its present form.) It leads to the cloister, to which there is a door near the entrance to the cell. The kitchen is in this same passageway, with its entrance opposite the wall of the inner cell.

There is a storeroom running north around the corner from the head of the kitchen. It has a door with a key to the cloister and makes an inside corner. An old room runs from the wall that stands at the head of the cloister here, and beyond it Father Rodríguez made two new ones. The entrance to all is through the door of the old room. On the side of the building around the corner facing north there is a very high adobe wall the length of the rooms. The drain is beneath it, and it ends at the corner of the sacristy.

There is a cloister, and in accordance with the above description it has three sides: one as we enter and one on either side. On the left it runs along the old church to the sacristy, which I have already said stands at the head of it. On the right it runs to the office and the rooms attached to it. It is entirely enclosed and has several windows for light, with a little door near the upper corner on the right-hand side, which gives on the bare patio.

ITS FURNISHINGS: Four tables, one of which has an ordinary cover. Two chairs. Two benches. Four old bronze candlesticks. Sixteen books of various sizes and dates, which deal with diverse subjects by various authors. They were left here by some fathers. There is an inventory of them, and, in addition, those I will mention in the writ of visitation are missing.

ITS SERVICE: All together, a chief fiscal, four subordinates, ten sacristans, ten cooks, eight bakers. But weekly, one fiscal, two sacristans, two cooks with two big girls to carry water, and two bakers per week as has been said in other places. In addition, a herder for the sheep, horse, or other animals if there are any. Carting of wood as needed. For the church—the musicians, drummers, and buglers.

ITS LANDS AND FRUITS: The lands consist of six small plots on the very meadows of the river, which are a little above the church, three on one side and three on the other. They are reasonably good, are watered by the river itself, and although they are limited because the river has been eating them away, they produce adequate crops. One of them serves as a kitchen garden and has some thirty vinestocks of very good grapes, which are used only for eating. Since they do not cultivate them, there are not enough to make a little wine. The necessary amount of green vegetables is raised. The pueblo does the sowing and takes care of them through harvest.

MISSION FATHER

At the time of my visitation Father Fray Mariano Rodríguez de la Torre exercised the apostolic ministry here. He was also Vice-Custos. He is a native of Mexico City, fifty-one years of age, thirty-six in profession, twenty-four as a missionary in the Custody, divided as follows: Jémez, two years; Zuñi, one year, during which period he apostoli-cally entered the province of Moqui;[3] Santa Clara, fifteen years, during which he did the things already well described; Santo Domingo, at the time of the visitation, six years. He holds general faculties from Durango revocable at will.

ADMINISTRATION OF THE MISSION: Mass at a regular hour on feast days, and before or after it the catechism is recited on some occasions and the rosary on others. Saturdays, the rosary and the Litany of the Blessed Virgin Mary are chanted. Every day, morning and evening, the unmarried people to catechism. And on all these occasions mentioned the father joins the Indians, to whom he gives the necessary instructions, using an interpreter. (They know how to speak Spanish, but the father considers this method better.) Fridays of Lent, *Via Crucis,* with a short exhortation on this subject.

NOTE: One league to the north on the same plain there is a rancho of a citizen and his family.[4] For this reason the amount collected there is so slight that obventions and first fruits are not counted. Although the Indians make no contribution of that kind, they do have their devotions, and some pay for Masses and make obsequies (see San Juan) for their dead. In addition to these offerings, they make small offerings from their harvest. Therefore something goes to the missionary for expenses.

EXPENDITURES: Food consumed by the household is not counted. A fanega and a half of wheat for altar breads is given annually. Some of these are allotted to the missions of Cochiti and San Felipe, for they are made in this mission. Wax for administra-

3. In 1770, Father Rodríguez wrote an account of his *Entrada en la provincia de los Moquis, 1755.* H. H. Bancroft, *History of Arizona and New Mexico* (San Francisco, 1890), p. 265n.

4. "Rancho de José Miguel de la Peña" is the name given in the Santo Domingo registers from 1777 to 1780; then "Rancho de Peña" in 1791, and from 1792 on it is "Rancho de la Peña Blanca." José Miguel de la Peña (II) was a native of Santa Fe who received his lands above Santo Domingo as a grant. See NMF.

tion, 30 to 40 ordinary candles. About 12 cuartillos of wine.

How He Acquires Necessities: By exchange like all those mentioned before, and this friar does not indicate anything special.

Convent Provisions: They have been designated, and, to establish them on a firmer basis, recorded in the inventory and authorized by the following

WRIT OF VISITATION

Mission of Our Father Santo Domingo and June 1 of the year 1776. In prosecution of the juridical visitation which our Reverend Father Fray Francisco Atanasio Domínguez, one of the appointed preachers in the Convento Grande of Our Father St. Francis of Mexico City and Commissary Visitor of this Custody for our Very Reverend Father Minister Provincial Fray Isidro Murillo, is making of this Custody, his Reverend Paternity proceeded to examine and did examine this inventory. Although it agrees with what exists and belongs to church and sacristy, with regard to the items belonging to the convent, the following books are missing: A *Cuaresma* by Niseno. *Oraciones Evangélicas*, by Fray Diego Malo. *Manojito de Flores. Vida del Padre Margil.*[5] Therefore the

present mission father, Fray Mariano Rodríguez de la Torre, or his successor, is ordered and commanded never to permit any friar to remove books from the mission or from the library of the Custody, which is kept here, without first leaving a signed memorandum of the books he may take so that their whereabouts may be known and they can be recovered.

Proceeding to the convent provisions, his Reverend Paternity orders and commands that they be the following: 10 fanegas of wheat, 10 of maize, 10 sheep, 6 strings of chile, half a fanega of frijol, a jar of ordinary lard, 12 tallow candles, 50 onions, 2 wax candles, a bottle of wine. In regard to all this the Reverend Custos and his Vice-Custos cannot dispense with anything, but only, indeed, add what they may consider necessary for the benefit of the mission and missionary. If the latter finds anything lacking when he takes over, he shall give notice of it, and we therefore order the Reverend Custos or Vice-Custos to make it good immediately, for this is the intention and will of our Very Reverend Provincial Superior, who so orders and commands *ratione officii,* and therefore validly for all time. Our Reverend Father Commissary Visitor so provided, ordered, and signed before me, the undersigned secretary, to which I attest. Fray Francisco Atanasio Domínguez, Commissary Visitor. In my presence, Fray José Palacio, secretary.

The parish books were inspected, approved, etc., without there being any need for comment. They are rather new. Father Rodríguez gave them. They are clean and their foliation is complete. The same is true of the books of Inventory and Patents, and the said father provided them.

Addition: In the sacristy of this mission there is a chest containing various necessary articles for the Navajo missions, which the King gave as is shown by the memorandum signed by the prelates which is kept there in the same place. Some copper baptismal fonts

---

5. Fray Diego Niseno (Hieronymite), (d. 1656), one of the most eloquent preachers of his time, published several books of Lenten sermons, some of which are translated into French, Italian, and Latin. The *Oraciones Evangélicas y Ferias principales de Quaresma* by Dom Diego Malo de Andueza, O.S.B. (d. 1673), was in two volumes published in Madrid, 1661-1664. Fray Juan Nieto's *Manogito de flores* (Madrid, 1723) has been described as a book of popular character, interesting chiefly because of the exorcisms it includes. The first biography of Father Margil appeared a decade after his death, when Fray Isidro Félix de Espinosa published *El peregrino septentrional Atlante* (Mexico, 1737). In 1747 Espinosa published *Nuevas empressas del peregrino Americano septentrional Atlante.* This was followed by Fray Hermenegildo de Vilaplana's *Vida portentosa del americano septentrional apóstol* (Mexico, 1764; Madrid, 1775).

and six broken bells which are kept separately also belong to the same lot.

The library of this Custody is also in the said sacristy, and another chest serves as the archive. All of it will be recorded in good order in a separate place rather than digress here.

PUEBLO

The pueblo is located very near the Río del Norte on a plain on the east bank flanked by hills which, as we face due south, run straight in this direction on our left, with some cañadas and arroyos between them. And as this ridge of hills winds down the highway, it draws near the meadows of the said river in some places and recedes from them in others. Accordingly, those near this pueblo must be about a middling artillery shot from it. It has a very fine view in all directions, made pleasant by the river and its woods and poplar groves.[6]

The pueblo consists of six blocks, or buildings, of dwellings. Of these, two stand one after the other below the right corner of the new church, and face due east overlooking the church and convent to their left side on the north and to the south on their right side. The four remaining blocks face due south with their backs to the church and convent. They are all separate from one another, with a street in the form of a cross dividing the four. The houses have upper and lower stories like those I described at Tesuque, and these are better arranged than the ones there, with a beautiful plaza overlooked by the last ones mentioned between their façades and those of the church and convent.

The whole pueblo is surrounded by a rather high adobe wall with two gates; this is for resistance against the enemy [Indians], for day by day they show more daring against the natives of this kingdom. This pueblo lies in such a location, or situation, in relation to the whole kingdom that it is necessary to go to it on the highway going up or down. As a result there are plenty of travelers who bring or carry away news according to whence they come or where they are going.

ITS LANDS AND FRUITS: In relation to the location of the pueblo, there are as many farmlands above as below it, and the same is equally true on the opposite bank, as well as on either side of the pueblo. With the exception of some up the highway to Santa Fe to the east which are dependent on rain, all the rest are watered by the Río del Norte, from which they take some deep irrigation ditches, this being necessary for many reasons.

These lands are very fine, and as such they produce corresponding crops of everything sown in them (without exception) and in such quantity that the proceeds provide clothing. There are small trees of very tasty peaches and apricots; there is also an abundance of very delicious melons and watermelons.

The natives of this pueblo are called Queres (we shall see seven pueblos of this nation), whose native tongue they speak in a rather feminine tone of voice. Here they are commonly called Chachiscos, because most of the expressions have *Cha, Chis, Cos, Cañè.* As a curiosity, here is an example: They meet a Spaniard, who necessarily addresses them in Spanish; and if they do not or do not wish to understand, they say *Chachiscacañè,* which means, *I do not understand you,* or synonomously, *I do not hear.* Truly it is the prettiest and easiest of all the languages in these regions. In speaking Spanish they are just like the Teguas. With regard to their customs in particular, what has been said in the above note will indicate that they are good. Here is the

---

6. The present pueblo is an eastward extension of the old one after the western part and the old churches and convent were carried away by the Río Grande in 1886. This flood was so strong that it washed away to river level the high embankment on which these buildings stood. Old-timers recall seeing the bodies from the cemetery floating away.

CENSUS

136 families with 528 persons

Since the rancho administered by this mission is up the plain, it is obvious that it enjoys lands, crops, and water like those of the pueblo. Therefore I do not stop to describe it in detail. The owner is a Spaniard, with servants of low class who speak the usual Spanish. All are included in the following memorandum.

1 family with 11 persons

Sandia

From Santo Domingo one travels south some 7 leagues downstream along the whole meadow of the Río del Norte, which is on the east, in sight of the said river. The ridge of hills which I mentioned in the aforesaid pueblo is always to the left, and at this point the hills run along below the foot of the sierra and in front of it. At the end of the said 7 leagues one finds the pueblo and mission of Nuestra Señora de los Dolores de Sandia.[1] It is 16 good leagues from Santa Fe and is south, quarter south-southwest, of the villa, on the highway like the foregoing mission.

The mission is new, founded for the Indians of the province of Moqui who were reduced by Father Menchero in the year 1746.[2] It stands in the middle of the plain on the same site as the old mission which was destroyed in the general uprising of this kingdom. To the east is a sierra called Sandia because there is a pueblo and mission of this name here. Although it does have a connection with the sierra of Santa Fe very high up (via some little hills and mounds), we cannot properly take it to be a continuation of the latter in view of the great distance and few indications; rather we shall call it a Sierra Madre, since it spreads down for a long way with the characteristics of a mother range. The Río del Norte is about half a league to the west among poplar groves.

CHURCH

The church at this mission is unusable, being in such a deplorable state that it truly saddens the soul to see the marks of the barbarities they say have been perpetrated here. Since it has been ruined, it has no roof, and only the walls remain to indicate what the temple was like. These measure 46 varas long from the mouth to the center, 12 wide, and 6 high. It is said the old ceiling was *artesonado*.[3] On the inside and joined to the old walls there are some half walls of adobe which Father Menchero built with the intention of restoring the church to its former state. But he soon realized that it was useless and that everything was going to fall flat together. So it remained as it was. It faces east and has two small towers dating from that time; and in one of these there are two bells which the King gave, and they are now well broken.

For the present, the room that used to be a baptistery in those days is kept in service as the church. As we enter the ruined church it stands to our right on the corner and outside the walls, extending to the north. Therefore its door is inside the ruins. It looks like a coach house and measures 12 varas long by 5 rather long varas wide and 3½ high. It has fifteen carved beams with small corbels. There are two poor windows in the Epistle wall which face east, and the door is like that of a coach house with no other lock than a thong to tie the leaves, or sides, together.[4]

ADORNMENT: A great adobe table serves for an altar. Two gradins of the same rise from it like a throne, and at the top there is a box which looks like a badly-made niche. In this there is a tiny Our Lady of Sorrows in the round, whose clothing I shall describe later. There is no record of the donor of this Lady and other things. Therefore I shall only indicate what the King gave and an occasional item of which the donor is known. The following is arranged on the gradins: A small carved St. Anthony with his Holy Child and a little silver diadem. Six very ragged bouquets of painted paper. A tiny bronze crucifix on a wooden cross and pedestal. Arranged about the wall are six small canvases and six middle-sized prints, all in dreadful shape. On the altar table there are an altar stone, two small brass candlesticks, which the King gave. And since there is no dais, there is a very poor little frieze carpet on the earth floor.

The following are in this whole room: A great ugly wooden confessional. A chair for the priest. The baptismal font in a corner. The processional cross, the holy-water pot, and some old poles. There is no sacristy. Therefore, in one of the cells, under the missionary's eye, there are some chests designed and made like the counters of cheap shops,[5] but they are not as high nor do they have a key. Moreover, since there is no lock in the chapel, the things that it might be risky to leave there alone are kept in the

1. In the Sandia registers the title is also given as "Our Lady of Sorrows and St. Anthony." Unlike other missions where the entries followed one another as they came, here the books were divided into sections for Spanish and Indian people. Later, when Bernalillo built its church, it was called "Our Lady of Sorrows," while that at Sandia continued as "St. Anthony." Hence Our Lady of Sorrows seems to have been the patronal title of the Spanish folk while St. Anthony was the Indians' patron.

2. See SANM, 1: no. 848, on the refounding of the mission and pueblo, 1748; F. V. Scholes, "Notes on Sandia and Puaray," *El Palacio*, 42 (1937): 57-59.

3. "The term *artesonado* does not specify the type of structure other than by geometrical form: it signifies a coved or concave ceiling, regardless of material or technique." G. Kubler, *Mexican architecture of the sixteenth century* (New Haven, 1948), 1: 181.

4. These appear to have been the ruins of the pre-Revolt church. At about this same period Fray Sebastián Fernández proceeded to build churches at Picuris and Sandia without proper authorization, going against the wishes of his prelate, Vice-Custos Fray José Medrano, who succeeded Fray Mariano Rodríguez de la Torre in that office in July, 1776. See pp. 321-24 *infra*. The church now in use at the pueblo dates from the 1890's.

5. "Tiendas de tlacos."

cell. All have been inventoried as follows.

Vestments: A usable chasuble of white lustrine and fine gold fringe with all necessary accessories, which the King gave. Another like it of mother-of-pearl lustrine trimmed with galloon like the foregoing, with accessories, which the King gave. Another of the same description which serves for green. Another of purple lamé with a complete set of accessories which, like those mentioned, the King gave. Another of black lustrine with accessories of the same description as the aforesaid. A cope to match the first chasuble, which the King gave. A small cape to match. A cross sheath like this last. And the King gave them all. A white banner like the aforesaid. A cope to match the black set of vestments. A very old frontal of black velvet with imitation galloon; it is not known whether the King was the donor. A cross sheath exactly like this frontal, and the same is true with regard to knowing who gave it. A white humeral veil to go with the first chasuble mentioned. A separate old stole of blue velvet. An old altar cover of black velvet.

Linen: Two old Brittany amices. Two more usable ones of the same material. An old Brittany alb. A new one of Rouen. An ordinary altar cloth. A usable Brittany surplice. A usable pair of double corporals of Brittany. Two purificators. A cotton cincture. A cap for baptisms. And perhaps everything came from the King.

During his visitation in the year 1772 the Reverend Custos Hinojosa gave this mission a fine Brittany amice, without lace, and an alb of the same material, but with lace of medium quality.

Silver and other metal: Chalice with paten and spoon. A small ciborium. Three small vials with the holy oils, and they are kept in a little cedar box without a key. Two cruets with little bell and plate. A shell for baptizing. Three small coins which serve for arras. A medium-sized monstrance, which I am informed the R. Seijo, who was Procurator of these missions, remitted to the Reverend Custos Hinojosa in the year 1767 with the information that it had been found in the Procurator's office. It is not known whether this piece came from the King, while it is known that all the foregoing did. And if this information should not be correct as I have reported it, the aforesaid Reverend Hinojosa will tell how it is.

Baptismal font with its cover. Holy-water pot. Thurible with accessories. Mold for making altar breads. A crowbar. All from the King. Processional cross from the same lord.

Other things: An altar stone which I mentioned with the altar and which the King gave. Another very small one, and perhaps it is one that the Procurator's office remitted to the aforesaid Reverend Hinojosa, without consecration, at the same time mentioned before. A missal with our saints, which the King gave. Another very old one. *Manual* by Osorio.

Note: Inasmuch as Father Menchero brought necessary items for the Navajo missions, provided by his Majesty (God keep him), it is essential to state here that everything mentioned in the account of this mission of Sandia as being from the King was applied to it out of that supply of necessary things.

CONVENT

The thing that bears this name here resembles nothing more than the old half-fallen houses that are usually found in Indian pueblos near Mexico City. Nevertheless, I say: It is joined to the ruined church on the Gospel side and runs to the south, the whole site of the building being on the east. The porter's lodge is at the lower corner of the said place, and it is a small portico in bad condition, as is the door. When we enter it, a galley, or storeroom, runs on the left, and near it on the same left side there are two rooms together around the corner, but there is no inside corner but a passageway between the head of the last one and a ruin which turns the corner to the former sacristy which adjoined the lost church on the Gospel side. And in this said place there is a very ugly square patio.

There is no entrance to the aforesaid patio from these rooms, but through another bit of wasteland which faces south. And the entrance to this ill-arranged convent is here. For greater clarity, I note that those rooms which form an inside corner against the storeroom at the said patio do not make a corner outside, but that from the head of the storeroom two rooms run to the south and consist of an inner cell near the aforesaid and a cell beyond it which ends in a wall. Therefore, there is a façade like a block of houses between the porter's lodge and the cell, which faces east. And toward the center of the front, which faces west, the aforesaid rooms stick out.

Therefore, there are two recesses, one at the patio against the church, and the other at the wasteland patio. In the latter there is a poor stairway which leads to two rooms over the ones I said jutted out, and the lower rooms are the kitchen and stable. As we enter the porter's lodge, there is a poor stairway on the right against the church, which leads to an azotea over the porter's lodge. There is the entrance to three cells, or to one of three rooms which are over those below. The description is labored and boring, but the poor arrangement of the place leaves no alternative.

NOTE

When I dealt with the adornment of the church, I deferred my description of the little adornments of Our Lady of Sorrows, and although I might have given the information along with the things pertaining to the sacristy, which does not exist, it slipped my mind. But since what might be subject to risk is kept in the missionary's cell (as I said in that place) it is not difficult for me to note them here, since my aim is to explain all. There are, then, two new little Brittany chemises and one old one. Two new little white Brittany petticoats. Two more old ones of the same material. An old little dress of half cloth. A similar small mantle of blue ribbed silk. A pair of small petticoats of mother-of-pearl ribbed silk. A similar buff-colored one. In addition to being old, it all has false fringe.

The following trifles are put on the little dress and changed: A small crystal rosary. Two small silver reliquaries. A pair of little hoop earrings with fine small pearls. Some strings of ordinary beads. A small silver badge of the Holy Office.

ITS FURNISHINGS: A table. Two chairs. Three benches. A bed. Two locks on the doors. A broken measure. And all the foregoing now old. Father Hinojosa provided a new table, chair, and small bench.

ITS SERVICE: All together, a chief fiscal, four subordinates, eight sacristans, eight cooks, four bakers. And weekly, a fiscal, two sacristans, two cooks, two bakers. Herders, whom the pueblo provides in turn, and carting of firewood as described elsewhere.

ITS LANDS AND FRUITS: There are two plots, one to the south below the convent and the other to the north above the church. If wheat is sown in the lower one, it takes about 2 fanegas, which ordinarily yield about 50; if maize, some 4 almudes, which yield almost the same amount mentioned for wheat. The results with regard to the upper plot are almost the same as with the other that has just been mentioned. In addition to those plots, there is a small kitchen garden which lies to the west near the convent. In it there are some small apricot and peach trees and a goodly number of vinestocks, all of which Father Menchero planted, and in a hollow on the wasteland a few chick peas are sown, which usually yield about a fanega. The fruit of the little trees and grapevines is seldom harvested, because they freeze most years. The sowing, cultivation, and harvesting are in charge of the pueblo.

MISSION FATHER

The one who is now engaged in the apostolic ministry at the time of the visitation is Father Fray José Medrano, native of the port of Veracruz, thirty-five years and some months of age, sixteen in profession, four years as a missionary in the Custody, all at Sandia. He holds faculties to hear confessions from the Most Illustrious and Reverend Lord [Bishop] Bravo for the period he may administer these missions.

ADMINISTRATION OF THE MISSION: The usual mission regimen, to which I refer, for there is no special feature.

OBVENTIONS AND FIRST FRUITS: For the means and amounts, see what has been said before from Santa Fe on. With regard to this mission in particular, they usually pay as obventions a cow, horse, or ewes, or a mixture of the foregoing with seeds, but the regular thing is grain, sackcloth, or blankets.

Some 6 or 8 fanegas of all kinds of grain together of first fruits, 3 or 4 strings of chile, small amounts of other things. As for cattle, there is usually some devout person who gives a little calf. Five or six small head of livestock. The Indians give nothing at all.

HIS EXPENDITURES: Food consumed by the household is not counted. About 4 pounds of wax a year, about 1 jug of wine, half a fanega of wheat for the altar breads made here.

HOW HE ACQUIRES NECESSITIES: The same things in the same form and manner as have been described in the other missions.

CONVENT PROVISIONS: These have been designated, and, to establish them on a firmer basis, authorized in the mission inventory by the following

WRIT OF VISITATION

Sandia, May 25 of the year 1776. In prosecution of the juridical visitation which our Reverend Father Fray Francisco Atanasio Domínguez, one of the appointed preachers in the Convento Grande of Our Father St. Francis of Mexico City and Commissary Visitor of this Custody for our Very Reverend Father Minister Provincial Fray Isidro Murillo, is making of this Custody, his Reverend Paternity proceeded to examine and did examine this inventory, which he found in accurate and legal agreement with what exists and what he inspected in his juridical visitation of this mission. Therefore his Reverend Paternity approved it and renders thanks to the Reverend Custos Hinojosa for the clarity and detail with which he recorded the things pertaining to divine worship. And he also thanks the present mission father, Fray José Medrano, for the cleanliness and neatness with which he preserves and keeps what belongs to the church and convent. And, proceeding to determine the provision, his Reverend Paternity orders and commands that it be the following in this mission: 7 fanegas of wheat, 5 of maize, 1 almud of salt, 10 strings of chile, 100 onions, a jar of local lard, 4 wax candles, a bottle of wine, 6 sheep, if the outgoing friar is taking over a mission that has them.

The outgoing friar must hand over all this as well as the necessary things for the church and the convent furnishings, and the incoming one shall receive it in accordance with the inventory. And if anything is missing, the Reverend Custos or his Vice-Custos shall be notified at once so that the lack may be supplied. The Reverend Custos or his Vice-Custos cannot dispense with any of this, but they may, indeed, add all they think necessary for the benefit of the mission and missionary, for this is the intention and will of our superior prelate, who so orders and commands *ratione officii,* and therefore validly for all time. Our Reverend Father Commissary Visitor so provided, ordered, and signed before me, the undersigned secretary, to which I attest. Fray Francisco Atanasio Domínguez, Commissary Visitor. In my presence, Fray José Palacio, secretary.

The parish books were examined, etc., and there is no need for comment. They are new; the Reverend Custos Hinojosa provided them when he was missionary of this mission. Each one comprises over a hundred leaves, and he assigned one hundred to the Indians and those left over to the Spaniards. The Inventory and Patent books are small new ones provided by the same father, and they are like the foregoing.

PUEBLO

In relation to the location of the church and convent, the pueblo lies to the east, but it is not opposite them. Rather it stands below their façade. It is arranged and built in three small blocks, or buildings, up in a northerly direction and two small plazas down somewhat to the south. Everything is made of adobe (like the foregoing) and distributed and arranged like the other missions. Inasmuch as this pueblo has Indians of two nations, like a microcosm, it is necessary to state that some (this is the majority) are Tiguas, and these are the ones who live in the above. The others (and they are very few) are Moquis, and they live in some small, badly-arranged houses above the church to the north. For this reason, and in view of their very small numbers, the present lord governor, Don Pedro Mendinueta, has ordered them to move and join the said Tiguas so that in this way they may resist any attack made by the enemy Comanche nation. One of these occurred in the year 1775, when about thirty sons of the pueblo died at the hands of the aforesaid. This did not, indeed, happen inside the pueblo, but perhaps their great daring can result in some harm to it. And keeping in mind that at the beginning I left this pueblo in the middle of the plain, etc., I shall not enlarge upon it further, since that indicates the view it must have, for the plain lies and continues below.

ITS LANDS AND FRUITS: In relation to the buildings I have mentioned up to now, this pueblo has lands above to the north and below to the south for the distance of a league in each direction. But there is not a corresponding amount on the opposite bank of the Río del Norte to the west. Although they are on the meadow, they are not equally good because the upper ones are rather sandy and the lower ones are good land. They are watered by the aforesaid river and produce their respective crops, which suffice all together. The Indians have a few small trees like the convent's.

Some of the people who have taken root in this pueblo and their progeny are Tiguas, and others (the proportions have already been mentioned) are Moquis. Each group speaks its native tongue, one group being distinct from the other, and they have different interpreters. Their Spanish is the same as that of the people of Our Father Santo Domingo. With regard to their special customs, I say that they somewhat resemble the aforesaid. And although there are the said different nationalities among them, since it is all one body they are included in one

CENSUS

92 families with 275 persons

This mission has charge of the administration of some citizens divided into two small groups. One up to the north, which is about 2 leagues away, is called *Bernalillo*, and it all consists of separate ranchos with not very good lands.[6] These are watered

6. Bernalillo had some haciendas in the seventeenth century, whose settlers escaped the 1680 massacre while their neighbors nearer to San Felipe and Sandia perished. HS, 1: 30. These settlers were members of the Chávez, Baca, Montoya, and González-Bernal families. The place did not get its name from descendants of Bernal Díaz del Castillo as frequently is stated, for no such people came to New Mexico. Bernalillo is a diminutive form of the Bernal family name. See NMF. Shortly after the Reconquest, 1700-18, according to church records, there was a church with friars' convent there with the title of "Our Father St. Francis" (also the title of the pre-Revolt pueblo of Sandia and of more ancient Puaray). When Sandia was refounded with new patronal titles, Our Lady of Sorrows became and has remained the patroness of Bernalillo, although there is a reference to the "Plaza de San Francisco de Bernalillo" as late as 1783.

with the aforesaid river and produce fairly reasonable harvests because of the cultivation those concerned give them. These citizens are considered Spaniards, and with regard to them all I reiterate what I have said of others to avoid delay. They are included in the following

CENSUS
27 families with 81 persons

The other branch is to the west on the side (of the river mentioned) opposite the one on which the mission stands. It is called *Upper Corrales*,[7] and the distance from the pueblo is the half league between it and the river plus the width of the river, and no more, for the ranchos are right there. The not very good lands are watered, cultivated, and taken care of as I have just described. Since the individuals are all exactly alike, I say the same as of all, and proceed to the

CENSUS
10 families with 42 persons

7. Santa Rosalia de Corrales was the full name in 1762. BL, N.M. Origs.

Albuquerque

The mission of the Villa of San Felipe Neri de Albuquerque is 4 leagues down the highway to the south on the same plain I have been mentioning from the mission of Our Father Santo Domingo on. It stands on the same plain and so near to the Río del Norte that the church and convent are about two musket shots from it. It is a very good 20 leagues from Santa Fe and lies to the south, quarter south-southwest of it. The arrangement, or plan, will be better described later.[1]

CHURCH

The church is adobe with very thick walls, single-naved, with the outlook and main door to the east. From the door to the ascent to the sanctuary it measures 32 varas long, 7½ wide, and the same high. The ascent to the sanctuary, which continues from the nave, consists of two small wrought-beam steps. The width being as given, it is 7 varas long to the center, and higher than the nave because of the clerestory. It has a choir loft like those described where there

are such. On the Gospel side there are two windows with wooden gratings facing south, and one to the east in the choir.[2]

The roof of the nave consists of thirty-nine beams, and the clerestory rests all along the one that faces the sanctuary. There are ten more in the sanctuary. These, like the others, are wrought and corbeled. The main door has two paneled leaves with a good

1. During the seventeenth century and after the Reconquest until 1706, the general area of Albuquerque was variously called "Bosque Grande," "Bosque Grande de Doña Luisa," "Estancia de Doña Luisa de Trujillo," and "Bosque Grande de San Francisco Xavier." This Bosque extended from the southern limits of Alameda pueblo lands south to the swamps of Mexía, and the original limits of Albuquerque were set within this general area from the lands of Elena Gallegos on the north to the swamps, also called "of Pedro López," on the south. Church registers; BL, N.M. Origs., 1727; SANM, 1: no. 297; HS, 1: 26. The Villa of Albuquerque was founded in the spring of 1706 by Governor Francisco Cuervo y Valdés. On April 23 of that year he certified to its founding. See L. B. Bloom, "Albuquerque and Galisteo, certificate of their founding, 1706," NMHR, 10 (1935): 48-50. Bloom translated the certificate from a manuscript in AGM, Provincias Internas, Tomo 36, Ramo 5, with a facsimile reproduction of the original. Another translation is in HB, 3: 379-81, from the Bandelier copy of the manuscript in AGI, Aud. de Guadalajara, leg. 116, together with further accounts of the founding of Albuquerque.

The official contemporary documents concerning the founding of Albuquerque state that there were

thirty-five families, with 252 persons, including adults and children. The early baptismal records indicate a population of at least this size. On the basis of the *Noticias* of Juan de Candelaria [NMHR, 4 (1929): 274-97], written some seventy years later when he was in his eighties, it is usually assumed that the Villa of Albuquerque was founded with twelve families and soldiers from Bernalillo. It is undoubtedly true that some of the first citizens of the Villa of Albuquerque came from Bernalillo, but more came from other districts. Both the Albuquerque and Bernalillo areas had Spanish settlers before 1680 and after the Reconquest. The older and correct spelling of the name is Alburquerque, and this was used by Domínguez, but we have conformed to the modern spelling.

2. Although the present church at Albuquerque faces south, Domínguez' description of the church and convent facing east is so consistent in every detail that it is hardly possible to ascribe the discrepancy to an inadvertent error on his part or that of his amanuensis. The church collapsed less than twenty years after he saw it (SANM, 2: no. 1226) and what must have amounted to a new building was begun in the 1790's. Nineteenth-century drawings and photographs of the church show considerable differences in the appearance of the façade, but in all of them it faces in the same direction as now. It would seem, therefore, that the change in orientation must have been made during the complete rebuilding undertaken in 1793.

lock. It is more than 3 varas high by 2½ wide. It is squared like those mentioned before. There is a small arch above this door, containing two middle-sized bells (one smaller than the other) which the King gave, and they are now broken. The cemetery is enclosed by a rather high adobe wall which has three gates. It begins at the front corner on the Epistle side and finishes the enclosure beyond the porter's lodge.

It is now obvious that the church is inside the cemetery, supposing that the convent is joined to the church on the Gospel side and extends to the south. Father Rojo made the said cemetery when he was minister of this villa, and he placed a large cross on an adobe pedestal in the center. The adornment of the church is as follows.

HIGH ALTAR: Father Fray Rafael Benavides installed an altar screen in perspective on canvas. It is very seemly. It consists (as it is painted) of two sections, and beginning at the gradin it rises about 6 varas across the width of the wall. The first section contains three pictures. The one in the center represents St. Francis Xavier, because this saint was firmly believed to be the titular patron. But I have now established and know for certain that it is St. Philip Neri.[3] I therefore ordered that an image of this saint be put in place, and it is a large oil painting on canvas in a wooden frame, which the King gave, and it is now in poor condition from age.

On either side of St. Francis Xavier, Our Father St. Francis and St. Anthony of Padua are painted (all as if they were in niches).

Near the middle of the second section (it is understood that all is painted), a crucifix, and on either side of it Lord St. Joseph and St. Augustine. At the top, the Eternal Father with an angel on each side. On the gradin at the foot of this altar screen is a rather seemly tabernacle with all necessary appurtenances. On it there is a middle-sized image in the round whose title is Our Lady of the Conception. She is clothed, and I shall describe her adornment (because it is changed) in the sacristy. A little in front of this Lady and at the edge of the tabernacle is a lacquer Child Jesus with a little linen shirt, a small jet rosary, and a little bronze reliquary.

The gradin is adobe, and on it there are a small iron cross, four bronze candlesticks, and four paper bouquets in wooden vases. The altar table is adobe with an altar stone which the King gave, wooden missal stand, ordinary cloths, pall to match, frontal like the altar screen. The carpet is of frieze, now old, and there are three small bronze bells.

3. In his certificate of founding, Governor Cuervo y Valdés stated that he gave Albuquerque "as titular patron the most glorious Apostle of the Indies San Francisco Xavier." In so doing he may have been happy to honor his own name saint, but he was also acting in accordance with an older tradition in the area. Cf. n. 1 *supra*. A document in HB, 3: 380, further informs us that "The same *junta general* [in Mexico City, July 28, 1706] notified the governor that he had acted wrongly in proceeding with this foundation without consulting his Excellency, and since a royal cedula of Señor Felipe [King Philip] V had already been issued directing the founding of a villa bearing his name, Cuervo was ordered to give the name to that of Albuquerque. Therefore, though its first title had been San Francisco Xavier, from the year of its foundation it bore that of San

Felipe." The last statement is open to question, for the confusion continued for years thereafter. The Albuquerque registers name the patrons as follows: San Francisco Xavier from the very first baptism on June 21, 1706, until August, 1709; then San Felipe Apostol (*sic*) from August 9, 1709, to January, 1711; San Francisco Xavier again from January 8, 1711, to April, 1777. At that time Fray Andrés García began using San Felipe Neri, following Domínguez' orders, and this has been the patronal title ever since. Outside the church registers, however, the town was usually referred to as San Felipe de Albuquerque, and occasionally as San Francisco Xavier de Albuquerque. The Provincial records in Mexico City (some of which are now in MN and BNM) have a single reference to the Villa of San Felipe Neri de Albuquerque in 1721 (MN, Asuntos, 259), and there are other references to San Felipe, or San Felipe de Albuquerque, but most of the eighteenth century records give the name as San Francisco de Albuquerque. Not until very late in the century do we find another reference to San Felipe Neri de Albuquerque, and even then San Francisco is still used in some documents.

Credence table for the chalice, etc., at solemn Masses, and a rough chair for the priest.

NAVE: On the right, or Gospel, side, there are two altars. The first, near the front, is a Holy Sepulcher. It consists of an ordinary image in the round with hinges in a casket of painted wood. The Lord has a loincloth and sheet of Brittany, a little quilt, two pillows, and a curtain made from a cloth *rebozo*. All are now worn. The furnishings of this altar consist of: A wooden niche containing a middle-sized Our Lady of Sorrows with an old dress of mother-of-pearl ribbed silk, a blue mantle of the same material, a silver radiance and dagger. On the wall hang an old oil painting on canvas a vara high and four small ones. The altar table is adobe and completely bare.

The other altar is below the aforesaid. It is dedicated to Our Father St. Francis, whose small image is dressed in a serge habit, with a cross in his hand and a diadem on his head; both of these are silver. There are five canvases on the wall like those mentioned above. The altar table like the aforesaid. The confessional stands between these two altars. It is badly made of wood. There are two poor benches on this same side.

There are two more altars on the left side. The first, near the front, is of Jesús Nazareno, whose image is an ordinary one in the round clothed in two tunics, one old and the other almost new, both of mother-of-pearl ribbed silk, carrying the cross on his back. There are four small old oil paintings on canvas arranged on the wall. The altar table like those mentioned above. The other altar is farther down. It is dedicated to St. Anthony of Padua, with a tiny image in the round, and it has a silver diadem. There is no other adornment. The altar table like those mentioned above, and on it a new middle-sized carved St. Francis Xavier. The pulpit is near the front on this same side. It is like the confessional. On the right near the corner by the door as we enter is the baptistery upon a small adobe table that serves

as a drain and holds the baptismal font. The floor of this church is the bare earth and its aspect is gloomy.

THIRD ORDER

Although it is founded in this church, what it has for its own uses is not known. It is all in a very poor state. Therefore this statement is all that can be concluded about it, as follows:

ITS FEASTS AND EXPENDITURES: Annually, St. Louis, King of France, procession, Mass, and sermon, 40 regional pesos. Our Father St. Francis, vespers, procession, and Mass, 15 pesos. Conception of Our Lady, vespers, procession, and Mass, 15 of the aforesaid. Anniversary of deceased brethren, with office of the dead, Mass, and responsory, 15 pesos. Monthly Sunday Mass, procession, and responsory, 6 pesos. For each newly deceased brother, three low Masses, 6 pesos. All the foregoing are paid for in chile, onions, *congas* blankets,[4] or other things.

This Third Order holds exercises only on Friday of Sorrows[5] and Good Friday, owing to the fact that all the brothers live so scattered that only on those two days do many of them assemble. Since everything is in very bad order, I commanded that a book be made. This has been done, and it consists of thirty-four leaves, not counting the first and last, and I recorded the following in it.

DECREE

In view of the fact that the brethren of the Third Order of this villa have no system whatsoever for their regimen and administration, our Reverend Father Fray Francisco Atanasio Domínguez, one of the appointed preachers in the Convento Grande of Our Father St. Francis of Mexico City and Commissary Visitor of this Custody for

4. "Frazadas congas." We have been unable to determine the meaning of "congas" as used here.

5. The Friday preceding Good Friday was called "Viernes de Dolores," honoring Mary at the foot of the Cross as described in the Gospel of St. John.

our Very Reverend Father Minister Provincial Fray Isidro Murillo, orders and commands the treasurer of this Third Order to record the monthly expenditures and receipts clearly and in detail in this new book, which he presented, consisting of thirty-four leaves (not counting the first and last). And at the monthly meetings he shall make an accounting to the Reverend Father Commissary Visitor and councillors so that in this way the state of this Third Order may be known and whether the brothers do or do not pay their dues, so that the penalties the Sacred Rule prescribes may be applied to those who default when they are able to pay.

And because, according to their rule, the tertiary brethren must be punctilious in their attendance at the devotional exercises, they are exorted to fulfil their obligations and charged to abandon the lethargy and laziness in which they have lived up to now, to the loss of many graces and indulgences. Our Reverend Father Commissary Visitor so provided, ordered, and signed before me, the undersigned secretary, to which I attest. Fray Francisco Atanasio Domínguez, Commissary Visitor. In my presence, Fray José Palacio, secretary.

CONFRATERNITY
OF THE POOR SOULS

It was founded in the year 1718 with the permission of the Ordinary, who was Father Fray Domingo de Araos, by Captain don Antonio Montoya, citizen of Bernalillo. And although it is all going from bad to worse, some alms are collected from the brethren, out of which the mission father is given 60 regional pesos for the Masses which are sung every Monday. This is not sufficient, for each one should cost 6 regional pesos.

FABRIC AND ITS RECEIPTS

The majordomo is one José Apodaca, who receives the payments, as follows: Bur-

ial in the cemetery, 2 pesos. From the door of the church to the center, 4 pesos. In the center, 8 pesos. From there to the sanctuary steps, 16 pesos. All is in the same commodities which have been described elsewhere, and from it is taken what is necessary for

Its Expenditures: Annually, 2 jugs of wine; of wax, if it is good, 50 candles, but if it is black, 100, and in either case the stubs are returned. He uses a fanega of wheat for altar breads, and he has an iron for making them which the King gave. He must also take care of repairs to the church building and of keeping the linen in the sacristy clean. For this he uses 16 small cakes of soap, which are worth 2 regional pesos.

SACRISTY

The sacristy is joined to the church on the right side near the sanctuary. It is an ordinary room, with a window facing west, an ordinary door without a lock to the church, and another to the convent with a good key. At the head of this room there is a board fastened in the side walls, which serves as a table where the priest vests. On the wall above it there is a small old oil painting on canvas of St. Rita with a print on either side. On one of the side walls there is a cupboard with doors used to keep what is necessary, and all this is as follows.

Vestments: A white satin chasuble, with all accessories, which the King gave. Another of mother-of-pearl satin, with all accessories. Another purple satin one with all accessories. Another of velvet (old) with two faces, one green with an orphrey embroidered in gold and the other mother-of-pearl with an orphrey of yellow lamé. Another of green velvet, and a mother-of-pearl orphrey, with stole and maniple, nothing more. Another of mother-of-pearl satin, its only accessory being a burse. Another of green ribbed silk with all necessary accessories. Another of mother-of-pearl satin without any accessories. Another of blue satin without accessories. Another of black damask with what is necessary. A white satin cope. Another of green satin. Another of mother-of-pearl satin. Another of black satin. A green satin humeral veil. Another of yellow damask.

Linen: Three usable Brittany amices. Four usable albs. Three altar cloths, now old. A pair of double corporals of Brittany. Four more of the aforesaid. Six purificators. Two finger towels. A surplice. Two starched ribbon cinctures. A cotta. Four palls.

Silver and other metal: Chalice with paten and spoon. Ordinary ciborium. A middle-sized monstrance, with only the rays gilded. Three small vials with the holy oils, and they are kept in a little cedar box without a key. A small pyx with its corporal. Two cruets without a plate. Shell for baptizing. All from the King.

Baptismal font and cover, all of copper. Holy-water pot. Thurible with accessories. Processional cross. All from the King.

Other things: A good missal. Two more old ones. *Manual* by Vetancurt. A very old white satin banner. A cross sheath, and it is white satin. Another of black satin. A white satin canopy. Two catafalques.

Adornments of the Virgin: Four Brittany chemises with lace, now worn. A plain dress of crimson flowered silk without a mantle. A tunic of white cloth, now worn, with very wide silver fringe and a mantle of blue ribbed silk. A wig of false hair. Silver-gilt crown. Seed pearl necklace in two strands with two silver pendants, each set with five small semiprecious stones. Rosary of silver filigree. Another of corals which has the Pater Noster in pearls. Two small metal crucifixes with Bohemian stones. Five small silver reliquaries. Two more of bronze set in gold.

NOTE: With the exception of the King, the benefactors from whom all the things mentioned up to here came are not stated or known. Therefore I do not mention them. And just as I specify what the King gave and the altar screen in perspective which Father Benavides made, I also state that after he left this mission for El Paso, the said father sent a set of vestments, which consists of chasuble, stole, maniple, pall, and burse of corporals. All this is of mother-of-pearl flowered silk trimmed with imitation silver galloon.

CONVENT

When I described the part of the church near the cemetery, I indicated that the convent extended to the south on the right side in the form of a square. There is a porter's lodge facing east near the front corner of the church, and it is a small portico 5 varas deep from the mouth to the center, 10 long and 3½ high. There are two little pillars with corbels in front, which make three arches and hold up the cross timber which supports the roof. There are small adobe seats around the wall inside, and the door is in the center of the façade. It is two-leaved, of medium size, and has no lock but the crossbar.

As we enter the porter's lodge, on our left there is a gallery which serves as a storeroom and has a key. Then the kitchen, which is on a corner. Around this corner there is a long room to store *tlazole,* or straw, and then the stable. At the head of the latter, against the wall on the side that completes the square, there is a passageway which faces south and leads to a corral we shall soon see. Beyond the passageway is the cell, with two inner cells, then an anteroom to the sacristy, which closes the square. There is no cloister, but just a bare patio.

The description of the passageway shows that the corral is beside the convent on the south. It has quite a high wall with a good large door to the east, with two leaves and a good lock. It extends from one end (or corner) of the convent to the other and is about 15 varas wide. It is new. Father Benavides made it completely.

ITS FURNISHINGS: Two chairs. A large table. A bench. The two locks mentioned. Another one in the minister's cell.

ITS LANDS AND FRUITS: Down to the south of the convent there is a milpa which is ordinarily planted with maize. It takes an almud, which usually yields 25 fanegas. Back of the convent on the Río del Norte there is a little swamp where the horse which the father uses in his ministry is kept. The father does his meager planting.

MISSION FATHER

Our Mother the Province maintains Father Fray Andrés García in this villa for the apostolic ministry. For the reason mentioned at Santa Fe, he receives no royal allowance. He is a native of Puebla de los Angeles, fifty-eight years of age, thirty-nine in profession, thirty as a missionary in the Custody, as follows: Galisteo, six months; Taos, two years; Pecos, one year; Acoma seven months; Zuñi, three months; Zia, five months; Acoma again, eight months; Albuquerque, thirteen days; Santo Domingo, twelve days; Taos again, one year; Jémez, one year; El Paso, in the villa, seven months; Realito of El Paso, two months; Taos again, four years; Nambe, twenty days; Taos again, eight years; Sandia, ten months; Santa Fe, one year, seven months; Picuris, six months; Cañada, six years; Albuquerque, again, three months; Laguna, two years, three months; Abiquiu, two months; Albuquerque again, and he is here now, six months. He holds general faculties from Durango, revocable at will.

ADMINISTRATION OF THE MISSION: The administration of this widespread, scattered population necessitates constant travel, both inside and outside the villa, and this will be evident from the description of its districts. In addition, doctrinal sermon in the afternoon on Fridays during Lent. Feast celebration on the Friday of Sorrows. A citizen called José Sánchez pays for it. He keeps a fund in ewes for the purpose, from which 15 sheep are given for the Three Hours' Agony Mass and sermon. He also provides the wax for this function. Good Friday, the Three

Falls, with a sermon for which the Third Order pays 25 pesos in the commodities available. On the same day, Descent from the Cross, the sermon being paid for by the collection of alms. Sermon of Our Lady of Solitude in the late evening of this same day, paid for as above.

OBVENTIONS AND FIRST FRUITS: In accordance with the general custom I described in Santa Fe. This friar says that they sometimes give him sheep; others give cows; and the usual contribution in seeds, chile, sackcloth, blankets, wool, etc. With regard to this, a legal instrument signed by the magistrate and other citizens of the place will be found elsewhere.

The first fruits of this mission of Albuquerque usually amount to 100 fanegas of maize, 50 of wheat, 16 of frijol alone, another 16 of other legumes mixed; about 30 strings of chile, about a cartload of onions. Of livestock, about 30 small head of sheep, about 10 kids, 5 to 7 calves.

SERVICE AND EXPENDITURES: These are just like those of the minister at La Cañada, to which I refer in order not to repeat the same thing at length. Moreover, the same method is used to collect the first fruits as at the said Cañada.

HOW HE ACQUIRES NECESSITIES: By exchange like all the mission fathers mentioned before, and there is no local characteristic such as I have noted in some of the aforesaid missions.

CONVENT PROVISIONS: These have been established and designated in the new inventory Father García has just made, authorized by the following

WRIT OF VISITATION

Villa of Albuquerque, May 23 of the year 1776. In prosecution of the juridical visitation our Reverend Father Fray Francisco Atanasio Domínguez, one of the appointed preachers in the Convento Grande of Our Father St. Francis of Mexico City and Commissary Visitor of this Custody for our Very

Reverend Father Minister Provincial Fray Isidro Murillo, is making of this Custody, he visited this mission, and, finding that the old inventory, in addition to being full, does not agree with what actually exists, he orders and commands the present mission father, Fray Andrés García, to record and set down the adornment of the church, the valuables of the sacristy, and the furnishings and other things pertaining to the convent in this same book which is now newly presented and consists of thirty-six leaves, not counting the first and last, with the clarity, order, and detail which he has seen used in this visitation, in order that it may agree with the one that is to be remitted to the Province. And on the occasion when Obedience transfers him to another mission, he shall hand these over in accordance with the new inventory alone.

And, proceeding to the provisions that this mission must have, he orders and commands that these be the following: 10 fanegas of wheat, 10 of maize, 12 sheep, 12 strings of chile, half a fanega of frijol, a jar of ordinary lard, an almud of salt, 50 onions. With regard to this and other dispositions, the Reverend Custos or his Vice-Custos are not empowered to dispense with or take away anything, but they may, indeed, add what is necessary for the benefit of the mission and missionary. When the latter takes over from the outgoing friar, he shall give a receipt and report to the Reverend Custos or his Vice-Custos if there is anything missing so that the lack may be supplied, for this is the intention and will of our Superior Provincial Prelate, who so orders and commands *ratione officii,* and therefore validly for all time. Our Reverend Father Commissary Visitor so ordered, commanded, and signed before me, the undersigned secretary, to which I attest. Fray Francisco Atanasio Domínguez, Commissary Visitor. In my presence, Fray José Palacio, secretary.

The parish books were examined, etc., and the only thing to be noted about them is that they are nearly full. I ordered Father García to apply to the Father Vice-Custos [for new books from the supply] from the Province. The aforesaid old ones remain at this mission. The book of Baptisms is so inadequate that, since it has 49 leaves, this Father García provided and began it in the year 1772, and he himself is finishing it this present year of 1776. The book of Marriages was begun in the year 1726 by Fray Andrés Ceballos and is now being finished by Father García. It has only 66 leaves out of the 143 that its decree of presentation mentions. The book of Burials was begun in the aforesaid 1726 by the same Ceballos and is being finished by the same García. It has only 81 leaves of the 143 it should have according to the decree.

VILLA

Some pages back it was said that it stands on the plain near the meadows of the Río del Norte. The villa itself consists of twenty-four houses near the mission. The rest of what is called Albuquerque extends upstream to the north, and all of it is a settlement of ranchos on the meadows of the said river for the distance of a league from the church to the last one upstream. Some of their lands are good, some better, some mediocre. They are watered by the said river through very wide, deep irrigation ditches, so much so that there are little beam bridges to cross them. The crops taken from them at harvest time are many, good, and everything sown in them bears fruit.

There are also little orchards with vinestocks and small apricot, peach, apple, and pear trees. Delicious melons and watermelons are grown. Not all those who have grapes make wine, but some do. The citizens are of all classes and walks of life as in the other places I have mentioned, and they speak the local Spanish. They are included in this

CENSUS

157 families with 763 persons

DISTRICTS

Before relating them, I note that since these lie off in various directions and not one after the other in the same general direction like the districts of the villas described before, I decided to describe them more independently than the others. To begin with, I say that *Alameda*[6] is upstream to the north. It is 2 long leagues from the mission, is a settlement of ranchos on the same plain formed by the river meadows, and the farms are like those of Albuquerque, on which they border. And I therefore refer to their description and say the same of these, since I find no reason to repeat myself.

There is a chapel of Our Lady of the Conception in this place. Don Juan González built it years ago with permission from the Ordinary, and later the Lord Bishop Tamarón ratified it for a son of the aforesaid, named Alejandro González Baz, who left this license to his son, Gaspar González, when he died. A copy of the license will be included elsewhere.[7] This chapel is small and faces south, with an ordinary two-leaved door and a good key. It has a little belfry with two small bells. Adequate cemetery. It is adorned by a high altar, on the wall of which there is a niche with an old yellow satin curtain on a rod. This holds a middle-sized image in the round of Our Lady of the Conception. Her head and hands are ivory,

and her adornment consists of a wig of false hair, a silver crown, gold earrings with pendants of fine crystal, a string of ordinary pearls, a rosary of black glass set in silver, and tombac bracelets of gilded metal.

There are six old canvases about a vara high arranged around the niche. There is a gradin with two small gradins above it, all of adobe. On them there are a rather middle-sized cross with relics and glass case, and eight paper bouquets. On the gradin there is another Our Lady of the Conception smaller than the aforesaid. It is in the round, and to clothe her they have four Brittany chemises, a complete little dress of ribbed silk, badly worn, a small silver crown, two strings of ordinary pearls, two bronze reliquaries plated with gold.

The altar table is adobe with an altar stone, a cross with a bronze crucifixion, three brass candlesticks, a wooden missal stand, a small bell, and a board dais. There is an ordinary wooden confessional in the little nave. There is a sacristy of ordinary size, and in it a table with a drawer in which are kept an old but usable brocade chasuble with complete accessories, including frontal; a white satin canopy for processions; amice, alb, cincture, corporals, purificator, altar cloths, finger towel; chalice with paten and spoon, all of silver, cruets of the same; a worn missal and a manual.

An annual feast in honor of the Immaculate Conception is held in this chapel with the Anniversary afterwards. For this the father is given 40 pesos in sheep, which come from the ewes the said Gaspar González holds and keeps as a fund. The titular image

6. The Tigua pueblo of Alameda was abandoned and burned after the Revolt of 1680. In 1706, "a new mission of Tiguas," La Alameda, was administered by the friar at Bernalillo. HB, 3: 375-76. On January 27, 1710, the Alameda tract was granted to Captain Francisco Montes Vigil (one of the settlers who came from Zacatecas after the Reconquest) by the governor, Marqués de la Peñuela. The boundaries were as follows: "on the north a ruin of an old pueblo, of two that there are, is the more distant one from the Alameda tract; and on the south a small hill, which is the boundary of Luis García; on the east the Rio del Norte, and on the west plains and hills for entrances and exits." SANM, 1: no. 605. On July 18, 1712, Montes Vigil conveyed the tract to Juan González, the founder of the chapel described below. SANM, 1: no. 302.

7. See pp. 253-54 *infra*. Apparently the structure described by Domínguez succumbed to time, or to one of the periodic floods that made the Río Grande change its bed, for the former González Baz chapel, now part of a house at Sandoval owned by Dr. J. E. Longhurst, faced east, with the sanctuary at the west. Although there have been extensive additions and changes in this house, the layout of the chapel is clearly visible, and it is impossible that it could ever have faced south as Domínguez says the 1776 chapel did.

of this chapel and everything in it belong exclusively to the heirs of the aforesaid Don Juan González because he, as the prime mover, gave most of it, and his relatives have given some small items. A forty-day indulgence has been conceded to the aforesaid most holy image to those who pray a Salve [Regina] on their knees before it. The Lord Bishop Crespo granted it. The Lord Bishop Tamarón granted the same for an Ave Maria prayed kneeling. The population of this Alameda consists of people of various classes and walks of life, as has been fully stated about that of other places. Their Spanish is the same. And this is the census of this little place.

CENSUS

66 families with 388 persons

On the same side of the river as the mission, down the highway to the south, is another small place called *Valencia*,[8] which is about 6 leagues from the church. It is a settlement of ranchos on the same meadow and plain we have been following from higher up. The farmlands, irrigation ditches, and crops like those of Albuquerque. Its population like the foregoing. Their Spanish the same. And here is the

CENSUS

17 families with 90 persons

Below this place and also to the south is *Tomé*,[9] which is about 10 leagues from the mission. It is a settlement on the plain and meadow mentioned (I noted this at the very beginning). Its farmlands, ditches, crops, citizens, and Spanish the same as the foregoing. The census will be inserted below, since it is necessary to state that there is a

chapel of Our Lady of the Conception in this Tomé, which the settlers have built, and it is all as follows.[10]

The chapel is adobe with thick walls, with the outlook and door to the west. It is 36 varas long, 8 wide, and the same high, with fifty-eight wrought beams. There is no choir loft. Two windows to the south on the Epistle side, and a little belfry with a cracked bell. The main door like that of the missions, with a wooden lock and key. There is no cemetery.

Its furnishings as follows: In the center of the upper wall there is a niche like an arch containing a middle-sized completely carved image in the round of Our Lady of the Conception. She has imitation lace on the edge of her mantle. Her wardrobe consists of six silver reliquaries, an escutcheon and medal of the same, a small reliquary and five medals of bronze, an ordinary rosary set in silver, another silver one. She has a crown of gilded cardboard on her head. Fine pearl earrings in her ears. Around her neck two strings of ordinary pearls. On her wrists bracelets of black jet. On her fingers twelve silver and copper rings.

There are two rather middle-sized mirrors above the arch, or niche, and fourteen old, but not torn, canvases arranged on the whole wall. There is a gradin, and on it stand a middle-sized Jesús Nazareno in the round in old clothes; a completely nonde-

8. Site of the seventeenth-century hacienda of Francisco de Valencia, who was born in Santa Fe some time after 1610 and was lieutenant general for the Río Abajo in the middle of the century. None of the Valencias returned to settle this area after the Reconquest. NMF.

9. Site of the seventeenth-century hacienda of Tomé Domínguez de Mendoza, son of Tomé Domínguez. Although members of his and his brothers' families escaped the massacre of 1680, none of them returned to New Mexico. NMF. In 1750, Tomé was called "the new village of Our Lady of the Conception situated on the post called 'of Tomé Domínguez.'" SANM, 2: no. 437.

10. Bishop Elizacoechea gave permission for this church in 1743. It was completed in 1750 and blessed by Vicar Roybal in 1754. Note in marriage register. In 1828 the priest and people of Tomé decided that their eighty-year old church needed rebuilding, and on a safer site away from the river. Governor Armijo endorsed the decision, but the people of Valencia refused to cooperate. AASF, 1828, no. 8.

script tabernacle with a key; a cross for Mass. The altar table is adobe with an altar stone, wooden missal stand, two bronze candlesticks, and a little bell. In the nave there is a badly-made wooden confessional.

There is a set of vestments consisting of a white satin chasuble with all accessories; amice, alb, cincture, altar cloths, pall, finger towel, corporals, purificator; chalice with paten and spoon, all of silver, small silver vials for the holy oils, which came from the King and are kept in a little tin-plate box; glass cruets on a Puebla plate. With the exception of what I specified as coming from the King, everything was provided by the settlers, who sometimes hold their Holy Week function in the chapel and always the annual feast of the titular patron, and the Christmas novena. For all this, alms are collected from these settlers, and they amount to seeds, chile, wool, sackcloth, and similar things. These are given to the father who comes to perform the aforesaid, who is usually not their own minister because he is extremely busy at the head mission. Here is the

CENSUS

135 families with 727 persons[11]

On what is the west bank of the river here at Albuquerque is the settlement they call *Atlixco*.[12] It is as far from Albuquerque as the distance between it and the river, which is about two musket shots, and the breadth of the river and no more, for the ranchos are right there on a beautiful sandy plain which comes down from more hills like those on the east bank. The farmlands of this little place are very sterile because they are sandy, and therefore they are cultivated with great labor, yielding reasonable crops in proportion. I say the same of its citizens as of the foregoing with regard to social classes and Spanish. They are counted in this

CENSUS

52 families with 288 persons

Above this Atlixco to the north there is another settlement of ranchos which is called *Lower Corrales*, and it borders on Upper Corrales, which pertains to Sandia. It is on the same sandy plain that I have just mentioned. Its farmlands, waters, crops, and settlers, their classes, walks of life, and language, as before. The individuals are included in their

CENSUS

26 families with 160 persons

SUM TOTAL

453 families with 2416 persons

11. Fray Andrés García wrote in the Albuquerque burial book that on May 26, 1777, he buried from the Tomé chapel twenty-one settlers massacred by the Comanches. On August 27, 1777, ten men and one woman of Albuquerque were killed by enemy Indians, and again at Tomé, June 3, 1778, thirty more persons suffered the same fate.

12. Like other sites near the Río Grande, Atlixco (Nahuatl, "upon the water," probably named for the Valley of Atlixco in Mexico), present Atrisco, had settlers from the seventeenth century on and was considered a good fertile site, because the river at this point flowed farther to the east. In 1662, Governor Peñalosa contemplated establishing a formal town and went so far as to gather fraudulent signatures at the hacienda of the Varelas. AGM, Inquisición, Tomo 507.

Cochiti

Down to the southwest of Santa Fe, across that cañada I mentioned at Cieneguilla and also across the mesa mentioned at the same place, taking a higher road than the one that leads to the Río Abajo along the said cañada and mesa, is the route to the pueblo and mission of San Buenaventura de Cochiti. It is established and located on the west bank of the Río del Norte, and it is across the river from Santa Fe. It stands on a fine plain in full view of the river, as I shall explain better later. It is 8 or 9 leagues from Santa Fe to the southwest.

CHURCH

The church[1] is adobe with walls about a vara thick, single-naved, with the outlook and main door due east. It is 30 varas long from the door to the ascent to the sanctuary, 7 wide, and 8 high as far as the bed molding. The ascent to the sanctuary consists of three steps made of wrought beams that mark it off, and it measures 6 varas to the center, with the same width as the nave because it is not closed in like the head of a transept as has been said of others. It is as much higher as is necessary because of the clerestory. There is no choir loft. On the Gospel side there are two poor windows facing south. The roof of the nave consists of thirty-four wrought and corbeled beams, and the clerestory rises all along the one opposite the sanctuary. The roof of the latter continues with eight beams like those mentioned.

The main door is squared, with a strong wooden frame instead of masonry. It has two roughly paneled leaves and a crossbar for a lock. It is about 3 varas high by 2 wide. There is a little belfry over it with a good

1. There seems to have been a seventeenth-century church at Cochiti, although the pueblo was usually a visita of Santo Domingo. We do not know how much it suffered during the Revolt and Reconquest periods. In 1696 one Laureano Gómez was killed at Cochiti and buried in the church there. NMF. In 1706 Father Alvarez made his usual statement: "The church is being built." HB, 3: 375. It is possible that the church described by Domínguez, perhaps the one still in existence, incorporates remnants of the seventeenth-century structure.

middle-sized bell that the King gave. The cemetery runs from the front corners with an adobe wall more than a vara high with three gates. It is 9 varas wide and 12 long. The church floor is the bare earth, its interior very gloomy, and its furnishings as follows.

HIGH ALTAR: In the center of the wall hangs an old, untorn canvas with a wooden frame, 2 varas high by a long vara wide, representing St. Bonaventure in oils, which the King gave. Above this canvas is another one measuring a vara, without a frame, which represents Our Lady of Guadalupe in oils. Still higher, another small oil painting of St. John of God. Arranged at intervals on either side of the chief painting are four great prints on paper of two Holy Evangelists and two Holy Doctors. Except for the painting from the King, it is not known who gave the rest.

The altar table is adobe with an altar stone given by the King. A small altar card with a rather large cross. Two small brass candlesticks, which the King gave. Three ordinary bells. There is no dais or carpet. I do not give any heading for the nave because there is so little in it that it amounts to two confessionals and a pulpit, all of wood and most unseemly.

SACRISTY: The sacristy is joined to the church on the Gospel side, and it is a room 5 varas square with a window to the west, an open arched doorway to the sanctuary, and an ordinary single-leaf door without a key to the cloister. In this room there is a wooden table with a drawer and key where what I shall soon mention is kept, and the necessary things are put on it when the priest vests. On the wall above this table hangs a very old middle-sized oil painting on canvas of Our Lady of Guadalupe, and above it a small wooden cross. In one corner there is a wooden stand like a rooster's leg upside down (here they called it a forked pole), and on it there is a large earthen bowl for a baptismal font, with a board cover. The contents of the table drawer follow.

Vestments: An old white damask chasuble with all accessories, which the King gave. Another old one of crimson damask with complete accessories, which the King gave. Another almost new one of black damask with false fringe and all accessories including cope and cross sheath, which Father Camargo gave.

Linen: Two new Brittany amices. Two new Brittany albs, one with lace and one without, which Father Marulanda provided. A good Brittany altar cloth without lace. A pair of good double corporals of Brittany. Two purificators. A finger towel. A cincture.

Other things: Another altar stone—it is not known whether it came from the King. A worn missal with thong bookmarks. A usable *Manual* by Osorio. A clay shell for baptizing. Two chasubles, amices, albs, and finger towels so old and useless that they are considered worn out.

CONVENT

The convent is joined to the church on the right side, extending to the south, where it forms a square. There is a porter's lodge, which is a very pretty little portico to the east without pillars in front because it is very limited. The floor of this little portico is paved with small stones of various colors, and in the center there is an eagle very well wrought in stones like those mentioned. There are adobe seats around this room, and the door is in the center of the wall. It is an ordinary two-leaved door with a crossbar for a lock. In front of the porter's lodge only, there is a little stairway of small beams with an adobe railing, and from it a little corridor goes up by the mouth of the said little portico. It is like the one mentioned at Santo Domingo, but this one does not reach the corner of the convent.

As we enter the porter's lodge, there is a beautiful room on our left, beyond which there is an inner cell on a corner. There is another inner cell around the corner, and then another room, at the head of which there is a passageway which faces south and leads to a corral I shall describe later. The entrance to the kitchen is from this passage, and the kitchen is around the corner on the side of the building that completes the square. Beyond this kitchen is a gallery that serves as a storeroom and ends at the sacristy. It has a three-sided cloister, which begins up against the church at the exit from the sacristy. It ends down at the porter's lodge, which it joins. There is a small patio between the sides of the cloister and the wall of the church. This cloister is entirely closed in and has only three windows, one on each side. It is so dark that it resembles a dungeon.

The corral is against the convent on the south, runs from the upper to the lower corner, and is about 8 varas wide. It has a rather high adobe wall and a great two-leaved door without a lock to the east. Against the south wall in this corral are the stable and strawloft, both very large rooms, which Father Cayuela built new.

ITS FURNISHINGS: Two chairs. A table. A bench. A large measure for grain.

ITS SERVICE: In all, a chief fiscal, three subordinates; eight sacristans and the chief sacristan; eight cooks, four bakers. Weekly, a fiscal, two sacristans, two cooks with two big girls to carry water. The bakers take turns. The pueblo brings the necessary firewood. Throughout the year the pueblo takes turns weekly as caretakers of sheep, cows, hens, pigs, and horses.

ITS LANDS AND FRUITS: On the east bank of the Río del Norte, opposite the mission, the convent has four beautiful milpas of great fertility. They are watered by the said river through very deep, wide irrigation ditches, and they yield such good and abundant crops that there are usually 80 or more fanegas of wheat at harvest time and 70 or more of maize. On the pueblo side of the river, in full view of the convent and almost on the river, there is a small plot for a kitchen garden, which yields many good green vegetables. The pueblo does the sowing, etc.

MISSION FATHER

Father Fray Estanislao Mariano Marulanda exercises the apostolic ministry in this mission. He is a native of Ozumba, forty-three years of age, twenty-six in profession, eighteen years as a missionary in the Custody, as follows: Pecos, one year; Zuñi, two years; Picuris, three years; Zia, seven years; Isleta, two years; Cochiti, where he is living, three years. He holds general faculties in Durango, revocable at will.

ADMINISTRATION OF THE MISSION: The same regime as the other missions, to which I refer, for there is no local peculiarity.

OBVENTIONS AND FIRST FRUITS: Although the settlers (we shall deal with them later) administered by this mission harvest small amounts, because of the lack of permanent water and because, at the same time, they are not landholders, nevertheless there are some obventions as has been said in other places. As first fruits, 6 or 8 fanegas of all kinds of grain together and small amounts of green vegetables usually are collected. Although the Indians make no contributions of this kind, they usually pay for Masses in the way I described at San Juan.

EXPENDITURES: Food consumed by the household is not counted. About 6 pounds of wax a year, about 2 jugs of wine. The altar breads are paid for by the pueblo; they give the chief sacristan of Santo Domingo a fanega of wheat a year.

HOW HE ACQUIRES NECESSITIES: I refer to the method used by the fathers mentioned before, since there is nothing new here.

CONVENT PROVISIONS: In the inventory Father Zambrano made in the year 1753 (and which still continues, although it is not in order) the following, made by the Reverend Custos Castro, appears on folio 7 v.: 10 fanegas of wheat, 10 of maize, 10 sheep, 6 strings of chile, half a fanega of frijol, half an almud of salt, a jar of ordinary lard. For the present this has been approved, and I added what is recorded in sufficient detail in the said inventory in the following

WRIT OF VISITATION

San Buenaventura de Cochiti, May 14 of the year 1776. In prosecution of the juridical visitation of this Custody which our Reverend Father Fray Francisco Atanasio Domínguez, one of the appointed preachers in the convent of Our Father St. Francis of Mexico City and Commissary Visitor of this Custody for our Very Reverend Father Minister Provincial Fray Isidro Murillo, is making, his Reverend Paternity proceeded to examine and did examine this inventory, which does not agree with the only belongings of church, sacristy, etc. that exist, for many of the things it records have been used up. Therefore his Reverend Paternity orders and commands the present mission father, Fray Estanislao Mariano Marulanda, to record on the blank pages that remain—with all clarity, detail, and order—the belongings, vestments, linen, etc. which really exist, so that in this fashion this inventory may agree with the one which is to be remitted to the Province and likewise so that when a change of missionary may occur, what should be received and handed over may be known, and so that in future the reverend prelates may be able to inspect these things without so much labor and confusion as has now been involved.

And inasmuch as this mission's provisions have been designated in this inventory by the Reverend Custos Castro, our Reverend Father Visitor orders and commands that they be maintained, kept, and observed punctiliously. And although for the present his Reverend Paternity adds 12 tallow candles, 4 wax candles, and a bottle of wine, after he is completely acquainted with the income of this mission and has taken into consideration whether it is truly as rich as it is said to be or not, he will add or take away what he thinks best, but for the present

abides by what has been ordered. With regard to all this and such orders as may be issued later, the Reverend Custos or his Vice-Custos shall not be able to make any dispensation, misrepresentation, or reduction, but only, indeed, add all they may think necessary for the benefit of the mission and missionary, since that is the intention and will of our Superior Provincial Prelate, who so orders and commands *ratione officii* and therefore validly for all time.

And in order that all the foregoing may have due effect, we order the incoming friar to report to the Reverend Custos or his Vice-Custos whether anything ordered here is missing at the time of the transfer, and the latter shall see that the lack is promptly supplied, as is proper. Our Reverend Father Commissary Visitor so dictated, not only with regard to the provisions but also concerning the belongings of church and sacristy and the convent furnishings which exist today. Before me, the undersigned secretary, to which I attest. Fray Francisco Atanasio Domínguez, Commissary Visitor. In my presence, Fray José Palacio, secretary.

The parish books were examined and approved, and the corresponding decrees were recorded in them, by which, because they are nearly full, Father Marulanda is ordered to take prompt measures to supply new books, and as soon as that is done, the old ones shall be remitted to the archive of this Custody, which is at the mission of Our Father Santo Domingo. These were started in the year 1726 by Father Esquer and are now being finished by said Father Marulanda. The said Inventory remains here and also a new book which Father Marulanda provided for Patents of Prelates.

PUEBLO

Having noted in the beginning that Cochiti is on a good plain, I reiterate that the pueblo and mission lie in full view of the Río del Norte on the west bank within a musket shot and a half of the river. The aforesaid plain spreads out to give an extensive view on all sides, for on the south it reaches beyond Santo Domingo; to the east, about 2 leagues to the mesa where the aforesaid roads are; to the north and west, about a league as far as a chain of hills and small wooded mesas which begin at the river canyon (this runs through the aforesaid mesa where the roads are on the north), and, making a curve down the plain, stand at the said river rather near the mission of San Felipe (I shall describe this sequence later).

Having considered this location, it remains to be said that the pueblo itself is toward the north in relation to the church, planned and arranged of adobe houses which form two small plazas with all their four blocks separate from one another. One is east of the others, and another to the west, with a tenement, or building, in between that faces south. The arrangement of doors, adornment, and alignment as in the other pueblos via ladders and *cois*.

ITS LANDS AND FRUITS: All the important farmlands which this pueblo owns lie on the east side of the river, downstream along the river, extending the breadth of the plain and down to join those of the pueblo of Santo Domingo. There are some milpas on the bank on which the pueblo stands, and very few up to the north on both banks. All take the water of the said river for irrigation through deep wide ditches. They yield very abundant crops of everything sown in them. There is an occasional peach tree.

The natives of this pueblo are Queres, whose native tongue they speak, and also Spanish, but brokenly. With regard to their particular customs, the same as those of Santo Domingo, and here is the

CENSUS

116 families with 486 persons

This mission has charge of the administration of a settlement which is located to the north in a cañada which the aforesaid hills (see the description of the pueblo) and small mesas offer from west to east. It is 2 long leagues from the mission and is called *Cañada de Cochiti*.[2] It is a settlement of ranchos throughout the canyon, with lands of good quality by nature, but since the very small river that runs through the middle of the said canyon in the same direction always fails at the best season, as a result the farming is usually in vain. This leads to scanty crops, and the people are obliged to seek grain elsewhere. The settlers are of all classes and walks of life and speak the usual Spanish. Of all those who live here today, only twenty-two families are old residents; the rest are newcomers, but they are included in the present

CENSUS

52 families with 307 persons

2. This name is first mentioned in the Cochiti baptismal register in 1760. It also appears in a civil document of 1762. BL, N.M. Origs., 1762. The village was abandoned in the twentieth century.

San Felipe

Four leagues south of Cochiti, along the plain downstream on the west bank, one comes to a great mesa (it is the one I mentioned a short time ago, and I shall soon speak of it at some length) which rises near the Río del Norte. It forces the road to run below at its foot, which is a league long. This, added to the foregoing 4, makes 5 leagues from Cochiti to the pueblo and mission of San Felipe de Jesús, which is located and established on a small level site like a nook at the foot of the said mesa against the river, from which the establishment is about 300 varas.

This resembles the site of the sanctuary of Our Lady of Guadalupe, because, like it, it is at the foot of a hill with a view of the river running in front of it. Thus this mission is at the foot of a mesa and overlooks the river which runs in sight of it. But although there is a resemblance in this respect, there is none with regard to the wide view the said sanctuary has, for this pueblo is like something tucked in a corner. Its only view is a little to the south, some hills to the east that meet the river, a little to the north, and none to the west because the mesa at the back obstructs it.[1]

The gossipy vulgar herd have always considered St. Philip the Apostle as the titular patron of this mission and have celebrated his feast as such on his day.[2] A European citizen of this kingdom, called Don Bernardo Miera y Pacheco, supported this opinion by selling to the Indians of this pueblo (at a high price in proportion to those of this land) an image of the said Holy Apostle, a large carved statue in the round, which he made himself. And although it is not at all prepossessing, it serves the purpose and stands on the high altar at this mission.[3] The pueblo under the present heading is 11 good leagues from Santa Fe, lying to the southwest of the villa. I will give other details later.

CHURCH

The church is adobe with thick walls, single-naved, with the outlook and main door to the east. From the door to the ascent to the sanctuary it is 35 varas long, 7 wide, and 6 high. The sanctuary is marked off by four steps made of wrought beams and measures 5 varas from the last of these to the center. It is as wide as the nave and as much higher as the clerestory demands. The choir loft is in the usual place and like those of the missions that have them. Its entrance is from the flat roof of the convent. On the right side there are three poor windows with wooden gratings which face south. And there is one in the choir to the balcony we shall see presently.

1. The pueblo of San Felipe apparently was moved to its present location sometime after the revolt of 1696 and before 1706, when Father Alvarez tells us that "the church and a new pueblo are being built, the latter having been moved down from a high mesa." HB, 3: 375. In 1681, the Spaniards had found the church and convent at the original pueblo on the Black Mesa in ruins and the pueblo abandoned. HS, 1: cl; 2: 260, 269. When de Vargas came in 1693, he found San Felipe at a new site on the mesa about a mile north of the pre-Revolt pueblo. An adobe church was built here in 1694, remnants of which may still be seen. The Spanish people and soldiers of Bernalillo were gathered here in 1696 when the rebellion began. Not only did they find a protected place, but they also prevented the San Felipe Indians from joining the rebels. AGI, Aud. de Guadalajara, leg. 141.

2. Domínguez undoubtedly is mistaken about St. Philip of Jesus, the Protomartyr of Japan, who was beatified in 1627, but not canonized until 1862. See GLOSS. St. Philip [the Apostle] was made the titular patron of this pueblo in 1598, the year following the martyrdom of Philip of Jesus. Tamarón, however, calls the pueblo San Felipe de Jesús (AT, p. 65), and Fray Francisco Xavier Dávila wrote "San Felipe de Jesús" in the parish books March to April, 1764. They were not the only ones to assume that Philip of Jesus had been canonized, for Father Francisco Javier Alegre, S.J., writing *c.* 1767 [*Historia de la Compañía de Jesús en Nueva España* (Mexico, 1841-42), 2: 177-78], described the celebrations held in Mexico City, February, 1629, to honor the "canonization" of San Felipe de Jesús "with the greatest solemnity that had ever been seen. . . . All the guilds took great interest in applauding this holy martyr, the first from these kingdoms and from this city to ascend to the altars." A document in AASF, 1798, no. 10, concerns the collection of alms in New Mexico for the canonization of Blessed Philip of Jesus.

3. Captain Don Bernardo Miera y Pacheco was a jack-of-all-trades. On one occasion he tried to recast some ordnance pieces at Santa Fe, but failed. He is, of course, best known as a cartographer. The large crude statue here described, heavily retouched, still occupies the central niche in the church at San Felipe.

The roof of the nave consists of forty wrought and corbeled beams, and the clerestory rises on the one that faces the sanctuary, which is roofed by seven beams like those mentioned. The main door is squared, with a wooden frame for masonry, has two paneled leaves, no lock, and is 3 varas high by 2 long ones wide. After we enter it, there is a small room on the right, which has an entrance under the choir loft and extends outside the church wall. It serves as a baptistery. It has a poor door and a worse window. In the center stands a small adobe pillar, which, hollowed out for a drain, holds a large earthen bowl as a baptismal font, covered with a board.

From the front corners of the church to near its door two tower buttresses jut out. Each one has a tiny tower with four little arches without gratings. There is a rather middle-sized bell which the King gave in the one on the right side. Between the tower buttresses and over the door there is a balcony like that at Santa Fe, and the exit to it is through the window in the choir loft that I have just mentioned. The cemetery juts out in proportion from the sides of the said buttresses. The wall is of stone and mud, and it is more than a vara high, extends 30 varas in a rectangle, and has three gates. The church floor is bare earth, its interior is dark, and its furnishings as follows.

HIGH ALTAR: A niche has been opened near the middle of its wall, and it contains the image of St. Philip the Apostle mentioned a little while ago. Above the niche hangs a large old oil painting on canvas with a wooden frame of St. Philip of Jesus, which the King gave. Still higher, a large old oil painting on canvas of Jesus tied to the column.[4] Its donor is not known, nor are those

4. The painting of St. Philip of Jesus is now in a later wooden reredos to the right of Miera's image of St. Philip the Apostle. Though crudely redone several times, the crucified young Franciscan and a Japanese soldier with a spear are still recognizable. On the opposite side, equally spoiled by time and repainting, is the scourging of Christ.

of the following. At the sides of the said niche, two large old canvases of St. Mary Magdalene and St. Benedict Abbot, both in oil. Above these, on either side of St. Philip of Jesus, two small old oil paintings on canvas of the Immaculate Conception and Lord St. Joseph.

There is a large, wide adobe gradin, on which stand: An ebony cross with a bronze Christus and a Mater Dolorosa of the same metal at the foot. Lacquer Child Jesus. Our Lady of the Conception in Michoacán paste. Two small brass candlesticks which the King gave and four wooden ones which a father provided. The altar table is adobe with a good altar stone which the King gave, a wooden missal stand, and two small bronze bells. There is no dais or carpet. The only thing in the nave is a wooden confessional, old but not one of the worst.

SACRISTY: The sacristy is joined to the church on the right side and is a room 6 varas long by 5 wide and more than 3 high, with a good roof, a window to the west on one side, an ordinary single-leaf door with-

and its accessories consist of frontal, stole, and maniple. Another old one of green velvet with stole and maniple only. Another old one of blue damask with stole and maniple. After the one mentioned as from the King, it is not stated whether the King or other persons donated the foregoing. Another almost new one of black damask with false fringe and accessories including cope and cross sheath, which Father Camargo gave.

Father Fray Tomás Murciano de la Cruz provided the following: A damask chasuble with two faces (white and crimson) trimmed with false galloon, with accessories. Cope and frontal of colored satin with fringe like the foregoing.

Linen: Said Father Murciano provided here a cambric amice with fine lace and good ribbons. A fine Brittany alb with good lace. An altar cloth like the alb. Father Fray

out a lock to the sanctuary, and a door of the same description with a wooden key to the convent through the cloister. Near the head wall there is an adobe table at which the priest vests, and on one side on some pieces of beam an old unpainted chest with a key, in which the following are kept.

Vestments: Two old damask chasubles each with two faces (white and crimson) trimmed with narrow silk fringe, with all accessories, which the King, of course, gave. Another old one of white satin without accessories. Another old one of crimson velvet with an orphrey embroidered with images,

Francisco Xavier Dávila has provided two plain amices of fine Brittany. Three purificators. A cotton cincture.

The old things: An old Brittany amice. An alb like it. Another of smooth linen stuff which Father Bermejo provided. An old Rouen altar cloth. A surplice like the altar cloth. A pair of double corporals of Brittany with lace, which Father Bermejo provided. Four more double ones, very old. Another of Brittany, double and without lace, which Father Lezaun provided. Sixteen purificators of various linens. An old white ribbon cincture with silk tassels at the ends. Another of thread and silk. Another of cotton. Four strips of thread and silk which Father Lezaun provided for amices. Several palls for the chalice. Two old palls. Cloth and cap for baptisms.

Silver and other metal: A very old chalice completely enameled and with twelve blue stones. It has a paten and spoon. It is said that the King gave it. Three small vials with the holy oils, which the King gave, and they are kept in a little cedar box with a key. Three reales used for arras, and the King gave them. Two large cruets.

Bronze thurible with incense boat and spoon. Plate for the cruets. A tin-plate processional cross. Shell for baptizing. Two copper rings for arras. Holy-water pot.

Other things: An old missal. A wooden box for altar breads. Three flageolets and two bassoons, all broken now, which Father Fray Angel García gave.

CONVENT

It is on the south, joined to the church on the right side, and forms a square there. In front of the part that faces east there is a little corridor like the one mentioned at Santo Domingo, which runs from one side of the cemetery, with a small stairway in front of the porter's lodge, and ends at the corner of the convent. The porter's lodge faces the cemetery, has a wide opening like the mouth of a portico, and runs like a gallery to the church wall. Its door is opposite the said mouth. It is an ordinary single-leaf one without a lock.

As soon as we enter this, a very long room runs to the left, which (according to the story) was formerly used for a church (together with the present porter's lodge) while the present one was being finished. The inner cell is on a corner and was once the sacristy. There is a good lock and key on the outside door. Beyond the inner cell are another cell and inner cell, and then the kitchen. Between the latter and the side of the building that completes the square there

is a passageway facing south, and it leads to a corral we shall soon see.

The side around this corner consists of two single cells, then a fine storeroom which ends against the head of the sacristy. There is a square cloister, all enclosed and very dark because each side has two very small windows. The corral is very large, with a very high stone-and-mud wall, a large door to the east, and a stable and strawloft near the west wall, now in bad condition, but they serve.

Its Furnishings: A large table, two benches. Three small chairs. Mortar without a pestle.

Its Service: All together, a chief fiscal, four subordinates; ten sacristans and two chief sacristans; ten cooks, six bakers. All take turns weekly. Herders and firewood provided by the pueblo in common, as has been said of other pueblos.

Its Lands and Fruits: The convent has a milpa of poor land upstream on the same side of the river as the pueblo. It ordinarily takes 2 fanegas of wheat, which usually yield 25 to 30. If maize is sown, it takes about 3 almudes, which yield 16 to 20 fanegas. There is another milpa farther down of the same description as the foregoing. On the bank across from the pueblo there is a large kitchen garden. Besides being used for green vegetables, which yield a reasonable crop in quality and quantity, legumes, such as broad beans, chick peas, and vetch are sown at the rate of an almud each, and 8 to 10 fanegas all together harvested. The pueblo sows, etc.

MISSION FATHER

The one who exercises the apostolic ministry at this mission is Father Fray Francisco Xavier Dávila, native of Florida, fifty-eight years of age, thirty-seven in profession, and twenty-six as missionary in the Custody, as follows: Socorro at El Paso, eight months; Zuñi, one year; Santa Ana, ten months; Zuñi again, one year and three months;

Pecos, one month; Zia, five years, during which time he built the church; Pecos again, nine months; Galisteo, one year, nine months; Santa Fe, two months; Zia again, nine months; Nambe, fifteen days; Jémez, nine months; San Felipe to the present, fourteen years. He has general faculties from the Lord [Bishop] don Pedro Tagle.[5]

ADMINISTRATION OF THE MISSION: The same regime as at the mission of Our Father Santo Domingo.

OBVENTIONS AND FIRST FRUITS: Taking the general rule for granted, what obventions there are usually consist of ewes, goats, wool, or sackcloth. The first fruits of grain are almost non-existent for the reason I shall give when I discuss the settlers—only small livestock, which usually amount to 12 little lambs and 3 or 4 kids.

EXPENDITURES: Food consumed by the household is not counted. About an arroba of wax. About 3 jugs of wine. About 300 altar breads, since he celebrates Mass almost every day, and he gives the chief sacristan of Santo Domingo half a fanega of wheat for them.

HOW HE ACQUIRES NECESSITIES: By exchange like the afore-mentioned fathers, without there being any local peculiarity.

CONVENT PROVISIONS: The Reverend Custos Fray Jacobo de Castro assigned the following: 10 fanegas of wheat, 10 of maize, 10 sheep, 6 strings of chile, half a fanega of frijol, half an almud of salt, a jar of ordinary lard. This is confirmed, and I added to it what is recorded in the inventory in accordance with the following

WRIT OF VISITATION

Mission of San Felipe and May 19 of the year 1776. In prosecution of the juridical visitation which our Reverend Father Fray Francisco Atanasio Domínguez, one of the appointed preachers in the Convento Grande of Our Father St. Francis of Mexico City and Commissary Visitor of this Custody for our Very Reverend Father Minister Provincial Fray Isidro Murillo, is making of this Custody, his Reverend Paternity proceeded to examine and did examine this inventory, which agrees with what exists at present. Therefore his Reverend Paternity orders and commands the present mission father, Fray Francisco Xavier Dávila, or his successor, to hand over and receive in accordance with it, and if anything is missing, the incoming friar must report it to the Reverend Custos or his Vice-Custos, who will have the lack supplied.

And since the provisions designated by the Reverend Custos Castro, which are on the recto of this folio 6 in this inventory, are in accordance with what this mission yields, our Reverend Father Commissary Visitor decided and dictated that these be observed and be the provisions which the incoming and outgoing friars must receive and hand over in this mission, adding to the aforesaid provisions two wax candles and a bottle of wine. With regard to all these, the Reverend Custos or his Vice-Custos cannot make any substitution or dispense with anything, but only, indeed, add all they may find necessary for the benefit of the mission and missionary, since that is the intention and will of our Superior Provincial Prelate, who so orders and commands *ratione officii,* and therefore validly for all time.

Our Reverend Father Visitor also orders and commands the aforesaid Father Dávila to erase completely in such a way that it can never be read the note that Father Junco made in this inventory, since it is indecorous, unbefitting our [religious] state, and extremely defamatory of our holy habit. Our Reverend Father Visitor so provided, ordered and signed before me, the undersigned secretary, to which I attest. Fray Francisco Atanasio Domínguez, Commissary Visitor. In my presence, Fray José Palacio, secretary.

5. Pedro Anselmo Sánchez de Tagle, Bishop of Durango, 1749-57.

The parish books were examined, etc., without need for comment in their decrees. The Inventory book is incorporated with that of Patents; the latter was approved as an adjunct to the former. With regard to the parish books, I note that all of them were started in the year 1726 by Father Ceballos. In the year 1727 they were presented by Father Irigoyen, each one consisting of 36 leaves; and it happens that Father Dávila has added enough to the book of Baptisms so that it consists of 109, not including the first and last; not so many to the other two, each of which consists of 71, not including the first and last.

PUEBLO

The location of this pueblo has been sufficiently described some pages back. Therefore I go on to say that it lies to the north in relation to the church and consists of a square plaza, whose tenements, or blocks, all are separate from one another. Below the said plaza and against the river there is another plaza arranged like the foregoing, but the tenement by the river is not complete on the south side. In the vicinity of both plazas on all sides some twelve small houses are scattered. The alignment, etc., such as I have been describing from Santo Domingo on.

ITS LANDS AND FRUITS: The Indians of this pueblo have lands for a league upstream and the same distance downstream on both sides of the Río del Norte. They are not, indeed, very wide, because near this pueblo the hills draw in on the east, and the mesa on the west, against the river. They are of every quality; they are watered by the said river through irrigation ditches not as deep as the ones mentioned before, and they yield many good crops of everything sown in them. There are some small fruit trees like those mentioned before. The natives are Queres, whose native tongue they use; and with regard to everything else, to be brief, they are like those described above. Here is their

CENSUS

95 families with 406 persons

A small settlement of ranchos looks to this mission for spiritual administration. It is about 2 leagues downstream from the mission on the same side of the river. It is on a small sandy level site (it will be better described in a note below) at the foot of some hills. It is called *Upper Bernalillo* to distinguish it from the Bernalillo I mentioned at Sandia. Its farmlands are extremely poor, because the sandy soil does not permit good irrigation ditches, and so the work of cultivation is continually lost, with the same results as have been fully stated with regard to the settlement near Cochiti. The people are of various classes and walks of life. They speak the current Spanish, and here is their

CENSUS

11 families with 63 persons

NOTE

Since it is my intention to convey, as far as possible, a reasonable understanding of what has been learned during my visitation, I find myself obliged to say that the mesa of this San Felipe runs far to the west, joining some broken hills and other small mesas, as far as a sierra they call the Sierra of Cochiti because it is in sight of the pueblo, although it is far from it in the said direction. At the same time this mesa runs about another league and a half to the south, with its lower slope turning west. A cañada opens right here, which runs from west to east and consists of the mesa and a chain of hills on the north side, and of hills alone, which come from very high up, on the south. Through its sandy center runs a river of very bad water and bottom.

This water is very salty and is so scanty and shallow that it hardly covers the horses' hooves. The bottom is so miry that at times it has played very tiresome pranks, wagons having been mired to the axle and other things of this kind. On the south bank of this river, where the said cañada opens, is the settlement I have just described. This river comes from Jémez, as I shall state there, and the missions of Santa Ana, Zia and Jémez are in this cañada, all on the north bank, as I am about to relate.

Santa Ana

One enters the cañada mentioned in the above note by traveling south downstream from San Felipe on the same side of the river, turning to the right. Sometimes [the road runs] at the very foot of the mesa, sometimes on little level sites like nooks along the Río del Norte. The pueblo and mission of Santa Ana is 4 leagues from the foregoing mission. It is all located and established on a little plain that hangs from the skirt of the said mesa, which is about a quarter of a league back of the site to the north. There is another road from San Felipe to this mission, and it is over the mesa. It is very flat and so direct that it is just a little more than 2 leagues long. Of course there are the steep slopes to climb from there and to descend here, and they are very troublesome. Santa Ana is 15 to 16 leagues from Santa Fe via the highway and lies southwest of the villa.

CHURCH

The church[1] is adobe with thick walls, single-naved, with the door to the east. It is 22 varas long from the door to the ascent to the sanctuary, 8 wide, and 7 high. The sanctuary is marked off by two steps made of wrought beams. From there to the center it measures 5 varas, with the same width as the nave. It is as much higher as the clerestory demands. There is a choir loft like those described before. On the right side there are two poor windows with wooden gratings facing south, and one in the choir loft. The roof of the nave consists of thirty wrought beams with small corbels, and the clerestory rests on the length of the one opposite the sanctuary. From here on there are seven beams in the sanctuary like those in the nave.

The main door is squared, has two poorly paneled leaves, no lock except the crossbar, and a wooden frame instead of masonry. It is more than 3 varas high by nearly 3 wide. At the front corners the walls jut out like tower buttresses, but they do not have towers or a balcony, but a sort of mirador which is open at the sides. There is an adobe arch on top, but it has no bell, since the one there was went to pieces. And today the necessary summonses are sounded by a war drum. The cemetery juts out an equal distance from the front corners. It is 30 varas square, with an adobe wall nearly a vara high. It has a wall on two sides only, one on the Gospel side and the other in front, each with a gate. The other side consists of the convent, as I shall explain later. The church floor, bare earth, its interior not very dark, and its adornment as follows.

HIGH ALTAR: Near the middle of the wall an old, untorn canvas 2 varas high and more than a vara wide, with a frame of painted wood and an old curtain of yellow ribbed silk, representing St. Anne in oils,[2] which the King gave. Six small oil paintings on canvas surround this painting, and the images of only two are recognizable. These are our fathers St. Francis and St. Dominic, and the other four are so old that they are indistinguishable. There are also four old prints on paper, too dirty to be recognizable.

There is an adobe gradin below, and on it an old wooden cross with the crucifix

worn off, four old bouquets of colored paper, a tiny carved Lord St. Joseph, and two small brass candlesticks, which the King gave. The altar table is adobe, with an altar stone given by the King, a wooden missal stand, a small bronze bell, and a small buffalo skin carpet on the floor, because there is no dais. There in the sanctuary are two old wooden processional candleholders, turned on a lathe, and six tin-plate candlesticks. In the nave there is an extremely unseemly wooden confessional.

SACRISTY: The sacristy is joined to the church on the Epistle side,[3] running along the wall outside like a small gallery, but it has a good deal of light from two windows facing north. It has a poor door to the sanctuary and another like it to the convent. The latter is in a narrow hall which runs along the whole Epistle wall of the church to below the convent. At the head of the sacristy there is a great adobe table at which the father vests, and on it a large old chest with a key. On the wall above the table hangs a large old oil painting on canvas with a saint who no longer is visible through the dirt. Above it, two crosses of ordinary wood, and an old print on either side of the painting. There is a small adobe pillar in a corner, holding a large earthen bowl for a baptismal font, with a board for a cover. The following are kept in the aforesaid chest.

Vestments: A usable white damask chasuble with accessories, including a damask frontal that serves for white and crimson. Another usable one of crimson damask with all accessories. Another old one of mother-of-pearl Madrid silk with stole and maniple, nothing more. Another old one of blue damask with stole and maniple only. Another old one of white damask like the ones I have mentioned. Another like them of green damask. Another very old one of white damask with only a stole. Another very old one of white lamé, the only accessories being

1. See AB-1634, p. 263, for the history of Santa Ana in the seventeenth century. The Indians of this pueblo settled at the present site during the Reconquest period, and in 1694 it became a visita of Zia. By 1706 a small church had been built. HB, 3: 376. In 1734 Fray Diego Arias de Espinosa rebuilt the church and convent. J. B. Salpointe, *Soldiers of the Cross* (Banning, Calif., 1898), p. 96. This must have been the church described by Domínguez, and it is still in existence. The present measurements of the nave and the number of newer vigas on the old corbels are the same.

2. This painting now hangs on a wooden reredos of later date. It is flanked by two oval paintings of St. John the Baptist and the Carmelite St. John of the Cross.

3. The sacristy no longer exists. The low doorway that formerly led to it from the nave is walled up.

stole, maniple, and frontal. Another almost new purple satin one with stole and maniple only. The donors of all this I have mentioned are not known, but the presumption is that they came from the King and some fathers.

An almost new black chasuble with all accessories. It is said that a father provided them, but his name is not given. Another one of black damask with accessories including cope and cross sheath, which Father Camargo gave. Another new one of green damask with all accessories, trimmed with fine gold galloon. It is said that Father Lezaun provided it.

Linen: A plain new Brittany amice which the Reverend Custos Hinojosa gave. An alb like this amice, with lace at the bottom, which the same reverend gentleman gave. Another almost new plain one of the worst quality Brittany. Two usable Rouen altar cloths. A pair of double corporals of Brittany, plain and worn. Two purificators. A very old finger towel. A new cotton cincture. Another old one of silk. Three good Brittany surplices.

Silver and other metal: Two chalices. Three patens and a spoon; perhaps they are all from the King. A thurible with incense boat and spoon; its donor is not known. Three small vials with the holy oils, which the King gave, and they are in a little cedar box with a key. Shell for baptisms; it is not known who gave it. Seven very old coins with rings, and they are used as arras here and at Zia.

An old holy-water pot. A plate for the cruets, which are glass. A processional cross with a crucifix. Mold for making altar breads, which the King gave.

Other things: A well-worn missal. A worn *Manual* by Osorio. Another by Vetancurt. Four new red wool cassocks for servers, and two more old ones.

CONVENT

The convent is not joined to any side of the church like those we have seen at the missions described earlier, but is located near the front corner of the church on the Epistle side, lying (in relation to it) to the north. It faces south and its corner joins the corner of the church. It forms a square there, and the porter's lodge faces south and stands outside the cemetery. It is a small portico without pillars at the opening, which is 5 varas square and correspondingly high. The door is in the middle of the center wall. It is rather large, has two leaves, and a crossbar for a lock.[4]

As soon as we enter this door, there is a spacious cell on the right, with an inner cell on a corner. Around the corner there is another cell with an inner cell between both rooms, and then the stable runs to the corner. At the corner on the third side there is a beautiful storeroom, privies, and a room on the other corner. On the last side, which

4. Three rooms extend west from the portico to where the sacristy stood. The passageway between them and the north church wall has filled up with dirt and sand, so that one can walk up the incline to the roofs of these rooms and of the portico and also to the church balcony. The cells that formed a square and cloister to the north are gone.

completes the square, there is a kitchen, a room for the metates, and another small room for guests. On the left of the entrance to the porter's lodge there is a tunnellike gallery which leads to the sacristy, as I said when I described it. There is a completely enclosed square cloister, and not very dark since it has three good windows with wooden gratings on each side.

Its Furnishings: A large table. Another small one. Four chairs. Two benches. A small old oil painting on canvas of Our Father St. Francis. Iron lock with its key on the storeroom.

Its Service: The same as at Cochiti, in order not to cause boredom by repetition. Herders and firewood also the same.

Its Lands and Fruits: For better understanding I shall describe them later under the pueblo.

MISSION FATHER

Father Fray Manuel Abadiano exercises the apostolic ministry at this mission. He is a native of the port of Veracruz, fifty-five years of age, thirty-two in profession, thirteen years and some months as a missionary in the Custody, as follows: San Juan at the Junta de los Ríos, two years; Guadalupe at that place, five years, all alone; El Paso, three months; San Ildefonso, six months; Santo Domingo, three months; Acoma, six months; San Juan de los Caballeros, three years, six months; Santa Ana, to now, two years, two months. He holds general faculties, revocable at will, in the diocese of Durango from the Lord [Bishop] Tamarón, and faculty [for the absolution of grave sins] reserved [to superiors] by the synodal decrees.[5]

Administration of the Mission: The usual regime, and I go on to

5. Less than a month later Domínguez wrote that Father Abadiano was so ill that it was not possible for him to carry on missionary work and that the sight of one eye was almost gone. He died at Santa Ana in January, 1777.

His Expenditures: Six pounds of wax a year in all administration; more than a jug of wine. The father gives here a fanega of wheat for the altar breads, and Zia and Jémez get theirs from here without giving any subsidy, nor does the father ask for it, although the father at Jémez did, indeed, once give a little wheat. Food consumed by the household is not counted.

How He Acquires Necessities: By barter as has been said of the others.

Convent Provisions: To establish these on a firmer basis, they have been designated and recorded in the inventory in accordance with the following

WRIT OF VISITATION

Mission of Our Lady Santa Ana, May 18 of the year 1776. In prosecution of the juridical visitation which our Reverend Father Fray Francisco Atanasio Domínguez, one of the appointed preachers in the Convento Grande of Our Father St. Francis of Mexico City and Commissary Visitor of this Custody for our Very Reverend Father Minister Provincial Fray Isidro Murillo, is making of this Custody, his Reverend Paternity proceeded to examine and did examine this inventory, which was made with very little care, since some things are listed which are not there and some of those which exist are not recorded. Therefore our Reverend Father Visitor orders and commands the present missionary, Fray Manuel Abadiano, to record in this same book on the following blank page the valuables, vestments, and other things extant today with the clarity, detail, and length that he saw used in the visitation, in order that it may agree with the one to be remitted to the Province. The said father is also charged to show as much energy as possible in doing this as has been suggested and not to leave the things pertaining to the church in the care of the Indians alone, but, in so far as he is able, to examine and care personally for what pertains to divine worship.

Going on to the provisions of this convent, his Reverend Paternity orders and commands the following: 6 fanegas of wheat, 3 of maize, 3 strings of chile, a small jar of lard, half an almud of salt, 2 wax candles, a bottle of wine. In addition to this, the outgoing friar must hand over and the incoming one receive: Two tables (small and large). Four chairs. Two benches. A small painting of Our Father [St. Francis]. The lock to the storeroom. The belongings of church and sacristy. And if anything is missing, the new friar shall notify the Reverend Custos or his Vice-Custos at once, and they shall carry out this order duly and completely. For this reason they cannot make any dispensations with regard to what has been decided; rather, indeed, add all they may find necessary for the benefit of the mission and missionary, since this is the intention and will of our Superior Provincial Prelate, who so orders and commands *ratione officii* and therefore validly for all time. Our Reverend Father Commissary Visitor so provided, ordered, and signed before me, the undersigned secretary, to which I attest. Fray Francisco Atanasio Domínguez, Commissary Visitor. In my presence, Fray José Palacio, secretary.

The parish books were examined, approved, etc. The book of Patents is new and contains none. It is approved. The Inventory has been seen. All these mentioned are quite new and were provided by Father Salas in the year 1771. He himself began them and Father Abadiano is continuing them up to now. The first three have 100 leaves each; Patents, 120; Inventory, 80.

PUEBLO

In view of the description in the preliminary note it seems to me that I have no more to say. Nevertheless, I again point out that the said cañada is so arid that even though it has the river mentioned, there are no poplar groves, osiers, meadows, or other pleasant things. The view is boxed in by mesas on one side and broken hills on the other. The pueblo itself consists of nine blocks of dwellings, or tenements, like those mentioned at Santo Domingo, for example. They are arranged as follows: There are four on the right side of the church, forming a poor plaza with a street between them and the church. The other five are behind the church, separate from one another and not in any order. Alignment of houses, etc., like the same ones cited.

ITS LANDS AND FRUITS: The Indians of this pueblo have a certain amount of land on both sides of the aforesaid cañada and in some small cañadas there are to the south between the hills, and to the north at the foot of the mesa. They are really dependent on the rains, because in addition to the inadequacy of the river, which sometimes helps irrigation when there is heavy rain, the uneven site, now uphill, now off at a distance, does not permit the formation of pools to quicken and fertilize the plants. This results in completely unfavorable crops. Formerly the convent had a good large kitchen garden with two milpas of the same quality on the same bank where it stands, below near the river, but the river carried them away and they were done for. The Indians suffered the same experience with those they had near it.

Finding themselves in this difficulty, the latter bought a good piece of ground from a citizen who owned it. This is about a league and a half to the east down the highway from Santa [Ana], occupying both banks of the Río del Norte, very extensive to the east and west, and running about a league from north to south. They do most of their farming here today, which is very good, both because of the good and fertile level sites and because of the handy and permanent irrigation offered by the aforesaid river. The purchase was made in the year 1767, and since then they have made use of it as owners, gathering many good harvests of everything they plant.[6] On the east side of the said river the natives have assigned to the convent a plot in which they sow wheat and maize, which amounts to 36 fanegas of wheat and about 20 of maize at most.

6. These are the present Ranchos de Santa Ana where the Indians now live the year round. The old pueblo is used only for the annual feast and for old ceremonials. Exact details of the purchase of the land are not clear. In 1763, Isidro Sánchez, lieutenant of Bernalillo and the pueblos of Jémez, Zia, and Santa Ana, certified that in 1734 Juan Márquez had sold a piece of land belonging to his wife, Magdalena Baca, to the natives of the pueblo of Santa Ana. No legal instrument had been executed because of lack of paper. The date must be incorrect, for the marriage between Juan Márquez and Magdalena Baca, widow, took place at Santa Fe, January 16,

The natives of this pueblo, Queres, whose native tongue they speak, and also Spanish, but brokenly. Their particular customs, the same as those of the other Queres. Here is the

CENSUS

102 families with 384 persons

1735. Márquez murdered his wife in February, 1741. In 1763 Cristóbal and Nereo Montoya, Magdalena's sons by her first husband, Diego Antonio Montoya, brought suit against Antonio Baca for illegal sale of land in the Ancón de Bernalillo to the Indians of Santa Ana. A compromise was reached under which the Indians retained possession of the land. SANM, 2: nos. 570, 572; NMF.

Zia

The pueblo and mission of Nuestra Señora de la Asunción de Zia is up the aforesaid cañada 2 leagues beyond Santa Ana, over rather broken hills and flat places. It is located and established on the middling-level site at the top of a hill of black stone like *tezontle,* but hard. They call it malpaís here.[1] It is about 18 leagues from Santa Fe via the highway, and in relation to this aforesaid villa it lies to the southwest, quarter west-southwest.

CHURCH

The church is adobe with very thick walls, with the door to the east. From the door to the ascent to the sanctuary it is 35 varas long, 8½ wide, and 9 high. The sanctuary is marked off by two steps made of wrought beams, and from there to the center it measures 6 varas, being as wide as the

nave and as much higher as the clerestory demands. Choir loft like those mentioned before. It has four windows with wooden gratings on the Gospel wall, facing south,

1. Literally, "bad land," malpaís is used in the Southwest to refer to lava beds. The New Mexican pronunciation, incorrect but universal, is *malpáis.* *Tezontle* is a kind of porous volcanic rock, frequently used in colonial buildings in Mexico.

and one in the choir. The nave is roofed with forty good corbeled beams, and the clerestory rises along the length of the one facing the sanctuary, whose roof consists of eight beams like the foregoing.[2]

The main door is squared, with a wooden frame instead of masonry, has two badly-made leaves, a crossbar for a lock, and is more than 3 varas high by more than 2 wide. Above it a little belfry in the form of an adobe arch containing a small bell, which the King gave, and it is now in bad condition. The cemetery begins at the front corners of the church and is square, with a mud-and-stone wall and two gates. The floor of the church, bare earth, its interior a well-lighted gallery, and its adornment as follows.

HIGH ALTAR: Near the middle of the wall hangs a large canvas, old but not torn, with a frame of painted wood, representing Our Lady of the Assumption,[3] which the King gave. Above this painting is a small old oil painting on canvas of St. Anthony Abbot. At the sides two small old oil paintings on canvas of St. Matthew and St. Bartholomew. Above each of these two small not very old paintings on buffalo skin of the Immaculate Conception and Our Father St. Francis. There is a wide adobe gradin and on it stand: A small cedar cross with a copper Christus and Mater Dolorosa; two small brass candlesticks, which the King gave. Lacquer Child Jesus, with a small piece of fine linen and three silver nine-rayed aureoles. A small carved Our Lady of the Assumption with a silver crown. A carved St. Anthony of Padua a vara high. Except for what the King gave, some fathers have provided the foregoing.

The altar table is adobe with an altar stone given by the King. A wooden lectern. Three small bronze bells. A dais of well-laid boards with a carpet. The nave is completely empty, for the confessional is always in the

SACRISTY: The sacristy[4] is joined to the church on the Gospel side, running along it from the front almost to the center. It is 12 varas long, 6 wide, and 4 high, with a good roof, good window to the west in the front wall, an ordinary single-leaf door to the church, and another like it to the convent

2. There was a convent of Nuestra Señora de la Asunción at Zia, of which Fray Cristóbal de Quirós was guardian, as early as 1613. *Relación verdadera que el P. P. Fr. Francisco Pérez Guerta de la Orden de San Francisco, guardián del convento de Galisteo, hizo al Rmo. Comisario General de la dicha Orden de la Nueva España de las cosas sucedidas en el Nuevo México . . .*, AGM, Inquisición, tomo 316. The Indians abandoned the pueblo at the time of the Revolt of 1680. Although de Vargas found Zia "in ruins" in October, 1692, and said that it had been "razed" by his predecessor, Don Domingo Jironza Petrís de Cruzate in 1689, the damage cannot have been as great as these terms imply, for he ordered the Indians "to reoccupy their said pueblo, since the walls are strong and in good condition, only lacking the wooden parts, which I ordered them to cut at the time of the next moon." J. M. Espinosa, *First expedition of Vargas, 1692* (Albuquerque, 1940), pp. 176-77. In 1706 Father Alvarez said that the church was "now at a good height." HB, p. 376. Domínguez tells us that Fray Francisco Xavier Dávila built the church during the five years he resided at Zia. The parish records show that Father Dávila was there June to December, 1752, September, 1754, to July, 1759, and November, 1761, to June, 1762. It is doubtful that he built an entirely new church, but extensive repairs, especially re-roofing of adobe structures, often gave those responsible for such the reputation of builders. Alterations have also been made since Domínguez' time, for his measurements vary considerably from those of the present church, there being a difference of about 34 feet in the length of the nave. The present number of closely laid vigas is twenty-two, while Domínguez counted forty. There is now only one large window in the center of the south nave wall, but an old photo (GK, fig. 167) shows this window and a higher walled-up one toward the choir.

3. This very much faded and decayed painting now hangs in the sacristy. For a few years after the Reconquest, the mission registers used the advocation of "Purísima Concepción," but in 1700-01, Fray Francisco de Alvarez again began to use the pre-Revolt title of "Asunción." The other paintings described have disappeared.

4. The sacristy still exists, with the adobe table at the west end and an adobe font in the northeast corner. Two later rooms flank its whole length on the south. None of the rooms of the old convent survive.

through the cloister. In one corner there is an earthen bowl on a small adobe stand for a baptismal font. At the headwall where the window is, there is a great adobe table at which the father vests, and on the wall on either side of the window, two middle-sized old paintings on buffalo skin. On the table an old chest of unpainted wood with a key, and in it the following.

Vestments: An old damask chasuble with two faces (white and crimson) with all accessories, which the King gave. Another old one of crimson damask with stole and maniple only. Another old one of green damask with stole and maniple, nothing more. Another blue one like these mentioned. Two more white ones like these last. Another black one like the same. The donor of all these is not given. An almost new black damask chasuble with accessories, including cope and cross sheath, trimmed with false fringe, which Father Camargo gave. An old humeral veil of crimson damask.

Linen: An old Brittany amice. Another new plain one of Brittany, which Father Burgos just provided. An old Rouen alb. Two more of Brittany. Another of Rouen and ordinary lace, which Father Ruiz provided. A fairly good Rouen altar cloth. Another old one of the same material. Three usable pairs of double corporals of Brittany. Seven purificators. A new cotton cincture, which Father Ruiz provided. Another old one. A finger towel. Two small cloths for the cruets.

Silver and other metal: Chalice with paten and spoon, which the King gave. Three small vials with the holy oils, which the same lord gave, and they are in a small box without a key. A cruet. A small plate. A pyx for the Viaticum.

Tin processional cross. Two incense boats. Three candlesticks. Tin-plate box for altar breads.

Other things: Two old missals. A worn *Manual* by Osorio. Two old ones by Vetancurt. Four small old satin mantles for the Lady in the round on the high altar. An old calamanco curtain for the large painting of Our Lady. Mother-of-pearl shell for baptizing.

CONVENT

The convent is joined to the church on the right side, where it forms a square, full of rooms and extending to the south. It is arranged as follows: The side that faces east has an ugly little portico in the center which serves for a porter's lodge. On the side against the church there is a cell with an inner cell, and there is no key. On the side running to the corner there is a single room, and it is on a corner. Around the corner, facing south, there is a cell with two inner cells, the rear cell being on a corner. Around the corner to the west there is a room for

metates (see Tesuque), then a passage which leads to a corral we shall soon see, and then the kitchen against the sacristy. The latter turns the corner as I have already hinted in its place, and below it there is a beautiful storeroom which stands against the little inner cell mentioned in the beginning.

There is a square cloister, completely enclosed and very dark, for there are two tiny windows on each side. The corral lies to the west. It has a rather large single-leaf door to the passageway and is completely enclosed by a stone-and-mud wall. The stable and strawloft are on the west wall.

ITS FURNISHINGS: A large table. Another small one. Two chairs. Three armless chairs. Two benches. Three metates.

ITS SERVICE: It troubles me to repeat myself, and therefore I refer to Cochiti.

ITS LANDS AND FRUITS: There is a milpa to the west down the hill on which the pueblo stands. If wheat is planted, it takes more than a fanega and a half, which yield about 30 fanegas; and, sown with maize, it takes about 5 almudes, which yield about 20 fanegas. Beyond this milpa there is a small plot for green vegetables, of which some are harvested. On the east and also down the said hill is another milpa like the above in every way. The large amount sown in them and the small crop show that they are not very good, but they help. They are irrigated from the river understood to be in the said cañada. The pueblo does the sowing.

MISSION FATHER

At present he is Father Fray José Burgos, native of Veracruz, forty-five years of age, twenty-eight in profession, twelve and some months as a missionary in the Custody, as follows: Santa Fe, four years; Nambe, nine months; Santa Fe again, two years; Taos, three months; Santa Fe again, a year; Pecos, seven months; Zia, two years; Albuquerque, eleven months; Zia again, and he resides here now, a year and some months. He holds

general faculties in Durango, revocable at will.

ADMINISTRATION OF THE MISSION: The usual one like those mentioned before, to which I refer.

EXPENDITURES: Food consumed by the household is not counted. Wax, about 7 pounds a year. About 2 jugs of wine. About 250 altar breads, which are given by the mission of Santa Ana, as was mentioned there.

HOW HE ACQUIRES NECESSITIES: By exchange, as has been told with regard to the foregoing fathers.

CONVENT PROVISIONS: The Reverend Custos Fray Jacobo de Castro assigned the same provisions here as has been stated elsewhere (San Felipe, for example), but at present this mission is in a very wretched state. Therefore I designated a moderate amount in the inventory, and this is of record in the following

WRIT OF VISITATION

Mission of Zia, May 17 of the year 1776. In prosecution of the juridical visitation which our Reverend Father Fray Francisco Atanasio Domínguez, one of the appointed preachers in the Convento Grande of Our Father St. Francis of Mexico City and Commissary Visitor of this Custody for our Very Reverend Father Minister Provincial Fray Isidro Murillo, is making of this Custody, his Reverend Paternity proceeded to examine and did examine this inventory, which does not agree with what actually exists, because many of the things it records have been used up. Therefore his Reverend Paternity orders and commands the present mission father, Fray José Burgos, to add sufficient paper to this Inventory and record in it anew the valuables of the church and convent and the convent furnishings in the form, manner, detail, and order which he has seen employed in this visitation so that after this fashion it may agree with the one to be remitted to the province. In accordance with the said new inventory, the present missionary will make the transfer, along with the provisions designated in this visitation, which are the following: 5 fanegas of wheat, 3 of maize, 6 strings of chile, half an almud of salt, a jar of ordinary lard, 2 wax candles, a bottle of wine.

Moreover, the outgoing friar must hand over and the newcomer receive two chairs, a large table, another small one, three armless chairs, two benches, three metates, and an old kneading trough. And if any of what has just been mentioned, or anything belonging to church and sacristy, is missing, he shall notify the Reverend Custos or his Vice-Custos at once, and they shall have the lack supplied. And the latter cannot dispense with anything determined here; rather, indeed, add what may be necessary for the benefit of the mission and missionary, since this is the intention and will of our Superior Provincial Prelate, who so orders and commands *ratione officii* and therefore validly for all time. Our Reverend Father Commissary Visitor so provided, ordered, and signed before me, the undersigned secretary, to which I attest. Fray Francisco Atanasio Domínguez, Commissary Visitor. In my presence, Fray José Palacio, secretary.

The parish books were inspected, etc. The two for Baptisms and Burials are new. Father Burgos began them in the year 1772; he himself is continuing them to the present, and each one has 133 leaves. Father Zambrano began the one of Marriages in the year 1727, and Father Burgos is continuing it today. One hundred thirty-four leaves are specified in the decree for this book, of which it now has only twenty-five, many entries being missing. Because this book is in such condition, I ordered Father Burgos to ask the Father Vice-Custos for one of those

that just came. Father Cayuela provided the Inventory in the year 1745.

PUEBLO

Beginning with the note I inserted before Santa Ana and repeated under that pueblo, the aridity, etc., of the missions located in this cañada has been sufficiently stated. Therefore there is no more to be said with regard to this pueblo of Zia than that its houses are of stone like the hill on which it stands. They are arranged and built in nine small tenements, or blocks, of dwellings. One of them is opposite the church and the rest are to the south in the form of two small plazas open at their four corners, and they are to the east and west of each other. Alignment, etc., as has been stated above.

ITS LANDS AND FRUITS: There are some [arable lands] in several small cañadas of the hills to the south, others near the mesa in the north, and the Indians of this pueblo have farm lands for a league upstream and a league downstream along the river of the aforesaid cañada, as wide as fit into it. The land in the small cañadas is always dependent on rain. Those along the river are watered from it when the rains are heavy; when they are not, there are difficulties. In view of this and because the said lands are very sterile, so little is harvested that when things go well, they make the most of that year. The natives are Queres, whose native tongue they speak, and also Spanish, but brokenly. Their particular customs are like those of the Queres mentioned before, and they are included in the following

CENSUS

125 families with 416 persons

Jémez

Two leagues up the cañada from Zia, turning little by little to the right in a northerly direction over an easier road than the earlier ones, which offers a good stretch of plain that falls in a short, gentle slope toward the site of the pueblo, is the pueblo and mission of San Diego de Jémez.[1] It is located and established on a reasonably good site between two sierras (that of Cochiti to the east and that of Jémez to the west) on either side of the pueblo, and the distance to the pueblo from the foothills of each is about half a league. I shall have more to say later. By the highway I have been traveling, Jémez is about 20 leagues from Santa Fe and lies to the west-southwest in relation to the villa.

When I came to this mission for my visitation, I took a road from Cochiti which runs along that chain of hills and wooded mesas mentioned then when I was describing that pueblo. This road is very near, but quite troublesome because of the broken terrain. Therefore I have deliberately abandoned it now in this narrative and am taking the highway. In view, then, of what I have been saying, I visited Jémez first, then Zia, and from there on as follows, and this is very obvious from the dates on the writs of visitation, because here I am following the highway.

CHURCH

The church[2] is adobe with thick walls, single-naved, and facing south. From the door to the ascent to the sanctuary it is 40 varas long, 8 high and 9 wide. The sanctuary is marked off by two steps made of wrought beams, has the same width as the nave, and measures 6 varas to the center, and is as much higher as the clerestory demands. The choir loft like those described before. There are three reasonably good windows with wooden gratings on the Epistle side facing east, and another like them in the choir. The nave has forty-six wrought beams without corbels in its roof, and the

1. The history and locations of the missions in the Jémez district are obscure and complicated. For discussions of the problem, see F. V. Scholes, "Notes on the Jemez missions in the seventeenth century," *El Palacio,* 44 (1938): 61-71, 93-102; GK, pp. 82-85; AB-1634, pp. 274-79; L. B. Bloom and L. B. Mitchell, "The Chapter elections in 1672," NMHR, 13 (1938): 89-109.

clerestory rises along the length of the one facing the sanctuary, whose roof consists of eight beams like those mentioned.

The main door is squared with a wooden frame instead of masonry, two poorly paneled leaves, a crossbar for a lock, and is 3 varas high by more than 2 wide. Above, there is a small adobe belfry containing two small cracked bells, and these came from the King. As we enter the door, the baptistery is

to our left under the choir and extending outside the church walls. It is a tiny room with a window to the south and an ordinary two-leaved door with a padlock, which Father Ruiz provided, to the church.

Near the center of this room there is a small wooden pillar, and on it the baptismal font, which is made of jasper. The said father provided this. It has a board cover, and it resembles the little fonts of holy water which are in very many churches outside this land. On one side there is an adobe table like an altar, on which stands a carved St. John the Baptist, pretty but old and rather small; on the wall a middle-sized painting on buffalo skin in an unpainted wooden frame of Our Lady of Guadalupe,

2. This church and convent were in ruins by 1887-88 when the present church was built on the same site, according to the recollections of old-timers. No traces of the earlier buildings remain.

and it is now old. The cemetery begins at the outside corner of the baptistery, and measures 15 varas square. It ends at the front corner of the church on the Epistle side. Its wall is adobe, more than a vara high, with three gates. The floor of the church is the bare earth, its interior not of the worst, and its adornment as follows.

HIGH ALTAR: Near the middle of the wall hangs a very pretty old oil painting on canvas, 2 varas high by a little more than a vara wide, with a frame of painted wood, of St. Didacus of Alcalá, which the King gave. Above it a small old painting of a crucifixion, on buffalo skin. On one of the side walls, an ordinary very old oil painting of St. Athenogenes. On the other wall, an ordinary old painting of Our Lady of Sorrows, on buffalo skin. The nave of the church is bare, and there is only a poor wooden confessional.

There is a gradin on the high altar, which is adobe, and on it stand a middle-sized cross of wood painted black, two small brass candlesticks, which the King gave. The altar table is adobe with an altar stone which the King gave. Ordinary lectern, two small bronze bells, dais and small carpet. On the Epistle side there is a small table to hold the things necessary for celebrating Mass.

SACRISTY: The sacristy is joined to the church on the Epistle side. It is a new room, of average proportions, which Father Ruiz built. It has a window to the west on one side, an ordinary single-leaf door to the church and another like it, without a key, on the other side leading to the convent through the cloister. At the head of this room there is an adobe table, and the said father put a drawer with a key in it. It serves as a place for the priest to vest, and the following are kept in the drawer.

Vestments: An old damask chasuble with two faces (white and crimson) with the necessary accessories, which the King gave. An almost new black damask chasuble with accessories, including cope and cross sheath, which Father Camargo gave. Another old one of white lamé with no accessories at all. A very old green lamé frontal. A yellow one like it. The King gave these last three items.

Linen: An old Brittany amice without ribbons. A reasonably good Rouen alb with lace. An altar cloth like this alb. Another very old one. A very old Rouen surplice. A reasonably good cotton cincture. An old finger towel. A bag in which the chalice is kept. Two small cloths for the cruets. Six purificators. Two reasonably good double corporals of Brittany.

Silver and other metal: Chalice with paten and spoon, which the King gave. Three small vials with the holy oils, which the said lord gave, and they are kept in a small box with a key. Eleven extremely old coins which the King gave for arras.

A thurible with accessories. Small plate for the cruets. A pitcher for baptizing.

Other things: An extremely old missal, and it does not have our [Franciscan] saints. Two more, in pieces and unbound, from those sent for the Navajo missions. *Manual* by Osorio. Woolen cassock for the sacristan who serves at Mass.

Note: Father Ruiz provided the following: A chasuble, now worn, of mother-of-pearl flowered silk with gold, with accessories consisting of stole, maniple, burse, and pall, all trimmed with fine gold lace and lined with crimson ribbed silk. A new Brittany amice with ribbons and lace. A cloth cincture with the ends trimmed with silk and gold over cardboard. Double corporals

of lawn. A pair of small silver mugs for cruets. A small pewter plate. All this (he says) came to him from the Procurator's office in the year 1769 for a charge of 130 pesos. In addition, two silver rings for arras. A violin and a guitar for the church. He acquired the latter here.

CONVENT

The convent is joined to the church along the Epistle side. It forms a square there between the head of the sacristy and the front corner of the church, extending to the east. It has two stories. The lower floor consists of a porter's lodge near the church wall, and this is a little portico 5 varas square and correspondingly high, with adobe seats around it, an ordinary two-leaved door without a key in the middle of the center wall. There are no pillars at the front, which faces south.

As we enter the porter's lodge, the stairway is on our right in a well in order not to encumber the cloister. And I defer the description of the upper story. Beyond the stair well on the lower floor there is a small cell with its inner cell on a corner. From there some rooms that serve as storerooms run the length of the side around this corner. There is a small room in the corner on the third side, and then a porter's lodge like the foregoing, which faces north, and then the sacristy. The cloister is square and open, with wooden pillars at regular intervals which leave archlike openings. Below there is an adobe railing around the cloister.

The stairway is made of small beams set in the walls of the stair well and ends at a sort of landing. On the right side there is a kind of mirador over the porter's lodge, but it does not face south. Instead it overlooks the flat roof of the cloister, serving as a passage to the choir and an entrance to the roof to reach other rooms that open on it, for there is no upper cloister.

As we ascend and pause at the top, the cell is on our left, with an inner cell on the corner and another inner cell around the corner. Then there are more rooms as far as the next corner, and they open on the roof. The kitchen is around this corner, then a mirador which extends to over the sacristy. This faces north on one side and the south rooms on the other. Father Ruiz has built all the foregoing by rebuilding the older structure.

By the wall of the convent facing east there is a beautiful adobe corral which begins at one corner of the said building and ends at another. Its length is that between the said corners, and it is 15 varas wide. The entrance is a good large two-leaved door without a key, which faces north, and on the east side there are a strawloft, stable, and a little pigsty for fattening pigs.

ITS FURNISHINGS: Two large tables in the cell. Another small one in the inner cell. Two benches. An armless chair. Two cupboards with doors. A table in the kitchen.

ITS SERVICE: All together, a chief fiscal, four subordinates; eight sacristans and the chief sacristan; six little singers; eight cooks, six bakers. They are allotted weekly as follows: One fiscal, two sacristans, a singer, who at the same time is learning to speak Spanish well and to read so that he may serve as interpreter and teacher for the other Indians, two cooks with two little girls to carry water. The pueblo takes turns as caretakers of small livestock, the horse, hens, etc., if there are any. Firewood in winter only, which the community carts, because in summer (this father says) to save carting, charcoal is brought, which two boys make every week in the forest.

ITS LANDS AND FRUITS: There are four plots of very reasonable fertility, although small, among the Indians' milpas. One of them is the most important because it is about 200 varas square. Three serve for wheat and maize, the usual annual harvest being about 60 fanegas of wheat and about 40 of maize. The other plot is used for a kitchen garden, from which they usually get 40 strings of chile, many onions, cabbages, and other miscellaneous vegetables. They are irrigated by the aforesaid river of the cañada mentioned above. The sowing, etc., by the pueblo.

MISSION FATHER

The one who is now exercising the apostolic ministry here is Father Fray Joaquín Ruiz, native of the pueblo of Mixcoac, fifty-one years of age, thirty-five in profession, ten as a missionary in the Custody, as follows: Picuris, two years, four months; Acoma, six months; Jémez, where he is living, seven years, four months. He holds general faculties in Durango from the Lord [Bishop] Tamarón.

ADMINISTRATION OF THE MISSION: The usual regime has special characteristics here in method, for one of the little singers, the one whose turn it is that week as mentioned above, takes the catechism and with it in his hand he recites the doctrine with the others. Moreover, an effort is made to have many married couples who do not know the doctrine—and they are very backward in this respect in spite of repeated efforts—come to recite as well.

OBVENTIONS AND FIRST FRUITS: With regard to the first, what has been fully stated at other missions. With regard to the second, some 3 or 4 fanegas of wheat, the same amount of maize, about 2 fanegas of all kinds of legumes together. No livestock. Nothing at all from the Indians.

EXPENDITURES: Food consumed by the household is not counted. About 5 pounds of wax per year for administration, about 2 jugs of wine, nearly 200 altar breads, and they are given by the mission of Santa Ana as I mentioned there.

HOW HE ACQUIRES NECESSITIES: By exchange as has been stated in full elsewhere with regard to the other fathers.

CONVENT PROVISIONS: These are of record in the inventory of this mission, in which I inserted the following detailed

WRIT OF VISITATION

San Diego de Jémez and May 15 of the year 1776. In prosecution of the juridical visitation which our Reverend Father Fray Francisco Atanasio Domínguez, one of the appointed preachers in the Convento Grande of Our Father St. Francis of Mexico City and Commissary Visitor of this Custody for our Very Reverend Father Minister Provincial Fray Isidro Murillo, is making of this Custody, he proceeded to examine and did examine this inventory, which he pronounced accurate and legal, since it is in agreement with what actually exists and was seen, examined, and inspected during this visitation. He therefore gave many thanks to the present mission father, Fray Joaquín Ruiz, as well as for the care, solicitude, and attention which he has paid to the convent building and the neatness and cleanliness with which he keeps the things pertaining to divine worship, and for the teaching and good management he uses with his Indians, whom he has reduced to a Christian and civilized way of life in so far as their capacity makes this possible.

His Reverend Paternity was also very gratified and pleased to see the little teachers of the catechism so learned and well instructed in Christian doctrine, reading, singing, and the manner of assisting at Mass, as well as [to observe] their decorum and modesty, for they resemble novices. For all this he gave many thanks to God and charged Father Ruiz to persevere and to continue the fine regime which he has observed up to now.

And proceeding to the provisions this convent must have, his Reverend Paternity orders and commands that these be as follows: 2½ fanegas of wheat, the same amount of maize, 5 strings of chile, half an almud of salt, 4 cuartillos of lard, 2 wax candles, 1 bottle of wine. In addition, the outgoing friar must hand over and the newcomer receive the convent furnishings recorded in this inventory, as well as the things belonging to church and sacristy. And if anything ordered to this point is missing, the Reverend Custos or his Vice-Custos shall be notified at once so that the lack may be made up duly and completely, putting this into effect. Therefore they cannot dispense with anything designated by us, since that is the intention and will of our Superior Provincial Prelate, who so orders and commands *ratione officii* and therefore validly for all time.

And inasmuch as our Reverend Father Visitor has observed that the regime and administrative system which Father Ruiz follows in this mission is the best and most suited to the guidance and instruction of the Indians, his Reverend Paternity orders and commands the friar who may come to serve at this mission in future, whatever his qualifications, under formal precept of holy obedience, to observe, keep, and follow the same method. A description of this will be given to the Reverend Custos, or his Vice-Custos, and to the Provincial, so that they may see to it that it is always observed and maintained, imposing penalties at their discretion on any friar who is remiss. And in order that no one may allege ignorance, Father Ruiz is ordered to write down on a sheet of paper a complete account of the regimen he uses with the Indians, large and small, the hours for recitation, and, in short, everything that the father and Indians were seen to do during the visitation. The said paper shall be affixed to a small board and be kept in the cell for the next friar so that he may maintain the system with the utmost punctiliousness.[3] His Reverend Paternity so ordered, commanded, and signed before me, the undersigned secretary, to which I attest. Fray Francisco Atanasio Domínguez, Commissary Visitor. In my presence, Fray José Palacio, secretary.

The parish books were examined; their entries were approved. And since they are

___

3. See pp. 308-15 *infra*.

nearly finished, Father Ruiz has been ordered by the decrees recorded in them to take prompt measures to provide new books, remitting the old ones to the archive. Father Fray Carlos Delgado began them all in the year 1720 and Father Ruiz is continuing them at present. None of them have the foliation mentioned in their decrees, many entries being missing, and no one knows what happened. The book of Patents is incorporated with the Inventory, and Father Ruiz provided them both in the year 1771.

PUEBLO

The floor of the cañada I have been taking from Santa Ana to this place is not so arid and barren here as the lower part of it I described. On the contrary, indeed, it is fairly pleasant. The view below spreads widely to the south, and higher up there is something to be seen to the north as well as on either side, for at this place the aforesaid cañada turns to the north (see the beginning of the description of this mission). The aforesaid site is almost oval east and west, and the pueblo is located near the center. It all stands behind the church and convent, extending to the north. It consists of five blocks, or tenements, all of adobe, and two of them stand at the ends, one on the east and the other on the west, because the other three run across between them, one behind the other, opposite the convent; and there are very good streets between them. Alignment, etc. like others I have mentioned.

The river I began mentioning lower down does not have such bad water and bottom as might be inferred from how bad both things are farther downstream. The said river has its source very high above the pueblo and is comprised of several springs that flow into two small canyons in the east-northeast and northwest, through each of which a little brook comes, and these are the ones that join to form the river of these pueblos. In the vicinity, higher up, at various short distances there are ruins of old pueblos. One of them is the former site of this mission, and even today it keeps the name of the old pueblo of San Diego.

ITS LANDS AND FRUITS: The Indians have very good lands for a league upstream and another league downstream on both sides of the river that flows through the cañada. Watered by the said river through adequate irrigation ditches, they produce very good and abundant crops of everything sown in them. Very many orchards of fruit trees like those I have mentioned elsewhere have been planted in the little canyons I spoke of above. As a result, this pueblo is much frequented by summer visitors. At the same time, some milpas are scattered through one of the said canyons because it is larger than the other. And all these are watered by the little streams that run through them.

The natives of this pueblo are called Jémez, like their town. The language they use (in this respect, but in no other, they conform with Pecos) also is called Jémez. It is very different from all the other languages of these regions, and its pronunciation is closed, almost through clenched teeth. They also differ greatly from the others in their characteristic customs, and what has been said about the regime imposed by the present father indicates that a certain rebelliousness demands great firmness. They speak Spanish in the manner described elsewhere, but not all of them use it, because they do not wish to. The following includes them.

CENSUS

102 families with 345 persons

This mission has charge of the administration of a very small settlement of ranchos, which is to the east-northeast in relation to the pueblo, a little way up one of the aforesaid small canyons. It is more than 2 leagues from the mission. It is called *Vallecito* and lies almost at the foot of the sierra of Cochiti, which is east of here.[4] They have fairly reasonable farmlands, watered by a stream that rises in the said sierra and flows through one of the canyons already mentioned. They do not produce as much as they might, because their owners are so poor that they do not have the strength to cultivate them well. These owners are of all classes and are all their own masters. They speak the local Spanish. Here is their

4. In 1768 Governor Mendinueta made a grant to six families at this place of "San José," which was called "Santo Toribio" three months later when actual possession was given on September 2, 1768. (1870 copy of Spanish grant no. 12, which is missing from SANM). Mendinueta ordered the settlement made in the form of an enclosed plaza as protection against the Navajos. A matrimonial investigation of 1778 refers to the place as "Santo Toribio del Vallecito," and to this day it is known as Vallecito de Santo Toribio.

CENSUS

11 families with 63 persons

Laguna

From Jémez to the pueblo and mission of Señor San José de la Laguna, a very twisting road runs 15 good leagues to the south across little hills in some places, cañadas (between mesas), some short, some long, and some of which are traveled from one end to another while others are crossed, and over long stretches of plain. By a lower and more direct road than the one I am describing (this one runs between missions) it is 30 leagues from Santa Fe and lies to the southwest of the villa, almost in a straight line with Albuquerque.

The pueblo and mission stand on the flat top of a little hill, which, spreading out a good deal toward the road I am taking from Jémez to this place, consists on the whole south slope of small whitish stones, very soft and sandy. The said little hill offers a reasonably good view, as we shall see later. For future reference I now point out that everything built here is made of the stone from this hill and mud. I also note that these three missions which follow—Laguna, Acoma, and Zuñi—were visited after my return from my journey to the new discovery,[1] and so I visited them in reverse order from that in which I am describing them; that is, Zuñi, Acoma, and Laguna.

CHURCH

The church[2] is stone with not very thick walls, single-naved, facing due east. From the door to the ascent to the sanctuary it is 25 varas long, 7 wide, and 7 high. The sanctuary is marked off by five steps made of wrought beams and measures 5 varas to the center, with the same width as the nave, and it is as much higher as the clerestory demands. Choir loft in the usual place, like those mentioned before. On the Gospel side there are two poor windows with wooden gratings facing south, and another in the choir facing east.

The roof of the nave consists of thirty wrought beams without corbels, and the clerestory rises along the length of the one opposite the sanctuary, the roof of which consists of seven beams like those mentioned. The main door is squared, with a wooden frame instead of masonry, two-leaved, small and narrow, and with no lock except the crossbar. Above it there is a triangular belfry containing two small bells, which the King gave, and they are entirely good. As we enter the main door, on our right under the choir, outside the walls of the church, is a small room like an alcove, which serves for the baptistery. It has a very small window to the east and a completely open doorway to the church. In the middle of this little room stands a small pillar hollowed out for a drain, and on it an earthen bowl for a baptismal font, covered with a board.

The cemetery, as seen from the door of the church to the front, is very short in length and long in width, for it is 9 varas long from the door to the front and 30 varas wide from beginning to end. Its wall begins at the outside corner of the baptistery and, turning a corner in the manner stated, it continues to join the upper corner above the convent, jutting out at the upper end. The foregoing shows that the porter's lodge and convent face the cemetery. The floor of the church, bare earth, its interior very gloomy, and its furnishings as follows.

HIGH ALTAR: Near the middle of the wall is a middle-sized wooden canopy, all painted blue, and in the center a large oil painting on canvas, with a wooden frame, of Lord St. Joseph, which the King gave. There is a stone gradin. It is wide and there are three small gradins of the same material above it, ascending like a throne, and the said canopy stands on the last one. On the middle step there is a medium-sized carved crucifix, and on the lower one a tabernacle completely painted in colors, as if in tempera. It has no key, and the single-leaf door has an octagonal mirror.

On the gradin are two brass candlesticks, which the King gave, with an altar card be-

1. His expedition into Utah with Fray Silvestre Vélez de Escalante.

2. According to Fray Juan Sanz de Lezaun, the mission of San José de la Laguna was founded by Fray Antonio Miranda, who "went throughout all the land, even to the most rugged sierras, collecting the wandering sheep of numerous nations. . . . They spoke many languages, but have all learned that of the Queres, forgetting their native tongues." HB, 3: 469. Hodge (AB-1634, pp. 287-88) suggests "that the nucleus of the Laguna population consisted of Queres who had fled to the Hopi country (Tusayán) during the great revolt or earlier. This is based on the fact that Kawaíka, the native name of Laguna, is identical with that of a village, now in ruins, not far from Awátovi, a former pueblo of the Hopi in northeastern Arizona." Bancroft, followed by later authors, states that about 1697 "the rebel Queres of Cieneguilla, Santo Domingo, and Cochiti formed a new pueblo four leagues north of Acoma, on the stream called Cubero." H. H. Bancroft, *History of Arizona and New Mexico* (San Francisco, 1890), p. 221. On July 4, 1699, this pueblo made formal submission to Governor Cubero and was named San José de la Laguna. A number of Queres Indians from other pueblos had taken refuge at Acoma during the revolt of 1696. This group began to settle at Laguna toward the end of the following year and formed part of the population of the mission established in 1699. In 1706 a church, which was administered from Acoma by Fray Antonio de Miranda, was under construction at the new pueblo. HB, 3: 376. This is probably the small church described by Tamarón in 1760 (AT, p. 67) and Domínguez in 1776. It is still in existence, but extensive repairs have been made through the years.

tween them. The altar table is stone, with an altar stone which the King gave, ordinary lectern, two small bronze bells, a well-made board dais, a small carpet dyed with cochineal.

NAVE: On the Epistle side a little below the sanctuary is an altar to Jesús Nazareno, whose image is a middle-sized one in the round with a white linen tunic. On either side hang two small old oil paintings on buffalo skin, and there is a very old yellow curtain at the back. The stone altar table is bare. Opposite this altar, over the door to the sacristy, hangs an old painting on buffalo skin. Down from this door are a bench and then a poor wooden confessional.

The canopy, but not the steps, the tabernacle, but not the mirror, the crucifix and the Jesús Nazareno were made and provided by Father Fray Andrés García, who is also responsible for the altar to Jesús [Nazareno]. The mission had the other things before, dating from the time when Father Padilla was missionary here.

SACRISTY: The sacristy is joined to the church on the right side, and it is a room 5 varas long, 4 wide, and 3 high, with round beams in the ceiling. It has a window on the west side, a narrow entrance without a door to the church, and a single-leaf door without a key to the convent through the cloister. At the head of the room there is a large wooden table which has a drawer with a key, and above it on the wall hangs a large old painting of Lord St. Joseph on buffalo skin. The following are kept in the drawer mentioned.

Vestments: An old damask chasuble, which the King gave, with two faces (white and crimson), the only accessory of which is the frontal. Another like it of white damask with the orphrey of crimson velvet, with accessories except for frontal; they say that Father Miranda provided it. Another old one of mother-of-pearl damask with stole and maniple only. Another almost new one of black damask with accessories including cope and cross sheath, which Father Camargo gave.

Linen: A worn amice of plain Brittany. An alb to match. Two altar cloths of Brabant linen with narrow lace. Two worn pairs of Brittany double corporals. A finger towel. A worn surplice of Brabant linen. Two old thread-and-silk cinctures. Three palls. Eight purificators.

Silver and other metal: Chalice with paten and spoon, which the King gave. Three small vials with the holy oils, which the King gave, and they are in a little cedar box with a key. Thirteen small old coins, which the King gave. A silver reliquary with four Bohemian stones, which Don Pedro Pino gave, and it serves as a monstrance at Corpus Christi, for which purpose it has a crystal base.

Thurible without accessories. Small plate for the ordinary cruets, which are broken. Tin-plate box for altar breads. Two rings for arras.

Other things: A small altar stone. A fairly good missal. Another old one. *Manual* by Osorio. An earthenware cup for an incense boat, and a spoon of the same. A small gourd cup for baptizing. Four old woolen cassocks for the sacristans.

CONVENT

In view of what I said when I discussed the cemetery, it is obvious that the convent is joined to the church on the right side, where it forms a square extending to the south. It is arranged as follows: Porter's lodge, which faces east and consists of a small portico, without pillars in front since it is very small. Stone-and-mud seats around it, and in the middle of the center wall, an ordinary single-leaf door with a latch which Father Claramonte provided. On our right as we enter, there is a little stair well with a stone staircase that leads to the choir. On our left there is a cell with its inner cell on a corner. There are two rooms around the corner and then a passageway which faces west and leads to the corral, which we shall see later. Around the corner from here there is a beautiful storeroom and then the sacristy. Father Claramonte rebuilt all that has been mentioned in the year 1766, for when he came to this mission, he found everything in bad shape, and so he installed many doors and windows.

There is a small square cloister, and although it is walled in, it is light, for when the said father rebuilt it, he arranged a beautiful window on each side. He also made a corral with a high stone-and-mud wall, and, leaving a fine two-leaved door with a latch to the south, sheltered by a portico inside, he fitted in a stable and strawloft on the north side. Much of this was accomplished at the cost of maize and wheat which he gave to poor people who came to beg.

This convent has a small upper story built by the Father Ex-Lector Fray Joaquín Rodríguez, and the approach to it is this: As we enter the porter's lodge and go to the left, there is a small stairway in the corner of the cloister which comes out (with no protecting roof above it) on the flat roof. It leads to the cell, which overlooks the cemetery to the east, and, with its two inner cells, runs to join the church over the porter's lodge. And they are very pretty rooms. With regard to the rest of the upper level, the flat roof over the lower rooms has nothing on it.

ITS FURNISHINGS: A large table. Another small one. Three armless chairs. Father Claramonte provided all this. A bench. A chair; Father Cuellar provided this.

ITS SERVICE: All together, a chief fiscal, three subordinates; eight sacristans and two chief sacristans; eight cooks, four bakers. The weekly allotment is: one fiscal, two sacristans, two cooks with two little girls to carry water, two bakers. Caretakers for the horse, for the pigs, if there are any, and for the little hencoop, and nothing more. Firewood, the pueblo in general.

ITS LANDS AND FRUITS: About half a league west of the pueblo at a place, or rancho, they call Santa Ana, belonging to the pueblo, there is a beautiful milpa of good level ground which is always sown with 3 fanegas of wheat, which usually yield 50 at most. It is watered by a brook that flows near it, which I shall describe at my leisure later. A few years ago they plowed up two good pieces near there for legumes and maize, but only in a year when it rains a good deal and the river is full of water does it irrigate the said plots. In relation to the first, they are uphill, and for that reason the river does not rise high enough to water them if the current is not running strong. Therefore what is sown there is always being lost. The pueblo does the sowing, etc.

Below the pueblo's hill, about two musket shots to the south, the convent has a kitchen garden, which yields something. There are some small peach trees in it, which Father Padilla planted, and it is all watered from the said river.

MISSION FATHER

Father Fray Patricio Cuellar exercises the apostolic ministry at this pueblo. He is a native of Tulancingo, forty-nine years of age, twenty-six in profession, ten as a missionary in the Custody, as follows: Santa Fe, three months; Nambe, four months; Santa Fe again, eight years; Galisteo, two months; Tesuque, nearly a year; Laguna, where he now is, five months. He holds general faculties in Durango, revocable at will.

ADMINISTRATION OF THE MISSION: The usual regime, to which I refer, for there is no local characteristic.

EXPENDITURES: Food consumed by the household is not counted. Annually, in administration, about 5 pounds of wax, nearly 2 jugs of wine, about 200 altar breads, which are brought from Acoma without expense to the father.

HOW HE ACQUIRES NECESSITIES: The father of this mission does not have as much trouble as those mentioned before, because here (the same is true of Acoma and Zuñi) the father is given a sheep a week, and frijoles, broad beans, eggs, lard, salt, flour, a tallow candle, and milk in the summer every day. The fiscal for the week collects all this from the pueblo, since he knows the order of the houses.

NOTE

I visited this mission on December 22 of last year, 1776. I did not record a writ of visitation there, because I did not think it necessary. But with regard to convent provisions, Father Cuellar has been instructed that these should be: 4 fanegas of wheat, 4 of maize, a jar of lard, a bottle of wine, 2 wax candles.

The parish books were inspected and since they are nearly full, I ordered Father Cuellar to apply to the Father Vice-Custos for three new ones out of those that came from the Province, remitting the old ones to the archive. I also ordered him to remit the very old ones of Inventory and Patents to the same place. And in order that there might be new ones for this purpose at this mission and another for Edicts of the Lord Bishop, I gave sufficient paper, and they have been authorized by me. The old parish books lack many old entries.

PUEBLO

In order to make its location clear, I state that a very wide cañada comes from the west. As it runs to the east, there are others on either side (although they are narrow and short). It is formed by a chain of mesas on the north, and on the south by mesas higher up, which, near the pueblo and even below it, end in broken, wooded hills. It keeps spreading out a good deal on both sides almost in a circle until it starts closing in again below the pueblo. And at this point the mesas on the north side turn toward it, as if they were going to form another cañada. There below the pueblo the broken hills on the south turn to the east where the circle seems to close, and little by little they diminish into a plain.

The outspread little hill on which the pueblo stands is almost in the center of the aforesaid circle. To the south it overlooks a sandy plain which comes from the foot of the hills and mesas visible in this direction; to the east the hills that run by it until they taper off; on the north the mesas; on the west up the cañada for a long distance to the Zuñi Sierra. The upper part of the cañada is as follows: A small river of very good water comes from very high up in it, flowing almost through the middle (when we travel to Zuñi, I will describe its source and other things). It flows in this way for about 4 leagues. About 2 leagues before Laguna it begins to be alkaline, both because some springs of bad water join it and because the terrain is alkaline.

Now salty, it flows down the cañada, and about a quarter of a league before it reaches the pueblo it empties into a beautiful lake, which is on the north side of the cañada near the mesas. It is almost round and very large, and is about 700 varas from the pueblo or a little more. Those who have observed this lake say that its bottom is more or less like a funnel and that its depth at the center is unknown, for since there are no canoes, it is not possible to go out to the middle to take soundings. Its funnellike contour is known because during periods of great drought the water has gone down so much (the inference from this is that it is not a spring but is formed by the river flowing into this hollow) that the pebbly bed slopes down such a long way that it must measure about 40 varas in depth.

To return to the river, after leaving water in the lake, it flows out on the south side again and, after running a short distance to the east, rather near the pueblo it falls musically about 300 varas. Then it continues to the east, and its course from there on turns in accordance with what has been said above, and it keeps on twisting, but always in an easterly direction. But it never reaches the Río del Norte, because in the long distance between them (it must be about 15 leagues) the little water it carries disappears. Humans do not drink from it (the animals do) but from a very delicious spring which has a good location among the rocks where the river falls, as I have just said. There are no poplar groves or anything of the kind as there are along other rivers. There are bulrushes like those in Mexico on one shore of the lake.

The pueblo itself consists of seven tenements, or blocks, of dwellings, four of which form two intricate little plazas in full view of the church and convent. Of the other three, one is next to the convent and extends to the south, facing east; another is farther down facing the plain to the south; and the third is behind the little plazas more or less to the north, rather far from the convent and facing south. The entrances to the dwellings are ladders and *cois*, but the interiors are always very clean and all the exterior walls are whitewashed so that the pueblo can be seen from afar on any road because it is so white.

ITS LANDS AND FRUITS: There are some irrigated lands and some dependent on the rains. The irrigated lands begin a league higher upstream on both sides of the river. They are not very wide because they cannot be. There are similar lands for a league downstream below the pueblo throughout the cañada where it turns to the north. Some of those dependent on rain are on little patches of the sandy plain which lies to the north; there are others in other directions, to be brief. It is understood that the first ones I mentioned above get water from the river; the others, of course, from the clouds.

North of the pueblo is a place called Cebolleta, which is about 2½ leagues from the pueblo.[3] The Indians have many good farmlands there, which they irrigate from two streams which rise in the Sierra de Navajo. Many good crops of everything sown in them are gathered from all together, in accordance with what I have said. The Indians also have many small peach trees scattered in various directions.

The natives of this pueblo are Queres, whose native tongue they speak. Very few use Spanish, and these in the way already described in other cases. With regard to their customs, I say that they are humble, timid, and obedient. Here is their

CENSUS

178 families with 699 persons

This mission has no settlement to administer, but the alcalde mayor and his family live in the pueblo. Moreover, two families of poor people, so destitute that they keep

3. See H. W. Kelly, "Franciscan Missions of New Mexico, 1740-1760," NMHR, 16 (1941): 60-67, for a summary of the history of the short-lived Navajo missions at Cebolleta and Encinal founded by Father Menchero in 1746. The Spanish settlement did not come into existence until 1804-08, its first people coming from the Belén area. SANM, 1: nos. 206, 207.

themselves alive by serving the Indians, are hangers-on at the pueblo. For this reason it is obvious that the obventions and first fruits collected from these families consist of the first fruit paid by the magistrate alone, which amounts to a fanega of all kinds of grain together, a little lamb, and a small calf.[4] The others, nothing, because

of their poverty. And this note includes them all:

3 families with 15 persons

4. This is a rare instance in which the Spanish alcaldes were allowed to reside in the pueblo. Bernabé Baca, married to Margarita Mata, was alcalde mayor of Acoma and Laguna in the third decade of the century and was most unpopular with the Indians and missionaries. He was followed by his son, Baltasar Baca, married to Manuela Rael de Aguilar, who was even more unpopular. A relative, Manuel Baca, married to Feliciana Chávez, was the alcalde mayor c. 1756-70. The Baltasar Baca who was making trouble for the friars and Indians in 1772-76 may have been the same Baltasar who had been alcalde earlier, or perhaps a younger man of the same name and family. He was succeeded by Pedro José Pino, as Domínguez notes later.

Acoma

South of Laguna, crossing the sandy plain that lies in this direction, then the wooded hills mentioned there, and then taking a long cañada with mesas on either side which runs from south to north, at a distance of 4 leagues over the above terrain one finds the pueblo and mission of San Esteban de Acoma. It is located and established on the flat top of a mesa 80 to 100 varas high. This resembles a cliff, and for this reason they call it the Peñol of Acoma. The ascent to this is a sandy and very difficult slope (there are many footpaths leading up, which only the Indians manage with skill). It begins on the west side of the mesa, ascends almost halfway, and from there on makes a number of boxed-in turns, so difficult that in some places they have made wide steps so that the pack animals may ascend with comparative ease.

The buildings are at the top of the said mesa, almost in the center, and they resemble the little shrine to St. Michael on the hill of Guadalupe in Mexico. The said mesa stands in the middle of the plain, which has some cañadas nearby in the south, east, north, and northwest. To the west and southwest a chain of mesas runs a long distance. This mesa has some crags around it, some of which rise to a third of its height and others halfway up, and there are some corrals for livestock on them, to which they climb by little paths which the Indians have made. In other places there are such horrible precipices that it is not possible to look over them for fear of the steep drop. This Acoma is 34 good leagues from Santa Fe via the highway and lies to the southwest of this villa.

Although I have not spent so much time at the beginning of my description of other missions as I have here, it is because there is no comparison with the situation here. The little I have said to begin with at those places indicates in brief to the judicious reader the nature of the buildings and transportation in relation to the nearby rivers and easy transportation of all necessities. The contrary is true here, for there is not even a brook, earth to make adobes, or a good cart road. Therefore it is necessary to prevent any preconception in order to achieve even a confused notion of this place. This makes what the Indians have built here of adobes with perfection, strength, and grandeur, at the expense of their own backs, worthy of admiration.

CHURCH

This church[1] was inaugurated in the year 1725. Father Miranda (they say) built it,

and it is of good adobe with walls nearly 2 varas thick. The main door faces east, and from there to the ascent to the sanctuary it is 36 varas long, 12 wide, and 14 high up to the bed molding. Six steps of wrought beams form the ascent to the sanctuary, which measures 6 varas from the last step to the center, with the same width as the nave. The height is the same because there is no clerestory. The choir loft is in the usual place, occupies the width of the nave, and projects 5 long varas into the church. It is supported by fourteen wrought beams

1. The exact date of the building of the Acoma church is not known, but the weight of the evidence indicates that the greater part of the structure described by Domínguez, and therefore of the present church, dates from the seventeenth century. The Acoma Indians were not converted until some years after the Spanish conquest of New Mexico, and in 1621 the pueblo was still a pagan refuge for malcontents from other pueblos where missions had been established. F. V. Scholes, *Church and State in New Mexico 1610-1650* (Albuquerque, 1937), p. 79. In the autumn of that year Fray Jerónimo de Zárate Salmerón, who claimed to be the first to undertake effective missionary work at Acoma, arrived in New Mexico. F. V. Scholes and L. B. Bloom, "Friar personnel and mission chronology," NMHR 20 (1945): 62. According to Zárate Salmerón (DHM, p. 4) he "alone conquered and pacified the Peñol of Acoma, which was at war with the Spaniards." Apparently this was after he had founded two missions at Jémez, the first at San José de Giusewa in the winter of 1621-22, and later the "pueblo de la Congregación," at or near the present mission of San Diego. The latter was abandoned temporarily in 1623, but it is not clear whether missionary work at San José was also interrupted. It is possible, however, that this was the period when Zárate Salmerón turned his attention to the Queres pueblos of Zia, Santa Ana, and Acoma. He makes an ambiguous statement about building "churches and convents," but we have no evidence that he did so at Acoma, nor do we know how long he spent there or how much he really accomplished. He returned to New Spain in the autumn of 1626 and was again at San José before that. F. V. Scholes, "Notes on the Jemez missions," *El Palacio*, 44 (1938): 61-71. In 1629 Fray Juan Ramírez renewed the missionary effort at Acoma and served for many years. Presumably the church was built under his auspices. Although Hodge (AB-1634, p. 287) believes that he built a church slightly to the north of the present edifice, he gives no convincing evidence. There are traces of foundations for a building running north and south at right angles to the present church. Tradition at the pueblo has it that after this work was started, it was abandoned and the church was built facing east. A 1664 copy of an earlier document mentions the extremely beautiful church on the

which rest on a strong cross timber imbedded in the side walls with corbels. Below, two pillars of carved wood reinforce it, and their position results in a semblance of three arches.

On the right side there are three beautiful windows with wooden gratings facing south, and one in the choir facing east. The whole roof consists of fifty well wrought and corbeled beams. The main door is squared, with a strong wooden frame instead of masonry, two well-paneled leaves, no lock except the crossbar, and is 4 varas high by 2½

wide. The tower buttresses jut out from the front corners and extend toward the center to hold two small towers, one on each. The one on the right contains two small bells which the King gave, and they are cracked. There is no balcony between them as in other places.

When we enter the main door, the entrance to the baptistery is under the choir to our left.[2] It is outside the church wall and is a very spacious room with a window to the east, a door with two completely grated leaves to the church, an ordinary one without a lock. In the center stands a small wooden pillar, hollowed out for a drain, with a large earthen bowl on top for a baptismal font, covered with a board. The cemetery is enclosed by a stone-and-mud wall. It begins at the corner of the baptistery, where it juts out like a head wall, and continues around to the front corner on the Epistle side. It is 40 varas square. The wall is more than a vara high and has two gates, one on each side. The dead are buried in it, for it has been deliberately terraced up with earth because of the steepness of the slope in relation to the area in varas. There are no burials in the church because the rock prevents this, and in order to cover it, it was filled with earth to a depth of about half a vara. This is the church floor. The interior is pleasant, although bare, and the adornment is as follows.

HIGH ALTAR: The whole wall is covered, as we shall see. Beginning with the gradin, I state that it is adobe and wide. There are

---

Peñol of Acoma. The date of the original is not given, but F. V. Scholes, who published a translation of it in 1929 ("Documents for the history of the New Mexican missions in the seventeenth century," NMHR, 4: 45-58), informs us that although he then assumed that this copy (in AGI, Aud. de México, leg. 306) was a supplement to the Zárate Salmerón *Relaciones,* further research and internal evidence in the document have led him to believe that this statement dates from *c.* 1641. In any case it is clear that a noteworthy building was erected sometime after 1629 and before 1641.

In 1672 the guardian of Acoma, Fray Lucas Maldonado Olasqueaín, considered his "church, convent, sacristy, and cemetery, one of the best there are in this kingdom." F. V. Scholes and E. B. Adams, "Inventories of church furnishings in some of the New Mexico missions, 1672," *Dargan Historical Essays* (Albuquerque, 1952), p. 34. This cannot have suffered great damage in the Pueblo Revolt of 1680, for when Acoma surrendered to de Vargas on November 4, 1692, he "went to inspect their holy temple, which is dedicated to St. Stephen. I found it to be very large, and it seemed to me even larger than the monastery of San Francisco, at that court [Mexico City], both in the length of the said church and in the height of its walls, which are almost a vara and a half thick, and they stand firm with the exception of the holes which were made in breaking the windows and the skylights of the said church." J. M. Espinosa, *First Expedition of Vargas, 1692* (Albuquerque, 1940), p. 194. Acoma joined in the revolt of 1696 and finally offered to make peace in 1698, making formal submission in July, 1698.

In 1700, Fray Antonio Miranda became minister of Acoma and Laguna and was at Acoma in 1706 when Father Alvarez made his usual statement: "The church is being built." HB, 3: 376. This must be taken to mean that the church was being repaired, for it is highly unlikely that the imposing

edifice described by de Vargas had been seriously damaged in the troubles of the 1690's after surviving the 1680 Revolt. But this does explain Domínguez' information that Father Miranda built the church. We cannot clarify his ambiguous statement that it was inaugurated in 1725. The great church at Acoma probably incorporates more of the original structure than any of the surviving seventeenth-century churches in New Mexico. In this sense, although it was not built as early as Isleta, it has a strong claim to consideration as the "oldest church."

2. The baptistery no longer exists, but the walled-up door is still visible.

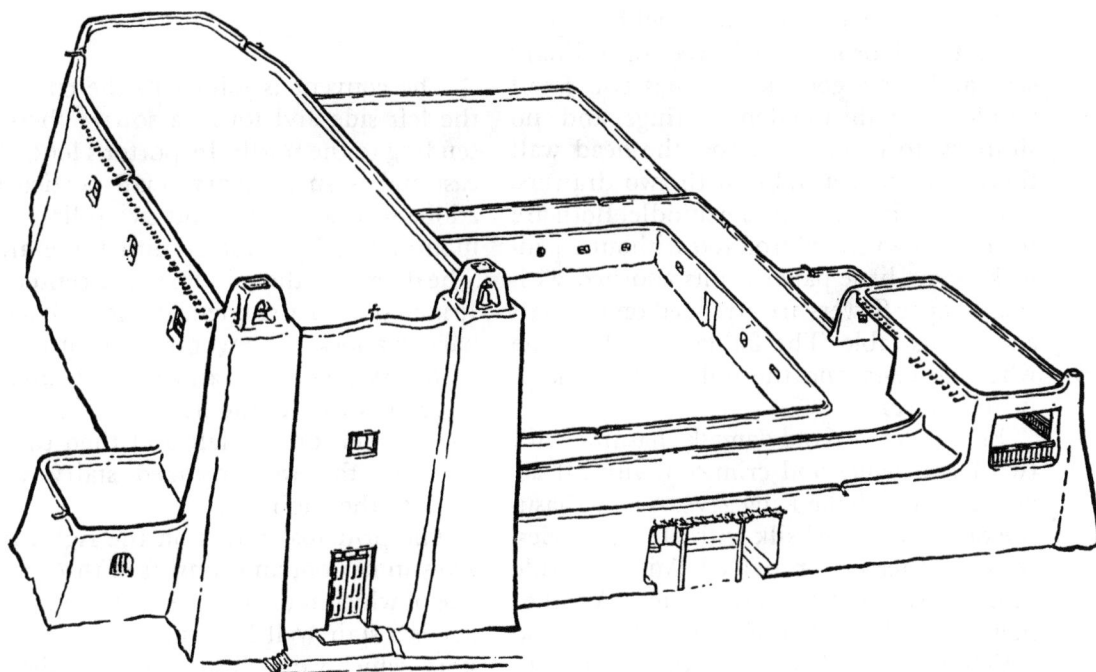

three ledges of the same material on it, ascending like a throne. On the top there is an ordinary painted wooden niche to hold a completely carved St. Stephen of rather medium size. The Indians bought this statue, or image, along with the niche. Above it hangs a large old painting on buffalo skin of St. Stephen's martyrdom, which Father Miranda provided in a painted wooden frame.[3] Above this is another buffalo skin picture without a saint, but there is a beautiful gilt paper cross on it and it is all spangled with little flowers made of painted paper.

3. The nature of this painting of the Protomartyr St. Stephen, which now hangs on the right wall of the sanctuary, leads one to suspect that he was the original patron saint of Acoma. The fact that his feast came in winter and close to Christmas (December 26) may be the reason that the celebration at Acoma was transferred to the feast of St. Stephen, King of Hungary (September 2). Domínguez makes no distinction between the statue and the painting, so it may be presumed that both represented the Protomartyr.

The whole area that I have been describing, up to the top, has arches painted with colored earth, executed by the Indians. The same is true of the saints at the sides which follow here. On either side of the niche hang two large oil paintings, now old. One represents St. Peter and the other St. Anthony of Padua. Above these are two paper prints surrounded by little painted paper flowers. The altar table is adobe with an altar stone given by the King on it. A cross of painted wood, two small brass candlesticks, which the King gave, and an ordinary missal stand. Below there is a small bronze bell, a board dais, and a beautiful carpet dyed with cochineal, which the Indians wove in Father Pino's time. The only thing in the nave is the confessional, which is adobe and resembles a bookstand.

SACRISTY: It is joined to the church on the Epistle side, but there is no door to the church, only to the cloister, in a corner of which it stands against the church. Running along the cloister, it is 10 varas long and 5 wide, and 3 long varas high with a good roof. The door is single-leaved, of ordinary size, and has a good key. It has two small windows, with wooden gratings and no shutters, to the west. Across the head wall there is a wooden table with two drawers, one above the other, in the middle. Both are secured by a vertical iron rod without a padlock. Some little paper prints adorned with small paper flowers are arranged on the wall above this table. The father uses the table when he vests, and the following are kept in its drawers.

Vestments: An old damask chasuble with two faces (white and crimson) with all accessories, which the King gave. A new chasuble of green ribbed silk with all accessories, which Father Pino provided. An old purple satin chasuble with accessories. Another new one of mother-of-pearl ribbed silk, which the said father provided. Another old white satin one with accessories. Another old mother-of-pearl satin one with accessories. Another very old black ribbed silk one with accessories. An old black damask cope. A green ribbed silk pall. Another mother-of-pearl one.

Linen: Three good Brittany amices. Three albs like them. Three altar cloths like the foregoing. A cloth cincture. Father Pino provided them all during the many years he lived here. Six pairs of double corporals of Brittany in fair condition. Several purificators. Four finger towels.

Silver and other metal: Chalice with paten and spoon, which the King gave. Three small vials for the holy oils, which the same lord gave. The arras and rings given by the said lord.

Thurible with accessories. Processional cross. Tin-plate box for altar breads. Mold for making altar breads, which the King gave.

Other things: A usable missal for secular priests. Another very old one. *Manual* by Osorio. Two ordinary cruets. A small gourd cup for baptizing. Many old poles, which are in the rear of the sacristy.

CONVENT

The convent is joined to the church on the left side and forms a square there, extending to the north. Its porter's lodge faces east and is an ordinary small portico with adobe seats around it and two pillars at the mouth, which divide it into three arches. The door is in the middle of the center wall. It is an ordinary single-leaf one with a crossbar for a lock. The whole convent is adobe with very good walls, all well made and very large. As we enter the porter's lodge there is a single cell on the left and then the stair well for the well-arranged stairway that leads to the choir.

The principal cell is on the right. It has a key in its door and consists of three rooms, one of which is on a corner. Around the corner is a stair well leading to a small upper story, which we shall soon see, and then two beautiful storerooms with wooden locks. Just before we turn the corner, there is a passage which leads to the corrals I shall soon describe, making two turns on the way. The kitchen is around the corner, then a storeroom, and then the sacristy. There is an enclosed cloister, lighted by three good windows on each side. On one side there is a door to the patio, in which there are some little peach trees which are watered by hand. And in one corner there is a small recess for certain necessary business. The door leading to either the sacristy or convent is on the side against the church in its very wall.

Let us proceed to the corners I left for future mention. The stair well in the first one was once a small cell, whose door remains today, but a small stairway is now fitted into the center with three short and very neatly made turns, for the steps are made of bricks with a railed banister. There is a railing at the top with a gate to match, which, when closed, prevents any sudden accident. It is all roofed over, with a closed wall to the north and completely open to the south over the whole flat roof of the first floor. As we emerge and face south over the flat roof, there is a well-arranged mirador to our left on the flat roof of the room on the corner. It faces north and east, with railings and pillars. It has an earthen floor, but hard, and on the south and west walls there are seats of well-wrought boards resting on small corbels. It has an ordinary single-leaf door without a key.

On the right there is a beautiful salon, the upper part of which is partitioned off with boards to make an inner cell. Father Pino made it all. In the other corner where the passage is, is the exit to the afore-mentioned corrals, and they are really one, with a third of it divided off. The said father made them, and they have a very high and thick stone-and-mud wall. The largest one has a good two-leaved door without a key to the north, and there are a stable and strawloft in it. The other is beside it to the south at the back of the church. It serves as a chicken yard and is narrow with a rather low door.

Its Furnishings: Two large tables. Three benches. Three armless chairs. An adobe stand for books.

Its Service: The same as has been described at Laguna, but here there are twelve Indian women who bring twelve small jars of water to be used daily. And as soon as they put them in the kitchen, they go home until the next day, when they do it again. The reason for such a large number of water carriers is that the water (as I shall explain later) is very far away, and to avoid frequent trips a good deal is brought at one time. When it is necessary to water the little trees mentioned above, the girls who come to catechism go with the weekly fiscal and bring a great deal all at once, even more than enough.

Its Lands and Fruits: There are no lands assigned to this mission as is the case in other missions, and I will explain the reason for this in detail when I describe the pueblo lands.

MISSION FATHER

The one who exercises the ministry at this mission is Father Fray José Mariño, native of San Miguel el Grande, thirty-six years of age, seventeen in profession, three years as a missionary in the Custody, as follows: El Paso, six months; Acoma, two years, six months. He holds general faculties in Durango, revocable at will.

Administration of the Mission: The usual regime, but carried out in a most exquisite manner which Father Pino taught the Indians, and this is: Sometimes the men put the questions of the catechism, other times the women; still others, the little boys, and others the little girls, and still others, the father. Sometimes they all put the questions to the father, sometimes at random, sometimes in sequence. And when the questions are put by the respective groups, as I have said, the other groups reply in the same way. Some explanation is always made, and the said Indians have many quaint customs that the said father taught them.

Expenditures: Food consumed by the household is not counted. About 6 pounds of wax a year, about 2 jugs of wine. A fanega of wheat is given to the chief sacristan for the altar breads used here and for those sent to Laguna when they ask for them.

How He Acquires Necessities: In this regard I refer to what was said at Laguna in a few well-chosen words.

NOTE

I made the visitation of this mission on December 17 of the past year of 1776, and no writ of visitation was left because I did not consider it necessary. Instructions were left for Father Mariño that the convent provisions should be as follows: 4 fanegas of wheat, 4 of maize, a jar of ordinary lard, a bottle of wine, 2 wax candles.

The parish books were inspected and approved. And since they are nearly full, I ordered the said father to ask the Father

Vice-Custos for three new ones from the supply that just arrived and to remit the old ones to the archive. I also ordered him to remit the old Inventory to the same place, and since the book of Patents is incorporated with it, the same is to be done with it as with its adjunct. I gave sufficient paper for new books for the Inventory, Patents, and an additional one for the Edicts of the Lord Bishop, and authorized them.[4]

PUEBLO

Although the site of this mission was described at the beginning, it still remains to be said that west of the buildings on the adjoining surface of the mesa which I mentioned in that place, there is a cistern which God made in the rock itself. Its opening must be about 40 varas in circumference, and it must be fully as deep. Rain water is caught in it, and when it snows, the Indians take care to collect all the snow they can in it. For this purpose, and in order that the rain water may be clean when it goes in, they are careful to keep the space around it swept, and there is a guard to prevent pollution.

The water collected in this usually half fills it. Because the rock is cold, it has never been known to become fetid, and it is always fresh, although turbid. The descent to it is a little stairway in a corner, made in the rock itself and very steep. When one goes to it, one travels a quarter or a third of a league from the pueblo, because one descends by the boxed-in road mentioned above, reaches the sandy slope, and, traveling up hill over the sand again, traverses a rocky stretch to it. After getting water, one returns the same way, and so home. This trip is made constantly, for although there are other cisterns in view of the pueblo on the site where it stands, they are no bigger than a vessel of a font, and therefore they do not last for more than eight or ten days.

In view of this, it is clear how much work must have been involved in building church and pueblo. The latter is north of the church, arranged and built in six tenements, or blocks, of dwellings constructed of stone and mud. Three face east, and three south, one behind another, with very wide streets between, forming, with the convent, a handsome plaza. They have upper and lower stories such as I have described in all the foregoing, and they are not as clean and well kept as at Laguna but like the rest.

ITS LANDS AND FRUITS: The Indians have lands wherever the cañadas in the south, east, north, and northwest mentioned above provide arable level ground. All are completely dependent on rain, for although there are two small springs, they only suffice as drinking water for some small livestock. They have made a low bank of earth around them for this purpose. When it rains these milpas do well, but if rain is completely lacking, there are hardships, as has been the case for three years now, when there has been great drought.

Three leagues up the cañada from Laguna and 5 or 6 north-northeast of Acoma (we shall see this again on our way to Zuñi) there is a place called Cubero in a cañada which runs between mesas from south to north. It is about a league long from south to north and about half a league wide from east to west. The Indians sow all they can in it on both sides of the river that flows to Laguna; they irrigate with it and harvest very reasonable crops. In this very place they plant for the convent wherever the father chooses, usually harvesting 40 fanegas of wheat, the same amount of maize, and a little of each kind of green vegetable. The natives are Queres (this completes the seven pueblos of this nation), whose native

4. The second book of Baptisms, begun in 1726 when Fray Antonio Miranda was missionary, contains two long lists of confirmations; 300 persons were confirmed by Bishop Elizacoechea on September 26, 1737, and by Bishop Tamarón 260 on June 30, and 252 on July 1, 1760.

tongue they speak. As for everything else, they are like the Laguna Indians. With regard to these Acomas, here is this

NOTE

Father Claramonte tells me that in the year 1768, when he was missionary of Laguna and was taking care of this Acoma mission because of Father Pino's death, the census of the Acoma Indians numbered 1,114. Only those whom we shall soon see now remain in the pueblo out of so large a number. The reason for this great decrease is that many have died since then, some from natural causes in epidemics or from other diseases, others at the hands of Apaches so insolent that if this pueblo were not by nature defensible, perhaps nothing would now remain of it. The present mission father also states that still others are wandering about and that some have fled to Moqui for fear of the famines and wars they have suffered in a few years.[5] The following lists those here at present.

CENSUS

135 families with 530 persons

There is no settlement under the administration of this mission, but only the lieutenant alcalde mayor and his family live here.[6] This note includes them.

1 family with 5 persons

5. Between 1760 and 1776 the population had declined from 308 families, with 1502 persons, to considerably less than half that number. AT, p. 69.

6. To all appearances, this assistant alcalde was young Pedro Bautista Pino, brother of Alcalde Pedro José Pino. His fame rests on the fact that thirty-five years later he was the one and only deputy from New Mexico to the Court of Madrid. At this time his wife was Manuela Gabaldón, whom he had married in Santa Fe on December 24, 1772. Two children were María Vicenta, born November 1, 1773, and María Gertrudis, July 9, 1775. The fifth member of this single Spanish family at Acoma may have been another child or a relative living with them. During his long life Pino had two subsequent wives and many children by both. The Pinos of Santa Fe were mostly children of the third wife. NMF.

Zuñi

Zuñi is 30 leagues west of Laguna up the cañada. The road to it is as follows: Three leagues from Laguna is Cubero, as I stated above. From Cubero one travels about 4 leagues through cañadas and finally encounters some rocks hidden among willows, and this is the source of the Laguna River. From here (now turning a little to the right) one travels about 3 leagues to a very good cañada running from south to north, in which there is a spring of delicious and very abundant water, so much so that its overflow forms a brook which runs through the middle of the cañada to the south until, after more than a league, it disappears at the foot of a mesa which cuts it off. The source of the Laguna River is presumed to be this hidden stream. The said cañada offers a good site for a middle-sized settlement with convenient irrigation for beautiful farmlands, pasturage for cattle, firewood for the taking, timber nearby and easy to transport, etc., but this cannot be made because at present the kingdom is so very subject to attack [by hostile Indians]. This spring is called El Gallo.

From here a sierra called the Zuñi Sierra runs. It is very variable to travel, with many cañadas, good pasturage, firewood, and small springs of good water. It must be about 4 leagues across, and before one leaves it, there is a very broad canyon with a good floor and some cliffs at intervals, below which there are some lava beds that look as if they were boiling on the fire. After leaving it one travels over several very good stretches of plain with arroyos at intervals and mesas on either side in many places. And about 3 leagues before one reaches the pueblo, in the middle of a little plain, there is a spring they call Zuñi. Although it runs in the direction of the pueblo, it does not reach it because its meager water disappears within a short distance.

Finally one reaches the pueblo and mission of Nuestra Señora de Guadalupe de Zuñi, which is located and founded on an ample plain surrounded by buttes and mesas on the east, north, and southeast. It is 60 leagues from Santa Fe via the highway. Although we might call this mission the last one since there is no other beyond it, it does not seem to me proper to do so, for in addition to the fact that the two foregoing ones are located in the vicinity, in relation to the Custody as a whole it lies on one side, although at a distance.

Nevertheless, in relation to the direction in which it lies from the capital, which I am considering the center, and considering it as one end of a square, it must be said that in relation to Santa Fe it lies to the west-southwest in latitude 35°7′ north, longitude 268°24′.[1] This pueblo has no river, but an arroyo which flows only in a very rainy season or when the snows melt. And when this does not occur, they open a number of wells in it, some of which have good water and others, bad. In this way I indicate the great labor necessary for the building of church and convent, for, water being scarce, the difficulties may be imagined. With regard to transportation of what is necessary, except water, it is understood that it would not be very troublesome, because of the flatness of the road, although the sierra where timber is obtained is distant.

CHURCH

The church[2] is adobe with walls nearly a vara thick, single-naved, facing east-north-

1. Cf. n. 1, p. 13 *supra*.

2. The present pueblo of Zuñi, formerly known as Halona, is the only survivor of the group of six Zuñi pueblos in existence at the time of the Spanish conquest of New Mexico, which have been called the "Seven Cities of Cíbola." Missionary work among the Zuñi, which was started in 1629, suffered frequent tragic reverses, but during the seventeenth century churches were built in three of the pueblos, Hawikuh, Halona, and Kechipauan. For divergent opinions concerning the date and builder of the

east. From the door to the ascent to the sanctuary it is 30 varas long, 9 wide, and 8 high. The sanctuary is closed in like the head of a transept. The ascent to it consists of four steps of wrought beams, at the top of which there is a railing. From here to the center it measures 5 varas square, being as much higher as the clerestory demands. There is a choir loft in the usual place, and it is like those described before. On the right side there are two windows with wooden gratings facing southeast, and one in the choir to a balcony overlooking the cemetery. The main door is squared, with a wooden frame instead of masonry, with

two paneled leaves, no lock except the cross-bar, and measures 3 varas high by 2 wide.

The nave is roofed by thirty-six wrought and corbeled beams, and the clerestory is at the very place where it reaches the mouth of the sanctuary, in which there are seven more beams to the center. As we enter the main door, there is an ordinary room on our right outside the wall of the church, which serves for a baptistery as described

---

church at Halona, see GK, pp. 95-97, and AB-1634, pp. 289-94.

Most of the pre-Revolt sources give the advocation of the Halona church as Our Lady of Candelaria (Purification) and that of Hawikuh as the Immaculate Conception. Nevertheless, on September 19, 1672, Fray Juan Galdo, who had been stationed at Halona for a year, with Hawikuh as a visita, referred to the convents of the "Immaculate Conception of Alona" and the "Purification of Aguico." F. V. Scholes and E. B. Adams, "Inventories of church furnishings in some of the New Mexico missions, 1672," *Dargan Historical Essays* (Albuquerque, 1952), pp. 35-36. At this time the Zuñi missions were in a very precarious state because of the increasing fury of the Apache raids, and Father Galdo was faced with the problem of maintaining soldiers as well as the Indians from supplies reduced to a minimum by drought and Apache thefts of livestock. His change of the titular patrons of the two missions may have been an inadvertent error, but his statement, a signed original, also raises another question, the date of the martyrdom of Fray Pedro de Avila y Ayala at Hawikuh, which is usually given as October 7, 1672. Some sources give the year as 1670, which is obviously wrong; the name of the pueblo has also been garbled and in at least one case mistaken for Abo. *Autos tocantes a socorros del Nuevo México*, 1677, AGI, Aud. de Guadalajara, leg. 138; AGM, Provincias Internas, tomo 37, exp. 5; Fray Agustín de Vetancurt, *Teatro Mexicano* (Mexico, 1870-71), 4: 346-47; Fray Francisco Antonio de la Rosa Figueroa, *Bezerro . . . 1764* (MS in Ayer Coll., Newberry Library, Chicago), pp. 314-15; HB, 3: 298; O. Maas, *Misiones del Nuevo Méjico* (Madrid, 1929), p. 52; F. W. Hodge, *History of Hawikuh* (Los Angeles, 1937), p. 99. Galdo's report and two other references which have been over-

looked indicate that Fray Pedro's death must have occurred sometime during the first half of 1673, for on September 19, 1672, Father Galdo alone had been in charge of Halona and Hawikuh for a year, and if Avila y Ayala was killed on the seventh of the next month, it must have been but a few days after his arrival. A marginal note on the manuscripts of Vélez de Escalante's *Extracto de Noticias* (AGM, Historia, vol. 2, f. 67 v. and BNM, leg. 3, doc. 2) reads: "The Apaches attacked Tahuicú de Zuñi in the year 1673. They captured almost all the women and children; they killed many Indians and Father Fray Pedro de Ayala; they burned the church, etc." This note was omitted from the printed version of DHM. On July 15, 1673, Governor Miranda issued to Don Juan Domínguez de Mendoza a title as *maestre de campo* in reprisals against the Apaches. This document states that these Indians had gone so far as "to have killed the friar minister of the pueblo of Aguico in the province of Zuñi," but the date is not given. Biblioteca Nacional, Madrid, 19258. Father Galdo went to Hawikuh the day after the tragedy and brought the body to Halona for interment. Perhaps both the Zuñi missions were abandoned for a time after these events, but Halona, at least, was reoccupied before 1680, when Fray Juan de Bal was martyred there. HS, 1: 111; HB, 3: 338. According to Vetancurt (3: 321), there was also a missionary at Hawikuh, who escaped. Hodge (*History of Hawikuh*, p. 102) recounts a Zuñi tradition of the adoption of the latter into the tribe. Both churches were burned. Hodge also suggests that Fray Juan Galdo and Fray Juan de Bal might have been the same person, but information from Figueroa's *Bezerro* makes this theory untenable, for a Fray Juan Val of the province of Castile was incorporated in the Mexican Province of the Holy Gospel in 1668 (p. 137), and Fray Juan Galdo, of Seville, professed in Mexico City on July 6, 1659 (p. 302).

In 1692, de Vargas found the Halona Indians living on Corn Mountain. They took part in the 1696 rebellion, and in 1699 most of them were still there, although some of them made formal submission to before, with an earthen bowl for a baptismal font. Above the main door there is a balcony like the one I described there at Nambe, and still higher an adobe arch containing two small bells, which the King gave, and they are good ones. The cemetery begins at the outside corner of the baptistery, and, enclosed by a low adobe wall with three gates, it ends on one side of the porter's lodge, which lies within it. It measures 20 varas square. The church floor is of earth, its interior dark, and its furnishings as follows.

HIGH ALTAR: It has a small new altar screen, as seemly as this poor land has to offer, which was paid for by Father Vélez and the Indians of the pueblo. It consists of two sections, as follows: In the center of the whole thing, almost from top to bottom, there is a framework lined with coarse brown linen and very well painted, in which a large oil painting on canvas with an old frame, newly half gilded, of Our Lady of Guadalupe, which the King had given before, hangs. Below this painting is

a very old lacquer Child Jesus vested as a priest, the clothing also old.[3]

The lower niches at the sides contain St. Michael on the right and St. Gabriel at the left, new middle-sized images in the round. In the two in the second section above those lower ones mentioned are our fathers St. Dominic on the right and St. Francis on the left, painted half life-size. Above at the top a bust of the Eternal Father in half relief. The gradin is below the little altar screen, serves as a base for it, and has a small tabernacle well placed in the center.

The altar table is adobe with an altar stone given by the King, two small brass candlesticks, which the same lord gave, four candlesticks which the fathers have provided, a middle-sized wooden cross with a lacquer crucifix, a new lectern, a frontal like the framework canopy, just now completed, an adobe dais, a small new colored rug, two small bronze bells. On the little railing there are a wooden processional cross and candleholders, all new and painted.

NAVE: On the walls which stand below the sanctuary in imitation of a transept there are two adobe tables (one on each side), whose adornment consists of: on the right side a large painting, on buffalo skin, of Our Father St. Dominic, and on the left another like it of Our Father St. Francis, both old. Farther down on one side an old and badly made wooden confessional.

SACRISTY: The sacristy is joined to the church on the right side and, running along its wall, which it adjoins, for 10 varas, it ends a third of the way down the nave. It is 5 varas wide and 4 high, with a good roof, a large window with gratings and shutters on one side, an ordinary door to the church and another to the convent through the cloister. At the head there is a beautiful

---

Governor Cubero on July 12. In the same year, Fray Juan de Garaicoechea persuaded them to return to Halona, for the fragments of the Zuñi parish books have entries made by him beginning October 22, 1699, and continuing until his death in August, 1706. To protect the pueblo against Apache raids, soldiers were stationed there. Their behavior was such that the Zuñis killed three of them, José Valdés, Juan Lucero, and Juan Palomino, when they were singing in the church choir on March 4, 1703. Note by Father Irazabal, June 17, 1709. According to DHM (pp. 181-84) the Zuñi withdrew to the peñol again for a time after this episode, although they continued to treat the missionary with respect and there is no indication that the church was harmed. Therefore Father Alvarez' routine statement in 1706 that the church was being built is unlikely to refer to an entirely new structure. HB, 3: 377. Indeed, it is quite possible that the original seventeenth-century structure had survived in part. Father Alvarez apparently was mistaken when he said that the patronal title of the Halona mission was the Immaculate Conception, for beginning with the Burial Book authorized on May 20, 1700, we find Nuestra Señora de Guadalupe de Alona used in the eighteenth century.

3. This probably is the Santo Niño of Zuñi which has been the object of local pilgrimages for many years. The statues of the archangels Michael and Gabriel mentioned in the next paragraph, acquired at Zuñi in the 1880's by Stevenson and Cushing, are now in the U.S. National Museum.

wooden table which the priest uses for vesting. It has two drawers, one above the other, with a key to the top one. An old painting on buffalo skin, of Christ crucified, hangs on the wall above this table. The following are in the drawer that has a lock.

Vestments: An old damask chasuble with two faces (white and crimson), with all accessories, which the King gave. Another

gave them all. A cruet, whose donor is unknown.

Small pewter plate. Spoon and incense boat for a clay censer made by the Indians. Mold for making altar breads, which the King gave.

Other things: An old missal. A worn *Manual* by Osorio. Four new red shalloon cassocks which Father Vélez provided for

very old one of blue damask, which the said lord gave together with its accessories. Another old one with two faces (green and mother-of-pearl), with accessories. Another (almost new) of black damask with accessories including cope, which Father Camargo gave. An almost new cope of white damask, which Father Murciano gave. A usable tapestry frontal woven in foliage design with narrow silver fringe.

Linen: An old Brittany amice. Two albs like it, but all usable. Another very old one. Two altar cloths like the albs and amice. An almost new Brittany surplice. Four pairs of good double corporals of Brittany. Seven purificators. Two old cloth cinctures. Another new one of silk. Two small cloths for baptisms. Two new palls of embroidered linen. Two more, worn out.

Silver and other metal: Chalice with paten and spoon. Three small vials with the holy oils, in a little box with a key. Thirteen old coins with their rings for arras; the King

the acolytes together with four new Brittany cottas.

Note: Last year, 1776, the things our Mother the Province sent to this mission for divine worship were received, to wit: A white flowered silk chasuble with all necessary accessories, trimmed with fine gold fringe. Another of mother-of-pearl flowered silk like the foregoing in every detail except color. A lawn amice with good lace and ribbons. A lawn alb with very good lace at the bottom a third of a vara wide.

CONVENT

The convent is joined to the church on the right side, forming a square there which extends to the southeast. Its porter's lodge, inside the cemetery, faces east-northeast, and it is an ordinary small portico with adobe seats around it and two pillars at the mouth which divide it into three small arches. The door is in the middle of the

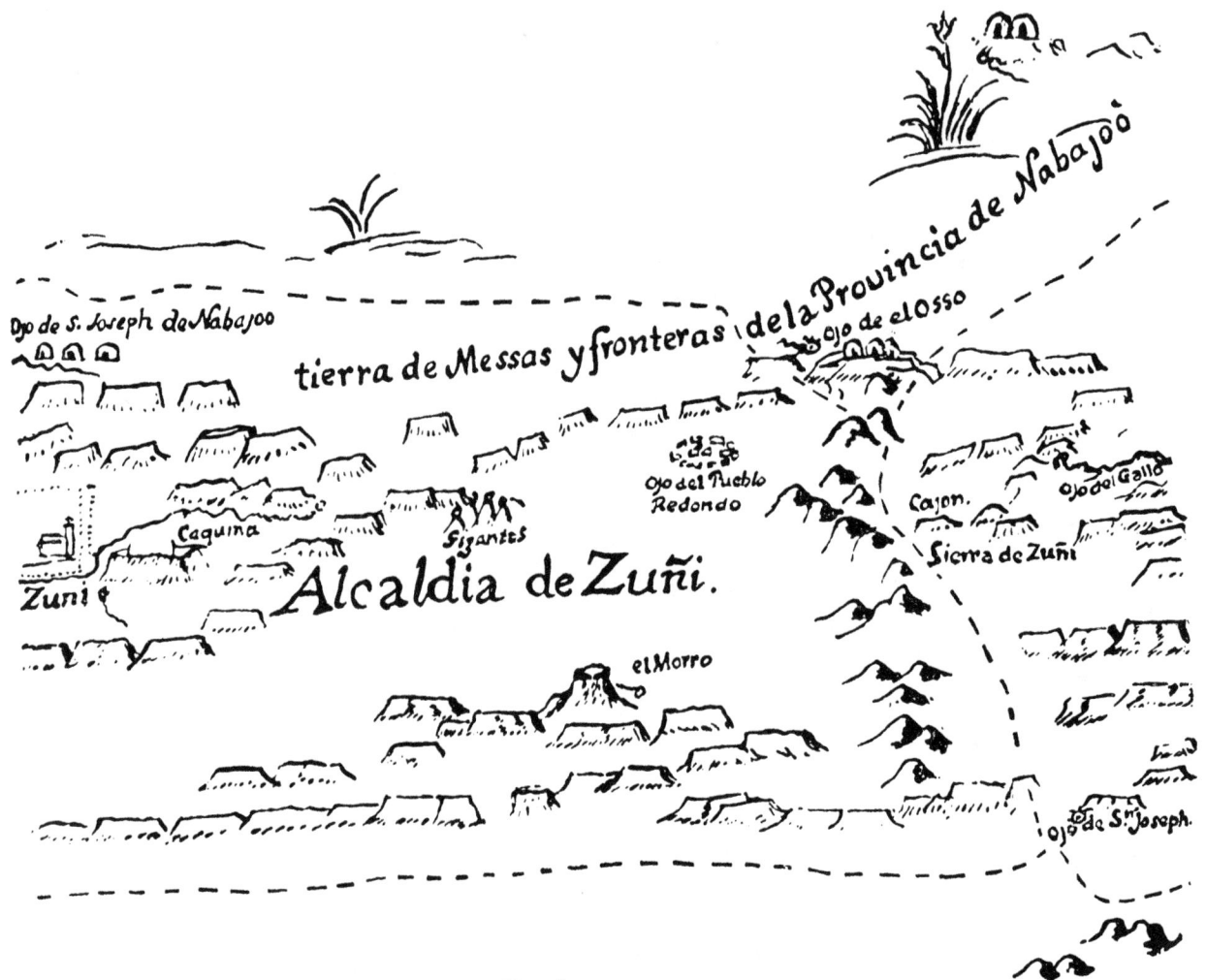

Ojo de S. Joseph de Nabajoo

tierra de Messas y fronteras de la Prouincia de Nabajoo

Ojo de el Osso

Ojo del Pueblo Redondo

Cajon.

Ojo del Gallo

Caquina

Gigantes

Sierra de Zuñi

Zuñi

Alcaldia de Zuñi.

el Morro

Ojo de S.ᵗ Joseph.

llanos de la Salina de Zuni

center wall, is of ordinary size and has two leaves with a crossbar for a lock. It is all badly made of adobe and small, but it suffices. As we enter the porter's lodge there is a cell on the left, whose door has a key, then an inner cell on a corner. Around the corner there is another cell with a small inner cell, then the kitchen and the stable, which is on a corner. It turns again with a passage to the street, for there is no corral and no place to make one. Beyond this there are two rooms used as storerooms, and they adjoin one side of the sacristy.

The cloister is enclosed and has three sides. It begins up against the side of the church, turns along the center of the convent, and joins the church again opposite the porter's lodge. It is rather dark because it has a single window on each side, and the patio is useless. The passageway to the street has an ordinary single-leaf door with a crossbar.

ITS FURNISHINGS: An ordinary table in each cell. Two benches distributed in the same way. A small chair in each cell.

ITS SERVICE: The same as stated at the Laguna mission.

ITS LANDS AND FRUITS: The lands which were assigned to this convent in the early days were very sandy, and in the course of time have become a sort of clay, and therefore useless. Therefore, at present the Indians sow for the convent some very small patches among others they have to the east on the small level sites there are near that little spring I mentioned 3 leagues before the convent. They are watered from the said spring, and something is harvested from them.

MISSION FATHERS

Fathers Fray Silvestre Vélez de Escalante and Fray Mariano Rosete exercise the apostolic ministry at this mission. The first is a native of Tresenio in the Valle de Bandalija of the Montañas de Santander, twenty-eight years of age, nine in profession, two years and six months as a missionary in the Custody. The second is a native of Puebla, twenty-eight years of age, ten in profession, a year and some months as a missionary in the Custody. Both hold general faculties in Durango, revocable at will.

ADMINISTRATION OF THE MISSION: The usual regime as described elsewhere, to which I refer.

EXPENDITURES: The little that is harvested is not counted, since it is consumed by the household. About 10 or 11 pounds of wax are used in administration, and about 4 jugs of wine, for since there are two priests who celebrate Mass nearly every day, this amount is used. One fanega of wheat a year suffices for the altar breads.

HOW THEY ACQUIRE NECESSITIES: I have spoken about this, beginning at Laguna, and this account suffices.

NOTE

The visitation of this mission was made on the ninth day of December of the past year, 1776. No writ of visitation was left, because it was not necessary, but the fathers have been well admonished that the convent provision shall be as follows: 4 fanegas of wheat, 4 of maize, a jar of ordinary lard, 2 wax candles, a bottle of wine.

The parish books were inspected, and since they are nearly full, I ordered that three of the new ones which came from the Province be given. The old ones remain at this mission, and many entries are missing. The old Inventory remains here also with the Patent book combined with it. I donated sufficient paper for new ones and for another of Edicts of the Lord Bishop, and after they were made I authorized them.

PUEBLO

Its location was sufficiently described in the beginning. Therefore, proceeding to its construction, I state that some houses are adobe and others stone-and-mud, all arranged around the church and convent, which stand in the middle of the pueblo. It consists of many tenements, some of which form a plaza in front of the church and convent, the latter making one side of the plaza. Others form a small plaza back of the aforesaid, which again make one side of the plaza. Still others form a small plaza beyond the one in front of the church and convent, and others make still another one on the left side of the church. In addition to these four plazas, which are small, there are more small tenements and separate houses round about which would be enough to make another plaza if they were all together. The neatness is not as great as that described at Laguna nor as little as elsewhere.

ITS LANDS AND FRUITS: The Indians have farmlands for a league above, a league below, and the same distance on either side of the pueblo. And all those mentioned are dependent on rain, for there is no river to use for irrigation. The only irrigation is at those little patches I mentioned under the convent's lands, referring to the small spring on the road. To crown these difficulties, there is the added drudgery of doing all sowing by hand, because there are no oxen in this pueblo. In spite of these handicaps, God deigns to grant them very reasonable crops.

The natives of this pueblo are Zuñi, whose native tongue they alone speak, because it is an entirely different language from all those known and observed in this kingdom. Few speak Spanish, and those brokenly. With regard to their particular customs, I state that they are of very docile and gentle disposition. The following includes them all.

CENSUS

396 families with 1,617 persons

Isleta

In relation to the location of all those mentioned before (and to those that remain to be described) this mission is so situated that it is the first one in this interior branch of the Custody, because it is the mouth, or entrance, of this kingdom. But the sequence which I have followed is the reason for giving it the next to last place in the narrative. Instead of traveling 17 good leagues from Laguna to there, we shall go to it from the nearest place, which is Albuquerque. From there, then, one heads west with the intention of crossing the Río del Norte. On the west bank one turns left to the south in sight of and downstream along the said river, on whose broad meadow (with hills to the right which extend down south about a league from the shore) one travels 4 leagues to the pueblo and mission of San Agustín de la Isleta, which is located and established in full view of the river on so small an elevation that it might pass for a plain. It is 24 good leagues from Santa Fe, lying to the south quarter south-southwest of the villa. It is in latitude 35° 3′ north, longitude 71° 8′.[1]

CHURCH

The church[2] is adobe with walls nearly a vara thick, with the door to the south. From there to the ascent to the sanctuary it is 34 varas long, 9 wide, and 8 high. The ascent to the sanctuary consists of four steps made of wrought beams, and from there to the center it measures 6 varas, with the same width as the nave and as much higher as the clerestory demands. There is a choir loft like those mentioned before. On the Epistle side there are three windows with ordinary

gratings facing east, and one in the choir. The main door is squared, with two new leaves installed by Father Junco's efforts, and no key. It is 3 varas high by 2 wide.

The nave is roofed by forty wrought and corbeled beams, and the clerestory rests there where it reaches the sanctuary. From there on, eight beams like those mentioned roof the sanctuary. As we enter the main door, the baptistery is to our right under the choir loft, extending outside the church wall. It is an ordinary room with a small window to the south and a two-leaved door without a key to the church. There is a small wooden pillar with a box of the same material, all painted up, in the middle of this room. It holds an earthen bowl like those elsewhere.

On top of each of the front corners of the church is a turret, one of which contains a middle-sized bell, which the King gave, and it is a good one. The cemetery begins at the outside corner of the baptistery, and, surrounded by a rather low adobe wall with three gates, it ends at one side of the porter's lodge. Its area is 30 varas square. The church floor, bare earth, its interior like that of a rather dark wine cellar, and its furnishings as follows.

HIGH ALTAR: A niche has been opened near the center of the wall, and it contains an old, completely carved image of St. Augustine, made outside the kingdom, vested (the clothing is carved) as a bishop, and a vara high. Above it hangs an ordinary

1. Cf. n. 1, p. 13 *supra.*

2. The seventeenth-century church at Isleta was built about 1613, and the titular patron of the mission was St. Anthony of Padua. When the Pueblo Revolt broke out in August, 1680, the Spanish survivors in the Río Abajo area assembled at Isleta. By the time Governor Otermín reached there early in September he found the pueblo deserted. In December, 1681, the Otermín expedition found the church and convent at Isleta "burned and ruined . . . and a cowpen inside the body of the church." When the Spanish force returned to El Paso the following January, they took 385 Indians from Isleta with them and burned the pueblo. HS, 1: 27; 2: 208, 357-58. The pueblo established for these Indians near El Paso was also called San Antonio de la Isleta, and the appellation of Corpus Christi was added later. Although the church at their former pueblo was burned twice, it was not completely destroyed, for when de Vargas reached the pueblo on October 30, 1692, he found it in ruins "except for the nave of the church, the walls of which are in good condition." J. M. Espinosa, *First expedition of Vargas, 1692* (Albuquerque, 1940), pp. 186, 286. Vélez de Escalante tells the story of the reoccupation of the old pueblo of Isleta as follows: "In addition to the Tigua Indians who, along with some Tano and Jemez Indians, were in Moqui, and in addition to those whom Otermín took out and settled at El Paso del Río del Norte, a number of families of the same Tigua nation had remained scattered in different pueblos and others among the Apaches. As soon as Father Fray Juan de la Peña became prelate of this Custody, he dedicated himself to collecting them from the pueblos and to getting the others away from the infidels. And when he had assembled them, he placed them on the site of Isleta. He gave them cattle for their maintenance and tilling the first year. And, having thus provided for their support, he re-established and refounded the old pueblo and mission of San Agustín of Isleta with

the consent and aid of the governor at the beginning of January, 1710." DHM, pp. 197-98. Fray Juan de la Peña was elected custos of New Mexico in the Chapters held in Mexico City on May 5, 1708, and September 7, 1709. BNM, leg. 9, no. 8. He died in 1710. The eighteenth-century documents continue to give the titular patron of Isleta as St. Augustine. The bulk of the historical and archaeological evidence indicates that Isleta was refounded at its former site, so it is quite likely that the church described by Domínguez—which is the one in existence today—dates from 1613, with, of course, extensive repairs and rebuilding, and has one of the best claims to be the oldest church in New Mexico.

old oil painting on canvas. Four middle-sized old paintings on buffalo skin are arranged at the sides. The gradin is adobe and holds a middle-sized cross with a lacquer Christus, now old, an image of the Immaculate Conception in Michoacán paste, and two small brass candlesticks, which the King gave. The altar table is adobe with an altar stone given by the King, an ordinary lectern, a small bronze bell, a board dais, and a poor carpet.

There are two altars in the sanctuary in addition to the high altar, one on each side. The one on the right is dedicated to Our Father St. Francis, whose image is a rather middle-sized one in the round, completely carved, placed without any artifice on a steplike gradin. On one side of this there is a lacquer Child Jesus. The altar table is adobe and completely bare. The other altar is of Our Lady of Sorrows, whose image is an ordinary one in the round dressed in the current fashion. And there is a middle-sized crucifix a little higher up. The altar table like the foregoing. Everything so described is old. The donors are not mentioned. The only things in the nave are a poor wooden confessional and five old oil paintings on buffalo skin on the walls.

SACRISTY: The sacristy is joined to the church on the Epistle side and is a room 8 varas long, 4 wide, and 3 high, with a good roof, a window to the north on one side, an ordinary door to the church, and another with a key to the cloister. Across the head of the room there is a wooden table with six drawers, all with keys, although poor ones, and in them the following.

Vestments: An old damask chasuble with two faces (white and crimson), with all accessories, which the King gave. Another old purple satin one with complete accessories. Another which serves for green. Another like them which serves for blue. Another, also like the aforesaid, which serves for black. The assumption is that they came from the King. An almost new black damask chasuble with accessories, including cope and cross sheath, which Father Camargo gave. A new white damask chasuble with complete accessories, pall of the same material, and a new cope of mother-of-pearl ribbed silk, which was paid for by Father Junco, Don Clemente Gutiérrez, Don Francisco Trébol, and Don Antonio Baca.

Linen: Two old Rouen albs. Three old Rouen altar cloths. Two pairs of double corporals of Brittany, usable. Four usable purificators. A woman's chemise for St. Augustine; it must be a dandy thing.

Father Junco says that he has provided the following: New amice and alb of Brittany with lace. Two new Rouen altar cloths. Two new cloth cinctures. Two Brittany purificators. A new Rouen surplice. Two Brittany finger towels.

Silver and other metal: Two chalices with their patens and spoons; it is not known whether both belong to the sovereign. A small ciborium. Thurible with accessories, and the donor is not mentioned. Three small vials with the holy oils, which the King gave, and they are in a little box without a key. Thirteen very old reales and two rings for arras, which the King gave.

A holy-water pot. The other metal objects have been mentioned already.

Other things: Two old missals. *Manual* by Osorio. Another altar stone; it is not known whether it came from the King. An old silk processional canopy. A humeral veil of the same description. An old frame for a [Holy Thursday] sepulcher. Nondescript catafalque of three tables. Wooden processional cross. A small gourd cup for baptizing. A new processional canopy of China satin, which those mentioned above paid for.

CONVENT

The convent is joined to the church on the Epistle side, where it forms a square extending to the east, with a great portico[3] of

3. This portico no longer exists, but a photograph dated *c.* 1881 shows it. GK (p. 75, fig. 99) suggests that it once served as an open chapel.

adobe arches in the porter's lodge, which faces south inside the cemetery. Although this convent is square, the plan is so intricate that if I describe it, I shall only cause confusion. It has upper and lower stories so

each, which usually yield, when wheat is planted in two of them, some 80 fanegas. Three almudes of maize can be planted in each milpa, and if maize is planted in three of them, 80 fanegas of maize are usually harvested from these three that remain. Obviously they are good. They are irrigated by

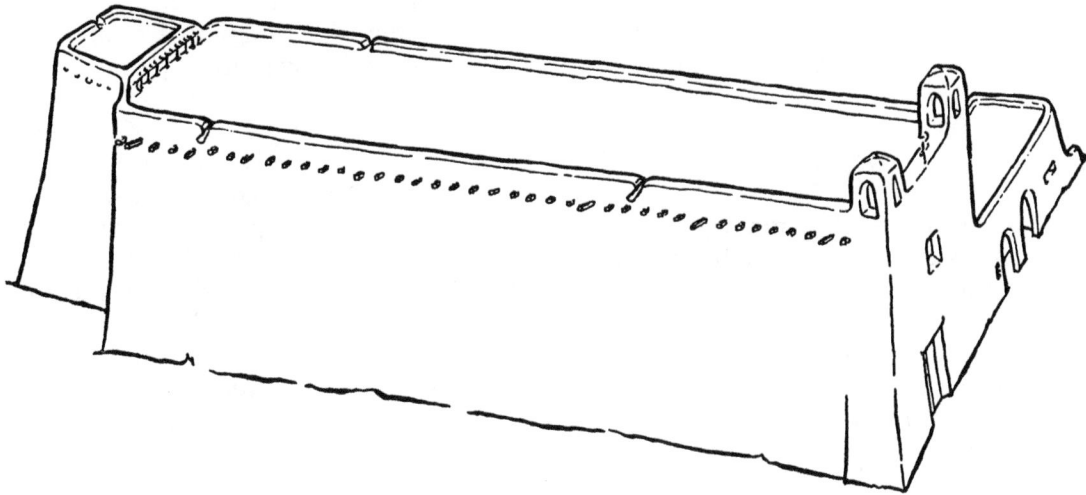

badly arranged and planned that in proof of the poor arrangement I reveal that the entrance to it all is by a stairway which gives on the corral.

This is beside the convent, also extending to the east. It is a very large square area with a very high adobe wall, a new two-leaved gate, which Father Junco installed, and on one side are the stable, strawloft, hencoop, and sty for fattening pigs.

ITS FURNISHINGS: Two large tables. Two benches. Two small chairs.

ITS SERVICE: The same as stated at the Sandia Mission.

ITS LANDS AND FRUITS: This convent has a beautiful kitchen garden among the Indians' lands, from which a large amount of green vegetables is gathered. There are vinestocks in it, but wine is not made because they are few. Cotton is also sown in it, and a small amount is gathered for candles. It has small peach trees. There are seven milpas. If wheat is sown, they take 3 fanegas

very deep wide ditches taken from the Río del Norte, and the pueblo takes care of everything, including depositing the harvest in the convent storerooms.

MISSION FATHER

Father Fray José Junco, native of Tlaxcala, forty years of age, twenty-six in profession, fourteen years as a missionary in the Custody, as follows: San Felipe, three months; San Juan, eight years, six months; Cochiti, two years; Isleta, three years and some months. He has general faculties issued by the Lord [Bishop] Tamarón in Durango and revocable at will.

ADMINISTRATION OF THE MISSION: The usual regime, to which I refer, since it has been stated in many missions.

OBVENTIONS AND FIRST FRUITS: With regard to the first, although the custom in these parts is the same everywhere, yet in this mission there are usually some small sheep, a cow, an ox, sheep, or horse. Although not all of this is given at once, there are always occasions when they are, or a mixture of the foregoing with seeds. As for the second, there are usually collected about 30 fanegas of wheat, the same amount of maize, and about 20 fanegas of all kinds of legumes together, many green vegetables, about 20 small head of livestock, about 10 small head of goats. There are some who devoutly give cattle, and there are usually some four little calves and as many colts or young mules.

NOTE

What has been said up to this point refers to general visitation matters, but no visitation of this mission was made because it was not expedient, since it proved necessary to use subterfuge here (and in many others) to attain the desired end. But as soon as it was accomplished, I watched for the opportune moment, and when I was again in this mission, I executed what is of record in the following

WRIT

Mission of San Agustín de la Isleta, July 8 of the year 1776. Inasmuch as our Reverend Father Fray Francisco Atanasio Domínguez, one of the appointed preachers in the Convento Grande of Our Father St. Francis of Mexico City and Commissary Visitor of this Custody for our Very Reverend Father Minister Provincial Fray Isidro Murillo, entered this mission on the twenty-second day of May of the present year, 1776, with the intention of making a juridical visitation of it and of its missionary friar, Fray José Junco, and inasmuch as he did not put this juridical visitation into effect because of more important considerations that impelled him to omit it (of which he will give an account to our Very Reverend Father Provincial), even though he was aware that the said mission required examination, now that he is in this mission of Isleta on business pertaining to the said Father Junco, he has taken a detailed report of the state of affairs at the mission from the present missionary, Father Fray Mariano Rodríguez de la Torre. And he learned from this report that it was exactly as his Reverend Paternity had suspected. Therefore, as soon as his Reverend Paternity assigned the said Father Rodríguez as missionary to this mission, he ordered him to make a new inventory, recording separately the things that really exist and are in usable condition pertaining to church, sacristy, divine worship, and convent furnishings. At the same time his Reverend Paternity promised the aforesaid father that he would turn over to him the provisions corresponding to this convent, and he did, in fact, hand over to him the following (after taking them from what Father Junco was keeping in a private house in the pueblo)[4]: 10 fanegas of wheat, 10 of maize, 10 sheep, 6 strings of chile, a jar of ordinary lard, an almud of salt, a bottle of wine, 2 wax candles.

The outgoing friar must hand over all these and the newcomer receive them, giving a receipt. And if any of these are missing, or anything recorded in the inventory, he shall notify the Reverend Custos or his Vice-Custos so that the lack may be supplied. And with regard to what has been determined here, the Reverend Custos or his Vice-Custos cannot dispense with or take anything away, but they may, indeed, add all they think necessary for the benefit of the mission and missionary, for that is the intention and will of our Superior Provincial Prelate, who so orders and commands *ratione officii,* and therefore validly for all time. Our Reverend Father Commissary Visitor so provided, ordered, and signed before me, the undersigned acting secretary, to which I attest. Fray Francisco Atanasio Domínguez, Commissary Visitor. In my presence. Fray Andrés García, acting secretary.

4. Father Junco was a "proprietor," a most grave fault in the Franciscan Order, because he kept and sold merchandise for his own use and profit.

I examined the parish books, which have very few folios. I provided three new ones out of the supply that came from the Province. And the foregoing writ is recorded in the new Inventory which Father Rodríguez made by my order.

PUEBLO

The little rise on which the pueblo stands is as small as I said in the beginning, and it lies on the very meadow of the Río del Norte, which sometimes overflows its bed up above the pueblo when it is very high and forms a very wide branch at a distance from it. This cuts off the settled part as if it were an island, which is doubtless the reason why it was named Isleta. This place stands, as has been said, on the very meadow, open to the plain which slopes down from those hills I mentioned at Atlixco of Albuquerque. And they start at the cañada mentioned in the note inserted before Santa Ana. This Isleta is about a musket shot and a half from the aforesaid river. It enjoys a very fine and pleasant view in all directions, especially downstream to the south, where a sierra which is some 20 leagues to the south can be seen. They call it the Sierra de la Magdalena.

The pueblo consists of three beautiful blocks of dwellings, separated from one another at the corners, which are located in front of the church and convent, and form a very large plaza there to the south of them. Outside the plaza at various distances all around there are some twenty houses which would be as large as one block, or tenement, of the plaza if they were all together. Everything is of adobe, very prettily designed and much in the Spanish manner. But in general there are *cois*, etc., such as I have been describing since Tesuque.

ITS LANDS AND FRUITS: The Indians of this pueblo have arable lands of every quality for a league upstream, a league downstream, and as far on either side as such lands extend. As has been said, they are irrigated from the afore-mentioned river, and from all of them they get very copious crops of everything planted. There are many orchards of fruit trees as well as vinestocks, and they usually make a little wine.

The natives are Tiguas, like those of Sandia, whose native tongue they speak, both pueblos speaking in similar fashion to those of Picuris and Taos, all of whom use substantially the same language, although in a different manner and with distinctive pronunciation. This makes it appear that there are four distinct kinds of languages among them all, but this superficial appearance, easily penetrated by a careful mind, does not alter the fact that they are the same. Adults and children, men and women, use, speak, and understand Spanish, but in the same way as has been said of those genízaros of Santa Fe and Abiquiu, to whom I refer. With regard to their particular customs, I say that they are well inclined to Spanish customs, for many use mattresses on their beds, and there are many bedsteads. Here is their

CENSUS

114 families with 454 persons

A very large number of settlers are administered by this mission, and they are as follows:

Pajarito is located 2 leagues north of the pueblo on the same plain and meadow along the road from Albuquerque to Isleta. It consists of ranchos with arable lands, mostly sandy like those at Atlixco of Albuquerque. They are irrigated from the aforesaid river through deep irrigation ditches (this is also true of other places I shall describe below) taken from it, and they produce reasonable crops of everything. The owners of this Pajarito are mostly Spaniards, with servants of low class, and all those here use the regional Spanish. Here is their

CENSUS

37 families with 214 persons

About a league downstream from the mission to the south some widely separated ranchos begin, located all over the river meadow downstream. They belong to a settlement of ranchos called *Belén* (it is opposite Tomé), which is 6 leagues from the mission. It lies on the river meadow mentioned so many times. It has good farmlands, which are irrigated from the said river, and they yield very good and copious crops of everything. The individuals are like those everywhere, not to be boring, and here is their

CENSUS

96 families with 593 persons

In this Belén there is a group of genízaros like those at Santa Fe.[5] And some of them have small plots of arable land, and others

5. This was in the settlement of Los Jarales. SANM, 2: no. 1092b.

have nothing, supporting themselves as their luck helps them (only they and God know whether they have managed to get their hands on what belongs to their neighbors). Here is their

CENSUS

49 families with 209 persons

Four leagues down the road to the south of this place, on the same meadow, is a settlement of ranchos like the above. It is called *Sabinal* and is 10 leagues from the mission. Their lands are good, even better than those of Belén. They are irrigated with the aforesaid river and yield proportionate crops and harvests. The individuals like all the rest, and here is their

CENSUS

51 families with 214 persons

Pecos

The pueblo and mission of Nuestra Señora de los Angeles de Pecos is 7 leagues southeast of Santa Fe at the foot and lower slope of the Sierra Madre mentioned at the said villa. It is located and established on a good piece of level ground offered by a low rock, which is easy to climb. This rock is more or less boxed in between a sierra and a mesa. The sierra lies to the east, about 3 or 4 leagues from the pueblo, and the mesa to the west, about a quarter of a league from it. The buildings are on the said rock, surrounded by a fence, or wall, of adobe, which I shall describe more fully later.[1] I reiterate that this pueblo is 7 leagues from Santa Fe and lies to the south of it.

CHURCH

The church is adobe with walls even more than a vara thick, with the outlook and main door to the west. From the door to the mouth of the formal transept it has, it is 36 varas long and 9 high and wide. From there to the mouth of the sanctuary the transept is 9 varas long, 15 wide, and as much higher as the clerestory demands. The ascent to the sanctuary consists of five steps made of wrought beams which occupy a long vara in the transept, and they have little railings on both sides coming up from below, but they do not continue across in front of the sanctuary. The sanctuary measures 6 varas square and is as high as the transept.

There is a choir loft in the usual place, and it is like those described before. In the end wall of the right arm of the transept there is a window with a wooden grating facing north, and there is a seemly tribune at the other end. There are three windows facing south on the Epistle side of the nave, and one in the choir to a balcony like the one at Nambe. All the beams in the roof are well wrought and corbeled and are distributed as follows: thirty-eight in the nave, twenty in the transept, and ten in the sanctuary. The following inscription is on the one facing the nave: *Frater Carolus*. The inference is that a friar of this name was the one who built the church, but it is impossible to identify him since the individual is not identified by his surname.[2]

The main door is squared, with a wooden frame instead of masonry. It has two paneled leaves with a crossbar and is 3 varas high by 2 wide. On top of the flat roof at both front corners there are two small towers with a small bell donated by the King in one of them, and it is a good one. The cemetery has a high adobe wall with a gate, but

1. Dr. A. V. Kidder, whose knowledge of Pecos is unequaled, has been kind enough to read this section of the manuscript and he considers Domínguez' description the best he has seen. He says: "The only mistake that I could find is the statement that the wall around the pueblo was of adobe, whereas it was of unshaped pieces of sandstone. It's possible, of course, that when Domínguez was there it was finished with adobe plaster. We found a great number of skeletons buried under the floor of the nave in the few pits we put down. These were evidently all of Indians, but in front of the altar steps there were the remains of two priests in wooden coffins. Their long woolen garments were quite well preserved. These and the other burials in the mission were replaced and we arranged to have the local priest from Pecos town conduct a service." Letter of A. V. Kidder to E. B. Adams, October 2, 1953.

2. Although Fray Francisco de San Miguel was assigned to Pecos in 1598, there is no evidence that he, or his companion, Juan de Dios, remained there for long or started any church building. In 1619 Fray Pedro Zambrano Ortiz became guardian and was succeeded by Fray Pedro de Ortega in the autumn of 1621. A year later Fray Andrés Suárez was in charge of the mission and remained there for at least ten years. F. V. Scholes and L. B. Bloom, "Friar personnel and mission chronology," NMHR, 19 (1944): 328; 20 (1945); 66. Benavides credits Suárez with the founding of "a convent and church of peculiar construction and beauty, very spacious, with room for all the people of the pueblo." AB-1634, p. 67. It is probable, however, that the work was begun before he arrived. Other seventeenth-century references to the church indicate that it was larger and more imposing than most. The documents for the 1680 Revolt and for the Reconquest do not make it clear what happened to the church. In 1706 Father Alvarez said, "The building of the church has been begun," but, as usual, it is difficult to determine the exact meaning of his statement. HB, 3: 373. We learn from Domínguez that there were two churches, the older one somewhat smaller than the one in use in his time. It seems likely that the new church was built after the Reconquest, but when it was started or how long it took is still a question.

The only friar named Carolus (Carlos, Charles) in all the Custody's history up to 1777 was Fray Carlos Delgado, who was stationed at Pecos early in the eighteenth century. His known entries there run from December 23, 1716, to October 30, 1717. See FRANCISCANS. Pecos, once one of the most populous pueblos of New Mexico, declined throughout the eighteenth century and was abandoned finally about 1838. AB-1634, p. 273. The ruins have been the subject of intensive archaeological investigations, first undertaken by the Department of Archaeology of Phillips Andover Academy in 1915, and the results have been published by A. V. Kidder and others.

only on two sides, the one that begins at the front corner on the right side and the one in front, for the façade of the convent makes the third side. This is all inside the cemetery, as we shall soon see. In accordance with this arrangement the cemetery measures 24 varas, almost in a square.

As we enter the church, on our right under the choir is the entrance to an old church outside the wall. The old building extends to the south, with the door where I said, and is joined to the convent on the Epistle side. And in order not to become involved, I state now that it is of a size to fit into the nave of the one we are describing and that it is falling down. As we enter this old church, outside its wall on the left is the sacristy now in use, and the baptistery now in use is on the right, also outside the walls, and the entrance to both rooms is from the old building.

I shall speak of the sacristy presently. With regard to the baptistery, I state that it is a small room with a window, a door, a small pillar and an earthen bowl like those I have described elsewhere. Before the entrance to this room there is a large door leading to the cloister. The interior of the church in use today is rather pleasant, the floor is bare earth, and its adornment as follows.

HIGH ALTAR: A little above the center of the wall hangs an old oil painting on canvas with a painted wooden frame of Our Lady of the Angels. Below this is another, which is similar in size and frame but not so old, and it is a well-painted representation of Our Lady of the Assumption.[3] The King

gave them both. Eight ordinary old oil paintings are arranged around those mentioned above. The images of three are undistinguishable, but the others can be made out, and they are St. Jerome, Our Lady of Solitude, Our Lady of Sorrows, St. Anthony, and Our Lady of Guadalupe.

The wooden altar table is movable, with an altar stone donated by the King, a small cross with a bronze Christus and INRI, altar card, lectern, and two small brass candlesticks, which the King gave. Below there is a board dais and two small bronze bells. On the right side of the sanctuary there is a small door to a little room used for storing some church belongings, and above this little door there is an old middle-sized oil painting on canvas of Jesús Nazareno. There is another painting opposite it, but on buffalo skin and so old that the image is undistinguishable.

TRANSEPT: There are two altars in the transept. The one on the Gospel side is at the end wall under the window mentioned above. It is dedicated to St. Anthony of Padua, whose image is an ordinary, fairly good painting on buffalo skin. There are five small old oil paintings around it. The other altar is under the above-mentioned tribune. It is dedicated to Our Lady of Guadalupe, with a painting on buffalo skin like the above, with four small paintings at the sides. The tables of these altars are wood and bare. The nave of the church has a very well made wooden pulpit in the usual place. There is a pretty wooden confessional on a platform on the Gospel side, and then a long bench with legs.

SACRISTY: I have already said above that it is on one side of the old church. It runs from there up along the wall of the present church, being 8 varas long, 4 wide, and 3 high. It has twelve beams with corbels in

---

3. These two paintings were not only similar in size, but undoubtedly much alike in pictorial treatment, for "Our Lady of the Angels" was St. Francis' own name for "Our Lady of the Assumption" at Assisi, mother church of the Franciscan Order. One of these two canvases survives in the Spanish parish of Pecos. It is said that the Pecos Indians, when they abandoned the pueblo in 1838, left it with the people of Pecos village, providing that they should keep on celebrating the feast of our Lady of the Angels on August 2. The Pecos villagers have ob-

served this feast ever since, in addition to their own patronal feast of St. Anthony of Padua on June 13. The painting was restored and framed by the Rev. Michael Dumarest and his two artist sisters in the 1920's.

the roof, a window to the south on one side, and an ordinary two-leaved door without a key to the said old church. All across the end wall there is a good wooden table that has five drawers without keys. There is a middle-sized wooden cross on the wall; below it are the prayers for vesting, in manuscript. For this purpose the table is completely covered by a painted buffalo skin. There is a good platform at the foot of the table, and on it two small chests like those in which the secular priests carry their vestments, and these have no locks. On one side there are four tablets with edicts of the Holy Office and a very neat wooden washstand, on which the bowl and towel are placed as is the custom outside of this land. The things pertaining to divine worship are kept in all the drawers mentioned, as follows:

Vestments: A usable damask chasuble with two faces (white and purple) with complete accessories, which the King gave. Another usable one with two faces (blue and mother-of-pearl), and its accessories lack burse and cloth [veil for the chalice?]; the King gave it. Another usable one with two faces (purple damask and striped mother-of-pearl silk), and its accessories consist of stole and maniple. Another usable one of calamanco embroidered with silver twist, with accessories. Another almost new one of black damask, with accessories including

cope and cross sheath, which Father Camargo gave. A usable white damask cope. An old humeral veil of mother-of-pearl ribbed silk.

Linen: A usable Brittany amice. Three albs like the amice. Another with the top half of Brittany and the lower half of Campeche lace. Two usable Brittany altar cloths. Two palls to match. A pair of usable double corporals of Brittany. Thirteen purificators. Three silk cinctures and one of cotton. A Brittany finger towel. A very tiny Brittany surplice. A cloth used for a cap in baptisms.

Silver and other metal: Chalice with paten and spoon. Three small vials with the holy oils in a little box without a key. Thirteen very old reales with their rings, for arras. The king gave it all.

A thurible with accessories. A broken holy-water pot. Two processional crosses. Two more small candlesticks from the King. A mold for making altar breads from the same lord.

Other things: Another altar stone, which must be from the King. A usable missal. Three old *Manuals* by Vetancurt. Another by Osorio, which the rats have completely raped with their teeth. Two glass cruets garnished with wax. Puebla plate for the foregoing. Two wooden processional candleholders. Box for altar breads of the same white stone as the reredos of Our Lady of Light at Santa Fe.

CONVENT

When I was describing the cemetery, I mentioned the location of the convent. It forms a square, has upper and lower stories, and, resembling our friaries of recollection, it is arranged as follows: The porter's lodge is inside the cemetery facing north, and it is a square portico measuring 10 varas divided equally. There is a strong cross timber in the center of the roof, and two wooden pillars at the mouth, which divide it into three arches, with railings in the ones at the sides. There are adobe seats around it and an ordinary two-leaved door with a crossbar in the middle of the center wall.

As we enter the aforesaid, there are two beautiful stables, each with a strawloft, on our right. One is on a corner, and around the corner is a stair well with stairs leading to the upper story, which we shall soon see. Beyond the stair well there is a cell, then a passageway I shall describe later, then another cell on the corner. There are six rooms around the corner as far as the inside corner against the old building, and of all these six, only one, which serves as a fine storeroom, has a door, but no key.

On the left as we enter, the wall of the baptistery extends to the inside corner of the old building and continues around the corner against the aforesaid old building to that inside corner where the six rooms are. In this corner, and in the cloister itself, is another stairway, which leads· to the upper story like the one mentioned above. The lower cloister is enclosed, with two windows on each side, making eight in all. The passageway I left pending further mention leads to a fortified tower which stands on one side of the convent. When there are enemies, a stone mortar is installed in it.

Whichever of the afore-mentioned stairways we ascend, we see rooms over the lower ones mentioned, but I note that those over the porter's lodge and its sides are in bad condition, as are those around the corner to the west. Only those that face south and are approached by the stairway in the corner of the cloister are usable. In these south rooms and in the ones on the west there are very good miradores, one on each side. The south one has a good railing. The other is bare because, according to what the Indians say, an alcalde who was here (and he still lives here, but is no longer alcalde), called Vicente Armijo, took the balusters to put them in the *casas reales*. The upper cloister is open, with railings between wooden pillars.

NOTE

Although there are no mission fathers at this mission and at the one I have yet to describe to whom my visitation may be made, the efficacious fulfillment of my duty obliged me to inspect both as if I were making one. Therefore I have examined the foregoing and what remains to be reported, deferring, as I should, what concerns the other mission to its proper place. With regard to this mission, I now continue. I took the small vials with the holy oils to *Santa Fe*, and I left the other things in care of the alcalde, Don José Herrera, with many admonitions.

The parish books date from the year 1727. Their writs record 200 leaves, but this number does not exist now. There is little missing from the book of Baptisms and the entries seem to be complete. The others have scarcely twenty leaves each, and their entries have been visited frequently by the mice.

I remitted these to the archive, which is at the mission of Our Father Santo Domingo (as has been said before). Three new ones from the supply that came from the Province remain in Santa Fe so that the mission father there may keep the records in the interval until there is a missionary at Pecos, whose Indians are baptized and married in said villa. With regard to burials, if an Indian dies, the others perform the offices, etc. Although there is no father, they still know that the children must go to the church daily to recite the catechism with the fiscal. In the mornings of Saturdays and feast days the whole pueblo goes to recite the rosary. Alcalde don José Herrera assured me of this.

ITS LANDS: There are five plots, some larger than the others, distributed as follows: There is a beautiful kitchen garden for green vegetables below the cemetery to the west. It is dependent on rain, and has a good wall attached to and entered from the cemetery. North of this kitchen garden are two separate large milpas. The one near the kitchen garden is dependent on rain, and the one beyond it gets irrigation from a river we shall soon see. There is another large milpa dependent on rain beyond the kitchen garden to the west. To the south, another like the aforesaid, also dependent on rain. Located in this way in the directions mentioned, they are about a quarter of a league from the pueblo, and I give no account of their crops because the Indians give me none. Indeed, they do say uproariously that wheat, maize, etc., are sown, except for chile, and that a sufficient amount is harvested. For the present the aforesaid plant them for themselves, and when there is a father, they do the work for him.

PUEBLO

I have already said that it is on a rather boxed-in rock. The adobe fence, or wall, which surrounds it is about 500 varas long and about 200 wide. There is plenty of room for all the buildings inside and separate from it. The only entrance is a gate facing north where the ascent to the pueblo is. A short distance from the entrance are some tenements, or blocks, all joined at the corners, which have a little plaza between them. The entrance to it is a door in the middle of the block that faces east. Of these four blocks, the two that face east and west are very wide and have dwellings in the center on the top that overlook both the little plaza and the outside. They are like

the top section of a long and narrow tomb.

To the south beyond this little plaza there is another block, or tenement, like the two described. The only difference is that it stands alone and extends a long distance from north to south. Everything appears very large and can only be seen in perspective up from the north and down from the south. On the west it is near the aforesaid mesa, and on the east near the sierra (this is no longer the Santa Fe Sierra) called Pecos because it is so near, as has been said, and it runs from the north very far to the south. Along the small plain between the sierra and the pueblo a very good river of good water and many delicious trout runs from north to south, but the water is not taken for use in the pueblo because it is about half a league away and there is very great danger from the Comanches. Therefore they have opened some wells of reasonably good water below the rock, and that is used for drinking and other purposes.

ITS LANDS AND FRUITS: The Indians have arable lands in all the four principal directions, but only those which lie to the north, partly east, enjoy irrigation. The rest are dependent on rain. These irrigated lands are of no use today because this pueblo is so very much besieged by the enemy, and even those dependent on rain which are at a distance cannot be used. Therefore, but a very small part remains for them. Since this is dependent on rain, it has been a failure because of the drought of the past years, and so they have nothing left. As a result, what few crops there usually are do not last even to the beginning of a new year from the previous October, and hence these miserable wretches are tossed about like a ball in the hands of fortune.

Today these poor people are *in puribus*, fugitives from their homes, absent from their families, selling those trifles they once bought to make themselves decent, on foot, etc. On the other hand, Governor don Pedro Fermín de Mendinueta, Knight [of the Order of Santiago], has come to their aid with twelve cows, which, added to eight old ones they had before (which were all the enemies had left them), make twenty. As for horses, they have twelve sorry nags all together when they once had a very great number. The natives of this pueblo and their native tongue are Pecos, the language agreeing *uno ore* with Jémez (as I said there). Most of them are good carpenters. The aforesaid sierra provides them with timber. With regard to their particular customs, I say that they are devout and have good inclinations. There is proof of this in what was said at the end of the above note. They speak Spanish very badly, and here is their

CENSUS

100 families with 269 persons[4]

4. Cf. AT, pp. 48 ff. In the sixteen years since Bishop Tamarón's visitation, the population apparently had declined from 168 families to 100. A complaint in 1815 states that Pecos, formerly one of the largest pueblos, had no more than forty persons of both sexes. AASF, 1815, no. 7. Tamarón mentions the excellent horsemanship of the Pecos Indians. AT, p. 50.

Galisteo

The pueblo and mission of Nuestra Señora de los Remedios de Galisteo is 6 leagues from Santa Fe toward the south-south-west over a beautiful plain with some depressions in it.[1] It is located and established on the same plain where we have been traveling. Near the pueblo it is very open to the east, north, and west. About two musket shots from the pueblo to the south is a craggy rock which has the shape of a cock's crest, and for that reason they call it Crestón; this runs a short distance from east to west, about half a league. The pueblo under the above heading is the said 6 leagues from Santa Fe, and lies in the direction already mentioned in relation to the villa. I shall have more to say about it later.

NOTE

The description of the church and convent at this mission finds no better expression than in the Lamentations of Jeremiah, for this is the situation: The church is small. Its walls are about to fall. Half of the roof is on the ground, and the rest is ready to lie on the floor. That is, half of it has fallen, and it will not be long before the rest does. The main door, which faces east, is always open, for if they move it to close it, it falls to the ground. In short, it is useless and needs to be completely rebuilt from the foundations. The sacristy is the least decayed. The plan of this room resembles an oratory of the Indians of Mexico, but its little adornment does not. I shall soon make a brief statement about its contents.

The convent is on the Epistle side of the ruins. There are only indications of what may have been there, for it is so uninhabitable that to live in it is to enter expecting death and to remain buried there as soon as one sits down, because it is so near to falling. It has eight ruined rooms. In one of them there is a chair without a seat, another without arms, and that is all. There is a great adobe table in the sacristy. On the wall above it hangs a large old oil painting on canvas of Our Lady of Remedies, which the King gave. Outside, a small broken bell from the King on some posts. The following are in an old unpainted chest in the sacristy.

Vestments: An old damask chasuble with two faces (white and crimson), with accessories, which the King gave. Another of the same description, but its faces are blue and green, given by the King. An old one of pure silk embroidered with silver twist, and its accessories do not include stole or frontal. Another almost new one of black damask, with accessories including cope and cross sheath, which Father Camargo gave.

Linen: A good cambric amice; the donor is not mentioned. Another old one of Brittany. Two albs like the last amice. An old Rouen altar cloth. Another of the same material, which Governor Mendinueta just gave. An old Rouen pall. Two old pairs of double corporals of Brittany. Three purificators. There are no cinctures.

Silver and other metal: Chalice with paten alone, which the King gave. Twelve extremely old coins with two rings for arras, which the King gave. A small cross.

A latten plate. Two small candlesticks, which the King gave, and they are broken. A broken processional cross. A bronze Christus on a small wooden cross, which is used on the altar. A small altar bell. A little spoon.

Other things: A very small altar stone. Usable missal. An old *Manual* by Vetancurt.

NOTES

First: There are no chrismatories at this mission because an Indian stole them (some time ago) but they have now turned up in the following manner. When I was making my juridical visitation at the Villa de la Cañada, one Bustos came to me to sell me two of them, and he gave me this explanation in substance: He had been waiting for the Lord Bishop in order to turn those cigar cases over to him, for one of his sons had bought them from an Apache who had them hanging from his horse. He had taken them to Father Rodríguez de la Torre and Father Fernández, but they neither bought them nor paid any attention. Now that I had come, he would sell them to me for 25 regional pesos. I immediately suspected mischief and took them from him with civility. I applied to the Knight Governor, who severely reproved the said Bustos and de-

1. The title of the Galisteo mission in the seventeenth century was Santa Cruz de Galisteo. F. V. Scholes, "Documents for the history of the New Mexican missions," NMHR 4 (1949): 53. The Tanos of this pueblo were among the leaders of the Rebellion in 1680, and it was they who occupied Santa Fe between 1680 and 1693 and whom de Vargas had to conquer in bloody battle in December, 1693, in order to regain the villa. They were resettled at San Cristóbal in the Santa Cruz-Chimayó district, only to incite a second rebellion in 1696. Subsequently these fierce people were returned to their own pueblo, which was refounded under the title of Nuestra Señora de los Remedios, the Virgin on the royal standard used by de Vargas. Evidently this title was given to this specific mission in memory of the triumph of the royal standard over the Tanos in the battle for Santa Fe. In a letter to the King, Governor Cubero calls the patroness of Galisteo Nuestra Señora de Gracia, but the context shows that he meant "Remedios." AGI, Aud. de Guadalajara, leg. 265. This is the name recorded in the oldest extant mission register, begun in 1711 by Fray Lucas de Arévalo when Fray Juan de Tagle was custos. The only images mentioned in a short inventory in this book were a canvas of Nuestra Señora de los Remedios 9 cuartas long by 6 wide in a gilt frame, a picture of Our Lady on paper about half a vara long, and a St. John in the round about 3 cuartas tall with its pedestal.

prived him of them. They are in my care, with the intention of leaving them in Chihuahua to be repaired.

Second: I found only one parish book. It is used for Marriages and Burials. Father Gabaldón started it in the year 1727, and the section which serves for Marriages ends on May 1, 1774, with the signature of Father Fray Patricio Cuellar. In the section for Burials there is this entry only: "I received this mission on the fourth day of May, 1774. Fray Patricio Cuellar." With regard to Baptisms, I found only a paper with six entries, four made by the Father Ex-Lector Rodríguez and two by the said Cuellar. I found two books of Inventory, one for the year 1753 and the other for 1759, and they show how much is missing. I admonished the Indians about this, and they replied substantially as follows:

With regard to the Baptismal book, they say that: That Armijo mentioned in my report on the Pecos convent, the one who took the balusters from the mirador, this same man and a lieutenant called Jerónimo Leiva (he is now dead) cut out and carried off the leaves of this book. And with regard to the other things that are missing, the said persons cut the ribbons from the amices and took them away.

Everything reported under Inventory up to here is all I saw and found at this Galisteo. With the exception of what the Indians have to say, there is no further information, because the fathers who have lived here and are still in the Custody make no statement about the many things that are missing according to the aforesaid inventories. The fact is that they are lost, and the reason is (without being rash, since there is proof) the great carelessness of those whose duty it was to watch over, see to, preserve, etc., the existence of these things.

Such zeal inspires me to remove the occasion for it. I therefore took with me to the Villa of Santa Fe all the ecclesiastical vestments still in existence, which have been mentioned. They are in the care of the mis-

sion father there, to whom I also gave three new parish books until there may be a friar at Galisteo, whose Indians are administered from Santa Fe like those of Pecos, as stated. Only the old chest for sacred vestments and a key to the convent, which has just been found, remain at Galisteo, all in the keeping of Lieutenant José Miguel Garduño. I also gave the mission father of the said Santa Fe sufficient paper for a new inventory.

LANDS: There are three small milpas of poor land below the pueblo to the west. These are irrigated with the water of a spring higher up, and it flows in an arroyo which comes from the canyon they call Pecos because it comes from that direction. They call the place where the spring is Nieto,[2] and only there is there water, for little runs in the arroyo. With regard to the harvest from these little milpas, the Indians make a confused statement, saying they yield wheat and maize, but now they do not even plant them for themselves.

PUEBLO

It has already been said that it stands on an open plain. Its description is as follows: A wall of adobes and stones in the form of a large square with a large gate to the south. At the southwest corner of this wall is the so-called church, with the convent beside it, and there is a fortified tower on this corner. The pueblo buildings are in the north section in two small plazas, each composed of four small tenements, or blocks, of dwellings, in as ruinous condition as the convent. There are three fortified towers on the three remaining corners of the fence, or wall, one on each.

ITS LANDS AND FRUITS: The Indians of this pueblo have as much land as can be compassed in each direction for a league down from the pueblo. Of them all, only those adjoining the convent lands have any

2. Members of the related Nieto and Leiva families living in the Galisteo basin were massacred or taken captive by the Tanos in 1680.

irrigation; the rest are dependent on rain. For this reason they have suffered greater disasters than the Pecos Indians, and they are enduring even more deplorable poverty than they are, for these Galisteos, unlike them, no longer have anything to sell in order to live. Most of the year they are away from home, now the men alone, now the women alone, sometimes the husband in one place, his wife in another, the children in still another, and so it all goes. Comanche enemies and great famine because of the droughts are the captains who compel them to drag out their existence in this way. The former have deprived many of them of their lives and all of them of their landed property. The latter drives them to depart, as has been said. And those who remain eat the hides of cows, oxen, horses, etc., in a sort of fried cracklings, and when they do not find this quickly, they strip the vellum from the saddletrees or toast old shoes. They do not have one cow; there is not a single horse. At present Governor Mendinueta, Knight [of the Order of Santiago],

has lent them seven yoke of oxen for their planting. In short, they are so discouraged that they have thought of abandoning the pueblo and dividing themselves as best they might among the pueblos with good supplies, but they have not done so for fear of the government.[3]

The natives of this pueblo are called Tanos. They speak the Tegua language, like the pueblos from Tesuque to San Juan. They speak Spanish in the same way as the other Tanos, whose particular customs they share. Here is their

CENSUS

41 families with 152 persons

3. The population had declined by nearly one half in the sixteen years since Bishop Tamarón's visitation. When he arrived they rode out to greet him and frightened the bishop's escort, who mistook them for Comanches. AT, pp. 53-54. According to a baptismal entry at Santo Domingo, Galisteo was still occupied in October, 1780, but by February, 1792, the pueblo of Galisteo is mentioned as extinct, with the remnants of the population living in Santo Domingo. SANM, 2: no. 1188.

SUMMARY

The group of missions that the interior branch of this Custody has in the Río Abajo is now complete, and we found the last pueblo and mission caught on a reef of misfortunes. This group numbers fourteen missions, including the Villa of Albuquerque and thirteen Indian pueblos, which, added to the Río Arriba group, make the sum of twenty-two which I enumerated in the beginning (the little pueblo of Pojoaque is counted). The description of these fourteen missions shows what I observed in them.

The number of 10,781 souls dwell in them under the care of eleven priests residing in them. (Due consideration justifies my passing over the fact that Pecos and Galisteo are administered from Santa Fe, since it makes no real difference whether they are

attached to the said mission or to one of the Río Abajo missions.) Although, in my general visitation, thirteen fathers were visited, one of them (this is Father Junco) is absent at provincial headquarters, and another died while I was drawing up this report of my visitation, and the latter is Father Abadiano. The said Río Abajo group has 3,301 more souls than the Río Arriba group. Adding the 7,480 souls in Río Arriba to the 10,781 of Río Abajo, they amount to (allowing for error) 18,261 souls who now live under the care of twenty priests distributed as has been seen throughout this interior branch.[1]

1. Including Santa Fe, the total of the figures given in the manuscript for the Río Arriba is 7,550 persons, and for the Río Abajo, including Pecos and Galisteo, 10,794, or a population of 18,344 in the interior missions.

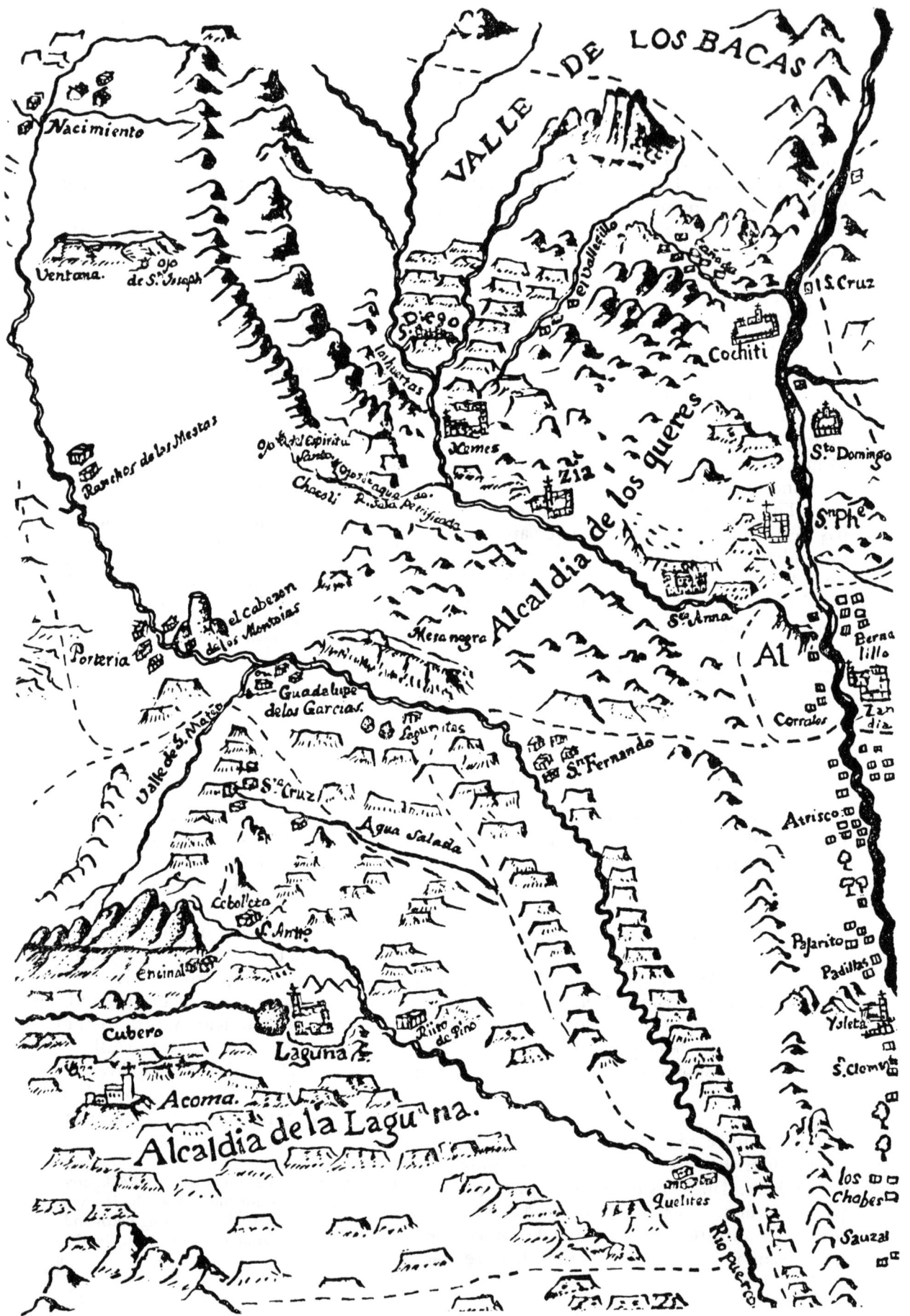

V. THE
LIBRARY & ARCHIVE
OF THE CUSTODY

ADDENDA: In my description of the mission of Our Father Santo Domingo, at the foot of the writ of visitation under the heading *Addition,* I said that there was a chest there containing things from the Sovereign for the Navajo missions, and the library and archive of this Custody. With regard to the contents of the chest, I consider it superfluous to stop to list them, because the signatures of the prelates acknowledging what they are prove that they are being cared for. And therefore I proceed to the remainder, without classifying the books or keeping sets together.[1]

The Library

IN FOLIO

[1] Four volumes of *Teologia moral* by Villalobos. [Fray Enrique de Villalobos, *Summa de la Theología Moral y canónica,* Salamanca, 1622. The 1788 Inventory lists eight copies of Pt. 1 and five of Pt. 2.]

[2] *Ortus Pastores.* The author is not given. [Not identified in 1788 Inventory.]

[3] *Questiones de Escoto contra Lombardo.* [John Duns Scotus.][2]

[4] Two *Panegiricos de Maria Santisima* by Fr. Martin Castillo. [Fray Martín del Castillo, *Commentaria in Debboram et Jahelem: sive Panegiricus de S. S. Maria, Domina nostra, in illis Veteris Testamenti heroicis et celebratissimis Faeminis adumbrata,* Seville, 1678. 1788 Inventory: "Yllustraon Penegirica Maria Debora Mistica. Otra."]

[5] *Discursos morales* by Almonaci. [Fray José de Almonacid, *Discursos para los domingos y ferias principales de la Quaresma,* Madrid, 1676. In 1788 Inventory under full title.]

[6] *Practica de curas y confesores* by Father Noidens, in two volumes. [Benito Remigio Noydens, *Práctica de curas y confesores y doctrina para penitentes,* Madrid, 1658. The 1788 Inventory lists three copies.]

[7] *Chronica de Dieguinos.* [Possibly Fray Baltasar de Medina, *Chronica de la Santa Provincia de San Diego de México de Religiosos Descalços de N. S. P. S. Francisco,* Mexico, 1682. Not identified in 1788 Inventory.]

[8] *Bocabulario* by Nebrija. [Antonio de Nebrija, *Dictionarium latino-hispanicum,* Salamanca, 1492. The 1788 Inventory lists two copies, one "without beginning, etc."]

[9] An *Expossitivo,* without beginning or end.[3]

[10] *Logica* by Rodrigues. [1788 Inventory: "Fr. Luis Rodriguez Noyens Comentar. in Logicam, Phisicam et metaphisicam D. Subt. Scoti."]

[11] *Propugnacion de verdades catolicas* by Torrecilla. [Fray Martín Torrecilla. 1788 Inventory: "Idem (Fr. Martin de Torrecilla) Propugnaculo ortodoxae fidei adversus quosdam veritatis hostes."][4]

[12] *Casos de conciencia* by Filguera. [Manuel Ambrosio Filguera, *Summa de casos de conciencia que se disputan en la Teologia Moral,* Madrid, 1667. Not identified in 1788 Inventory.]

[13] *Meditaciones de la vida oculta de Christo* by Salmeron. [Fray Marcos Salmerón, *El príncipe escondido, Meditaciones de la Vida oculta de Christo,* Madrid, 1648. 1788 Inventory: "Fr. Marcos Salmeron el Principe Escondido."]

[14] *Obras* of the Father Minister Juan de Avila. [Juan de Avila, *Obras,* Madrid, 1588. 1788 Inventory: "P. M. Juan Abila Tratados del SSmo. Sacramto. Spritu Sto. y M.ª SSma."]

[15] Another *Expositivo,* without beginning or end.

[16] Two volumes of *Chronologia de N. P. San Francisco.* [1788 Inventory: "Chronologia

---

1. This library has disappeared and may have been lost when the church and convent were swept away by the Río Grande in 1886. A vestment case in the present sacristy is filled with old volumes in disarray. An examination of them in 1942 revealed one small book printed in black letter, without cover or title page, apparently one of the *Decretales* of Gregory mentioned in this list. The remainder are old missals and breviaries.

While this volume was in press, a valuable manuscript came to light in AASF (1788, no. 8): *Imbentario Gral de la Libreria de esta Sta Cust.ª q.ᵉ esta en el Conv.to de N. P. Sto Domingo Año de 1788.* In so far as time and the bibliographical material at our disposal have permitted, we have collated Domínguez' list with the 1788 Inventory.

Domínguez' list comprises 256 entries, unclassified except by size. The actual number of volumes is somewhat larger, for he often listed sets or additional copies in a single entry.

The 1788 Inventory is classified according to subject and catalogued under seven headings: *Scriptura Sacra et Spositores Sacri, Scholasticos Totius Theologiae, Morales, Predicables, Historicos, Misticos, Diversos.* There are 384 entries. Since separate entries were frequently made for volumes of sets and for additional copies of the same work, the Library of the Custody had not increased nearly so much by 1788 as the figures might suggest. Domínguez does, however, list a number of liturgical books, a category not included in the 1788 Inventory.

Some thirty items listed by Domínguez have not been found in the 1788 Inventory, and a somewhat larger number listed in the 1788 Inventory cannot be positively identified with any of Domínguez' entries:

Scholasticos: "Decisiones Sacrae Rotae sin principio." "P. Fr. Ant.º Rubio Comentaria in Universam Aristhotelis Dialecticam idem in 8 Libr.ˢ Phicō audito seu ausculatioem." "Fr. José Nicolas Cavero Anti-Agredistae Parisienses Expugnati." "Fr. Miguel de Medina de Sacrorum hominum Continencia." "Roberto Belarmino Controversias Christianas de fe contra los Hereges de estos tiempos tom. 3." *Morales:* "1 tom. en folio sin princ. ni fin. Fr. Alonso de la Vega Suma llamada Practica del Fuero Interior." "1 Tomo en folio latino sin princip. ni fin." "Juicio sacramental etc. sin princ. ni fin. otra." "Busembaum Medula Theolog. Moralis." "Un tom. en 8 sin princ. ni fin latino." "Josefo Augustino Panormitano Brevis noticia de eorum quae scitu digna confesariis. P. Manuel Sa Aphorismi Confesariorum. P. Joann. Ant.º Oviedo Sucus Theologiae Moralis. otro." *Predicables:* "Cartagena Homilias de B. V. M. Latinas." "Fr. Fran.co Lizana Primera Escuela del hombre Dotrinas morales." "Serm.ˢ de S. Bernardo sin princ. ni fin." "Moreno Construcion Predicable." *Historicos:* "Hist. Pontifical. lo mismo (sin princ. ni fin.)" "Un manuscripto sin princ. ni fin." "Epictectorum Joann. Ravissi. Thomas Zovio de Signis Ecclae Dei." "Gerarquia Serafica sin princ. ni fin." "Mercurio Trimegisto Pimander de Potestate et sapi.ª Dei. Richelme Veritas pro modestia; Avendaño Tesaurus Indicus." "1 tomo latino sin princ. ni fin. otro lo mismo." *Misticos:* "Fr. Andres de Guadalupe Mistica Theologia. otro. otro. otro." "Sobre las virtudes Theolog.ˢ y 7 Viticios 1 tomo sin &." "Sucquett Via Vitae Eternae." "Mott. Manus Religiosorum." "De virtutibus sin princip. &. otro. Aphorismi Superiorum sin princ. &." *Diversos:* "Tesauro Latino. Miscelaneo de sentencias sin princip. &." "Bocabulario manual. otro. Pomey Explicacion de la Rectorica." "Compendio de Theologia. 1 de mathemicicas." See also the footnotes which follow.

In 1944, Adams published "Two Colonial New Mexico Libraries, 1704, 1776" (NMHR, 19: 135-67)

Historica Legalis de la Orn y Cap. Grales; 2.ª Parte de Chronicas de la Orn sin princ. ni fin."]

[17] Solorsano, *Gobierno de Yndias*, unbound. [Juan de Solórzano Pereira, *Disputationes de indiarum iure, sive de iusta Indiarum Occidentalium inquisitione, acquisitione et retentione*, Madrid, 1629. 1788 Inventory: "Solorzano de Iure Indiarum."]

[18] *Consultas Apologicas* by Torrecilla. [Fray Martín Torrecilla. 1788 Inventory: "Consult.ˢ de Torrecilla tom. 2; idem Consultas y Apologias Regulares y varias tom. 1 sin fin; idem Consultas & tomo 2."]

[19] Fourth, fifth, etc. parts to the eleventh, *Morales* by Diana. [Antonio Diana, *Resolutionum moralium pars prima et secunda*, Palermo, 1629. Ten more parts published 1636-56. The 1788 Inventory lists two copies of vol. 1, pts. 1, 2, and 3; two copies of vol. 2, pt. 4; one copy each of vol. 3, pt. 5; vol. 5, pt. 7; vol. 6, pt. 8; vol. 7, pt. 9; vol. 8, pt. 10; vol. 9, pt. 11. "Diana Compendio practicae resolutionum casuum 5 pars." Cf. 47.]

[20] *Monumentos antiguos seraficos acerca de la Virgen*, in two volumes, by Astorga. [Fray Pedro de Alva y Astorga, *Monumenta antiqua Immaculatae Conceptionis*, Louvain, 1664, 1665. 1788 Inventory: "Monumenta antiq. Ord. Seraph. pro immaculatae Concepcionis de Fr. Pedro de Alba y Astorga."]

[21] Second part of the *Suma* of St. Thomas. [St. Thomas Aquinas, *Summa Theologica*. 1788 Inventory: "Cardin.ˢ Thomas de Vio (Cajetan) in Summa S. Thomae Pars 1; idem Pars. 2.ª in

Prima 2ᵃᵉ; Prima Pars Div. Th. cum Comentaris Cardin. de Vio; Prima 2ⁿᵉ eiusdem; 2.ª 2ᵃᵉ eiusdem; otra 2.ª 2ᵃᵉ eiusdem; Prima Pars Div. Th. ut supra; Prima 2ᵃᵉ eiusdem; 3.ª Pars Divi Thom. Cum Comentariis eiusdem sin prin. ni fin; (In margin): 3.ª Pars in suma Div. Thomae letra antigua sin principio; Prima 2ᵘᵉ Div. Th. sin prin. ni fin letra antigua." Cf. 30, 56.]

[22] A volume of *Teologia escolastica*, without beginning or end.

[23] A *Biblia*, without beginning or end. [Four Bibles are listed in the 1788 Inventory, the same number as in the Domínguez list: "Biblia Sacra de letra antig. en fol. sin princ.; otra desquadern. sin princ. ni fin; 1.ª Biblia sin principio ni fin, otra del mismo modo." Cf. 45, 49, 162.]

[24] *Logica* by Soto. [Fray Domingo de Soto, *In dialecticam Aristotelis commentarii*, Salamanca, 1544. 1788 Inventory: "Fr. Dominicus Sotus in Dialecticam."][5]

[25] A volume of *Teologia* by Macedo. [Fray Francisco de San Agustín Macedo. 1788 In-

3. The 1788 Inventory is more specific about Holy Scripture and exegesis. Under the heading "Scriptura Sacra et Spositores Sacri Lit.," we find a number of items which may correspond to some of those noted by Domínguez in more general terms. Cf. 15, 39, 53, 54, 220, 222. The following list of works in the 1788 Inventory cannot be specifically related to Domínguez' entries.

"Glosa Ordinaria Part. 1 q.ᵉ contiene el Pentateuco. Idem 3.ª Part. sbr. el Psalt. Proverb. Eclesiastes, Cantica Canticorum, Sapientiae, et Eclesiasticum. Idem 5.ª Parte sup. 4.ᵒʳ Evang. Los 10 interpr. 1 tom. q.ᵉ contiene hasta el Lib. de Ester. Sin fin. Idem 2.º tom. q.ᵉ incluye desd. el Psalt. hasta la Epist.ª de S. Pablo ad Hebreos sin prin. ni fin. Il. D. Juan Fero anotac.ˢ in Joan. et in Ep.ª eiusd. et in Ep. B. Pauli ad Romam (Juan Feri, *In sacrosanctum Iesu Christi secundum Ioannem Euangelium Commentaria*, Alcalá, 1569; *Exegesis in Epistolam Pauli ad Romanos*, Alcalá, 1578). D.ⁿ Ludovici Ayllon et Quadros Elucubraciones Bibliae (Seville, 1676). D. Ambrosii (St. Ambrose) Commentaria in Sacram Scripturam sin principio ni fin. D. Joann. Chrisostomi (St. John Chrysostom) in Ep.ᵃˢ 2 ad Timotheum, ad Titum, ad Philomonem, et ad Hebreos."

4. The 1788 Inventory includes one item by Torrecilla not listed by Domínguez. "Summa mor. de Fr. Martin de Torrecilla tom. 1."

5. The 1788 Inventory includes one item by Soto not listed by Domínguez. "Idem (Fr. Dominicus Sotus) de Iure et Justicia."

based in part on Domínguez' account. We have now been able to identify more items, and the data in the 1788 Inventory are a useful supplement to Domínguez' contribution to our knowledge of the literature available to the eighteenth-century religious in New Mexico. The dates of publication given in our identifications are usually those of the earliest editions to which we have found reference.

2. The following Scotist items in the 1788 Inventory may correspond to some of Domínguez' entries, but the nature of the references does not permit positive identification with his list. "Fr. Antonio Higueo 3.ª Part. in Libr.ˢ 4ᵒʳ sentiarum Scoti; Idem in 5 Libr.ˢ Metaphicorum xª mentem Subt. Doct.; Scoto Quest.ˢ Reportadas in quatuor Libr.ˢ Sentenc.ʳᵘᵐ" "Fr. Mauritio de Portu sup Libr. Scoti in 5 Universalia Porfirii." "Fr. Hyacinto Fern.ᶻ de la Torre Curso Philosˢ Scotico 1 tom." Cf. 10, 33, 35, 38, 46, 67, 105, 148, 177, 179, 204.

ventory: "Schola Theologiae Positivae ad Doctrinam Catholicorum et Confutationem Hereticorum" (Rome, 1664).][6]

[26] Second volume, *Moral* by Bonacina. [1788 Inventory: "P. Martin Bonacina Operum Moralium tom. 2 in quo de legibus, de Preceptis Decalogi et Eccle. de Restitutione et Contratibus agit."]

[27] Second and third part of *Moral* by Corella. [Fray Jaime de Corella, *Suma de la Theologia moral,* Parte primera, Pamplona, 1687. The complete work consists of six parts, of which the first two were published before Corella's death; parts 3, 4, 5 edited by P. José de Cintruénigo, and part 6 by P. Francisco Xavier Cintruénigo. 1788 Inventory: "Fr. Jayme Corella Confer.[s] moral.[s] 1 y 2[a] P.; Ydem Confer.[s] moral.[s] 1 y 2 P.; idem Conf.[s] morales 1 y 2 P.; idem Sum. Mor.[l] 3.[a] Part.; idem Sum. Mor.[l] 3.[a] Part.; idem Practica del Confes.[o] 1 y 2 P.; otra; otra sin principio ni fin." Cf. 66, 94.]

[28] Two volumes of *Teologia,* without beginning.

[29] *Constituciones* of our Order by Fr. Gabriel Adongo. [Not identified in 1788 Inventory.]

[30] Third part of the *Suma* of St. Thomas. [Cf. 21.]

[31] *Bocabulario Mexicano.* [1788 Inventory: "Bocabulario de lengua Castellana y mexicana."]

[32] Second part of the *Comentarios* by Baeza on the Gospels. [Diego de Baeza, *Commentariorum moralium in Evangelicam Historiam,* 1624-27. 1788 Inventory: "Fr. Diego de Baeza Comentaria Moralia in Evang.[m] Hist.[m]"]

[33] Four *Comentarios* by Poncio on the theology of Scotus. [Juan Poncio, *Comentarii Teologici, in quibus Subtilis Doctoris Quaestiones in libros Sententiarum elucidantur,* Paris, 1661. 1788 Inventory: "Fr. Juan Pontio in 1 Sent.[rum] tomo 1 Scot.[s]; eiusdem in 1 Sent.[rum] tom. 1; Eiusdem in 2.[o] Sent.[rum] Pars 1; eiusdem in 2.[o] Sent.[rum] Pars 2; idem in 3[o] Sent.[rum] Pars. 1 idem in 3.[o] Sent.[rum] Pars 2."]

[34] *Fisica* by Soto. [Fray Domingo de Soto, *Super octo libros Physicorum Aristotelis Commentarii,* Salamanca, 1545. 1788 Inventory: "idem (Soto) super 8 Libr. Phicorum."]

[35] *Fisica* by Escoto. [John Duns Scotus. Cf. 3.]

[36] *Varios sermones* by Dr. Delgado. [Possibly Antonio Delgado Buenrostro, Bishop of Puebla de los Angeles, *Sermones varios,* Seville, 1696. The 1788 Inventory lists several volumes of sermons, author not given, under similar titles. Cf. 101.]

[37] *Concilio Mexicano.* [Probably Francisco Antonio Lorenzana, *Concilios provinciales primero y segundo celebrados en la muy noble y muy leal ciudad de México en 1555 y 1565,* Mexico, 1769; *Concilium mexicanum provinciale III celebratum Mexici anno 1585,* Mexico, 1770. Not identified in 1788 Inventory.]

[38] *Grammatica especulativa* by Escoto. [John Duns Scotus. Cf. 3.][7]

[39] Another *Expossitivo,* without beginning.

[40] *Conquistas de Filipinas.* [Gaspar de San Agustín, *Conquistas de las Islas Philipinas: la temporal, por las armas del Señor Don Phelipe Segundo el Prudente: y la espiritual, por los religiosos del Orden de Nuestro Padre San Agustín: Fundación, y progressos de su Provincia del Santíssimo Nombre de Jesús,* Parte Primera, Madrid, 1698. 1788 Inventory: "Conq.[ta] de Filipinas 1 Part."]

[41] *Exerciciòs quaresmales* by Balderrama. [Fray Pedro de Valderrama, *Exercicios espirituales para todos los dias de la Quaresma,* Seville, 1602. 1788 Inventory: "Valderrama exercicios spirit.[s] de reg.[s] p.[a] todos los dias de Quaresma; Idem." Cf. 88.]

[42] Sixty-five *Anales* by Ubadingo. [Luke Wadding, O.F.M., *Annales Minorum,* 1625-54. 1788 Inventory: "Uvadingo Annales minorum tom. 1; Fr. Franco Aroldi Epitome Annales de Vvadingo tomo 1; idem tom. 2." (Francis Harold, O.F.M., *Epitome annalium,* Rome, 1662.)]

[43] Third volume of the *Dispertador cristiano.* [José de Barcia y Zambrana, *Despertador Christiano de Sermones Doctrinales, sobre particulares assumptos,* 1678-84. 1788 Inventory: "Barcia despertador Quaresmal Tom. sin princ. ni fin; idem despertador xptiano; idem dispert. xptiano; idem Quaresmal sin princ. ni fin; idem lo mismo; idem lo mismo; idem Dispetador Eucharistico." "Barcia Serm.[s] de

---

6. The 1788 Inventory includes another work by Macedo not listed by Domínguez. "Fr. Fran.[co] de S. Agust.[n] Macedo Diatriba de la Venida de Santiago a España; otra."

7. Although this work has long been ascribed to Scotus, there is evidence that the actual author was Thomas d'Erfurt, O.F.M. E. Gilson, *Jean Duns Scot* (Paris, 1952), p. 672.

Quaresma; otro de lo mismo." "Barcia Dispert. Quaresm.¹ sin prin. ni fin." Cf. 70, 95, 136.]

[44] *Los Salamaticenses.* [*Colegii Salmaticensis FF. Discalceatorum B. Mariae de Monte Carmeli primitivae observantiae Cursus theologicus* . . . , Salamanca, 1631. Many editions of this work, which comprises a complete course in theology as given at the University of Salamanca during the seventeenth and eighteenth centuries. 1788 Inventory: "Tom. 2 del Curso Theologico de los Salmanticenses."]

[45] A *Biblia.*

[46] Second volume of the *Sentencias* of Escoto. [John Duns Scotus. Cf. 3.]

[47] *Resoluciones morales* by Diana. [Cf. 19.]

[48] A *Moralista,* without beginning or end.

[49] *Biblia,* without beginning or end.

[50] *Historia sagrada de Susana.* [1788 Inventory: "Hist.ᵃ Sacra de Susana sin princ. ni fin Latina; Otra; otra."]

[51] One volume of *Questiones regulares, y canonicas.* [Gerónimo Rodríguez, *Quaestiones Regulares et Canonicae enucleatae,* Salamanca, 1628; or Fray Manuel Rodríguez, *Quaestiones regulares et canonicae,* Salamanca, 1598-1602. The 1788 Inventory includes copies of both works and another volume "Fr. Man.¹ Rodriguez Resolutiones de las qq. Regulares." Cf. 108, 168.]⁸

[52] Fourth part of the *Monarquia Ecclesiastica,* without beginning or end. [Fray Juan de Pineda, *Los treinta libros de la Monarquia Ecclesiástica,* Salamanca, 1588. 1788 Inventory: "Monarquia Eccla sin prin. ni fin."]

[53] Another *Expossitivo,* without beginning or end.

[54] Three more, like the foregoing.

[55] Fr. Tomas Ubaldense, *De sacramentos.* [Thomae Ubaldenis Anglici, *De sacramentis et sacramentatilo,* Salamanca, 1557. 1788 Inventory: "Il. P. Fr. Thomas Uvaldensis de Sacramtis contra Hereticos."]

[56] Two volumes of the *Suma de Teologia* by St. Thomas. [Cf. 21.]

[57] *Bocabulario Ecclesiastico,* without the end. [Rodrigo Fernández de Santaella (Maese Rodrigo), *Vocabularium ecclesiasticum,* Seville, 1499. 1788 Inventory: "Bocabulario Ecclo Letra antigua." Cf. 126.]

8. The 1788 Inventory includes a work by Rodríguez not listed by Domínguez. "Fr. Man.¹ Rodriguez Suma de Casos de conciencia."

[58] *Concordancias de la Biblia.* [1788 Inventory: "Concordan. de la Biblia."]

[59] *Controversias Teologicas,* without beginning or end. [Fray Juan de Rada, *Controversiae Theologicae inter S. Thomam et Scotum,* Paris, 1589. 1788 Inventory: Fr. Juan de Rada Controversias Theolog.ˢ in D. Thom. et Scot. 1 P.; El mismo 2 part. sin princ. ni fin." Cf. 3, 67.]

[60] *Marial* by Quirós. [Fray Juan de Quirós, *Rosario Inmaculado de la Virgen,* Seville, 1650; *Marial, o segundo tomo de los mysterios y gloria de Maria,* Seville, 1651. 1788 Inventory: "Fr. Juan de Quiros Marial."]

[61] Two volumes, *Moralistas* by Father Tomas Sanches, Jesuit. [Tomás Sánchez, *Disputationem de Sancto Matrimonii Sacramento,* Genoa and Madrid, 1602-05. 1788 Inventory: "Thomas Sanᶻ Disputaciones del Sto Sacramto del matrimº; Otro tom. del mismo sobre el mismo asumpto tom. 1; Otro tomo lo mismo; El mismo tomo 2 de los Impedimtos del matrim.º"]

[62] *Silva racional, y espiritual de los divinos oficios.* [1788 Inventory: "Paprana, Silva Racional y Espir.¹"]

[63] Ledesma: *Moral.* [Fray Pedro de Ledesma. 1788 Inventory: "1ª Parte de la Sum. Moral de Fr. Pedro de Ledesma; idem 2ª Parte de la Sum.; idem 1 Part.; idem Segunda Parte" Cf. 79, 194.]

[64] First part of the *Moral* by Fr. Manuel Rodrigues. [Fray Manuel Rodríguez, *Obras Morales en Romance,* Madrid, 1602. 1788 Inventory: "Fr. Man.¹ Rodriguez Obras Mor.ˢ en Romanze."]

[65] A *Mistico,* without beginning or end.

[66] *Conferencias morales* by Sintrseenigo (*sic*). [1788 Inventory: "Fr. Fran.ᶜº José Cintruenigo Sum. de la Theologia Moral 4 P.; idem 4 Part.; idem 5 Part." Cf. 27.]

[67] *Controversias Teologicas* by Father Rada. [Cf. 59.]

[68] *Historia de Ester* by Father Bolaños. [Juan de Bolaños. *In sacram Esther historiam Commentarius* . . . , Seville, 1701. 1788 Inventory: "Fr. Juan Bolaños in Sacram Ester Historiam Comment. Liter.¹ y Moral."]

[69] *Tiara simbolica de S. Pio quinto.* [Fray Tomás de Granda, *Tiara simbólica de San Pío, papa quinto en tres libros,* Salamanca, 1715. 1788 Inventory: "Fr. Thomas de Granada (*sic*) Tiara Simbolica de S. Pio V."]

[70] Another *Dispertador cristiano*. [José de Barcia y Zambrana. Cf. 43.]

[71] One volume of *Sanctoral serafico*. [1788 Inventory: "Santoral de Tobar." Possibly a Franciscan martyrology by Fray Pedro de Tovar Aldana, author of *Excelencias de Nuestra Señora y de los Santos*, Barcelona, Madrid, 1633-35.]

[72] Solis, *De Yndias*. [Probably Antonio de Solís y Rivadeneyra, *Historia de la conquista de México, población y progressos de la América septentrional, conocida por el nombre de Nueva España*, Madrid, 1684. Not identified in 1788 Inventory.]

[73] Six *Expossitivos* by Salmeron. [P. Alfonso Salmerón, S. J., *Opera, Commentarii in Evangelicam historiam & in Acta Apostolorum*, 16 vols., Cologne, 1602-04. 1788 Inventory: "Salmeron Tom. 1 y 2 in Vnibers. Sacr. Scrip.; idem tom. 3 y 4; idem, tom. 5 y 6; idem, tom. 9 y 10; idem tom. 11 y 12; idem tom. 13 y 14."]

IN QUARTO

[74] *Vida de Fr. Sebastian de Aparicio*, in Latin. [Nicolaus Plumbensis (Franciscus Olovchich, Bishop of Bosnia), *Opusculum vitae virtutum et miraculorum Ven. servi Dei Fr. Sebastiani ab Apparitio*, Rome, 1696. 1788 Inventory: "Vida del V.e Sebastian de Aparicio; Otra sin prin. ni fin."]

[75] *Discursos predicables* by Father Rota. [1788 Inventory: "Fr. Pedro de Rota Discursos Pred.ˢ Latinos."]

[76] *Tesoro de la doctrina* by Furlot. [Not in 1788 Inventory.]

[77] Three *Artes de lengua Mexicana*. [1788 Inventory: "Arte de lengua mexicana; otro, otro." Cf. 189.]

[78] *Camino del cielo*, in Mexican. [Fray Martín de León, *Camino del cielo en lengua mexicana*, Mexico, 1611. 1788 Inventory: "Fr. Martin de Leon Camino del Cielo en lengua mexicana."]

[79] Four volumes, *Morales* by Ledesma. [Fray Pedro de Ledesma. Cf. 63.]

[80] A *Moral* by Fr. Anselmo Gomes. [Fray Anselmo Gómez, *Tesoro de la sciencia moral, y suplemento de las sumas más selectas y modernas*, Valladolid, 1668? 1788 Inventory: "Fr. Anselmo Gomez Tesoro de la Sciencia Moral; idem." Cf. 109.]

[81] Seven books which discuss the proposi-tions condemned by the Popes. [1788 Inventory: "Fr. Raymundo Lumbier Navarro Not.ˢ Theolog. Morales acerca de las proposition.ˢ Conden.ˢ por Innoc 11 y Alexandro 7; Idem Noticia de las 65 Proposit.ˢ Conden.ˢ por N. SS. P. Innoc. 11; Otro de lo mismo." (Fray Raymundo Lumbier, *Noticia de las sesenta y cinco proposiciones nuevamente condenadas por nuestro Santísimo Padre Inocencio XI, mediante su decreto de 2 de Mayo del año 1679*, Zaragoza, 1680, and later editions. *Séptima impresión, añadidas las cuarenta y cinco proposiciones de Alejandro VII*, Lisbon, 1683.) "Fr. Valentin de la Madre de Dios Compilatio Moralis in propˢ dagnatte Alexandro 7 Innoc. 11 y Alexandro 8; Otro de lo mismo; Otro de lo mismo; Fr. Mathias Rodriguez Explic.ᵒⁿ de las 65 Prop.ˢ dagn. de Innoc. 11; Otro sobre el mismo asumpto sin princ. ni fin; Otro lo mismo." "Fr. Thomas de Velasco Breviloquio Moral practico; otro." (Fray Tomás de Velasco, *Breviloquio Moral practico, en que se contienen las sesenta y cinco proposiciones prohibidas por Inocencio XI declaradas por via de impugnacion etc.*, Mexico, 1681.) Cf. 87.]

[82] A *Libro de Christo, y Maria* by Fr. Fernando Peralta. [Fray Fernando de Peralta Montañés, *Libro de Cristo y María*, San Lúcar de Barrameda, 1626. 1788 Inventory: "Serm.ˢ de Xpto y M.ª por el M. Fr. Hernando Peralta Montañes."]

[83] Echarri, *Moral*. [Fray Francisco Echarri, *Directorio Moral*, Valencia, 1770. 1788 Inventory: "Fr. Fran.ᶜᵒ Echarri Directorio Moral Añadido."]

[84] Acosta, *Sermones quaresmales*. [Acosta's name does not appear in the 1788 Inventory, but there are two similar anonymous entries: "Serm.ˢ Quaresmales sin prin. ni fin." "Serm.ˢ Quaresmales sin princ. ni fin." Cf. 91.]

[85] *Discursos predicables* by Pauleti. [Cf. 147.]

[86] *Teologia escolastica* by Uberto. [Not identified in 1788 Inventory.]

[87] Two volumes of *Proposiciones condenadas por N. P. Innocencio 11*. [Cf. 81.]

[88] *Exercicios quaresmales*. [Fray Pedro de Valderrama. Cf. 41.]

[89] *Sumulas de Moral*. [Fray Simón de Salazar, *Sumulas de moral e indice de vocablos*, Zaragoza, 1671, 1684. 1788 Inventory: "Sumulas de Moral, y indice de los Vocablos del Comp.ᵒ de Fr. Simon de Salazar."]

[90] Six *Dispertadores de noticias morales.* [Fray Clemente de Ledesma, *Dispertador de Noticias de los santos sacramentos,* Primer tomo, Mexico, 1695; *Compendio del Despertador de noticias de los Santos Sacramentos,* Mexico, 1695; *Despertador de Noticias Theológicas morales que apuntan y despiertan las letras del A, B, C, al Cura y al Confesor,* Segundo tomo, Mexico, 1698. 1788 Inventory: "Fr. Clemente de Ledesma Despertador de Sacramtos t.1; Idem tom. 1; Idem tom. 1; Idem tom. 1; Idem tom. 2; Despertador de Noticias Morales; Idem Tom 2; Idem tom. 2; Idem tom. 2; Ydem Compendio de las Notic.ˢ Morles; Idem Compendio; Idem Compendio &." Cf. 113, 195, 206.]

[91] *Sermones quaresmales.* [Similar entries in 1788 Inventory: "P. Jacobus Suares a Sta Maria Serm.ˢ de Quaresma Latinos." "Adviento y Dominc.ˢ hasta Quaresma de Fr. Juan de Mata." "Serm.ˢ de Quaresma en lengua mexicana." Cf. 84, 240.]

[92] *Meditaciones del amor de Dios.* [Possibly Fray Diego de Estella (Fray Diego de San Cristóbal), *Meditaciones devotísimas del amor de Dios,* Salamanca, 1576, 1578. 1788 Inventory: "Meditac.ˢ del Amor de Dios sin princ. ni fin."]

[93] *Ceremonial de los Papas.* [Not in 1788 Inventory.]

[94] One volume of the *Suma* by Corella. [Fray Jaime de Corella. 1788 Inventory: "Prim.ᵃ parte de la Suma de Corrella en 4.º" Cf. 27.]

[95] One volume of the *Quaresma* by Barcia. [José de Barcia y Zambrana. Cf. 43.]

[96] *Explicacion de la Crusada.* [Fray Manuel Rodríguez, *Explicación de la bulla de la Sancta Cruzada,* Alcalá, 1589. 1788 Inventory: "El mismo (Fr. Man.¹ Rodriguez) Explicacion de la Bula de la Cruzada."]

[97] *Addiciones* to that *Explicacion.* [Fray Manuel Rodríguez, *Adiciones a la explicación de la Bula de la Cruzada,* Salamanca, 1598, 1601. 1788 Inventory: "El mismo (Fr. Man.¹ Rodriguez) addiciones a la Explic.ⁿ de la Vula de la Cruzada."]

[98] *Concilio Tridentino.* [1788 Inventory: "Exposicion sobre el Concilio de Trento de Marzilla." (Pedro Vicente de Marzilla, *Decreta Sacrosancti Concilii Tridentini ad suos quoque titulus secundum Juris methodum redacta, adjunctis Declarationibus Auctoritate Apostolica,*

Salamanca, 1613.) "Concilio de Trento; Otro; Otro; Otro; Otro." Cf. 181, 248.]

[99] Two volumes of *Sermones latinos.*

[100] *Certamen Mariano* by Arbiol. [Fray Antonio Arbiol y Díez, *Certamen Marianum Parisiense, ubi veritas examinatur in splendoribus Sanctorum et opus mirabile Civitatis Dei,* Zaragoza, 1698. 1788 Inventory: "Arbbiol Certam Marial Parisiense."]

[101] Twelve volumes of *Varios Sermones.* [Similar entries in the 1788 Inventory: "Miscelaneo de Serm.ˢ Varios; Serm.ˢ desde la Dñica 1 de Adviento asta S. Blas varios; P. Man.¹ Naxera sermones varios penegiricos." (Manuel de Nájera, *Sermones varios,* Alcalá, 1643.) "Serm.ˢ de todas las Dominicas despues de Pentecostes sin princ." "Miscelaneo de serm.ˢ varios." "Miscelaneo de serm.ˢ Varios." "Serm.ˢ Varios sin prin. ni fin." "Serm.ˢ Varios sin princip. ni fin." "Serm.ˢ de Dñicas sin princ. ni fin; Miscelaneo de Serm.ˢ Varios; Serm.ˢ de Dñicas sin princip. ni fin." "Serm.ˢ Varios Panig.ˢ sin princ. ni fin; Otro de lo mismo sin princ. ni fin." Cf. 36]

[102] One volume of *Selectos de la Escriptura* by Pereiro. [Benedicto Pereyra Valentino, *Selectae disputationes in Sacram Scripturam,* Lyon, 1604-10. 1788 Inventory: "Benedicto Pereyro Valentino Disput.ˢ Select.ˢ in Sacr. Script. tom. 3."]

[103] Two volumes of *Discursos morales.* [Not identified in 1788 Inventory.]

[104] *Laurea evangelica.* [Fray Angel Manrique, *Laurea Evangélica,* Salamanca, 1605. 1788 Inventory: "Laurea Evangelica sin prin. ni fin."]

[105] *Fisica* by Merinero, two volumes. [Fray Juan Merinero, *Commentarii in duos Libros Aristotelis de Ortu et Interitu rerum naturalium juxta ... Joannis Duns Scoti mentem, una cum disputationibus et quaestionibus, hoc tempore, agitari solitia (Tomus posterior commentariorum in octo libros Aristotelis de physico auditu, seu auscultatione,* etc.), 2 vols., Madrid, 1659. 1788 Inventory: "D. Fr. Juan Merinero Coment. in 8 Libr. Phisicor. Pars. 1; Idem Pars 2." "Idem in 8 Libr. Phisicorum Pars 1." Cf. 3, 150.]⁹

9. The 1788 Inventory includes two items by Merinero not noted by Domínguez. "Idem (D. Fr. Juan Merinero) de Visione Dei et peccatis sin principio; Idem de Scientia et voluntate et Predestinatione etc. sin princ. ni fin."

[106] Five volumes of sermons by Dias. [Possibly Felipe Díez Luistano (d. 1601). 1788 Inventory: "Fr. Felipe Diez Quaresma tom. 1; Idem Quaresma tom. 2; Idem de Dñicas del año tom. 3; Idem de lo mismo tom. 4."]

[107] Two *Manuales* by Cerra. [Fray Angel Serra, *Manual de administrar los santos sacramentos a los españoles y naturales de esta provincia de los gloriosos Apostoles S. Pedro y S. Pablo de Mechuacan conforme a la reforma de Paulo V y Urbano VIII*, Mexico, 1681. Not in 1788 Inventory.]

[108] *Questiones regulares*, 2 volumes. [Cf. 51.]

[109] *Tesoro de la ciencia moral*. [Cf. 80.]

[110] Two volumes of *Sermones* by Niceno. [Fray Diego Niseno, *Asuntos predicables para todos los Domingos del primero de Adviento al último de Pascua de Resurrección*, Barcelona,

Lisbon, 1632; *Asuntos predicables para todos los Domingos después de Pentecostés*, Barcelona, Madrid, 1630. 1788 Inventory: "Fr. Diego Niseno Asumptos Predicables desde Adv.to asta Resurreccion; Idem de todas las Dñas desp.s de Pentecostes." Cf. 173.]

[111] *Teologia simbolica*. [Andrés de Azitores, *Theologiam Symbolicam, sive Hierogliphicam pro totius Scripturae Sacrae juxta primarium & genuinum sensum commentariis*, Salamanca, 1597. 1788 Inventory: "Fr. Andres de Acitores Theologia Simbolica tom. 1."]

[112] *Recopilación de los privilegios de los Menores*. [1788 Inventory: "Privilegia Fratrum minorum."]

[113] *Dispertador republicano*. [Fray Clemente de Ledesma, *Despertador Republicano que por las Letras del A, B, C, Compendia el Segundo Tomo del Despertador de Noticias*

THE 1788 INVENTORY

Theológicas, Mexico, 1699; *Despertador Re-publicano que por las letras del A, B, C, Compendia los compendios del Primero y Segundo Tomo del Despertador de Noticias Theológicas*, Mexico, 1700. 1788 Inventory: "Idem (Fray Clemente de Ledesma) Despertador Republicano; Idem." Cf. 90.]

[114] *Epistola exortatoria* by Barcia. [José de Barcia, *Epístola exhortatoria*, Puebla de los Angeles, 1693. Not identified in 1788 Inventory.]

[115] Various offices of our [Franciscan] saints. [Not in 1788 Inventory.]

[116] Various of the same of Augustinian [saints]. [Not in 1788 Inventory.]

[117] *Diceptacion mistica*. [Fray Antonio de la Anunciación, *Disceptacion mystica, de Oratione et Contemplatione*, Alcalá, 1689. 1788 Inventory: "Fr. Ant.º de la Anunciacion Disceptacio Mistica."]

[118] *Varios sermones* by Guerra. [Fray Manuel Guerra y Ribera, *Sermones varios de Santos*, Madrid, 1677-80. 1788 Inventory: "Fr. Man.ˡ de Guerra y Ribera Serm.ˢ Varios de Stos."]

[119] *Celo Pastoral*. [Bernardo Hozes, *Zelo pastoral con que N. S. P. Ynocencio XI ha prohibido sesenta y cinco proposiciones, reformando algunas materias*, Seville, 1683, 1687. 1788 Inventory: "Fr. Bernardo de Hozes Zelo Pastoral con q.ᵉ N. SS. Innc. 11 proh.; Idem."]

[120] *Flores de questiones Teologicas*. [Fray José Anglés, *Flores Theologicarum quaestionum in libros Sententiarum*, Calari, 1575-76. 1788 Inventory: "Fr. José Angles Valentino Flores Theologic.ˢ"]

[121] Two volumes of *Sermones* by Garcés. [Francisco Garcés, *Varias metaforas, ideas sagradas o evangelicos assumptos*, Valladolid, 1679, 1686. 1788 Inventory: "Fr. Fran.ᶜᵒ Garzes Varias metaphoras è Ydeas sagradas Evangelic.ˢ"]

[122] Various offices of Mercedarians. [Not in 1788 Inventory.]

[123] *Casos morales*. [Fray Juan Enríquez, *Questiones practicas de casos morales*, Sanlúcar de Barrameda, 1643. 1788 Inventory: "Fr. Juan Enriquez qq.ˢ practicas de Casos morales; Idem."]

[124] Two volumes, *Decretales*, without beginning or end. [1788 Inventory: "Sexto Decretalium, Clementinarum et extravagantes."][10]

[125] Two Montenegros, *De Yndios*. [Alonso de la Peña Rivas y Montenegro, *Itinerario para párrocos de indios*, Madrid, 1668. 1788 Inventory: "Illmo. Montenegro itenerario de Parrocos de Indios; Otro; Otro;" "Montenegro itinerario de curas de indios."]

[126] Three old *Bocabularios Ecclesiasticos*. [Cf. 57.]

[127] *Dialogo entre confesor, y penitente*. [1788 Inventory: "Dialogo entre el Conf.ʳ y el Penit. sin princip. ni fin."]

[128] *Manual* of D. Juan Palafox. [Juan de Palafox y Mendoza, *Manual de los Santos Sacramentos, conforme al ritual de Paulo Quinto*, Mexico, 1642. Not in 1788 Inventory.]

[129] *Exaltacion de la Betlemitica Rosa*. [Pedro Muñoz de Castro et al., *Exaltacion magnifica de la Betlemitica rosa de la mejor americana Jerico, y accion gratulatoria por su plausible Plantacion dichosa; nuevamente erigida en Religion sagrada por la Santidad del S.ʳ Innocencio XI. P. N. que Celebro en esta Nobilissima Ciudad de Mexico, el Venerable Dean, y Cabildo de esta S. Iglesia Metropolitana, y Sacratissimas Religiones, con assistencia del Ex.ᵐᵒ Señor D. Joseph Sarmiento Vallardares, Virrey de esta Nueva-España, y Del Illmo. Señor D.ᵒʳ D. Francisco de Aguiar Seyxas, y Vlloa, Arçobispo de esta dicha Ciudad . . .*, Mexico, 1697. 1788 Inventory: "Seyxas y Vlloa exaltacion magnifica Belethmitica."]

[130] *Disputas Teologicas*, without author. [Not identified in 1788 Inventory.]

[131] Two volumes of *Platicas* by Miranda. [Fray Luis de Miranda, *Pláticas y colaciones espirituales*, Salamanca, 1617, 1618. 1788 Inventory: "Fr. Luis de Miranda Platicas y Colaciones Espir.ˢ 3 pte. idem 1 Part." "Colationes Spirituales sin princ. etc." Cf. 138.]

[132] *Erudicion cristiana*. [Fray José Luquián, *Erudición christiana, en veinte y cinco discursos devotos muy provechosos para el alma*, Tarragona, 1594. 1788 Inventory: "Erudicion Christiana sin prin. ni fin."]

[133] *Discursos predicables*.

[134] *Instruccion de Predicadores*. [1788 Inventory: "Fr. Juan Ferrones instruccion de Pred.ʳᵉˢ y alg.ˢ Serm.ˢ lo mismo."]

[135] *Varios sermones* by Cespedes. [Antonio

10. Additional entries of legal nature in the 1788 Inventory: "Tractatus de Curia Pisana." "Synopsis Iuris Canonici; Instituciones de Justiniano."

de Céspedes, *Sermones varios*, Madrid, 1677. 1788 Inventory: "Serm.ˢ Varios del P.ᵉ Ant.º de Cespedes."]

[136] *Dispertador Cristiano.* [Jose de Barcia y Zambrana. Cf. 43.]

[137] *Abecedario espiritual y ley de amor.* [Fray Francisco de Osuna, *Abecedario espiritual*, First part, Seville, 1528. The entire work consists of six parts, of which there are many editions. *Cuarta parte o Ley de Amor*, 1530. 1788 Inventory: "Leyes del Amor sto de Dios p.ᵃ predicarlas."]

[138] *Platicas, y colaciones espirituales.* [Cf. 131.]

[139] *Año Apostolico.* [Not in 1788 Inventory.]

[140] A book consisting of separate offices. [Not in 1788 Inventory.]

[141] *Triunfos de la gracia, y gloria de los Santos.* [Not in 1788 Inventory.]

[142] A volume of *Oraciones Evangelicas.* [Not in 1788 Inventory.]

[143] *Apologia de confesores regulares.* [Gabriel Novoa, *Apología de confesores y predicadores regulares. Respuesta a una consulta en derecho regular, en la que se tratan y deciden todas las dificultades que suelen ocurir entre los regulares con los obispos y más ordinarios en materia de aprobación y licencias de confesar y predicar.* 2ᵃ Imp., Salamanca, 1705. 1788 Inventory: "Fr. Gabriel de Noboa Apologia y deffensa de Confessores de Regular.ˢ"]

[144] A book of *Teologia* without beginning or end.

[145] *Lexicon Ecclesiasticum.* [Fray Diego Jiménez Arias, *Lexicon ecclesiasticum latino-hispanicum ex sacris Bibliis, Conciliis, Pontificorum, etc.*, Salamanca, 1565. 1788 Inventory: "Lexicon Eclesiastico; otro."]

[146] Two books of *Sermones en Mexicano.* [Fray Juan Bautista, *Sermonario en Lengua Mexicana*, Mexico, 1606. 1788 Inventory: "Fr. Juan Bapta Serm.ˢ de Adviento en Lengua Mexicana."]

[147] *Discursos predicables* in Latin. [1788 Inventory: "Discursos predicables, o serm.ˢ de todas las Dnicas del año y algunas festiv.ˢ de Christo y M.ᵃ sin princ. ni fin en Latin." Cf. 85.]

[148] Two volumes of *Tentativas Complutensis.* [Fray Francisco Félix, *Tentativae Complutensis . . . Duns Scoti mens . . . elucidatur . . . Angelici Doctoris doctrina sponitur . . .* , Al-

calá, 1642-46. 1788 Inventory: "Fr. Fran.ᶜᵒ Felix Tentativa Complutense 1 Part. idem 2 part." Cf. 3.]

[149] A *Tratado de voto.* [Not identified in 1788 Inventory.]

[150] One volume *De ortu, et interitu.* [Cf. 105. 1788 Inventory: "Idem (Fray Juan Merinero) in 2 Libr. Aristhot de Ortu, e interitu."]

[151] *Los dos estados de la espiritual Jerusalen.* [Fray Juan Márquez, *Los dos estados de la espiritual Hierusalem sobre los psalmos CXXV y CXXXVI*, Medina del Campo, 1603. Not in 1788 Inventory.]

[152] *Declaracion de los siete psalmos penitenciales.* [Fray Pedro de Vega, *Declaración de los siete Psalmos Penitenciales*, Alcalá, 1599. 1788 Inventory: "Declar.ⁿ de los 7 Psalmos Penitenc.ˢ del P. Pedro de la Vega."]

[153] *Orden Judiciario* by Miranda. [Fray Luis de Miranda, *Liber ordinis iudiciarii*, Salamanca, 1601. 1788 Inventory: "Miranda Ordinis Iudiciarii."]

[154] *Sermones* by Segura. [Nicolás Segura, *Sermones quadragesimales*, Madrid, 1729; *Sermones varios*, Mexico, 1742. 1788 Inventory: "P. M. Nicolas de Segura Serm.ˢ Quadragesimales; El mismo Serm.ˢ Varios Panegire.ˢ" Cf. 239.]

[155] *Conceptos predicables*, without beginning, &a. [1788 Inventory: "Conceptos politicos y morales sin princ. ni fin."]

[156] *Panegiricos* by Oviedo. [Juan Antonio de Oviedo, *Panegyricos sagrados en honra y alabanza de Dios, de Maria Santissima, etc.*, Madrid, 1718. 1788 Inventory: "P. Juan Pedro (sic) Oviedo Serm.ˢ Panigiricos Varios."]

[157] Two *Fueros de la conciencia.* [Fray Valentín de la Madre de Dios, *Fuero de la conciencia y compendio Salmanticense Moral*, Madrid, 1702. 1788 Inventory: "Fr. Valentin de la Madre de Dios Fuero de la Conciencia; idem; idem illustrado Tom. 2."]

[158] *Tesoro de confesores.* [Dr. Juan Daza y Berrio, *Tesoro de confesores y Perla de la conciencia para todos estados*, Madrid, 1648. 1788 Inventory: "Dr. Juan Daza y Berrio Tesoro de Conf.ʳᵉˢ y Perla de la Conciencia."]

[159] *Apologia en defensa de nuestro orden.* [Gabriel de Guillixtegui, *Apología en defensa de la Orden de Penitencia de San Francisco*, Bilbao, 1643. 1788 Inventory: "Guillistigui Apologia en defensa de la 3.ᵃ Orn de N. S. P. S. Fran.ᶜᵒ"]

[160] *Resumen moral* by Machado. [Juan Machado de Chávez y Mendoza, *Suma moral y resumen brevísimo de todas las obras del doctor Machado,* Madrid, 1661. 1788 Inventory: "Suma Mor.¹ y Resumen de todas las obras de Doct.ʳ Machado; Idem."]

[161] *Vida de Cristo* by Villalobos. [Possibly an edition of Fray Ambrosio Montesino, *Vita Christi cartuxano romançado por fray Ambrosio,* Alcalá, 1502, 1503 (trans. from Ludolphus of Saxony). 1788 Inventory: "Vida de Christo 3 P. de Montesinos."]

[162] A *Biblia,* without beginning or end.

[163] *Tratado de anima.* [Fray Juan Merinero, *Commentaria in libros Aristoteli de anima,* 1659. 1788 Inventory: "idem (D. Fr. Juan Merinero) in 3ˢ Libros de Anima."]

[164] *Naturalesa, y virtudes de las plantas.* [Francisco Hernández, *Cuatro libros de la naturaleza y virtudes de las plantas y animales que están recibidos en el uso de Medicina en la Nueva España,* Mexico, 1615. (Trans. from Latin by Francisco Jiménez.) Not in 1788 Inventory.]

[165] *El superior predicando,* without beginning. [1788 Inventory: "el Superior Predicando sin princ. ni fin."]

[166] Two volumes of *Discursos Evangelicos,* without beginning. [1788 Inventory: "Discursos Evangelicos de Xpto. M.ᵃ y los App.ˢ y otros; Lo mismo." "Discursos Evang.ˢ de Christo y del SSmo Sacramto sin pr. ni fin."]

[167] A volume of the *Platicas* of Father Parra. [Juan Martínez de la Parra, *Luz de verdades católicas y explicación de la doctrina cristiana, que según la costumbre de la casa profesa de la Compañia de Jesús, todos los jueves del año se platica en su iglesia,* Mexico, 1691. 1788 Inventory: "Platicas del P. Parra."]

[168] *Tratados del modo de corregir.* [Possibly an edition of *Quaestiones regulares et Canonicae* by Fray Manuel Rodríguez. *The British Museum Catalogue of Printed Books* (Ann Arbor, 1946) describes one copy of this work as: "Editio ultima, prioribus . . . auctior, *etc.* (Praxis criminalis Regularium Saeculariumque omnium . . . a Patre F. P. Berti . . . nuncupata Quaestionum Regularium tomus quartus.) 4 tom. Antverpiae, 1616. fol." 1788 Inventory: "Berti Praxis Crimin. Regularium." "1 tom. en 4 sin princio ni fin. q. trata de practica Criminal." Cf. 51.]

[169] *Directoriis decisiones regulariis.* [Fray Antonio de Hinojosa, *Directorium decisionum Regularium,* Madrid, 1627. [1788 Inventory: "Fr. Ant.º Hinojosa Directorio de las decisiones Regulares."]

[170] A *Moralista,* without beginning or end. [Not identified in 1788 Inventory.]

[171] *Soliloquios de las cosas divinas.* [Casparus Barthius, *Soliloquiorum rerum divinarum, Liber primus. Ejusdem Anacreon Philosophus,* Frankfort, 1623. 1788 Inventory: "Casp. Barthi Soliloquios."]

[172] A *Logica.*

[173] Two volumes of sermons by Niceno. [Fray Diego Niseno. Cf. 110.]

[174] *Tratos, y contratos de mercaderes* by a Dominican. [Fray Tomás de Mercado, *Tratos y contratos de mercaderes y tratantes,* Salamanca, 1569. Not in 1788 Inventory.]

[175] Two *Grammaticas de lengua griega.* [Fray Martín del Castillo, *Gramática de la lengua griega en Idioma Español,* Lyons, 1678. 1788 Inventory: "Fr. Martin del Castillo Grammatica de la Lengua Griega en Castellano."]

[176] *Phisica* by a Jesuit. [Not identified in 1788 Inventory.]

[177] *Moral by Delgadillo.* [Fray Cristóbal Delgadillo, *Duo tractatus: alter de Incarnatione; de adoratione alter, in quibus legitima subtilis, Dr. J. Duns Scoti,* Alcalá, 1653; *Bipartitus de Poenitentia tractatus,* Alcalá, 1658. 1788 Inventory: "Fr. Christobal Delgadillo De Yncarnac.ᵉ et adoratione; idem Tractatus Bipartitus de Penitencia." Cf. 3, 179.]

[178] *Apologia de las obras de Tertuliano.* [Fray Pedro Manero, *Apologia de Quinto Séptimo Florente Tertuliano, presbítero de Cartago, contra los gentiles, en defensa de los cristianos,* Zaragoza, 1644. 1788 Inventory: "Yllmo. Manero Apologia a las obras de Tertuliano; idem sin princ. ni fin."]

[179] Delgadillo, *De Incarnatione.* [Cf. 177.]

[180] *Sermones varios,* in Latin.

[181] *Concilio Tridentino.* [Cf. 98.]

[182] A *Biblia.*

[183] *Oraciones Ecclesiasticas.* [Fray Diego de Arce, *Miscelanea primera de Oraciones Eclesiasticas desde el Domingo XXIV despues de Pentecostes hasta la vigilia de Navidad,* Murcia, 1605. 1788 Inventory: "Fr. Diego de Arce Miscelaneo de Orac.ˢ Ecclas."]

[184] *Questiones morales.* [José de Alfaro (Antonio Charlas), *Disputatio Theologica de*

opinionum Delectu in Quaestionibus Moralibus, Rome, 1695. 1788 Inventory: "Ant.º Charlas QQ.ˢ Morales."]

[185] *Regla de nuestra religión*. [Fray Martín de San José, *Breve exposición de los preceptos que la Regla de los Frayles Menores obligan a pecado mortal, según la mente de los Sumos pontífices, y de San Buenaventura*, Zaragoza, 1638; or Fray Pedro Navarro, *Exposición de la regla de Nuestro Padre San Francisco*, Madrid, 1636. 1788 Inventory: "Fr. Martin de S. Josè exposicion de la Regla de S. Fran.ᶜᵒ seis 6." "Navarro Expos.ⁿ de la Regla; otro." "1 Exposion de la regla sin princ. ni fin." Cf. 207, 208.]¹¹

[186] Various separate offices. [Not in 1788 Inventory.]

[187] *Sermones varios*, without beginning.

[188] Twenty-two *Morales* by Larraga. [Fray Francisco Larraga, *Promptuario de la Theologia Moral*, Madrid, 1765, Puebla de los Angeles, 1766. 1788 Inventory: "Fr. Fran.ᶜᵒ Larraga 25 Tom.ˢ]

[189] *Arte Mexicano*. [Cf. 77.]

[190] *Triunfos Evangelicos*. [Fray Isidoro de San Juan, *Triunfo Evangélico de Christo y sus Santos*, Madrid, 1672. 1788 Inventory: "Fr. Isidro de S. Juan Triunpho Ev. de Xpto y sus Stos."]

[191] The third volume of *El hijo de David perseguido*. [Dr. Cristóbal Lozano, *El Hijo de David más perseguido*, Madrid 1740. 1788 Inventory: "El hijo de David mas perseguido."]

[192] Some *Discursos morales*, without beginning or end.

[193] *Arte de sermones* by Velasco. [Fray Martín de Velasco, *Arte de sermones, para Saber hazerlos y Predicarlos*, Cádiz, 1677, Mexico, 1728. 1788 Inventory: "Fr. Martin de Velasco Arte de serm.ˢ p.ª hazerlos y predicarlos."]

[194] *Moral* by Ledesma. [Fray Pedro de Ledesma. Cf. 63.]

[195] *Dispertador moral* by the same. [Fray Clemente de Ledesma. Cf. 90.]

[196] Second part of the *Monarquia mistica*. [Lorenzo de Zamora, *Monarquía mística de la Yglesia, hecha de hieroglyficos, sacados de humanas y divinas letras*, Segunda parte, Alcalá, 1601. 1788 Inventory: "Monarquía mistica 2.ª parte."]

11. Cf. another entry in 1788 Inventory: "Fr. Ant.º Diaz Comp.º de la Doctrina Xptiana y preceptos de N. Sta. Regla; Idem."

IN OCTAVO

[197] Two volumes of *Sermones* by the Granatense. [Fray Luis de Granada, *Primus tomus Concionum de Tempore*, Lisbon, 1573; *Secundus . . . , Tertius . . . , Quartus . . . ,* Lisbon, 1575. 1788 Inventory: "Fr. Luis de Granada serm.ˢ de tempore 1 tom. idem serm.ˢ de Tempore 2 tom. idem 2 tom. Sant.ˡ idem de lo mismo tom. 4." Cf. 230.]

[198] *Casos de conciencia* by Burgraber. [1788 Inventory: "Adamo Burghaber Centuriae Selectorum Casuum Constientiae."]

[199] Four volumes of *Advertencias para confesores de Yndios*. [Fray Juan Bautista, *Advertencias para los confesores de los indios*, Mexico, 1599. 1788 Inventory: "Fr. Juan Bapta advertencias p.ª Conf.ʳᵉˢ de Naturales. idem . . . otra sin princ. ni fin."]

[200] *Manual de confesores* by Ascargota. [Fray Juan de Ascargota, *Manual de Confesores*, Madrid, 1713. 1788 Inventory: "Fr. Juan de Ascargota Manual de Confesores; Otro, Otro; Otro; Otro sin princip. ni fin."]

[201] *Consideraciones espirituales*, in Latin. [Fray Juan de los Angeles, *Considerationum Spiritualium super librum Cantici Canticorum Salomonis in utraque lingua, Latina et Hispana*, Madrid, 1607. Not identified in 1788 Inventory.]

[202] *Questiones Teologicas*. [Not identified in 1788 Inventory.]

[203] *Dubia regularia* by Portel. [Laurentius de Portel, *Dubia regularia tam ad subditos quam ad praelatos, in utroque foro attinentia, fere per compendium resoluta*, Rome, 1712. 1788 Inventory: "Portel Dubia Regularia sin princ. ni fin."]

[204] Five *Morales* by Escoto. [John Duns Scotus. 1788 Inventory: "Scotus Moralis; idem; idem; idem." Cf. 3.]

[205] *Manual de confesores* by Ledesma. [Fray Clemente de Ledesma? Cf. 63, 90, 206, Not identified in 1788 Inventory.]

[206] Two *Dispertadores morales* by the same. [Fray Clemente de Ledesma. Cf. 90, 205.]

[207] Seven *Exposiciones de nuestra regla* by Fr. Martin de San Jose. [Cf. 185.]

[208] Two more by Navarro. [Cf. 185.]

[209] Two *Morales* by Ascargota. [Fray Juan de Ascargota? Not identified in 1788 Inventory.]

[210] *Manual* of Contreras. [Fray Pedro de Contreras Gallardo, *Manual de administrar los*

Santos Sacramentos a los españoles y naturales desta Nueva España conforme a la reforma de Paulo V, Mexico, 1638. Not in 1788 Inventory.]

[211] *Declamaciones de la Virgen.* [Possibly Fray Luis de Carvajal, *Declamatio expostulatoria por inmaculata Conceptione Genetricis Dei Marie*, Paris, 1541. Not identified in 1788 Inventory.]

[212] Two *Manuales de sacerdotes* by Arbiol. [Fray Antonio Arbiol y Díez, *Manuale sacerdotum Sacris Scriptoris et Sanctorum Patrum sententiis Illustratum*, Barcelona, 1711. Not identified in 1788 Inventory.]

[213] *Examen de confesores* by Blanco. [Not identified in 1788 Inventory.]

[214] *Oraciones latinas,* without beginning. [Not identified in 1788 Inventory.]

[215] Two *Morales* by Salazar. [Fray Simón de Salazar, *Promptuario de materias morales*, Alcalá, 1674. 1788 Inventory: "Fr. Simon de Salazar promptuario de materias morales; otro; otro; otro; otro; otro; Otro añadido y corregido por el P.ᵉ Fr. Fran.ᶜᵒ de Castro."]

[216] Another by Allosa. [Juan de Alloza, *Flores summarum sive alphabetum morale*, Lyons, 1665. 1788 Inventory: "Alloza Flores Summarum seu Alphabetium Morale."]

[217] *Catecismo* of St. Pius V. [Not in 1788 Inventory.]

[218] *Sermones de S. Pedro Crisologo,* without beginning or end. [Probably Fray Martin del Castillo, *Divi Petri Chrysologi Sermones,* Lyons, 1676. 1788 Inventory: "Serm.ˢ de S. Pedro Chrisologo sin princ. ni fin."]

[219] *Moral* by Remigio. [Benito Remigio Noydens, *Prontuario moral de questiones prácticas y casos repentinos en la teologia moral, para examen de curas y confesores,* Valencia, 1661. 1788 Inventory: "Noydens Protuario de qq.ˢ y casos de conciencia."]

[220] *Declaracion de las Epistolas de S. Pablo.* [Not identified in 1788 Inventory.]

[221] Three *Manuales de Confesores* by Villalobos. [Fray Enrique de Villalobos, *Manual de Confesores*, Salamanca, 1628, Valladolid, 1628. 1788 Inventory: "Villalobos Man.ˡ de Confesores; otro; otro; otro; otro sin princip. ni fin; otro de la misma suerte."]

[222] *Tratado de las siete palabras de Christo en la Crus.* [Not identified in 1788 Inventory.]

[223] Two *Explicaciones de la syntaxis.* [1788 Inventory: "Explicacion de la sintaxis; otro; otro." Cf. 245.]

[224] *Tratado del bien estado religioso.* [Hieronymus Platus, *De Bono Status Religiosi* (Span. trans. by Francisco Rodríguez, *El libro del bien del estado religioso*, Medina, 1595). 1788 Inventory: "Hieronimi Plati de Bono Status Religiosi."]

[225] Two *Moralistas* in Latin, without beginning or end.

[226] *Compendio de los Concilios.* [Not identified in 1788 Inventory.]

[227] Two little books of the *Epistolas de S. Geronimo.* 1788 Inventory: "Epist.ˢ de S. Geronimo 1.ᵃ et 2.ᵃ part."]

[228] *Practica de confesores* by Escobar. [Antonio de Escobar y Mendoza, *Examen de Confesores y practica de Penitentes. En todas las materias de Theulugia moral,* Pamplona, 1630. 1788 Inventory: "P. Ant.º de Escobar Examen y Practica de Confesores y Penitentes."]

[229] *Itinerario Catolico* by Gusman. [Fray Juan Focher, *Itinerarium Catholicum Proficiscentium, ad infideles convertendos.... Nuper summa cura et diligentia auctum, expurgatus, limatum ac praelo mandarum per fratrem Didacus Valadesium.... Ad Reverendissimum Patrem F. Franciscus Guzmanum, omnium Indiarum maris Occeani Commissarium generalem,* Seville, 1574. Not in 1788 Inventory.]

[230] *Sermones latinos* of the Granatense. [Fray Luis de Granada. Cf. 197.]

[231] *Geografia* by Cluberi. [Philip Cluver, *Introductio in universam geographiam tam veteram quam novam,* Leyden, 1624. Not in 1788 Inventory.]

[232] *Tratado del confesor solicitante* by Fr. Antonio Escoto. [Fray Antonio Escoto, *Scutum Confessionis contra nefarios Sacordotes in Sacramento Poenitentiae ad turpis provocantes,* Mexico, 1703. Not in 1788 Inventory.]

[233] *Suma de las virtudes.* [Not identified in 1788 Inventory.]

[234] *Virgilio.* [1788 Inventory: "P. Vergilii Mayronis; otro."]

[235] *Versos latinos,* without beginning or end. [Not identified in 1788 Inventory.]

[236] *Epistolas* in Latin verse, without beginning. [Quintus Horatius Flaccus, *Epistles.* 1788 Inventory: "Q. Oracio Flacci Epistolas."]

[237] *Compendio moral*, without beginning. [Francisco de la Mota, *Compendio de la suma*

añadida del reverendo P. Fr. Martín de To-
rrecilla, con addiciones del tomo de proposi-
ciones condenadas y del de Obispos y otros,
Madrid, 1698. 1788 Inventory: "Fr. Fran.^{co} de
la Mota Compendio a la Sum. de Torrezilla."]

[238] *Ceremonial de la Provincia.* [Probably
Fray Isidro Alfonso Castaneira, *Manual
Summa de las ceremonias de la Provincia de el
Santo Evangelio de México,* Mexico, 1702,
1703. Not in 1788 Inventory.]

[239] *Sermones* by Segura. [Cf. 154.]

[240] *Sermones feriales de quaresma.* [Cf.
91.]

[241] *Practica de confesores de Monjas* by
Borda. [Fray Andrés de Borda, *Práctica de
confesores de monjas,* Mexico, 1708. 1788 Inventory: Fr. Andres Borda practica de Confesores de monjas."]

[242] *Practica de Exorcistas.* [Benito Remigio Noydens, *Práctica de exorcistas y ministros de la iglesia,* Madrid, 1660. Not in 1788
Inventory.]

[243] Ovidio. [Publius Ovidius Naso, *Meta-
morphoses.* 1788 Inventory: "Compendio de las
Transform.^s de Ovidio."]

[244] *Humildad del corason.* [Not identified
in 1788 Inventory.]

[245] *Explicacion del arte de Nebrija.* [Cf.
223.]

[246] *Advertencias de la grammatica.* [Pos-
sibly Bernardino de Llanos, *Advertencias de
Gramática,* Mexico, 1645. Not identified in
1788 Inventory.]

[247] *Ceremonial Romano.* [Not in 1788
Inventory.]

[248] *Concilio Tridentino.* [Cf. 98.]

[249] *Manifiesto chronologico, y satisfatorio.*
[Alonso López Magdaleno, *Manifiesto crono-
logico y satisfactorio,* Madrid, 1679. 1788
Inventory: "Fr. Alonso Lopez Magdaleno Ma-
nifiesto Apologetico p.^r la Relig.ⁿ Sca."]

[250] *Instruccion de Presbiteros.* [Francisco
de Toledo, *Summa casuum sive instructio
sacerdotum,* Lyons, 1599. (Spanish trans. by
Diego Enrique de Salas, *Instrucción de sacerdotes y suma de casos de conciencia.)* 1788 Inventory: "P. Fran.^{co} de Toledo, instruc.ⁿ de
sacerdotes."]

[251] A separate volume of *Teologia.*

[252] *Manual de confesores* by Navarro.
[Martín Azpilcueta (Dr. Navarro), *Manual de
confesores y penitentes,* 1552. 1788 Inventory:
"Navarro Man.^l de Confessores; Compendio
del Man.^l de Navarro." "Compendium prelu-
diorum Manualis Navarri."]

[253] *Sermones de adviento* by Castro. [An-
tonio de Castro, *Adviento con los sermones de
sus quatro Dominicas, y las Fiestas de su
tiempo, hasta los Reyes,* Burgos, 1681. 1788 In-
ventory: "Serm.^s de Adv.^{to} y festiv^{des} asta Reyes
del P. Ant.^o de Castro."]

[254] Third volume of the *Historia de la
alma.* [Not identified in 1788 Inventory.]

[255] Twelve old *Breviarios.* [Not in 1788
Inventory.]

[256] One volume, *Quaresmal* by Fr. Diego
López Andrade. [Fray Diego López de An-
drade, *Tractados sobre los Evangelios de
Quaresma,* Madrid, 1615. 1788 Inventory: "Fr.
Diego Lopez Serm.^s de Quaresma."]

The Archive

A large chest with a lock serves this purpose. What we shall soon see is in it, and so completely mixed up that considerable time and space would be necessary to put it in the proper order. Its present disorder is the reason it is not listed systematically; it therefore follows the order in which I examined it.[1]

Six bundles of matrimonial investigations, and they date from 1619 to the present year, 1776.

One bundle of patents.

Seven quarto volumes of baptismal records.[2] The missions from which they came and the years when they began are unknown because the entries give no information about this. They do not have many leaves, because the largest one has thirty-three folios and the others progressively less down to the last, which has six leaves.

Thirty-one loose sheets folded once, with baptismal records; and they are similar to the seven volumes mentioned above.

Eight quarto leaves like the folded sheets.

Three quarto volumes like the foregoing.

Thirty-seven folded leaves and nine quarto leaves, all with burial records, and they are kept in a parchment cover.

Three small volumes of leaves with a single fold, with burial records. One has five leaves; it begins in the year 1750 with Father Lezaun's

signature and ends in 1770 with the signature of Father Rodríguez de la Torre; it pertains to Santo Domingo. Another has sixteen leaves; it begins in the year 1726 with Father Araos' signature and ends with the signature of Father Lezaun in the year 1750. The mission from which it came is not known. Another has seventeen leaves; it begins in the year 1729 with Father Esquer's signature and ends in 1764 with the signature of Father Zamora; it pertains to Santo Domingo.

Five quarto volumes with burial records. One has seventeen leaves; it begins in the year 1702 with Father Garaicoechea's signature and ends in 1720 with the signature of Father Irazabal; from Zuñi. Another with ten leaves; it begins in 1707 with Father Alvarez' signature and ends in 1725 with the signature of Father Cruces [de la Cruz]; from Nambe. Another with ten leaves; it begins in 1701 with Father Mata's signature and ends in 1709 with the signature of Father Broton [Brotons]; from Taos. Another with fifteen leaves; it begins in 1716 with Father Arévalo's signature and ends in 1726 with the signature of Father Mirabal; from San Juan. Another with twenty-three leaves; it begins in 1701 with Father Chavarría's signature and ends in 1720 with the signature of Father Delgado; from Jémez.

Thirty separate sheets folded once, with baptismal records, place not given, and they are wrapped in a piece of buffalo hide.

Five quarto volumes with marriage records, and they are in another piece of buffalo hide. One has twelve leaves; it begins in 1699 with Father Chavarría's signature and ends in 1724 with the signature of Father Irazabal; from Cochiti. Another with eight leaves; it begins in 1711 with Father López' signature and ends in 1725 with the signature of Father Pino; from Cochiti. Another with ten leaves; it begins in 1699 with Father Mata's signature and ends in 1712 with the signature of Father Montaño; the mission is not known. Another with six leaves of writing and five blank; it begins in 1698 with Father Chavarría's signature and ends in 1714 with the signature of Father Muñiz; from San Felipe. Another with fifteen

1. Cf. pp. 259-65 *infra*.

2. In 1934 all the known volumes of baptismal, marriage, and burial records, as well as the matrimonial investigations, were collected and deposited in AASF. The early "Diligencias matrimoniales," which would help to solve many problems of that period, are missing, for there are only two pre-Revolt items, dated February, 1678, and April, 1680, a hundred for the years 1681-93, forty-four for the year 1694 (post-Reconquest marriages), and 122 for 1695-1700. Although there are more for the eighteenth century, there are still many gaps. Many mission records also have disappeared, and others are fragmentary. The earliest Santo Domingo registers are missing and may have been destroyed in the nineteenth-century flood; the later ones were at Peña Blanca. Perhaps the surviving records were not sent to Santo Domingo as ordered by Domínguez, and so escaped destruction.

leaves; it begins in 1726 with Father Araos' signature and ends in 1760 with the signature of Father [Manuel] Miñagorri; from Santa Ana.

Six folio volumes with baptismal records. One with sixteen leaves; it begins in 1713 with Father Miranda's signature and ends in 1728 with the signature of Father Zambrano; from Bernalillo, but the mission is not designated. Another with thirteen leaves; it begins in 1708 with Father Muñiz' signature and ends in 1720 with the signature of Father Delgado; from Cochiti. Another with twenty-two leaves; it begins in 1703 with Father Miranda's signature and ends in 1725 with the signature of Father Ceballos; from San Felipe. Another with twenty-three leaves; it begins in 1700 with Father Garaicoechea's signature and ends in 1711 with the signature of Father Irazabal; from Zuñi. Another with eight leaves; it begins in 1722 with Father Irazabal's signature and ends in 1724 with the signature of Father [Manuel de] Sopeña; from La Cañada. Another with sixteen leaves; it begins in 1702 with Father Colina's signature and ends in 1716 with the signature of Father Araos; from Zia.

Two folio volumes with baptismal records. One with seventeen leaves; it begins in 1694 with Father Alpuente's signature and ends in 1712 with the signature of Father Miranda; from Santa Ana. Another with ten leaves; it begins in 1694 with Father Alpuente's signature and ends in 1701 with the signature of Father Alvarez.

Seven loose sheets folded once; on them are the names of those whom the Lord [Bishop] Tamarón confirmed at various missions.

Nine folio volumes of patents.

Thirty-four sheets folded once, and on them scraps of patents, entire writs of visitation, expenditure and receipts of missions are visible.

A volume of leaves with a single fold containing patents.

Three folio volumes which comprise inventories and convent dispositions of various missions.

Three quarto volumes which deal with the same subject.

Seventeen loose sheets folded once, with the same.

Nine quarto leaves with the same.

Seventy-seven papers with various matters pertaining to this Custody; I am taking them with me.

The decree of the Lord Viceroy of Mexico with regard to the four villas of this Custody; I am taking it with me.

Four papers which Father Rodríguez de la Torre handed over, which pertain to the foregoing seventy-seven; with me.[3]

A paper in the hand of the same Father Rodríguez, which pertains to him and contains various information; with me.

The instrument of the Province which the Reverend Father Dozal issued concerning the royal alms for the mission fathers of this Custody remains in the archive.

Two folio volumes with marriage records. One has nine leaves; it begins in 1712 with Father Miranda's signature and ends in 1736 with the signature of Father Delgado. Another with nine leaves; it begins in 1694 with Father Alpuente's signature and ends in 1711 with the signature of Father [Pedro] Montaño. The first is from Bernalillo and the mission [Santa Ana?] is not stated. The other is from Santa Ana.

3. AASF (1772), nos. 3, 4, 5, 6.

WATERMARK FROM PAPER
USED BY FATHER DOMINGUEZ

BOOKS

Three in folio with various patents.

Six in folio which concern inventories and convent disposition of various missions.

Two in quarto containing patents. Three in folio with burial records. One with sixty-five and a half folios; it begins in 1727 with Father Zambrano's signature and ends in 1772 with the signature of Father Burgos; from Zia. Another with twenty-one and a half folios; it begins in 1707 with Father Arranegui's signature and ends in 1727 with the signature of Father Gabaldón; from Pecos; and when it was presented, it had thirty-four leaves. Another with nineteen leaves; it begins in 1700 with Father Muñiz' signature and ends in 1727 with the signature of Father Irigoyen; from Santo Domingo.

Two in quarto with marriage records. One with ten leaves; it begins in 1707 with Father Alvarez' signature and ends in 1724 with the signature of Father Lezaun; from Nambe. Another with forty-six leaves, and its beginning and end are curious and thought-provoking, for it begins in 1716 with Father Arévalo's signature and the same finished it in 1715; from Taos.

Three folio books with marriage records. One with seventeen leaves; it begins in 1728 with Father Esquer's signature and ends in 1770 with the signature of Father Rodríguez de la Torre; from Santo Domingo; and when it was presented it had 158 leaves. Another [Pecos] with seventeen leaves; it begins in 1706 with Father Arranegui's signature and ends in 1727 with the signature of Father Gabaldón; when it was presented it had twenty-eight leaves. Another [San Ildefonso] with ten leaves; it begins in 1700 with Father Farfán's signature and ends in 1724 with the signature of Father Tagle; these last two do not give their missions.

Four folio books with baptismal records. One with forty-seven leaves; it begins in 1698 with Father Farfán's signature and ends in 1725 with the signature of Father Miranda; from Acoma. Another with eleven leaves; it begins in 1710 with Father Lara's signature and ends in 1721 with the signature of Father Delgado; from Picuris. Another with thirty-one leaves; it begins in 1703 with Father Farfán's signature and ends in 1725 with the signature of Father Esquer; from San Ildefonso. Another with ten

leaves; it begins in 1711 with Father Arévalo's signature and ends in 1727 with the signature of Father Gabaldón; from Galisteo.

Three quarto books with various records. One with baptismal records has thirty-one leaves; it begins in 1714 with Father Arévalo's signature and ends in 1725 with the signature of Father Mirabal; from Taos. Another with marriage records has six loose sheets; it begins in 1765 with Father Guzmán's signature and ends in 1766 with the signature of the same; from Santa Ana. Another with burial records has six leaves; it begins in 1765 with Father Guzmán's signature and ends in 1771 with the signature of Father Salas; from Santa Ana.

The same Guzmán presented these two last from Santa Ana before the Father Vice-Custos Hinojosa in the year 1766 with 146 leaves each; but Guzmán himself performed the good work of using all their paper to make cigarettes, and, according to what they tell me, he was inclined to smoke even his breviary.

Three folio books; in each of them there are baptismal, marriage, and burial records.

The first has twenty-two leaves in the section which concerns baptisms; it begins in 1694 with Father Díez' signature and ends in 1727 with the signature of Father Guerrero. In the section of marriages it has eight leaves; it begins in 1694 with Father Díez' signature and ends in 1724 with the signature of Father Guerrero. It has twelve leaves for burials; it begins like the foregoing with the same signature and ends in 1724 with the signature of Father Guerrero; from Nambe.

The second has eleven leaves in the section for marriages; it begins with successive entries as follows: *Don Felipe Antonio with Angelina María; their sponsors were Juan de Yé and Antonia María;* he keeps the records in this manner as far as a note which says: "The Father Preacher and Minister Fray Diego Seinos married all those mentioned from 1694 to 1695, when the Father Preacher Fray Juan Alpuente took over the mission. He married the following." And it continues in the manner I have just described, ending in 1706 with the signature of Father Arañaga [Arranegui]. It has twenty-eight leaves in the baptismal section; it begins in 1694 with Father Seinos' signature and ends in 1700 with the signature of Father Arañaga. The section for burials has thirteen leaves; it begins in 1695 with Father Alpuente's signature and ends in 1706 with the signature of Father Arañaga; from Pecos.

The third book is from Sandia; its entries begin with Father [Juan José] Hernández' signature, and they end with that of Father Hinojosa, as follows: The section pertaining to marriages has sixteen written leaves and four blank; it begins in the year 1748 and ends in 1769. The baptismal section has fifty-three leaves; it begins in 1748 and ends in 1771. The burial section has twenty-five written leaves and three blank; it begins in 1748 and ends in 1768.

Three folio books with baptismal records. One has thirty-six written leaves and three blank; it begins in 1740 with Father Zambrano's signature and ends in 1771 with the signature of Father Rodríguez de la Torre; from Santo Domingo; and when it was presented it had 171 leaves. Another with seventy-six leaves; it begins in 1727 with Father Araos' signature and ends in 1770 with the signature of Father Burgos; from Zia; and when it was presented it had 204 leaves. Another with 172 leaves; it begins in 1720 with Father Pérez' signature and ends in 1774 with the signature of Father Salas; from San Juan; and when it was presented it had 206 leaves.

NOTE

Throughout most of the context of my visitation, decisions ordering mission books (now old) to be remitted to the archive may be found. But when I visited the archive, which was on June 1 of the past year of 1776, only the following had arrived:

Three, in folio, from Picuris. The baptismal book with forty written leaves and four blank; it begins in 1750 with Father [Juan José] Hernández' signature and ends in 1776 with the signature of Father Claramonte. That of marriages has twenty-two leaves; it begins in 1726 with Father [Juan] Sánchez' signature and ends in 1775 with the signature of Father Claramonte. That of burials has thirty-one leaves; it begins in 1728 with Father Irazabal's signature and ends in 1776 with the signature of Father Claramonte.

When these books were presented they had: the first, 206 leaves; the second, 155; the third, 104. With regard to these discrepancies, Father Claramonte says that when the Comanches sacked his convent in the year 1769 (the sack is described under Picuris), these books were lost, and an Indian found them and brought them back torn.

Three, in folio, from Cochiti. That of baptisms with 109 leaves; it begins in 1726 with Father Esquer's signature and ends in 1776 with the signature of Father Marulanda; it formerly had two hundred. That of marriages with thirty-six leaves; it begins in 1726 with Father Esquer's signature and ends in 1776 with the signature of Father Marulanda; it once had 153. The other with sixty-seven leaves; it begins in 1729 with Father Esquer's signature and ends like the foregoing; it used to have 153 leaves.

One, in folio, from Zia; it is of marriages with twenty-four leaves; it begins in 1725 with Father Zambrano's signature and ends in 1776 with the signature of Father Burgos; it formerly had 134.

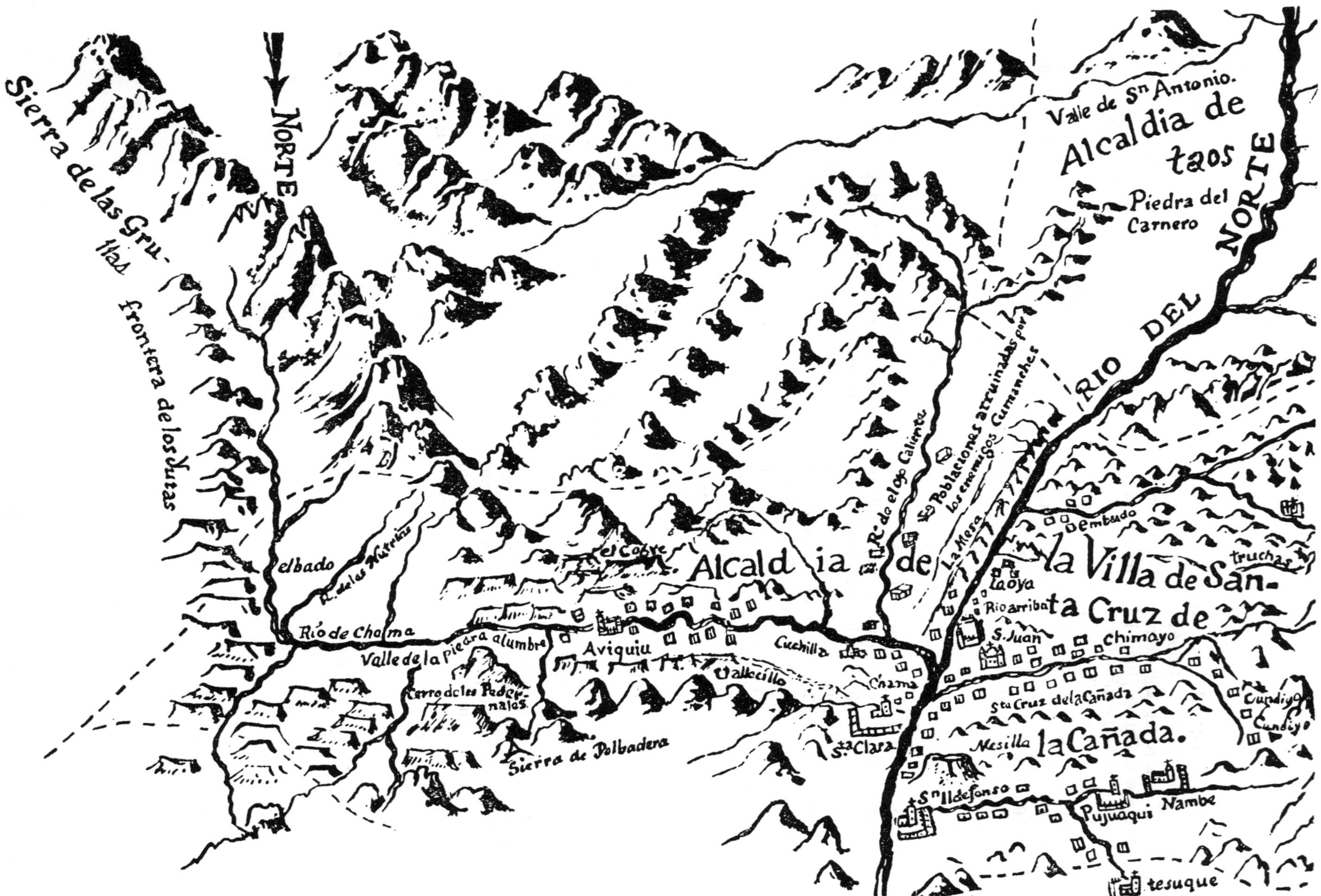

Sierra de las Grutas
frontera de los Yutas
NORTE
Valle de Sn Antonio.
Alcaldia de taos
Piedra del Carnero
RIO DEL NORTE
Poblaciones arruinadas por los enemigos Cumanches
La Mesa
Ro de el ojo Caliente
elbado
R. de las Nutrias
el Cobre
Alcaldia de
Río de Chama
Valle de la piedra alumbre
Cerro de los Pedernales
Sierra de Polbadera
Aviquiu
Cuchilla
Valleçillo
Chama
Sta Clara
embudo
truchas
la Villa de Santa Cruz de la Cañada.
la Oya
Rio arriba
S. Juan
chimayo
Sta Cruz de la Cañada
Mesilla
Cundiyo
Sn Ildefonso
Pujuaqui
Nambe
tesuque

VI.
MISCELLANEOUS
INFORMATION

Various items

which, during the description of my visitation, I have left pending for discussion in this place (so as not to digress). I shall take them up in the same order as the places to which they refer.

In my introduction to the account of my visitation, I mentioned the fact that there is no holy patron of this kingdom and that Our Lady of the Rosary is considered such by unfounded popular opinion, this popular error having been fortified by statements from the pulpit. All this arises from events (as I said in that place) dating from 1770 to the present. During this period a most solemn function (in so far as pomp is possible in this kingdom) in honor of Our Lady under the said title or advocation has been celebrated annually in the month of October. The nature and cause of all this is as follows:

On the thirty-first day of August of the year 1769, Don Nicolás Ortiz died in active battle against the Comanches (at a place called the Cerro de San Antonio, which is about 6 leagues north of Abiquiu). He was then in command of the Christian troops, with the rank of lieutenant governor (called lieutenant general here). Governor don Pedro Fermín de Mendinueta, Knight [of the Order of Santiago], therefore went to present his condolences to the widow. For this reason the conversation there concerned the seriousness of the hostilities in this kingdom, and a woman who took part in it said she knew that in all Christian places there was a sworn patron saint, but there was none in this land. When the conversation was over, the said knight took his leave.

After this incident the said gentleman decided to celebrate a function in honor of Our Lady of the Rosary that very year. He actually did celebrate it with the utmost solemnity, entirely at his own expense. In the following year, 1771, the citizens Don Carlos Fernández, Don Antonio José Ortiz, Don Manuel Pareja, and three others presented themselves before the lord governor with a writing in which they begged his permission to solicit alms for the purpose of solemnizing the said Our Lady and proclaiming her as patron. He granted it, and when the alms had been collected another magnificent function was celebrated in the year 1771, but there were no ceremonies pertaining to her as a patron saint. And a majordomo was elected to serve in future.

In the following year, 1772, the celebration was at the majordomo's expense, and since then new majordomos have been elected, who sometimes out of their own pockets, sometimes from the collection of alms, sometimes both, have continued to outdo one another in solemnizing Most Holy Mary of the Rosary, imploring her aid and intercession against all the enemies who attack these regions. These functions have always been celebrated with vespers, procession, Mass, sermon, procession through the streets reciting the Rosary; and the governing body has always attended and authorized the function, beginning with the vesper services, accompanied by the royal garrison under the standard, marching and firing salvos. The citizens do their bit with salvos of shots and *luminarias*. Many good fine white wax candles have been placed on the altar; last year, 1776, there were three hundred lights. There are three days of festivity, with performances of Moors and Christians, tilts, a comedy, and bullfights.

These functions as I have described them are the reason Our Lady of the Rosary is considered the patron saint. But all this is nothing more than a devotion to her Majesty for the help mentioned above. There has been no formal agreement between the citizens and the government nor any notification of the Ordinary preliminary to avowing and making oath to the Most Holy Lady as patron saint. In short, the necessary requisites for an oath of patronage have not been observed. The aforesaid Mendinueta and other persons of standing, who all maintain that there has not been, nor is there, any such oath of patronage, have assured me of this fact.[1] The father is given 35 regional pesos in sheep and other commodities for the church function; the preacher, 25 pesos of the same kind.

SANTA FE

In my account of the Third Order I mentioned a certification by the chief brother. It is accurate, and since the original document is included, it will be better to put it at the end (here it is in the way). In my report on the Confraternity of the Blessed Sacrament I cited another; the circumstances are the same, and these papers will be put in the same place. With regard to what remains to be said about this confraternity, the following statement is made: There are 173 members, whose debt to it is 456 pesos. Each member gives 3 pesos when he is enrolled, and 1 peso annually.

The capital this confraternity has today consists of 200 ewes farmed out at interest, which amounts to 32 sheep per year. This receipt is insufficient to cover expenditures. Therefore, the Vicar don José Lorenzo Rivera, by his decree of May 20, 1776, determined and ordered substantially as follows: That the weekly Masses be suspended and that only those of the fixed annual feasts be said until such time as the livestock may be recovered. It is of record in this same decree that this confraternity owes the former father minister of Santa Fe, Fray Francisco

1. Cf. n. 7, p. 8 *supra*.

Zarte, 500 pesos, none of which has been paid up to this very day. The said decree is recorded in this confraternity's book of expenditures and receipts on folios 47 and 48, attested by the notary named José Maldonado.

This confraternity has two books. One for expenditures and receipts with 131 leaves, authorized on May 16, 1735, by Vicar don José Bustamante.[2] The other is for the enrollments of the members, with 136 leaves, and although there is no record of authorization, it evidently dates from 1729, when it was provided. The aforesaid Father Zarte canceled 100 pesos of the amount due him, and so 400 are still owed.

After I spoke of this confraternity I dealt with the Poor Souls. The following concerns this devotion. Its capital, or principal, comes down to 300 stolen or lost ewes, which are farmed out at interest at 48 sheep per year, which does not cover expenditures; and this has been stated in the proper place. Therefore, after paying the sum of said 48

2. In 1730 Bishop Crespo declared that he had established a secular benefice in New Mexico and conferred orders on "the natives of the capital of Santa Fe." One of these was Don Santiago Roybal, the first secular vicar of New Mexico. See n. 59, p. 35 supra. The only other secular priest in the region in those times was Don José Bustamante. He does not seem to have been a native of Santa Fe, but was probably born or reared at Guadalupe del Paso, where there was a large family of this name. Some of them came to Santa Fe with Governor Domingo de Bustamante. We do not know how the priest was related to the governor or to his lieutenant, Don Bernardo de Bustamante. Don José was vicar in Santa Fe from 1733 to 1736, when Roybal went down to El Paso in the same capacity. This exchange of vicariate may have been arranged by Governor Bustamante. Vicar Bustamante's term in Santa Fe was shortened by his undue meddling in a poor boy – rich girl marriage case which became a cause célèbre in the controversy between Bishop Crespo and the Franciscans over ecclesiastical jurisdiction. We hear no more of him. NMF; Chávez, "A Romeo and Juliet story in early New Mexico," New Mexico Quarterly, 20: no. 4 (Winter, 1950-51), pp. 471-80.

sheep, there is still something owing, and the majordomo devoutly makes up the difference out of his own pocket.

Don Diego Arias Quirós was the founder of this. He left a house in Santa Fe in order that after the death of his wife, Doña María Gómez (both were citizens of the aforesaid villa), it should be sold and the proceeds invested so that the interest might be used for suffrages for souls in Purgatory. The lady died in the year 1752, and in 1753 the foregoing was sold for 300 pesos in hard cash. Don Juan Gabaldón, also a citizen of the said villa, received them, and as security for the said amount and the interest on it he executed a writing before the alcalde mayor of Santa Fe, Don Nicolás Ortiz, under date of November 7, 1753, and mortgaged his house and farmlands which are near it. This document was filed in the archive of the ecclesiastical court, and I have read it several times.

The Most Illustrious Lord don Pedro Anselmo Sánchez de Tagle, Bishop of Durango, was informed about this guarantee and instrument, etc. And by a decree of June 21, 1754, his Most Illustrious Lordship decided that the interest of 15 pesos produced by the aforesaid 300 should be used for Masses for the Poor Souls. I did not see the original of this decree, but I did see a copy, which is in the book of expenditures and receipts of the Confraternity of the Rosary on folios 3 v. to 4. The Masses: For some time fifteen were paid for by the said Gabaldón, and his receipts from the priests who said them are with the aforementioned instrument. In the end, both the above principal and interest were lost. Therefore the aforesaid individual made it good with what he had mortgaged.

The mortgaged house now belongs to Don José Calves, citizen of this villa, who bought it from Vicar don Santiago Roybal, who executed the deed before Don Felipe Tafoya, alcalde mayor of the said place. And he gave for the above house and lands 300 ewes which one Antonio Chaves, citizen of

Atrisco at Albuquerque, owes him. By a paper dated October 13 (and the year is not given), which he executed before José Apodaca, lieutenant of Albuquerque, the said Chaves acknowledges his debt of 300 ewes to the aforesaid Calves. When the majordomo of the Poor Souls demands them from said Chaves, the latter replied, and always will reply, that he is insolvent.

This is the condition of the Devotion of the Poor Souls at the present time. Its majordomo is Don Diego Antonio Baca, citizen of Santa Fe, who has in his possession the instrument I have just described and another whose content is as follows: "In this Villa of Santa Fe on February 26 of the year 1772, the election of the majordomo of the Poor Souls was held. Vicar don Santiago Roybal presided, with the assistance of the Reverend Father Fray Patricio Cuellar, minister of the same villa. Don Diego Antonio Baca was elected majordomo of the Poor Souls by unanimous vote of all those present, and he accepted the said office with pleasure. And in order that he may know the expenses he must bear and make it his business to meet them throughout the year, they are set down for him clearly and in detail here. In the first place, on the first Tuesday of every month, sung Mass with tolling of the bell and chanted responses. The aforesaid shall pay 8 pesos to the father minister and one to the singer. Item:" It continues in this fashion with the expenditures, and these are as stated in my description of the villa as far as: "Twelve pesos are assigned to the majordomo for his work, to be taken from the income in his care. And if any money is left over, let it be used for as many low Masses for the Poor Souls as it will pay for. And the said majordomo will make a satisfactory accounting by presenting the receipts [for the Masses]. And in order that this may be of record, the said vicar and the said father minister signed it on the said day, month, and year. Br. Santiago Roybal, Fray Patricio Cuellar. In my presence, José Campos Redondo, notary appointed."

When I discussed the Confraternity of the Rosary, I referred to a separate report about it, and here it is: There are 225 members, who owe it 626 pesos among them. Each new brother gives 3 pesos upon enrollment and 1 peso per year. The capital it has today consists of 200 ewes, which are farmed out at interest at 32 sheep per year, insufficient income for the expenses it has. Therefore Vicar don José Lorenzo Rivera, by his decree of May 22, 1776, decided and ordered substantially as follows: That the weekly Monday and Saturday Masses be suspended and that only the feasts of Our Lady and the monthly Sunday Masses be celebrated, because of the small amount that accrues to the Confraternity from the livestock. And although the deficit could be covered by the back dues which the brothers owe, nevertheless, in view of the fact that there is no income for the present year which might support greater expenses than the aforesaid functions, his grace decided that no more should be undertaken until the debt is covered, *in order to avoid charges.* This provision was made in Santa Fe in the presence of the notary appointed, José Maldonado.

This decree is in the book of expenditures and receipts of this Confraternity of the Rosary on folios 39 and 40. The same vicar states in the decree that the Confraternity owes 533 pesos to the former father minister of Santa Fe, Fray Francisco Zarte, to the singer, and to the majordomo. The said confraternity has two books. One for expenditures and receipts, which also serves for the inventory of the valuables of the Virgin; it has 100 leaves and carries authorization for the aforesaid purposes by the Father Vice-Custos and Ecclesiastical Judge Fray Domingo Araos, dated January 20 of the year 1729. The other is used to list the members; it has 198 leaves and carries an authorization like the above. In both decrees of approval the said Father Araos orders that the old books be filed in the archive of the Custody. I have searched it thoroughly and they are not there, nor do they turn up in the archive of the ecclesiastical tribunal, which I have also examined to my satisfaction.[3] The aforesaid Father Zarte released this confraternity from paying 100 pesos, and the rest is still owing him.

Now, in accordance with the decrees of the said vicar, both in this case and that of the Confraternity of the Blessed Sacrament, the weekly Masses of both have been and still are suspended. And although he orders in the aforesaid decrees that the annual functions be held, should this be in effect, I will report to my Mother the Holy Province in order that she may be fully informed.

When I discussed obventions under Santa Fe, I promised the schedule for them in this kingdom. Therefore:

Accurate and legal copy of the schedule for parish obventions which the Most Illustrious Lord don Benito Crespo, Bishop of Durango, left during the visitation he made of this kingdom.[4] It is of record in his lengthy decree making provision in this matter under date of August 29 of the year 1730. And it is as follows:

Nuptials: For a marriage of Spaniards, 16 pesos 4 reales; arras and candles, with the specification that the arras of any marriage must be thirteen coins of large or small denomination, and that if the marriage be elsewhere than in the principal church, the fees are to be doubled. For a marriage of free mulattoes, 6 pesos; arras and candles. For a marriage of

mulatto or negro slaves or service Indians, 5 pesos, arras and candles.[5]

Burials: For burial of Spaniards with a sung Mass by obligation, 16 pesos 4 reales, and there must be an offering of bread, wine, and wax, whatever the parties may wish to offer. And if the burial should be elsewhere than the principal church, the fees are to be doubled; and with regard to the offering, the parties will make an agreement with the minister. The minister is to collect 2 pesos for the use of the cope at any funeral, and one of them is to be applied to the church fabric. He must also charge two half-pound candles for every funeral of Spaniards, negroes, mulattoes, and service Indians. For a funeral of free mulattoes and negroes, with a sung Mass by obligation, 8 pesos; and if it is not to be sung, 6 pesos. For a funeral of negro and mulatto slaves and service Indians, 5 pesos with a low Mass by obligation, and 7 pesos if sung. For the funeral of a Spanish child with tall cross and cope, 8 pesos; with small cross and cope, 6 pesos. For the funeral of a mulatto or negro slave child or a service Indian child, 3 pesos, and if it be with tall cross and cope, 5 pesos. Let it be noted with regard to the funerals of Spaniards who die intestate without designating a burial place that double fees must be paid even though the deceased be buried in the parish church.[6] *With assistants:*[7] Each assistant at any funeral shall collect one peso and his candle, and the priest assisting, 2 pesos and his pound candle. The singer, one peso and his candle. *Novenas:* For a novena of sung Masses, 6 pesos for each Mass; if it be with a vigil, 10 pesos. At the last Mass there must be an obligatory offering, and at the others as the parties wish. For a novena of successive low Masses with obligatory responses at each, 2 pesos for each Mass. With regard to the wax placed on altars and catafalque at funerals,

3. Some of the old books of the Conquistadora Confraternity were in the possession of a quondam majordomo, Don Bernardino de Sena, who mentioned them in his will of 1758. SANM, 1: no. 860. In 1782 Custos Fray Juan Bermejo declared them unserviceable and ordered that they be "filed where they belonged." The Sena family apparently returned them after Domínguez' time in very battered condition. Scattered fragments of them dating between 1684 and 1726 were found in recent times and used as the basis for Chávez, *Our Lady of the Conquest* (Santa Fe, 1948).

4. A translation of two letters by Bishop Crespo relating the events of his visitation is in AT, pp. 95-106.

5. These regulations covered the entire diocese of Durango. In those times the rich and important people liked to be married at home or in their private chapels, a practice which was discouraged. There were very few negro and mulatto slaves in New Mexico, but they were more common in Nueva Vizcaya.

6. To encourage the making of wills in good time. Spaniards of the period usually waited until they felt themselves dying.

7. "Acompañados." Possibly these were official paid mourners.

obsequies, and novenas, half of it goes to the minister and the other half to the church fabric. For Masses specified in wills, with obligatory responses at the end of each one, 1 peso 5 reales each. For obsequies and anniversary with vigil, 10 pesos, and these must be an obligatory offering of bread and wine; to the deacon and subdeacon, 1 peso each; candles to the priest and ministers. For the vigil and Mass which is said for the confraternity in its communion for the deceased, 13 pesos. For a sung Mass in memory of the dead, 6 pesos.

Let it be noted that for each sung Mass of communion in accordance with the founding of a chaplaincy the minister must be paid 6 pesos, and if it be with vigil or vespers, 10 pesos. For a low Mass, one peso. For the low Masses said on Mondays for the Confraternity of Poor Souls, 3 pesos. For a sung Mass for the confraternity, 3 pesos, and the confraternity pays for the rest. For processions, 10 pesos each, and 2 more for the deacon and subdeacon. For taking part in the Holy Thursday, Good Friday, and Easter Sunday processions, 16 pesos 4 reales each, and 2 pesos more for the deacon and subdeacon. For marriage banns of Spaniards, one peso for each reading. For other people, 4 reales each.

Sacristan: For tolling for a Spaniard, 1 peso. For carrying the tall cross, 1 peso and its candle. For the censer, 1 peso. For other classes, at the rate of 4 reales. For the tolling at a novena, 2 pesos. For reading a censure, 1 peso.

Let it be noted that all the foregoing fees which are hereby regulated must be collected in reales or their equivalent according to the prevalent custom. Thus far the schedule, and it goes on to forbid formal stops in funeral processions and to order that it be proclaimed in the villas and their districts.[8]

When I discussed the Third Order and how the father minister of Santa Fe acquires necessities, I promised a brief statement, or explanation, of the pesos of this land in terms of things used in trade, and by way of summary I say: A fanega of wheat, or of maize, is worth 4 pesos; a fanega of chick peas, 12 pesos; a fanega of any other legume, 8 pesos; a cow with calf, 25 pesos; one without a calf, 20; an ordinary bull running wild, 15 pesos; a tame bull which serves under yoke, 20 pesos; a tame ox (here they call them *de Só, y Para* [Soh! and it stops]), 25 pesos; a yearling calf, 6 pesos; one head of livestock, whether it be sheep, ewe, nanny goat, or he-goat, is worth 2 pesos; a fowl, 4 reales; an ordinary she-mule, 40 pesos; a fine jenny, 100 pesos and sometimes more; an ordinary he-mule, 30 pesos; a fine jack, according to the individual animal; with regard to horses, the same as the jennies; a vara of ordinary linen, 2 pesos; a pound of chocolate, 2 pesos; a pound of sugar, 1 peso; a pair of shoes, 2 pesos; a deerskin, 2 pesos; a fat pig, 12 pesos; 20 eggs, 1 peso; a string of chile, 2 pesos in Río Arriba, 1 peso in Río Abajo; 4 fleeces of wool, 1 peso in Río Abajo, in Río Arriba, 2 fleeces for 1 peso.

There are various other things (as is taken for granted) a detailed account of which would be impertinent rather than careful, since this account suffices in brief. Moreover, I think that what has been said is more than enough prudently to convey complete understanding of the situation here. Nevertheless, for greater clarity, I provide an example: A fine she-mule is worth 200 pesos, and the following is given in ex-

---

8. Funerals, it has been said, are more for the benefit of the living than of the deceased, and this saying is illustrated by the universal tendency toward display and ostentation by the bereaved. Minor extra displays over and above the plain funeral service, which could be refused to no one because of poverty, were the use of a tall cross in the procession instead of a small one, of the thurible and incense, and of extra mourners. A major show were the *pasos*, or stops with special ceremonies, at various stages of the funeral procession; the richer the person, the greater the number of *pasos*. When the priest refused these extras to those who could not pay for them, ill feeling and scandal resulted, and he was accused of refusing Christian burial except at a high price. The bishop was making an unsuccessful attempt to abolish such things. Cf. Chávez, "Doña Tules, her fame and her funeral," *El Palacio,* 57 (1950): 233-34.

change: 2 fanegas of wheat, 8 pesos; 2 of maize, 8 pesos; 1 of chick peas, 12 pesos; 1 of any other legume, 8 pesos; a cow with her calf, 25 pesos; a cow without calf, 20 pesos; an untamed bull, 15 pesos; a tame bull, 20 pesos; an ox, 25 pesos; a calf, 6 pesos; 2 ewes, 4 pesos; 2 nanny goats, 4 pesos; 2 sheep, 4 pesos; 2 hens, 1 peso; 40 eggs, 2 pesos; 2 varas of linen, 4 pesos; 2 pounds of chocolate, 4 pesos; 2 deerskins, 4 pesos; 2 pairs of shoes, 4 pesos; a fat pig, 12 pesos; 10 pounds of sugar, 10 pesos; the sum total, 200 pesos.

When I spoke of the chapel of Our Lady of Light, I deferred the description of its confraternity for this place. It consists of 236 persons, who owe nothing. And when a new brother joins, he gives 2 pesos for enrollment; he says, or has a Mass said, for the living brethren and another for those who have died. He presents the receipts for them and gives 1 peso annually. He takes oath (at the hands of the chief brother, whether he be an ecclesiastic or a layman) to defend the mystery of the Immaculate Conception, since this is one of the constitutions of the confraternity. The capital this confraternity has today is 1,070 ewes farmed out at an interest of 214 sheep and 12 fleeces of wool per year, a sufficient income to cover the expenditures for the feasts of its chapel which I mentioned above.

The prime mover and founder of this chapel and its confraternity was Don Francisco Antonio Marín del Valle, former governor of this kingdom. And during that same period when he held office, he performed what I am about to relate. Out of his own pocket he bought the site where the chapel now stands; he made the reredos of fine white stone; he sent to Mexico to have the canvas with the sovereign image of Our Lady of Light painted; he has given everything as shown in the inventory in the description of this chapel; he established a capital fund of 530 head of ewes for the confraternity; he drew up the constitutions of the confraternity, which are in proper form.

At the very time that the foregoing was done, which was in the year 1760, the Lord Bishop Tamarón was in this kingdom making a visitation. Therefore, on the third day of June of the aforesaid year, the constitutions were presented to his Most Illustrious Lordship, who approved them and conceded certain graces and indulgences for the benefit of those who should join the confraternity. On the fifth of the aforesaid month and year, the first meeting of this confraternity was celebrated. Its beginning, or founding, dates from that day. The said Lord Bishop presided. In his hands both the said Lord Marín and Vicar and Ecclesiastical Judge don Santiago Roybal, and others who became brothers, took oath to defend the Immaculate Conception of Most Holy Mary. At the same time and on that very day the election of the officers the said confraternity had to have and has, in accordance with its constitution, was held in the presence of the same Lord Bishop. And Lord Marín was elected chief brother. His Illustrious Lordship [Tamarón] approved both this election and that of the other officers. He charged them to be fervent in their new devotion, to persevere in it, and he gave them his holy blessing.

This meeting and election were held in the sacristy of the chapel of which I am speaking. And since it was not yet finished, there was no church function until the following year, 1761. On the afternoon of May 23 of that year, Vicar don Santiago Roybal blessed the chapel in the presence of the Reverend Custos Fray Jacobo de Castro; his Vice-Custos, Fray Manuel Zambrano; six religious; the governor at the time (it was now another), Don Manuel Portillo Urrisola, with the garrison of the royal presidio in formation; the members of the confraternity, and other distinguished persons.[9]

On the following day, May 24, the said Vicar celebrated Mass with deacon and subdeacon; the said Reverend Custos preached

9. Don Manuel Portillo Urrisola was governor *ad interim* from January, 1761, to February, 1762.

because of the illness of Father Fray Tomás Murciano de la Cruz, to whom the sermon for this day had been assigned. On the twenty-fifth, the aforesaid Reverend Custos celebrated the Mass with deacon and sub-deacon, and Father Fray Miguel Campos preached. On the twenty-sixth, the Father Vicar and Ecclesiastical Judge of the Villa of Albuquerque, Fray Manuel Rojo had the altar, and Father Fray Francisco Guzmán preached. On the twenty-seventh, obsequies for the brethren who had already died were held, the Mass being sung by Father Fray Joaquín Jerez. On all these days eighty large candles of fine wax burned on the altar. The aforesaid Lord Marín paid for everything on the first day. On the first three days there were comedies in the afternoon. The constitutions have now been printed with the necessary licenses in Mexico City by Don Felipe de Zúñiga y Ontiveros at Lord Marín's expense. They are in the little archive of the confraternity.[10]

For the spiritual benefit of this confra-

ternity the aforesaid Lord Marín obtained from Our Most Blessed Father Lord Clement XIII a brief in which His Holiness grants plenary indulgence and remission of all their sins to persons (of both sexes) who, after confessing and receiving communion and praying for the extirpation of heresies, etc., should visit this said chapel on one of the feasts of Our Lady designated by the Ordinary (the fifteenth of August has been designated); and on the other six feasts of Our Lady, after confession and communion, praying for the same as above, the faithful may obtain seven years and seven times forty days of pardon; all the foregoing for the period and duration of fifteen years. This brief was issued in Rome on March 22, 1764. It was passed upon by the Council, the Commissary of the Crusade, and the Mitre of Durango, Lord Marín bearing all the necessary expenses.

Among the papers of this confraternity there are two books. One is in folio with 95 leaves, into which the constitutions are copied, along with the approval of Lord Bishop Tamarón, first election, and members. The other is in quarto with 139 leaves; it serves for expenditures and receipts. Today this is the best organized confraternity, the one that has good capital and is in no way in debt.[11] It depends from the Sacred Mitre, to whose vicar in this kingdom it renders accounts every three years. And it holds its meetings without the intervention of any ecclesiastic as presiding officer. But, although it is good in the foregoing way, it has its abuses, in proof of which I refer to the long note I recorded above when I described the chapel and confraternity. And since I promised a patent there, here is its copy:

Fray Francisco Atanasio Domínguez, of the Regular Observance of Our Seraphic Father

10. *Constituciones De La Congregacion De Nuestra Señora De La Luz, Erigida en la Villa de Santa Fee Capital de la Provincia de la Nueva Mexico, y aprobada del Ilmó Señor D. Pedro Tamaron Obispo de Durango. A sus expensas las dà al publico D. Francisco Antonio Marin del Valle, Governador, Capitan General que fue de dicha Provincia, Hermano mayor de su Congregacion. Dedicanse A la misma Emperatriz Soberana.* Impresas En Mexico, con las licencias necesarias, Por D. Phelipe de Zuñiga, y Ontiveros, en la calle de la Palma, año de 1766. "8°, title, with a cut of Nuestra Señora de la Luz on the verso, 5 pages of dedication to Soberana Señora, 4 pages to the Ilmõ Señor, and 45 pages of *Constituciones,* 7 pages of *aprobación* dated Santa Fe, June 3, 1760, signed by Pedro Obispo de Durango, 7 pages of the minutes of the meeting for the election of officers, 2 pages of *notoriedad,* 2 pages of *diligencias,* and 2 of license, or, besides the title leaf, a total of 74 pages, all unnumbered." H. R. Wagner, *The Spanish Southwest, 1542-1794* (Albuquerque, 1937), pp. 446-48. A copy of the booklet was discovered in Mexico City by W. B. Stephens, who sent a photostat copy to Wagner. The latter presented the photostat to the Historical Society of New Mexico. Bishop Tamarón refers to the founding of the confraternity in his report of his visitation. AT, p. 47. Cf. n. 52, p. 33 *supra.*

11. Unlike other confraternities, it was composed of the more affluent among the military and elite of Santa Fe. Within two decades this society was dead, and by 1846 the military chapel itself was in ruins.

St. Francis, Preacher General *de jure,* Commissary Visitor, Custos, and Servant, etc. To the Father Vice-Custos and minister of Santa Fe, Fray José Medrano, and to those who may be ministers of this Santa Fe in future, greeting and peace in Our Lord Jesus Christ.

Since one of the principal obligations of our ministry is to watch over and see to the exact observance of the sacred rites and ceremonies which Our Mother the Church has holily established and ordained for the decorum of the sacerdotal functions and administration of the sacraments, especially those which most directly and immediately pertain to the veneration and respect which we all must have for their Most Holy Author, and since, by virtue of this obligation, we must not permit in this our Custody that anything be done in contradiction of or beyond said sacred rites and ceremonies, and we must uproot the abuses we find, however introduced, we order under holy obedience by virtue of the Holy Spirit and command for all time that your Reverend Father Custos, as such minister of Santa Fe, and all those who under our Rule may succeed him in this ministry:

First, they shall never take the Blessed Sacrament from the principal church to the Chapel of Our Lady of Light to expose it there publicly for the veneration of the faithful on the feast days that either private devotion or that of the members of the confraternity of said chapel and advocation may celebrate, even though it be done with the greatest solemnity, and not even on the very feast day of Our Lady of Light.

Second, not even on the fifteenth day of August (on which the faithful can win the plenary indulgence which our Most Holy Father Clement XIII conceded to those who should visit the altar, or altars, of the said chapel after confession and communion, which concession is temporary, for fifteen years only, and comes to an end in the year 1779) may they expose the Blessed Sacrament or permit It to be exposed, not even during Mass. Not only is this unnecessary for the attainment of the indulgence, but there is no authentic license from the Lord Bishop of Durango for such exposition, and therefore it must not be made, and we, as has been said, strictly forbid it, as pertains to our office.

Third and last, when the Blessed Sacrament is carried in procession, either on the day of Corpus Christi or to the sick, the priest who carries It shall not stop on any pretext of attention to any being whatsoever nor bless with the Sacrament the people or the banner or the royal arms or any house, to whomever it may belong, whether there may or may not be a custom of doing so, for such a custom deserves not the name of custom but of abuse.[12]

We so order and command in perpetuity by these our letters patent, signed by our hand, sealed with the great seal of this our Custody, and countersigned by our undersigned acting secretary. Issued in this our mission of Our Father St. Francis of Santa Fe on April 11 of the year 1777. Fray Francisco Atanasio Domínguez, Commissary Visitor and Custos. By order of his Reverend Paternity, Fray Silvestre Vélez de Escalante, acting secretary.

CAÑADA

The circumstances about the site on which the church of the Villa of La Cañada stands today are as follows: Father Fray Antonio Gabaldón was missionary of this villa in the year 1741. In his presence, in that of the alcalde mayor of that place, Don Juan José Lobato, and in that of Francisco Valdés y Bustos, citizen of the same town, a widow called Antonia Serna declared and stated that of her own free will she was giving the necessary land for the church which had already been started, since it was for the religious, and that for their protection and that of the church she was giving sufficient land in order that in all four directions the citizens might build the houses they liked in the form of streets, with the church *in the middle.* This is the substance of the very long report which the aforesaid Valdés gave just now during my visitation.

To this information I add a copy of a lit-

---

12. Except on the feast of Corpus Christi, benediction and processions with the Blessed Sacrament were much more restricted than now, and, as at present, reserved to the discretion of the bishop.

tle instrument which has just been executed, and here it is:

I certify, in so far as I am able to do so and the law allows, that there is no other legal instrument concerning the donation which Antonia Serna left for building the church of Santa Cruz de la Cañada than the legal instrument I remitted by the father minister of this mission (he speaks of, or means, of Abiquiu) to the Reverend Father Fray Francisco Atanasio Domínguez. The donation of land to build the church by the aforementioned benefactress was made verbally to the Reverend Father Gabaldón and to me, her testamentary executor. And in order that it may be of record, I signed it on April 16, 1776. Juan Pablo Martín Serrano, lieutenant alcalde mayor.

In my discussion of this Cañada I spoke of the Confraternity of Carmel founded there. And here I reiterate that it had its beginning and founding in the year 1710, with license for it given by the Reverend Provincial of the Carmelites, Fray Miguel de Santa Teresa, by his patent of April 3, 1710. Later the Most Illustrious Lord [Bishop] Tamarón, at the time of his visitation in the year 1760, when he visited this confraternity, by his decree of June 17 of the same year, 1760, re-erected the aforesaid in these words:

Moreover, his Illustrious Lordship said that although this Confraternity of Our Lady of Carmel has been founded as such, as is of record in the patent of the Reverend Father Provincial of the Discalced Carmelites of New Spain, and the constitutions that were drawn up for it were approved and accepted by the founding members of the confraternity, nevertheless, in order to avoid doubts and confusion as to its erection and founding, in case not all the necessary prerequisites were fulfilled, his Illustrious Lordship said that he would interpose and did interpose his authority and that he would and did re-erect it as such confraternity in order that its members might enjoy and partake of all the graces and indulgences. He therefore entrusted to and charged the Reverend Father Francisco Campo Redondo, missionary minister, vicar and ecclesiastical judge of this villa, with the publication of the said indulgences so that the faithful members of the said confraternity might be aware of them and take steps to gain them.

He continues by ordering the secretary to examine the rest.

Those who belong to this confraternity today are more than 700, for there are members even in El Paso. They give 2 pesos at enrollment and 1 peso per year. Most of them have been in arrears for a long time. Its capital at present is 300 ewes, with the income from which, along with seeds, they cover expenses. The majordomo is Don Juan Bautista Vigil, who has in his possession two books in folio, one with 195 leaves which serves for recording decrees and decisions concerning the confraternity. The other has 144 leaves and is used for expenditures, receipts, and inventory of what belongs to it. Both are new and have been authorized by the Father Vicar and Ecclesiastical Judge Fray Francisco Campo Redondo on July 8 of the year 1761.

The original of the certification by the alcalde mayor of this Cañada concerning obventions there will be sent along with those of Santa Fe mentioned above. With regard to the convent provisions of this mission of Cañada, I state that these have already been established by a new decree and that they are in accordance with the produce of said villa. With regard to the former school, I state that it has come to an end because the schoolmaster died and it seems that there is no other available.

PICURIS

Accurate and legal copy of the writ of visitation which the Lord Bishop Tamarón left in the book of Baptisms of this mission under the heading of the year 1760:

In the pueblo and mission of San Lorenzo de Picuris on the ninth day of the month of June of the year 1760, the Most Illustrious Lord, Dr. don Pedro Tamarón, Bishop of Durango and of the New Kingdoms of Vizcaya and Mexico, provinces of Sonora, Sinaloa, Pimas, Moqui, and Tarahumara, of his Majesty's Council, etc., my lord. While engaged in the visitation of this pueblo of San Lorenzo de Picuris, he inspected its church, high altar, sacristy, and holy oils, all of which were found in proper condition, as well as the necessary vestments it has for use in divine worship. And he also found that the Indians were instructed in Christian doctrine and that the present missionary minister, the Reverend Father Fray José Noriega, shows every care and attention in this regard. As a result of his zeal and fervent labor, his Illustrious Lordship hopes that he will induce these Indians to confess at least once a year, since they do so only on the point of death. And he must dedicate himself to this important ministry with the greatest fidelity, whether by arranging for them to confess as best they may in the Spanish language or by working out an interrogatory for confession in their language, overcoming the difficulties encountered in so doing, for the Divine Spirit will show him the way to attain it. And we grant our authority to said father minister or to the one who may succeed him so that he may celebrate Mass on a portable altar in order to administer the Most Holy Viaticum to the sick who may be in the country ranchos, and if he should stay there another day to be with him, provided it be done with proper decorum. And he may also apply for the benefit of his ill parishioners who may be in danger of death a plenary indulgence which his Illustrious Lordship is empowered to grant by apostolic authority. He also has this authority to concede three plenary indulgences on three different days of each year, and in this pueblo he designated for one the Friday of the fifth week of Lent, on which the Sorrows of Most Holy Mary are observed; for another, St. Lawrence's day, August 10; and for the third, December 8, when the Immaculate Conception of Our Lady is celebrated. These indulgences will be gained by those who, after confession and communion, shall visit the church of this pueblo on these days. Next his Most Illustrious Lordship in-

spected this book of baptisms, the entries of which are in order. And he rendered and gave thanks to the said father for the care and vigilance which he shows, both in this and in the other matters pertaining to his ministry, and charges him, as soon as it may reach him, to conform to the edict his Illustrious Lordship dispatched for the whole diocese under date of July 7 of last year and to put it into practice in this his pueblo.[13] And he is to prepare a book in which the persons whom his Illustrious Lordship has confirmed in this pueblo are to be recorded along with those who may be confirmed in future. His Most Illustrious Lordship so decreed, to which I attest. Pedro, Bishop of Durango. In my presence, Br. Felipe Cantador, secretary.

Accurate and legal copy of the license for the founding of the chapel of the Señor San José de Gracia in Las Trampas, jurisdiction of Picuris, which the Lord [Bishop] Tamarón left; and it is and always has been in the possession of the mission father.

We, Dr. don Pedro Tamarón, by the grace of God and of the Holy Apostolic See, Bishop of Durango and of the kingdoms of Nueva Vizcaya and New Mexico, and provinces of Sonora, Sinaloa, Pimas, Moqui, and Tarahumara, of his Majesty's Council, etc.

Inasmuch as we are occupied in our general visitation of this kingdom of New Mexico and have reached the settlement of Trampas, jurisdiction of Picuris, the citizens of the said place petitioned and begged us to be pleased to concede our license so that they might build there a chapel and church with the title and advocation of Lord St. Joseph of Grace and of Most Holy Mary Immaculate in the first instant of her being, in order that the Holy Sacrifice of the Mass may be celebrated there along with all the other sacraments, since there is a large number of citizens in the said place and it is 2 leagues from the said pueblo by an enemy-infested road. In response to this petition and supplication, and considering the greatest service to God and consolation of souls, along with other reasons of spiritual fitness, we have de-

13. Edict translated in AT, pp. 81-85.

cided to order the issuance of these presents, whereby we grant our license for the building of the said chapel and church in the place mentioned. And for the blessing of its first stone we give our license and authority to the Reverend Father Fray José Noriega, of the Regular Observance of Our Father St. Francis and missionary minister of the mission of Picuris, to whose jurisdiction the place of Trampas pertains. And when the chapel has been finished, and provided that it is seemly, clean, and otherwise as required (at such time we commit its inspection in that regard to the said mission father or his successor), and after the blessing of the chapel according to the dispositions of the Roman Ritual (which is also entrusted to him and will be recorded formally after this license), the Holy Sacrifice of the Mass may be celebrated there every day by the missionary minister who is or may be in future at the aforesaid Picuris, or by any other secular or regular priest. And those who hear it on days of obligation do thereby comply with the respective precept. Moreover, the sacrament of penance may be administered by any priest licensed to hear confessions in this our diocese; burials of the dead and baptisms may be performed by the said reverend father, the present missionary parish priest, or by his successors, or by another priest to whom the missionary may give his license, because this has been found to be fitting and necessary, but always with the understanding that the parish right is reserved. And we charge the citizens of the place to try to maintain the aforesaid chapel with all possible seemliness and cleanliness so that the devotion of the faithful may thus be aroused to frequent it and so that they may find in it the spiritual consolation which is the aim of our pastoral zeal. And let this be valid for the duration of our pleasure. Issued in this pueblo and mission of Picuris, signed by us, sealed with our arms, and countersigned by our undersigned private, administrative, etc., secretary, on June 15 of the year 1760. Pedro, Bishop of Durango. By order of his Most Illustrious Lordship the Bishop, my lord, Br. Felipe Cantador, secretary.

NOTE

Although I made no note to this place in my description of the two pueblos which follow (Taos and Abiquiu), nevertheless, my thoroughness does not permit me to pass over in silence what I am about to state briefly.

TAOS

Throughout the Taos valley and in the vicinity of the pueblo there are a number of ruins of very good ranchos with many good qualities for farming. They were abandoned in the year 1760 because on August 4 of that year the Comanche nation, with (so it is said) a very large force of its men, attacked the valley and, as they demonstrated by overrunning the whole region in a number of troops, their intention was to finish the pueblo and the aforesaid ranchos to avenge the fact that two months earlier they had danced under their eyes with twenty-four scalps of their people (I shall soon describe this dance). But all the fury broke out at the house of one Pablo Pando (he was away; his family and property were all lost), which stood in the middle of the plain. There, then, was the brunt of the battle, which lasted most of the day because of the great resistance only seven men offered with bullets to more than three thousand heathens. The latter finally had recourse to opening breaches in the walls. Through them they won the house, killed those seven men (who had killed more than a hundred Indians, some inside and some outside) who had put up such great resistance. After taking the house and killing them, they killed a number of women, who had fought like men, and when they were dead, they insolently coupled them with the dead men. They sacked the house and set fire to it. They went off and took more than fifty captives with them (many have now returned), leaving seventeen Christians dead and the farms for the most part destroyed.[14]

What I have related shows the barbarity, excessive cruelty, insolence, etc., of these in-

14. Bishop Tamarón also describes the Comanche attack of August 4, 1760. AT, pp. 58-59. See also p. 4 *supra*.

domitable beasts, so execrable an extreme of evil that the Catholic arms of our beloved Sovereign alone will be able to destroy it. Yet while they reach this extreme of evil, they are also extremely good when they are in the mood. Therefore time alone sets them a middle course between such great extremes. The foregoing clearly shows that they are as bad enemies as they are good friends. The proof of the first has already been given; here is the proof of the second.

When they are on their good behavior, or at peace, they enter Taos to trade. At this fair they sell buffalo hides, "white elkskins," horses, mules, buffalo meat, pagan Indians (of both sexes, children and adults) whom they capture from other nations. (In Father Claramonte's time Christians from other places were also ransomed. He astutely cultivated the Comanche captain, his great friend, in order to get them out of captivity, for otherwise they carry them off again.) They also sell good guns, pistols, powder, balls, tobacco, hatchets, and some vessels of yellow tin (some large, others small) shaped like the crown of the friars' hats, but the difference is that the top of the hat is the bottom of the vessel. These have a handle made of an iron hoop to carry them.

They acquire these articles, from the guns to the vessels, from the Jumanas Indians, who have direct communication and trade with the French, from whom they buy them.[15] The Comanches usually sell to our people at this rate: a buffalo hide for a *bel-*

duque, or broad knife made entirely of iron which they call a trading knife here; "white elkskin" (it is the same [buffalo] hide, but softened like deerskin), the same; for a very poor bridle, two buffalo skins or a vessel like those mentioned; the meat for maize or corn flour; an Indian slave, according to the individual, because if it is an Indian girl from twelve to twenty years old, two good horses and some trifles in addition, such as a short cloak, a horse cloth, a red lapel are given; or a she-mule and a scarlet cover, or other things are given for her.

If the slave is male, he is worth less and the amount is arranged in the manner described. If they sell a she-mule, either a cover or a short cloak or a good horse is given; if they sell a horse, a poor bridle, but garnished with red rags, is given for it; if they sell a pistol, its price is a bridle; if both together, a horse is given for them. This is the usual, and a prudent judgment of how everything must go can be based on it. They are great traders, for as soon as they buy anything, they usually sell exactly what they bought; and usually they keep losing, the occasion when they gain being very rare, because our people ordinarily play infamous tricks on them.[16] In short, the trading day resembles a second-hand market in Mexico, the way people mill about.

ABIQUIU

Every year, between the end of October and the beginning of November, many heathens of the Ute nation come to the vicinity of this pueblo. They come very well laden with good deerskins, and they celebrate their fair with them. This is held for the

15. For discussions of the identity and activities of the so-called Jumano Indians, see F. V. Scholes and H. P. Mera, "Some aspects of the Jumano problem," Carnegie Institution of Washington, *Contributions to American Anthropology and History,* no. 523 (Washington, D. C., 1940), and AB-1634, pp. 311-15. Their contact with the French apparently dated from the 1680's. For trade with the French, see also H. Folmer, "The Mallet expedition of 1739 through Nebraska, Kansas, and Colorado to Santa Fe," *The Colorado Magazine,* 16: no. 5 (September, 1939), and detailed comments on it by L. B. Bloom in NMHR, 15 (1940): 89-94; Folmer, "Contraband trade between Louisiana and New Mexico in the eighteenth century," NMHR, 16 (1941): 249-74;

Folmer, *Franco-Spanish rivalry in North America, 1524-1763* (Glendale, 1953), pp. 297-303.

16. Earlier in the century it was the practice of some governors and officials to reserve this trading for themselves, punishing the ordinary people who sought to gain some profit at these fairs. F. Ocaranza, *Establecimientos franciscanos en el misterioso Reino de Nuevo México* (Mexico, 1934), pp. 185-89.

sole purpose of buying horses. If one is much to the taste and satisfaction of an Indian (the trial is a good race), he gives fifteen to twenty good deerskins for the horse; and if not, there is no purchase. They also sell deer or buffalo meat for maize or corn flour. Sometimes there are little captive heathen Indians (male or female) as with the Comanches, whom they resemble in the manner of selling them. They usually sell deerskins for belduques only, and they are given two of the latter for a good one of the former. With the exception of firearms and vessels, the Utes sell everything else as described with regard to the Comanches, but they are not so fond of trading as has been said of the latter.

ALBUQUERQUE

When I was discussing the obventions of this mission, I promised a certification like those mentioned at Santa Fe and Cañada. And since the one to which I now refer is, like them, in the original, it will be included with them. I discussed the chapel that has been built at Alameda, jurisdiction of this Albuquerque, when I began to describe the mission districts, and because I promised there a copy of the license which Gaspar González holds for this chapel, here it is:

We, Dr. don Pedro Tamarón, by the grace of God and of the Holy Apostolic See, Bishop of Durango, of the kingdoms, Nueva Vizcaya and New Mexico, and provinces of Sonora, Sinaloa, Pimas, Moqui, and Tarahumara, of his Majesty's Council, etc. Inasmuch as we have been engaged in our general visitation of this kingdom of New Mexico and have visited in it the chapel which exists on the farming hacienda of the place called Alameda in the parish of the Villa of San Felipe de Albuquerque, dedicated to Most Holy Mary Immaculate in the first instant of her being, the property of and belonging to Don Alejandro González Baz, citizen of said villa, he has petitioned and begged us to be pleased to issue our license to him so that the Holy Sacrifice of the Mass may be celebrated in the said chapel, along with the other sacraments, as a parish auxiliary of the

aforesaid villa, because there are many people on the said hacienda and many ranchos of citizens near it, and the hacienda and ranchos are rather far from the villa. And we, in view of his request and because, during our visitation, we found this chapel quite ample, seemly, and provided with what is necessary, and also heeding the greater service of God and consolation of souls, with other motives of spiritual fitness worthy of attention, and because the licenses the said chapel obtained are very old, we have decided to order the issuance of these presents whereby we grant our license so that the Holy Sacrifice of the Mass may be celebrated in the chapel mentioned by any secular or regular priest on every day of the year. And those who hear it on holy days of obligation thereby comply with the respective precept. Moreover, the sacrament of penance may be administered there by any priest licensed to hear confessions in our diocese. Consequently, with the license of the parish priest, baptisms and burials may be performed there. Finally, all other parish functions may be celebrated in it which have been celebrated there up to the present time, with the understanding that the parish rights of the Villa of San Felipe de Albuquerque, to which it pertains, are reserved in every way. And we charge the owner of the hacienda to maintain the chapel with all possible seemliness and cleanliness so that it may accordingly inspire the devotion of the faithful to frequent it and attain the spiritual profit which is the aim of our pastoral zeal. And because the aforesaid owner of the chapel has told us that the vestments and some valuables, all the property of the said chapel, are scattered among several churches, we order the Reverend Father Fray Manuel Rojo, missionary minister of Albuquerque and our vicar and ecclesiastical judge, immediately and without delay, to have them collected and handed over to the aforesaid Don Alejandro González Baz, owner of the chapel, for which they were bought out of his private means. And let him keep them and have them always ready for such functions as may be held. And let this our license be valid for the duration of our pleasure and without prejudice to the parish rights. Issued in the pueblo and mission of Señor San José de la Laguna, signed by us, sealed with our seal, and countersigned by our undersigned private, governmental, and visitation secretary on the twenty-eighth day of the month of June of the year 1760. Pedro, Bishop of Durango. By order of his Most Illustrious Lordship the Bishop, my lord, Br. Felipe Cantador, secretary. Recorded in the book of visitation.

A few years ago, in addition to the large population of which the mission father of Albuquerque now has charge, the size of which is clear from the description of its districts, the following districts were administered by this mission:

Carnué, which is 2 leagues east of the mission on the same side of the Río del Norte, located in the middle of the Sandia Sierra.[17] And it was a settlement of ranchos like those everywhere, with very good farmlands irrigated from a stream of their own in that place. It was abandoned in the year 1772 because of the continual Apache raids.

Nutrias,[18] which is 14 leagues south of the mission on the same side, along the same meadow of the aforesaid river, where the ranchos of the settlement are, with good farmlands they used to irrigate from the above river. Cattle and livestock were easily raised here, but the Apaches attacked all of it and its people. It was abandoned at the same time as Carnué.

Río Puerco, which is located 6 leagues northwest of Albuquerque (on the opposite bank from the mission).[19] And these ranchos were for cattle breeding only, because, although they used to plant, they seldom got any harvest on account of the lack of water in the river. The individuals maintained themselves by buying grain with the cattle they raised. It is called Río Puerco because its water is as dirty as the gutters of the streets, since its bed is of black clay and its

bottom very treacherous with mire. It was abandoned in the year 1774 because of a Navajo uprising, as I will tell in what follows.

Navajo, which is 11 leagues from the mission in the same direction as Río Puerco. And it was a settlement of ranchos exactly like those of Río Puerco which I have just described. It is called Navajo because it belonged to Navajo Apache Indians. It was abandoned at the same time as said Río Puerco. And the origin and beginnings of this was that years ago the aforesaid Navajos (they used to live almost in the midst of the citizens of these places) used to steal many of the herds. When the owners realized this, they entered a complaint to the governor against the offenders. He summoned them and, their crimes having been very clearly proved, admonished them several times to make restitution as they had seen restitution made to them when they asked for justice. But their reply was to flee, and within a short time they repeated their crimes so openly that they now made it clear that they were enemies. The government attacked them as such. This resulted in quasi-civil wars, because the said Navajos live almost in the midst of our people, who, in view of these things, feared greater evils and abandoned their lands, distributing themselves among the places to which they could go.

INDIANS

Even at the end of so many years since their reconquest, the specious title or name of neophytes is still applied to them. This is the reason their condition now is almost the same as it was in the beginning, for generally speaking they have preserved some very indecent, and perhaps superstitious, customs. Of these, I mention the following: As Christians, a saint's name is given them in holy baptism as is the custom in our Holy Mother the Church, but they value it so much that they do not mention it among themselves nor are they known by it, but

17. Apparently of Indian origin, the name later became Carnuel.

18. The name of a South American rodent applied in New Mexico to the North American broadtailed beaver.

19. For the land grant of "Nuestra Señora de la Luz, San Fernando y San Blas," and later settlements at this place, 1753 and 1772, see SANM, 1: no. 277.

rather by appellations according to the custom handed down from their ancestors.

They use these to such an extent that most of them do not know their saints' names and those who know them do not use them, and when we call them by their saints' names they usually have their joke among themselves, repeating the saint's name to each other as if in ridicule.[20] They have no surnames by family or descent, but in relation to their Christian names the aforesaid appellations have come to be used as such, one for each individual. Among themselves they are distinguished, called, and known by them. Therefore, if there are two or more persons with the same appellation (let us call it bad name), to avoid confusion they add to it or modify the pronunciation or the kind of letters and vowels.

All this will be clearer when I state that each bad name they use has a meaning; and some mean decent things and others, indecent. Let us leave the latter veiled by the shame that even thinking of them arouses. I say that some of the decent ones mean stick, stone, cat, dog, little bird, wheat, maize, water, earth, sierra, etc. And just as there are varieties in each species down to the least subspecies, this is where the distinguishing feature comes in, with the use of a different pronunciation, by adding or diminishing.

I elucidate further: If two are called *Stick*, and there are many of this name, they call one *Pine-Branch*, for example, and the other, *Piñon-Branch*. They make a similar distinction if the name is *Cat*: one is called *Black Cat*, another *White Cat*, and so it all goes. Very many usually take Spanish surnames, but it is not by inheritance but capriciously according to their whim or taste; perhaps because the Spanish surname seems pretty to them or because they are on close terms with some Spaniard, or for some other reason, and thus they appropriate surnames.[21]

Their repugnance and resistance to most

Christian acts is evident, for they perform the duties pertaining to the Church under compulsion, and there are usually many omissions. They are not in the habit of praying or crossing themselves when they rise or go to bed, and consequently they have no devotion for certain saints as is customary among us. And if they sometimes invoke God and His saints or pray or pay for Masses, it is in a confused manner or to comply in their confusion with what the fathers teach and explain. For example, they pay the father for a Mass, and he asks them what the intention is in terms adjusted to their understanding, and they reply: *You know, that saint what more good, more big, him you make Mass. I not know, maybe him Virgin, maybe St. Anthony*, etc., not to weary ourselves by more. And the father applies it with a good direct intention, as he knows that he must do.

They do not confess annually. If the fathers find some who know how to make a proper confession, and there are few, there is rarely anyone capable of receiving communion. When in danger of death they do indeed confess, most of them through an interpreter, since out of all the pueblos only those of Isleta, Nambe, San Juan, and Abiquiu do not make use of one, with very rare exceptions (except at Abiquiu which is Spanish-speaking),[22] for the fathers find it necessary for clearer explanation.

21. Spanish surnames among the Pueblos, as the registers show, began sporadically, much sooner in some pueblos than in others. They were first taken from the early landowners and alcaldes in the vicinity of each particular pueblo, some of whom frequently acted as godparents, like Roybal, Vigil, Martínez, and Luján in the Río Arriba; or García, Chávez, Abeyta, and Sánchez in the Río Abajo. Names of popular Spanish governors, such as Vargas or Cachupín, or of padres, like Toledo and Chavarría, were also adopted. Other surnames are translations of Indian words, like Calabaza and Pajarito, or else the phonetic spelling of Indian terms, like Waquiu and Chuina.

22. As genízaros (See GLOSS.), the Indians of Abiquiu were forced to employ Spanish as a common language and hence became more proficient in it.

20. Even today some Pueblo Indians think twice when asked their Christian names.

They are exceedingly fond of pretty reliquaries, medals, crosses, and rosaries, but this does not arise from Christian devoutness (except in a few cases) but from love of ornament. And these objects are always kept for special occasions, and only when the friars admonish them for not wearing them all the time do they wear them until that little scolding has been forgotten. Then they put them away again until another reproof, and so it goes. They are extremely grasping. They are very happy to take everything that is given them, but if they make a gift once in a while, it is not in the liberal spirit with which they received, for one must give them something in return.

To eat their ordinary coarse hash, many (without regard for persons) gather around the bowl or trough and put their filthy hands in it, and so they eat in brotherly fashion and without disgust, although there may be nastiness. Their only napkin for wiping themselves is to shake their hands right over it. If their noses run, they wipe them off with their dainty hand and throw it to the ground right before everyone; they half wipe it off on their shoe, the ground, or their clothing, and back goes the paw into the bowl or trough. The men's clothing consists of a deerskin coat or a woolen jacket (on festive days it is something else again), and their breeches, etc., are the same. The women use woolen blankets.

They use estufas, of which some pueblos have more, others less.[23] There are sometimes nine in one pueblo, as at Pecos, and one in others, as at Nambe. Some of them are underground, and others are above ground with walls like a little house, and of them all, some are round while others are rectangular. But the entrance is always through a *coi*, or trap door on the roof, as has already been said some time ago. These estufas are the chapter, or council, rooms,

and the Indians meet in them, sometimes to discuss matters of their government for the coming year, their planting, arrangements for work to be done, or to elect new community officials, or to rehearse their dances, or sometimes for other things.

Their customary dances usually resemble contredanses or minuets as danced in Spain, or they are scalp dances. And for any of these dances they make preparations as follows: Just as our Spaniards bathe before putting on their gala finery, so these Indians bathe before bedizening themselves with filthy earths of different colors (only the men, the women do not) with which they paint their nakedness from head to foot, covering their private parts with a breechclout like a loin cloth. They usually paint half the body lengthwise with one color and half with another, or sections of the whole body in the same way.

One foot, one color, the other, another; one leg one color, the other, another; one thigh in one way, the other in another; and so bit by bit they reach the head. As a result they are unrecognizable, because they completely disfigure their features, and they can only be recognized after careful scrutiny. Moreover, they tie a tortoise shell to one leg, hanging near it many little cloven hooves of deer, sheep, or similar animals, so that all this rings and sounds with the movement of the body like little bells. They also tie on some of these *cascabeles,* or other small bells, and it all serves to make music.

Although the women bathe, they do not undress, or paint anything except their cheeks with carmine, using make-up to supply what nature failed to give them. Both women and men go barefoot, let their hair hang loose. The men tie a small handful of macaw feathers on their heads, and the women put on some little painted boards trimmed with a few feathers and latticed with agave fiber. Not only does this resemble a halo, but it looks something like those small lattices found in gardens or flower pots. They put on good blankets and

23. Domínguez and other Spanish observers used the descriptive word *estufa* for this structure. The Hopi name "kiva" also is used today. See AB-1634, p. 226.

hang about their necks as many rosaries, crosses, or medals as they can, and all hanging from ribbons.

When they are decked out in this way, either twelve or more men dance, or the same number of women alone, or eight of each, or a couple like a minuet. There is a musical instrument and chant for these dances. The instrument is one they call *tombé*[24] (there is no other), and this is nothing more than a kind of *teponastle,* whose outline, form, or shape is a hollow log like a middle-sized barrel with both openings covered with skin like the head put on a barrel or cask of chocolate, and it is played with a small stick like a drum.

The chant is a gabble of echoes without pronunciation of words. Many form a chorus for this, as when a music master has his pupils echo in chorus the high, middle, half, low notes, etc. of the scale, accompanied by the soft beating of the tombé. Sometimes they do sing words, but it actually amounts to metered prose, for they are incapable of composing verses. They use these dances for ceremonial days of the year, and they do not appear to conceal further malice or superstition beneath the superficial trappings.

The scalp dance is as follows, and it is described from the beginning since there are special features. The Christians kill one or many heathen enemies, and even before they are quite dead the Indians remove their scalps along with the hair, and sometimes with the ears, for even for that they have principles or regulations (the heathens do the same thing to the Christians). This is a token of victory, and they dance with it to avenge after a fashion the grievances suffered. Whether they take one scalp or many, the Indians who took part in the war give and share them liberally with those who did not, and the latter share with others, and so all the pueblos participate in the pleasure, if only in a small way.

This dance is their most solemn festival,

because (as the saying runs) they jump into the frying pan and shoot the works.[25] When they draw near the pueblo, they signal with smoke; the people see it, get excited; men, women, children, and old folk bedeck themselves and go out to meet it [the scalp]. There they make such unseemly demonstrations that when I say that the women scornfully touch their private parts with the scalp, nothing more needs to be said, for they go to such execrable extremes.[26] They paw, fondle, flatter, and overwhelm with thanks the one who brings it. (He puts on very severe, vain, triumphant, etc., airs.)

The place where this reception is held is usually about half a league from the pueblo, and from there they bring the scalp home in a sort of triumphal procession, singing on the way about the events of the battle. All this with much babbling in broken meter, howls, leaps, shouts, skirmishes, courses back and forth, salvos, and other demonstrations of rejoicing over so infamous a relic. Even though the distance is so short, they usually take about three hours to go from the meeting place to the pueblo. They arrive at the pueblo; they abandon the scalp as if they had thrown it away; and they go to the church as if to give thanks. This lasts about as long as three Credos. They leave; they go to the place where they left the precious thing; and they parade it around the pueblo in the same fashion as they brought it there.

Then they put it in the accursed reliquary where they keep the old scalps and leave it there. That night, or the next day, there is a confabulation, of the men only, in the estufa, and at that meeting the day of the feast is appointed. This is held with the attend-

24. *Tombé,* onomatopoeic, like "tom-tom."

25. "Se echan a freír y echan el resto." *Echar el resto* is a gambling term which signifies to bet everything one has on the table.

26. For similar features connected with the present "rabbit hunts," part of the game also used to "feed" the scalps, see L. A. White, "The Pueblo of Santo Domingo, New Mexico," *Memoirs of the American Anthropological Association,* no. 43 (Menasha, Wis., 1935), pp. 144-48.

ance of guests from other pueblos who are near enough to come and to whom they show great courtesies. The dance is organized as follows: A pole is fixed in the ground in the middle of the plaza or other public place, and the new relic is placed on it along with the old ones. The tombé is placed at the foot of the pole, and the singers gather there and the dance continues at their pleasure, all in sight of the relics. This usually lasts three days.

There are other general customs observed by the Indians of these regions, but I have mentioned only the most noteworthy. I note, indeed, that although I stated above that the contredanses, or minuets, do not appear to be essentially wicked and are usual on solemn occasions during the year, here in the scalp ceremonial the dances are tainted by the idea of vengeance. The fathers have been very zealous in their opposition to this scalp dance, but they have only received rebuffs, and so the fathers are unable to abolish this custom and many others, because excuses are immediately made on the ground that [the Indians] are neophytes, minors, etc.[27]

27. The estufas and the dances which were lumped by the padres under one term, "cachinas," were a major feature in the constant quarrels between the missionaries and the civil officials from the beginnings of New Mexico history. The Franciscans tried to insist on their complete abolition if the Pueblos were to be thoroughly Christianized. A great number of Spanish governors and their followers opposed the friars for their own political or commercial advantage, and some even encouraged the Indians. Just prior to 1680, when some governors sided with the fathers, their opposition to these practices was one of the factors that led to the Pueblo Rebellion of that year and the martyrdom of twenty-one missionaries. The Inquisition records of this period are full of this topic, amply referred to by F. V. Scholes in *Church and State in New Mexico, 1610-1650* (Albuquerque, 1937), and *Troublous Times in New Mexico, 1659-1670* (Albuquerque, 1942). Governor Otermín continued the policy of abolition in 1681. See HS, *passim*. Governor Mogollón also had estufas in various pueblos destroyed. BL, N.M. Origs., 1714. A private venture in the opposite direction was Juan de Tafoya's tricky

Under such pretexts they will always be neophytes and minors with the result that our Holy Faith will not take root and their malice will increase. May God our Lord destroy these pretexts so completely that these wretches may become old Catholics and the greatest saints of His Church.

NOTE

The Indians of Picuris and Taos outdo all the rest in all the general customs. Without describing their excesses in each particular, I shall only tell about two as the most noteworthy, and they will serve as a basis for imagining the ones I omit. They are so notably opposed to Christianity that they cannot even look at Christian things, for they are unwilling to give charity (those of Taos do give alms) or lodging to a Spaniard. If they see a Spaniard, they hide; if he is the father (this is the worst in their eyes), they are as terrified as if they were to see Lucifer himself and they would like to make themselves invisible. They flee from him like the devil from the cross, and the children even cry, running as if from their cruelest enemy.

Perhaps the little ones may be playing in the street, now in the pueblo, now a little way off, but within sight, and as soon as the bell rings they forget their game and run to take refuge in their nest. Therefore it is necessary for the fiscales to order them to come to Mass or catechism by the town crier's voice. And if there is no such summons, the bell may break [with ringing for all the attention they pay to it]. On their way to church, whether they be old or young, they go mincing along one by one, but when they leave, first comes first, be-

offer to the Indians in 1712, when he promised to get permission from the viceroy for them to keep their estufas if they supplied him with a great quantity of deerskins. SANM, 2: no. 171. The conflicting views on the subject continued up to Domínguez' time, but, as he here observes, by then the Pueblos were in full use of their estufas and everything connected with them, as they are today.

cause they fall over one another like sheep leaving the corral for pasture.

They are so shameless that the men constantly go about naked with only a breech-clout and a skin or blanket to keep them warm, being thus naked even when they go to church. And although the father scolds them for their indecency, they go on as before, for the malice of these minors is so great that there is no remedy. And this is because they do not wish to clothe themselves, not because they lack the wherewithal. The little boys and girls, absolutely *in puribus* until they are twelve to fourteen years old. In this regard Father Claramonte forced them to half cover themselves by whipping them, and as a reward for this good work, he was accused of imprudence with minors.

The Indians of Abiquiu do not adhere to any of the foregoing customs, because they were brought up among Spaniards and they are therefore Hispanicized in this respect. But even though they are not given to that practice, they are weak, gamblers, liars, cheats, and petty thieves.

NOTE

In the memorandum of the archive given some pages back, I said that I was taking with me 77 papers with various matters pertaining to this Custody: "The decree of the lord viceroy . . . Four papers of Father Rodríguez . . . A paper in his hand . . ." But I am not taking them away from the Custody, but only removed them from the archive until I should master their content. And having done so, I find the following useful.[28]

28. A similar list is in MN, Asuntos, 198. It appears to be in Domínguez' own hand and bears the heading "Memorandum of the papers pertaining to the affairs of this Custody which are in the archive of the interior missions of New Mexico." This memorandum lists 82 papers, or groups of papers, instead of the 52 given in the report of the visitation. All except one of those listed above are included, but the order, and sometimes the wording of the description, does not always correspond. At

A representation made to Viceroy [José Sarmiento de Valladares], Conde de Moctezuma, on January 14, 1698, with regard to the small number of religious this Custody had, asking him for thirteen more and a chaplain for the presidio. This is unsigned, and the governor

the end of this memorandum there is a statement indicating that all the papers remaining in the archive at Santo Domingo, with the exception of the mission registers, are included. The items not mentioned in the report are as follows:

Act of obedience which Custos Fray Francisco Vargas issued to Fathers Fray Agustín Colina and Fray Joaquín Hinojosa so that they might go to the discovery of the Jumanos as chaplains. [Cf. letters in AASF, 1691, no. 2, 1691, no. 4.] § Decree and reply to it concerning the state of the missions at the Junta de los Ríos. [AASF, 1693, no. 6.] § Copy of a letter written to Custos Fray Francisco Vargas by Fray José Arbisu, in which he gives an account of the mission of San Cristóbal. [Cf. n. 32, *infra*.] § Petition of Admiral D. José Chacón [governor of New Mexico, 1707-12] to Father Custos Fray José de Haro, asking what motive he had for opening two letters in the dispatches that came to him. § Possession (in addition to those already mentioned) of the site on which the convent and church of Santa Fe is built, which was given to Fray Miguel Muñiz. [Cf. n. 64 *infra*.] § Schedule of obventions which Fray Juan de la Cruz made. § Exhortatory letter by Father Miranda. This father holds an opinion about this; I mean, he died holding that opinion, as I will relate in its place. § Directive letter by Father Fray Pedro Marín. § Two patents of Provincial Fray Manuel Vigil [1708-10] consoling the religious in their corporeal needs. [AASF, 1708, no. 1; 1709, no. 3.] § Patent of Provincial Fray Martín de Aguirre [1710-11] so that they may beg God for a successful outcome for Governor D. Francisco Cuervo y Valdés, benefactor of this Custody. [AASF, 1710, no. 2; 1711, no. 1.] § Patent of Fray Fernando Alonso González [Commissary General of New Spain, 1723-34] to the effect that the religious are not to interfere in governmental matters nor write to the governors. § Letter of congratulation from the Duque de Alburquerque to Custos Fray Juan de la Peña upon the rebuilding of the mission of Isleta; and he promises him vestments. [AASF, 1709, no. 1. Cf. n. 2, p. 203 *supra*.] § Letter of Fray Salvador de San Antonio summoning the fathers for the expedition into New Mexico. § Opinion of the friars in favor of applying to the syndic of Parral, Don Martín Salvasa, for succor because of the delay of the dispatch. § Letter of Fray Antonio Aparicio to Custos Fray José de Haro, in which he advises him who made it is unknown.[29] § Opinion of Father Fray Joaquín Hinojosa that the Mansos Indians should be brought to El Paso and that a new mission should not be founded for them.[30] § Representation by Father Custos Fray Juan Tagle and the council members of this Custody in favor of the Indians of this kingdom against their paying tribute. Made to the Duque de Linares [Fernando de Alencastre Noroña y Silva, viceroy of New Spain, 1711-16].[31] § Letter of

Father Fray José Arbisu to the Father Custos Fray Francisco Vargas in which he notifies him that he is leaving the mission of San Cristóbal because it has been abandoned and because the governor is unwilling to provide an armed escort and an uprising is expected for certain.[32] § Opinion of the fathers of this Custody that the wagon train should be given up. Year 1694.[33] § Opinion of the missionary religious of the Junta de los Ríos that the said missions could not survive, and a letter of Custos Fray Nicolás López on the same subject.[34] § Appearance of Father Fray Juan de la Peña before the Custos for investigation as to whether it was true that he incited the citizens of La Cañada to write against Governor Cubero [1697-1703]. The investigation came out in Father Peña's favor.[35] § Representation by Governor Cuervo Valdés [1705-07] to the Duque de Alburquerque [Francisco Fernán-

---

of the convocation of Utes, Comanches, and Apaches. § Letter from Fray José Arbisu to Custos Fray Francisco Vargas in which he informs him why he left the mission. [AASF, 1696, no. 2. Cf. n. 32 infra.] § Patent of the commissary for the removal of the schedule [of obventions, etc.] which Fray Nicolás López made, which is to be remitted to him. § Patents of Fray Salvador de San Antonio in which he exhorts the religious to learn the [native] language. § Certification which the cabildo of Santa Fe gave to Custos Fray Salvador de San Antonio that he had entered the foothills of the mountain where the apostate Indians were. § Petition which Brother Fray Miguel de la Cueva made to Custos Fray Juan Tagle that the religious should state what they owed to the syndic of Parral. § Petition to the Duque de Alburquerque for the new reduction of Isleta. They ask him for vestments, bells, etc. § Petition made by Fray Joaquín Hinojosa and repeated by Fray Francisco Vargas to obtain possession of churches and convents which the ministers of this Custody have built during twelve years. [AASF, 1692, no. 1. See also O. Maas, *Misiones de Nuevo Méjico* (Madrid, 1929), pp. 155-81.] § Letter of the friars to Vice-Custos Fray José Pedraza in which they ask that the wagons be traded in because this is advisable. [Cf. a letter of Father Pedraza, Vice-Commissary of the Indies, to the Custody, Mexico, February 28, 1716, AASF, 1716, no. 1.] § Petition of Fray Juan Alvarez to Governor Cubero asking the latter to inform the viceroy about the vestments and other things lacking at Pecos, Santa Fe, and other missions. [HB, 3: 369-78.] § Letter of Vice-Custos Fray José Pedraza to the religious forbidding them to make any statement in writing without his permission. § Decree of the Lord Bishop D. Manuel de Herrera [1686-89] to the effect that the friars may grant dispensations of impediments to marriage and that the lay population may apply to them. [Cf. AT, pp. 12-13.] § Certification which Governor D. Pedro Cubero gave to Father Fray Francisco Farfán that the latter had ascended the Peñol of Acoma to reduce the Indians. [1698] § Requisitory edict of Governor D. Pedro Cubero asking for a minister for Moqui because the pueblos of Acoma, Laguna, and Zuñi had been re-

conquered and an Indian had come to ask for a father.

29. Cf. HB, 3: 370. BNM, leg. 4, no. 13, contains a copy of a certification by Governor Cubero dated at Santa Fe, February 12, 1698, made at the request of the Father Procurator Fray Buenaventura de Contreras. The content indicates that it refers to the same paper of which Domínguez apparently found a draft. The governor states that when he entered Santa Fe on July 2, 1697, there were 34 Franciscan priests and 4 lay brothers serving in the New Mexico missions and in the El Paso district. The 1696 rebellion, in which five of them had suffered martyrdom at the hands of the apostates, had not turned them from their evangelical labors. Since the rebellion, there had been 12 priests administering the sacraments and one lay brother acting as procurator, under conditions of the utmost difficulty and hardship, for 21 had left for reasons of health. He had therefore informed the viceroy that 13 additional friars were needed.

30. Fray Joaquín Hinojosa became president *in capite* of the Custody of New Mexico in April or May, 1692, because of the death of Fray Diego de Mendoza, who had been elected Custos at the Chapter of June 2, 1691. This opinion is dated at Senecu, April 23, 1693. AASF, 1693, no. 6. The Manso Indians had rebelled in 1684, and in April, 1691, Custos Fray Francisco de Vargas, after two years of effort, reduced some of them to a pueblo he founded 8 or 9 leagues from El Paso, called San Francisco de los Mansos. *D. Diego de Vargas to the Viceroy, Conde de Galve, El Paso del Río del Norte, August 14, 1691*, AGM, Historia, vol. 37. This

dez de la Cueva, viceroy of New Spain, 1702-11] with regard to the scarcity of religious, their poverty, and that of this whole kingdom, dated January 15, 1706.[36] § Account of the spirit in which some religious of this Custody died at the hands of the Indians on the fourth day of June, 1696.[37] § Report of Father Fray Miguel

Muñiz about Governor Peñuela's [Admiral don Joseph Chacón Medina Salazar y Villaseñor, Marqués de las Peñuelas, 1707-12] removal of several *regidores* without cause; and his reason for demolishing part of the fortifications of the stronghold. § Report of Father Fray Juan Alvarez on the same. § Report of Father Fray Juan Tagle on the same.[38] § Writing of Father Fray Francisco de Ayeta[39] presented to Governor don Antonio Otermín as syndic of this Custody for the conversion of 1,490 head of cattle into silver for buying wine, wax, and other necessary items for the religious. Year 1681. § Appearance of the Special Father Procurator of this Custody, Fray Diego

---

pueblo appears in a list in a petition of Father Vargas to Governor de Vargas dated August 30, 1691, but it was not included among the missions of which de Vargas gave formal possession to Fray Joaquín de Hinojosa in May, 1692. Maas, *Misiones de Nuevo Méjico*, pp. 157, 164; AGI, Aud. de Guadalajara, leg. 139.

31. Fray Juan de Tagle was already custos in October, 1710. AASF, 1710, no. 3. He was re-elected in the Chapters held in Mexico City on October 24, 1711, and April 29, 1713. He appears to have been at odds with the Marqués de la Peñuela, governor of New Mexico 1707-12 and who made complaints against him to the Duque de Linares. DHM, pp. 198-99. The subject of this representation was a controversial one of long standing.

32. See FRANCISCANS for the story of Father Arbisu, one of the martyrs in the 1696 rebellion.

33. For the origins and seventeenth-century history of the supply service, see F. V. Scholes, "The supply service of the New Mexico missions in the seventeenth century," NMHR, 5 (1930): 93-115, 186-210, 386-404.

34. The reference is probably to the missions founded during the expedition into Texas made in 1683-84 by Fray Nicolás López, then Vice-Custos of the New Mexico Franciscans, and Captain Juan Domínguez de Mendoza. Fray Antonio de Acevedo and Fray Juan de Zabaleta remained at La Junta for a few months, but were forced to flee for their lives. In a certification dated at El Paso, August 18, 1685 (BNM, leg. 2, no. 14), Governor Domingo Jironza Petris de Cruzate stated that Custos Fray Salvador de San Antonio, who had arrived in El Paso in March, 1685, had found Zabaleta and Acevedo in Parral and had brought the latter to El Paso with him. In spite of the extremely critical state of affairs in El Paso in the years immediately following the Pueblo Revolt, Fray Nicolás López was most optimistic about the future of the missions at La Junta and the conversion of the Texas tribes. In September, 1684, he summoned the friars to Senecu, and they agreed that he should go to Mexico City to give a true report to their prelates. AGM, Provincias Internas, vol. 37. He was also anxious to further Domínguez de Mendoza's efforts to secure the governorship of New Mexico. Some of the many documents concerning the Texas expedition and López'

petitions to the authorities in Mexico City and Spain have been published in the following: H. G. Bolton, *Spanish exploration in the Southwest, 1542-1706* (New York, 1916), pp. 310-43; HB, 3: 20-22, 354-65; Maas, *Misiones de Nuevo Méjico*, pp. 109-19.

35. See FRANCISCANS.

36. See HB, 3: 366-83 for translations of some of the representations on this subject made in the time of Governor Cuervo y Valdés.

37. This may be a two-page incomplete manuscript copy in AASF, 1698, no. 1 [14], entitled: *Mex.º Mayo 20 de 1698 años Rason con el espiritu que murieron los 5 Ministros Misioneros de la S.ta Cusstt.a de la nueba Mex.º a manos de los Yndios el dia 21 [sic] de Junio año de 1696*. It is a series of rhetorical questions, perhaps part of a sermon delivered in Mexico City, apparently in answer to someone who had impugned the spirit of all the friars of New Mexico at this time.

38. Reports probably made *c.* 1707, when Father Alvarez was custos, Father Muñiz, vice-custos, and Father Tagle, secretary, of the Custody. On July 7, 1708, the Viceroy, Duque de Alburquerque, issued two orders relating to the subjects mentioned to the Marqués de las Peñuelas. SANM, 2: nos. 140, 142. These documents are partly illegible, but in both the Viceroy begins by referring to communications received from New Mexico which had been reviewed in council in Mexico City. With regard to the appointment of *regidores*, the New Mexico governor was ordered to remit copies of the royal or viceregal order empowering him to take such action. As for the fortifications, the Viceroy wished to know "whether he had an order from H. M. to pull down and demolish the said castle, the reasons he had for demolishing it, the length of time the new building and construction would take," etc.

39. See FRANCISCANS.

Párraga, before Governor don Antonio Otermín so that he might make a juridical investigation as to whether the convent of El Paso or
any friar has taken a milpa, eggs, fowl, etc.,
from the Piros Indians.[40] § Writings in which
the cabildo of this kingdom revokes the testimony against the religious of this Custody.
Year 1703.[41] § Decrees and proceedings concerning the false charge made by the Mansos
Indians against Father Fray Francisco González and sentence in his favor. Year 1712.[42]
§ Letter of Father Fray Francisco Corvera in
which he advises Father Custos Fray Francisco
Vargas that the Indians may rebel and that he
does not intend to leave his mission of San Ildefonso even though they may kill or carry him
off. Year 1695. This Father Corvera knew the
Queres language well.[43] § Certification concerning the bones of Father Fray Juan de Jesús,
found near an estufa in the pueblo of Jémez.
In duplicate.[44] § Case of two Piros Indians.
Year 1692.[45] § Instrument of the second act of
taking possession of the Peñol of Acoma, Zuñi,
and Moqui in favor of our Province [of the
Holy Gospel] and [Franciscan] Order. Year

40. See FRANCISCANS.

41. Cf. HB, 3: 495; J. M. Espinosa, *Crusaders of
the Río Grande* (Chicago, 1942), pp. 342-46.

42. A "Fray Francisco de Gonzales" was minister-
ing "to the Indians of the Mansos and Piros nations
and to the new conversion of the Xanos" in 1706.
HB, 3: 377. He was also commissary of the Inquisition. He resigned the mission of Guadalupe del
Paso, February 1, 1712. AASF, 1712, no. 6. Cf.
FRANCISCANS.

43. BNM, leg. 4, no. 10; AASF, 1695, no. 3.

44. Two seventeenth-century martyrs at Jémez
have been confused in later accounts because of the
similarity of their names. Fray Juan de Jesús was
one of the martyrs of August, 1680. HS, 1: 31, 56,
110. During a Jémez Valley campaign in 1694, Governor de Vargas located and unearthed the bones of
Fray Juan on August 8 and placed them in a box
which he kept in his tent until his return to Santa
Fe, where they were interred under the altar of the
parish church. AGM, Historia, vol. 39, ff. 216-18;
AASF, 1694, no. 3. On June 4, 1696, Fray Francisco
de Jesús also was martyred at Jémez. A letter of
Fray Francisco de Vargas dated at Santa Fe, July 21,
1696, states that when the soldiers went to the
pueblo, they found that animals had eaten Fray
Francisco's body, but they gathered some of his
bones and buried them in the church at Zia. BNM,
leg. 4, no. 13. See FRANCISCANS.

45. AASF, 1692, no. 7.

1692.[46] §Instrument for the rebuilding of the
pueblo and mission of San Agustín de la
Isleta.[47] § Copy of the legal instrument for the
act of taking possession of the convent and
church of Santa Fe. Year 1692.[48] § Copy of a
cédula of Charles II ordering the governors to
see to the reduction of the nearby pagans and
to help the ecclesiastics to achieve this.[49]
§ Warning of Father Fray Salvador de San Antonio to Governor Vargas that the Indians were

46. *Año de 1692, diciembre 18. Posesión que en
virtud del pedimento presentado del Reverendo
Padre Misionero Fray Francisco Corvera, presidente
de los capellanes que fueron con el susodicho real
ejército para la conquista del Reino de la Nueva
México, que en su villa y cabeza de Santa Fe se le
dió asimismo de la feligresía de dichos naturales y
administración de los santos sacramentos, y habi-
endo pasado a la reducción del peñol de Acoma,
provincias de Zuñi y Moqui, se le dió en la misma
forma, reproduciendo el tenor en esta presente por
el señor Don Diego de Vargas Zapata Luján Ponce
de León, gobernador y capitán general de este dicho
Reino de la Nueva México y castellano de su fuerza
y presidio por S. M. BNM, leg. 4, no. 2. Fragment
also in AASF, 1692, no. 3.

47. Cf. n. 2, p. 203 *supra*.

48. *Septiembre a 14 de 1692 años. Posesión que
a favor de la Santa Custodia de Nuestro Padre San
Francisco dió Don Diego de Vargas Zapata Luján
Ponce de León, gobernador y capitán general de
este Reino y Provincia de la Nueva México y castellano de su fuerza y presidio por su Majestad, del
sitio para la iglesia y santo templo y convento y lo
demás anexo y perteneciente en la Villa de Santa
Fe, cabecera del Reino de la Nueva México, acabada
de reducir y conquistar nuevamente en dicho día,
mes y año, ut supra, etc. BNM, leg. 4, no. 1.*

49. The royal cédula dated Buen Retiro, May 14,
1686, addressed to the Viceroy of New Spain, the
Audiencias of Guadalajara and Guatemala, and the
governors of those provinces concerning the reduction and conversion of pagan Indians in their districts. It states that the heathen tribes begin 24
leagues from Mexico City and extend through the
provinces of New Spain, New Galicia, New Vizcaya,
New Mexico, and the New Kingdom of León as far
as Florida without interruption, and that there are
also pagan Indians between Campeche and Guatemala. The authorities have been neglecting their
conversion and reduction, although it is the chief
duty of their offices. Upon receipt of this cédula
each one is to undertake in his district "their reduction and conversion by the most gentle and effective
means at your disposal, entrusting this to ecclesiastical persons of whose virtue and courage you are
completely satisfied, as is necessary for so essential a

desirous of rebelling. Year 1693.⁵⁰ § Opinion
submitted by order of the lord viceroy (neither
his name nor his title are given) as to what
should be done with the Apaches who were
ransomed. It has no signatures. Year 1715.⁵¹
§ Decree of Governor don Pedro Rodríguez
Cubero requiring the father custos (it does not
say who he was) not to remove the father ministers of Acoma and Zuñi.⁵² § Original decrees
of an ecclesiastical visitation. Consultation and
opinion, with a decree of remission. It is of
record in these proceedings that the governor
was excommunicated (it does not say who he
was) and later absolved.⁵³ § Reply to a cédula
of Philip V in which he asks the religious of
this Custody for a donation; notification of the
cédula by [Governor] Marqués de Peñuela.
The reply was: that *nemo dat quod non habet.*
Year 1711.⁵⁴ § Copy of a letter of Father Fray
Diego Chavarría in which he informed Governor don Pedro Cubero that after his journey
to Zuñi and Moqui had been decided upon, he

found out that Bartolomé Ojeda, who was to
accompany him, had gone forth against the
Gileños. He asks what he shall do.⁵⁵ § Decree
and legal instrument of the Bishop of Durango,
Don Fray Manuel de Herrera [1686-89], in
which he makes Father Custos Fray Francisco
de Vargas chief parish priest of these mis-
sions.⁵⁶ § Certification of Governor Cubero in
favor of Father Farfán.⁵⁷ § Copy of the act of
possession of this Custody from the Río del
Sacramento.⁵⁸ § Certification by the cabildo of
Santa Fe in favor of the fathers of this Custody.
Year 1693. With it there is a little separate
paper from Juan Lucero de Godoy in which he
certifies under oath that he has never heard
the Indians say that they want black fathers
[i.e., secular priests or Jesuits] or of any other

matter as this, giving them whatever assistance,
favor, and aid may be necessary . . ." AGM, Reales
Cédulas Dup., vol. 30, ff. 181-83. This was received
in Mexico City on September 21, 1686, and copies
forwarded to the appropriate local authorities.
AASF, 1686. no. 3.

50. Petition of San Antonio and the other friars
in New Mexico dated at Santa Fe, December 18,
1693. DHM, pp. 142-43; AASF, 1694, no. 1.

51. Fernando de Alencastre Noroña y Silva,
Duque de Linares, was viceroy of New Spain
1711-16. There were a number of campaigns against
the Apaches in New Mexico at this period.

52. Possibly in 1702 or 1703, when there was a
precarious state of affairs at Zuñi. At this period
Fray Juan de Garaicoechea was at Zuñi and Fray
Antonio de Miranda, at Acoma. The custos was
probably Fray Juan de Zabaleta. Cf. n. 2, p. 196
supra.

53. The description of this document is too vague
to permit positive identification. In New Mexico
the Franciscans made use of this powerful weapon
more than once in their controversies with the governors. De Vargas was excommunicated for usurping
ecclesiastical jurisdiction during his dispute with
Father Hinojosa in 1692. BNM, leg. 4, no. 4; AASF,
1692, nos. 4, 5.

54. The *donativo,* or contribution to the royal
exchequer, especially when war or other circumstances necessitated extraordinary expenditures, was
customary in Spain from early times. According to
legal theory, it was a voluntary donation by individuals or corporations, although as time went on it

sometimes degenerated into a tax. The monarchs
made requests of this kind from their subjects in the
Indies as well as in Spain. The occasion for this particular one was probably the War of the Spanish
Succession. See F. de Fonseca y Urrutia, *Historia
general de Real Hacienda* (Mexico, 1845-53), 4:
429-50.

55. Father Chavarría was at Zia on November 27,
1701, when the mission records show that he performed a marriage there. It is possible, therefore,
that this is the period when he contemplated a
journey to Zuñi and Moqui, for Bartolomé de
Ojeda was the governor of Zia who served as a faithful adherent and ally of the Spaniards during and
after the Reconquest period. Governor Cubero had
made an expedition to Moqui early in 1701. Cf.
Espinosa, *Crusaders of the Río Grande,* pp. 347-49.

56. A certified copy of this document from the
original, dated at Durango, October 24, 1688, in the
archive of the Custody was made by Fray Antonio
de Acevedo by order of Custos Vargas and is now in
BNM, leg. 3, no. 3. See AT, pp. 12-13.

57. See FRANCISCANS.

58. After the refugees from the Pueblo Revolt in
New Mexico settled in the El Paso area in 1681,
jurisdictional disputes over the limits between New
Mexico and Nueva Vizcaya arose and continued for
some years. The older controversy over ecclesiastical jurisdiction between the New Mexico Franciscans and the Bishops of Durango also helped to
complicate the situation. See AT, pp. 1-19. On July
28, 1682, a *junta general* in Mexico City, presided
over by the viceroy, defined the boundary between
New Mexico and Nueva Vizcaya as the "Río del
Nombre de Dios, or the one called Sacramento, and
from here the district of the government of New
Mexico begins." AGI, Aud. de México, leg. 53. The
Río del Sacramento runs a short distance to the
north of the city of Chihuahua.

color except blue.[59] § Petition of the lay brother Fray Miguel de la Cueva (overseer of the wagon train) to the father custos to have the father certify to the alms they received from him.[60] § Petition of the fathers of this Custody to the cabildo of Santa Fe that it certify that they have not been the cause of the soldiers' collecting their pay. The cabildo issues a certification in favor of these fathers.[61] § Act of possession and grant of the convent and the lot on which it stands of the mission of Santa Fe made by Governor Cubero to the Father Custos Fray Juan Alvarez as its head. Year 1697. The Santa Fe convent was built at this Governor Cubero's expense.[62] § Grant of a piece of land, which is upstream from this villa, which Governor Cubero made in favor of the convent of this villa. § Possession of the convent, church, and lands in Santa Fe to our Sacred Order, which Governor don Diego de Vargas granted on September 14, 1692.[63] § Petition of Father Fray Joaquín de Hinojosa to the governor (it does not say who he was) for the possession of the convents, church, and lands of certain missions. The said father states that he made a favorable reply, but it is not of record.[64] § Writing of the Father Custos Fray Juan Tagle to Governor don José Chacón [Marqués de las Peñuelas] asking him to hand over a writing which was made against the fathers and presented to the cabildo. And also for another writing against the priests that they

placed in the hands of an image of Most Holy Mary which was venerated in the church of Santa Fe. Year 1712. Although the writings did not turn up, their author was known, but there is no record of his punishment.[65] § Copy of a cédula of Charles II with a decree of the Duque de Alburquerque granted to Father Fray Alonso Benavides so that the custos and his religious might see to it that the Indians should not be burdened by the governors or alcaldes with plantings and services for a week at a time, etc., and inform the viceroy of all violations. Year 1709. This is also in the secular church archive.[66] § Legal instruments for the defense with regard to the uprising of the Indians of this kingdom. Year 1695. The original was remitted to the Province, but the year

64. Maas, *Misiones de Nuevo Méjico,* pp. 158-59: AGI, Aud. de Guadalajara, leg. 139.

65. April 23, 1712. Santa Fe. Testimonies defending the friars against libelous statements, before the cabildo of Santa Fe, by Fray Juan de Tagle and others. 18 pp. M. J. Geiger, *Calendar of documents in the Santa Barbara Mission Archives* (Washington, D. C., 1947), p. 262. This complaint concerns an unsigned letter placed in the hands of La Conquistadora.

66. Fragment in AASF, 1686, no. 2. The problem of personal service was a subject of continual controversy throughout the Indies. The Crown issued cédula after cédula forbidding the flagrant abuses committed by officials, encomenderos, and others, but to no lasting effect. This situation was even more acute in unproductive areas like New Mexico, where the exploitation of Indian labor was the best available source of profit to governors and settlers alike. See Scholes, *Church and State* and *Troublous Times* for an unbiased picture of the situation in the seventeenth century. The details of Domínguez' description of the cédula obtained by Fray Alonso de Benavides are puzzling, for the dates are inconsistent. In 1635, or earlier, Benavides presented petitions asking that the Indians be exempt from tribute and personal service for ten years after their conversion. The decree on the document, dated January 19, 1635, applies earlier cédulas on the subject to the Indians of New Mexico, and this decision was embodied in a cédula to the viceroy dated January 30. AB-1634, pp. 168-77, 187-89. Although this cédula does not quite answer the description in the above list, it is not unlikely that Benavides also obtained one in these terms. It may later have been reissued by Charles II, probably when some specific charges or complaints were made, and still later remitted to New Mexico again on a similar occasion with a covering decree by the

59. Individual Franciscan groups in Spain and America, probably influenced by Mother María de Agreda and the Conceptionist Franciscan nuns, began to wear blue habits instead of the ordinary gray in honor of the Immaculate Conception of Mary. The New Mexico friars, as shown here, had been wearing blue and presumably continued using this color until the end of the Custody after 1800. The incorrupt corpse of Father Padilla, examined by Custos Fray Francisco de Hozio in 1819, wore a habit that crumbled into blue-colored dust when exposed to the air. See FRANCISCANS, Fray Juan José de Padilla. Old Spanish statues and New Mexican santos of St. Francis and St. Anthony of Padua show them dressed in blue.

60. Cf. n. 28 and 33 *supra.* We have found no other references to Fray Miguel de la Cueva, who seems to have been overseer when Fray Juan de Tagle was custos, *c.* 1710-13 or 1720.

61. Since this is undated, it is difficult to identify. There was more than one episode of this nature.

62. See n. 43, p. 27 *supra.*

63. See n. 48 *supra.*

when it was sent is not stated.[67] § Presentation of Father Custos Fray Juan de Alvarez to Governor don Francisco Cuervo y Valdés asking for vestments and other necessary items for the missions. Year 1706. The original is in the archive of this government.[68] § Appearance of Father Eusebio Francisco Kino, Jesuit priest, before the Audiencia of Guadalajara, asking that newly converted Indians not be forced to go to the mines. The reply was favorable. Year 1686.[69] § Appearance before the Marqués de la Nava y Bracinas, governor of this kingdom, by Father Fray Juan Alvarez, asking him to take statements under oath from the citizens who were driven from New Mexico in the year 1680 by the general uprising whether at that time he succored them all with food, cattle, and livestock, and that for their maintenance the said father used from what he had at his mission ten or eleven thousand head, wheat, etc. They all certified that this consumption actually occurred.[70] § Patent of the Father President *in capite* of these missions, Fray Joaquín de Hinojosa, asking for the fathers' opinions as to whether conversion of the infidels by the religious alone or with the aid of the arms of the King would be better. The fathers replied favoring religious alone. But both the patent and

the fathers' replies are so involved that I cannot unravel or understand them.[71] § Dispatches of Viceroy Fonclara [Pedro Cebrián y Agustín, Conde de Fuenclara, 1742-46] with regard to the erection of four Navajo missions. Year 1746.[72] § Copy of the fiscal's opinion and the decree of the Lord Viceroy de Croix [Carlos Francisco de Croix, Marqués de Croix, 1766-71] that the four villas of this Custody continue to be missions, but without royal alms or allowance.[73] § Copy of the presentation which the Reverend Dozal made concerning the lump sum of the royal allowance for the missionaries of this Custody so that the missionaries of the aforesaid villas may share accordingly.[74] § Copy of an instrument in which the annulment of a marriage at the pueblo and mission of Taos is of record. This was executed by my order on July 18, 1776, and the chief offender was absolved from the censure. § Copy of an instrument and matrimonial proceedings with regard to a marriage suspected of being null and therefore completely investigated by my order. It was revalidated and dispensation *ad cautelam* granted, both because of the difficulty in having recourse [to superior authority] and because of the doubt; and also because the contracting parties love each other and are mostly Indian. On July 18, 1776. The originals of these copies, or recent transcripts, are in the book of Marriages of Taos. § Patent of Custos Fray Francisco Atanasio Domínguez to the mission father of La Cañada, Fray Manuel Rojo, with regard to the exchange of land belonging to the mission for another piece nearer the convent. § Original writ of said exchange on April 21, 1777.[75]

second Viceroy Duque de Alburquerque, which would explain the date 1709.

67. A reference to some of the letters, petitions, to Governor de Vargas for military protection of the missions, and other writings of the Franciscans in 1695-96, when they were aware of the imminence of the 1696 rebellion and seeking to forestall it. AASF, 1695, no. 2, with 1696, no. 1 and letters of missionaries, 1695, no. 3, 1696, no. 2; BNM, leg. 4.

68. HB, 3: 369-72.

69. See H. E. Bolton, *Kino's Historical Memoir of Pimería Alta* (Berkeley and Los Angeles, 1948), pp. 107-09, for a translation of Father Kino's account of his efforts to obtain this cédula, with an abridged version of the cédula. Complete cédula, dated at Buen Retiro, May 14, 1686, is in AGI, Aud. de Guadalajara, leg. 69.

70. At the *junta de guerra* in El Paso on August 25, 1680, Fray Francisco de Ayeta said that he would leave the guardian of that convent, Fray Juan Alvarez, "in charge of the relief of those refugees who might arrive, and he hoped that this ready supply of cattle and grain would give us strength." On October 15, in a letter to the viceroy, Alvarez mentioned the "1,600 head of beef cattle and another portion of provisions," provided by Ayeta until relief should come from New Spain. HS, 1: 34, 203.

71. Probably related to the bitter dispute between the Franciscans and Governor de Vargas over administration of the Indians in 1692. See AASF, 1693, no. 4; AGM, Historia, vol. 37; BNM, leg. 4; AGI, Aud. de Guadalajara, leg. 139; Maas, *Misiones de Nuevo Méjico*.

72. See HB, 3: 416; BL, N.M. Origs., 1745-49.

73. *Testimonio del original remitido a este oficio, para que los Religiosos de San Francisco de la Nueva México se mantengan en las cuatro misiones, que se habían mandado secularizar a petición del Illmo Señor Obispo de Durango. 1768.* BNM, leg. 9, no. 1. This was part of the aftermath of Bishop Tamarón's visitation. AASF, 1768, no. 1 (a).

74. Fray Juan Dozal was procurator general of New Spain in 1769. MN, Asuntos 165.

75. See pp. 318-21 *infra*.

RELATED MATERIALS

Map labels:

Sierra de la Magdalena — Sierra escura — Sn Pasqual — paraje — Mesa de Senecu — Contadero — NORTE — Sierra de Sn Mateo — Frai Christóbal — R. de los Nogales — Mal pais — Jo de Anaia Puerto — Sierra blanca — Principia la Provincia de Sta — canon del Muerto — Sierra de F. — JORNADA DEL MUERTO — Sierra del Caballo — Perrillo — Arroyo de S. Matheo — Siete Rios — avitacion de Apaches — Sierra del Sacramento — las Petacas — Sierra de Guadalupe — LLANOS SIN AGUA — Begas de Sta Barbara — Sn Diego — Presidio proiectado — la Florida: — Cerros de Robledo — Sierra de Robledo — Sierra de los Organos — Mesilla — Rancheria grande — el Brazito — los frijoles — Zeja — Rancheria del Capitan arruinada — Chilecito — Sn Lorenzo — Senecu — Ysleta — Cerro hucco — Cerro del Aire — Socorro — tiburcas — Tuias Caldas — hazda de Sn Ant. despoblada — Passo del Rio del Norte — Sierra del Passo — Rio de el Norte — Zeja — ojo de la Casa — Sierra del Puerto — ojo de Sn inalaiuca — Sierra del Gito — Medanos — Guadalupe despoblado — Puerto de Guadalupe — Sierra de la toma — Pto S. Elceareo — S ojo del Cartizo

Legend text:

Plano del Rio del Norte desde S. Elceareo hasta el paraje de Sn Pasqual, por D. Bernardo de Miera y Pacheco. En donde se demarcan, sus Margenes, Sierras y angosturas, Se mira el paraje de Robledo, proiectado poner Presidio, en donde se hace dificil su planteo, para su establecimiento por la angostura que tiene entre Sierra y Lomas, y no tener saca de Agua cinco Leguas Rio abajo están dos situaciones frente una de otra, para todo comodas y explaiadas, que son la Mesilla de la banda de el Passo, y la Rancheria grande de la otra, distantes de dicho Pueblo del Passo quinze ó dies y seis Leguas. Rio arriba saliendo de las angosturas de dho Robledo, a las seis Leguas empiezan las Begas espaciosas de Santa Barbara con buenas sacas de Agua para labores y muchas combeniencias de pastos, Leña y Maderas de la banda de dicho Pueblo del Passo. Su fundación se precissa sea mui fuerte por estar en el centro de las havitaciones de los enemigos Apaches, y efectuado que fuera se les cortaba la Comunicación, con los de Sierra blanca y Natabajees, y los pusieron en gran consternación y siendo dable poner otra fuerza en la propria banda, frontero del paraje de S. Pasqual se facilitaba poblarse dicho Rio desde el Nuebo Mexico hasta el Passo, y no se tenia que pasar dicho Rio haciendose mas comodo su transito. y el Copitan de dicho Pressidio de Sta Barbara combenia que tubiera el mando en politico y Militar en los Pueblos y Jurisdicion de dho Passo para que tubiera mas fuerza para el castigo de los enemigos, y puebla de los parajes que intermedian.

1 2 3 4 5 — 10 — 20

Escala de beinte Leguas.

MAP

of the Río del Norte from San Elzeario to the Paraje de San Pascual, by Don Bernardo de Miera y Pacheco, on which are traced its borders, sierras, and narrows. The Paraje de Robledo, proposed site for a presidio, is shown, where there are obstacles to establishing it because of the narrow space between sierra and hills and the lack of a water supply.

Five leagues downstream are two locations facing each other, ample and extensive enough for every purpose. These are La Mesilla on the El Paso bank and La Ranchería Grande on the other side, 15 or 16 leagues from said pueblo of El Paso. Six leagues upstream, beyond the narrows of said Robledo, begin the spacious meadows of Santa Bárbara, with good water resources for farming and many convenient places for pasture, firewood, and timber, on the same side as said pueblo of El Paso.

This establishment must necessarily be very strong because of its location in the midst of the habitations of the enemy Apaches. And if it were put into effect, it would cut their communications with the Indians of Sierra Blanca and with the Natajes and throw them into great confusion. And if it were feasible to place another fort on the same side, opposite the stage at the Paraje de San Pascual, then the said river could easily be populated all the way from New Mexico down to El Paso, and it would not be necessary to cross the river, since travel along it would become more convenient.

And the captain of said Presidio de Santa Bárbara should have political and military command over the pueblos and jurisdiction of said El Paso so that he might have greater strength to punish the enemy and to settle the intervening stages.

Scale of twenty leagues.

[*1770's*]

LETTERS AND OBSERVATIONS

Letters

of Fray Francisco Atanasio Domínguez, 1775 to 1795.

I

To Provincial Fray Isidro Murillo
El Paso, November 4, 1775[1]

Most benign and my greatly venerated father and lord:

Monday, September 4, marked my fortunate arrival at this mission of Nuestra Señora de Guadalupe del Paso del Río del Norte. On Wednesday, the sixth of the same month, a letter from your Very Reverend Paternity dated July 28 of this year, 1775, reached me. Its contents sorely grieved me, for I infer the surprise and worry which the almost unintelligible letter of the Father Custos must have inspired in your Reverend Paternity.[2] The sweeping terms in which this father writes and by which he forebodes the ultimate extermination of this Custody arise from a justifiable fear which worries him greatly and keeps him (like all those who live in these regions) in a state of miserable panic because of the repeated assaults the barbarous Apache Indians are making on this whole New Kingdom. In addition to the outrages and hostilities they commit against every kind of traveler on the roads, they enter the pueblos, steal from them all the horses and mules they find, make captives of the little ones who fall into their hands, and leave their parents, if not completely dead, without the better half of their lives, which is their children.

The said enemies were in this pueblo a few days before my arrival, and they carried off the little singer of this mission, leaving his parents in this sad and lamentable misfortune. This is not the only misfortune that the settlers at El Paso have suffered. Many more have arisen from the thefts, the murders, and the fierce inhumanity of these same enemies.

Since my sole purpose in this letter is to reply to that of your Very Reverend Paternity and to explain what the Father Custos meant by his, I shall not stop to relate in detail the strong expressions which the Father Vice-Custos Fray Mariano Rodríguez uses to convey to the Father Custos the extent of the persecution of New Mexico by the Apaches, Comanches, and so many other enemy nations. In the letter [the Custos] received from him during the month of September, he tells him how the Comanches attacked the missions of Sandia, Belén, and others and left them completely devastated; that in one of these encounters he was in danger of being killed by the enemy; that he considers the Father Visitor [Domínguez] foolhardy to want to enter at a time when those regions are so besieged; and that the enemies have assembled in such squadrons against that whole kingdom that it will doubtless suffer hopeless defeat. Your Very Reverend Paternity may now see what inspired the Father Custos to say: "This Custody is on the point of suffering its last agony."

Nevertheless, it may now have some relief and attain peace by means of the general campaign against the Apaches, which started September 21 and still continues. It is true, however, that the three hundred men who left this pueblo with forty soldiers from the Presidio of San Elzeario killed (they say) only forty Apaches, seized three hundred horses, and brought in thirty-one captives. The captives consisted of thirty-one Indian women with their small children, including two Indian women and a little boy whom the enemies had captured in the vicinity of Chihuahua. The three hundred men from this pueblo and the forty soldiers from the Presidio of San Elzeario arrived here on Friday, October 27, but Colonel don Hugo O'Conor and the officer from Sonora are still pursuing the enemy in the field. The

two forces together must consist of over a thousand men. May it be God's will that they intimidate and check the enemies.

For our part, we have done everything possible. On September 21 before the troop left, there was a solemn high Mass attended by all from the chief officer to the last soldier. I gave them a brief sermon on the theme of what constituted a just war and the means that assure victory. Almost all the professional soldiers and their captains confessed and received communion before they set forth. Afterwards we made a novena to Most Holy Mary of Guadalupe with sung Masses, all for the intention of the successful outcome of the campaign. We did even more. Father Fray Cayetano Bernal went as chaplain of the said troop, and Father Rosete took charge of his mission. Two things have been accomplished as a result. The most important and pleasing to us was that Father Bernal baptized in the field a little Indian boy newly born to an Apache woman. Although the child reached here alive, his condition is such that his death is expected hourly. The other was that Colonel don Hugo O'Conor showed in a thousand ways his gratitude to Father Bernal for accompanying the troop, and his lordship decided to come to this pueblo to thank me as soon as he concludes his task. As many beans and tortillas as we can spare are taken daily from the mission to feed the Indian women and children.

Although a solemn high Mass was sung on Sunday, October 29, as a thanksgiving for the advance made by the citizens of this pueblo and the soldiers of the Presidio of San Elzeario, there was no sermon, because I am deferring this to the end of the campaign and a greater blow against the enemies.

I assume that the New Mexico fathers have probably done the same with regard to the campaign the governor of that kingdom is making against the Comanches and other opponents. I believe so because I know that a missionary friar has gone as

1. BNM, leg. 10, no. 22.
2. The custos was Fray Juan de Hinojosa.

chaplain on other occasions and that they all do everything they can for the greater service of God and the king.[3]

Because of these campaigns, there have been difficulties about my entering New Mexico up to now, but I hope in God that when the garrison in this pueblo is reinforced and the little cordon which is now on the way to Chihuahua for the alms of the Virgin returns,[4] that I may be able to induce the lieutenant governor to raise a cordon of fifty or more men to accompany me to New Mexico. The citizens are very anxious for this because they lack meat to eat at present, as well as other necessaries of life, and it is to be obtained only in that kingdom. I long for it with impatience so that I may soon carry out the superior orders of your Very Reverend Paternity and take last year's royal allowance to my brother missionaries, for so far they have not received even one tablet for lack of anyone to bring it. Usually, by the time the provision reaches them, they owe far more than the amount of the whole royal allowance combined. I am a witness to the fact that in the month of September Father Fray Rafael Benavides wrote to the mission father at this mission of El Paso to send him a barrel of wine for Mass, and he has not yet been able to send it to him. What will this friar have done to obtain it? And if he has had the luck to find it (which is somewhat difficult), what will they make him pay for it? According to what I am told and to what I see in this pueblo as far as the merchants are concerned, I do not hesitate to tell your Very Reverend Paternity that his whole royal allowance will not pay for it.

3. For a summary of the campaigns against the Indians at this period, see the introduction to A. B. Thomas, *Forgotten frontiers* (Norman, 1932). See also E. González Flores and F. R. Almada, eds., *Informe de Hugo de O'Conor sobre el estado de las Provincias Internas del Norte, 1771-76* (Mexico, 1952).

4. Possibly a reference to alms and dues sent to the Conquistadora Confraternity by the families of former New Mexicans who did not return with the Reconquest and settled in the Chihuahua area.

Now when I speak to our Very Reverend Paternity about the situation in the interior missions, that in this pueblo, and about the trade between them, I will make you see the iniquitous manner of carrying on trade, buying and selling, by all the traders and merchants of this New Kingdom. I defer the subject until then, for it involves so many entanglements and so much confusion that some time will be necessary to explain it properly.

Therefore I conclude by saying that although New Mexico is as the Father Vice-Custos describes it in his aforesaid letter, which was received in September, and although these regions are in the state I have described in this one, I am taking the risk of entering to make my juridical visitation because I trust in God that the enemy will be subdued and routed by our people during the said campaigns. Moreover, I will endeavor to safeguard my person with the armed escort I shall ask the chief commanding officers to give me. I do not doubt that they will grant it in view of the letters which the Most Excellent Lord Viceroy deigned to give our Very Reverend Paternity in my favor, and also because it will be of great benefit to the population. In this way I shall manage to undertake my task and succor the need of my indigent missionary brethren.

Today, Friday, November 3, two citizens of this place arrived from the Presidio of Carrizal (30 leagues from this pueblo). They are Vicente Ruiz and Ramón Orcasitas. Both went to Carrizal to take up the milpas they had there. The two of them say that while they were at the presidio, Captain San Vicente arrived there with the news that the Apaches had killed sixty men in the vicinity of Chihuahua, that they stole all the herd of horses at the Presidio of Janos, and that at the Presidio of Carrizal itself they killed three men, including Alférez don Manuel Delgado's caretaker. And when they were on their way back to this pueblo, fourteen Apaches on horseback confronted them and there were more at a distance, although they could not make out the number, who cut them off; and perhaps because the Indians delayed to change horses, they had an opportunity to gain ground on them and make their escape.

This, then, our father, is the way our people attack or pursue them. What will it be like when the campaign is over? But if when they seek them in one place, they are already in another, how are they going to grapple with them?

Finally, I beg your Very Reverend Paternity with all possible humility to remember us constantly in your prayers and to beseech the Lord to fill us with His holy love and His great zeal for the good of the souls in our charge, and to inspire the commanders to the greatest success in the subjugation of these infidels. May He grant your Very Reverend Paternity many years of life for me, as I pray, for all my veneration and help. Mission of Nuestra Señora de Guadalupe del Paso del Río del Norte and November 4, 1775.

Our Very Reverend Father Minister Provincial,

Your most reverent subject and son who loves and esteems you kisses your hands.

Fray Francisco Atanasio Domínguez
(rubric)

II

To Provincial Fray Isidro Murillo
El Paso, November 8, 1775[5]

Most benign and my greatly venerated father and lord:

Once again I trouble the religious ear of your Very Reverend Paternity in order to deal separately with affairs that are most particularly for your consideration alone and because your orders for the better government of this your Custody depend upon your knowledge of these things. For this reason and because I am endeavoring to make matters clear, you will countenance the duplication of my letters and forgive the errors I commit in everything.

I therefore inform your Very Reverend Paternity that the Father Custos has appeared before me in due legal form with a lengthy and full accounting of the distribution and final settlement of Father Polanco's spolia. Finding his accounting in agreement with and confirmed by the legal instruments I enclose, which I examined more than three times, and also public knowledge, as he states, I pronounced it satisfactory, accurate, and legal, but ordered that it be remitted to your Very Reverend Paternity so that you might see it and make what decision you please. Indeed, I must point out that Father Polanco himself left a signed memorandum of his spolia in his own hand for the Father Custos, and that this does not agree with the one he gave your Very Reverend Paternity. Most of what it lists was not his property and has been returned to its legitimate owners, as is of record in their receipts.

With regard to the complaint against the mission fathers of this Custody which the Most Illustrious Lord Bishop of Durango presented to your Very Reverend Paternity, I state that I have seen and read a letter written by his Most Illustrious Lordship to the Father Custos, dated July 7 of this year, 1775.[6] In it he gives him a thousand thanks for his zeal and care for the benefit of the souls in his charge and grants him full authority to revalidate *in facie ecclesiae* a marriage contracted *nulliter*. The case was that one of our friars in the New Mexico missions, being under a misapprehension, inadvertently married *in facie ecclesiae* persons related in the third and fourth degree. Within a short time he discovered his error and informed his prelate immediately so that the situation might be remedied without delay. Thereupon the Father Custos sent a report of the whole affair to the Lord

---

5. BNM, leg. 10, no. 23.
6. Bishop Antonio Macarulla, 1774-81.

Bishop and humbly and religiously begged his dispensation. In view of the just reasons for this request, his Most Illustrious Lordship granted it, and in addition to giving him authority to revalidate the aforesaid marriage, he fervently expresses his gratitude in the letter I have cited and even takes for granted in it that the Father Custos keeps him informed of all the occurrences pertaining to his jurisdiction and episcopal office. In view of this and because I am aware that during the very month that he complained to your Very Reverend Paternity he wrote to thank the Father Custos for keeping him fully informed and showing him due respect, I have reasoned with myself that his Most Illustrious Lordship's excessive zeal and delicate conscience do not permit him to suffer any error whatsoever of any kind. We must all follow this course, and may God strongly imprint such zeal and delicacy on our hearts. But when the error does not arise from malice or even from culpable ignorance, it seems to be excusable. In any case I know that his Illustrious Lordship has been given all the information that seemed necessary and that the same will be done in future, thus showing the veneration we have for him and the obedience we always render to the superior orders of our Very Reverend Paternity.

With regard to your suggestion that I suspend any friar whom I find without faculties, I inform you that Fathers Llanos and Zarte entered this Custody without those permitting them to hear confessions and preach because of the deviation from the route when they came to the missions. In view of this and of the plausibility of the case, the Father Custos had recourse (as was his duty) to Don Fray José Vicente Díaz Bravo, may he rest in peace, who was then Bishop of Durango.[7] In reply to the Father Custos' letter, this lord granted him authority to give them the faculties and habilitate them completely for service in the missions. Accordingly the aforesaid fathers have been and are still hearing confessions,

preaching the Gospel, and administering the Holy Sacraments to the faithful. The reason why these fathers did not present themselves in Durango and get the faculties there was truthfully given to the Lord [Bishop] Bravo as the Father Custos understood the matter. The bishop's attention was directed to the real need for ministers and his Most Illustrious Lordship willingly desired and ordered the Father Custos to give them faculties and to habilitate them, and he himself designated them subjects *quod per alios facimus per nos facere videtur*. Moreover, the present bishop (for the same reasons that any bishop can do so in his territory) has not revoked, or even demanded the presentation of, any faculty to hear confessions, etc., issued by his predecessor in person or by another with his authority, because the need for ministers that existed then still exists, to say nothing of the difficulty of the very lengthy and extremely dangerous journey and the fact that the fathers cannot leave the missions at which they are stationed even once a year because there is no armed escort available and no one can venture forth without one. I therefore ask your Very Reverend Paternity whether the order you gave me applies to the aforesaid fathers.

Also, what should be done with the vestments and the articles of silver, copper, and iron listed in the memoranda I enclose in the letter I am writing to the Reverend Father Procurator Fray Nicolás Téllez Xirón (so as not to make this one any bulkier).[8] Some of these things are in the pos-

7. Bishop Tamarón's successor, 1769-72. H. H. Bancroft [*History of the North Mexican States and Texas* (San Francisco, 1886) p. 684] questioned whether he ever took office after being consecrated in Puebla in 1770, but the statement here indicates that he did.

8. The R. P. Fr. Nicolás Téllez Girón appears on a list of friars of the Province of the Holy Gospel dated October 6, 1772, with the following description: Creole, *predicador general*, apostolic notary and notary of the Holy Office, ex-definitor of this province and secretary general, and father of the

session of the Father Vice-Custos Fray Mariano Rodríguez and others in that of Don Clemente Gutiérrez, a citizen of New Mexico. The memoranda which I cite and am remitting to the Reverend Father Téllez clearly state which are in the hands of the former and which in the possession of the latter. This whole wagon train was brought at the King's expense and paid for by his royal treasury. Father Menchero brought it with the intention of establishing four missions in Navajo and settling the Indians of that tribe in them. But at the very outset of this undertaking, when the Navajo, or Navajores, Indians had been subdued and had come to an agreement with the same Father Menchero, their inconstancy and fickleness compelled them to get on their high horse, retire to their old hiding places, and abandon all that had been started. Nevertheless, Father Menchero always kept with him the vestments and the articles of silver, copper, and iron he had brought for the establishment of the aforesaid four missions in Navajo. Some of these vestments were taken to supply two missions that were founded later. These are Sandia and Abiquiu. After Father Menchero's death, the care of the remaining vestments and the existing copper and iron fell to the Reverend Father Fray Jacobo de Castro, as Custos, and he transferred the responsibility to his Vice-Custos, Fray Juan José de Hinojosa. As soon as this reverend father was made Custos, he handed them on to Father Fray Mariano Rodríguez, present Vice-Custos. In this way the care of these things has been passed along, but Father Menchero always expected the viceroys to demand recovery of or reimbursement for the foregoing. The Reverend Father Fray Jacobo de Castro gave

the same impression to the present Father Custos, who assures me that this is so. Since the said effects were bought with the King's money, and because the four missions for adornment of which they were given were not erected, it is reasonable to fear recovery and reimbursement. Furthermore, when Don Tomás Vélez Cachupín was governor of New Mexico, he wanted to collect them and take them out of our keeping. This is the complete account which the Reverend Father Custos has given me about this matter.

And I, without undertaking to inquire whether the scruples felt up to now about allotting the said effects to the needy missions are justified or not, shall present for your Very Reverend Paternity's consideration the following reflections: Whether Governor Vélez Cachupín only threatened to seize the said effects or whether he actually did so? If the first, then did he know that he could not take them from the fathers? For it is not difficult to believe that such an intrepid man, a man with but little liking for us, would have done so if he could have found a reason to justify and uphold his decision.[9] If the second, then was some very powerful reason given for not handing them over to him? In fact, in spite of all Vélez Cachupín intended, they were then and are now in our possession and keeping. Cannot this same reason be given to any other governor who might want to collect them? Moreover, in spite of all the fear of recovery and reimbursement, they nevertheless dared to give what was necessary out of these same vestments to the missions of Sandia and Abiquiu, and as a matter of fact these missions were not any of the four to be established in Navajo. But let us go on. I strongly suspect that the reason for not having allotted the said effects to the poor missions is because it is feared that the twelve thousand pesos they apparently gave from the royal treasury to Father Menchero were

Province of Zacatecas; fifty-eight years old, forty-two in the [Franciscan] habit. Procurator of New Mexico. MN, Asuntos 165. Inventory of church furnishings for the Navajo missions, which had been kept at Sandia since the days of Father Menchero, and record of their transfer to Governor Anza, April 15, 1782, in AASF, 1782, nos. 2, 3.

9. Cf. AT, p. 24.

not spent for them. Supposing they were not all spent, can reimbursement be made while the said effects are kept? Will we be able to conceal any fraud (if I can believe that there is any) by remaining oblivious of such things? There is even more to fear. Can there be reimbursement of the royal treasury for the sum of pesos which were given for the adornment of the four missions which were to be founded in Navajo and were not founded? Indeed there can be, but will it not be very well known in the royal treasury that the amount of pesos was for the purpose of making vestments, etc.? Then, proving to them that the effects for which the amount of pesos was designated still exist also serves as a complete accounting for the money they gave. But here lies the difficulty (says fear). Whether the effects that exist, including those given to the missions of Sandia and Abiquiu, are worth all the money that was given from the royal treasury for them. This doubt will be easy to resolve by finding out the full amount of pesos given and appraising (by a qualified person here or in Mexico City, for it is easy to determine the value in the usual manner for silver, iron, etc.). This doubt, I say, can easily be resolved by learning fully what amount of pesos was given and by valuing the existing effects. Note that they should not be valued at their present worth, but at what they cost when they were made, since it is normal for them to have diminished and deteriorated (as they have), and they may be worth much less now than what they cost when they were made. The expense of bringing them from the old Mexico to the New must necessarily be included in this accounting. Then, after a prudent and careful accounting of everything has been made, it will show whether there is any balance against the Custody in favor of the royal treasury. If so, our Holy Province will be informed, but not without first finding out how long it has been since the King our lord has given a single vestment or chalice or anything at all for use in Divine Worship

in the churches of these missions. And, knowing absolutely and certifying to all that the missionary brethren have done at the cost of their sweat, royal allowance, and labor, our Province will know what decision to make in the case. Because to expect the mission friar to furnish his church out of the 300 pesos the King gives him annually is contrary to his royal intention and to the condition imposed by the Lord Alexander VI on the Catholic Kings: "that they should be able to seek these unknown kingdoms and very distant lands under the obligation of giving from their royal exchequers all the necessary furnishings for their churches, etc."[10]

All the foregoing, our father, is for the sole purpose of learning what should be done with these effects. My only motive for discussing the matter at such length and wearying your attention is lest they should be completely destroyed. There is no presumption whatsoever in me, nor even less has it crossed my mind that I might be able to give more information than the Father Custos. I know what the Reverend Father Castro was, and I realize the great enlightenment conferred upon the Reverend Father Hinojosa. And I surely realize and blush to consider that your Very Reverend Paternity's wise mode of thinking may render all my reflections useless and vain, but let your benignity deign to receive them as the result of my activity and the fulfillment of my duty.

I had more to say and to tell your very Reverend Paternity, but I will do it through the Reverend Father Procurator to avoid greater expense in the mail with many bulky letters.

I wish your Very Reverend Paternity the best of health, and I beg Our Lord to preserve for me in all prosperity your very important life for the many and completely happy years I desire for my veneration and

10. Apparently a reference to the Bull *Eximiae,* December 16, 1501, granting the tithes of the New World to the Catholic Kings under this condition.

help. Mission of Nuestra Señora de Guadalupe del Paso del Río del Norte, November 8, 1775.

Our Very Reverend Father Minister Provincial,

Your most reverent subject and son who loves and respects you kisses your hand.

Fray Francisco Atanasio Dominguez
(rubric)

III

To Provincial Fray Isidro Murillo
Santa Fe, June 10, 1776[11]

Most benign and venerated father and my lord:

Let your Very Reverend Paternity not be surprised by the handwriting. A violent headache prevents me from writing in my own, but since the hand belongs to the father who has served as my secretary during this visitation, I have not refused to tell your Very Reverend Paternity in his hand part of what he witnessed.

I left El Paso on March 1 with fathers Rosete and Palacio, and we entered this villa of Santa Fe on March 22, going directly to the house of the lord governor, by whom we were well received and up to now treated with special attention and courtesy. From then until April 10 we all continued to receive the favor of his table and conversation. In the private conversations we two had during those days he asked me for a friar for the Pecos mission, giving me good reasons, among them the long time those souls have gone without spiritual nourishment. I agreed and immediately assigned Father Rosete to the said mission. He was already on the point of departure when a letter came from Father Vélez Escalante in which he asked me for him as his companion at the Zuñi mission. I showed this letter to the governor, and in view of it he told me that it was very just to accede to Fray Silvestre's re-

quest and also that the other friar who had come with me should accompany me as secretary during my visitation. Therefore the mission of Pecos remained as before and Father Rosete left on April 25 for Zuñi, where he now is.

I started my visitation on April 10, beginning with the northern missions of the interior as far as the last one, which is San Jerónimo de los Taos to the north. I spent twenty-six days on the visitation of these missions, including the day I reached this villa, which was May 5. Because of matters which came up here, I could not leave for my visitation of the other missions until May 13, beginning with the one mentioned in the aforesaid series which I enclose. In each and every one of these missions I observed your Very Reverend Paternity's instructions punctiliously and made clear notes, of which I am now making a fair copy to remit to your Very Reverend Paternity under safe-conduct by the hand of the most trustworthy bearer I may find, because the mail is useless since my narration of everything amounts to a folio volume. Your Very Reverend Paternity, who gave me my instructions and ordered me to observe them to the letter, will easily realize how great my work has been and how large a volume all of it will fill. I say this lest my remitting now only my itinerary with the list of religious, their ages, etc. be considered an omission or carelessness, for neither the length of the journey nor the great toil nor the impetuous manner in which the Spanish population is now leaving for El Paso because of minor risk permit more.

I should like to remit to your Very Reverend Paternity on this occasion a detailed account of the content of the archive of these interior missions. It amounts to nothing more than matrimonial proceedings, patents of prelates, and other such papers pertaining to this Custody. And I shall extract the corresponding information from it as your Very Reverend Paternity orders me in

11. BNM, leg. 10, no. 34.

your letter of November 7, 1775, which I received on May 23, 1776, but I am not sending it because it covers three complete folded sheets of paper. I am sorry, because it would make your Very Reverend Paternity aware of the great carelessness there has been in regard to the parish books, for everything comes down to loose leaves, half-books—and, in a word, if one should ask for an affidavit of a baptism, for example, for the year 1760 or earlier, it could not be issued with due certification. My regret because this memorandum does not go is not because your Very Reverend Paternity may not learn how ill you have been served, but just because you might give a rule for us to follow in case a lord bishop asks for the parish books in the archive during his visitation. If he sees them as they are now, what must we reply? Or what must we do to avoid the shame that can result from such an incident? I am apprehensive about this because the people of this kingdom are malicious and not well-intentioned, and they have seen the fathers' windows covered with—or with blinds made of—baptismal records. In so far as I was able, I labored to put the archive into some kind of order, and I will work harder to see how I can partially remedy so great an evil. The same was done with the library. It will make your Very Reverend Paternity laugh to see the books it contains and the state it is in. I now go on to relate the rest.

In each mission the corresponding amount of provisions was designated in accordance with what it produces, and with express orders that this be punctiliously observed because your Very Reverend Paternity so commands. The inventories of valuables, vestments, convent furnishings, and utensils left at each mission were corrected to agree with those which I am to remit to your Very Reverend Paternity. They are in accordance with what I saw, examined, and what actually exists. An investigation of what each of the three villas in the interior actually produces has been

made, and the report of this is also lengthy. No provision has been assigned to La Cañada, which is a villa, for the father stationed there feigns a thousand expenses, so I left it until the truth should be known. Father Fray Andrés García sold the farmland [this mission] held in the King's name to a layman in order to use the price to roof the church. He asked permission to do this from Father Custos Fray Andrés Varo, who granted it, and the original of the license and of the bill of sale are in the possession of the layman who is now owner of the land. I made a literal copy of everything and have it in my possession to remit to your Very Reverend Paternity, for I used a ruse to ask the said layman for the papers and made a copy of them. It was my opinion that Father Fray Andrés could not sell such land, and therefore I had thought of summoning the aforesaid layman and making him sell it to me under the pretext that I needed it for the mission, even though it might mean buying it at an increase in price, but I have not decided to do so since I do not know whether your Very Reverend Paternity would approve or not. Therefore I await your advice and will act in accordance with it.

I took from the archive of the secular priest who is ecclesiastical judge of this kingdom an instrument drawn up by a religious to found a Confraternity of Poor Souls with the alms which one of the settlers owed him. By this he obligated the religious who might be missionary there in future to thirteen Masses annually. This without license from his prelate and with the despotism of a layman and absolute owner of property. The layman who owes the alms, which consist of some ewes the friar had farmed out to him at interest, obligated himself to give the alms for the thirteen Masses annually in such good produce as the religious might want from a mill and other properties he has. In a word, the instrument is the same as if it had been made between two laymen. It will remain in my possession until I find out from your Very

Reverend Paternity what I must do to prevent the religious from complaining about me. For now, this is what occurs to me that is worth passing on to your Very Reverend Paternity.

For the rest, I must tell you that I kept a separate book for the juridical visitation. In it I have recorded the state in which I found the mission and the religious and the reply he made to the juridical questions usually asked in such cases. And for now I inform your Very Reverend Paternity that Father Fray Manuel Abadiano is so extremely ill that it is not possible for him to fulfill his duties as a missionary minister. For this reason I found everything pertaining to Divine Worship in the sole care of the Indians without the father's knowing what there was or what was missing. His sight is almost gone in one eye, and although he has asked me for the mission of Santo Domingo, I cannot grant his petition, for if he were there, the archive would be completely lost. Father Hermida is no less ill than the aforesaid father, but the old woman who is taking care of him (there are no other physicians here) has told me that he will get well in a milder climate. Since El Paso has this, I will send him down to the mission of San Lorenzo del Realito (if your Very Reverend Paternity agrees).

I also notify your Very Reverend Paternity that Father Rodríguez is going to the mission of Isleta [New Mexico] in place of Father Junco, but he is also ill and so feeble that he will not be able to cope with such an extensive jurisdiction. Therefore I think that Father Fray Joaquín Ruiz should occupy it permanently. In the administration of his mission at Jémez he maintains such good order that I have ordered in the writ of visitation that the same system be followed by any religious who may enter there, and I even favor establishing it in all the missions, for truly I have not seen any other so suited to the Christian instruction of the Indians or the civilization and culture which the Sovereign wishes for them. I have

in my possession a copy of this system of administration to remit to your Very Reverend Paternity on another occasion. I think that the aforesaid father will know how to remedy and rectify Father Junco's errors. Finally, our father, I am speaking to your Very Reverend Paternity as an eye witness.

It must be pointed out, however, that everyone has pretensions to this mission of Isleta, and it is said that this father pestered me in Chihuahua with requests for it. This is false. And the Father Guardian Fray Angel López only asked me for Isleta at El Paso for Father Ruiz. This is a very different mission from the one I am speaking of. If he is stationed there [Isleta, New Mexico] (for in my conscience I consider it just) something can be hoped for. Therefore I now acquaint your Very Reverend Paternity with the justice I wish to do.

For similar just reasons I transferred Father Fray Ramón Salas from the mission of San Juan de los Caballeros to San Antonio de la Isleta at El Paso. He will start his journey there on the fifteenth of June with the settlers who are leaving here.

The missions of Pecos, Galisteo, and Tesuque are without fathers. The lord governor deplores this, but he is satisfied with the reasons I have given him to persuade him that not everything can be as we should like. Nevertheless, on one occasion when we were speaking of sending friars farther into the interior to discover lands and win souls, he said to me: "If there are not enough fathers for those already conquered, how can there be any for those that may be newly conquered?" An expression of opinion which can chill a spirit ardently burning to win souls, so I made up my mind on the spot to pass it on to your Very Reverend Paternity for your guidance.

I have already said at the beginning that I received your Very Reverend Paternity's esteemed letter of November 7, 1775, on Thursday, May 23 of this year of 1776. Father Rosete was then already in Zuñi at Father Escalante's request. Therefore I did not assign Father Palacio to that mission, but if your Very Reverend Paternity wishes this father and not the other to be at Zuñi, you will so advise me in order that your command may be exactly carried out.

I already had a copy of the paper which your Very Reverend Paternity enclosed in the aforesaid letter. I made it from one your Very Reverend Paternity sent to Father Escalante. From that time I began to gather information and to see with my own eyes what I could, and I have already written this down. But it is necessary that the information acquired from the reports of others go too, as your Very Reverend Paternity has commanded me, in legally attested form. This will mean considerable work, for the people here are very light in their speech and there is no rhyme or reason to what they say. This means that any information I may furnish your Very Reverend Paternity must first be tested by the fire of close investigation (if possible), reason, and actual proof.

Even before Father Morfi wrote to the lord governor so that he would give Father Vélez Escalante access to his archive, I had already undertaken the necessary preliminaries to seeing and examining it. And although the lord governor has replied to him (and also to me) that it contains nothing but old fragments and that he will find all he needs for his purpose in the captaincy general, nevertheless it will be examined and your Very Reverend Paternity will be notified of what is found.[12]

His Excellency the Viceroy has written to the lord governor asking for information concerning what Father Escalante wrote. The latter (says the Viceroy) promised to discover the route to Monterey with twenty men. I am expecting him hourly and also hoping to see what comes of this.

Your Very Reverend Paternity must excuse the diffuseness of this letter, but your sagacity will realize how necessary it has been and will forgive its having been written in two hands, for when I got well, my secretary, Father Palacio, fell ill.

May Our Lord bless, prosper, and keep your Very Reverend Paternity for me many years more as I beg Him, for all my veneration. In this mission of Our Father St. Francis of the Villa of Santa Fe, June 10, 1776.

Our Very Reverend Father Minister Provincial,

Your most reverent subject and son who respects and loves you kisses your hands.

Fray Francisco Atanasio Dominguez
(rubric)

[P. S.] I am serving at this mission until Father Benavides arrives from El Paso.

During my visitation I have not given any expense to the friars except for my food, and this poor, as I commanded. I took with me chocolate for the secretary, a servant, and myself, and the mission father also shared it. I did not even accept paper from them to record the location, etc. Everything is of record in certifications each of the religious gave me and which I am keeping.[13] I have traveled on mounts provided for my use. The subsyndic gave Father Junco 100 pesos on my account. I gave Father Salas three pack and one saddle mule for his journey: the three pack mules out of what I received for Masses, and the saddle mule is one used by the Father Custos, who loaned it to me.

I am writing your Very Reverend Paternity two letters from this Villa of Santa Fe and both during this month of June. The one that mentions Father Junco is dated the fifth, and this one about my visitation dated the tenth.

---

12. The notes Father Vélez de Escalante made for Father Morfi were published in part in DHM, anonymously; there are manuscript versions in AGM, Historia, vol. 2, and BNM, leg. 3, doc. 2. A translation of Morfi's *Geographical description of New Mexico* is in Thomas, *Forgotten frontiers*, pp. 87-114.

13. See pp. 324-25 *infra*.

IV

To Provincial Fray Isidro Murillo
Santa Fe, July 29, 1776[14]

Our Father:

On April 15 of this year, 1776, when Father Fray Mariano Rosete, second minister of that mission, was going to Zuñi, I wrote a letter in the form of an order to

14. BNM, leg. 10, no. 26. This letter and enclosures, the Vélez de Escalante letter of the same date (p. 307 *infra*) and other related papers have been published in O. Maas, *Viajes de misioneros franciscanos a la conquista del Nuevo México* (Sevilla, 1915), from copies in AGI.

Father Fray Silvestre de Escalante telling him to come to me as soon as he received it to discuss some matters pertaining to the commissions entrusted to me by your Very Reverend Paternity in your instructions, and before that, to the religious of this Custody in your letters patent.

Father Fray Silvestre arrived at this mission of the Villa of Santa Fe on the night of June 7, and I immediately asked him whether he had any news of a letter which the Reverend Father Garcés had written from the junction of the Gila and Colorado Rivers to the missionaries of this Custody. He replied that he had no news of it, but that even without this new commission, just

PORTION OF A LETTER OF JUNE 10, 1776, IN WHICH THE HANDWRITING
CHANGES FROM THAT OF FRAY JOSE PALACIO, WHO FELL ILL,
TO THAT OF FRAY FRANCISCO ATANASIO DOMINGUEZ

his own strong wishes and the fulfillment of the superior order of your Very Reverend Paternity in your letters patent had led him to decide to make a journey to Monterey and to undertake it during this present summer if I considered it fitting.

In my judgment it was so necessary and proper that from that very night we made a pact for the two of us to undertake the journey and to seek out persons who might be useful to us in the enterprise. But we first communicated our intention and decision to the lord governor, who, as one so eager for all that might be to the greater service of both Majesties [divine and human], not only applauded our plan but also opened his heart and his hands, giving us supplies and everything we might need for the journey.

The date was set for the fourth of this month of July, for we had already seen the interpreters and the few men we needed. But on June 20 the troop of this Royal Presidio went out in pursuit of the Comanche enemies who [had] killed ten at the post of La Ciénega, and I sent Father Fray Silvestre with them to exhort and confess the soldiers. This scouting expedition lasted ten days in a row, and although Father Fray Silvestre returned tired and worn out, after three days he again set out for Taos on urgent business which I could not attend to without neglecting to finish other business that summoned me to San Agustín de Isleta.

From there I had to hasten to Taos, because so acute a pain in his side seized Father Fray Silvestre there that it put him in great distress. When I reached Taos, the father was already out of danger, but without strength enough to travel. Therefore I ordered him not to leave for the Villa of Santa Fe until a week had passed.

Our journey was put off because of these necessary and unavoidable delays. And in the interval the Reverend Father Fray Francisco Garcés came from the mouth of the Colorado River to the pueblo of Oraybi in Moqui. He wrote from there to the father minister of Zuñi and sent him the letter by an Indian of the pueblo of Acoma, called Lázaro, who had been a fugitive in that province [of Moqui] since winter.

Father Fray Mariano Rosete, second minister of Zuñi, received the Reverend Father Garcés' letter from the Indian Lázaro at the said mission. And after he had put various questions to the Indian about the aforesaid Father Garcés, he recorded them all for me with the replies in the letter he writes me enclosing the original letter of Father [Garcés].

I enclose with this for your Very Reverend Paternity a literal copy of the latter and of Father Rosete's letter, so that you may be completely acquainted with the matter.

Father Fray Silvestre and I conferred about this new development, and since the Reverend Father Garcés states in his letter that he came to Moqui from the mouth of the Colorado River, we believed that our journey would still be useful. For even if we should not attain our end, which is to discover a route to Monterey from this kingdom, the knowledge we could acquire of the lands through which we traveled would represent a great step forward and be of great use in the future. Moreover, we intend to return via Cojnina in order to confirm that nation's good decision to become Christian and to divorce it completely (if God favors us) from the Moquis, who are so strongly opposed to their conversion and that of the others.

At the foot of the last copy, which is the one of Father Rosete's letter, is the plan of our trip and the persons who accompany us, to whom we are giving mounts, which, together with the mules to carry the supplies, I have acquired by my efforts along with all the other things which I will explain to your Very Reverend Paternity upon my return from the journey.

Now I only advise you that this very day, Monday, July 29, we are leaving this Villa of Santa Fe on our journey, and we leave happy and full of hope, trusting only in your fervent prayers and in the fact that you as our father will have our brethren in that Holy Province of mine remember us in their sacrifices and prayers, for we do not forget them or your Very Reverend Paternity in ours. We beg God Our Lord [to grant] you the greatest enlightenment and best success in order that, being an Elias as you have been up to now, we, your subjects, may all be Eliseus, clothed in the spirit of Elias, our father, your Very Reverend Paternity.[15] And may God keep your very important life for us many years more for all my reverence. Mission of our Father St. Francis of the Villa of Santa Fe and July 29, 1776.

Our Very Reverend Father Minister Provincial,

Your most useless subject and most favored son, who esteems you, etc., kisses your Very Reverend Paternity's hands.

Fray Francisco Atanasio Domínguez
(rubric)

ENCLOSURES

Letter of Fray Francisco Garcés
Moqui, July 3, 1776[16]

In Jesus' name.
Very Reverend Father and most dear brother:

After traveling along the Colorado River from its mouth to latitude 35° and among the nations who inhabit the country along the river as far as Sonora, and as far as the new establishments of Monterey, I have come to this pueblo of Moqui. Here they have shown me no courtesy, nor have they even been willing to come near me although the other tribes have outdone one another in their attentiveness to me, and five tribes along the Colorado River are well disposed to receive fathers, as well as those of the Pima nation on the Gila River, etc. I would gladly have gone that way [i.e., to New Mexico], but since these Moquis are displeased, it would be necessary to return with troops and Christian Indians and to bring gifts. Therefore I should have had to wait for a reply from the lord governor.

I will rejoice to hear that your Paternity enjoys perfect health. We shall have a means to communicate with one another by the establishment of a presidio on the Colorado, and also to send cattle from that province [New Mexico]. And it may be possible to make trade with Sonora safe, because the Apaches who can prevent it are friends of the Yumas and Jomajabas, who, I believe, may soon have fathers, and they say that they do not reach the Spaniards nor do the latter reach them.

There is no occasion [to say] more. I beg your Paternity to advise the lord governor with this letter or its content. I truly commend myself to him, knowing that he governs that province to the satisfaction of all; and the same to the Very Reverend Father Custos. Moqui and July 3, 1776. Your least brother kisses your Paternity's hands. Fray Francisco Garcés.

To the Reverend Father Minister of Zuñi.

Letter of Fray Mariano Rosete
to Fray Francisco Atanasio Domínguez
Zuñi, July 6, 1776

Our Most Reverend Father Commissary Visitor:

After greeting your Reverend Paternity, I go on to give you the news and a complete account of the present episode, so greatly desired by your Paternity. An Acoma Indian, called Lázaro, has arrived in this pueblo of Zuñi. He came traveling post

---

15. IV Kings 2. The Hebrew and King James (II Kings 2) forms of these names are Elijah and Elisha.

16. See E. Coues, *On the trail of a Spanish pioneer, the diary and itinerary of Francisco Garcés* (New York, 1900). See pp. 380-81n for a copy of Father Garcés' letter transcribed from a different copy certified by Domínguez in AGM, *Historia*, vol. 25.

from the province of Moqui with the enclosed letter from the Reverend Father Garcés, alumnus of the College [of Propaganda Fide] of Our Lady of Guadalupe of Zacatecas.[17] I am sending it on by the same hand that brought it to me. And since the letter is as laconic as it is unintelligible, I took the following statement from the bearer:

In the first place, I told him to tell me in God's name the whole truth in answer to all my questions. He promised me that he would, and I immediately asked him to describe the habit of the father who had given him the letter. He replied that it was gray (pardo) and that all his other clothing was of the same color;[18] that he was as young as I and that he also had a large black book and another small one which he read, like ours (that is, Breviary and Book of Hours). He told me that on the first day of the present month he [Garcés] reached the province of Moqui with the cacique of the Cojninas and four others belonging to this tribe, who brought the father to Moqui; that the father wanted to go to Santa Fe to greet the lord governor, and that the Cojninas, in order to take the father to their land sooner, put many obstacles in his way, emphasizing the very bad road from Moqui to Santa Fe. Therefore the father changed his mind. I asked the aforesaid [Indian] whether he was very friendly with this father. He replied that so much so that during the two and a half days the father was in Moqui he never left him. The father told him that he brought with him many Spanish people, men, women, boys and girls, and many Christian Indians and some soldiers. They had not come to Moqui with his Paternity because their mounts were in a very bad way. He also told him that the Cojninas were very fine people, and also the Yumas; and that all the people he had

brought with him were planting on the meadows of the Colorado River and that the Cojninas were helping them in everything, for they liked them very much. They were so pleased with the Spaniards that they even took care of their horses.

Your Reverend Paternity is aware that on the many expeditions the religious of this Custody have made to the province of Moqui, its inhabitants have received them very well, but they have received the friar under discussion as infamously as I shall relate. On June 30 he sent two Cojninas to Oraybi to announce his arrival to the cacique and the others of whom their government is composed. The Moquis were astonished by this announcement, asking how the father could have come via Cojnina, to say nothing of so many Spaniards; that the father must be lying, for there are no Spaniards in that direction, that perhaps they might be Apaches. The friar reached the pueblo of Oraybi on the following day. No one came out to meet him; on the contrary, indeed, they were so overbearing that they did not even give him a pitcher of water. But why do I say water, when they did not even give him a house to rest in, for they left him in the plazas? And the Acoma Indian heightens this by saying that the plaza where the father lodged was full of rubbish and ordure, etc. On July 2, before the sun rose, the cacique proclaimed that he did not want anyone to become Christian, that he would punish anyone who went near the father. And they all obeyed his mandate, not even being willing to hear the father when he gave them gifts, for the cacique said: "The father wants to deceive us by bringing us gifts, and therefore let no one accept anything." And young and old did [as he said] with blind obedience.

When the father called to any Moquino, adult or child, man or woman, they fled like roe deer and went into their coises, or houses. When he saw that his apostolic zeal had no effect, the father decided to return with the cacique of Cojnina and the other

17. The College of Guadalupe at Zacatecas was founded in 1707 by Fray Antonio Margil de Jesús.

18. The Indian apparently noticed the difference in color, for the New Mexican friars wore blue.

four who had brought him. They took him to the place where the other Spaniards and the Indians who accompanied him were. The cacique of Oraybi was very angry with the Cojninas, asking them why they had brought that father there. The Cojninas replied that he was coming to baptize them. Then the cacique of Oraybi said that if they liked the father so much, they should take him back to their land. The Cojninas were very happy to do so, and off they went to Cojnina. All these are the words of the Acoma Indian whom I examined about the whole course of events, in his own language by means of an interpreter and in our Castilian, which he does not speak badly, and it all came out the same. With regard to other things your Paternity knows, I suppose that you will take a more precise statement from him. I have taken it with regard to what is most important, which is what I am writing; moreover, I am trying not to molest your attention unduly with my unpolished style. God keep your Paternity many years. Your Reverend Paternity's convent of Zuñi and July 6, 1776. Your most humble and useless subject kisses your Very Reverend Paternity's hands. Fray Mariano Rosete y Peralta.

To our Reverend Father Commissary Visitor Fray Francisco Atanasio Domínguez.

[P. S.] I am also writing to the governor and I am sending him a copy of the Reverend Father Fray Francisco Garcés' original letter. And I am also telling him that your Reverend Paternity will give him complete information, since I am writing you at more length and in more detail. Your Reverend Paternity will forgive the defects of this letter; there are several, due to haste. I remit the Reverend Father Fray Francisco Garcés' letter, and because his hand is rather poor, some expressions have been corrected in the copy of it which I am sending to the lord governor, as your Reverend Paternity will see.

CERTIFICATION

I certify that the preceding copy of the letter which the Reverend Father Francisco Garcés wrote from Oraybi to the father minister of Zuñi is faithful and to the letter. I also certify that the other one, which also precedes this, is a faithful and literal copy of the letter which the father minister of Zuñi, Fray Mariano Rosete y Peralta, wrote to me when he remitted the aforesaid original letter of the Reverend Father Garcés and that the report he includes in it by the Indian of the pueblo of Acoma, called Lázaro, agrees with the one the same Indian made to the lord governor, to Father Fray Silvestre Vélez de Escalante, and to me, since we all examined him with special care. The two original letters mentioned are in my possession. Villa of Santa Fe and July 28, 1776.

Fray Francisco Atanasio Domínguez
(rubric)

And inasmuch as we are about to leave tomorrow, the twenty-ninth of this month, there is no time to write at further length, and since it is necessary that your Paternity have some previous information about our intention, I am setting down the people who are going with us and the project of our expedition, which I shall announce to your Paternity in the letter with which I shall enclose this, under date of the twenty-ninth of the present month. And we have already given it to the lord governor so that he may inform his Excellency [the viceroy]. It is as follows:

PROJECT FOR THE JOURNEY

We are leaving this capital for the north-northwest with the aim of finding out, if possible, what nations in addition to the Yuta inhabit the regions between here and Monterey in the aforesaid direction, even though it may involve a roundabout route because it is necessary to go down to reach said port. And on our way back [we hope to discover] the tribes who dwell from west to east as far as Cojnina, where we intend to go in order to strengthen the people of this nation in their good intention of becoming Christians, and in order to give the most careful and accurate report possible about the region they inhabit and the sites it may offer adapted to and convenient for settlements. Also, if no insuperable obstacle intervenes, we will proceed direct to Moqui, exploring as much as possible the country in between and the environs of Moqui in order to give information about any suitable sites there may be to which the Moqui pueblos can be moved in case of their conversion, or to establish another, or others, which may be available.

People who voluntarily accompany us, and for the sole purpose of serving God and our Sovereign, God keep him:

1. Don Juan Pedro de Cisneros, alcalde mayor of the pueblo of Zuñi. 2. Don Bernardo Miera, citizen of the Villa of Santa Fe. 3. Don Joaquín Laín, citizen of the same villa. 4. Lorenzo de Olivares, citizen of the pueblo of El Paso del Norte. 5. Andrés Muñiz, citizen of the post of Bernalillo. 6. Juan de Aguilar, citizen of the same post. 7. Antonio Lucrecio Muñiz, citizen of the post of Embudo. 8. Simón Lucero, servant of the said alcalde of Zuñi.

Fray Francisco Atanasio Domínguez
(rubric)

V

To Provincial Fray Isidro Murillo
Zuñi, November 25, 1776[19]

Our Very Reverend Father Minister Provincial Fray Isidro Murillo.
Most benign and my venerated father and lord:

In the letter I wrote to your Very Reverend Paternity dated July 29 of this year of 1776, I not only enclosed a literal copy of the letter the Reverend Father Fray Francisco Garcés wrote from Oraybi in Moqui to the Father Minister of this mission of Zuñi, but

I also remitted to you a copy of the one concerning the same matter which the second minister of this mission, Father Fray Mariano Rosete, wrote to me, and I gave you prompt notice of the journey, and on the same twenty-ninth of July Father Fray Silvestre Vélez de Escalante and I ventured forth.

And in fact it was in accordance with the plan of it I presented to your Very Reverend Paternity in the letter mentioned, to the north-northwest of the Villa of Santa Fe, although at first we traveled nearly 100 leagues to the northwest through territory of Yutas, Payuchis, Muhuachis, and Tabeguachis. After 199 leagues, we reached the Yutas Sabuaganas, to whom we proclaimed the Gospel. The first Sabuaganas whom we saw were a little beyond the northern end of the Sierra de la Grulla and almost in 40° of latitude. They made many difficulties and tried to hinder us in the prosecution of our journey, but, praise God, all the difficulties they made were overcome without offending them.

Among them there were six Laguna [Utah lake] Indians who are called Tympanogotzis, or Tympanocuitzis, in their language. With two of these for guides, we continued our way on through the Yutas and through territory of the Comanches Yamparicas, and at the last great river that divides the Yuta

19. AGM, Historia, vol. 52, exp. 9. With this letter there is another of the same date addressed to Governor Pedro Fermín de Mendinueta and signed by both Domínguez and Vélez de Escalante. Except for the opening and closing paragraphs and an occasional minor difference in wording, these letters are almost exactly the same. Apparently it was a joint composition. In the letter to the governor they mention their weariness and the excessively cold weather, which prevented them from proceeding to Santa Fe at once. These letters, of course, summarize the account given at much greater length in their diary of the expedition, for which and for a detailed discussion of the expedition, the reader is referred to H. E. Bolton, *Pageant in the wilderness* (Salt Lake City, 1950). See also O. Maas, *Viajes de misioneros franciscanos*, and *Documentos para la historia de México*, Sér. 2, vol. 1 (Mexico, 1854).

nation from the Comanche and other nations on the north and northeast, and which we named San Buenaventura, we found ourselves in 41° 19′ of latitude, the highest to which we ascended during the whole journey.

After crossing this last river, we traveled west, quarter west-southwest, and at 316 leagues from the Villa of Santa Fe we reached the great valley and lake of the Tympanocuitzis, which we named Nuestra Señora de la Merced because we arrived there on the day of this advocation of the Most Pure Virgin [September 23]. Here we found the most docile and affable nation of all that have been known in these regions. We proclaimed the Gospel to them with such happy results that they are awaiting Spaniards and religious so that they may become Christians. They accepted all our proposals with pleasure, and in proof of their sincerity they gave us a sign on a piece of chamois in order that we might show it to the lord governor, and they gave us two Indians to come here with us. One of them returned because of an unexpected contingency, after having traveled with us more than 40 leagues from his land, and the other went on and has come here with us. This has sweetened the inevitable bitter things that so long a journey offers, because we have now assured the safety of this soul.

The said valley is on the west side of an extensive sierra that comes from the northeast and the land of the Yamparicas and in latitude 40° 49′. Five rivers, which enter a great lake abounding in fish, which is in the center of the valley, water it. Around it dwell the Tympanocuitzis and another nation whom we were unable to see. This valley is so spacious, with such good land and beautiful proportions, that in it alone a province like New Mexico can be established and can be maintained there well supplied with every kind of grain and cattle, as your Very Reverend Paternity will see at more length in the Diary which I will remit in due course. The Sabuaganas call these Indians Come-Pescado (Fish Eaters), and it is true that they have good fish.

From the Valley and Lake of Nuestra Señora de la Merced of the Tympanocuitzis, we took our route toward Monterey, traveling south, and mostly to the southwest. We encountered many people of the same docility and simplicity as the Lagunas. We preached to them as well as the fortuitous difference in the language permitted, and they all received the Gospel with pleasure. These Indians whom we discovered beyond the Lagunas generally have as thick and dense a beard as the Spaniards. Most frequently they remove it, and some wear it so long that they look like Capuchin Fathers or Bethlehemites. In addition to this distinction from all the rest, the cartilage of their noses is pierced, and they wear a little bone through the hole. They resemble the Spaniards in their physiognomy. They use the language of the Lagunas. It is a widespread and numerous nation. The last of them whom we saw and instructed as much as possible became so fond of us that when they took leave of us, they burst into tears, and until we lost them from sight we heard their tender sobs and lamentations. The special name of these Indians is Tyrangapui in their language, and the valley in which they live, which is very extensive, is in 39° 35′ of latitude.

From these Yutas Barbones [full-bearded] (we call them this because they use the Yuta language, although with noticeable difference) we proceeded to the southwest toward Monterey, and after six days' journey we found ourselves already with very little food, for although the Lord Governor supplied us with sufficient for the whole journey, it was necessary for us to use a great deal among the Yutas, especially among the Sabuaganas. And therefore, although we killed two buffaloes and bought a fardel of very good dried fish at the lake, it failed us at the critical time. Besides this, there was a heavy snowfall, with almost intolerable cold. For these and other reasons which your

Very Reverend Paternity will see in the Diary, we considered our reaching Monterey unattainable for now, and so from 38° and minutes of latitude we took a new route for the Río Grande de Cojnina, Moqui, and Zuñi.

Beyond the Barbones Indians we found other nations, and all so wild and cowardly that we had great difficulty in getting them to come near us so that we might instruct them, in so far as the difference in language permitted, through the Laguna and the interpreter. Among those nearest the Río Grande there are some who now sow maize and calabashes. They are called Parussis and they are the farthest north, at 37° and minutes of latitude. The climate of the territory they inhabit is more hot than cold, according to what we experienced.

In none of the nations mentioned did we find any information whatsoever about the Spaniards of Monterey. Before we reached the Río Grande, and among the Parussis, our food supply ran out completely. We were unable to obtain a guide among all these people, and therefore we suffered many deviations from our route, delay, and such hunger that many days we ate grass seeds, tuna [prickly pear] cake, *nopal chico* [another variety of prickly pear], and finally six horses from those we had been using. We reached the Río Grande in 36 and more than a half degrees, having come down before as far as a full 36½°. We did not find a ford here, and so we traveled upstream, with great difficulty because the terrain is almost impassable, until we found a ford in 36° 55′ of latitude.

A little more than 8 leagues after we crossed the river, we found a ranchería of Yutas Payuchis, of the most western ones, but as cowardly and wild as the Indians mentioned on the other side. We spent two days urging them to approach us to see whether we might buy some supplies from them and have them give us information about Cojnina and Moqui, but they hardly saw us before they returned to the crag where they were with great speed. They gave the information we were seeking to the Laguna and the interpreter and the marks of the road that led to Moqui and of the one that went to the Cojninas, whom they said were far in the interior gathering piñón. We took the road to Cojnina through very good terrain.

We went down to 35° through Cojnina territory. We found a small, but beautiful, farm, and a rancho of these Indians, but we did not see any of them. Perhaps they were in the nearby sierra gathering piñón. On the said farm, which has several springs of good water to irrigate it, they had sown maize, frijol, watermelons, melons, and calabashes this year, for there were remains of all these. In addition to the huts

SIGNATURE OF BERNARDO DE MIERA Y PACHECO

made of palisades, there was a small house well made of stone and mud. [In these and in subterranean granaries were][20] the baskets (cuévanos) and other utensils of these Indians.

From here we went toward Moqui. We traveled by extensive plains on which the herds of cattle and horses of Moqui graze, and after three days, which was on the sixteenth of this November, we reached Oraybi, where we were well received, although the populace detained us for a short time at the entrance to the pueblo. We went to all the pueblos. We preached the Gospel to all, and none of them is willing to receive it. The brevity of this letter and the scarcity of time does not permit me to inform your Very Reverend Paternity of all that happened in Moqui, especially in Gualpi, but your Very Reverend Paternity will see it all in the Diary.

The Navajos and Yutas have killed, captured, and robbed the Moquis, and they are now at war with them. We had such bad weather at Moqui that it was impossible to make observations of latitude either by day or by night.

Finally, we reached this mission of Nuestra Señora de Guadalupe de Zuñi on the twenty-fourth day of this month, having traveled in the whole journey nearly 600 Spanish leagues. From the lake to near the Río Colorado there is an extremely beautiful road, and entirely free from enemies. With regard to Monterey, according to what we observed and through all the land we traveled from the lake, it is possible to travel safely with a very small force.

This is the substance of what happened on our journey and what I can tell your Very Reverend Paternity for now with the necessary brevity. May Heaven prosper your life for many years to my honor. Mission of Nuestra Señora de Guadalupe de Zuñi and November 25, 1776.

Our Very Reverend Father Provincial, Your Very Reverend Paternity's least subject and most favored son who loves and respects you kisses your hands.

Fray Francisco Atanasio Dominguez
(rubric)

VI

To Provincial Fray Isidro Murillo
El Paso, May 21, 1777[21]

Our Very Reverend Father Minister Provincial Fray Isidro Murillo:

In my letter of June 10 of last year, 1776, I informed your Very Reverend Paternity about everything that then seemed necessary to me, and I also advised you that only the three missions of Laguna, Acoma, and Zuñi remained for me to visit. Their visitation has now been made as of the month of December of the same year. And although your Very Reverend Paternity has replied to my aforesaid letter of June 10 in one dated August 9, giving me the instructions I must observe with regard to setting fees and to recording accurately the missing baptismal entries by making use of the citizens to find out from them with method and subtlety the day, month, and year when their children, relatives, or acquaintances were baptized, I say that I am unable to carry out such an order for various reasons. Sometimes because, generally speaking, the people of this kingdom are so simple that they do not even know the day on which they were born; or else their malice is so great that they will misrepresent matters in such a way that they raise a lot of confused gossip, out of which it costs a good deal to get at the truth. Moreover, these same people have seen the complete entries used to stuff the windows. And finally, a number of alcaldes and lieutenants of the pueblos have removed the parish books from some missions, and their leaves have been used to

---

20. Supplied from the letter to the governor mentioned in n. 19 *supra*.

21. BNM, leg. 10, no. 42.

make cigarettes, as the Indians who have witnessed this aver. There is no further remedy, in my opinion, in case the matter comes up, than [to answer with] something that at any rate really did happen and this is: In the year 1764 some women possessed by the devil broke loose in this kingdom. By order of the Lord Governor don Tomás Vélez Cachupín, and in accordance with the opinion of some religious, they were shut up in the cell then used for the library and archive of this Custody. And in their fury, or for some reason I know not what, many books were used to smoke with and they burned all the parish books there were. This episode is quite public and well known in the whole kingdom, but even so, it does not cover all that is necessary to give a satisfactory answer to a lord bishop who may want to know all there is and pertains to his Sacred Mitre. The more so because there are many books after 1764 in which it is obvious that there are entries missing. Therefore, in order to direct attention elsewhere, it is necessary to conceal the books that are in the archive and only show those which now exist at the missions. I am taking great pains with the latter, and I firmly believe that if the prelates of this Custody had examined the said books carefully in their juridical visitations, the remedy would have been imposed long before now. I also reflect that when the lord bishop is shown the books now in use, he may ask for the earlier ones, and then we fall into the same deficiency, because there are entries missing from many of them. I do not want to be held responsible on this point, nor do I wish to lack instructions about it. Will your Very Reverend Paternity please give me the most suitable instructions?

Neither can I carry out your Very Reverend Paternity's order concerning the land pertaining to the mission of La Cañada. Its present minister is sunk in such great poverty and wretchedness that it has been necessary to succor him with some necessities. The aforesaid land which Father Fray An-drés García sold to Juan Bautista Vigil cannot be returned to the mission because its owner has built houses on it. It became necessary, therefore, to look for a piece of land near the mission and say to Juan Bautista: "You buy that land in your name; take the 125 regional pesos they want for it and draw up the purchase papers in your name." As soon as this was done, and after some days had passed, the syndic of these missions, Don Clemente Gutiérrez, and Juan Bautista Vigil appeared together before the alcalde mayor of La Cañada, and the syndic said: "Mr. Juan Bautista Vigil, do you wish to exchange the land you have near this mission for the land which this mission has near the old church? Since you have a house in the vicinity, you can cultivate it more easily, which the missionary cannot do because of the long distance." [Vigil] replied that he did so wish, and, the parties being in agreement, the writ of exchange was made according to law and in conformity with our institute and rule. I am remitting a copy to your Very Reverend Paternity for your further information about this procedure.[22]

Your Very Reverend Paternity will also have evidence of what was done to abolish completely the Devotion of the Poor Souls which Father Fray Sebastián Fernández founded *auctoritate propia* with excessive assumption of authority. The capital, or principal, could not be obtained because the debtor does not have it at present, and he only gave a legal bond to the syndic as such to give 300 regional pesos a year in wheat, maize, etc., until the sum of 588 ewes he owes is complete. I am also remitting a copy of this to your Very Reverend Paternity. The original remains in the possession of Syndic don Clemente Gutiérrez. The document which Father Fray Sebastián Fernández drew up for this Devotion was thrown into the fire because it deserved to be.

And for the same reason I placed Father Fray Joaquín de Jesús Ruiz at the mission

22. See pp. 318-21 *infra*.

of Isleta even before I received your Very Reverend Paternity's letter of August 9, 1776, in which you again order me to do so, telling me there are higher reasons for this.

The one I had was no less, for my conscience pricked me to take away part of Father Junco's property and deposit some of it with our brother syndic, Don Clemente Gutiérrez, as I told your Very Reverend Paternity in my letter of July 29, remitting to you a copy, or memorandum, of the aforesaid property. I have not yet had a reply to this letter of July 29, and today is May 2, 1777. In this same letter I informed your Very Reverend Paternity that Father Fray Ramón Salas was going and had gone to the mission of Isleta at El Paso; that Father Fray Juan de Llanos escaped from going to the mission of Laguna for a certain reason and that he remained at that of Sandia; that Father Fray Mariano Rosete remained at that of Zuñi; that Father Fray Mariano Rodríguez de la Torre was resigning and did resign as vice-custos, and that I put in his place Father Fray José Medrano, who, during the journey I made with Father Vélez, remained as prelate and vice-custos, not as visitor as the Reverend Father Téllez charges against me in a letter of January 10, 1777, telling me that I had left Father Rosete as visitor and that in order partly to remedy so invalid an act, he was remitting a patent to the Reverend Hinojosa so that he might govern the Custody until I returned to it. I never thought of such a thing, and how was it possible for me to leave Father Rosete [in the office] when I had reported that he was at Zuñi? This must have slipped the Reverend Father Téllez' mind, for I also advised him of this, and for that reason and also because the charge against me is false and because I have not been accused by your Very Reverend Paternity, by whom alone (in case it were true) I should have been and should be judged, I say no more about the matter. But if I see the patent the Reverend Téllez tells me about, indeed it will be necessary for me to speak of

it, as I will do, more to satisfy your Very Reverend Paternity than to convey that I know how to perform my duty.[23]

I again return to my letter of July 29, and I state that in it I promised to give a report on other money matters of certain religious. And in fact, 1,020 silver pesos were taken from Fray Juan José de Llanos. He had them in Don Diego de Borica's keeping, and they were used by the latter for expenses of the journey which Father Vélez and I made and for other things. Not only will your Very Reverend Paternity find them in the documents I am remitting about this, but I will now make a brief statement in this letter. Some little property of the large amount he had was taken from Father Fray Sebastián Fernández, and the amount he had will be obvious from what the same father has done.

Without license from and against the judgment and opinion of the Father Vice-Custos Fray José Medrano, his legitimate prelate, he decided to build the two churches of Picuris and Sandia, giving for their cost to two different individuals of this kingdom mules, cattle, deerskins, and other things he has acquired by illicit trade, a business he has habitually engaged in since he has been in this kingdom. For the said fabric of churches and the transfer of the property referred to, he made two writings before the lieutenant alcalde mayor of his pueblo of Abiquiu, and he framed them in the same way as a layman who is absolute owner of his property. At this time I was engaged in my visitation of Zuñi, and for that reason the Father Vice-Custos tolerated it, leaving it to me to straighten everything out. This was not done as it should have been, which would have meant taking from the laymen the property which the father had given them, because not only would that have given a scandalous shock to the whole kingdom, but I was taking a middle course

23. The reference seems to be to the procurator, Fray Nicolás Téllez Girón. See n. 7 *supra*.

for the sake of your Very Reverend Paternity's honor and my own, since from the time I arrived and even before those of this kingdom knew me it was said that you were sending me to collect the alms from the field. The terms of this expression indicate that it emanates from religious, and I feel no embarrassment in saying that this same Father Fray Sebastián has been desirous of beclouding my good name, for I have irrefutable proof of this. But since my honor is as shining and great as the sun, Father Fray Sebastián's little cloud has not been able to darken its light and its rays. Finally, lest I tire your Very Reverend Paternity's attention with the deeds of a disobedient friar, one who scorns the letter patent of his prelates, an owner of property and merchant like this father, the two writings for the fabric of said churches were made anew before a qualified judge with the intervention of the syndic and in terms proper to our state in life and our extreme poverty, as will be evident to your Very Reverend Paternity from the copies of the two writings which I am remitting to you. The originals remain in the hands of the syndic of these interior missions, Don Clemente Gutiérrez.[24]

He, as well as other individuals, was paid in its entirety all that some friars owed him. The reason I had for this was to take away from some of them the trade they have been carrying on illicitly and from others the scandalous and injurious dealings with women who are not only suspect but leading notoriously evil lives with these same friars. For some years this has been one of the chief causes of great affliction in this whole Custody, discredit to our habit, and imponderable harm to the souls of parishioners and ministers. But I must confess that all this effort, inspired by my zeal and desire to merit your Very Reverend Paternity's trust in me, has cost me means, steps, and even risk to my own life. I have seen it undertaken and put into effect within a very short time. There

has been no scandal nor noisy publicity, nor censures nor formal precepts of obedience, but pleas, supplications, affability and sweetness, and if there has been any who has delayed longer than the appointed time in casting from himself and his mission the infamous connection, I have showed myself ill disposed toward him and have written with sternness and superiority. Thank God, this is now exiled at distances such that they cannot see or communicate with one another. I have assigned an old woman in cases where I have learned that they need attendance. No suspicion can arise from this, and I have first informed myself about their age, life, and customs. I have done the same in the case of the men servants they must have, in order to assure in this way, first, the security of our consciences, second, the veneration and respect due those who are ministers of the Most High, third, all the help it is lawful for the missionaries to have, and finally, to remove with ease all that may be prejudicial to the liberty and good upbringing of the Indians in our charge. I have found no other means more suited to the abolishment of the aforesaid errors, for first it was necessary to pay the debts the friars had incurred by their earlier slips, to help them out with something for the transportation of the obligations they had contracted and for the succor of these women. Otherwise, I am sure that in addition to not attaining our end, serious scandals would result, and since I must avoid all noisy judicial proceedings and not take such steps except as a last resort, I decided on the course I have already indicated.

The aforesaid debts of the religious, then, have been satisfied out of the produce of the property of Father Junco, that of Father Fray Sebastián, from Father Llanos' money, and from part of the spolia of Father Abadiano. I will give a clear, separate, and very detailed account of all this in the documents I am remitting to your Very Reverend Paternity, among which there are receipts from the persons to whom payment has

24. See pp. 321-24 *infra*.

been made and various signatures of those who have witnessed the very thing they sign. And I am keeping a copy of everything for my own protection, and I will hold the copies until I have a letter from your Very Reverend Paternity in which you tell me specifically that you have received everything. I eagerly await this so that I may get rid of so large a quantity of paper which embarrasses and humiliates me. I also hope that in the same reply your Very Reverend Paternity will tell me your feeling with regard to each and every one of my decisions. So far I have believed and do believe that I have pleased your well-known zeal and ardent desire for the good of this Custody and your religious sons who compose it. It can well be that there are defects in all I have done and have now related to your Very Reverend Paternity, but if there are, they are unblamable and have arisen solely from my imperfect understanding and the great lack of spirit, of which, as a friar, I must have a great deal in order to carry through God's and your Very Reverend Paternity's plans in the office of custos which you have conferred upon me beyond my merits. And I beg the chapter to relieve me and remove me from the office, which I resign, although I do not exempt myself from this or any other task but am ready to work at everything I am ordered to do. And the reason I have for renouncing the office is the same one Our Father St. Francis gave when he renounced the one he held, saying, *Nolo esse carnificem fratrum meorum,* for although I have personally experienced the docility of some religious of this Custody, others of insolent and haughty spirit are not lacking. And if I continue in office, I find myself obliged to take steps against their insolence and audacity. But for this digression I have committed, what has been said suffices, because I hope from your Very Reverend Paternity's kindness that you will grant my petition and remove me from the office of custos.

Continuing, then, to speak of my visitation, I made a juridical visitation of all the religious of these interior missions, excepting, as I did except from juridical proceedings, the missionaries of Laguna, Acoma, and Zuñi, because the bad weather and the inherent difficulties of these places so required. But I did examine their convents, churches, valuables, etc., and I found everything in accordance with the account I give in the narrative I am making of each mission. I am remitting this exactly as your Very Reverend Paternity orders me in your instructions, with such good fortune that even with regard to the order given me in these same instructions about inquiring for or acquiring the Reverend Father Fray Francisco Garcés' letter, I remitted to your Very Reverend Paternity a copy of the original which the same Reverend Father wrote to the missionary of Zuñi.

From the same narrative to which I refer and which I am sending to your Very Reverend Paternity concerning the missions, their directions, distances, locations, and the information about the characteristics of each one in particular and of all in general, you will know very well the care and nicety with which I have carried out your orders and the pleasure I take in acquainting you with all the sierras, woods, waters, and other things this interior kingdom contains by means of that map [*país*] which I am remitting to you and which I humbly dedicate to your diversion along with all the rest I report and enclose pertaining to the visitation I have made of these interior missions of New Mexico.

I left them on the fifth of this month of May because of the opportunity offered by the departure of Don Diego de Borica at the summons of the new Commandant Inspector, for otherwise my departure would have been delayed longer for lack of a cordon, which leaves but once a year. I reached this mission of El Paso on the eighteenth of the same month of May with poor health and many troubles but ready to do in these missions the same as in those of the interior, and with the same detailed description and efficacy.[25]

I wanted to send all the documents, description of missions and the others I cite in this letter with the Reverend Hinojosa, thinking he might leave in haste, but his genius will move him to make the journey when God so wills. I find no convoy with whom to send the foregoing, and since all it contains is of some weight and worthy of your Very Reverend Paternity's attention, I have decided to send it by post and at the expense of this Custody, both because it now has the wherewithal to do so in Chihuahua and also because there is something remaining in the interior missions. If I err in this, I ask pardon. And I go on to list the papers I am sending.

A book in folio of what the missions contain, their directions, distances, etc. A map [pais] of the whole kingdom in three parts. Account of the property which was taken from Father Junco, its produce and distribution. Account of the 1,020 pesos of Father Llanos and their distribution. Account of the property which was taken from Father Fray Sebastián Fernández. Account of the spolia of Father Abadiano. Receipts of the laymen to whom the religious owed and whom I paid with letters of the indebted fathers. I note that only Don Pedro Pino's receipt for 200 silver pesos and 1 real which I paid for Father García is lacking, and it is missing because the said person lives a long distance away and could not give it at the time, but he remained responsible for the satisfaction of said receipt. Account of the expenses I have had, and I did not put down 57 pesos 4 reales which this journey from Santa Fe to El Paso, accompanied by Father Hermida, who is very ill here, has cost, or

an account of the loan [dependencia] I have in Chihuahua with Don Francisco Duro, which increases more and more every day, for I was not aware of the debt, which I have another reason for wishing to liquidate, and let your Paternity tell me how. I have not had nor do I have a mission, nor is it fitting that the one who may be custos should have one if he wants to fulfill his duty. Three juridical instruments pertaining to the three interior villas, in which it is of record that the religious who administer them cannot support themselves with the obventions they yield. The book of the visitation. The diary of our journey in two parts.

During this journey, a she-mule and a horse were lost from those of Father Junco. Therefore I am responsible only for five she-mules of this father and for a he-mule and a she-mule of Father Abadiano, for three blankets and four buffalo [skins].

Father Fray Silvestre de Escalante remained in the interior missions as vice-custos. He is the only person who can carry out my just plans and decisions. And [he is] at the mission of San Ildefonso.[26] Fathers Dueñas, Fernández, and Velasco are ready to go to the interior. It will be necessary to provide them with the necessary supplies for their journey. Father Hermida remains here very ill and incapable of serving his office at present, and it is also necessary to succor him with all he needs.

I have much more to say to your Reverend Paternity, but the haste with which Don Diego Borica is leaving for Chihuahua does not permit more and I leave it for another occasion. In order not to increase costs in the mail, I include in the portfolios mentioned the certifications by the fathers for the collection of their royal allowances and other letters which your Reverend Pa-

---

25. Don Teodoro de Croix became Commandant of the Interior Provinces in 1777. Don Diego de Borica, lieutenant governor of New Mexico, had participated in O'Conor's campaigns of 1776 by order of Governor Pedro Fermín de Mendinueta, and continued his military service on the frontier under Croix and Juan Bautista de Anza.

26. At San Ildefonso on August 17, 1777, Father Vélez de Escalante, Vice-Custos, announced his forthcoming visitation of the Custody in the name of Domínguez, Provincial Visitor recently made Custos. AASF, 1769 (Patentes, 1769-1807) no. 2, doc. 5.

ternity will see, and you will be kind enough to deliver them to those to whom they are addressed. I earnestly entreat you to put the one for Don Hugo O'Conor in his own hands. It is from our beloved lieutenant governor of this pueblo, and if said O'Conor is not in Mexico City, let it be sent to him wherever he may be.

I have not yet received any reply to the two letters dated July 29, and, in view of their importance, I am surprised. And I have a reply only to the one I wrote upon my return from the journey. I thank you from my heart for the expressions in it, as I should, and for such great good I beg God to prosper, make happy, and keep you many years more than me in the greatest exaltation for my veneration.

Mission of your Very Reverend Paternity of Nuestra Señora de Guadalupe del Paso del Río del Norte, and May 21, 1777.

Our Very Reverend Father Minister Provincial,

Your most favored son and reverent subject, who esteems you, kisses your hands.

Fray Francisco Atanasio Domínguez
(rubric)

VII

*To Provincial Fray Isidro Murillo
El Paso, June 26, 1777* [27]

Our Very Reverend Father Minister Provincial Fray Isidro Murillo.
Most benign father and lord of all my veneration:

Under date of the twenty-first of the month of June which is now coming to an end I have written to your Very Reverend Paternity and remitted to you a detailed account of all you order me in your instructions and of all that happened and was decided in the juridical visitation of the interior missions of this Holy Custody. May it be God's will that they have reached your Very Reverend Paternity's hands safely and

that you have received them with your usual kindness.

The juridical visitation of these five missions of El Paso del Río del Norte is entirely finished with regard to the legal formalities, but what pertains to the material realm of the missions, their valuables, etc., directions, and waters, remains to be written down. This will be done soon, and I will remit it all to your Very Reverend Paternity in the first convoy. [28]

If there was great reason to grieve and to sorrow in the interior missions, in these there are also motives enough to do likewise. There is no teaching of the Indians, and consequently no care taken to have them attend catechism and learn it. Their ministers (this does not refer to all of them or to all the missions) aspire only to possess many temporal goods and to obtain them at the cost of the poor Indians' sweat and labor. In a single mission I found the books of Marriages and Burials without a single entry recorded in them for a period of five years. What grave carelessness! What injurious omission! The religious delinquent in this respect has already been judged by God. And he did this so openly that he left a blank space in the book of Baptisms for entries he failed to record. Just as I drew up a directive for the administration and government of the Indians of the interior missions and ordered its punctilious observance by the missionaries, I have sent the same for these missions and given the same order. Because both here and in the interior missions it seemed as if we were living among Latins and Greeks according to the different methods of teaching the Indians used by those who did teach them. To remedy partially the omission of entries, the parishioners of that mission are being questioned subtly about how old they are, in which missionary's time and in what year they were mar-

---

27. BNM, leg. 10, no. 49.

28. We have not found Domínguez' formal report of his visitation of the El Paso area, although he mentions it in his letter of August 16, 1777, p. 299 *infra*.

ried, who their sponsors were, and in this way I will see whether I can remedy so grave a fault. And when the truth has been established, the handwriting of the signature of the religious who should have made the entries will be counterfeited. At present I find no other way out, and your Very Reverend Paternity will deign to tell me if I am doing right, or what I ought to do.

In these missions there are also plenty of debts incurred by the religious who administer them. Among them all there is one that troubles me most, both because it amounts to 736 pesos and 1 real and because it belongs to the Durango tithes, and the *jueces acreedores* are now pressing for their money. The religious who contracted it prevailed upon the Ecclesiastical Judge don Lorenzo Rivera to give him the administration of the tithes of this jurisdiction and the collection of the seeds, and besides doing so, he came to owe and owes the said amount. The stewards are now remonstrating with the above ecclesiastical judge about the money he owes them, which amounts to more than seven thousand pesos, and in order to reply and render his accounts, it is necessary for him to state the amount the friar owes him. The latter is insolvent on the one hand, and on the other, it is known that he keeps a *volante* with which he furnishes the presidios with seeds, etc., and that he is a very wealthy father. All his wealth comes down to being in debt to *many* and in a large amount, as I have proof, for I have put my hand in this and taken charge of everything, as is my duty. I am completely absorbed in thinking of ways to get out of this and not at the expense of our habit or the honor of the Custody. Let your Very Reverend Paternity suggest a dignified way out to me and take charge of the major part of this affair, which is simply what I am explaining to you, for in order to tell you in detail the course of this matter, much time and more paper would be necessary, confiding to the pen what I keep locked in my breast because it cannot stand the light.

Nor is this all that I have encountered during my visitation. In order to do my duty and silence the outcries of my conscience, I have arranged here for moral lectures every two weeks, and the same in the interior missions. I forgot to mention this in my letter of June 21. I have banished from the missions the service by women cooks, and one of them is leaving for Chihuahua on the date of this letter. Her husband appeared before the vicar of that villa, stating that such and such a father had unmarried her. In this regard several letters requisitorial came from the same vicar at different times, as I have now learned, and since no attention was paid to them, they have left all the mortifications for me. *Plue Jupiter super me calamitates,* but with the favor of Heaven I keep insisting that there is a remedy for everything and that it can be applied without making a din.

It is indeed true that in order to key this down and avoid in future having so much evil spoken of this Custody as has been said up to now, it is sometimes necessary to use the greatest severity, and I do not know but what some public juridical proceedings as well. There are depraved, disobedient, bold characters and brothers who carry knives and blunderbusses as if they were highwaymen. In my presence one of them took the liberty of drawing his knife from his pouch and speaking his mind. And I well know that to avoid this I must first use love and kindness (which is my nature), pleading and entreating, begging, insisting, arguing, obsecrating, but I have also learned from St. Augustine that *via deveniendi ad medium est declinare in extremum.* And what nature will be necessary for this? That of a Nero or a Caligula, not my own tender and compassionate one which truly loves my brethren. Someone like me who lives in constant fear of falling into greater absurdities, and who makes every allowance he can for human frailty and [the temptations] every son of Adam is exposed to, is not suited to that. This obliges me to submit, as I humbly do submit to your Very Reverend Paternity, once, twice, and thrice, my resignation as custos and submissively to beg you to accept it as a prelate who heeds the greatest good and benefit of his subjects. I hope in your well-known clemency for the benign reception and quick dispatch of my petition. I will count this favor among the many I owe your Very Reverend Paternity which I shall never know how to repay except by giving complete satisfaction with my procedure in the offices your Very Reverend Paternity has entrusted to me, being ready to respond on every occasion to all you may wish to order me.

The Reverend Father Hinojosa is leaving for the province on the date of this letter, both because he has your Very Reverend Paternity's consent and also because his ailments do not permit him to linger in these regions any longer. Father Fray Rafael Benavides accompanies him as far as Chihuahua. He is going to said villa for treatment because he is seriously ill and it is necessary to do everything possible to restore his health and to find out whether he will be able to continue as a missionary. Father Fray Buenaventura Hermida, who is better and determined to serve as much as he can, is at the mission of Senecu, where the Reverend Father Hinojosa was residing. Fathers Fernández and Velasco are now in New Mexico, but Father Fray Francisco Dueñas resisted going, and after the bad turn he did me by his unwillingness, he is now assistant to the missionary of Socorro.

It is impossible to inform your Very Reverend Paternity about many things that I still have to tell you, but I will do so as convoys become available.

I wish your Very Reverend Paternity every happiness and I beg God to keep you for me many years more for all my veneration. Paso del Río del Norte and June 26, 1777.

Our Very Reverend Father Minister Provincial,

Your most obedient subject and most favored son who loves you kisses your hands, etc.

Fray Francisco Atanasio Dominguez
(rubric)

VIII

To Provincial Fray Isidro Murillo
August 16, 1777 [29]

Our Very Reverend Father Minister Provincial Fray Isidro Murillo.
Our Father:

In reply to your Very Reverend Paternity's letter of last July 2, in which you inform me about the rumors which malice and ignorance are sometimes wont to start and that they have assured you *de facto* that claims have been made to the Caballero de Croix with regard to the despoliation, I must tell you that such assertions to your Very Reverend Paternity arise from a letter a friar of this pueblo of El Paso wrote to another friar of that province, carried away by the lies they told him, as a result of which he wanted to plan a motion or complaint. But as soon as he was undeceived, he undertook to satisfy me and to tell me, as he did, all he had written. Nevertheless, if this was not the motive and if it was the whole truth (I have serious reason to doubt it), I am ready to reply to and satisfy all your Very Reverend Paternity may order me, with the assurance that I will make it lucid enough to show clearly my special eagerness to serve God and the King more. I remain, then, in hope of the outcome and that your Very Reverend Paternity will inform me about it completely as you promise in your aforesaid letter of July 2.

Meanwhile, I can do no less than tell you with holy ingenuousness that the expression your Very Reverend Paternity uses in speaking to me of the solution for my [difficulties in fulfilling] my obligation: "by all means without creating unrest among the reli-

29. BNM, leg. 10, no. 46.

gious," grieves me. And when have I upset them for the purpose of solving my affairs? Do not the certifications from each of the friars I visited, which I have remitted to your Very Reverend Paternity, suffice to prove my disinterest and religious behavior? Does it not suffice that I have even taken off my shirt, as I will prove, and my undercloth-ing to succor the indigence of some of them; that I have been burdened with Masses for some time in order to relieve the friar who owed them; that I have applied [my fees for] Masses at missions where I stayed several days to take care of the possible cost of the poor meals served me; that I have not ac-cepted even chocolate, and have made them all take some of what I had with me; that I have favored the friars sometimes with cigars, sometimes with chocolate, sometimes by giving them all they asked me for? Does not this suffice, I say, to remove even the slightest suspicion there may possibly be against my good conduct?

Surely, our father, I should prefer to have been abandoned by your Very Reverend Paternity in a dark prison and loaded with chains than to have seen imprinted in your letter an expression which implies some-thing that has never even crossed my mind. The precept, *curam habe de bono nomine*, obligates even religious, and even though they have renounced their will, yet they can-not renounce their honor. Therefore, I sub-missively beg your Very Reverend Paternity to condescend to give me your permission to send a formal statement of my procedure in every matter in terms legally valid as evi-dence, and most especially with regard to the implication of the phrase: *By all means without creating unrest among the reli-gious.* Otherwise your Very Reverend Pa-ternity cannot be satisfied about my good conduct nor can I have the serenity and peace of mind which I so greatly need. It is indeed true that if you reread the afore-said certifications and make a careful exam-ination of the accounts, receipts, and other papers I have sent, and if you take into con-

sideration their formality, efficacy, and the religious and lay witnesses in whose pres-ence everything was done, and that these men are still alive and ready to reiterate all they saw, witnessed, and received, I think that I must justly receive the glorious good name of a disinterested religious and that that "by all means without," etc., will con-sequently be taken for a slip of the pen.

I now go on to speak of other matters, such as the faculties to hear confessions which were granted me for the period of my visitation only. Before I finished it I had occasion to notify the Holy Office by letter that they were expiring and that during the period it would take me to have them coun-tersigned in Chihuahua I would not give spiritual nourishment to the faithful. The same thing is true of Fray José Palacio. His Illustrious Lordship put off his reply be-cause of his illnesses, and this obliged me to leave here August 12, leaving Father Mar-tínez in my place with a patent as vice-custos. But two days on my way, at the Ojito of Samalayuca, I met Father Benavides, who was returning, having recovered from his ailment, which was cured in Chihuahua. And he was bringing me a letter in reply from his Illustrious Lordship with faculties for Father Palacio and for me, the latter's for two years and mine for all the time I might stay in this Custody. He tells me that he is issuing an order to Vicar don José Lo-renzo Rivera in order that, with my consent, a friar satisfactory to me may be appointed vicar and ecclesiastical judge in the interior missions; and that when he hears from him and from me, he will issue the correspond-ing title. It makes me realize that because of the irregular refusal of my predecessor, who was unwilling for the religious to be vicars, souls have suffered the evils I have felt. For the vicarship (there will be two, as there have always been) I find no friar better qualified than Father Vélez and Father Dueñas, if the latter does not leave me, pro-vided he cannot go to the interior. Your Very Reverend Paternity will tell me if I am right or not in my choice, for I await your opinion.

At the said Ojito of Samalayuca I received your Very Reverend Paternity's letter of July 2, and in that very place I finished, with poor ink and a worse pen, the one I had started. Its content is for the purpose of satisfying your Very Reverend Paternity with regard to the commission you give me concerning Father Rodríguez and to bring to your attention nine serious points which I need to resolve for the sake of my administration. I enclosed with said letter the visitation book pertaining to these five missions of El Paso del Río del Norte. With this I satisfy the substantial and legal part of it, for the description of locations, etc., besides not being substantially necessary, is almost impossible for me to remit at present since I do not have the assistance of an amanuensis and my eyesight is nearly gone, especially in my left eye which I think is going to lose it, thanks to God. I also included with that letter the juridical certification of what this mission of El Paso brings in, and the restoration of the royal allowances can be put into effect now because the Caballero Croix knows about the great poverty of this kingdom.

For my guidance and protection I give your Very Reverend Paternity this memorandum: Since the remission of the packages I have written three letters: The first, dated June 26, in which I notify you of the many missing marriage and burial records in the old books (I provided new ones) of the mission of Socorro [at El Paso] from the year 1769 to 1776. And I now inform you that if I proceed as I said I would do in the same letter in order to supply so much that is missing, I know that I shall certainly find many invalid marriages because this population is all interrelated. I will advise your Very Reverend Paternity of the outcome. In the same letter I tell you of the loan of 736 pesos which Father Fray José Gómez owes from the tithes he appropriated. And the *jueces hacedores* of Durango are pressing for payment with great acrimony so that I no longer have a head to read letters written to me petitioning me for payment from the said father. The second letter was finished at the aforesaid Ojito under date of August 10, and it is the one which contains the satisfaction and points mentioned. The third is this one, dated today, August 16, and it contains the following addition to what has already been written. I received a letter from the Caballero de Croix, the content of which is the following:

"I thank your Reverence for the congratulations you give me in your letter of last May 31 concerning the new office the King's clemency has deigned to confer upon me. And since I must make every effort toward the best justification of this trust, I hope that your Reverence will cooperate in so far as it concerns you for the success of my good desires, which are all directed to the service of both Majesties [divine and human]. I am equally hopeful that your Reverence will inform me about the state of the missions and pueblo of El Paso with the purity and truth that befits your sacred calling. God keep your Reverence many years. Mexico, July 9, 1777. El Caballero de Croix. To the Reverend Father Fray Francisco Atanasio Domínguez."

Before replying to that letter and making the report requested, I await your Reverend Paternity's order and the manner in which I should make it so that it may be based on mature consideration and be to your satisfaction. I will address it, as is proper, through your religious hands. I have an idea that the governor will ask for the same report, and I know that on this occasion he is satisfied with my administration and that he has proof that I have remedied all his Lordship discussed and asked for. Nevertheless, let your Very Reverend Paternity tell me what I must do about everything, and let this be as soon as possible. For now I enclose a letter for the Caballero de Croix, which you will give to him if you think it advisable to do so, and if not, no.

These five missions are indeed in poor condition. Father Salas lives all the whole week in this pueblo of El Paso in the house of a married woman at whose side he goes night and day before the eyes of a whole pueblo and of some military men who are now here. Father Terán leads an unruly life, trading at the cost of the Indians' sweat, full of a thousand debts, and so valiant that Captain of Militia don Miguel Espinosa is on his way to Chihuahua to tell the Caballero Inspector about the drubbing with a stick the said father gave him. All this and more about which I keep silence with regard to those and other friars I cannot rectify with love and kindness. If I must let them be thus, your Very Reverend Paternity will so advise me.

I reply in this letter to that of your Very Reverend Paternity dated June 9 with regard to the list of friars who are now resident in this Custody, and they are:

Fray Francisco Atanasio Domínguez; Father Vice-Custos Fray Silvestre Vélez de Escalante; Father Fray Andrés García, old and ill; Father Fray Manuel José Rojo, the same; Father Fray Francisco Xavier Dávila, sicker than all the others; Father Fray Mariano Rodríguez de la Torre, old, ill, and what I have stated in my letter of August 10; Father Fray Estanislao Marulanda, blind and therefore incapable of administering; Father Fray Patricio Cuellar, a notorious drunkard; Father Fray José Burgos, the same; Father Fray José Manuel Mariño, incorrigible and with public scandal; Father Fray Sebastián Fernández, not at all obedient to rule and trader with infidels; Father Fray José de Olaeta, old and ill; Father Fray Francisco Ignacio Zarte; Father Fray Juan José Llanos; Father Fray Andrés Claramonte; Father Fray Joaquín de Jesús Ruiz; Father Fray Mariano Rosete, not at all obedient to rule and agitator of Indians; Father Fray Tomás Fernández; Father Fray Carlos de Velasco; Father Fray Manuel de la Vega; Father Fray José Medrano; Father Fray José Palacio; Father Fray Francisco Dueñas;

Father Fray Ramón Salas, as described; Father Fray José Gómez Terán, as described; Father Fray Cayetano Bernal; Father Fray Damián Martín, very ill and disconsolate; Father Fray Rafael Benavides, ill; Father Fray Buenaventura Hermida, ill.

IX

To Provincial Fray Juan Bautista Dozal El Paso, October 12, 1778[30]

Beloved father and lord of all my veneration:

In your letter of last August 24 your Very Reverend Paternity tells me that because the friars were delayed in El Paso seven were not certified, and you impute this omission to my negligence. Although your Very Reverend Paternity can inform yourself about this from the Lord [Governor] Mendinueta, who is in that city [of Mexico], I must also tell you that in order to go to the interior, the friars need a cordon to conduct them, or an armed escort. This is obtainable but once a year, and it usually comes in November, returning to New Mexico in February at the earliest. This is why a friar who enters El Paso in September, for example, does not leave there until March, as happened to Father Rosete and me as well as to many others. If the commanding officers had been requested (as I have suggested) to have a squadron or force here to escort the fathers as soon as they reach El Paso, they would not tarry here nor would this failing be noted. This is a sea of land, and, just as there are delays of six or more months in Cádiz for lack of a ship, or convoy, so there is also a delay here for lack of a cordon.

The friars who came from Spain reached this pueblo with the Lord Governor Anza on the twenty-seventh of last month, and they have not left by this date, nor is it known when they will leave for the in-

30. BNM, leg. 10, no. 53.

terior.[31] Shall we say that the Lord [Governor] Anza or I have detained the fathers in this pueblo? Their delay is because the horses which are to be taken to New Mexico are expected, and they are waiting for them because if they were not being taken there now, they would be kept here for a whole year. And if this happens in the case of those who can give despotic orders for raising a force to escort them, what is a poor custos, who has no authority for this and finds no other expedient, to do? Fathers Dueñas, Velasco, and Fernández reached here in April, and by the rare coincidence that Captain Borica had come out in May, they had the good fortune to leave in June and they entered New Mexico in July. By a similar lucky chance fathers Carmona and Narro arrived in September and went to the interior at the end of January of this year of 1778. Was it possible to certify them in less than a year? Lord [Governor] Mendinueta promised that if the friars entered by March, he would certify them at the end of the year as if they had started in January. The first father mentioned arrived in July, and he was unwilling to certify them even though Father Vélez and I gave him reasons he might use in order to be able to do so without detriment to his conscience or defrauding the King. Fray Silvestre served the King by spending some time in searching the government archive, and although Lord [Governor] Mendinueta wanted to certify to this, the father did not permit it because of the rumors that many of the religious were al-

ready spreading about this. Let your Very Reverend Paternity realize that the lack of certifications for seven religious is not my fault but results from long-standing neglect with regard to what pertains to the benefit of the Custody and its religious. And although I have proposed the means in truthful reports, I have not seen anything under way yet.

I have delivered to the Reverend Father Custos all the accounts for dispatches and spolia of deceased friars. I have been deeply perturbed by the realization that my faithful conduct [is considered] superfluity; and in accordance with the most authentic testimonies, the Custody is not (as has been thought) in debt, indeed it has the sum of 196 pesos 4 reales absolutely clear. And although the failure to report the spolia of the deceased Father Salas was an omission, the reason was that Father Dueñas, who took care of the matter and has the records, has not been able to come. But this will be done with the same exactitude as the other. I have in my possession a certification of everything and one which will always protect my good name.

May Our Lord felicitate your Very Reverend Paternity in the greatest exaltation many years for my veneration. El Paso and October 12, 1778.

Our Very Reverend Father Minister Provincial,

Your humblest subject and most favored son, who venerates and loves you, kisses your hands.

Fray Francisco Atanasio Domínguez
(rubric)

X

To Provincial Fray Martín Francisco de Cruzealegui
Real Presidio de Janos, May 1, 1795[32]

Our Father:

Because I have been serving the King and my province as missionary in New Mexico

---

31. In 1778, Fray Juan Bautista Dozal, to whom this letter is addressed, brought forty-six friars from Spain. Eighteen of them were assigned to the Custody of New Mexico and made the journey there with Juan Bautista de Anza, who had been appointed governor in May, 1777. BNM, leg. 27, exp. 2; MN, Asuntos 188; see also Thomas, *Forgotten frontiers.* In a letter dated at Mexico City, May 23, 1778, Fray Juan Bautista Dozal, Minister Provincial, asked Custos Hinojosa for a report on the Custody and that the latter get information from Domínguez. AASF, 1769 (Patentes, 1769-1807), no. 2, doc. 6.

32. MN, Asuntos 238.

and as a chaplain in presidios of Nueva Vizcaya for twenty years, I now seek shelter under the beneficent shadow of your Very Reverend Paternity's wing and beg you with the greatest possible humility that, as a consequence of your compassion, you show it to me in the forthcoming chapter of 1796 so that by your means and powerful influence the status and exemptions of definitor may be granted to and obtained for me, since I deserve it for said period. And although my Holy Province has never been unaware of my merits and services and also of my religious procedures, there are in my possession documents to prove my claims in and out of court. But I have not known how to ask the fathers custos for any. Therefore,

I urgently entreat your Very Reverend Paternity to deign to instruct me on this point and to believe that my gratitude and acknowledgment of this new and conspicuous benefit will be as eternal as the profound respect with which I have the honor to be of your Very Reverend Paternity.

Our father, your most unworthy subject,

Fray Francisco Atanasio Domínguez
(rubric)

Real Presidio of Janos, May 1, 1795.
To our Very Reverend Minister Provincial Fray Martín Francisco de Cruzealegui.

Received on the twenty-seventh of the same month.

Letters

of Fray Silvestre Vélez de Escalante, 1775 to 1776.

I

To Fray Fernando Antonio Gómez
Zuñi, August 18, 1775[1]

Very reverend and beloved Father Fray Fernando Antonio Gómez:

Your Paternity will already know from two letters preceding this one that Fray Damián [Martín], obliged to do so by his infirmities, left me alone in Zuñi and returned to El Paso. And by the date of this letter he must be at least as far as Chihuahua on his way to the Province, according to what the Father Custos says in a letter which I have just seen. And surely, since he cannot live in Zuñi, he has done very well not to

remain in the Custody, and his return has given me the greatest satisfaction, because tranquillity is not achieved away from Zuñi as it is here in this mission, for it is the best one in the kingdom, and the only disadvantage it has is being 30 leagues from the nearest one. This is bad for one who lacks a companion, like myself at present because Fray Damián has left me alone on account of his illnesses. Therefore I desire a companion to come as soon as possible. In my opinion, the most suitable is Father Oyarzábal, who has written me that he is seeking to come, unless he has perhaps changed his mind. Let your Paternity encourage it, for you will thereby do great service to God, because in accordance with his character and other circumstances he is very suited to joining me in said mission.

In the month of June I entered Moqui, where I remained for a week, well attended by those wretched infidels, obstinate in their foolish libertinism, especially those who govern, who impede with terrible threats the conversion of their inferiors and subjects because they fear *(et non temere)* that they will be abused and almost enslaved by the Spaniards if they submit. A falsehood in which the demon succeeds in holding them by some sadly undeniable truths. I pointed out to them the good for which they were created and the eternal evil to which their infidelity is leading them, but for my great sins I achieved only the sorrow of leaving them in their obstinacy, although I did succeed in my intentions in other matters.

The first pueblo of Moqui is a little more than 46 leagues to the west of Zuñi. Today the province of Moqui has seven pueblos in an area of somewhat less than 5 leagues. The last pueblo to the west (which is called Oraybe) is the largest one there is in these regions. It is arranged like a chessboard, with well made and open streets in all directions. It has eleven rather long blocks two stories high, not counting more new buildings that are being added to it. In this pueblo alone there must be nearly four thousand souls. The Moquinos have many flocks of sheep; they harvest maize in the greatest abundance; they also gather cotton, etc. They are governed in quite a civilized fashion, and most of them are affable and well-inclined. They have all they need, and therefore they harm no one if they are not first given provocation. This suffices for your Paternity to have some information about said province and to commend to God

1. AGM, Historia, vol. 52, exp. 14. We include this letter to clarify the letters of May 21 and July 29, 1776, which follow, as well as Vélez de Escalante's reasoning about the route to Monterey and the possibility of reaching there.

the repair of such lamentable perdition.

One of the principal motives for my expedition to Moqui was to find out everything possible with regard to the communications those at Monterey seek with those of New Mexico. Therefore it was my intention to go on to Cosnina if the information should promise any favorable discovery, but since it was not as I had thought, I did not put this into effect. When I reached the first pueblo of Moqui, a Cosnina was there. After seeing me he promptly left to notify his ranchería, and its captain decided to come to see me with his people. When they were already near Oraybe, the Moquinos made them go back, saying that I had already left Moqui. Therefore they returned, and the captain sent one to see whether he might overtake me, as he did, for I had not left Moqui. I discussed the matter with him, and the account that he gave to me was the following:

The land where the Cosninas dwell is six days of bad road west of Oraybe, although there are already some rancherías of them three days away. Beyond the last rancherías (about nine days' travel from Oraybe) there is a very high sierra which stretches more than 100 leagues from northeast to southwest, tending toward the west, at the north skirt of which the Río Grande (de los Misterios) runs west, impassable by the Cosninas and those bordering on them. The Cosninas do not know what people there are on the other side of the river, nor even whether there are any, since they never cross it nor have they seen signs of them.

On this side, near the sierra, nine days' journey west of this Cosnina, there is a nation which speaks the same language and is called Jomascabas. Fourteen days from these are others whom they call Chirumas. They are warriors, thieves, and savages, because they eat the human flesh of those they kill in their campaigns. The Cosninas have learned from these Chirimas [sic] that there are Spaniards in that direction, although at a distance, because the said Chirumas go raiding in the lands of those Spaniards. This is what the Cosnina told me, agreeing with the information the Moquinos had given me earlier. The said Río Grande is a confluence of several rivers that come down from the Yutas and join before they reach the sierra of Cosnina, perhaps going on to join the Río Gila before entering the inlet, or estuary, which divides California from this continent, and which they call Río Colorado for another name. The Chirumas, I believe, are those they call Choromas in Sonora, and the Spaniards of Sonora those whom they rob and attack. The fact that I heard from the Cosnina the same thing about the Chirumas that is experienced and suffered in Sonora from the Cholomas gives rise to this conjecture; as well as the similarity of the name, the fact that both they and the aforesaid Spaniards are on this side of the river and in the direction where Sonora ends. And therefore the way to Monterey is not and cannot be, in my opinion, via the province of Moqui, which, as I have said, is west of Zuñi. I judge that the route must be sought through the Yutas, to the west northwest of them.

And although my Mother the Province has urged and does urge us to promote this discovery, not all the means under discussion are practicable, because one of the chief ones would be by letter, availing ourselves of some bordering tribe. I do not consider this attainable, because none will be found who can reach there unharmed or who will dare to take it to Monterey, since by special providence of the Most High, all the majority of the infidel nations are enemies. Moreover, so far as I can judge, it is at the very least 400 leagues from New Mexico to Monterey.

The method, if I am not mistaken, which would be suitable would be for his Majesty to bear the expenses of twenty men, or a few more, giving them the same amount daily as the soldiers of this land for three months at least, in order that, led by some intelligent person who would take the enterprise to heart, they might reach said Monterey and reconnoiter the intervening provinces. There are men of valor here, unencumbered by wives and children, who would undertake the journey for the said daily wage alone. There is also a *paisano* here, called Don Bernardo Miera, clever enough for the affair, and even I would sacrifice myself for such an undertaking. Here it is believed that the Spaniards or white people whom the Yutas say they have seen many times may be descendants from those 300 soldiers whom Captain Alvarado left when he entered by the Río Colorado at the beginning of the conquest.[2] I do not give great weight

2. Evidently a reference to Captain Hernando de Alvarado of the Coronado expedition, and to a legend Vélez de Escalante found current among New Mexicans. This tradition, however, does not agree with anything we know about Alvarado's activities. See G. P. Hammond and A. Rey, *Narratives of the Coronado Expedition* (Albuquerque, 1940) and H. E. Bolton, *Coronado on the Turquoise Trail* (Albuquerque, 1949).

A related, and equally unsubstantiated, eighteenth-century tale has been perpetuated to the present day. This is the story that the suburb of Analco at Santa Fe was originally settled by Tlascalan Indians who came with the "first Spaniards." See Urrutia Plan, p. 10 *supra*. Vélez de Escalante evidently read Tlascalan instead of "Mexican," in the 1680 Revolt journals of Otermín (DHM, pp. 117-18; HS, 1: 99; Twitchell translation, SANM, 2: 271) and so helped to preserve the legend. The earliest reference we have found to Mexican Indians living in the vicinity of the church of San Miguel (we do not find the name Analco until later) is dated 1640. AGI, Patronato, leg. 244, ramo 7. Since the voluminous Oñate papers make no reference to Mexican auxiliaries, we can only assume that these Indians, from the Valley of Mexico and vicinity, had come to New Mexico in the wagon trains, perhaps in the entourages of officials, or perhaps brought by the Franciscans in accordance with an old policy of "seeding" newly conquered areas with Christianized Indians to facilitate the work of conversion. The Mexican Indians did not return to New Mexico after the Pueblo Revolt, and in 1776 the inhabitants of Analco were genízaros. The Alvarado legend appears to be another version of the old New Mexico myth about the Spanish and Tlascalan deserters from Coronado's army who were believed to have settled in "Tiguex." Cf. n. 64, p. 37 *supra*.

to this opinion, but if it were true, this discovery would be of the utmost utility and service to both Majesties [Divine and human].

The kingdom is lost, both for lack of supplies and because of the continual incursions of the Comanches and Gileños who are finishing off the people and their property. A general campaign has been proclaimed for the second day of October next; perhaps it will be able to check the enemies somewhat.

An exact account of Monterey and its limits and of the Indians who are known on the east and south would be very useful to me.

I had some things to consult your Paternity about, but the urgency of the present mail does not permit me to do so. And therefore I remain begging Our Lord to preserve your Paternity's important life for me. Mission of Nuestra Señora de Guadalupe de Zuñi and August 18, 1775.

I kiss your Reverend Paternity's hands.

Fray Silvestre Vélez de Escalante

II

To Provincial Fray Isidro Murillo
Zuñi, May 21, 1776[3]

Our Very Reverend and beloved Father:

I have received the highly valued communication which your Paternity deigned to write me on November 6 of last year, and I thank your Paternity for the paternal love with which you instruct my simplicity and correct my ignorance, while overlooking my defects as much as possible. I trust in your religious zeal that having begun this without being asked by me, you will continue to do so at my request, enlightening me abundantly so that even in the most difficult matters I shall be sure of finding the proper solution. And therefore I shall take pleasure in carrying out the orders your Paternity

3. BNM, leg. 10, no. 25.

gives me in the letter I have cited. I might well finish my reply at this point, but the filial love I profess for your Paternity does not permit me to leave you as uneasy and suspicious as you have reason to be with regard to my conduct, especially in the matter alluded to. Therefore I now explain to your Paternity, as my father and prelate, the manner in which I have proceeded.

In the first place, I say that the reason why I have not addressed my letters to the Provincial office was that I received no order or request about these things from it. On the contrary, it was the Reverend Father Gómez and no other who suggested them to me on behalf of my most beloved Mother the Province and who has furnished all the relevant information he has been able to acquire. Therefore it never occurred to me that I would be guilty of disrespect in signifying my obedience through the same channel and in the same way that I was notified of the command. But I now realize that I proceeded without due reflection in matters of great moment, and henceforth I will act in conformity with the prudent orders of your Paternity in so far as God grants me the means to do so.

Before entering Moqui I wrote to the Reverend Father Vice-Custos asking permission, which he granted, as is of record in two of his letters which I have kept. Although he did not give me any help of Indians or settlers, the governor knew about my intention beforehand, for Don Diego Borica showed him a letter in which I notified him of it. Although seventeen Zuñis and their alcalde mayor accompanied me, they went voluntarily to trade under the license which suffices for this purpose according to local custom. To write the report, of which your Paternity will have seen a copy, I also obtained permission beforehand from the Reverend Father Vice-Custos.

With regard to the friendship and good relations which your Paternity says we should endeavor to cultivate with Don Diego Borica, I have already conveyed your Paternity's admonition to the religious I have been able to see. Long before this I had formed a close friendship with him, and I am trying to keep it with this gentleman and with the lord governor. And to both I owe unequivocal expressions of the most sincere affection and friendly confidence. Indeed, if I am to speak with due frankness, I should prefer that it were not so great, for my youth and lack of talent do not compass the discretion necessary to marry politics with the religious state and the priesthood. Moreover, it usually deprives me of the peace I thought I should find in this out-of-the-way place.

And although it might be considered necessary to present to his Excellency [the viceroy] the copy I enclosed in my letter to the Reverend Father Gómez, since it may not have been presented because of the need to copy it in another hand, I now remit for the purpose another ordinary one with the date of the original only so that even if it is presented with another paper that I am also remitting about the same affair, it may be possible to say that the copy was delayed on the journey; and if the other has been presented, I say in this second paper that I had already sent it. In this way, in my opinion, the contradiction which might otherwise be noted is in any event avoided. After my report was read here, an extract of most of it was made except for what I say in regard to the reduction of the Moqui Indians. And because the copy his Excellency remitted, which I am also keeping—it concerns what Captain Don Francisco Antonio Crespo did last year—took the reduction of the Moqui for granted since I have already explained that it is possible, it was feared that if my complete report should reach his Excellency's hands, the reduction would be undertaken in the only manner by which it can be obtained if we do not expect miracles, thereby not using the methods which should be tried first. And as a result of ill-founded fear of unusual difficulties, the very reflections I impugn in the aforesaid paper were

represented to his Excellency, showing great ignorance of how much our missionary brethren have labored to reduce those rebels. It is falsely stated that they are docile people ready for reduction by those who might wish to undertake it, and that they will be more easily subdued by gentle measures than by subjecting them first. Is this not the same as saying that the religious of this Custody have not made the effort they should to reduce the Moqui? His Excellency praises my expedition in hyperboles, and in so doing he implies that no one has labored to this end before. Let your Paternity not forget the reports which have gone from this kingdom against our brothers and which are preserved in the Royal Archive of Mexico, for if we are silent now, what judgment will his Excellency form of us? What will the Royal Tribunal think? What the Council? What our Catholic Monarch? This, our father, is the reason I have taken my pen in hand to start at the very beginning to relate what I have been able to find out for certain about the diligence with which the religious of this Custody have sought the eternal welfare of the Moqui Indians. I set down all the considerations to the contrary as they have occurred to me in order to remove any possible suspicion that some spirit of partiality may have inspired the replies, and to make these more acceptable. God indeed knows that my only purpose is that His Majesty be better served and worshipped where He is insulted and outraged. There is no need for me to represent to your Paternity how important any possible activity in this matter is to the greater glory of God, benefit of so many poor wretches, and honor of our teaching, for your Paternity knows this far better than I.[4] And so I only beg God to bestow His grace upon you and to

4. On April 30, 1776, Vélez de Escalante had sent his Moqui Diary to Murillo with a covering letter. O. Maas, *Viajes de misioneros franciscanos á la conquista del Nuevo México* (Seville, 1915), pp. 64-80. He had previously given his report and diary to Governor Mendinueta on October 28, 1775, and the

preserve your important life in it for many years.

Mission of Nuestra Señora Guadalupe de Zuñi and May 21, 1776.

Your Very Reverend Paternity's most affectionate godchild and subject, who venerates you, kisses your hands.

Fray Silvestre Vélez de Escalante (rubric)

III

To Provincial Fray Isidro Murillo
Santa Fe, July 29, 1776[5]

Our Very Reverend Father Minister Provincial Fray Isidro Murillo.
Our venerated and very beloved father:

Being in this Villa of Santa Fe by order of the Reverend Father Visitor to discuss certain matters of importance to the Order and the Crown, which I do not stop to mention because said Reverend Father Visitor is communicating them to your Paternity in the letter he is now writing to him, the lord governor of this kingdom told me what the Most Excellent Lord Viceroy wrote to him on March 20 about the proposal I made in August of last year: That is, that with twenty men properly equipped, etc., the desired discovery which we are undertaking at present could be carried out. And in order for his lordship [the governor] to give his Excellency [the viceroy] the opinion he requests about the number of men and auxiliaries that would be necessary to make this attempt with some probability of success, he discussed the matter with me, not, in my

opinion, because he finds the necessary talent in me, for I do not have it, but just because he knows that I am daily trying in every possible way to acquire helpful information. By virtue of this I replied to his lordship as follows and as I have already indicated at the end of my report.

Monterey is more than [400] leagues from this capital. The direction in which the intervening territory can be crossed is not known, for although there is some information about the country the Yutas occupy as far as the Río del Tizón and about the tribes who are on the other bank of this river, it is not all credible, for long experience has shown that not only the infidel Indians, but even the Christians, in order to raise themselves in our esteem, tell us what they know we want to hear, without being embarrassed by the falsity of their tales.[6] With regard to the proposal I made to my prelates, which is that the said discovery could be accomplished with twenty men, I state that I proposed this number as sufficient to find out whether the Spaniards whom the Yutas and others say are on the other side of the Río del Tizón are really there and who they are, but not to go as far as Monterey, which is doubtless much farther, and the character and number of the intervening tribes are unknown.

With regard to Don Bernardo de Miera, I state that, if I am not mistaken, I merely said in my letter that he would be useful as one of those who were to go, not to command the expedition, but to make a map of the terrain explored. And I state that only for this do I consider him useful.

And although I confess that my letter, with no other preceding it, indicates that my idea envisions the possibility of reaching Monterey with twenty men, I state that this has never seemed attainable to me with so few men and that I did not convey my mean-

---

governor had made use of them for his own reports and opinions. AGM, Historia, vols. 25, 52. On May 6, 1776, Vélez de Escalante wrote to Murillo expressing in very strong terms his opinion that the Moquis could only be reduced by force of arms and that the use of such force could be legally justified on the ground that they were rebellious vassals of the Crown. Maas, *op. cit.,* pp. 81-88. The letters of October 28 and May 6 [16?] are translated in A. B. Thomas, *Forgotten frontiers* (Norman, 1932), pp. 150-66.

5. BNM, leg. 10, no. 32.

6. Father Vélez de Escalante lays the finger on a practice which had misled Spanish explorers and missionaries from the days of Coronado and Fray Marcos de Niza on.

ing more clearly to my prelates because their paternities, according to the letter in which they exhorted and commanded the religious of this Custody to make every possible effort to further this matter, believe that the aforesaid Spaniards [near the Río del Tizón] are the ones at Monterey.

This is, our father, almost literally what I replied to the lord governor, and I explain it to your Paternity so that you may know in full what I am doing and saying in fulfillment of your orders and desire for the salvation of souls. On this basis, although I do consider the journey we are beginning today proper and useful, and although I am not without hope of reaching Monterey, all I explained in the above opinion is the truth; for although I say that it has never seemed possible of attainment with so few men, I do feel that there is enough probability of success in the latter to risk expense

to the royal treasury, which must always be incurred in the least doubtful matters; not because in going without noise of arms (which usually terrifies the tribes encountered on the way, and therefore there must be a sufficient force or none at all) I may not have conceived some probable hope that God will facilitate our passage as far as befits His honor, glory, and the fulfillment of the will of the All High that all men be saved. The shortness of time and the many very necessary occupations of this day permit me to say only this.

I shall be gratified that your Paternity enjoys good health and that God keeps you in it many years in His grace. Santa Fe and July 29, 1776.

Our Very Reverend Paternity, your least subject kisses your Reverend Paternity's hand. Fray Silvestre Vélez de Escalante.

Observations

on the Administration of the New Mexico Missions, by Fray Joaquín de Jesús Ruiz, missionary at Jémez. 1776.[1]

In the course of his juridical visitation of these interior missions of [the Custody] of the Conversion of St. Paul of New Mexico, Our Reverend Father Commissary Visitor Fray Francisco Atanasio Domínguez visited this one of San Diego of the Jémez Indians. Having seen the manner of administration, both spiritual and temporal, he commands me (by a decree which will be found on leaves 4 and 5 of the book of the Directive) to affix to a board the whole system of ad-

ministration and to make a copy of this and remit it to him. Duly carrying out this order, I have done so, and it is as follows:

MASS

The bell is rung at sunrise.[2] The married men enter, each one with his wife, and they kneel together in a row on each side of the nave of the church. Each couple has its own place designated in accordance with the census list. When there are many, the married couples make two rows on each side, the two men in the middle and the women at the sides. This may seem a superficial matter, but it is not, for experience has taught me that when these women are together they spend all the time dedicated to prayer and Mass in gossip, showing one another their glass beads, ribbons, medals, etc., telling who gave them to them or how they obtained them, and other mischief. Therefore the religious who has charge of the administration must have a care in this regard. After all, it is a house of prayer, not of chitchat.

The widowers and widows form another row, the widows on the Gospel side and the widowers on the Epistle side, leaving the passage from the altar to the door of the church free for the ceremonies of Asperges and [nuptial] veiling.[3]

From the pulpit to the altar on the Epistle side are seated in order the boys receiving instructions in doctrine, as I shall explain below. The girls are on the Gospel side. Beside them are the two fiscales mayores and their subordinates, six in number, so that they may not permit them to play games and laugh (which they do even under this regime) or play pranks or fall asleep or draw unseemly things upon the wall.

The petty governor and his lieutenant have their places at the door so that the people may not leave during the hour of prayer and Mass.

When all are in their places, the fiscal mayor notifies the father, who comes down with his census lists and takes attendance to see whether everyone is there, whether they are in their proper places, and whether their hair is unbound. If anyone is missing, the petty governor goes to fetch him. If he is not in the pueblo, it is indicated by the thong and he is punished on the following Sunday or holy day of obligation. If the truant is a woman, her husband is sent to fetch her.

Three of the little choirboys and two assistants are rehearsed, and the chief one intones half-chanting and the accompanists reply in ordinary fashion. Lest the devotions become burdensome, one day they recite (with a pause) from "Every faithful Christian" to the Articles; the next day from the Commandments to the Confession. On both days they end with the Angelic Salutation, and also on the third day when they recite the declaration of the principal Mysteries as far as the explanation of the Sacrament of the Eucharist. According to the judgment of the father minister, before or after the devotions the interpreter may give a little sermon leading to some understanding of what they have recited or are about to recite. But let it be brief, for if this wearies them, what would a long sermon do?

On Sundays, after they finish the devotions, the little choirboys ascend to the choir for the Asperges; and while the father is putting on his chasuble they descend to their appointed place, which is the same as for the devotions.

All the little sacristans are in front of the altar with their arms crossed, and all make the responses and serve at Mass. The musicians play until the elevation of the chalice and sing the hymn in praise of the Most Holy Trinity, and the people make the response.

After Mass is over, if the minister thinks that some have left, he summons them in accordance with the list and punishes anyone who does such a thing. He severely reprimands the petty governor who permits it.

If there is a baptism to be performed, let it be before Mass so that the mother (who

1. BNM, leg. 10, nos. 20, 21. A translation of the version of this in AGM, Historia, vol. 25, is in HB, 3: 502-06. There is also another shorter version in BNM, leg. 10, no. 12, which does not go into so much detail with regard to the management of the mission, but does make some statements about the behavior of certain alcaldes not included in the official fulfillment of Domínguez' order translated here.

2. BNM, leg. 10, no. 12: "The bell is rung when the sun is as high as two pikes, so that Mass begins at eight."

3. BNM, leg. 10, no. 12: "leaving the passage free for the entrance of the settlers, Asperges, etc."

always comes) and the godmother may hear Mass and pray. Do not entrust the key of the baptistery to the sacristans. Take great care lest they steal the holy oils and the consecrated water for their superstitions. Remove the water from the font in winter so that the bowl may not be damaged by ice.

Keep your cloth vestments in your cell, for even if the chest in the sacristy is good, there are many mice.

The lists of married men and widowers are so arranged that if any one is guilty of absence, this is indicated by the thong. In case they are usefully employed in the royal service or their own affairs, each married man or widower has a hole drilled in his card and there are some little pegs at the top of the board which fit into the holes, and in this way those on legitimate business are distinguished from the truants.

RELIGIOUS INSTRUCTION

In the morning the bell is rung at the same hour as for Mass, and in the evening, before sunset.[4] All the unmarried people come, even if they are old, and some young married women who have not yet borne children or who were married (for urgent reasons) before they knew the Christian doctrine well, and all the children over six years of age. In the summer they gather at the north portal; in the winter, in the cemetery. Some will say that it is unsuitable to have them come here to these places because the church is intended for this purpose and these functions are held in the church in all the missions. Moreover, they will say that it is cold in winter, the cemetery is full of snow, and it is an unkind thing. With my fathers' permission I shall say that when I came to this mission and went down to the church at the hour for devotions, I saw youths and girls romping, laughing, and

pulling one another around by the fringe of their buckskins or blankets, and the women by their girdles, and, during a certain prayer, a nude fiscal with his private parts uncovered performing many obscene acts. So if one has compassion, they do not pray; and since they only behave this way when there is comfort, let him not grieve for them. And if they have no pity in their dances, especially one they call the arrow dance, during which youths and old men remain kneeling attentively even when the snow is half a vara deep, with the chief female dancer in the middle, dancing in a cross, leaping from one side to another, melting the snow with her feet, why should it be pitiful for them to take part in the Divine Offices in the cold or snow?

They all gather in the places mentioned, and the boys form three rows according to age so that the little ones are in front, separated from one another to prevent them from talking. The women take their places in similar fashion. In front of the women are the little choirboys in the same manner as at the Sunday services at the church, and they divide the prayers in the way already described. After they are ended in the afternoon with the hymn in praise of the Sacrament and the Salutation, they sing the response and the minister intones the verses and prayer. For this occasion there is a sacristan in the tower, and he tolls the bell.[5]

4. BNM, leg. 10, no. 12: "In summer the bell is rung at sunrise, and in winter when it is as high as a pike."

5. BNM, leg. 10, no. 12: "The catechumens assemble in the cemetery. Each one has his appointed place, and the fiscal mayor endeavors to prevent them from changing places so that the father minister may easily see who is absent and not have to take time to use the census list. For recitation, all the little ones, both the little men and the little women, are placed at the front, about half a vara apart to prevent them from talking and amusing one another with gestures that distract attention. The girls are placed behind them in the same way, with their faces uncovered. They are not allowed to cover their faces with their blankets, for then they keep eating grains of toasted maize and chewing some nasty stuff they are addicted to. Behind them are the youths in the same order. Two choirboys stand with the catechism in their hands and begin reciting aloud, and

GOVERNMENT OF CHOIRBOYS AND LITTLE SACRISTANS

There are six choirboys. On their boards they have the office of sung Masses, the Introits, Graduals, Offertories, and Communions. The daily Masses follow the missal. Five of them know how to read, and although the sixth cannot, he sings the same as the other five. After breakfast they come to the convent, go over the reading or singing, and depart. The father minister does not let go of their hands until they are men, for if he turns his back, all his labors are lost. The Latin language should be emphasized, for this is the principal goal. They read this better than Castilian. They have the burial service for adults written down on boards, and that for children on a card. On the aforesaid they also have the responses for the Day of the Dead and the manner of receiving the prelate. When there is a burial, whether of an adult or a child, the office for the dead is performed at the door of the church, and from there to the grave.

The little sacristans come with the choirboys, go over their rehearsal or lesson for serving at Mass, and depart. Both these and the choirboys are the ones who repair the cells, shell the maize, or perform other manual chores that occur to the ministers,

---

all make the responses. . . . After prayers, the choirboy of the week assembles the sacristans and the little girls who serve in the convent with the fiscal of the week and hears them say the prayers in the order in the catechism. After this the father minister endeavors to appoint and dismiss the cooks, not permitting them to sleep in the convent under any pretext whatsoever. Neither should he allow them to consort with the sacristans and other youths in the kitchen, but be stern with them without beating them. For a second offense, have the fiscal punish them. At the ringing of the Ave Maria these [sacristans] come to the cell to recite the Angelic Salutation with the minister. When there is some plastering, whitewashing, or other work to be done in the convent, do not allow them to work together, for they do not behave as they should and there are unfortunate results."

and as a result there is no uproar or restlessness, and it helps them to perfect themselves in the Spanish language.

When a settler is to be buried and his people desire a solemn ceremony, the parties are asked to pay two long pesos for the choirboys, for they are very much in their debt. If the mourners do not dig the grave, they give the fiscal for the week a peso. It is true that this happens once in a century, for those who have something to live on seem to be an immortal breed, and only those wretches die who, instead of bringing something, oblige the father minister to pay for *atole*, for the mourners are feebler than the dead.

KITCHEN

There are two, summer and winter. The cooking is done with charcoal winter and summer; this makes things much easier for the people, since the little loads of coal that two boys, who are assigned each week, bring at the hour of evening doctrine would not be matched [in wood] by using the whole pueblo. The food is better; the cooks are not troubled, and filth does not fall into it. They have their little brick ovens with a grate, and if the father does not care for them himself, he will eat poorly, the pueblo will work carting wood, and he will live in impatience. He should not permit the sacristans to remain in the kitchen or to enter it except for fire or to summon one of the cooks; in the first place, because they do so for wanton dalliance, and in the second place, to eat up the dinner.

The sacristans have their own little separate oven for making chocolate, which is in their quarters at the father's door. These ask permission to go to dinner or supper. Let him keep them within bounds at the door of the cell, for otherwise they are apt to remain in their houses and there will be no one to light the fire, etc.; or there is a confession to hear and they are not ready. Together with the cooks, the water carriers, and the fiscal for the week, they assemble at the stroke of twelve for prayers at the cell and repeat the Angelic Salutation. As soon as the cooks have seasoned the supper, all those mentioned assemble with the chief choirboy to recite the prayers and commandments. Do not excuse them from this and keep your eye on them.

WOOD FOR WINTER

On Sunday when they come to Mass, all without exception bring two logs for the father, the sacristans, and the cooks. Keep this wood in a room, for if you do not, they will take it away again and you will congeal with cold before they bring it back. The sacristans and choirboys bring it up from the cemetery every afternoon during this period. Each boy (and also the women) brings a small log for the kitchen, which is usually in need of it. They do not hand this wood over until after devotions, when they do so one by one. The same system is observed in summer with regard to fodder for the animals, for they each bring a handful and deliver it in the same way as the wood. They bring wood from October until mid-May, and fodder from the latter month up to the time when they take in the maize tops, or husks.

HARVEST

One day they bring the wheat to the north portal. Do not permit them to carry it on their heads or their backs, or let the women come, but have them make carts to bring it in. If you do not watch the fiscales, they will

OBSERVATIONS BY FRAY JUACHIN (JOAQUIN) DE JESUS RUIZ

take it to the threshing floor, either with the intention of carrying it off that night or of letting it get wet and damaged so that they may have an excuse to take it, for they use it in this condition for the bread they make. If there is a fresh breeze early the next day, have them take it to the threshing floor, which is opposite, and keep all the boys and women away, for they will carry it all off, pretending it is chaff. Urge them on to finish the job that day, for otherwise you will be left without enough to eat. As soon as it is clean, all the little sacristans and choirboys put it in the granary. If the fiscal undertakes to have those children under instruction help, give it all up for lost. Those mentioned are enough, and let them be watched. Let them put the maize in carts with the husks on and have the said boys take it up to the roof of the cloister. Here let these same boys husk it, even if it takes three days. Spread it out to dry here on some racks on the roof so that it may not be soiled with mud in rain or snow. And if you do not watch this place, the sacristans and other officials will carry loads of it away. By no means allow the women to take part, for if they go to the cornfields to weed, they cover the grass and join the older youths in wanton and wicked dalliance. If they have anything to do with bringing in the wheat, the fiscales themselves turn their backs to their thefts, and the same is true with regard to the maize.

Two little boys take care of the hogs; and if you overlook it the first time they bring one to you dead, you will never have lard, for what they do is to keep them shut up in one of the houses of the pueblo until they die, and when they don't die of this, they kill them on purpose; and they do many wicked things to the sows, which cause their death. If the shepherd brings you a dead sheep, do not give it to him to eat, for he will not leave you one. If you send for the sheep you have bought, warn them that they are to carry in any that die, for this is the medicine that will ensure the arrival of the

full number. If you pass over these incidents without censure, you will perish.

Do not entrust letters to the fiscal, but to the one who is to carry them. Let him leave directly from the convent for the place to which he is to take them. If not, they will delay or lose them.

Let the father minister realize that these Indians are very tumultuous, daring, and great talkers. Let him always show them a severe countenance and endeavor not to have them come into his presence muffled up, for they are very treacherous. If they see that the minister has spirit, they are subdued, as has happened to me. On one occasion one of them raised his hand against me and struck me in the face. Because I wished to punish him, the pueblo rose against me, and some brought war clubs *(macanas)* and stone axes surreptitiously, so that I had to master them. When our aforesaid Reverend Father Visitor was making his visitation, they raised a tumult to have him remove me, for I had already been there many years.[6] Consider complaints to the alcalde

6. Father Ruiz gives further details about his experiences at Jémez in BNM, leg. 10, no. 12: "I went on to the Jémez mission. They are rebellious and daring Indians, and the Indian who did not attack me or my predecessors thought himself despicable. During the first two years I had some bad times with them, for on three occasions they showed disrespect for me, and the last time this happened, when one went so far as to strike me in the face, Alcalde [Bartolomé] Fernández came to the pueblo by coincidence, and left proclaiming that I was a liar, that no such thing had happened. But God, Who watches over those who endeavor to see that the honor His Majesty deserves is paid Him, wreaked stern justice on the alcalde mentioned, for within two months, in my own cell, his mouth was twisted, he lost his wits, he fell from favor with the government, and he died without recovering. José Miguel de la Peña came in his place. This man set out to skin the Indians, demanding sheep, pregnant cows, maize, etc., in the governor's name, laying such a burden on the six pueblos under his command that the Indians cried out. The ministers were unable to speak up, for the officials are swollen with importance and the ministers unheard, and he who interfered in such cases came out with the decrees at his haunches."

futile, for the one who comes to remedy them or to order tasks done for the support of the missionary cannot punish or reprove. Rest assured that he alone must do the work, as he alone will also receive God's reward.

To enable the father missionary to put the above system of administration into effect in quiet, peace, and tranquillity, it would be necessary to withdraw the alcaldes from the pueblos, for the aim of these gentlemen is to support themselves at the expense of the perdition of the Indians. From this one may infer the divergent goals, the aim of the fathers being to give the Indians spiritual nourishment, and that of the aforesaid gentlemen, to take away even their temporal nourishment, and therefore their spiritual. Since these aims are so opposed, the priests are unable to exercise their ministry, fearful that both the Indians and the chiefs will conjure up a quarrel with them (as they do) and that they will lose their peace of mind. It is no argument to say that I have established a halfway rational and Christian way of life at the Jémez mission, where there is an alcalde, for to attain this I have found it necessary to carry on a war with this man, and although I am a resolute man, I have found myself at the point of abandoning the mission. I have not done so because God has subjected my will to His. I deduce that there is not a father in the Custody who holds a different opinion, for all suffer what only God can tell.[7]

Therefore I say that if what I have seen done in some missions in the Sierra Gorda on the borders of Pimería in Huasteca were done here, the Indians of this kingdom would become as well behaved and indoctrinated as those. The practice in the said missions is as follows. Each mission has a head man. He is a quiet and courageous individual. His duty is to set out on horseback when the bell rings either for Mass or doctrine and make the rounds of the huts of the Indians without leaving out a single soul (unless they are incapacitated). He and the father count them together, and so everyone comes. If, as here, there are pagan Indians nearby, he does not permit them to fraternize without or within the pueblo so that they may not witness their accursed rites and so that they may forget what they professed when they were heathens. He does not allow gatherings at untimely hours, and when there are any, let them be public. He does not permit indecent dances. He endeavors to keep a watch lest they use caves for idolatrous purposes (like these Jémez Indians). Any Indian who leaves, notifies and gives his reasons to the father. He does not allow the settlers to sleep in the houses of the Indians, but in the community house. He does not permit the settlers to annoy, mistreat, or harm the Indians.

If he knows how to read, he sets up a school and has some boys for teaching. Some fools will say that this is the father's duty, but I reply that the King does not pay the

7. The version in BNM, leg. 10, no. 12, enlarges upon this point with specific examples. At Picuris, the alcalde and his lieutenant planted, but the alcalde never showed his face in the pueblo except when he went to collect the harvest. At Acoma, the lieutenant, a half-breed called "El Entenado," forced the Indians to give him a sheep, lard, frijoles, and tortillas weekly. The alcalde mayor of the Acoma–Laguna area made the Indians shear, and took the wool. His successor, Baltasar Baca, so abused Fray Joaquín Rodríguez, minister of Laguna, that he nearly died of hunger and thirst, wandering lost in the hills for three days. Baca's successor, Don Pedro [José] Pino, had not been on peaceful terms with any minister and behaved with the ostentation of a royal judge. Fray José Mariño was at odds with him for three or four years and left the Custody on his account. Conditions at Isleta were even worse, and Alcalde don Francisco Trébol obliged the Indians to do an excessive amount of work on his farm. "All the foregoing is but little and suffices for a rough idea. What the Indians get from the alcaldes is mistreatment and punishment, because I have never seen them do them justice or defend them, either their persons or their property, from their enemies. Therefore it is unprofitable for the pueblos to be governed by the aforesaid [alcaldes], for the Indians will never be civilized, God will never be served, and the sovereign will live under a misconception." Cf. AT, pp. 30-31.

father minister to be a reading master but to be a master of doctrine and to administer the sacraments. If this were anyone's duty, it would be that of the secular priests who have fat incomes. We see that elsewhere pueblos have a schoolmaster, and the community pays the said master for teaching. The result of this is that the Indians are Hispanicized and reach the point of becoming priests. It is more equitable for a schoolmaster to levy some tax on the Indians than for the alcalde to make them work and to pluck them merely because he holds the office of alcalde. But I can only say that it is very hard that they should be pensioned by virtue of their title, as they are, when they yield nothing for the benefit of the aforesaid Indians, as is our Sovereign's intention.

The aforesaid head man sees to it that the herds of horses are kept together and guarded, that the gates are inspected, and (according to the population of the pueblo) he has Indians assigned weekly so that when he hears of a raid, he has them mount and take the horses far enough from the pueblo so that they will not return, and he himself goes back to the pueblo.

The only officials the pueblo should have are the petty governor and his lieutenant, and the chief captain and his lieutenant, for if there are many captains, as there are here, for there are twelve to sixteen, they are youths and negligent, and they think of nothing but riots. This horde of captains intimidates the petty governor, and they take over command and there is no order. Therefore, do not blame the minister when he does not do what he ought to, but blame the one who goes to the lords governor and tells them that said officials are necessary. It is all in their own interest, trampling on the devotion owed to God.

The head man is chosen in consultation with the father minister, and he is immediately subject to the lord governor, who gives him his title and imposes a tax for his support. He cannot increase this by one grain of maize or wheat. This levy is kept in the convent for his maintenance. For example: Each house at Jémez can contribute a *cuartilla* of maize; if there are two families, a quartern of beans, and so in proportion salt, wood, and water. This to be administered by a *topil* [alguacil]. Finally, let him be given a cook, and with this he will have no reason to bother the Indians in their sowings, chores, or herding. The minister has charge of this; therefore the tax assessment is given to him.

They are not permitted to have mills, textile works, or farms; therefore those who exercise the office of head man are poor. And if this is not put into practice, God will never be served and the Sovereign will be deceived.

Fray Joaquín de Jesús Ruiz (rubric)

Yo Fr. Andres Garcia certifico, q. N. R. P. Visitador Fr. Fran.co Atanacio Do
minguez se ha manejado en esta Mission como en las anteriores, sin
hacer mas gasto, q.e el de una comida religiosa trayendo consigo asta
el Chocolate, y sin mas familia, q. la de su Secretario, y un moso, y las
Bestias respectivas, y por ser asi verdad lo firme en esta Mission de la
Villa de Alburquerque à 24 de Mayo de 1776.

Fr. Andres Garcia

Yo Fr. Jose Mediano certifico, q.e N. R. P. Visi
tador Fr. Fran.co Atan.o Dominguez se ha mane
jado en esta Mission, como en las anteriores
sin traver mas gasto, q.e el de una comida
Religiosa, trayendo consigo hasta el chocola
te, y sin mas familia, que la de su Secretario,
y un moso, y las Bestias Respectivas, y por ser
asi verdad lo firme en esta Miss.n de N. S. de
los Dolores de Sandia en 25 de Mayo de 1776.

Fray Jose Mediano

Yo Fr. Mariano Rodriguez de la Torre Certifico q.e
N. R. P. Visitador Fr. Fran.co Athan.l Dominguez, ha
sido su porte en esta Mission como en todas, sin Fra
ser mas gasto, que el de una Comida ordinaria, lo que
aun para q. los relig.s no se estuvieran mando en su
Parente Cordillera para q. assi se execurara, expresando no
sea su orden de estampilla sino real y verdadero
como lo acredita su accion pues el Chocolate que
toma lo trae consigo para su Secretario, y moso que
le acompaña, y aun queria yo mirara un andarse pa
ra su Caminara para q. la hiciera con mas alivio, no
admitio el Convite de q. se pruena su Desinteres, y Religion
lo que por ser verdad lo firme en esta Mision de
N. P. S.to Domingo en treinta de Mayo de mil Sete-
cientos Setenta y Seis.

Fr. Mariano Rodriguez de la Torre

CERTIFICATIONS OF FATHER DOMINGUEZ' GOOD CONDUCT
BY FATHERS ANDRES GARCIA, JOSE MEDRANO,
AND MARIANO RODRIGUEZ DE LA TORRE

DOCUMENTS

Papers

concerning the Sale and Exchange of Lands at La Cañada.[1]

Original paper of sale of the land belonging to the mission of La Cañada made by Father Fray Andrés García, and bought by Don Juan Bautista Vigil. Original license for doing this from the Reverend Father Custos Fray Andrés Varo.

Copy of the writing of exchange of said land and copy of the patent issued beforehand for that purpose. The originals of the writing and patent are in the archive of these interior missions.

In my letter of June 10, 1776, I informed our Father Provincial Murillo about this, and his Paternity ordered me that the said land should be recovered at the expense of the mission of La Cañada. Neither part of this order could be put into effect, because the present minister of the said mission, Fray Manuel Rojo, is steeped in the greatest poverty. Although it is voluntary, it is not praiseworthy, and it has been necessary to give him succor for the alleviation of both ills. Nor [could] the land [be recovered] because Don Juan Bautista Vigil, who bought it, was in possession and had built houses on it. In order, then, to fulfill the order and to remove papers which should not appear in court, this was done:

Land near the convent was sought; the amount asked for it was ascertained (Juan Bautista Vigil did all this at my request); and after the sum of 125 regional pesos in goods the settler wanted had been agreed upon, this amount was given to Vigil, and he was told: "Buy this land in your name; draw up a paper and attend to all the other particulars." When all was done and some days had passed, the syndic went and, appearing before the alcalde with Vigil, he made a proposal to the latter, asking whether he was willing to trade that land of his which is near the convent for the land belonging to the convent, adjoining the old church. Vigil said yes, and the aforesaid was done.

The land cost 125 pesos in regional pesos.

Reduced to silver, they amounted to 61 pesos 7 [tomines] 6 [granos].

As is of record in the papers of accounts of Don Diego de Borica.

For the Province.

Literal copy of the deed of exchange which was made in the mission of Santa Cruz de la Cañada.

In the Villa Nueva de Santa Cruz de la Cañada on the twenty-first day of the month of April of the year 1777, before me, the alcalde mayor and war captain of the jurisdiction and district of said villa, Don Salvador García de Noriega, there appeared Don Clemente Gutiérrez, citizen of the post of Pajarito and syndic of these interior missions of St. Francis, party of the first part, at the request and opinion of the Reverend Father Fray Francisco Atanasio Domínguez, Custos of this Custody of the Conversion of St. Paul of New Mexico, and in the name of the Apostolic See,[2] and Juan Bautista Vigil, party of the second part. And they said that they are agreed and in accord to make, as they did make, a mutual exchange of two pieces of land in this way:

Don Clemente Gutiérrez said that inasmuch as the land belonging to the convent of the said Villa of La Cañada is near the old church and at a distance from the new one, and therefore inconvenient for the mission father of the said villa to be able to harvest some grain from it, in accordance with the request and opinion of said Reverend Father Custos, in the name of the Apostolic See as syndic, administrator of ecclesiastical property, and administrator of all the temporalities pertaining to said missions and to the use of their religious, he exchanged

1. BNM, leg. 10, no. 44.

2. The Franciscan Order may not hold or transfer property under its own name, but under that of the Holy See.

and did exchange the said land for another piece which is next to the new church of said villa on the west and northwest with its owner and legitimate possessor, Don Juan Bautista Vigil, giving him in the name of His Holiness the Roman Pontiff full and incontestable ownership and free possession of the said land pertaining to the said convent and situated in the vicinity of the old church and adjoining on the east lands belonging to Juan José Sandoval and the same Don Juan Bautista Vigil, in such a way that right to, possession, or use of the said land may never be nor can be alleged on behalf of the said convent. And in the same way he received and did receive the other land mentioned near the new church, receiving right to and possession of it in the name of His Holiness.

Don Juan Bautista Vigil said that he willingly accepted and did accept the exchange, receiving for himself and his heirs the said land pertaining to the convent, and that he gave and did give the aforesaid land for it, with full legal ownership, usufruct, and possession, free of ground rent, mortgage, or any other lien, to said Don Clemente Gutiérrez as such syndic, administrator of ecclesiastical property, and administrator for the Holy See, in such a way that neither he nor his heirs may ever allege any right to the said land in or out of court.

It is next to the new church on the west and northwest and runs, after taking out the 40 varas pertaining to the immunity [of ecclesiastical edifices], 54 ordinary Castilian varas in a straight line to the north. This straight line to the north is exactly opposite the west corner of the chapel of Our Lady of Carmel and ends at the point where the 54 aforesaid varas meet another piece of land (which it adjoins here) belonging to Don Juan Pablo Martín, citizen and lieutenant of the pueblo of Abiquiu. From this point the boundary and dividing line runs in a straight line to the west from the aforesaid and from that of the above Don Juan Pablo Martín as far as the *acequia madre* [main irrigation ditch], which serves as the boundary line on the west. On the south it borders on land belonging to Manuela López from the aforesaid irrigation ditch to the wall of the church, the termination and boundary line of both being the foot of the hill on which the house and land of the said Manuela López are.

I inspected all this with the parties and the undersigned witnesses. This land, with the extent and boundaries described, Don Juan Bautista Vigil said that he exchanged and did exchange for that of the convent mentioned above. And the aforesaid syndic, as such, received this same land in the manner stated, whereupon they remained in agreement and content. And after all the above was read to them to the letter, they said it was true and that they firmly ratified the exchange in accordance with every legal form. And in order that it may be of record whenever and wherever necessary, they signed it with me, the said alcalde mayor, and corroborating witnesses with whom I am acting as the court for lack of a notary, because there is no notary of any kind in this kingdom, on the said day, month, and year. Salvador García de Noriega, *juez receptor*.[3] Juan Bautista Vigil. Clemente Gutiérrez, syndic. Francisco Valdés y Bustos, witness. Juan Ignacio de Mestas, witness.

Literal copy of the patent which preceded the writ of exchange.

Fray Francisco Atanasio Domínguez, etc. To the Father Preacher Fray Manuel José Rojo, missionary of Santa Cruz de la Cañada.

Greeting.

Your Reverence has informed me that the grainfield pertaining to that mission is extremely distant, which leads to serious inconvenience and great expense. I therefore immediately ask and beg the syndic of these missions, Don Clemente Gutiérrez, for charity's sake in Our Lord, to exchange the said land for another piece nearer that mission and equally useful, or to take the most fitting action according to law, for the mission will thereby benefit and we shall be favored.

Issued in this mission of Nuestro Padre San Francisco de la Villa de Santa Fe, signed by my hand and name, sealed with the great seal of this Custody, and countersigned by the under-

signed acting secretary, on the ninth day of April, 1777. Fray Francisco Atanasio Domínguez, Custos. By order of his Paternity, Fray Silvestre Vélez de Escalante, acting secretary.

The originals of this patent and of the writing are in the archive of these interior missions of New Mexico.

Villa de Santa Cruz de la Cañada and June 16 of the year 1770. Having seen the permission granted by our Very Reverend Father Fray Andrés Varo, Custos of this Holy Custody of the Conversion of St. Paul of New Mexico, which is of record in the enclosed letter, in accordance with said blessing and license, I proceeded to put into effect the exchange of the piece of land pertaining to this mission in the presence of two witnesses, who were Francisco Valdés y Bustos and Juan Fresquies, who had proof that the said piece of land is on the other side [of the river] at the place and site of the old church, the said land adjoining the rancho of Señor Juan Bautista Vigil, who gave alms in the amount of 100 regional pesos for the fabric of this new church. And it is understood that I have proof that said piece of land pertains to this said mission. And in order that it may be of record for all time that said exchange has been put into effect and that I have received the said alms from said Juan Bautista Vigil, I issued this writing so that in case of litigation he may appear before any royal judge. And in order that it may be of record, I signed it with the two witnesses in the said villa said day, month, and year.

Fray Andrés Garcia (rubric). At the request of Juan Fresquies, *Manuel de Arteaga* (rubric).[4] Witness, *Francisco Valdés y Bustos* (rubric).

I, Juan Bautista Montes Vigil, state that it is true that I have bought from the Very Reverend Father Fray Andrés García the land he mentions above, pertaining to the convent of this Villa Nueva de Santa Cruz de la Cañada, as it is of record that the transfer and assurance of said piece of land has been made to me. And I declare as a Christian that the aforesaid land belongs to my son, Miguel, and that none of

3. The *juez receptor* was a notary commissioned to preside over and record certain legal proceedings, and in this case García de Noriega was acting as such for lack of a notary. Under these circumstances, he was required by law to have two *testigos de asistencia*, or corroborating witnesses, to act with him.

4. Apparently Fresquies did not know how to write.

my [other] sons have any right to said land because they have proof that it was bought with his money, although I was the agent. And in order that it may be of record that this is true and so that none of my sons may be able to make any allegations now or at any time, I state that the land mentioned is his, and in order that it may be of record that this is the truth, I signed it today, September 7 of this present year of 1772.

Juan Bautista Montes Vigil (rubric).

My reverend and esteemed Father Fray Andrés García:

Friend and namesake: I received your esteemed Paternity's good wishes, in accordance with which I arrived safely at these missions of El Paso. And rejoicing to hear of your Paternity's good health, I place mine at your disposition.

And with regard to the report your Paternity gives me about the land claimed by José Antonio López, and with greater right by Juan Bautista Vigil, I say that your Paternity's action was very well taken, since it should be so because of Vigil's better right and the larger contribution he makes for the benefit of the church. And finally, your Paternity will act as one who has the matter at hand, for I will approve everything, provided it is just.

And since I have nothing further to say, I go on to beg God to keep your Paternity many years. Senecu and January 22, 1770.

Your affectionate friend and namesake kisses your Paternity's hands.

Fray Andrés Varo, Custos (rubric).

Papers

concerning the Devotion of the Poor Souls and the Fabric of the churches of Sandia and Picuris.[1]

Copies—two—of the writings that were made regarding the fabric of the churches of Nuestra Señora de los Dolores de Sandia and San Lorenzo de Picuris, in order that those Father Fray Sebastián Fernández made for this purpose, without consulting the prelate and against the opinion of the Father Vice-Custos Fray José Medrano, might be removed, as they were removed and burned. With these are also included the bond of José Martín, citizen of Abiquiu, to pay the 588 ewes he owed said Father Fray Sebastián, who, by his own authority, had founded with that fund a devotion of the Poor Souls, obligating the minister of that mission to a certain number of Masses per year. And although, in his letter of August 7, 1776, our Father Provincial orders me to abolish said devotion and to send the capital, or principal, to the procurator general, the second could not be done because of the insolvency of the debtor, and we shall accept what he promises in this bond, which was made in re-

1. BNM, leg. 10, no. 45.

ligious terms in order that the ewes at least may not be entirely lost, and in order to remove the writing said father made in this regard. It was proper to an absolute master of his own property, and, as I said to our Father Provincial in my letter of June 10, 1776, I abstracted the said writing from the archive of the secular ecclesiastical court. The same father had given it to the ecclesiastical judge, Don Lorenzo Rivera, in person, telling him that said writing pertained to his archive. This is nothing in comparison with the many other greater follies of this friar, who can be proved at any time to be disobedient, owner of property, and a trader, one of the shrewdest who has come to this kingdom.

For the Province.

In the Villa of Santa Fe of New Mexico, on the nineteenth day of the month of April of the year 1777, José Martín, citizen of the pueblo of Santa Rosa Limana of Abiquiu, appeared before me, Lieutenant General don Diego de Borica. And he said that inasmuch as he owes 588 breeding ewes pertaining to the use of the religious of St. Francis of these interior missions, he obligated and bound himself to pay for them to the syndic, Don Clemente Gutiérrez, as such syndic of these religious, or to the syndic general, Don Francisco Duro, citizen and member of the merchant guild of the Villa of Chihuahua, and to those who may succeed him as syndic, within the peremptory period of four years, which shall be counted from the date of this bond, by giving 300 regional pesos a year in maize, or wheat, or mules, or any other regional commodity. For the fulfillment of this he obligated his person and property, both real and movable, present and future, submitting himself to the royal justices for the execution of the payment, renouncing, as he does renounce, the laws in his favor.

And in order that it may be of record, and so that this bond may have due force according to law, I authorized it and signed it with two corroborating witnesses, in whose presence it was made for lack of a notary, because there is none of any kind in this government, on said day, month, and year. Diego de Borica. Clemente Gutiérrez. Witness, Carlos Fernández. Witness, Antonio Moreto.[2] At the request of José Martín, Diego Antonio Baca.

This agrees with the original, which remains in the possession of the syndic of these interior missions, Don Clemente Gutiérrez.

Domínguez (rubric).

In the Villa of Santa Fe of New Mexico on the eighteenth day of the month of April of the year 1777, there appeared before me, Lieutenant General don Diego de Borica, Don Clemente Gutiérrez, syndic of these interior missions of St. Francis, party of the first part, in name of the Apostolic See and at the request and opinion of the Reverend Father Fray Francisco Atanasio Domínguez, Custos of this Custody of the Conversion of St. Paul of New Mexico, and the party of the second part, Don Cristóbal Vigil, lieutenant of militia and lieutenant alcalde mayor of the jurisdiction of the Villa de Santa Cruz de la Cañada. And they said that they have concluded and come to an agreement in this way:

Don Cristóbal Vigil said that he obligated and bound himself to the said syndic as such, and to his successors, or to the syndic general of this Custody, Don Francisco Duro, citizen and member of the merchant guild of the Villa of Chihuahua, and to those who may succeed him as syndic, to proceed with the church of the pueblo and mission of Nuestra Señora de los Dolores de Sandia, which is already started, roofing it in four naves and putting four pillars on each side of the interior, not in the body, or center, of the floor, but a short distance from the lateral walls along the length of the church for greater stability and security of each one of the string boards which are to support and divide the naves; with choir loft, doors and windows, two board ceilings, round beams, corbels, belfry, and the said two windows with gratings. And he obligated and bound himself to do this, under the condition that they must give him twenty-five Indians of the same pueblo

---

2. Not a New Mexico settler, but a member of the governor's staff. SANM, vol. 1, no. 460.

twice a week to help make the block, not the adobes, and to raise this and the timber; but all this not to be in the season when they have work to do on their farms or cultivating the land, nor can he force the said Indians to go to the sierra or give oxen or other help for the said building.

And he said that in accordance with the foregoing he obligated himself to hand over the said church completely finished within the peremptory period of two years, which shall be counted from the date of this bond, in exchange for the amount said syndic is giving and gave him in the name of His Holiness the Roman Pontiff. And the same Don Cristóbal Vigil said that he has already received it and is content with it. It is as follows: 30 head of cattle, 2 mules, 210 deerskins, 25 fanegas of wheat. For the fulfillment of this bond he obligated his person and property, both movable and real, present and future, submitting to the royal justices in everything pertaining to said fulfillment. The aforesaid syndic, Don Clemente Gutiérrez, said that in the name of the Apostolic See he had given to Don Cristóbal Vigil the effects mentioned above, and that in the name of the Holy Apostolic See he accepted and did accept Don Cristóbal Vigil's bond as contained above, in accordance with which both parties remained in agreement and accord. And in order that it may be of record, they signed it along with me and the corroborating witnesses, with whom I am acting for lack of a notary, for there is none of any kind in this government, on said day, month, and year. Cristóbal Vigil. Clemente Gutiérrez. Diego de Borica. Witness, Domingo Lavadia. Witness, Bernardo de Miera y Pacheco.

This agrees with the original, which remains in the possession of the syndic of these interior missions, Don Clemente Gutiérrez.

Domínguez (rubric).

In the Villa of Santa Fe of New Mexico on the eighteenth day of the month of April of the year 1777, there appeared before me, Lieutenant General don Diego Borica, Don Clemente Gutiérrez, syndic of these interior missions of St. Francis, party of the first part, in the name of the Apostolic See and at the request and opinion of the Reverend Father Fray Francisco Atanasio Domínguez, Custos of this Custody of the Conversion of St. Paul of New Mexico, and the party of the second part, Don Salvador García de Noriega, alcalde mayor and war captain of the Villa Nueva de Santa Cruz de la Cañada and its districts. And they said that they have concluded and come to an agreement in this way:

Don Salvador García de Noriega said that he obligated and bound himself to the said syndic as such, and to his successors, or to the syndic general of this Custody, Don Francisco Duro, citizen and member of the merchant guild of Chihuahua, and to those who may succeed him as syndic, to construct the church of the pueblo and mission of San Lorenzo de Picuris, of the size of the old church, with transept, walls, 40-inch guide lines [for the walls], door, and two windows to the east, choir loft with board [floor], corbels, and round beams. And because some beginning has already been made on the site where this church is to be built, I obligate myself, in addition to the above, to build three covered rooms for a dwelling for the missionary religious in such a way that the outside walls of the said rooms may join the church with the pueblo, but I do not obligate myself to put doors or windows on the said three rooms. And he said that he obligated and bound himself to hand it over completely furnished within the peremptory period of a year and six months, which shall be counted from the date of this bond, in return for the sum which said syndic is giving and gave him in the name of His Holiness the Roman Pontiff. And the same Don Salvador García de Noriega said that he has already received it and is content with it. It is as follows: 12 cows, 12 yearling calves, 25 ewes with a stud ram, a fine she-mule, 100 fanegas of maize and wheat, 100 pounds of chocolate.

For its fulfillment he obligated his person and property, both movable and real, present and future, submitting to the royal justices in everything pertaining to said fulfillment. The said syndic, Don Clemente Gutiérrez, said that he had given Don Salvador García de Noriega the foregoing effects in the name of the Holy Apostolic See, and that in the name of the same

Holy See he accepted and did accept the said Don Salvador García de Noriega's bond as contained above, in accordance with which both parties remained in agreement and accord. And in order that it may be of record, they signed it with me and corroborating witnesses, with whom I am acting for lack of a notary, because there is none of any kind in this government. Salvador García de Noriega. Clemente Gutiérrez. Diego de Borica. Witness, José Miguel Tafoya. Witness, José Francisco Maese.

This agrees with the original, which remains in the possession of the syndic of these interior missions, Don Clemente Gutiérrez.

Domínguez (rubric).

Certifications

of Father Domínguez' Good Conduct. 1776.[1]

I, Fray Andrés García, certify that our Reverend Father Visitor Fray Francisco Atanasio Domínguez has behaved at this mission in the same way as at the ones before it, without causing more expense than a religious diet, even bringing chocolate with him. And his family consisted only of his secretary and a servant and their respective animals. And because this is true, I signed it in this mission of the Villa of Albuquerque on May 24, 1776.

Fray Andrés García (rubric).

I, Fray Mariano Rodríguez de la Torre, certify that our Reverend Father Visitor Fray Francisco Atanasio Domínguez has conducted himself at this mission, as at all the missions, without causing more expense than an ordinary diet. And in order that the religious might not exceed in this respect, he even sent his patent to this effect ahead by relay, stating that his order was not for form's sake but sincere and true, as his behavior has verified, for he brings with him for himself and his secretary and the servant who accompany him the chocolate they drink, and even when I wanted him to take a saddle horse for his excursion, he did not accept, which is proof of his disinterest and scrupulousness. Because this is true, I signed it in this mission of Our Father Santo Domingo on May 30, 1776.

Fray Mariano Rodríguez de la Torre (rubric).

I, Fray Juan José de Llanos, missionary in this mission of Our Father San Francisco de Nambe, certify that our Father Commissary Visitor

Fray Francisco Atanasio Domínguez entered this mission on the tenth day of April of this year, 1776, for the sole purpose of making his juridical visitation. He made it in three full days, and he brought with him only the Reverend Secretary and a servant, and also four animals, one of which carried his bed linen and that of his secretary. The only expense he caused this mission was his food, which was the diet of a religious and the same as I have every day. He brought chocolate with him, and he was not even willing to cause this expense. Not even animals for going back and forth were given him from this mission, but he came and went on his own. Because all this is true, I freely and spontaneously certify to it and sign in said mission on April 12, 1776.

Fray José de Llanos (rubric).

1. BNM, leg. 10, no. 31. There are fifteen of these original certifications, all 1776, signed: Fray Andrés García, Albuquerque, May 24; Fray José Medrano, Sandia, May 25; Fray Mariano Rodríguez de la Torre, Santo Domingo, May 30; Fray Juan José de Llanos, Nambe, April 12; Fray Manuel Rojo, Cañada, April 17; Fray Ramón Salas, San Juan, April 20; Fray Andrés Claramonte, Picuris, April 22; Fray José de Olaeta, Taos, April 25; Fray Sebastián Fernández, April 29; Fray Buenaventura Hermida, May 2; Fray Manuel de la Vega, San Ildefonso, May 5; Fray José de Burgos, May 17; Fray Manuel Abadiano, Santa Ana, May 19; Fray Estanislao Mariano de Marulanda, Cochiti, May 14; and Fray Francisco Xavier Dávila, San Felipe Apóstol, May 20. They are very similar in content, and often in wording, and we have translated here only four examples.

I, Fray Andrés Claramonte, missionary in this mission of San Lorenzo de Picuris, certify in so far as I can and should that our Reverend Father Visitor Fray Francisco Atanasio Domínguez entered said mission on Saturday, April 20, and remained in it three days, making his juridical visitation with the greatest efficiency with regard to everything pertaining to it. During the said three days his Reverend Paternity took the necessary nourishment with the scarcity and poverty that the country permits, since I partook of the very food his Reverend Paternity was bringing for his own use, although, indeed, to my extreme mortification, but his prudence, affability, and manner obliged me to accept and receive the favor that his Reverend Paternity deigned to do me. His baggage and family were strictly religious, because all they had came down to four necessary riding beasts, one for his Reverend Paternity himself, one for the Father Secretary, one for the servant, and the other for the bedding to which was added the little linen of the Father Secretary. After this same fashion his Reverend Paternity left for the mission of Taos on Monday, April 22, when his Reverend Paternity was unwilling to take a meager supply of food for the journey. From this action one may infer how great his Reverend Paternity's disinterest must be even in more important matters. I should like to say more, but I do not wish to mortify his religious modesty, etc. And because this is what I feel about the present matter, I issue this on April 22, 1776.

Fray Andrés Claramonte (rubric).

Feligreses de esta Yglesia, Naturales, y moradores al
presente de esta Villa, à quienes adverti su oblig.on
y espiritual parentesco. Y para q conste lo firmè d.ho
dia, mes, y año ut supra.

fray Fran.co Atan.o Dominguez
Miño.

En esta Yglesia de N. S. P. S. Fran.co de la Villa de Santa fee
veinte, y tres dias del mes de Iulio de este año de mil sete
cientos Setenta y seis, Yo Fr. Silvestre Velez de Esca
lante, por encargo del R. P. Fr. Fran.co Atanasio Domin
guez, Baptizè Solemnem.te y puse los santos Oleos à
una Criatura, q nació el Domingo catorce de este
mes de Iulio, y año de Setenta y seis, Hijo legitimo
de Iosè Crespin, y de Gertrudis de Oriosk, Españoles,
feligreses de esta Yglesia, Nativos, y moradores de esta
Villa, y legitimam.te Casados: à quien puse por nombre
Buenaventura de Jesus. Fueron sus Padrinos Blas
Apodaca, y su muger Maria Guadalupe Montaño,
Españoles, feligreses de esta Yglesia, Naturales de esta
Villa, en la qual habitan al presente, à quienes
aduerti su obligacion, y espiritual parentesco. Y
para q conste lo firmè dicho dia, mes, y año ut supra.

Buenaven
tura de Jesus.

fray Fran.co Atan.l Domin.z
Miño.

Fr. Silvestre Velez de Escalante
Baptiz.

PAGE FROM THE BOOK OF BAPTISMS, SANTA FE, JULY 23, 1776,
SIGNED BY FRAY FRANCISCO ATANASIO DOMINGUEZ
AND FRAY SILVESTRE VELEZ DE ESCALANTE

FRANCISCANS
AND SETTLERS

Franciscans

Most of the religious mentioned by Father Domínguez who served in New Mexico are identified in the following list. The material has been accumulated by the authors in the course of their investigations in the extant mission records in New Mexico, the Spanish Archives of New Mexico, the Provincial records and other relevant material preserved in American, Mexican, and Spanish archives and libraries, and standard sources. We have not attempted here to collate or interpret this scattered information nor to cite specific references. In cases where the mission and provincial records do not agree with regard to assignments, the mission records, of course, take precedence, for it was not always feasible to carry out assignments made at headquarters in Mexico City when circumstances in the Custody dictated other arrangements. In some cases, however, one of the pueblos may have been a visita, with the same friar in charge. See INDEX for data given elsewhere in this volume.

ABADIANO, FRAY MANUEL. *Mission:* Entries at San Ildefonso, Feb. 26–Aug. 31, 1769. Zuñi, Dec. 28, 1769–June 23, 1770, probably visiting there from Acoma, for he baptized over 75 persons on May 5, 1770. San Juan, Sept. 16, 1770–April 30, 1774. Santa Ana, May 18, 1774–Jan. 7, 1777. D. Santa Ana, Jan., 1777. *Provincial:* Guadalupe (Junta de los Ríos), 1765. 56 years old, 38 in habit, missionary N.M., 1769. Creole, *padre predicador*, 59 years old, 41 in habit, missionary N.M., 1772. Cochiti, 1772. Picuris, 60 years old, 42 in habit, *c.* 1773. San Juan, 1776.

ACEVEDO, FRAY ANTONIO. Native of Veracruz, professed in Puebla, June 29, 1674. Secretary, Isleta, May, 1682. Expedition to La Junta de los Ríos with Fray Nicolás López and Captain Juan Domínguez de Mendoza, 1683-84. Forced to flee to Parral and returned to El Paso with Custos Fray Salvador Rodríguez de San Antonio, March, 1685. Secretary, Isleta, Dec., 1685. Controversy over validity of his ordination, 1689. San Lorenzo, Dec., 1691, and Jan., 1695. Definitor of Custody, 1695. Nambe, 1695. Santa Fe, Nov., 1695–Nov. 1696; he conducted a small school for boys at this period. Petition, Feb. 7, 1702, citing more than 10 years service in N.M.

AGUILAR, FRAY JUAN. *Provincial:* Pecos, Oct. 26, 1737. Santo Domingo, n.d. (possibly 1731 or 1749). Procurator of N.M. missions, 1760, 1765.

AGUILAR, FRAY PEDRO DÍAZ DE. *Mission:* Entries at Laguna, Jan. 1, 1726–April 26, 1728. Zia, Nov. 22, 1728–Aug. 28, 1729. Albuquerque, Dec., 1733–Jan. 1734. Santa Ana, April 14, 1737. *Provincial:* Laguna, 1729. Zia, 1731. Jémez, 1733. San Cristóbal (Junta de los Ríos), 1736. San Felipe, 1740, 1743.

ALPUENTE, FRAY JUAN. To N.M. with de Vargas and Custos San Antonio, 1693. Chaplain of army, 1694. Zia and Santa Ana, 1694. Pecos, entries Nov. 25, 1695–May 1, 1696. Chaplain of army, 1696.

ALVAREZ, FRAY JUAN. *Mission:* Entries at Tesuque, Oct. 12, 1698–Jan. 14, 1699, Nov. 25, 1704–April 20, 1705, May 8–Nov. 21, 1706.

San Ildefonso, Feb. 2–Aug. 18, 1704. Nambe, Feb. 7, 1707–Nov. 11, 1708. (Tesuque was a visita of Nambe at this period.) *Provincial:* Native of Puerto de Santa María, professed in Puebla, Sept. 8, 1659. Elected custos, Chapter May 24, 1698. Commissary of Inquisition and missionary at La Concepción del Socorro, 1699. Asked exemptions as ex-custos, Feb. 13, 1702. Elected custos, Chapters Aug. 11, 1703, Aug. 8, 1705. *Other:* El Paso, definitor, 1680. Appointment as vicar by Bishop Escañuela, 1681 (see AT, pp. 10-11). San Antonio de Senecu, Aug., 1695. Report of visitation, 1706 (HB, 3: 372-78).

APARICIO, FRAY ANTONIO. Pecos, July, 1714.

ARAÑAGA. See Arranegui.

ARAOS (ARAUZ), FRAY DOMINGO DE. *Mission:* Entries at Albuquerque and Bernalillo, Oct., 1706–Dec., 1708. Zia, May, 1710–Feb., 1718. Jémez, March, June, 1721. Zia, Feb., 1724–May, 1727. Santa Ana, May, 1726–Nov., 1729, residing at Bernalillo. Secretary of visitations by fathers Tello, 1716, Barreda, 1720, Juan de la Cruz, 1721, 1722, Guerrero, 1723. *Provincial:* Professed in Puebla, Aug. 1, 1699. Granted *jubilación de hebdómada* for length of service in N.M. by Chapter, July 5, 1730. *Other:* At Zia before 1706 and ill in El Paso that year. Jémez, July, 1714. Vice-custos and ecclesiastical judge, 1729. D. at Santa Ana, 1731, possibly from poison.

ARBISU (ARBIZU), FRAY JOSÉ. Native of Mexico City, professed in Puebla, Feb. 23, 1679. Martyred at San Cristóbal, June 4, 1696.

ARRANEGUI, FRAY JOSÉ DE. *Mission:* Entries at Pecos, Aug. 12, 1700–Aug. 28, 1708. *Provincial:* Professed in Mexico City, April 20, 1695.

AYETA, FRAY FRANCISCO DE. Native of Pamplona, received habit in Mexico City, Nov. 26, 1659, at age of 19; professed, Nov. 27, 1660. Elected custos of N.M. by Provincial Chapter of July 29, 1676. Elected procurator general of N.M., 1679. Elected procurator general of New Spain, 1679; because of urgency of N.M. affairs, did not go to Madrid until 1683. For his activities in N.M., see HS. As procurator general he displayed great energy in the interests of his Order, obtained many cédulas in favor of the religious, and published a number of works in defense of the Franciscans of various areas. He died in the convent at Madrid about 1700.

BARROSO, FRAY CRISTÓBAL ALONSO. Accompanied de Vargas expedition, 1692. Santa Fe, Feb., 1698—Nov., 1699.

BENAVIDES, FRAY RAFAEL. *Mission:* Albuquerque, March 13, 1774—Nov. 30, 1776. Isleta (El Paso), Dec. 5, 1798—Feb. 23, 1803. D. El Paso, April, 1807. *Provincial:* C. 1771-73, creole, assistant at El Paso, 32 years old, 13 in habit. Zuñi, 1788. Vice-custos at El Paso, *c.* 1778-79. Santa Ana, 1791. Senecu and San Antonio Isleta, 1797, 1800.

BERMEJO, FRAY MANUEL. *Mission:* Zia, May 28, 1750—March 5, 1752. Picuris, May 16, 1753 —May 8, 1755. San Felipe, June, 1755. *Provincial:* Zia, 1750. Cochiti, 1752. *Other:* One of 18 friars who came from Spain to New Spain, 1743. Collaborated with Fray Juan Sanz de Lezaun on reply to charges made by Juan Antonio de Ornedal y Maza, 1750.

BERNAL, FRAY CAYETANO JOSÉ IGNACIO. *Mission:* San Felipe, May 14, 1779—April 12, 1780. Isleta, April 24, 1780—March 22, 1793. Tomé, 1793-95. Belén, 1795-1806. D. at Belén or Tomé April, 1807. *Provincial:* Native of Mexico City, son of Province of Holy Gospel. C. 1771-73, creole, Realito (de San Lorenzo, El Paso), 28 years old, 11 in habit. Isleta del Nuevo México, 1778-79. San Antonio Senecu, San Antonio Isleta, 1788. Custos, 1791, at San Antonio Senecu; 1793, at Santa Fe; 1794, at Belén. Definitor, 1797, 1800, Belén. (Since the mission records place Father Bernal at San Agustín Isleta in N.M., 1780-93, possibly the two Isletas were confused in the Provincial records; as custos, however, it may be that he visited the El Paso area.)

BROTONS (BROTONCO, BROTONI), FRAY FRANCISCO. Santa Fe, August, 1707. Taos, *c.* 1709, 1712.

BURGOS, FRAY JOSÉ DE. *Mission:* Entries at Santa Fe, Sept., 1760—Oct., 1767. Zia, Dec. 15,

1771—July 2, 1772. Aug., 1772, baptized 100 persons at Zuñi. Laguna and Acoma, Dec., 1772. Albuquerque, March 28, 1773—March 6, 1774. Santa Fe, Oct. 24, 1780—Feb. 26, 1781. Pojoaque and Nambe, Jan. 28, 1781—Feb. 27, 1784. Santa Fe, April—July, 1784, July, 1787—Aug., 1788. *Provincial: Lector de gramática,* Santa Fe, 1772.

CAMARGO, FRAY ANTONIO. *Mission:* Entries at Tesuque, Aug. 1 and 7, 1699, Sept. 24, 1700, Nov. 24, 1708—April 25, 1709, May 9, 1712, May 21—Nov. 26, 1713, March 17, 1714. Nambe, Nov. 29, 1708—April 7, 1709, Jan. 19, 1716— May 6, 1718. *Provincial:* Native of Valle Camargo, professed in Mexico City, June 3, 1697. Elected custos, Chapters Feb. 1, 1716, May 4, 1726. Elected procurator, Chapters June 19, 1723, Oct. 14, 1724. Isleta, 1729. Taos, 1731. Acoma, 1733. Guadalupe (Junta de los Ríos), 1736, 1737. *Other:* Procurator, 1706 (HB, 3: 378).

CAMPO REDONDO, FRAY FRANCISCO. *Mission:* Entries at Jémez, April 10—May 27, 1757. Secretary to visitor of missions, 1759. Santa Cruz de la Cañada, April 19, 1760—Dec. 14. 1765. *Other:* Appointed vicar and ecclesiastical judge of district of Villa of La Cañada by Bishop Tamarón (AT, p. 64).

CARMONA, FRAY JOSÉ MARÍA. *Mission:* Entries at Santo Domingo, May 10, 1778—Jan. 30, 1779. *Provincial:* Apparently returned to New Spain, 1779, and went to Puebla as *lector.*

CASTRO, FRAY JACOBO DE. *Provincial:* Elected custos, Chapters May 2, 1752, June 9, 1755, Oct. 23, 1756, Jan. 14, 1758. Custos at El Paso, 1760, 1765. 1769, 50 years old, 34 in habit, *ex-lector* of theology, ex-custos for about 22 years of the two Custodies of Tampico and N.M., for which the Province granted him exemptions of definitor, and present vicar of the Monjas de Santa Isabel of Mexico City. 1772, *ex-lector* of theology, ex-definitor, synodal examiner of the Dioceses of Puebla and Durango, and present secretary of the Province, 53 years old, 37 in habit. *Other:* March 25, 1765, mentioned at Santa Ana as "Custos and thrice vicar and ecclesiastical judge for the Bishopric of Durango." See also AT, pp. 25-26, 29, 48-49, 79.

CAYUELA. See Gómez Cayuela.

CEBALLOS (ZEVALLOS), FRAY ANDRÉS. *Mission:* Entries at pueblo of San Felipe, Jan. 14–March 3, 1726. Albuquerque, May, 1726–April, 1732. Pueblo of San Felipe, Aug., 1732–Feb., 1741. *Provincial: Predicador y ministro presidente* of Villa of San Felipe Neri de Albuquerque, 1721. San Felipe, 1725. San Francisco de Albuquerque, 1731, 1733. Granted *jubilación de hebdómada,* 1730. Santo Domingo, 1740, 1743. Asked incorporation of Province of Holy Gospel, Oct. 7, 1745. Albuquerque, 1749.

CHAVARRÍA, FRAY DIEGO DE. *Mission:* El Paso, 1690. Commissary at Socorro, 1693. Santa Cruz de la Cañada, 1697. Notary at Santa Fe, April, 1698–April, 1699. Tesuque, June 15, 1701. Zia, Nov. 27, 1701. *Provincial:* Professed, Mexico City, March 6, 1679. San Felipe, 1698. Cochiti, 1699. Jémez, 1701–. *Other:* Native of Tacuba, took habit Mexico City, Nov. 11, 1677, at age of 16. San Lorenzo, chaplain of Confraternity of La Conquistadora, 1689. Taos, 1695-96. Santa Fe, 1696. Chaplain of expedition to Acoma, 1696. San Felipe, 1697. Acting custos in absence of Fray Francisco de Vargas, *c.* 1698. Santa María Magdalena, Sumas, 1706.

CLARAMONTE, FRAY ANDRÉS. *Mission:* Entries at Picuris, April 13, 1764–May 15, 1765. Laguna, June 1, 1765–July 25, 1768. Visited Acoma and Zuñi from Laguna. Taos, July 2, 1770–Feb. 20, 1774. Picuris, Dec. 15, 1770–Feb. 3, 1776 (end of register). Nambe, June 23, 1776–May 17, 1777. Taos, July 7, 1777–Dec. 28, 1778. *Provincial:* Santo Domingo, 1765. Santa Fe, 1772. Picuris, 1775, 1776. Oct. 6, 1772, creole, *padre predicador,* N.M., 35 years of age, 14 in habit. *C.* 1773, Acoma, 36 years of age, 15 in habit. *C.* 1779, returned to New Spain, at Huejotzingo. *Other:* D. 1800. The BNM copy of Domínguez' report is in Claramonte's hand.

COLINA, FRAY AGUSTÍN DE. *Provincial:* Elected custos, Chapter Oct. 9, 1706. *Other:* Junta de los Ríos, 1687. El Paso, 1692. Zia, 1702. Jémez, Zia, 1706.

CORVERA, FRAY FRANCISCO. *Provincial:* Creole, native of Manila, professed Mexico City, Feb. 8, 1684. *Other:* El Paso, 1691, apostolic notary, 1692. Accompanied de Vargas to N.M. 1692. Baptisms at Pecos, 1692. Returned to El Paso and accompanied de Vargas to N.M. again, 1693. Assistant at Santa Fe, 1694. Assigned to San Ildefonso and Jacona, Oct., 1694. Martyred at San Ildefonso, June, 1696.

CRUZ, FRAY JUAN (SÁNCHEZ) DE LA. *Mission:* Entries at Taos, Jan. 16, 1719–Oct. 1, 1720. Nambe, as custos, Feb. 2, 1722–Dec. 28, 1724, Jan. 6, 1726–May 27, 1727. Picuris, Dec. 20, 1736–Sept. 29, 1738. San Ildefonso, April 9, 1727–Aug. 22, 1729. San Juan, Sept. 13, 1729–Feb. 12, 1746. *Provincial:* Elected custos, Chapters Sept. 14, 1720, Jan. 14, 1722. San Ildefonso, 1729. Granted *jubilación de hebdómada,* July 5, 1730. Assigned to San Juan, Chapters Oct. 27, 1731, June 2, 1733. To Socorro, Chapter Aug. 25, 1736. To Junta de los Ríos, Chapter Oct. 26, 1737. Santa María de la Redonda (Junta de los Ríos), 1740, 1743.

CUELLAR, FRAY PATRICIO. *Mission:* Entries at Santa Fe, Aug. 23, 1766–Feb. 27, 1774. *Provincial:* 1769, 36 years of age, 21 in habit, missionary in N.M. Oct. 6, 1772, creole, *padre predicador,* missionary N.M., 40 years old, 23 in habit. D. *c.* 1779?

DÁVILA SAAVEDRA, FRAY FRANCISCO XAVIER. *Mission:* Entries at Zuñi, June 7, 1751–June 18, 1752. Zia, June–Dec., 1752. Zuñi, May 13–July 24, 1754. Zia, Sept., 1754–July, 1759, Nov., 1761–June, 1762. San Felipe, March 11, 1764–April 17, 1779. Wrote in Zuñi burial register, Feb. 3, 1752, that the Zuñis blamed him for death of three runners, killed by Apaches, whom he had sent to Acoma; that the Zuñis showed no respect for their missionary, were becoming more and more disobedient about going to church and catechism, and had even told him to leave the pueblo, but he stayed on "because the Lord gives us strength to be able to suffer for His love." *Provincial:* Jémez, 1752. Zia, 1760. Galisteo, 1765. Isleta, 1772. 1769, 54 years old, 31 in habit, long a missionary in N.M. Oct. 6, 1772, creole, *padre predicador,* 59 years old, 36 in habit. Mexico City *c.* 1779.

DELGADO, FRAY CARLOS JOSÉ. *Mission:* Entries at Pecos, Dec. 23, 1716–Oct. 20, 1717. Laguna, 1718. San Diego de Jémez, Aug. 4, 1720–Jan. 25,

1721, Oct. 18, 1722–Feb. 27, 1724, April 14, 1727–Aug. 8, 1730. From the fall of 1728 to Dec., 1729, Indians dying like flies from *sarampión* (measles?); on Dec. 26, 1728, he noted that the entire kingdom was afflicted by these "passages of blood and coughing;" the Indians of Jémez, Zia, Santa Ana, and Cochiti had rebelled and fled to the sierra with all their belongings, and Governor Bustamante's foresight had prevented other pueblos from doing likewise. The rebels returned of their own accord, and the governor welcomed them back with "very Christian and edifying addresses." *Provincial:* Jémez, Cochiti, 1720. San Lorenzo de Picuris, notary of Holy Office, 1725. Jémez, 1729, Chapter Oct. 27, 1731. Granted *jubilación de hebdómada,* July 5, 1730. Taos, Chapter June 2, 1733. Feb. 5, 1734, given title of *predicador jubilado* for 25 years' service in N.M. missions. Santa Ana, 1736. Taos, Chapter Aug. 25, 1736. San Pedro Alcántara (Junta de los Ríos), Chapter Oct. 26, 1737. Isleta, 1743. Oct. 7, 1745, asked incorporation in Province of Holy Gospel. Isleta, 1745, 1749. *Other:* At Acoma in May, 1713, when he was forced to leave by the Indians. 1745, expedition to Moqui with fathers Irigoyen and Toledo. Statement by citizens of El Paso, Oct. 31, 1749: *Predicador general jubilado,* commissary of Holy Office in N.M., apostolic notary and notary of Holy Office, missionary in N.M. for 40 years; had come from Santa Fe to El Paso missions, where he lived two years, when Don Antonio Valverde Cosío was captain and alcalde, and acted as chaplain in the latter's campaign.

Díaz de Aguilar. See Aguilar, Fray Pedro Díaz de.

Díez, Fray José. One of the friars from the College of Santa Cruz of Querétaro who went to N.M. with de Vargas and Custos San Antonio in 1693. He was assigned to Tesuque, formerly a visita of Santa Fe, in Nov., 1694. He left N.M. on May 17, 1696.

Domínguez, Fray Francisco Atanasio. See Historical Introduction and *passim.*

Dueñas, Fray Francisco. *Mission:* Entries at San Antonio Isleta, Jan. 13, 1792–March 26, 1793. *Provincial:* Oct. 6, 1772, creole, *padre*

predicador, missionary in N.M., 39 years old, 22 in habit. *C.* 1773, San Antonio de la Isleta. *C.* 1779, Socorro del Paso. 1788, San Ildefonso. 1791, 1793, Albuquerque. *Other:* Nov., 1791, petition of pueblo of Isleta (N.M.) for his removal and substitution of Father Bermejo.

Escalante, see Vélez de Escalante in Historical Introduction and *passim.*

Esparragoza y Adame, Fray José. *Mission:* One baptism at Nuestra Señora de la Concepción de Fuenclara (Tomé) and one at Albuquerque, Dec., 1763. Nambe, Jan., 1764– (rest of register missing). One baptism at Albuquerque, March, 1765. Zuñi, 21 baptisms on April 8, 10, 28, 1766. *Provincial:* Cochiti, 1765.

Esquer, Fray Pedro Antonio. *Mission:* Galisteo, Nov. 22, 1724–April 4, 1725. San Ildefonso, June–Oct., 1725. San Felipe, May, 1728 –Jan. 29, 1731. Pecos, April 10, 1731–Sept. 27, 1732, May–Aug., 1734. Santa Clara, Oct.–Dec., 1734. Zia, Jan.–March, 1735. Acoma, Dec., 1735–Aug., 1736. Zia, May, 1737–July, 1738. Acoma, 1738-40. Very scattered entries in Río Abajo pueblos until last known signature at Zia, Sept. 9, 1749. *Provincial:* San Ildefonso, 1725. Cochiti, 1726. Santo Domingo, 1728, 1729, Chapters Oct. 27, 1731, June 2, 1733. Pecos, Chapter Aug. 25, 1736. Senecu, Chapter Oct. 26, 1737. Santa Clara, 1740, 1743. San Pedro Apóstol (Junta de los Ríos), 1749.

Ezeiza (Exija, Seisa, Zeiza), Fray Juan Antonio. *Mission:* Entries at San Ildefonso, Jan. 25–Sept. 1, 1730, Nov. 17, 1733–March 14, 1734, Sept. 10, 1742–Oct. 4, 1762, also baptisms Nov., Dec., 1739, Feb. 25, 1740. Picuris, Sept. 6, 1730–July 8, 1732. Santa Cruz, March 26– April 15, 1734. Santa Fe, April 23–Aug. 1, 1735. Zia, Nov. 27, 1735–Oct. 27, 1736. Nambe, Jan. 3, 1737–July 30, 1741. *Provincial:* Senecu, Chapter Aug. 25, 1736. San Antonio Isleta, Chapter Oct. 26, 1737. San Ildefonso, 1749, 1750, 1760. Santa Clara, 1752. *Other:* Governor Vélez Cachupín to Viceroy, June 28, 1762, "incapacitated."

Farfán, Fray Francisco. *Mission:* At El Paso missions, 1681-83. Entries at Santa Ana, Nov. 24, 1697–Jan. 6, 1698. Pecos, Oct. 13,

1698—July 4, 1699. Tesuque, Oct. 15, 1699—March 10, 1700. San Ildefonso, March 10, 1700—March 11, 1701. San Felipe, Nov., 1699. *Provincial:* Native of Cádiz, professed in Mexico City, July 7, 1662. Acoma, 1698. San Ildefonso, 1703. *Other:* Took habit, Mexico City, July 1, 1661, at age of 18. In N.M. at time of 1680 Revolt. Procurator, Mexico City, 1693, and took group of colonists to El Paso; reached Santa Fe, June, 1694. Vice-custos, 1701, when he ordered the friars to publish the excommunication incurred by those who offend against ecclesiastical immunity.

FERNÁNDEZ, FRAY SEBASTIÁN ANGEL. *Mission:* Entries at Santa Clara, May 6, 1772—Nov. 11, 1773. Laguna, Jan.—May, 1775. Three baptisms at Zuñi, July 20, 1777 (scratched out). Abiquiu, Oct. 7, 1777—Oct. 3, 1781. *Provincial:* Oct. 6, 1772, Galician, took habit in Mexico City, 33 years old, 14 in habit, missionary in N.M. Galisteo, 1772. *C.* 1773, Zia, 32 years old, 14 in habit. Santa Clara, 1776. Santo Domingo, San Felipe, Cochiti, 1788.

FERNÁNDEZ, FRAY TOMÁS SALVADOR. *Mission:* Entries at Laguna, Oct. 23, 1777—Jan. 16, 1779. Acoma, Feb. 17—Oct. 20, 1778, Sept. 4, 1781—Sept. 15, 1782, March 31—Nov. 30, 1786, Sept.—Oct., 1787. Taos, March 9—Sept. 25, 1780. Sandia, Nov. 8, 1784—Feb. 13, 1786. San Juan, Jan. 28—Aug. 26, 1787. *Provincial:* Sandia, *c.* 1779.

GABALDÓN, FRAY ANTONIO. *Mission:* Entries at Galisteo, June 22, 1723—July 12, 1724; turned Galisteo over to Father Esquer, Nov. 22, 1724, and got it back April 4, 1725; turned it over to Father Irigoyen, July, 1725, but stayed on; received it again from Fray Juan Sánchez, Nov. 9, 1728, and consigned it to Fray Juan George del Pino Aug. 6, 1729. Pecos, Jan. 8, 1724—May 27, 1727, March 14—Nov. 14, 1728, Jan. 3—March 12, 1734. Nambe, July 29, 1731—July 29, 1732, with Father Sopeña. San Ildefonso, May 4, 1732—Oct. 9, 1733, Sept. 9, 1736—July 12, 1741, Aug. 19, 1743—Feb. 26, 1744. Zia, May 12, 1734—Jan. 7, 1735. Santa Clara, Feb. 19, 1735—May 3, 1736. Santa Cruz, May—June, 1743, and with Fray Juan José Hernández, March 29, 1744—March 29, 1760. Secretary to fathers Camargo, visitation of 1728, Varo, 1729,

1730, Menchero, 1730, 1731. *Provincial:* Pecos, Galisteo, 1727. Pecos, Chapters Oct. 27, 1731, June 2, 1733. Aug. 22, 1736, granted *jubilación de hebdómada* for more than 10 years' service in N.M. Cochiti, Chapter Aug. 25, 1736. Taos, Chapter Oct. 26, 1737. *Lector de gramática,* Guadalupe del Paso, 1740, 1743. Cañada, 1749, 1750, 1752.

GARAICOECHEA (GARAYCOECHEA), FRAY JUAN DE. *Mission:* Two baptisms at Zia, Sept. 19, 1699. Zuñi, Oct. 22—Dec. 6, 1699, July 3, 1701—July 26, 1706. D. at Zuñi, comforted by Father Miranda, and was buried on Epistle side of sanctuary, Aug. 9, 1706. *Other:* To Moqui, 1700, 1701.

GARCÍA, FRAY ANDRÉS. *Mission:* Entries at Pecos, Oct., 1747. Picuris, Sept., 1748. Pecos, Nov. 28, 1749—Feb., 1750. Acoma, Aug. 4, 1749—Aug. 8, 1750. Visits to Zuñi, Nov. 11, 1749—May 11, 1750. Zia, Dec., 1749—Feb., 1750. Jémez, April 3, 1751—March 18, 1752. Zia, Dec. 2, 1759—July 19, 1760. Picuris, Oct. 12, 1761—Jan. 3, 1762. Santa Fe, April, 1763—May, 1765. Picuris, June, 1765—Feb., 1766. Santa Cruz, July 28, 1765—May 19, 1768. Santa Clara, Dec. 9, 1770—May 11, 1772. Albuquerque, to March 15, 1773. Laguna, March 19, 1773—Nov. 28, 1775; baptized 29 Navajos, June, 1775. Baptisms and marriages at Acoma, April 17, 18, 1773. Zuñi, July—Aug., 1773, nearly 100 baptisms in two weeks and 19 marriages on one day. Albuquerque, Dec. 5, 1775—end of 1780. *Provincial:* Navajo conversion, 1749. Isleta, 1752. Taos, 1760, 1765. 1769, 49 years old, 34 in habit, long a missionary in N.M. Oct. 6, 1772, creole, *padre predicador,* missionary in N.M., 52 years old, 37 in habit. *C.* 1773, Santa Clara, 53 years old, 38 in habit. Albuquerque, 1776. After 1779, d. as chaplain of the infirmary (Mexico City).

GARCÍA, FRAY ANGEL. *Mission:* Secretary of visitation to Father Menchero, May, 1743. San Felipe, Nov. 26, 1747—Jan. 28, 1749. *Other:* Entered El Paso as missionary in 1745, according to statement he made in favor of citizens there, Oct. 29, 1749. In Mexico, 1761.

GARCÍA DE NORIEGA, FRAY JOSÉ. *Mission:* Three guest entries: baptisms at Santa Fe, May

4, June 27, Santa Cruz, June 9, 1756. Zuñi, Jan. 23—May 26, 1758. Pecos, Aug.—Dec., 1758. Zia, July 21—Nov. 14, 1759. Picuris, March 25—July 13, 1760. Zia, July 30—Nov. 19, 1760. Laguna, March 3, 1764—April 22, 1765. Last known entries at Albuquerque, June—July, 1775.

GÓMEZ CAYUELA, FRAY MIGUEL. *Mission:* Entries at Nambe, Feb. 28, 1756—May 5, 1757, July 26, 1762—March 7, 1763. Santa Ana, Sept., 1745. San Felipe, Nov. 16, 1745—Oct. 26, 1747. Albuquerque, March 24—July 26, 1748, Jan. 24—March 24, 1751. Pecos, March—May, 1754. Albuquerque, Aug. 18, 1754—May 5, 1755. Pecos, Nov.—Dec., 1755. Jémez, May 3, 1761—March 7, 1762. *Provincial:* One of 18 friars who came from Spain to New Spain, 1743. Zia, 1745. Santa Ana, 1749. Taos, 1750. Nambe, 1752, 1760, 1765. 1769, Andalusian, 70 years old, 44 in habit, which he took in Province of Cartagena; long a missionary in and triennial custos of N.M.

GONZÁLEZ, FRAY FRANCISCO DE LA CONCEPCIÓN. *Mission:* Entries at Santa Fe, July 15, 1743—March 3, 1744. Nambe, Dec. 26, 1744—March 1, 1746. Pecos, June, 1749—Feb., 1750. *Provincial:* San Juan, San Cristóbal (Junta de los Ríos), 1749. Pecos, 1750. (Two men of this name? See n. 42, p. 262 *supra.*)

GUERRERO, FRAY JOSÉ ANTONIO. *Mission:* Entries at Tesuque, July, 1714—Jan., 1717. Santa Cruz (first part missing), July—Sept., 1721. Tesuque, April, 1724—July, 1726. Santa Fe, Jan., 1726—Feb., 1734. Scattered entries at Nambe, Nov., 1734—Nov., 1736, Jan.—May, 1738. Santa Fe, Nov.—June, 1738, Sept., 1739—July, 1742. Commissary visitor, 1723. Secretary of visitation, 1724. Vice-custos and visitor, 1725. Visitor general, 1727. Custos and visitor, 1728. *Provincial:* Nambe, 1724, 1727, Chapter Oct. 27, 1731, 1732. Granted *jubilación de hebdómada,* July 5, 1730. Santa Fe, Chapter Aug. 25, 1736. Laguna, Chapter Oct. 26, 1737. Zia, 1740, 1743. *Other:* Santa Fe, 1714.

GUZMÁN (GUSMÁN), FRAY FRANCISCO (XAVIER MIGUEL). *Mission:* Entries at Jémez, Oct. 20, 1760—Nov. 15, 1761. Santa Ana, March 29, 1765—Sept. 21, 1767. Scattered entries at Zia

during Jémez term and again Feb. 23, April 17, 1763. Santa Clara, Jan. 21, March 4, 1757. Isleta, Nov.—Dec., 1758. Albuquerque, Feb.—April, 1759. Zuñi, May—June, 1759. San Ildefonso, Sept., Nov., 1768. *Provincial:* San Ildefonso, 1740, 1743. Guadalupe del Paso, 1749. Zuñi, 1760. 1769, creole, 49 years old, 34 in habit, long a missionary in N.M.

HERMIDA (ERMIDA), FRAY BUENAVENTURA. *Mission:* Entries at Santa Clara, March 11, 1774—Jan. 30, 1777. Pojoaque, Feb. 9, 1779—May, 1780. *Provincial:* Appears in 1769 list under *Estudiantes,* 29 years old, 8 in habit. Oct. 6, 1772, Galician, took habit in Mexico City, 34 years old, 13 in habit, missionary in N.M. *C.* 1773, Cochiti, 33 years old, 12 in habit, Guadalupe del Paso, 1772.

HINOJOSA (INOJOSA, YNOJOSA), FRAY JOAQUÍN DE. *Provincial:* Professed in Puebla, May 5, 1677. *Other:* To Junta de los Ríos with fathers Colina and San Miguel, Feb., 1687, and remained there a year and 8 months. El Paso, March, 1689. Socorro, 1690, 29 years old. Became president *in capite* of Custody, April, 1692.

HINOJOSA (INOJOSA, YNOJOSA), FRAY JUAN JOSÉ. *Mission:* Vice-custos and missionary at Sandia, March, 1765. Presented register at Santo Domingo, Dec. 13, 1770, as custos. Custos and recent missionary at Sandia, March 13, 1771. Entry in marriage book at Pojoaque, 1779, refers to him as ex-custos twice and present custos. Entries at San Ildefonso, Feb. 8, 1779—March 27, 1780, with Nambe. San Felipe, April 24, 1780—April 28, 1781. *Provincial:* Jémez, 1765. Sandia, 1768, 1769, 1771. 1769, 43 years old, 24 in habit, missionary in N.M. Oct. 6, 1772, creole, custos of N.M., 46 years old, 27 in habit. *C.* 1773, custos of N.M., Santa Fe, 47 years old, 28 in habit.

INIESTA (YNIESTA), FRAY AGUSTÍN DE. *Mission:* Entries at Pecos (incomplete) Dec., 1743, Jan.—April, 1744. Isleta, July, 1747, with Father Delgado. Baptisms at Zia, Oct. 14—Dec. 3, 1749. San Felipe, Jan., Oct., 1750, Feb., June, 1751, Jan. 12, 1753—April 20, 1755. Jémez, Jan. 20, 1756—Feb. 6, 1757. Isleta, June 3, 1759—April 4, 1770. Visitation at Albuquerque, 1767, probably as vice-custos. *Provincial:* Cochiti, 1749. San Felipe, 1750. Sandia, 1760. Isleta, 1765. 1769, creole, 60 years old, 35 in habit, long a missionary in N.M.

IRAZABAL, FRAY FRANCISCO. Zuñi, 1707, 1711, 1713, 1720. To Moqui twice. Santa Fe, 1721, 1730, 1731, 1732. Cañada, 1722. Cochiti, 1724. Picuris, 1728, 1729.

IRIGOYEN (YRIGOYEN), FRAY JOSÉ DE. *Mission:* Galisteo, July 1, 1725—Oct. 14, 1726, with Father Gabaldón. San Felipe, Oct., 1726—July 26, 1727. Isleta, Nov. 23, 1727—Sept. 24, 1728. San Ildefonso, Sept. 30, 1730—April 21, 1732, Aug. 16—Nov. 17, 1734, June 17, 1735. Santa Cruz, with Fray Manuel de Sopeña, May, 1735 —March, 1741. Santa Clara, Feb. 24—Sept. 29, 1737. Acoma, May—Sept., 1741. Zia, June 1, 1742—Feb. 5, 1743. Jémez, May 12, 1743— March 2, 1745. Albuquerque, April, 1745—Feb. 12, 1748, May 18, 1749—Aug. 24, 1750, April 14 —Nov. 14, 1751. *Provincial:* Santo Domingo, 1727. Isleta, 1729. Guadalupe del Paso, Chapters Oct. 27, 1731, June 2, 1733. Aug. 22, 1736, granted *jubilación de hebdómada* for more than 10 years service in N.M. Jémez, Chapter Aug. 25, 1736. Picuris, Chapter Oct. 26, 1737. San Juan Bautista (Junta de los Ríos), 1743. 1750, son of Province of Holy Gospel, *predicador general jubilado,* apostolic notary and notary of Holy Office, *discreto* of Custody of Conversion of St. Paul, minister of Albuquerque. Cochiti, 1760. *Other:* Cañada, 1732. San Felipe de Albuquerque, 1745, petitioned to go to Moqui with fathers Delgado and Toledo.

JEREZ. See Rodríguez de Jerez.

JUNCO Y JUNQUERA, FRAY JOSÉ ELEUTERIO. *Mission:* San Felipe, Oct. 29, 1762—Feb. 28, 1763. San Juan, March 8, 1763—Aug. 8, 1770. Isleta, Aug. 27, 1772—May 22, 1776 (end of register). *Provincial:* San Francisco de Albuquerque, 1765. 1769, 32 years old, 17 in habit, missionary in N.M. San Felipe, 1772. Oct. 6, 1772, creole, *padre predicador,* missionary in N.M., 35 years old, 19 in habit. *C.* 1773, Taos, 36 years old, 20 in habit. *C.* 1779, returned to New Spain and sent to Tampico.

LEZAUN. See Sanz de Lezaun.

LLANOS, FRAY JUAN JOSÉ. *Mission:* Entries at Nambe, Oct. 20, 1771—June 12, 1776, with Pojoaque and Tesuque as visitas. Sandia, Oct. 6, 1776—Jan. 4, 1777. Santo Domingo, June, 1777. Santa Fe, July 15, 1777—Oct. 27, 1780, May 12— Oct. 14, 1781. *Provincial:* Oct. 6, 1772, creole, *padre predicador,* N.M., 36 years old, 19 in habit. *C.* 1779, chaplain at San Elzeario near El Paso. Possibly d. at this period.

LÓPEZ, FRAY NICOLÁS. In El Paso area at time of 1680 Revolt and sent to Mexico City by Fray Francisco de Ayeta to make report. 1681, secretary to Ayeta, 1683-84, vice-custos, expedition into Texas with Captain Juan Domínguez de Mendoza. Elected custos, Chapters June 23, 1685, Jan. 25, 1687. In Mexico City 1684-85 to make reports on Texas, etc. D. 1692.

MARIÑO, FRAY JOSÉ MANUEL. *Mission:* Entries at Acoma Nov. 7, 1773—Jan. 8, 1777, July 19—Dec. 21, 1777 (register incomplete), probably residing at Laguna. Visited Zuñi, 1774, 50 baptisms between June 23 and July 6. *Provincial:* C. 1771-73, creole, Senecu, 36 years old. C. 1779, returned to New Spain and sent to Tampico.

MARULANDA, FRAY ESTANISLAO MARIANO. *Mission:* Entries at Zuñi, June, 1759—Sept., 1760, probably visiting from Laguna. Picuris, Jan., 1761—April, 1763. Pecos, Oct., 1761—Jan., 1762. Zia, June 24, 1763—Aug. 12, 1770. Santa Ana, Aug. 2, 1768—June 26, 1770. Isleta, Aug. 24, 1770—Aug. 25, 1772. Cochiti, May 22, 1776 —March 2, 1778. Secretary of visitations, 1761, 1769, 1770. *Provincial:* San Felipe, 1760. Picuris, 1765. 1769, 35 years old, 20 in habit, missionary in N.M. San Juan, 1772. Oct. 6, 1772, creole, *padre predicador,* missionary in Tampico *(sic),* 38 years old, 22 in habit. *C.* 1773, Pecos, 39 years old, 23 in habit. *C.* 1779, in the Province.

MEDRANO, FRAY JOSÉ. *Mission:* Entries at Albuquerque, Jan., 1772. Sandia, May, 1772— June 23, 1776. Santa Fe, July 29, 1776—July 11, 1777. Santo Domingo, July 19, 1777—Nov. 11, 1784. Cochiti, May—Oct., 1778. San Felipe, Dec., 1783—July, 1784. *Provincial:* Oct. 6, 1772, creole, *padre predicador,* N.M., 34 years old, 13 in habit. *C.* 1773, Queres, 35 years old, 14 in habit. *C.* 1779, has come (to Mexico City) and is going to Toluca.

MENCHERO, FRAY (JUAN) MIGUEL. Took habit Province of Holy Gospel. Procurator of New Mexico missions, 1729-31. Aug. 22, 1736, given title of *predicador general,* his 3 years' service as procurator in N.M. being counted against the year and a half he lacked to win this title. Elected procurator, Chapters Aug. 25, 1736, Oct. 26, 1737; custos, Chapter Jan. 31, 1739; procurator, Chapters July 16, 1740, Oct. 27, 1741, Feb. 16, 1743. Navajo missions, 1747-49.

MINGUES, FRAY JUAN. Chaplain of Santa Fe Presidio, 1706, and accompanied two small expeditions to Moqui, 1707. With Cuervo y Valdés at founding of Albuquerque, and baptized 4 infants there on July 24, Aug. 10, 1706. Entries at Taos, Oct. 9, 1707—Jan. 1, 1708. Zia, end of 1708—May 2, 1709. Santa Cruz, Oct. 19, 1710—Dec. 17, 1719, with scattered entries at Nambe and San Ildefonso. Secretary of visitation to Father Tagle, 1714. Santa Cruz, Jan., 1720, succeeded by Father Sopeña by April. Galisteo, April 17—June 15, 1720. Joined Villasur expedition as chaplain and perished with forces massacred by French and Pawnees summer 1720, although there is a story that he escaped.

MIRABAL. See Pérez de Mirabal.

MIRANDA, FRAY ANTONIO DE. *Mission:* Entries at Laguna, Jan. 10, 1700—April 10, 1711 (visited Acoma and Zuñi), Sept. 28, 1721—Sept. 17, 1723. Acoma, June 25, 1725—Nov. 1, 1729. Zia, May 20, 1730—June 24, 1731. *Provincial:* Acoma and Laguna, 1721. Acoma, 1729. July 5, 1730, granted *jubilación de hebdómada.* Nambe, Chapter Oct. 26, 1737. *Other:* Acoma, 1700. San Felipe, 1703. Santa Ana, 1712. Acoma, 1714. Vice-custos, 1716. Various references to his studies of Queres language. Brother of settler Matías de Miranda, native of Sombrerete.

MUÑIZ DE LUNA, FRAY MIGUEL. *Mission:* Entries at Zia, Aug. 13, 1697—Feb. 2, 1698. Pecos, Sept. 18, 1699—June 27, 1700. Secretary of visitation to fathers Diego Padilla, 1699, Zabaleta, 1700, Guerra, 1702, 1703, Peña, 1709, Vice-Provincial Aguirre, 1711, Camargo, 1716,

Barreda, 1719, Camargo, 1729. *Other:* With de Vargas expedition, 1692. Santo Domingo, 1700. Cochiti, 1706, 1708. Vice-custos, 1707. Lieutenant commissary visitor, 1711. San Felipe, Santo Domingo, 1714.

MURCIANO DE LA CRUZ, FRAY TOMÁS. *Mission:* Entries at Santa Fe, Jan. 13, 1753—March 26, 1757, probably assistant to Fray José Urquijo. Secretary of visitation, 1753, 1754. Visiting missionary at Zuñi, Oct. 26, 1756—March 20, 1758. San Felipe, Oct. 28, 1758—May 9, 1762. *Provincial:* San Pedro de Alcántara (Junta de los Ríos), 1752. *Other:* Linguistic studies (AT, pp. 48-49).

NARRO, FRAY ANDRÉS PÉREZ. *Provincial: C.* 1779, has come (to Mexico City) and is in Tehuacan.

NORIEGA. See García de Noriega.

OLAETA, FRAY JOSÉ DE. *Mission:* Entries at Taos, Jan. 6, 1774—March 19, 1775. San Ildefonso, Nov. 23, 1778—April 16, 1780. Pojoaque, Aug. 4, 1780—March 31, 1781. San Ildefonso, Jan. 6—April 9, 1782. He died on Jan. 6, 1785, and was buried in Santa Fe. *Provincial: C.* 1771-73, creole, assistant at Socorro, 44 years old, 20 in habit.

ORDOÑEZ Y MACHADO, FRAY FÉLIX. First missionary at Abiquiu, 1754; entries May 7, 1754—Feb. 2, 1756. One entry at Laguna, April 25, 1756. In 1766 an Indian girl of Abiquiu claimed he had been killed through the witchcraft of a certain genízaro and his wife.

PADILLA, FRAY JUAN JOSÉ DE. *Provincial:* Picuris, Chapter June 2, 1733. La Junta, Chapter Aug. 25, 1736. Zia, Chapter Oct. 26, 1737. La Cañada, 1740, 1743. Laguna, 1749, 1750. Zuñi, 1752. *Other:* On Feb. 5, 1756, Father Padilla, who was then missionary of Laguna, died and was buried at Isleta after receiving the last rites from Father Pascual Sospedra. In 1775 his incorrupt body rose to the surface of the church floor in Isleta and was re-buried on June 26. In recording this, Father Junco (See INDEX) wrote that Father Padilla had been beaten or stabbed to death, although Father Sospedra did not mention any violence in the original burial entry. Subsequently, periodic risings and re-burials of the corpse made Father Padilla a source of legend, and for a long time he was identified with the martyred Father Padilla of Coronado's time. It may be significant that Father Domínguez failed to mention so recent and curious a phenomenon (Cf. p. 282 *supra*). For full accounts of this mystery, see Chávez, "The mystery of Father Padilla," *El Palacio*, 54 (1947): 251-68, "A sequel to 'The mystery of Father Padilla,'" 59 (1952): 386-89.

PALACIO, FRAY JOSÉ. *Mission:* Entries at San Juan, June 9, 1776—Jan. 8, 1779. Santa Cruz, Jan. 17—May 16, 1779. Taos, Oct. 28, 1780—April 6, 1781. Albuquerque, as assistant, May 12, 1781—Oct. 27, 1782, as pastor, Dec. 12, 1782—May 12, 1783. Sandia, May 23, 1783—Oct. 14, 1784. He died at Bernalillo, April 23, 1785, en route to his mission at Zuñi.

PÁRRAGA, FRAY DIEGO DE. Native of Mexico City who took Franciscan habit there Aug. 21, 1648, at age of 23. Accompanied to N.M. in 1652 by his widowed mother, who lived with him at Tajique for some time. Difficulties with Nicolás de Aguilar. One of survivors of 1680 Revolt.

PEÑA, FRAY JUAN DE LA. *Mission:* Notary at El Paso, Nov., 1698. Baptism at Bernalillo, Jan. 13, 1701. Marriage at Nambe, Nov. 11, 1708. *Provincial:* Elected custos, Chapters May 5, 1708, Sept. 7, 1709. *Other:* At San Antonio de la Isleta, 1706. Refounded San Agustín Isleta, Jan., 1710. D. 1710.

PÉREZ DE MIRABAL, FRAY JUAN JOSÉ. *Mission:* Entries at Taos, Oct. 26, 1722—July 29, 1727, and during this period Apaches who settled on Río de las Trampas in Taos Valley asked for him as missionary; request was granted. Santa Cruz, Oct. 27, 1732, Feb. 2, 1735—Nov. 3, 1736. Pecos, Dec., 1738—Jan., 1739. Scattered entries at Picuris, Oct. 4, 1732—Sept., 1733, May 3, 1739—Feb. 15, 1746, Oct. 5—Dec. 3, 1752. San Ildefonso, Nov. 13, 1735—May 10, 1736, Feb., March, 1763. San Juan, March 6—Oct. 9, 1746, April 25, 1747—Feb. 26, 1763. Santa Clara, July 10, 1756—Jan. 2, 1757. *Provincial:* Taos, 1725. San Juan, 1726. Taos, 1729, Chapter Oct. 27, 1731. Zia, Chapter June 2, 1733. Aug. 22, 1736,

granted *jubilación de hebdómada* for more than 10 years service in N.M. Socorro, Chapter Oct. 26, 1737. Picuris, 1740, 1743. Elected custos, Chapter Jan. 14, 1747. Custos, at San Juan, 1749. *Other:* Jicarilla Apache mission, 1733. Ex-custos, *predicador jubilado*, ex-vicar, San Juan de los Caballeros and Nuestra Señora de la Soledad del Río Arriba del Norte, 1750. Governor Vélez Cachupín to Viceroy, June 28, 1762, "incapacitated."

PINO, FRAY JUAN GEORGE DEL. *Mission:* Entries at San Ildefonso, Sept. 20, Oct. 21, 1717. Galisteo, Aug. 30, 1718—Feb. 26, 1722. Pecos, Dec. 22, 1718—Oct. 29, 1722. Galisteo, May, Sept., 1724. Santa Clara, Feb.—Aug., 1726. Galisteo, Aug. 6, 1728. Scattered entries Santa Fe, Jan. 18, 1728—Aug. 2, 1729. San Felipe, Feb. 8, 1731—May 1, 1732. Jémez and Zia, Oct., 1732—Feb., 1734, noting smallpox epidemic at Jémez, 1733. Albuquerque, June—Sept., 1732, May—June, 1734. Santa Clara, Nov. 26, 1735—April 22, 1736. Santa Cruz, Nov. 11—Dec. 27, 1735. Jémez and Zia, Feb. 15—June 13, 1737, Sept. 15, 1739—May 20, 1742, apparently visiting from another mission. Laguna, March, 1743. Albuquerque, April 7—June, 1743. Santa Cruz, July 21, 1743—Feb. 25, 1744. Albuquerque, Sept. 14—Dec. 22, 1750, May 1, 1751—Sept. 4, 1752, apparently visiting Jémez, for he turned Jémez registers over to Father Rodríguez de la Torre, Nov. 26, 1752. Nambe, Dec. 9, 1752—July 25, 1753. *Provincial:* Nambe, 1729. Granted *jubilación de hebdómada* July 5, 1730. Zuñi, Chapter Oct. 26, 1737. Pecos, 1740, 1743, 1752. Santo Domingo, 1749, 1750.

PINO, FRAY PEDRO IGNACIO. *Mission:* Entries at Zia, Aug. 2, 1741—May 13, 1742, June, 1745. Acoma, May 23, 1745—June 15, 1749, Aug. 20, 1750—Nov. 20, 1767. Zuñi, Nov. 12, 1752, May 30—Oct. 26, 1756, May 14, 15, 1762. D. at Acoma Dec. 9, buried at Albuquerque, Dec. 12, 1767. *Provincial:* Zuñi, 1740, 1743. Acoma, 1748, 1749. Taos, 1752. Acoma, 1760, 1765.

POLANCO (POLLANCO), FRAY JOSÉ ANTONIO DE LA CRUZ. *Mission:* Entries at Santa Fe, Feb. 4—Aug. 25, 1762. *Provincial:* Oct. 6, 1772, creole, *padre predicador*, N.M., 35 years old, 18 in habit. *C.* 1773, Guadalupe del Paso, 36 years old, 19 in habit.

QUINTANA, FRAY JOSÉ GABRIEL DE LA. *Mission:* Santa Fe, assistant to Fray Andrés García, 1765-66, and to Fray Patricio Cuellar, 1766-69. Zuñi, May, 1765. *Provincial:* Santa María de la Redonda (Junta de los Ríos), 1760. San Juan, 1765. 1769, creole, 39 years old, 23 in habit, missionary in N.M.

RODRÍGUEZ, FRAY JOAQUÍN ILDEFONSO. *Mission:* Entries at San Ildefonso, April 10, 1763—Aug. 21, 1768. Laguna, Sept. 17, 1768—May 17, 1772. Acoma, baptisms in batches, Sept., 1770—March, 1772. Zuñi, Sept., 1771. Pestilence at Laguna, Jan. 4—March 31, 1772, when he blamed Alcalde Baltasar Baca for much Indian suffering. At Pecos, Sept., 1772, wrote to Vicar Roybal complaining of Vice-Custos Rodríguez de la Torre, Father Junco, and Baltasar Baca; apparently out of his mind as result of real or imagined persecutions. *Provincial:* San Felipe, 1765, described as *ex-lector* of theology. Laguna, 1772.

RODRÍGUEZ DE JEREZ, FRAY JOAQUÍN. *Mission:* Pecos, July 20-28, 1755, May, 1756, March, 1757. Jémez, Dec. 5, 1757—Sept. 4, 1759. Albuquerque, Aug., 1758, March—May, 1761. *Provincial:* San Felipe, 1765. 1769, 55 years old, 40 in habit, *ex-lector novenal,* former guardian of "las Amilpa" and for many years a missionary in N.M. Laguna, 1772. Oct. 6, 1772, creole, *padre predicador general,* missionary in N.M., 58 years old, 43 in habit. *Other:* Pecos, 1760 (AT, p. 52).

RODRÍGUEZ DE LA TORRE, FRAY MARIANO. *Mission:* Secretary to Custos Hinojosa visitations 1771, 1772. Entries at Jémez, Nov. 26, 1752—June 26, 1754, Dec., 1775, Jan., 1756. Zuñi, July 24, 1754—Nov. 6, 1755. Santa Clara, Feb. 15—June 24, 1756, April 20, 1757—Aug. 16, 1760. Santo Domingo, minister, and secretary to Custos Hinojosa, Dec. 13, 1770; entries, Jan. 12, 1771—April 7, 1776. *Provincial:* San Antonio de la Isleta, 1752. Santa Clara, 1760, 1765, 1772. 1769, 44 years old, 29 in habit, missionary in N.M. Oct. 6, 1772, creole, *padre predicador,* missionary in N.M., 47 years old, 32 in habit.

RODRÍGUEZ DE SAN ANTONIO, FRAY SALVADOR. In N.M. proper as early as April, 1664, when he gave his age as about 25, native of Puebla de los Angeles. Had worked among the Mansos. 1672, minister of pueblo of Alamillo. Not in N.M. at time of 1680 Revolt, but later testified that he had worked there for 12 years before it, and then had great success among the Sumas, Mangas, and Jumanos. Appointed custos, 1684, and reached El Paso early spring of 1685. Elected custos, Chapter Nov. 22, 1692, and accompanied de Vargas on entradas of 1692, 1693. Resigned as custos, Palm Sunday, 1694, and returned to El Paso.

ROJO (ROXO), FRAY MANUEL JOSÉ. *Mission:* Entries at Pecos, Aug., 1751. Albuquerque, with Tomé, Nov. 22, 1751—March 28, 1752, Oct. 1, 1752—Aug. 3, 1754, May 6, 1755—Oct. 31, 1772. Santa Fe, Nov. 24, 1754—Jan. 30, 1755. Santa Cruz, Nov. 11, 1772—Jan. 14, 1779. *Provincial:* San Felipe, 1752. 1760, missionary of San Francisco de Albuquerque, vicar and ecclesiastical judge (Cf. AT, p. 44). Santa María del Socorro, 1765. 1769, 51 years old, 34 in habit, long a missionary in N.M. Oct. 6, 1772, creole, *padre predicador,* missionary N.M., 55 years old, 37 in habit. C. 1773, San Juan, 56 years old, 38 in habit. C. 1779, deceased?

ROSETE Y PERALTA, FRAY JOSÉ MARIANO. *Mission:* Entries at Santa Ana, May 4, 1777—Dec. 30, 1778. Laguna, Jan. 20, 1779—Sept. 2, 1781. Albuquerque, Sept. 30, 1781—Oct. 20, 1782. Acoma, Dec. 29, 1782—Dec. 10, 1785. Sandia, March 3, 1786—April 12, 1789. Acoma, April 25, 1789—Feb. 28, 1793. Laguna, March 19, 1789—March 3, 1793. Santa Ana, March 7, 1793—Jan. 1, 1795. Nambe, March 30—Nov. 22, 1795. Santa Cruz, Dec. 16, 1795—Jan. 7, 1802. Santa Ana, March 8—Sept. 3, 1798. Jan., 1802, turned Santa Cruz over to secular priest from Durango, Don Juan José de Lombide. San Ildefonso, Jan. 14, 1802—Jan. 18, 1805. D. at Santa Cruz, Dec. 23, 1805, when Fray José de Castro was pastor there, the secular priest having returned to Durango. *Provincial:* 1769, on list of "Hermanos Choristas Phylosofos," 20 years old, 4 in habit. Oct. 6, 1772, creole on list of "Hermanos choristas, theologos, philosophos y gramáticos," 22 years old, 6 in habit (the "hermano" before his name has been changed to "P[adre]" in another hand.) Galisteo, 1776. C. 1779, Acoma. Isleta, 1788. Sandia, 1791. San

Lorenzo del Realito, 1793. Jémez, with Santa Ana and Zia, 1794. Santa Cruz de la Cañada, 1797.

RUIZ, FRAY JOAQUÍN DE JESÚS. *Mission:* Picuris, April 13, 1765—May 17, 1768. Acoma, July—Aug., 1765, with trip to Zuñi last week of Aug. Jémez, March 29, 1769—April 28, 1776. Isleta, Sept. 25, 1776—April 22, 1778. *Provincial:* San Juan Bautista (Junta de los Ríos), 1765. 1769, 44 years old, 29 in habit. San Felipe, 1772. Oct. 6, 1772, creole, *padre predicador*, missionary N.M. *C.* 1773, San Felipe, 48 years old, 33 in habit. *C.* 1779, deceased?

SALAS, FRAY RAMÓN. *Mission:* Jémez, June 15, 1765—Jan. 16, 1769. Acoma, Sept.—Dec., 1768, Feb. 5—Dec. 1, 1769. Zia, Sept. 28, 1770—Nov. 2, 1771. Santa Ana, Nov. 2, 1771—March 13, 1774. Sandia, May 26, 1771—May 1, 1772. San Juan, April 5, 1774—April 29, 1776. *Provincial:* Galisteo, 1760. San Felipe, 1765. 1769, Andalusian, son of Province of Holy Gospel, 45 years old, 21 in habit, missionary N.M. Santa Ana, 1771. Santo Domingo, 1772. Oct. 6, 1772, Andalusian who took habit in Mexico City, 50 years old, 26 years in habit, missionary N.M. *C.* 1773, Galisteo, 49 years old, 25 in habit. San Juan, 1774.

SAN ANTONIO. See Rodríguez de San Antonio.

SANZ DE LEZAUN (LESAUN), FRAY JUAN. *Mission:* Entries at Zia, April, 1748—Feb., 1749. San Felipe, June—Aug., 1749. Santa Ana, June 16, 1750—April 23, 1752. Sept., 1752, blessed graves of scores of people at Zia who had died "while I was away on business of the Custody." San Felipe, Sept. 8, 1756—May 5, 1758. *Other:* San Felipe, 1757. Three entradas to Junta de los Ríos, 1759-60. In Mexico City, Nov., 1760, to attend Provincial Chapter, and apparently did not return to N.M. *Informe*, 1750; *Noticias lamentables*, 1760 (HB 3: 468-79).

TAGLE, FRAY JUAN DE. *Mission:* Entries at San Ildefonso, April 26, 1701—Nov. 17, 1726. Nambe, Aug. 10, 1714—Nov. 10, 1715, Sept. 29, 1718—Jan. 29, 1719, from San Ildefonso. *Provincial:* Elected custos, Chapters Oct. 24, 1711, April 29, 1713. Custos and commissary of Inquisition, 1720. *Other:* San Ildefonso, Santa

Clara, 1706. Secretary of Custody, vice-custos, and ecclesiastical judge ordinary, 1705-06.

TOLEDO, FRAY JUAN JOSÉ. *Mission:* Entries at Acoma, July 14, 1743—March 14, 1745. Isleta, Nov. 23, 1745—April 27, 1746. Jémez, March 9—Feb. 3, 1749. Visits to Zuñi throughout 1744-49. Pecos, Feb. 9, 1752—March 11, 1753. Nambe, Oct. 22, 1753—Oct. 24, 1755. *Provincial:* 1745, Alona and Zuñi; petition to go to Moqui with fathers Irigoyen and Delgado. Jémez, 1749, but went with Father Menchero to Navajo. Galisteo, 1750. Picuris, 1752. Guadalupe (Junta de los Ríos), 1760. San Francisco de la Junta, 1765. 1769, 53 years old, 38 in habit, long a missionary in N.M. Cañada, 1772. *Other:* Abiquiu, 1754, succeeding Father Ordóñez. Abiquiu, 1760, 50 years old (AT, p. 64.)

VARGAS, FRAY FRANCISCO DE. *Provincial:* A Spanish Franciscan who was incorporated in the Mexican Province of the Holy Gospel in 1665 (or, according to another source, a native of Toluca, who took the habit in Mexico City on Dec. 7, 1673). Elected custos, Chapters June 12, 1688, April 8, 1690. Custos, 1696 (succeeded Rodríguez de San Antonio, 1694). Later, definitor. *Other:* In El Paso at time of 1680 Revolt and one of three friars selected to go north with relief party. Was vice-custos at El Paso when he succeeded Rodríguez de San Antonio as Custos, and went to interior N.M. with 4 missionaries, reaching Santa Fe, Nov. 1, 1694. Considerable correspondence regarding 1696 Revolt. Went to Mexico City, 1697-98, where he spoke in defense of Governor Diego de Vargas.

VARO, FRAY ANDRÉS. *Provincial:* A native of Andalusia, born about 1683, who took the habit in the Franciscan Province of Santiago (Salamanca) about 1709. Came to Mexico with a group from Spain as *predicador general*. Elected custos of N.M., Chapters Jan. 18, 1729, Oct. 28, 1731, April 23, 1735, Aug. 25, 1736. *Jubilación de hebdómada*, July 5, 1730. Feb. 3, 1734, title of *predicador general* for 15 years' service in N.M., 4½ as custos. Santa Fe, 1737. San Antonio Isleta, 1740. San Antonio Senecu, 1743, 1749. Guadalupe del Paso, 1752. San Antonio Senecu, 1760, 1765. 1769, custos, *definidor habitual*, 86 years old, 60 in habit. *Other:*

1749, *predicador general jubilado,* commissary of Holy Office, apostolic notary, ex-definitor, ex-custos. Very active and a prolific polemic writer in controversies between the civil and ecclesiastical authorities in N.M. and those between the Custody of N.M. and the Bishopric of Durango. For published material, see HB and AT.

VEGA, FRAY (JOSÉ) MANUEL (MARTÍNEZ DE LA). *Mission:* San Ildefonso, Sept. 24, 1769—May 2, 1777. Pecos, June, 1764—April, 1766, apparently visiting there from Santa Fe. Also at Santa Fe, Nov., 1769—Feb., 1770, Dec., 1774, Jan., 1775. Santa Clara, May, 1777 through 1778. Albuquerque, May 30, 1779—June 13, 1780. D. 1789 as chaplain of the Presidio of Anamiquipa. *Provincial:* Santa Fe, 1765, *lector de gramática.* 1769, 35 years old, 17 in habit, missionary N.M. Albuquerque, 1772. Oct. 6, 1772, creole, *padre predicador,* N.M., 38 years old, 19 in habit. *C.* 1773, creole, Laguna, 39 years old, 20 in habit. *C.* 1779, chaplain at Goajoquilla. Zuñi, 1788. D. April 10, 1789.

VELASCO, FRAY CARLOS. *Mission:* Entries at Nambe, June 30—Sept. 18, 1777. San Ildefonso, Sept. 25, 1777—Oct. 18, 1778. Acoma, Nov. 21, 1778—Jan. 11, 1779. *Provincial: C.* 1779, has come (to Mexico City) and is in "Guaqueoholac."

VÉLEZ DE ESCALANTE, FRAY SILVESTRE. See HISTORICAL INTRODUCTION and *passim.*

ZABALETA (ZAVALETA), FRAY JUAN DE. In N.M. at time of 1680 Revolt. Minister at Isleta, 1682. Expedition to La Junta, 1683-84, with Fray Nicolás López and Juan Domínguez de Mendoza; forced to flee to Parral and returned to El Paso with Custos Rodríguez de San Antonio early in 1685. Isleta, 1687. To N.M. with de Vargas, 1693. Commissary of Holy Office, 1694. Taos, 1695. Santa Fe, 1699. Elected custos, Chapters July 11, 1699, Jan. 22, 1701. Entries at Tesuque, May—Aug., 1699, Oct., 1700—May, 1701. Bernalillo, Jan. 9—Dec. 1, 1702, June 16,

1703, Aug. 19, 1703—April 26, 1706. Bernalillo, Alameda, 1706.

ZAMBRANO, FRAY MANUEL. *Mission:* Entries at San Felipe, Sept., 1727. Galisteo, Oct. 24, 1732, received mission records. Zia, May 30—Aug. 11, 1727, March 4—Oct. 13, 1728. March, 1729, baptisms at Laguna, Acoma, and Zuñi; Aug., Oct., 1734, at Jémez. Isleta, Oct. 20, 1734—Oct. 25, 1736. Many scattered entries at Santa Fe, Oct., 1727, April—May, 1738, Sept. 5, 1747—July 29, 1749, April 9—Nov., 1752, Jan. 18, 1758—Feb. 15, 1762, Sept., 1762. Nambe, Aug. 26, 1749—May 21, 1752. *Provincial:* Zia, 1725, 1727, 1729. Cochiti, Chapters Oct. 27, 1731, June 2, 1733. Aug. 22, 1736, granted *jubilación de hebdómada* for more than 10 years service in N.M. Acoma, Chapter Aug. 25, 1736. San Felipe, Chapter Oct. 26, 1737. Santo Domingo, 1740. Guadalupe (Junta de los Ríos), 1740, 1743, *padre predicador jubilado.* Santa Fe, 1749, *padre predicador.* San Ildefonso, 1752. Santa Fe, 1760. *Other:* Governor Vélez Cachupín to Viceroy, June 28, 1762, "incapacitated because of poor health."

ZAMORA, FRAY ANTONIO. *Mission:* Entries at Santa Cruz, April 1, 1741. Jémez, Aug. 20—Nov. 26, 1742, June, Aug., 1745, Jan., 1746. Zia, Aug., 1745, July 3, 1746—Feb. 20, 1748. Nambe, May 1, 1748—June 23, 1749. San Felipe, April 8, 1751—March 12, 1752. *Provincial:* Santa Ana, 1740, 1743. Nambe, 1749. Cochiti, 1750. Galisteo, 1752. Santo Domingo, 1760, 1764. *Other:* Governor Vélez Cachupín to Viceroy, June 28, 1762, "incapacitated."

ZARTE, FRAY FRANCISCO IGNACIO. *Mission:* Entries at Santa Fe, March 2—Nov. 30, 1774, Jan. 17, 1775—June 3, 1776. Santo Domingo, June 14, 1776—Jan. 6, 1777. Began new baptismal book at Abiquiu, Feb. 18, 1777, his last entry in it Sept. 13, 1777. Nambe, Nov. 10, 1777—Aug. 29, 1779. *Provincial:* Jémez, 1772. Oct. 6, 1772, creole, *padre predicador,* N.M., 33 years old, 12 in habit. *C.* 1779, has come (to Province) and is in Puebla.

Settlers

In general terms, Domínguez and other contemporary sources usually referred to the Hispanic population of New Mexico as *vecinos* (citizens, neighbors) in contradistinction to the Pueblo Indians. We have rendered *vecinos* as "settlers." These settlers of the province included *españoles* (people of predominantly Spanish blood, whether creoles or Europeans), *gente de razón* (Hispanicized mixtures, including mestizos, mulattoes, and other castes), and sometimes genízaros.

This list contains all the settlers mentioned by Domínguez. Most of the information is taken from *Origins of New Mexico Families* (NMF), with additional material discovered in similar sources after publication of NMF. Non-settlers and secular priests are discussed in footnotes. See INDEX.

It is well to keep in mind that most surnames were spelled differently on occasion, or underwent changes in later generations, and that individuals with multiple Christian names or compound surnames sometimes used only part of them. By Domínguez' time most people had simplified their family names and omitted the preposition "de." Although this list is necessarily confined to details relevant to this work, it does illustrate such name changes and the close relationships among groups of these people.

AGUILAR, JUAN DE. Río Arriba native, born near Santa Clara. Remained in Bernalillo and married Isabel Gutiérrez, Sept. 24, 1781.

ALINI, MIGUEL DE. Misspelling of Miguel de Alire (Aliri). Native of Mexico City who married Isabel de la Vega y Coca of Santa Fe, May 18, 1728. Died a widower, May 15, 1798.

APODACA, JOSÉ DE. Married Petrona García, Albuquerque, March 22, 1745. Captain, 1772, when son Juan Antonio married Lucía Romero.

ARGÜELLO, JUAN [DE]. Native of Zacatecas, married Juana Gregoria Brito at Santa Fe in 1715. His family and the in-laws of his children composed the greater number of the original settlers of Trampas.

ARIAS [DE] QUIRÓS, DIEGO. Native of Asturias and officer of the Reconquest. Married Ana (María) Montoya, or Pacheco, widow of Nicolás Márquez, Santa Fe, July 20, 1694. Received important land grants. Second marriage to María Gómez Robledo (q.v.), aunt of Vicar Roybal, July 28, 1714. In 1746 his widow sold his Santa Fe estate to Bernardino de Sena (Cf. Tomás Antonio de Sena).

ARMIJO, [BÁRBARA] GERTRUDIS. Only child of Antonio Durán de Armijo II and Bárbara Montoya, married Manuel Vigil (q.v.). As her mother had first been married to Diego Romero, father (by a previous wife) of the Romeros of Taos, she and her Vigil husband acquired lands on the Río de las Trampas, or Ranchos de Taos.

ARMIJO, VICENTE. Pecos. There were several contemporaries of the same name, in Santa Fe and the Río Abajo, descendants of four Armijo brothers from Zacatecas. This man was most likely from Santa Fe.

ARTEAGA, MANUEL [DE]. Native of Mexico City, who came prior to March 29, 1761, when he married Isabel López, or Gabaldón, at Santa Cruz. Majordomo of the combined confraternities of the Rosary and the Blessed Sacrament at Santa Fe in 1774. Had moved down to Belén by 1797 when he married Ursula Durán

y Chaves of Los Padillas. Alcalde mayor of Albuquerque as late as 1805.

ATIENZO, FRANCISCA. Not identified. Original family name, "Atienza," evolved into present "Atencio."

BACA, ANTONIO. Eldest son of Josefa Baca of Pajarito, married Mónica Durán y Chaves at Albuquerque, June 16, 1726. Father-in-law of Clemente Gutiérrez (q.v.) and Francisco Trébol Navarro (q.v.).

BACA, BALTASAR. See INDEX.

BACA, DIEGO ANTONIO. Son of Antonio Baca and Mónica de Chaves. Married Juana Sáenz de Garviso (q.v.) in Santa Fe, Oct. 17, 1759. A majordomo of the Confraternity of La Conquistadora prior to 1776 with brother-in-law Francisco Trébol Navarro (q.v.)

BERNAL, ANTONIO. Santa Clara jurisdiction. May have been a man of this name who was living at La Cañada in 1729.

BUSTAMANTE, BERNARDINO [DE]. Correct full name, Bernardo de Bustamante y Tagle. Lieutenant governor of N.M. under Don Juan Domingo de Bustamante (q.v.), and possibly the latter's son or nephew. Still in Santa Fe in 1745 when he deposed that he was a native of Spain and 37 years old. Sold some Santa Fe lands in 1767. Married to Feliciana [de la Vega y] Coca (q.v.). Two daughters were: Josefa Bustamante (q.v.) who was the second wife of Nicolás Ortiz III (q.v.), and Rosa Bustamante, who married Antonio José Ortiz (q.v.), son of the same Nicolás III by a previous marriage.

BUSTAMANTE, JOSEFA. Daughter of Don Bernardo de Bustamante, married a Santa Fe widower, Nicolás Ortiz III (q.v.), Feb. 6, 1751. Was instrumental in reviving the Confraternity of La Conquistadora after her husband's death in 1769. D. Sept. 15, 1810.

BUSTAMANTE, JUAN DOMINGO [DE]. Governor of N.M. two terms, 1722-31. Nephew and son-in-law of interim Governor Valverde y Cosío (q.v.). He was lieutenant governor at Guadalupe del Paso before his promotion to Santa Fe. Relatives of the same name, natives of Spain, followed him to N.M.

BUSTOS, JUAN JOSÉ. Not identified.

CALVES, JOSÉ. Military officer and majordomo of the Confraternity of La Conquistadora in 1775. Lived in Santa Fe with his wife María Miera, very likely a daughter of Bernardo Miera y Pacheco *(q.v.)*.

CAMPOS REDONDO, JOSÉ. Native of Mexico City, and 37 when he joined the Santa Fe Presidio in 1777. Married Feliciana Ortiz Bustamante, daughter of Nicolás Ortiz III *(q.v.)* and Josefa Bustamante *(q.v.)*.

CHAVES, ANTONIO. Perhaps Diego Antonio Chaves, affluent sheepman of Atrisco, who married Juana Silva, Dec. 14, 1740. Or possibly Diego's first cousin, Antonio Chaves, also of Atrisco, who married Bárbara Padilla in 1750.

CISNEROS, JUAN PEDRO. Probably son of Nicolás Cisneros, who married Casilda Mestas of Río Arriba in 1714, for in 1754 Juan Pedro Cisneros and Casilda Mestas jointly sold some Chama property.

COCA, FELICIANA [DE LA VEGA Y]. Daughter of Miguel de la Vega y Coca, colonist from Mexico City in 1694. Married Don Bernardo de Bustamante *(q.v.)*. Sister-in-law of Miguel de Alini *(q.v.)*

DELGADO, MANUEL. Native of Pachuca, married Josefa García de Noriega at Guadalupe del Paso. Later transferred to the Presidio at Santa Fe. Second marriage to Ana María Baca in 1814. D. Aug. 13, 1815.

DOMÍNGUEZ, ANTONIO. Not identified.

DOMÍNGUEZ, MARÍA. In all probability the Indian woman of this name, who was 34 and single in 1740 when she testified in a Santa Fe trial, and whose nickname was "La Sacristana."

FERNÁNDEZ, BARTOLOMÉ. Son of Juan Fernández de la Pedrera and María Hurtado, married Luisa Tenorio de Alba in Santa Fe, May 8,

1740. Charter member of the Confraternity of Our Lady of Light.

FERNÁNDEZ [XIRALDO], CARLOS. Native of Zamora, Spain, married as early as 1744 to Juana Padilla, granddaughter of Sebastián Martín Serrano *(q.v.)*, through whom she acquired land in the Taos Valley; hence, this is probably the man after whom the later town of Fernández de Taos was named, there having been no Fernández people in Taos previously. Alcalde of La Cañada 1762-63, when he received a commission at the Santa Fe Presidio. A first majordomo of the revived Confraternity of La Conquistadora.

FRESQUIES, JUAN. Not identified. A Flemish name spelled "Fresqui" and "Fresquis" in the seventeenth and eighteenth centuries, and now "Frésquez."

GABALDÓN, JUAN [MANUEL]. Native of Puebla. In N.M. as early as 1731. Married Antonia Juliana Archibeque, niece of Vicar Roybal, July 26, 1735. Probably a nephew or younger brother of Fray Antonio Gabaldón.

GARCÍA [DE NORIEGA], JUAN ESTEBAN. Moved to Río Arriba area and at San Ildefonso married Luisa Gómez del Castillo, June 23, 1721. Ex-Governor Valverde *(q.v.)* was sponsor at the wedding.

GARCÍA DE NORIEGA, SALVADOR. Most likely a son of Juan Esteban. Wife María Martín had twins baptized at San Juan in 1760. In same year Salvador married Polonia Sandoval, widow of Manuel Tenorio, at Santa Fe.

GARDUÑO, JOSÉ MIGUEL. Grandson of Bartolomé Garduño, Reconquest settler from Querétaro who married Catalina Durán in 1695. José Miguel was a soldier of the Presidio by 1752.

GARVISO, JUANA. See Sáenz de Garviso.

GÓMEZ [ROBLEDO], MARÍA. Daughter of Andrés Gómez Robledo, officer killed in siege of Santa Fe, 1680, and Juana Ortiz. Aunt of Vicar Roybal. Married Spaniard, Alonso Romero, 1693; latter proved a bigamist and marriage annulled. In 1714 she married another

Spaniard, the widower Diego Arias de Quirós (*q.v.*). D., Santa Fe, May 21, 1752.

GONZÁLEZ [BAZ, BAS], ALEJANDRO. Son of Juan González Baz II and in charge of the chapel at Alameda as early as 1759. Married to Teresa Fernández de la Pedrera, probably a sister of Bartolomé Fernández (*q.v.*).

GONZÁLEZ [BAZ II], JUAN. Son of Juan González Baz I and María López del Castillo, who returned with the Reconquest and built family chapel at Alameda. Born at Alameda, Jan. 10, 1710. Evidently the man of this name whose wife was Manuela Baca.

GUTIÉRREZ, CLEMENTE. A Spaniard from Aragón who married Polonia Baca at Isleta, Oct. 13, 1755. Son-in-law of Antonio Baca (*q.v.*) and brother-in-law of Francisco Trébol Navarro (*q.v.*).

HERRERA, JOSÉ. Pecos. Most likely a José de Herrera, son of Miguel de Herrera and Antonia de Archuleta, born shortly after his father was murdered in 1712.

HURTADO, JOSÉ. See Mónica Martín.

HURTADO, JUAN MANUEL. Not identified.

LAÍN [HERREROS], JOAQUÍN. Native of Santa Cruz, near Coca in Castilla la Vieja. Married Josefa Tafoya of Santa Fe in 1768. Second marriage to Micaela Sánchez of Río Abajo. D. 1799.

LAVADIA, DOMINGO. Native of France, married Micaela Padilla, sister of Juana Padilla (*q.v.*), Santa Fe, Nov. 2, 1766. In 1790 census of San Juan, when he gave his age as 52.

LEAL, NICOLÁS. Appears as a witness at Chimayó, Aug. 18, 1752. Married to Ambrosia Martín. Son, Juan Domingo, born Aug. 5, 1755, married Verónica Cortés.

LEIVA (LEYBA), JERÓNIMO. Not identified.

LOBATO, JUAN JOSÉ. Married Elena Martín at San Juan, Nov. 27, 1733. Son, Juan Agustín, was born at Ojo Caliente and baptized at Santa Clara, Sept. 5, 1746.

LÓPEZ, ANTONIA. Not identified.

LÓPEZ, CARLOS. Perhaps the seventeenth-century New Mexican of this name who returned with the Reconquest to resettle the Río Arriba country. Wife, María González de Apodaca, died in 1712, and he married Juana de Cedillo in 1716.

LÓPEZ, JOSÉ ANTONIO. Married María Roybal, daughter of Bernardo Roybal and Margarita Martín, at San Juan, 1758. María was a niece of Vicar Roybal, half-sister of Juana Padilla (*q.v.*), and granddaughter of Sebastián Martín Serrano (*q.v.*).

LÓPEZ, MANUELA. Not identified.

LUCERO, SIMÓN. Not identified.

LUCERO DE GODOY, JUAN. Born in Santa Fe *c.* 1624, eldest son of Pedro Lucero de Godoy and his first wife, Petronila de Zamora (Montoya). *Sargento mayor* and alcalde of Santa Fe when the capital was captured by rebel Indians in 1680, he escaped with large family. Returned to Santa Fe in 1693 with third wife, Isabel de Salazar, whom he married at El Real de San Lorenzo, Jan. 14, 1689.

MADRID, CRISTÓBAL. Very likely a man of this name who made his will in 1765.

MAESE, JOSÉ FRANCISCO. Not identified.

MALDONADO, JOSÉ. A soldier of Santa Fe, who married María Luisa Tenorio, March 19, 1754. Second in command of the Presidio in 1789 when he made his will. D. June 14, 1789.

MARTÍN. Individuals of this name belonged to the numerous Martín Serrano family of the Río Arriba area. The name is now erroneously designated as "Martínez." It is difficult to identify them because there were so many contemporaries with the same baptismal and family name.

MARTÍN, ANTONIO. See Catalina de Villalpando.

MARTÍN, DIEGO. Not identified.

MARTÍN, JOSÉ. Resident of Santa Rosa de Abiquiu, bought and sold Río Arriba lands in 1764. Very likely the man of this name married to Micaela Valdés.

MARTÍN, JUAN PABLO. In 1728 a youth of this name, son of Miguel Martín Serrano of La Cañada, was the accusing witness in a celebrated morals case.

MARTÍN, MARCIAL. Eldest son and chief heir of Sebastián Martín Serrano (q.v.) of La Soledad in Río Arriba. His wife was Lugarda Medina.

MARTÍN, MÓNICA. Widow of Francisco Xavier Romero (d. 1768), nephew of Ana María Romero (See Catalina de Villalpando). In 1770, Mónica's second husband was a José Bustamante, alias Mirabal, who probably was the José Hurtado mentioned by Domínguez.

MARTÍN [SERRANO], SEBASTIÁN. Famous landowner and Indian fighter. Son of Pedro Martín Serrano de Salazar, seventeenth-century New Mexican who returned with family and relatives to reclaim Río Arriba lands. Sebastián's widow, María Luján, made her will in 1765.

MARTÍNEZ, RITA. Not identified.

MESTAS, JOAQUÍN. Son of Juan de Mestas Peralta, seventeenth-century New Mexican who returned with the Reconquest. First wife, Teresa Tafoya, had a son baptized at Santa Clara, 1742. Married second wife, Victoria Sánchez, at La Cañada, May 16, 1756.

MESTAS, JUAN IGNACIO. Son of Ventura Mestas.

MESTAS, VENTURA. Younger brother of Joaquín Mestas, married Catalina Jurado, who died in 1767 and left one son, Juan Ignacio. He died in 1771, shortly after his marriage to María Juana Vigil. The family name is now wrongly spelled "Maestas."

MIERA Y PACHECO, BERNARDO. Soldier and cartographer. Native of Valle de Carriedo, Montañas de Burgos. Came with his family from Chihuahua to El Paso in 1743, thence to

Santa Fe in 1754-56. Married to Estefania Domínguez de Mendoza of Chihuahua. Two sons, later prominent, were Cleto and Manuel. D. Santa Fe, April 11, 1785.

MIRABAL, CARLOS [JOSÉ PÉREZ]. Settled in Santa Clara area at the time Fray Juan José Pérez de Mirabal was missionary among the Río Arriba pueblos. Hence, possibly a younger brother of the latter. Married Beatriz Tafoya, moved to Santa Fe by 1758, thence to the Río Abajo.

MONTAÑO, ANA. Not identified.

MONTES VIGIL. See Vigil.

MONTOYA, ANTONIO. Son of Diego Montoya and Josefa de Hinojos. He returned to N.M. in 1693 with his parents and many relatives. Married Bernarda Baca in Bernalillo, May 20, 1707. Was the captain in charge, 1731, of alms distribution from church tithes and flocks. Moved to Santa Fe, 1732, there married a second time. D. Santa Rosa de Abiquiu, where he had established an hacienda, Aug. 8, 1754.

MONTOYA, LUGARDA. Not identified.

MORENO, [JUAN] JOSÉ. Native of Spain, junior officer at Santa Fe Presidio in 1732. Married Juana Roybal (q.v.), at San Ildefonso, July 8, 1732.

MUÑIZ, ANDRÉS. Not identified.

MUÑIZ, ANTONIO LUCRECIO. Not identified.

OLIVARES, LORENZO DE. El Paso settler. Not identified.

ORCASITAS, RAMÓN. El Paso settler. Not identified.

ORTIZ, ANA [MARÍA]. Wife of José Reaño II (q.v.), was one of several contemporaries of this name in Santa Fe. Most likely a daughter of Francisco Ortiz and Francisca Montoya.

ORTIZ, ANTONIO JOSÉ. Born Sept. 6, 1734, son of Nicolás Ortiz III (q.v.) by first wife, Gertrudis Páez Hurtado. Married stepmother's younger sister, Rosa Bustamante, Dec. 31, 1754 (See Josefa Bustamante). D. August, 1806. Succeeded Carlos Fernández (*q.v.*) as majordomo of the Confraternity of La Conquistadora in 1771, and at the turn of the century rebuilt and enlarged nave and south chapel of the Santa Fe Parroquia, also renovating its original sanctuary and the north Conquistadora Chapel. Likewise, restored the sanctuary of San Miguel, and erected famed Rosario Chapel shortly before his death.

ORTIZ, JUAN [ANTONIO]. Probably the younger brother of Antonio José Ortiz. Married María Loreta Ribera, Dec. 13, 1755. Through a son, Juan Rafael, grandfather of Don Juan Felipe Ortiz, Vicar in Santa Fe when the U.S. occupied N.M. in 1846.

ORTIZ [III], NICOLÁS. Son of Nicolás Ortiz II and Juana Baca. On May 28, 1730, married Gertrudis, daughter of interim Governor Juan Páez Hurtado (1704-05, 1717). Among five children were Antonio José and Juan Antonio (*q.v.*). Second marriage, Feb. 6, 1751, to Josefa Bustamante (*q.v.*), one of their daughters becoming wife of José Campos Redondo (*q.v.*). After his death in battle near Abiquiu, his body was brought to Santa Fe and buried on Sept. 4, 1769.

PADILLA, JUANA. Daughter of Juan Padilla and Margarita Martín, married Carlos Fernández (*q.v.*). Grandchild of Sebastián Martín Serrano (*q.v.*) and sister-in-law of Domingo Labadía (*q.v.*)

PANDO. See Villalpando.

PAREJA, MANUEL [GARCÍA]. Native of Tembleque near Toledo, married and widowed before coming to N.M. Married Rosalía Abeyta at San Juan, Nov. 4, 1755.

PEÑA, JOSÉ MIGUEL DE LA. See INDEX.

PINO, PEDRO [JOSÉ]. Son of Mateo José Pino, member of a Río Abajo family that came from Mexico City. Eldest brother of Pedro Bautista Pino, remembered as only delegate from N.M. to the Spanish Cortes. The latter was his brother's teniente at Acoma. See INDEX.

REAÑO [II], JOSÉ [DE]. Only son of José de Reaño y Tagle, Spaniard from the Montañas de Santander, and María Roybal, a sister of Vicar Roybal. Married Ana María Ortiz (*q.v.*) in Santa Fe, June 14, 1747. Demented after fall from a horse, was confined at the Presidio in Feb., 1763. He ran away with a young first cousin of his wife and four genízaro servants. Their bones were found on the eastern plains the following summer.

ROMERO, RITA. Not identified.

ROMERO, TEODORA. Not identified.

ROYBAL, JUANA. Wife of Juan José Moreno (*q.v.*) and a sister of Vicar Roybal. Daughter of Ignacio de Roybal and Francisca Gómez Robledo, and niece of María Gómez Robledo (*q.v.*).

RUIZ, VICENTE. Settler of El Paso. Not identified.

SÁENZ DE GARVISO [GARVISU], JUANA. Born in Santa Fe, Dec. 1, 1742, daughter of Manuel Sáenz de Garvisu, a native of Spain, and Ignacia Lucero de Godoy. Both her father and her husband, Diego Antonio Baca (*q.v.*), served as majordomos of the revived Confraternity of La Conquistadora.

SALAS, MARÍA IGNACIA. Not identified.

SÁNCHEZ, FRANCISCO. Not identified.

SÁNCHEZ, JOSÉ. Not identified.

SANDOVAL, JUAN JOSÉ. Son of Juan de Dios Sandoval Martínez, 1694 colonist from Mexico City. Married María Fernández at La Cañada in 1720.

SANDOVAL, MIGUEL. Most likely a son of Miguel de Dios Sandoval Martínez and Lucía Gómez Robledo, the latter an aunt of Vicar Roybal and sister of María Gómez Robledo (*q.v.*). Nephew of Juan José Sandoval (*q.v.*).

SENA, TOMÁS [ANTONIO] DE. Only son of Bernardino de Sena, 1694 colonist from Mexico City, and his first wife, Tomasa Martín González. Armorer and blacksmith. Married María Luisa García de Noriega in 1723. In 1763 registered a mine, *N.S. de los Dolores,* south of the hill called "Turquoise." D. in Santa Fe, Feb. 11, 1781.

SERNA, ANTONIA. Daughter of Felipe de la Serna and Isabel Luján, New Mexicans who returned to N.M. with the Reconquest. Wife of Matías Madrid (d. Feb. 18, 1727). However, the woman mentioned by Domínguez could have been a daughter or niece of the elder Antonia.

TAFOYA, FELIPE. Son of Antonio de Tafoya Altamirano, Reconquest colonist. Married Margarita González de la Rosa in 1728, and Teresa Fernández in 1750. Practiced medicine to some extent. Served as alcalde of Santa Fe and lieutenant governor.

TAFOYA, JOSÉ MIGUEL. Not identified.

TORRES, JUAN [DOMINGO]. Son of Marcial Torres of Taos by second wife, María Martín, the latter a daughter of Antonio Martín and Catalina de Villalpando *(q.v.).* A sister of Juan was killed by the Comanches, and his mother and two sisters were taken captive and never seen again.

TRÉBOL [NAVARRO], FRANCISCO. Newcomer to N.M., married María Ignacia Baca, sister-in-law of Clemente Gutiérrez *(q.v.),* Oct. 9, 1765. Commandant of the Santa Fe Presidio when he made his will in 1785. Shortly thereafter he died in Río Arriba, perhaps during an Indian campaign, and was buried in the military chapel, Santa Fe, June 10, 1785.

VALDÉS Y BUSTOS, FRANCISCO. Natural son of José Valdés and Josefa de Ontiveros, who later married a certain Bustos. Married Lugarda Martín in La Cañada, Oct. 11, 1723. Second marriage to Tomasa Benavides. In 1752 he registered a cattle brand at La Cañada.

VALVERDE Y COSÍO, ANTONIO. Interim governor of N.M. (1717-22). Uncle of Governor Juan Domingo Bustamante *(q.v.).* Following the Reconquest he lived at different times in Santa Fe, El Paso, and at the Roybal rancho near San Ildefonso, but finally settled permanently at El Paso, where he died, Dec. 15, 1728.

VEGA Y COCA. See Coca.

VIGIL, CRISTÓBAL [MONTES]. Probably the man of this name living in La Cañada with wife Teodora Medina. They had four sons who enlisted in the N.M. militia between 1761 and 1781.

VIGIL, JUAN BAUTISTA [MONTES]. A man of this name and his wife, Candelaria Medina, lived in La Cañada. Two of their sons enlisted in the N.M. militia in 1779 and 1787.

VIGIL, MANUEL [MONTES]. Husband of Bárbara Gertrudis Armijo *(q.v.),* and son of Juan Montes Vigil and Inez López of Santa Fe. Second marriage to Magdalena Valdés of Abiquiu, May 8, 1777.

VILLALPANDO, CATALINA DE. Wife of Antonio Martín of Embudo, and daughter of Juan de Villa el Pando, a Reconquest soldier who married Ana María Romero in Santa Fe, June 2, 1694. Her husband could well be the Antonio Martín at Ojo Caliente mentioned by Domínguez.

VILLALPANDO, PABLO [DE]. Brother of Catalina de Villalpando. Like the closely related Romero and Martín people of Embudo, resided variously at Taos or at Ojo Caliente, depending on the seriousness of the Comanche menace. He owned the largest house in the Taos Valley, which was attacked by Comanches on Aug. 4, 1760. His wife was killed while fighting. Having left on business that day, he escaped the massacre and capture of his family and neighbors.

GLOSSARY

ACCESSORIES, *avíos*. The matching pieces accompanying the chasuble, or largest Mass vestment, including the stole, maniple, chalice veil, and burse, and sometimes the cope, dalmatics, and the altar frontal. The term also is used for the incense boat and spoon as *avíos* of the thurible.

ACOLYTE, *acólito*. Liturgically, one of the Minor Orders, or steps leading to the priesthood, the special office of the acolyte being to assist the celebrant at solemn functions. Since ordained acolytes seldom were available, their duties were taken over by laymen and boys, and so acolyte was a synonym for "server," even in Domínguez' time.

ADOBE. Sun-dried brick. Also applied in English to the earth from which adobes are made.

ALB, *alba*. A loose-fitting white linen gown completely covering the priest's cassock or habit and brought together at the waist by the cincture. It is a necessary foundation for the rest of the Mass apparel.

ALCALDE MAYOR. In N.M., a subordinate official appointed by the governor to administer a subdivision of the province.

ALL SAINTS, *Todos los Santos*. A major feast day of obligation (Nov. 1) to honor all the saved or saints in heaven.

ALMUD. As a dry measure the almud varies greatly according to the locality; it can be from 3 to 23 liters.

ALTAR, *altar:* The altar table proper, or mensa, but also applied to whatever superstructures it may have, such as gradins *(sotabancos)*, a reredos or retable, or free-standing niches (which Domínguez calls *capillitas*, "little shrines"). The high altar *(altar mayor)* is the focal point of a church or chapel, in the sanctuary toward the rear wall opposite the main entrance. "Side altars" are those along the walls of the nave or transept. Domínguez referred to these as "coraterales" *(colaterales)* and also applied the term to any altar screen *(q.v.)*. In Spanish America *colateral* (side altar) was frequently used for any altar, even the high altar.

ALTAR BREAD, *hostia.* The bread or wafer to be consecrated at the Sacrifice of the Mass, host. *Hostiario,* box for altar breads, or host box; *hierro molde de hostias,* iron for baking altar breads.

ALTAR CARDS. Three tablets, usually framed, which contain certain prayers as an aid to the priest's memory. These cards were optional in Domínguez' day and therefore absent from most of the missions.

ALTAR CLOTH, *palia.* Three long linen cloths were required for the altar table on which Mass is celebrated, the top one hanging to the floor at either end. *Palia* can also mean tabernacle veil and usually does when the context shows that it was of silk or any fine material other than linen; in the latter case it is probably an altar cloth. Domínguez often uses the expression, "tabla de manteles," which originally meant the set of three cloths.

ALTAR COVER, *palio.* Like the feminine form, *palia,* the word is used for different kinds of altar coverings, as well as the chalice veil (Cf. Pall). It can also mean the canopy *(q.v.).* (The liturgical meaning for the special insignia of an archbishop does not apply in Domínguez.)

ALTAR RAIL, *barandal del presbiterio.* A railing separating the sanctuary from the nave, or body, of the church. Domínguez also uses *barandal* for the railing on the choir loft and the one on the porch above the main entrance, as well as *antepecho,* which is more properly a parapet, or breastwork. The altar rail is also called the communion rail in English.

ALTAR SCREEN, *retablo, colateral.* Reredos; a decorative screen or structure behind an altar.

ALTAR STONE, *ara.* The stone slab which covers the top of the altar table and is the essential part of a Catholic altar. It has a small sealed cavity in the center containing relics of early Christian martyrs, and is consecrated by a bishop. In lesser churches and in the missions, the stone is a small slab, in all respects like the large one, inserted in the center of the wooden top of the altar. It is then called a portable altar.

AMICE, *amito.* A linen cloth which the priest places on his head before putting on the alb, fastened by two ribbons crossed over the breast and tied around the waist. The secular clergy, using the biretta, or peaked cap, tuck the amice around the neck immediately thereafter. Members of the old Religious Orders, who wear a hood, continue to use the amice over the head or on the hood.

ANNIVERSARY OF THE FAITHFUL DEPARTED, *Aniversario de los difuntos.* Celebrated on Nov. 2, after the feast of All Saints, to remember the faithful departed in Purgatory; called All Souls in England, and also referred to as Poor Souls *(q.v.).*

ARRAS. Thirteen small coins used in wedding ceremonies to symbolize the endowment of the bride by the groom. The ring came to be considered part of the arras. These were kept in church in eighteenth-century N.M. because few people could afford to bring their own.

ARROBA. A weight of approximately 25 pounds, or a liquid measure of about 4 gallons.

ASCENSION, FEAST OF THE, *La Asención.* A major feast day of obligation commemorating the final bodily departure of Christ from this earth forty days after the Resurrection. Since it always falls on a Thursday, it is also called *Jueves de la Asención.*

ASPERGILLUM, *hisopo.* A sprinkler for holy water. The use of the terms aspergillum and hyssop in Latin and other languages was inspired by the Psalm recited in this ceremony: *Asperges me hyssopo.*

ASSUMPTION OF OUR LADY, *La Asunción.* The taking up of Mary's revived body into Heaven shortly after her death, as distinct from Christ's spontaneous Resurrection and Ascension. Feast, Aug. 15.

ATOLE. A gruel, or thin porridge, made of corn meal.

BACHILLER. The first degree taken in various disciplines, but not precisely equivalent to the English degree of bachelor because of the differences in the educational systems. "Br.," the abbreviation, frequently used by secular priests, has sometimes been mistaken for "Fr." (Fray) in Spanish manuscripts.

BANNER, *guión, pendón, estandarte.* Distinct terms often used interchangeably in the same way that the English words, guidon, pennant, and standard, frequently are confused. Both civil and religious banners apparently hung down vertically from a transverse bar on a staff.

BAPTISMAL HOOD, *capillo*. A tight hood placed on infants after their birth. Attached to the child's white dress at the ceremonies of baptism, the *capillo* gave its name to the entire garment as well as to the fee or offering.

BELLS, *campanas*. This term is used for all bells. In N.M., even those with clappers were not swung. The clapper was struck against the bell by pulling a thong attached to it. This is still done in Spanish country churches. Bells without clappers were struck on the outside with metal bars or with stones, as is still done in most Indian pueblos. The dimunitive, *campanita,* refers to small hand bells used at the altar, either singly, or several attached to a hoop or wheel *(rueda de campanitas).*

BETHLEHEMITES. An order of hospital brothers under the advocacy of Our Lady of Bethlehem, founded in Guatemala by a Capuchin Tertiary, Pedro de Bethancur (Bethencourt), who died in 1667.

BLESSED SACRAMENT, *Santísimo Sacramento,* also called *el Santísimo* or *el Divinísimo.* In English "Blessed" is preferred to "Holy" in this connection.

BLOOD OF CHRIST, *Sangre de Cristo.* Feast (July 1) commemorating Christ's shedding of His Blood in His Passion and Death, and the consecrated Blood in the Eucharist. The increase of devotion in this regard toward the end of the eighteenth century gave the name "Sangre de Cristo" to the mountain range running from Santa Fe into Colorado, called the "Sierra Madre" in Domínguez' time.

BREVIARY, *breviario*. A compendium of the Divine Office with the Psalms for each day, lessons from the Bible according to the Church seasons, short lives of the saints for each day, etc. The Franciscans had the privilege of inserting the lives of the beatified and canonized members of their Order into the body of the Roman Breviary. Hence the *breviario con nuestros santos* is a reference to the *Breviarium Romano-Seraphicum.*

BURSE, *bolsa.* A small square pouch in which to carry the corporal for the Mass, covered with material to match the chasuble. It is placed over the veil-covered chalice before and after Mass.

CAÑADA. See p. 41 *supra.*

CANDLEHOLDER, *cirial.* A portable or stationary candlestick for *cirios,* large thick candles, used in processions. Domínguez also used *arandela,* which means the top part of a candlestick, a low dishlike candlestick of the same shape, or even a sconce.

CANDLESTICK, *candelero.* A large stationary candlestick. *Candeleros* was applied by Domínguez to the six liturgical ones on the main altar. Smaller ones are called *blandoncitos,* which also means the squarish wax candles that they hold.

CANON LAW, *sagrados cánones.* A loose collection of universal Church legislation accumulated through the centuries, condensed and codified in modern times in the *Codex Iuris Canonici.*

CANOPY, *palio.* A portable shade borne on four poles with ornamented cloth ceiling and side valances, held over the Blessed Sacrament in processions. *Baldoquín* designated the stationary pillared or hanging canopy over the tabernacle, and sometimes a throne for dignitaries, such as the bishop (or in N.M., the governor), consisting of a dais, chair, hanging curtains, and a canopy of the same material, the name of the whole sometimes used for any of the parts.

CAPE, *capa.* A cape of any size or shape, such as the large mantle used by priests, religious, and laymen of former times; also specifically the *capa pluvial,* or *de coro.* See Cope. The diminutive, *capilla,* refers to short shoulder capes that were a part of the friars' habits next to the hood or capuche, or to ornamental capes worn by Mass-servers over the surplice or rochet. In one instance Domínguez uses *muceta,* the shoulder cape worn by a bishop, but here the reference must be to a server's cape.

CAPUCHINS. A reform branch of the Franciscan Order which separated from the Observants in Italy in 1525. A long beard and a long pointed hood, or capuche, were distinctive marks of this order from the very start.

CASAS REALES. "Royal palace." In N.M., the residence of the royal governor and the headquarters of the government in Santa Fe. The term is also used, in the singular or plural, for a building owned and maintained by many Indian pueblos for the accommodation of officials, merchants, travelers, or others who had reason to spend any time in the pueblo, and as a place in which to transact business with them. For the protection of the Indians, Spanish law discouraged the presence of outsiders in Indian pueblos. The plural usually denotes a more pretentious or larger edifice. These are also called *casas de comunidad* (community houses), or *mesones* (inns.)

CATAFALQUE, *tumba, monumento.* The *tumba* was a frame covered with a black cloth to simulate a casket placed in the aisle in front of the altar rail at special Masses for the dead. The cloth was usually embroidered with white or silver crosses and trimmings, and even with skulls and crossbones (now forbidden). The *monumento* was a pyramidal frame with several steps, draped and decorated like the *tumba,* erected in the center aisle near the entrance at Anniversary Masses.

CATHEDRA. The official throne of a bishop, and, by extension, of other high dignitaries.

CELEBRANT, *celebrante.* The priest who performs a liturgical function, especially the Mass. If alone, he is also called the minister *(ministro),* but this word refers more specifically to his assistants, deacons, subdeacons, etc., when the function is performed by several clergymen.

CEMETERY, *cementerio.* The consecrated churchyard used for burials, and in later usage, any graveyard. Domínguez applied *campo santo* to an extra churchyard at Santa Fe (p. 15 *supra*).

CHALICE VEIL. A square piece of material to match the chasuble, placed over the chalice, paten, and pall, and under the burse, before and after Mass.

CHANTERS, SINGERS, *cantores.* Those who chant the ordinary and proper parts of the Mass, or the office in choir, whether clergy or laymen.

CHASUBLE, *casulla, ornamento.* The outer vestment of the celebrant at Mass. The color chosen depends upon the feast or season. Domínguez frequently mentions chasubles with two faces, which made it possible for one garment to serve for two of the liturgical colors.

CIBORIUM, *copón.* The chalice-shaped vessel, with a tight-fitting lid surmounted by a cross, in which the consecrated Hosts are kept. The old Spanish type had a paten, or circular plate, inside.

CIÉNEGA. In N.M., a small marsh surrounded by arid land. Archaic form of *Ciénaga.*

CINCTURE, *cíngulo.* A long girdle with which the priest binds the loose alb about the waist and secures the stole.

CIRCUMCISION, *La Circuncisión.* A major feast day of obligation (Jan. 1), celebrating the octave of Christmas, and the Circumcision of Christ.

CLOISTER, *claustro.* Used specifically by Domínguez to designate the covered walk, sometimes completely enclosed except for windows, sometimes with railings or pillars, surrounding the court or patio of the convent.

COMMISSARY, *comisario.* One to whom a special task is committed. Used in this sense in Domínguez' title as Commissary Visitor empowering him to act for his Provincial in the formal visitation of the New Mexico missions. The offices of Commissary General of the Indies and Commissary General of New Spain and of Peru were instituted after the discovery of the New World, the first to reside in Madrid and have general supervision of all the Franciscan Provinces of the Indies under the Minister General of the Order and in accordance with the royal patronage; and the others to reside in America and exercise supervision over the areas assigned to them, subject to their superior in Spain. The title of Commissary is now also used in place of Custos *(q.v.)* with the single exception of the Custos of the Holy Land.

CONFRATERNITY, *cofradía.* A local church society, independent or affiliated to a larger group, to promote the glory of the society's patron, aid the pastor in parish affairs, assure suffrages for deceased members, and engage in charitable works. The erection of a confraternity needed the official approval of the bishop.

CONVENT, *convento.* From Latin, *conventus* (gathering), the official name for a Franciscan dwelling. St. Francis was against his followers' having even a dwelling-place, but necessity soon dictated the adoption of humble "convents" as distinct from the large, and often sumptuous, monasteries. A less permanent dwelling was a *hospitium* (hospice), called *ermita* in Spanish. Officially today, a formed or mature Franciscan house is a *conventus*, while an unformed house is a *residentia* (residence); a less important dwelling is a hospice. The term "friary" was coined in Mediaeval England. The term monastery has been used in the United States, but some attempt is being made to return to the old English term, since English-speaking Franciscans shy away from the old official term, convent, because of its association in modern times with the dwellings of female religious. The Franciscan influence in N.M. was so strong that to this day a secular priest's rectory is called a *convento,* and his housekeeper a "conventera."

CONVENT OF RECOLLECTION, *convento de recolección.* A convent set apart purely for contemplation, where the rule was strictly observed without the distraction of outside duties with seculars. This is not to be confused with the Franciscan "family" of Recollect friars.

CONVENTO GRANDE. The Convent of St. Francis in Mexico City, mother house of the Franciscan Order in New Spain, and headquarters of the Province of the Holy Gospel. Established in the 1520's.

CONVERSION OF ST. PAUL. Feast (Jan. 25) commemorating the incident related in the Acts of the Apostles when lightning struck St. Paul from his horse and he heard Christ saying, "Why persecutest thou Me?" Paul answered, "Lord, what wilt Thou have me do?" The seal of the Custody of the Conversion of St. Paul of New Mexico showed a man falling from a rearing horse, with Paul's reply, *Domine, quid me vis facere,* inscribed around the edge. Reproduced on title page, *supra.*

COPE, *capa pluvial, capa de coro.* A hooded cape originally used by vested priests in processions outside. It developed into a liturgical vestment for use in solemn functions in choir or at the altar.

CORPORAL, *corporal.* The square piece of linen on which the Body of Christ is laid at Mass.

Domínguez usually speaks of *corporales dobles,* and it is not clear whether he means folded *(doblados),* double-weave or thickness, or possibly of double size so that one end could be folded over the chalice in lieu of a pall *(q.v.).*

CORPUS CHRISTI. Feast of the Holy Eucharist occurring on the Thursday after Trinity Sunday. Usually in June.

CROSS, *cruz.* Technically, a cross without the figure of Christ, but often used to designate a crucifix. Here the reference is to the Latin cross on church pediments and towers, graves, hills, and fields. Inside the churches, large crosses served to hang the hinged figures of Christ on Good Friday; there were also small processional crosses on staffs, so called although these were usually crucifixes *(q.v.).*

CROSS SHEATH, *manga de cruz.* A sleeve-like sheath of fine cloth which was tied on a processional cross and hung from the point where the staff meets the cross or crucifix proper. In Spanish countries it has a cylindrical frame so that it resembles a peaked tubular umbrella or a lamp-shade.

CRUCIFIX, *crucifijo.* A plain or ornamental cross with the image of Christ Crucified attached to it. The altar crucifix had a base like that of the candlesticks. A crucifix is also often called a *Cristo.* Domínguez describes many crucifixes with an INRI, or Dolorosa, or both. The INRI, found at the top of most crucifixes, stands for *Iesus Nazarenus Rex Iudaeorum* (Jesus of Nazareth, King of the Jews). The Mater Dolorosa, or Dolorosa, was an image of Mary sorrowing at the foot of the cross as recorded in St. John and paraphrased in the poem of the Franciscan Jacopone da Todi, *Stabat Mater Dolorosa.* See Our Lady of Sorrows.

CRUETS, *vinajeras.* Two small vessels of glass or metal, one for the wine and the other for the water used at Mass.

CUARTILLA. As a liquid measure, usually about 25 liters; as a dry measure, 12 cuartillos *(q.v.).*

CUARTILLO. As a liquid measure, about half a liter; as a dry measure, about 2 liters.

CUSTODY, *custodia.* When his followers became so numerous that they had to be divided into groups, St. Francis chose this term in preference to "abbey" or other more formal designations. After his time the larger groups adopted the term "province," using "custody" for smaller groups dependent on a full-fledged province. This was the status of the Custody of the Conversion of St. Paul in N.M., which was dependent on the Province of the Holy Gospel in Mexico City for more than two centuries.

CUSTOS, *custodio.* The head of a Franciscan Custody. The term is used officially today for the vice-provincial. The eighteenth-century title of custos is equivalent to the modern commissary.

DALMATICS, *dalmáticas.* A pair of wide-sleeved, square-cut vestments of the same material as the chasuble, worn by the deacon and subdeacon assisting the celebrant at a solemn function. The subdeacon's garment is properly called a tunicle.

DEFINITOR, *definidor.* A member of the four-man council of a provincial or an old-time custos.

DEVOTION, *devoción.* An informal association of members without officers or bylaws for the promotion of some pious project.

ECCE HOMO. The words of Pilate when he presented Christ to the populace after He had been scourged, crowned with thorns, a red robe thrown over His naked shoulders, and a reed placed in His bound hands for a scepter. This is the specific image to which Domínguez refers. Some of these were seated figures. Many of them had hinged arms and, when attached to a cross, were called *Cristos;* dressed in a long rope-girdled robe, with a large cross placed over one shoulder, such an image became a *Jesús Nazareno (q.v.);* or laid out as for burial, it was called a *Santo Sepulcro* (see Holy Sepulcher.)

EPISTLE SIDE, *lado de la epístola.* The right side of the altar as one faces it, where the Epistle of the Mass is sung or recited; hence, the entire right side of the church.

EXALTATION OF THE HOLY CROSS, *Exaltación de la Santa Cruz.* Feast (Sept. 14) commemorating the rescue of the True Cross from the Persians by Heraclius. De Vargas took peaceful possession of Santa Fe on this day in 1692, and from then on it became the patronal title of the New Mexican troops to the end of the Spanish period.

FABRIC, *fábrica. Fabrica ecclesiae,* which includes not only the funds necessary for church construction, but the repair and maintenance of the building, the funds necessary to defray these expenses, any income applied for these purposes, and the persons in charge of administering church property, who were usually laymen, sometimes entitled *fabriqueros,* or *mayordomos de la fábrica.*

FANEGA. A dry measure of more than 1.5 to more than 2.5 bushels, according to the locality.

FIRST FRUITS, *primicias.* A voluntary annual offering from the harvests and herds, seldom requested from the poor and never from the Indians.

FISCAL MAYOR. As used here, an Indian official appointed to assist the father and see to it that the Indians performed their religious duties.

FRAY. A contraction of *fraile* (friar) used only as a title, never as a substantive and never apart from the first, or religious, name. It may be used with the full name of a friar, but not with the surname alone. For centuries it has been abbreviated as "Fr." in many languages. The use of the same abbreviation for Father in English has led to confusion.

FRIARS MINOR, *frailes menores.* The official name of the Franciscans, Order of Friars Minor, abbreviated as O.F.M.

FRONTAL, *frontal.* The front facing, plain or decorated, of an altar table; also a decorative curtain hung before it, an antependium.

GENÍZARO. See n. 72, p. 42 *supra.*

GOSPEL SIDE, *lado del evangelio.* The left side of the altar as one faces it; where the Gospel of the Mass is read, and the entire side of the church corresponding to it.

GUARDIAN, *guardián.* A friar who headed a convent, called "warden" in obsolete English.

HOLY CHILD, *Santo Niño, Niño Jesus.* The Christ Child. Domínguez never specifies any special advocacy or title. The Santo Niño de Atocha and the Santo Niño de Praga may have been introduced later.

HOLY FACE, *Verónica, Santo Rostro.* The bloodstained Face of Christ as impressed, according to a very ancient legend, on the veil of Veronica, a kind woman who wiped the Saviour's Face with it on His journey to Calvary.

HOLY OILS, *santos óleos.* The olive oil and chrism blessed by the bishop on Holy Thursday for use at baptisms, confirmations, and the anointing of the sick. These separately consecrated liquids were kept in *crismeras,* three metal cylinders with screwed-on lids.

HOLY SEPULCHER, *Santo Sepulcro.* A representation of Christ lying dead and naked, except for a loin cloth, on a mat with its pillow, sometimes in a shallow casket. If the statue had a movable jaw, a face band was tied under the chin and over the head. The phrase may also refer to the Repository of Holy Thursday *(q.v.).* Cf. Ecce Homo.

HOLY TRINITY, *Santísima Trinidad.* Represented as Christ the Son seated at the right hand of the Father, with the Holy Ghost in the form of a dove. In N.M. some examples of a flagrant abuse in pictorial representation of the Triune Deity of Christian belief have survived. These show the Three Persons like Three Christs, or identical human triplets.

HUMERAL VEIL, *almaizal.* A long shawl-like vestment worn over the tunicle or dalmatic by the subdeacon while holding the paten during part of a solemn Mass; also worn over the chasuble or the cope by the celebrant when carrying the Holy Eucharist in procession or to the sick, or when blessing the people at Benediction.

IMMACULATE CONCEPTION, *Concepción, Limpia Concepción, Purísima Concepción.* The belief that Mary, since she was to provide the Saviour with His human body, was, in the first instant of her own conception, preserved free from Adam's sin by God's special favor and through the foreseen merits of the Redemption. Feast, Dec. 8.

INDULGENCE, *indulgencia, perdón.* The application of merits by which the Church, as having the power of the "Keys of the Kingdom," remits or forgives wholly or in part the penance that a person must do for past sins, even though already forgiven. Also the granting of an indulgence on certain occasions or at certain places; the fact that an offering was sometimes requested when an indulgence was granted has led to the erroneous impression that indulgences are bought and sold. A parallel example in everyday speech is the expression (also used by Domínguez) to "pay for" a Mass, baptism, etc., when the reference is to an offering made on such an occasion.

JERUSALEM CROSS, *cruz de Jerusalén.* A heraldic emblem, "cross potent," which originally was an equilateral cross with a short transverse bar at the tip of each arm. An emblem of the Franciscan Custody of the Holy Land was a similar cross with small identical crosses at each of the four angles formed by the arms, the total of five crosses representing the Five Wounds of Christ.

JESÚS NAZARENO. Not "Jesus of Nazareth" here, but derived from Nazarite, a term applied in the Old Testament to certain persons especially consecrated to God, whose chief identifying mark was their untrimmed hair (e.g., Samson and Samuel). Such men were believed to be prototypes of Christ in His Passion, and the name was applied to statues of Him bearing His Cross, robed in a red or purplish gown, crowned with thorns, and with long matted hair and beard. See Ecce Homo.

JÍCARA. A gourd, or a cup or vessel made from a gourd.

JUECES ACREEDORES, JUECES HACEDORES. Here, the officials who administered the funds pertaining to the bishopric.

KINGS, FEAST OF THE, *La Fiesta de los Reyes, Epifanía.* Epiphany (Jan. 6).

LEAGUE, *legua.* In Mexico and N.M., about 2.6 miles.

LECTOR. A lecturer or teacher in a college.

LUMINARIAS (always feminine; usually plural in N.M.). Small firewood bonfires to outline flat rooftops and procession routes on festive occasions. The term is now often misapplied to improvised lanterns made of candles in sand-filled paper bags, a relatively recent innovation, which are properly called *farolitos* (little lanterns).

MAESE (MAESTRE) DE CAMPO. Obsolete title of a top-ranking Spanish army officer of field grade, equivalent to colonel, or even to major or lieutenant general, depending upon the number of troops under his command. Like *sargento mayor,* the title of a lesser field commander ranking from major to colonel, or even major general, it continued as an honorary title in Spanish America long after

Spain had adopted more modern designations. Related titles, such as *alférez* (ensign or lieutenant) and *capitán* (captain), also denoted relative degrees of rank, depending upon their responsibilities. A simple *alférez* was ordinarily the lowest ranking commissioned officer, but the coveted position of *alférez real* often was given to high-ranking officers.

MAJORDOMO, *mayordomo.* Steward. In church societies, the head of the governing board, who usually served as president, secretary, and treasurer. Cf. Fabric.

MANIPLE, *manípulo.* An ornamental band worn hanging from the priest's left forearm when vested for Mass; originally a kerchief used to wipe the face, it later became a symbolical vestment of the same precious material as the chasuble and its other accessories.

MANUAL, *manual.* A ritual, or handbook of rites.

MARRIAGE YOKE, *yugo.* A thick cord of cotton or other material placed over and around the shoulders of the bride and groom immediately after marriage. They stayed thus "tied" throughout the Mass, and the term *enlace* for marriage is related to this ceremony. Another term, *velación,* originated in an earlier custom of placing a veil over the heads of the couple at their espousals, but later came to mean the solemnization of the marriage at Mass. The Pueblo Indians still cling to the old Spanish ceremony of the marriage yoke, an old Mass stole being generally used.

MATER DOLOROSA. See Crucifix.

METATE. A rectangular stone with a concave surface used for grinding maize and other grain with a flat or cylindrical stone (mano).

MILPA. Plot of cultivated land, especially one used for growing maize.

MINISTER, *ministro.* Liturgically, an assistant to the celebrant, like the deacon and subdeacon. Also applied to a priest administering any of the Sacraments, and specifically in N.M. to the Franciscan priest in charge of a mission. In Franciscan terminology, the term is used for the heads of major groups. Therefore the head of the Franciscan Order is a Minister General, and the head of a province, a Minister Provincial.

MISSAL, *misal, libro de misa.* The large book containing everything pertaining to the Mass and its celebration, together with the Scriptural passages and prayers proper to the saint in whose honor the day's Mass is offered. *Misal de clérigos:* the Roman Missal used by secular priests of the Roman rite everywhere. *Misal con nuestro santos:* The Roman Missal incorporating Masses in honor of Franciscan saints not contained in the universal tome. It is called *Missale Romano-Seraphicum.*

MISSION. See Parroquia.

MITRE, *mitra.* Used here, and in Mexico to this day, as a synonym for bishopric.

MONSTRANCE, *custodia.* The metal receptacle in which the Holy Eucharist was kept as well as displayed for public adoration.

NATIVITY OF OUR LADY. The feast of Mary's birthday (Sept. 8).

NAVE, *cuerpo de la iglesia, cañon.* In N.M., the body of the church as distinct from the sanctuary, and the transept where there is one.

OBVENTIONS, *obvenciones.* Offerings received for baptisms, marriages, funerals, and other spiritual ministrations, in accordance with a fixed schedule *(q.v.).*

OCOTE. New Mexican term for pitch-pine wood, used for candles, kindling and for fiesta *luminarias (q.v.).*

ORDINARY, *ordinario.* The person exercising ecclesiastical jurisdiction by virtue of his office and not by delegation, such as a bishop over his diocese, or the Franciscan Provincial over his friars.

ORPHREY. A band, usually embroidered, affixed to ecclesiastical vestments. Domínguez used *escapulario* in this sense.

OUR LADY OF THE ANGELS, *Nuestra Señora de los Angeles.* The principal feast of the Franciscans (Aug. 2) because it is the title of their Mother Church near Assisi.

OUR LADY OF CARMEL, *Nuestra Señora del Carmen;* or *del Monte Carmelo.* Mary as patroness of the Carmelite Order (feast, July 16), ordinarily depicted wearing the cream mantle and brown habit of the Carmelites, with the Holy Child in her arms, and releasing souls from Purgatory.

OUR LADY OF GUADALUPE, *Nuestra Señora de Guadalupe.* The famous painting of the Virgin venerated in Mexico since 1531. As patroness of Mexico, and of the Americas, her feast is celebrated on Dec. 12, the day of the apparition.

OUR LADY OF THE KINGS, *Nuestra Señora de los Reyes*. An image of the Virgin and Child in the Capilla Real of the cathedral of Seville.

OUR LADY OF LIGHT, *Nuestra Señora de la Luz*. A representation of the Virgin in a white robe and blue mantle, with the Holy Child on her left arm, rescuing a youth from the demon. Originally painted for a Jesuit preacher in Sicily, it was brought to Mexico City in 1707 and was donated to the city of León in 1732, whence its devotion spread and was introduced into N.M. by Governor Marín del Valle.

OUR LADY OF LORETO, *Nuestra Señora de Loreto*. Mary's house at Nazareth, believed to have been transferred by angelic power to the town of Loreto in Italy. Feast, Dec. 10.

OUR LADY OF THE PILLAR, *Nuestra Señora del Pilar*. The famous image of the Virgin at Saragossa, traditionally believed to have been set upon its pillar by St. James the Apostle.

OUR LADY OF REMEDIES, *Nuestra Señora de los Remedios*. The image of the Madonna and Child with this title at Toltepec, brought to Mexico by a soldier of Cortés' army.

OUR LADY OF THE ROSARY, *Nuestra Señora del Rosario*. The feast of the Rosary was founded by St. Pius V to be celebrated on the day of the victory at Lepanto (the first Sunday of Oct., 1571), which was attributed to the intervention of Our Lady of the Rosary, patroness of the Spanish fleet.

OUR LADY OF SOLITUDE, *Nuestra Señora de la Soledad*. The Mother of Sorrows commemorated in her solitude following the Descent from the Cross, a purely Spanish devotion which originated at the royal court. Her dress was black.

OUR LADY OF SORROWS, *Nuestra Señora de Dolores*. A commemoration of Mary's sorrows as a bereaved Mother at the foot of the Cross, observed on the Friday before Good Friday. She is represented in a somber mantle, usually dark blue, with a silver heart on her breast pierced by seven swords. When at the foot of a crucifix *(q.v.),* this image is called a Madre Dolorosa, or simply La Dolorosa.

OUR LADY OF VALVANERA, *Nuestra Señora de Valvanera*. An ancient seated statue of the Madonna and Child at the shrine of this name in Navarre. The statue was found in a hollow oak after the expulsion of the Moors.

PALL, *palia, palio, hijuela, paño de cáliz*. Specifically, the square linen cloth with two thicknesses, sometimes reinforced with cardboard, placed over the chalice during Mass. Formerly the corporal served the purpose, one end being folded over the chalice. As in English, the ecclesiastical word "pall" *(palia, palio)* has been used in many senses, and the translation usually depends on the context. Cf. Altar Cloth, Altar Cover.

PARROQUIA. Parish church. The church of an officially erected congregation usually self-supporting. The churches in the Indian pueblos were neither officially erected congregations nor self-supporting, and were called mission churches. In Domínguez' time even the parish churches (in Santa Fe, La Cañada, and Albuquerque) were still referred to as mission churches.

PATEN, *patena*. A slightly concave metal dish, gold-plated on top, to hold the Host for the Mass.

PAX, *portapaz*. A wooden tablet or metal disk used for the "kiss of peace" at a solemn Mass.

PESO. In N.M., where there was little hard money available, the peso was usually reckoned in certain commodities, as Domínguez explains. The silver peso or dollar (piece of eight) was worth 272 *maravedís*, or 8 reales or tomines of 34 *maravedís* each.

POOR SOULS, *ánimas benditas del Purgatorio*. In Spanish *alma* means the soul of a living person, and *ánima,* a departed soul being purified in Purgatory *(q.v.).* To accelerate this process, the living make suffrages *(sufragios,* "votes," petitions") for them in the form of prayers, Masses, and indulgences gained in their behalf.

PRESIDIO. A garrison, or a place where a garrison was stationed.

PROCURATOR, *procurador*. A legal representative; a supply officer.

PROVINCE, *Provincia*. See Custody.

PROVINCIAL, *provincial*. The head of a Franciscan province.

PUEBLO. People, a community of people, any town. In N.M., except for the villas *(q.v.).*

the loosely grouped Spanish ranchos were generally referred to as *poblaciones,* or, if the population consolidated for mutual defense, as *plazas.* Hence the use in N.M. of *plaza* and *placita* meaning town or village.

PURGATORY, *Purgatorio.* A place where the souls of the just are completely "purged" of minor faults and of penalties due for forgiven past sins, before reaching Heaven, "where nothing defiled can enter." Cf. Poor Souls.

PURIFICATION OF OUR LADY, *Purificación, Candelaria.* Candlemas. Feast (Feb. 2) commemorating the Purification of the Virgin Mary and the Presentation of Christ in the Temple. On this day candles are blessed to commemorate Christ as the Light of the World.

PURIFICATOR, PURIFIER, *purificador.* A linen cloth folded twice lengthwise to form a small narrow towel used to clean and dry the chalice after the Communion.

PYX, *pixide, rodalito.* A little metal case with a lid, usually round, for keeping the Eucharist in the tabernacle and for taking Holy Communion or the Viaticum to the sick. Domínguez sometimes uses the word *rodalito* (a small radiance, or halo) for this.

REAL. A monetary unit of 34 *maravedís,* or one-eighth of a silver peso *(q.v.).*

REGULARS, *regulares.* Priests or lay brothers who follow the Rule of an Order, as distinct from secular priests *(clérigos seculares).*

RELIGIOUS, *religioso.* A member of an Order or Congregation.

RELIQUARY, *relicario.* A receptacle like a miniature monstrance to display some personal remembrance of a saint. Also sometimes called *rodalito* by Domínguez (cf. Pyx). Some *relicarios* were in the form of lockets.

REPOSITORY, *depósito.* An especially prepared altar shrine for depositing the consecrated Host after the Mass on Holy Thursday, where the Eucharist is adored continually until the Mass of the Presanctified on Good Friday. Also called *repositorio,* or *monumento.* When Domínguez uses *monumento,* it is often difficult to determine whether he means a representation of the Holy Sepulcher, a catafalque *(q.v.),* or a repository.

REREDOS. See Altar Screen.

RESIDENCIA. An accounting required of a public official, usually upon the completion of his term in office.

RESPONSORY, *responsorio.* Extra prayers for the dead, in the vernacular, with responses by the people, after the liturgical Latin prayers.

ROSARY, *rosario.* A circlet of beads arranged in decades, each denoting an *Ave Maria,* with a larger single bead between each decade, denoting the *Pater Noster.* At each decade an event, or "mystery," in the life of Christ or His Mother is meditated on.

ROYAL PATRONAGE, *real patronato.* The powers in ecclesiastical affairs exercised by the Crown of Spain in the New World by virtue of papal bulls granted to the Catholic Kings shortly after the discovery of America.

SACRISTAN, *sacristán.* The person in charge of the sacristy, and, by extension, of the cleanliness of the entire church. Often used in N.M. to refer to Indian boys selected to assist the priest and to receive special instruction.

SACRISTY, *sacristía.* A room, usually adjacent to the sanctuary, where the sacred vessels and vestments, and sometimes other paraphernalia, are kept, and where the priest and his assistants vest for Divine Services.

ST. ANNE, *Santa Ana.* The mother of Mary. Feast, July 26.

ST. ANTHONY ABBOT, *San Antonio Abad.* One of the famed Fathers in the Desert, the founder of Christian monasticism in the third and fourth centuries. Sometimes represented in a Franciscan-like habit, but more correctly in a long ragged shirt or a sheepskin over a hair shirt. Feast, Jan. 17.

ST. ANTHONY OF PADUA, *San Antonio de Padua.* A native of Lisbon who joined the Franciscan Order in the days of St. Francis and died at Padua in 1231; a Doctor of the Church, but popular as a youthful wonderworker. Portrayed as holding a playful Christ Child in his arms from a legend to this effect. Feast, June 13.

ST. ATHENOGENES, *San Atenógenes.* A bishop who suffered with ten disciples in Armenia in the days of Diocletian. Domínguez may have applied this name by mistake to an image of St. Acacius (San Acacio), who was also martyred in Asia Minor with several companions and is still honored in N.M.

ST. AUGUSTINE, *San Agustín.* Bishop of Hippo in the fourth century and the greatest of the

Fathers and Doctors of the Church. Usually represented in pontifical robes, but sometimes in a garment resembling the habit of the Augustinians. Feast, Aug. 28.

ST. BARTHOLOMEW, *San Bartolomé*. One of the Twelve Apostles, believed to have been flayed alive in Armenia and represented in classical gown and mantle, holding a flaying knife. Feast, Aug. 24.

ST. BENEDICT ABBOT, *San Benito Abad*. The founder of Western monasticism in the sixth century. Usually represented as an aged man with a long beard and the monastic tonsure, dressed in the choir cowl of the Benedictine monks, and wearing a pectoral cross. Feast, March 21.

ST. BONAVENTURE, *San Buenaventura*. Pioneer Franciscan, baptized as John, but called Bonaventura because St. Francis had held him as an infant and prophesied a good fortune for him. Minister General and reformer of the Franciscan Order, Bishop of Albano, and Cardinal. A Doctor of the Church, known as the "Seraphic Doctor." Usually represented in his Franciscan habit, wearing a pectoral cross, and with a bishop's mitre or a cardinal's hat.

ST. CLARE, *Santa Clara*. Co-founder with St. Francis of the Franciscan Second Order, the nuns called Clarisas in Spanish and Poor Clares in English. Represented wearing a gray or brown Franciscan habit with a black veil over a white wimple, and holding a monstrance. The Franciscans refer to her as *Nuestra Madre,* Our Mother St. Clare. Feast, Aug. 12.

ST. DIDACUS, *San Diego*. A Spanish Franciscan lay-brother who died at Alcalá in 1463. Some earlier writers of N.M. history have confused San Diego de Alcalá with Santiago (St. James the Apostle, *(q.v.)*; Twitchell invariably writes "Santiago" in SANM, even when the document plainly reads "Diego." Both Diego and Iago are derived from *Jacobus* (James). Old Feast, Nov. 12.

ST. DOMINIC, *Santo Domingo*. Spanish founder of the Order of Preachers, or Dominican friars. Because of his friendship with St. Francis, he is called "Our Father St. Dominic" by the Franciscans. He is represented in the white habit and black mantle of his Order, sometimes holding the black and white fleur-de-lis cross, the emblem of his Order, and sometimes with a little terrier carrying a burning torch. Feast, Aug. 4.

ST. FRANCIS OF ASSISI, *San Francisco de Asís*. Founder of the three Orders of Franciscans. Called "Our Father," "Our Father St. Francis," and "Our Seraphic Father" in the documents. In N.M. he was represented wearing a blue habit, with a cross in one hand and a skull in the other, or the skull at his feet. Feast, Oct. 4.

ST. FRANCIS SOLANO, *San Francisco Solano*. Sixteenth-century Spanish Franciscan missionary in South America. Usually represented in the act of baptizing an Indian. Feast, July 24.

ST. FRANCIS XAVIER, *San Francisco Xavier*. A Spaniard and charter member of the Society of Jesus and missionary in the Orient. Usually depicted in the act of preaching, wearing a surplice and stole over his black cassock and raising a crucifix aloft. Feast, Dec. 2.

ST. GABRIEL, *San Gabriel*. One of the Archangels, greatly revered by the Franciscans. Feast, March 24.

ST. IGNATIUS, *San Ignacio de Loyola*. Spaniard and founder of the Society of Jesus. Represented in Mass vestments or in a black cassock and high-collared cape, with a crucifix or the book of his Rule in his hand, and the emblem IHS on the book or elsewhere in the picture. Feast, July 31.

ST. ILDEPHONSE, *San Ildefonso*. A Spanish monk of the seventh century who became Archbishop of Toledo. Represented in the pontifical vestments of a bishop, holding a book and quill. Feast, Jan. 23.

ST. JAMES THE APOSTLE, *Santiago Apóstol*. Called the Greater or the Elder in the Gospels to distinguish him from the younger Apostle James; always regarded as the Apostle of Spain, where his tomb at Compostela was the major pilgrimage spot of mediaeval Europe. Represented in Spanish iconography wearing the cape and large hat with cockleshells of the pilgrims, or on horseback with upraised sword, trampling Saracens, from his reported apparitions during the wars with the Moors. Feast, July 25.

ST. JEROME, *San Jerónimo, San Gerónimo*. Fourth-century Doctor of the Church and a great Scriptural scholar and translator.

Sometimes represented in a cardinal's robes, or else half-naked in an animal skin to denote his asceticism while he lived in a cave at Bethlehem. Often depicted with a lion. Feast, Sept. 30.

ST. JOHN THE BAPTIST, *San Juan Bautista.* Precursor of Christ, and most honored saint in the early church after the Virgin and the Apostles Peter and Paul. Feast, June 24.

ST. JOHN CAPISTRAN, *San Juan Capistrano.* An Italian Franciscan missionary and Crusade preacher usually represented in his Franciscan habit and holding a banner with the emblem IHS. The unusual statue described by Domínguez (p. 16 *supra*) has him wearing a Crusader's white open gown over his habit, and a steel corselet; the "demon" at his feet is actually a Turk, while his upraised hand originally held a banner, and later a sword. This stood in the central niche of the Castrense reredos while it was kept in the old cathedral sanctuary and was therefore wrongly believed to have belonged there originally, especially in view of its military features. Feast, Oct. 23.

ST. JOHN OF GOD, *San Juan de Dios.* A fifteenth-century Spaniard, founder of the Hospital Brothers of St. John, the habit of whose Order was a dark robe, usually black, with a hood and scapular of the same color. Feast, March 8.

ST. JOHN NEPOMUCENE, JOHN OF NEPOMUK, *San Juan Nepomuceno.* A fourteenth-century Bohemian canon martyred by King Wenceslaus IV. Represented wearing a biretta and a canon's fur cape over his surpliced cassock, holding his forefinger to his lips. The bridge and river in the background refer to the finding of his body. Feast, May 16.

ST. JOSEPH, *Señor San José.* Spouse of the Virgin seldom referred to in Spanish without the prefix *Señor* (Lord), and often with *Patriarca* before or after this prefix. Usually represented as a bearded man past middle age, dressed in classical gown and mantle and holding the Holy Child on one arm, with a tall staff crowned with flowers in the other hand. Feast, March 19.

ST. LAWRENCE, *San Lorenzo.* A Spanish deacon roasted to death in Rome in the year 258 and considered the first Spanish martyr. Usually represented in a deacon's alb and dalmatic,

holding a martyr's palm and a gridiron. Feast, Aug. 10.

ST. LOUIS, KING OF FRANCE, *San Luis Rey.* Louis IX of France, Crusader and pioneer member of the Third Order of St. Francis, of which he is the principal male patron saint. Usually represented in royal robes or crusader's armor, sometimes holding the crown of thorns. Feast, Aug. 25.

ST. MARY MAGDALENE, *Santa María Magdalena, La Magdalena.* The famed penitent of the Gospels, sister of Martha and of Lazarus. Usually represented in rags or an animal skin as a hermit-penitent, contemplating a cross or skull, or both. Feast, July 22.

ST. MATTHEW, *San Mateo.* Apostle and Evangelist. Represented in classic gown and mantle, and holding a spear to denote his martyrdom; or with a book and quill, the winged head or body of a man nearby, all symbolizing his Gospel's emphasis on the Humanity of Christ. Feast, Sept. 21.

ST. MICHAEL, *San Miguel.* The Archangel who led the heavenly hosts against Lucifer and to whom St. Francis was particularly devoted. Usually represented as a winged figure in the uniform of a Roman soldier, holding a sword or spear over the prostrate demon. Feasts, May 8 and Sept. 29.

ST. NICHOLAS OF TOLENTINO, *San Nicolás de Tolentino.* A thirteenth-century member of the hermits or friars of St. Augustine. Represented in his black Augustinian habit, with a star above him or over his breast and a lily or lily-garlanded crucifix in his hand. Feast, Sept. 10.

ST. PAUL THE APOSTLE, *San Pablo Apóstol.* Represented in the classical robe and mantle, his dark hair and longer beard distinguishing him traditionally from St. Peter with his shorter gray and whitish beard, he usually holds the book of Epistles as well as the long sword of his martyrdom. Chief feast, with St. Peter, June 29; commemoration, June 30. See Conversion of St. Paul.

ST. PETER THE APOSTLE, *San Pedro Apóstol.* Represented in classical gown and mantle like St. Paul and the other Apostles, holding the distinctive crossed Keys of the Kingdom. Chief feast, June 29.

ST. PHILIP THE APOSTLE, *San Felipe Apóstol.* Believed to have been crucified in Hierapolis, hence the cross is his emblem. The crude statue by Miera y Pacheco at San Felipe shows him with a long black beard, holding a book in his left hand and a long staff resembling a thin cross in his right. Feast, May 1, with St. James the Less.

St. Philip of Jesus, *San Felipe de Jesús.* Born in Mexico City. The only native of North America canonized so far. The Franciscan Protomartyr of Japan, beatified in 1627, but not canonized until 1862. Feast, Feb. 5.

St. Philip Neri, *San Felipe Neri.* Sixteenth-century founder of the Oratorians. Represented as a white-bearded priest in a black cassock and turned-down collar. Feast, May 26.

St. Raphael. Archangel who accompanied the youth Tobias. Represented as an angel holding a fish, or accompanied by the smaller figure of Tobias with the fish. Feast, Oct. 24.

St. Rita, *Santa Rita.* A young Italian widow of the fifteenth century who died as an Augustinian nun in Cascia. Shown wearing a black robe with a black veil over a white wimple, contemplating a crucifix; sometimes wearing a crown of thorns, or at least the mark of a thorn on her brow. Feast, May 22.

St. Rose of Lima, *Santa Rosa de Lima,* or *Limana.* The first canonized saint of the New World. Represented in the Dominican habit (she was a Dominican tertiary), with a crown of roses on her head, and with a cross or crucifix and a scourge. Feast, Aug. 30.

St. Stephen, *San Esteban.* One of the original deacons of the Church and the first Christian martyr. Represented in the alb and dalmatic of a deacon with the martyr's palm in one hand and sometimes a stone in the other. Feast, Dec. 26.

St. Stephen of Hungary, *San Esteban de Hungría.* King of Hungary, 998-1038, who spread the Gospel there. Feast, Sept. 2.

St. Thomas the Apostle, *Santo Tomás Apóstol.* One of the Twelve Apostles. Represented in classical gown and mantle, sometimes holding a spear as the supposed instrument of his martyrdom. Feast, Dec. 21.

St. Vincent Ferrer, *San Vicente Ferrer.* A famous Spanish Dominican preacher of the fourteenth century. Ordinarily represented in his black and white habit in the act of preaching, he was also shown with two large angelic wings, from the contemporary belief that he was the Angel of the Apocalypse announcing the Day of Judgment. Feast, April 5.

Sanctuary, *presbiterio.* The area in a church next to the altar, occupied by the clergy; in N.M. separated from the nave only by a low railing.

Schedule, *arancel.* List of minimum fees assigned by the bishop for spiritual ministrations, always with the proviso that necessary ministrations be gratis in cases of poverty.

Seraphic, *seráfico.* Pertaining to the qualities of six-winged heavenly spirits distinguished for their ardor in adoring the Deity. Applied to St. Francis because Christ Crucified appeared to him in the guise of a winged Seraph when He imparted the stigmata to him; therefore he is often called the Seraphic Saint, the Seraphic Patriarch, the Seraph of Assisi, and his brethren inherited the designation, e.g., the Seraphic Order, the Seraphic Family.

Sermons of Holy Week, *Sermones de Semana Santa.* According to the traditional Spanish practice, the "Three Falls" on Holy Thursday, the "Descent from the Cross" on the afternoon of Good Friday, and "Our Lady of Solitude" in the evening. The first and last accompanied the service of Tenebrae *(q.v.).*

Server. See Acolyte.

Server's Cassock, *opa. Opa* is an obsolete term for the cassock worn by a Mass-server.

Server's Surplice, *sobrepelliz, roquete.* The short white garment worn by servers over their cassocks.

Spolia, *espolios.* The property of a deceased prelate; sometimes used loosely, as by Domínguez, to designate the property left by any clergyman.

Stole, *estola.* A long band, or scarf, of the same material as the chasuble, used by the celebrant in all liturgical functions.

Suffrages. See Poor Souls.

Surplice, *sobrepelliz.* A wide-sleeved garment of white linen or lace reaching to above the knee, used by the clergy in choir, or over the cassock at certain functions. Actually an abbreviation of the alb *(q.v.),* as are the related rochet and cotta.

Syndic, *síndico.* In this connection, a layman appointed to administer the finances of the

Franciscans, who were not permitted to handle money or transact business.

TABERNACLE, *tabernáculo, sagrario*. The veiled ark or box affixed to the altar table, in which the Eucharist is kept.

TENEBRAE, *tinieblas*. The offices of Matins and Lauds of the last three days of Holy Week, so called because of the darkness that followed the extinction, after each psalm, of twelve candles set in a candelabrum *(tinieblera)* before the altar. The thirteenth candle at the top and center represented Christ among the Apostles and was removed and extinguished. Then followed a tremendous racket made with *matracas* (razzle-dazzles) and the rattling of chains, to represent the thunder at the moment of Christ's expiration. The *matraca* was also used to summon the faithful to church during these days, for the bells were not rung from the Gloria of the Mass of Holy Thursday until that of Holy Saturday.

THIRD ORDER, *Tercera Orden*. So called because it followed the founding of the First Order of Franciscan priests and lay brothers and the Second Order of Franciscan nuns, or Poor Clares. See St. Clare. It was meant for men and women who wished to be followers of St. Francis *(q.v.)*, but who were counseled to remain in their homes and civil pursuits and there to practice his ideals of ardent piety, detachment from worldly vanities, and humble brotherly love. Originally the Tertiaries wore a modified form of the Franciscan habit over or underneath their regular clothing, but now a token scapular and cord. Other Orders have since established their own "Third Orders."

THURIBLE, or CENSER, *incensario*. A metal receptacle with a perforated lid, suspended from a ring by chains, for burning incense in church ceremonies.

TIERRA CALIENTE. "Hot country." Often applied more or less specifically to various tropical and subtropical regions.

TITHES, *diezmos*. The matter of the collection of tithes in N.M. is not entirely clear and requires further research.

TOMÍN. One real *(q.v.)*; one-eighth of a silver peso *(q.v.)*.

TRIBUNE, *tribuna*. A gallery in a church for the musicians, or for persons of high rank.

VARA. A linear measure of about 33 inches; a staff of office.

VESTMENTS, *ornamentos*. In Spanish, *ornamentos* is used to refer to liturgical vestments in general, or to the chasuble in particular. Often translated elsewhere as "ornaments."

VIA CRUCIS. Way of the Cross. A devotion commemorating the route of Christ's Passion from Pilate's Palace to Golgotha and the Holy Sepulcher. The number of stations varied considerably, but was fixed at fourteen by Clement XII in 1731.

VIATICUM, *Viático*. The name for the Holy Eucharist when taken as Holy Communion to the gravely ill.

VICAR, *vicario*. One to whom ecclesiastical authority has been delegated by the bishop or by his superiors, except for certain major offices, like that of vicar general, which carry ordinary authority by law.

VIGIL, *vigilia*. Sometimes used in Spanish as a synonym for Vespers preceding a feast; also, the Divine Office (Matins and Lauds) prayed for the dead.

VILLA. A town of relative importance. As the capital, Santa Fe alone enjoyed this title during the seventeenth century. By Domínguez' time there were three more villas: Cañada, Albuquerque, and El Paso. Cf. Pueblo.

VISITA. A mission administered by a priest residing at another parish or mission in the vicinity.

VISITATION, *visita*. An official inspection, or judicial inquiry, civil or ecclesiastical. The inspector was called visitor *(visitador)*. By a special commission from his Provincial, Fray Francisco Atanasio Domínguez served as a Commissary Visitor.

INDEX

A

Abadiano, Fray Manuel, 86, 87, 169-70, 217, 279, 292, 294, 325n, 329.

Abiquiu, 23n, 78n, 119, 120-26, 150, 207, 240, 249, 251, 252-53, 255, 259, 275, 276, 291, 319, 321-22, 336; church *illus.*, 121.

Abo, 197n.

Accessories, def., 350.

Acevedo, Fray Antonio de, 261n, 263n, 329.

Acolytes, 199; def., 350. *See* TEXT: Service.

Acoma, pueblo, xvii, 38n, 88, 150, 169, 179, 182, 183n, 186, 188-95, 236, 260n, 262, 263, 282, 283, 289, 293, 332; church *illus.*, 191; language, 285.

Adobe, def., 350.

Agave fiber, 7, 256.

Agricultural implements, 124.

Agriculture, 256, 288, 303, 312-13. *See also* Chile, Cotton, Food, Farmlands, Grains, Irrigation, Legumes, Livestock, Milk, Plants, Ranchos, Seeds, Vegetables, Wool. *See* TEXT: Lands and Fruits, Obventions and First Fruits.

Agua Fría, 41n.

Aguico, *see* Hawikuh.

Aguilar, Father, 131, 132.

Aguilar, Juan de, 286, 342.

Aguilar, Fray Juan, 329.

Aguilar, Fray Pedro Díaz de, 329.

Aguirre, Fray Martín, 259n.

Alameda, pueblo, 145n, 152n.

Alameda, Spanish settlement, 152-53, 253-54.

Alaska, xii.

Alb, def., 350.

Albuquerque, 80, 144-54, 174, 182, 202, 207, 217, 243, 253-54, 324, 325n, 336, 363; church *illus.*, 145.

Alburquerque, Duque de, 259n, 260, 261n, 264.

Alcalde mayor, 313-14, 315; def., 350; Acoma and Laguna, 187-88, 195, 314n; Cañada, 73n, 81, 248, 249, 290, 323; El Paso, 80n; Isleta, 314n; Jémez, 313n; Pecos, 212, 213; Picuris, 314n; Pojoaque, 62n; Santa Fe, 242, 350; Taos, 104, 105, 113; Zuñi, 286, 305.

Alexander VI, 276.

Alini, Miguel de, 19, 342.

All Saints: def., 350; feast, 21.